Stay on a farm

D1393579

JARROLD
PUBLISHING

Northern Ireland
Tourist Board

SCOTLAND

ENGLISH
TOURIST BOARD

BWRDD CROESO CYMRU
WALES TOURIST BOARD

1/97

Published by Jarrold Publishing, Whitefriars,
Norwich NR3 1TR
in association with the Farm Holiday Bureau (UK) Ltd,
the English Tourist Board and the National Tourist Boards
of Scotland, Wales and Northern Ireland
© Farm Holiday Bureau UK 1997
National Agricultural Centre, Stoneleigh, Warwickshire
CV8 2LZ

ISBN 0 7117 0997 1

The information contained in this Guide has been
published in good faith on the basis of the details
submitted by the proprietors of the premises listed.
These proprietors are current members of the Farm
Holiday Bureau and have paid for their entries in this
Guide. Whilst every effort has been made to ensure
accuracy in this publication, neither the publisher, the
Farm Holiday Bureau, the National Tourist Boards nor
their agents can guarantee the accuracy of the
information in this Guide and accept no responsibility for
any error or misrepresentation. All liability for loss,
disappointment, negligence or other damage caused by
reliance on the information contained in this Guide, or in
the event of bankruptcy, or liquidation, or cessation of
trade of any company, individual or firm mentioned is
hereby excluded.

The Farm Holiday Bureau of the United Kingdom
gratefully acknowledges the continuing assistance and
advice offered by the National Tourist Boards, the
Farming and Rural Conservation Agency (FRCA) of the
Ministry of Agriculture, the Scottish Agricultural
Organisations Society Ltd, and all those who seek to
maintain a balance in the rural community.

Produced for the Tourist Boards by The Pen and Ink
Book Company Limited, Huntingdon, Cambridgeshire

Printed and bound in Great Britain

Contents

Stay on a farm

Gift Tokens

FOR A PRESENT TO REMEMBER

FARM HOLIDAY BUREAU

'Stay on a Farm'
Gift Token

£5

£5

SEE REVERSE FOR CONDITIONS OF USE

FARM HOLIDAY BUREAU

'Stay on a Farm'
Gift Token

£10

£10

REVERSE FOR CONDITIONS OF USE

FARM HOLIDAY BUREAU

'Stay on a Farm'
Gift Token

£20

£20

SEE REVERSE FOR CONDITIONS OF USE

Available from

Farm Holiday Bureau (UK) Ltd,
National Agricultural Centre, Stoneleigh Park,
Warwickshire CV8 2LZ

Telephone: (01203) 696909
Fax: (01203) 696630

Welcome to the Farm Holiday Bureau

The Bureau is a national network of farming families who provide value for money, good food and a warm welcome in quality bed and breakfast and self-catering accommodation.

All members belong to one of 91 local Farm Holiday Bureau Groups, who, together with the National Tourist Boards, help ensure high standards for you.

We hope you enjoy your stay on a farm, and would like to ask you to help us provide an even better book for your use. Please send us your views and ideas.

Thank you for choosing to stay on a farm. We all hope you enjoy the opportunity to discover our countryside.

Farm Holiday Bureau
National Agricultural Centre
Stoneleigh Park
Warwickshire
CV8 2LZ

Telephone (01203) 696909
Fax (01203) 696630
e-mail: admin@fhbaccom.demon.co.uk
http://www.webscape.co.uk/farmaccom/

Stay on a Farm –
with Paul Heiney

In my travels around Britain, I have consulted many guides to accommodation of all shapes and sizes, but Stay on a Farm *is the one to which I will always return. There are several reasons why, but let us deal with an important one first.*

This book is so packed with accommodation of such good value that I sometimes have to look again to make sure I have not misread the prices quoted! Quite frankly, there are so many bargains to be found here that I cannot imagine why anyone would ever pay to stay in higher priced city hotels. If you are travelling with a family, the savings made on a farm can be huge.

But value is not the most important reason for staying on a farm. If you are a town or city dweller seeking a breath of country air, and a taste of freedom from the pressures of urban life, here is an invitation to another world, a chance to see the countryside as those who live and work there see it. Staying on a working farm gets you closer to true country living than any other way I can imagine.

And rest assured the welcome will be warm. I cannot recall how many welcoming cups of tea I have consumed and how much I have learnt about country life as it is really lived by talking to farmers, many of whom are only too happy to show you what they do, and why they do it. For children, this is very important, for the new generation seems to be growing up in a climate where the workings of farmers seem increasingly mysterious, and it is in the interests of all that as wide a section of the population as possible understands how farming works.

All that apart, these are relaxing places to stay: always clean, always comfortable and always restful. Some are tucked away in little corners of Britain that you never knew existed, others just in the right spot to break a long, cross-country journey. And apart from the farmers and their

wives, you will meet a wide variety of people staying on a farm. They are increasingly used by businessmen tired of staying in towns, and by families whose children appreciate the free side-show that livestock farms can provide.

Be warned, you will make friends if you start staying on farms. These farms will become a home from home, and you will find yourself returning year after year to pick up on old aquaintanceships.

I also feel duty bound to mention the traditional farmhouse breakfast. But on second thoughts, I will let you find out for yourself. You will not be disappointed!

Paul Heiney

How to use the guide

Selecting your farm...

The guide lists all the members of the Farm Holiday Bureau (UK) Ltd in the countries of England, Scotland, Wales and Northern Ireland. Members belong to one of 91 Farm Holiday Bureau Groups: key maps in the section entitled, Where to Go on pages 10–12 will tell you which counties and areas the individual FHB Groups cover. Arranged within countries, each Group has a numbered section in this guide which opens with a description of the area and an outline map showing the location of each farm. The Group contacts can help you find suitable accommodation if you wish.

Properties in each Group section are listed alphabetically under Bed and Breakfast, Self-Catering, and Camping and Caravanning. All entries feature a brief description and a line illustration, along with an indication of prices for bed and breakfast, self-catering and for evening meals where available. Clear symbols (see page 15) indicate what further facilities are provided.

A comprehensive index at the back of the guide (page 385) shows those members who offer facilities for camping and caravanning and those who welcome business travellers (with meeting room capacity where provided) and who offer en suite facilities.

The index also indicates those farms who have invited the National Tourist Boards to inspect the facilities they offer to wheelchair users and those who have difficulty walking. Each has been awarded an access category rating which is indicated by the Accessible Symbol (explained on page 14). Please check at the time of booking if you have special needs.

How to book...

All you have to do is telephone the farm of your choice. If the accommodation you want is not available, the owner will be happy to refer you to similar alternative FHB accommodation. **Alternatively, the Group Contact will be happy to help you find the right accommodation, and can usually provide you with a local group leaflet.**

Many members also offer a 'book a bed ahead' service to their guests. If you are touring, just tell your host where you wish to visit next, and he or she can make the booking for you.

PLEASE REMEMBER TO MENTION *STAY ON A FARM* WHEN MAKING A BOOKING

When making a booking...

• Mention the guide.

• Specify your planned arrival and departure dates.

• Specify accommodation needed and any particular requirements, eg twin beds, family room, private bath, ground floor, cot.

• Specify terms required, eg. B&B, evening meal etc. Evening meal times vary and high tea may be available for children. Farms offering evening meals do not necessarily do so all year round so do check.

• Specify special requirements, eg special diets, facilities for disabled people, arrangements for children, dogs.

• Check prices and any reductions that may be offered.

• Check whether a deposit is payable and, if so, what charges will apply if the booking is cancelled (see 'Cancellations' opposite).

• Check method and date of payment.

• Check whether B&B access is restricted through the day. Many farms are happy for visitors to stay in the house all day, but on some farms this is not practical and guests are asked to be out of the farmhouse between 10.30am and 4.30pm. Remember, it is essential that children are carefully supervised at all times on and around the farm.

• Check the best time to arrive and ask for directions to the farm. When you are near your destination, look out for the Farm Holiday Bureau member sign at the end of the drive. Your host will be glad to direct you by phone if you get lost.

• Give your name, address and telephone number.

NB We recommend that, time permitting, all telephone bookings are confirmed in writing, specifying exactly what you have booked and the price you expect to pay.

Payment and deposits
For reservations made in advance a deposit is usually payable and this will be deducted from the total bill. When you book please check when and how payment should be made.

Cancellations
Once a booking has been agreed, on the telephone or by letter, a legally binding contract has been made with the host. If you cancel a reservation, fail to take up the accommodation or leave prematurely (regardless of the reasons), the host may be entitled to compensation if it cannot be relet for all or a good part of the booked period. If a deposit has been paid it is likely to be forfeited and an additional payment may be demanded.

Insurance
Travel and holiday insurance protection policies can be taken out to safeguard visitors in the event of cancellation or curtailment. Insurance of personal property can also be sought. Hosts cannot accept liability for any loss or damage to visitors' property, however caused. Do make sure that your valuables are covered by your household insurance before you take them away.

Compliments and complaints

Many visitors write to the Farm Holiday Bureau saying how much they have enjoyed their stay. If you feel that something or someone deserves acknowledgement, or if you have a suggestion on how to improve the guide, please write to the Farm Holiday Bureau (UK) Ltd, National Agricultural Centre, Stoneleigh Park, Warwickshire CV8 2LZ, or ring (01203) 696909.

If you are dissatisfied, please make your complaint to the host there and then. This gives an opportunity for rectifying action to be taken at once. It is usually difficult to deal with a complaint if it is reported at a later date. If the host fails to resolve the problem, please write to the Farm Holiday Bureau who will be happy to help.

Where to go

The Farm Holiday Bureau has 91 local Groups, each of which has a section in this guide. The maps show the location of each Group and their position in the countries. Page numbers are indicated in *italic*; Group numbers are in red.

Shetland Islands

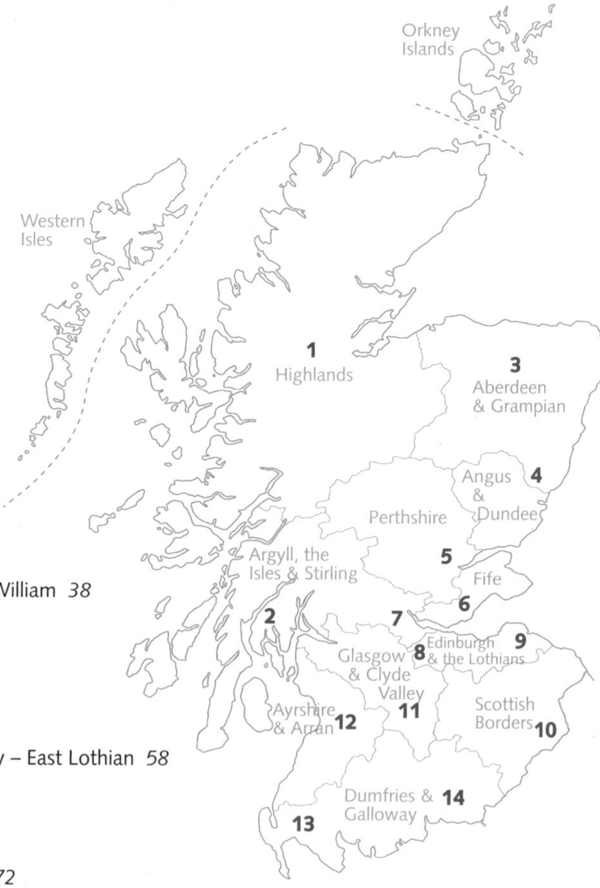

Orkney Islands

Western Isles

1 Highlands

3 Aberdeen & Grampian

Angus & Dundee **4**

Perthshire

Argyll, the Isles & Stirling

5 Fife

2

7

6

Glasgow & Clyde Valley **8** Edinburgh & the Lothians **9**

Ayrshire & Arran **12**

11

Scottish Borders **10**

Dumfries & Galloway **14**

13

Scotland

England

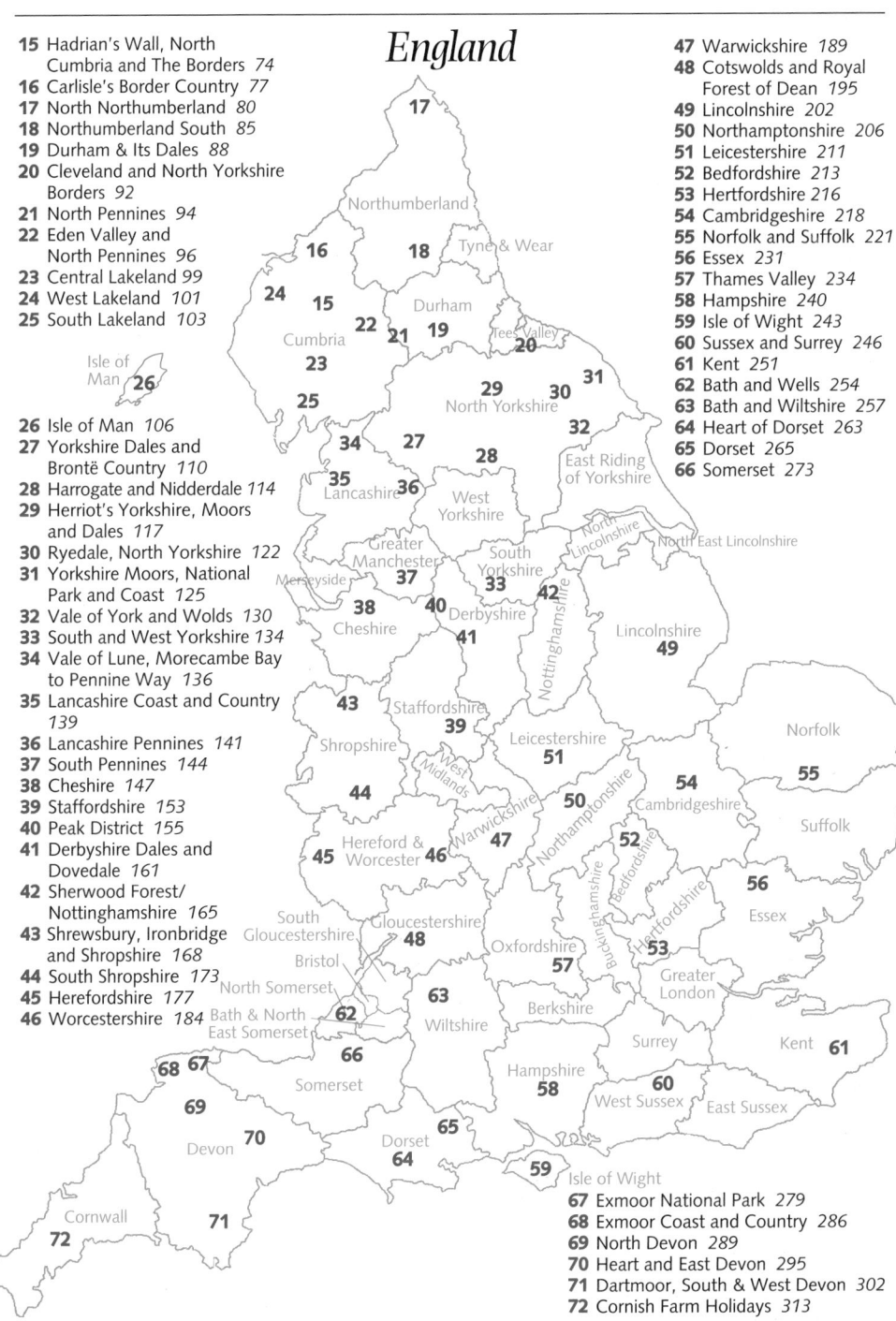

Wales

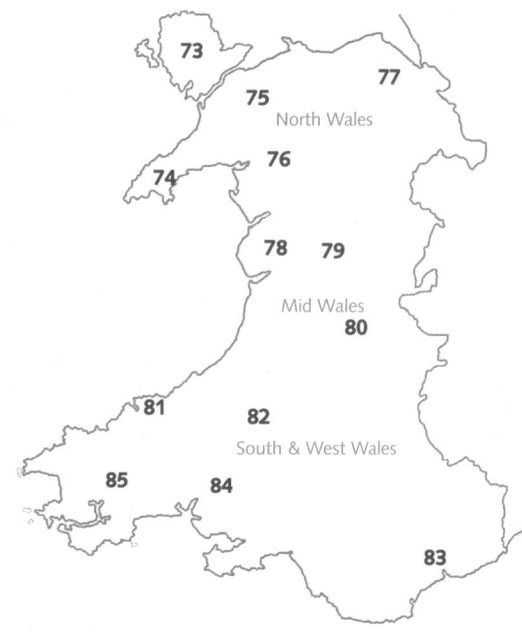

Northern Ireland

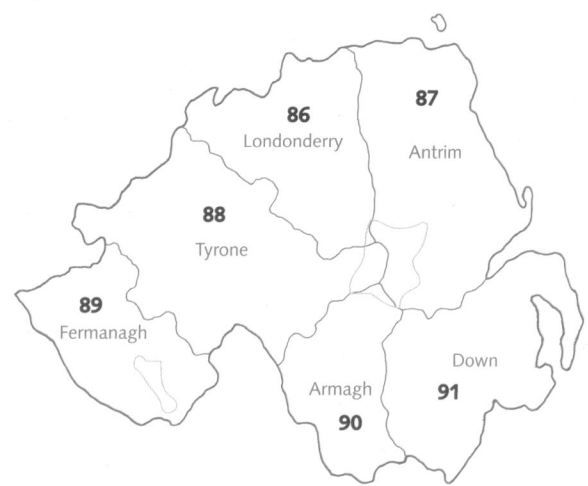

Accommodation classification and grading

Farm Holiday Bureau members are inspected by their Groups to ensure that a high standard of cleanliness, courtesy and service is maintained. All members must also be inspected by their National Tourist Board, agree to meet the Tourist Board's Minimum Standards and observe the Tourist Board's Code of Conduct.

Listed/ ☐

Crown classification and grading scheme for serviced accommodation
The National Tourist Boards for England, Scotland and Wales operate a common classification and grading scheme for serviced accommodation including farmhouses. Each member has a thorough annual inspection by the Tourist Board and is classified, according to the range of facilities provided, within 6 bands from 'Listed' and then from **1–5 Crowns** for England and Scotland, and from **'Welcome Home'** ☐ or **1–5 Crowns** for Wales. The more Crowns, the more extensive the range of facilities.

Quality grading
Classified establishments are also assessed for a separate quality commendation of '**Approved**', '**Commended**', '**Highly Commended**' or '**De Luxe**'. The quality commendation appears alongside the classification.

Self-catering holiday homes
All Bureau members who offer self-catering accommodation must have been inspected by the Tourist Boards or have applied for an inspection.

⚷ England

🐝 Scotland

🐉 Wales

Those inspected in England and Scotland are classified according to the range of facilities they provide (**1–5 Keys** in England, **1–5 Crowns** in Scotland). Holiday Homes with higher quality standards have the term 'Approved', 'Commended', 'Highly Commended' or 'De Luxe' alongside the classification. In Wales quality standards are indicated on a scale of **1–5 Dragons**.

Northern Ireland
All visitor accommodation is inspected annually by the Northern Ireland Tourist Board under a statutory system, and all the farms listed offer a high standard.

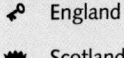

British graded holiday parks scheme
The National Tourist Boards operate a common quality grading scheme for holiday caravan, camping and chalet parks. The scheme grades parks according to the relative quality of what is offered, in a range of 1–5 ✓s. The more ✓s the higher the quality.

Wheelchair accessibility symbols

All the places that display one of the symbols shown here have been checked by a Tourist Board Inspector against standard criteria that reflect the practical needs of wheelchair users.There are three categories of accessibility:

 Category 1:
Accessible to all wheelchair users including those travelling independently.

 Category 2:
Accessible to a wheelchair user travelling with a helper.

 Category 3:
Accessible to a wheelchair user able to walk short distances and up three steps.

Please check at the time of booking if you have special needs.

Inspected accessible schemes have been developed throughout the UK as part of the nationwide Tourism for All campaign in conjunction with the Hotel and Holiday Consortium and are designed to provide disabled travellers with reliable information on standards and facilities. Additional help and guidance on finding suitable holiday accommodation for those with special needs can be obtained from: Holiday Care Service on (01293) 774535.

Welcome Host

The National Tourist Boards recently launched a Welcome Host scheme. Service and hospitality are as important as good accommodation and good food. The Welcome Host training programme places the emphasis on warm hospitality and first-class service. Recipients of the Welcome Host certificate or badge are part of a fine tradition – a tradition for friendliness.

Look at the entries to find those farms participating in the Welcome Host scheme.

 Scotland

 England

 Wales

 Northern Ireland

Taste of Wales

The Taste of Wales Hospitality Scheme promotes the use of fresh local food produce, and where better to find the freshest, most local food than down on the farm. Farmhouses have always played a great part in the Taste of Wales scheme, and in many regions they are the backbone of the local economy. The Farm Holiday Bureau promotes the best of farmhouses, and many Taste of Wales members are included in this guide.

Symbols

Symbol	Explanation	French	German
⌃(3)	Children welcome (minimum age)	Enfants bienvenus (âge minimum)	Kinder willkommen (Mindestalter)
🐕	Dogs by arrangement	Chiens autorisés sous réserve d'accord préalable	Hunde nach Vereinbarung
⚭	No smoking	Non fumeurs de préférence	Nichtraucher bevorzugt
▥	Credit cards accepted	Cartes de crédit acceptées	Kreditkarten werden akzeptiert
♟	Business people welcome	Facilités pour hommes d'affaires	Geschäftsreisende willkommen
♟	Waymarked walks on farm	Visite de fermes avec indication d'itinèncuies	Wanderwege gezeichnet
�’	Foreign language(s) spoken	Langues étrangères parlées	Hier werden Fremdsprachen gesprochen
☗	Riding on farm	Randonnée à poney ou équitation	Reiten auf Ponys oder Pferden
➡	Fishing on farm	La pêche à la ligne	Angeln
⊜	Country house, not a working farm	Manoir (pas une) exploitation agricole)	Landhaus, kein aktiver Bauernhof
⚑	Camping facilities	Camping	Camping – Einrichtungen
⛺	Caravanning facilities	Caravaning	Caravan – Einrichtungen
	Prices	**Prix**	**Preise**
B&B	price per person per night for bed and breakfast	Prix par personne par nuit pour chambre + petit déjeuner	Preis pro Person pro Nacht für Bett und Frühstück
EM	price per person for evening meal	Prix par personne pour repas du soir	Preis pro Person für Abendessen
SC	price per unit per week self-catering	Prix par location par semaine	Preis pro Einheit pro Woche bei Selbstversorgung
Tents	price per tent pitch per night	Prix par tente par nuit	Preis pro Zeltaufstellung pro Nacht
Caravans	price per caravan pitch per night	Prix par caravane par nuit	Preis pro Caravanaufstellung pro Nacht
	All prices include VAT and service charge if any.	Tous les prix tiennent compete de la TVA et du service, le cas échéant.	Alle Preise inklusive MWSt und Bedienungsgeld, wenn überhaupt

Further information

These official Tourist Boards will be happy to supply you with further general information on their areas.

National Tourist Boards

English Tourist Board
Thames Tower, Black's Road, Hammersmith, London W6 9EL
☎ (0181) 846 9000

Northern Ireland Tourist Board
59 North Street
Belfast
BT1 1NB
☎ (01232) 246609 Fax (01232) 312424

Scottish Tourist Board
23 Ravelston Terrace, Edinburgh EH4 3EU
☎ (0131) 332 2433

Wales Tourist Board
Brunel House, 2 Fitzalan Road, Cardiff CF2 1UY
☎ (01222) 499909

Regional Tourist Boards

Cumbria Tourist Board
(covering the county of Cumbria)
Ashleigh, Holly Road, Windermere, Cumbria LA23 2AQ
☎ (015394) 44444

Northumbria Tourist Board
(covering Durham, Northumberland, Tees Valley and Tyne & Wear)
Aykley Heads, Durham DH1 5UX
☎ (0191) 384 6905

North West Tourist Board
(covering Cheshire, Greater Manchester, High Peak District of Derbyshire, Lancashire and Merseyside)
Swan House, Swan Meadow Road, Wigan Pier, Wigan WN3 5BB
☎ (01942) 821222

Yorkshire Tourist Board
(covering East Riding of Yorkshire, North Lincolnshire, North East Lincolnshire, North Yorkshire, South Yorkshire and West Yorkshire)
312 Tadcaster Road, York, North Yorkshire YO2 2HF
☎ (01904) 707961

Heart of England Tourist Board
(covering Derbyshire, Gloucestershire, Hereford & Worcester, Leicestershire, Northamptonshire, Nottinghamshire, Shropshire, Staffordshire, Warwickshire and West Midlands)
Woodside, Larkhill, Worcester, Hereford & Worcester WR5 2EF
☎ (01905) 763436

East of England Tourist Board
(covering Bedfordshire, Cambridgeshire, Essex, Hertfordshire, Lincolnshire, Norfolk and Suffolk)
Toppesfield Hall, Hadleigh, Suffolk IP7 5DN
☎ (01473) 822922

London Tourist Board
(covering the Greater London area)
6th Floor, Glen House, Stag Place, London SW1E 5LT
Written enquiries only.

West Country Tourist Board
(covering Bath & North East Somerset, Bristol, Cornwall, Devon, North Somerset, Somerset, South Gloucestershire, Isles of Scilly, Western Dorset and Wiltshire)
60 St David's Hill, Exeter EX4 4SY
☎ (01392) 76351

Southern Tourist Board
(covering Berkshire, Buckinghamshire, Eastern Dorset, Hampshire, Isle of Wight and Oxfordshire)
40 Chamberlayne Road, Eastleigh, Hampshire SO5 5JH
☎ (01703) 620006

South East England Tourist Board
(covering Kent, East Sussex, Surrey and West Sussex)
The Old Brew House, Warwick Park, Tunbridge Wells, Kent TN2 5TU
☎ (01892) 540766

Britain On-Line
Information about all aspects of holidaying in Britain can be found on the British Tourist Authority Website: www.visitbritain.com

Tourist Information Centres

There are over 800 Tourist Information Centres (TICs) throughout the United Kingdom and they are there for you to use both before your holiday and during it. Look in your local telephone directory under 'Tourist Information' to find your nearest centre, or for locations and telephone numbers of any TIC in England, simply call Freepages on 0800 192 192. TICs can give you details about local attractions, events and accommodation and many will even be able to book it for you. Look out for the information sign.

Farm Holiday Bureau (UK) Ltd
National Agricultural Centre
Stoneleigh Park
Warwickshire CV8 2LZ
☎ (01203) 696909 Fax (01203) 696630
E-mail: admin @ fhbaccom.demon.co.uk
http://www.webscape.co.uk/farmaccom/

MAP OF GREAT BRITAIN

KEY TO MAP SECTIONS

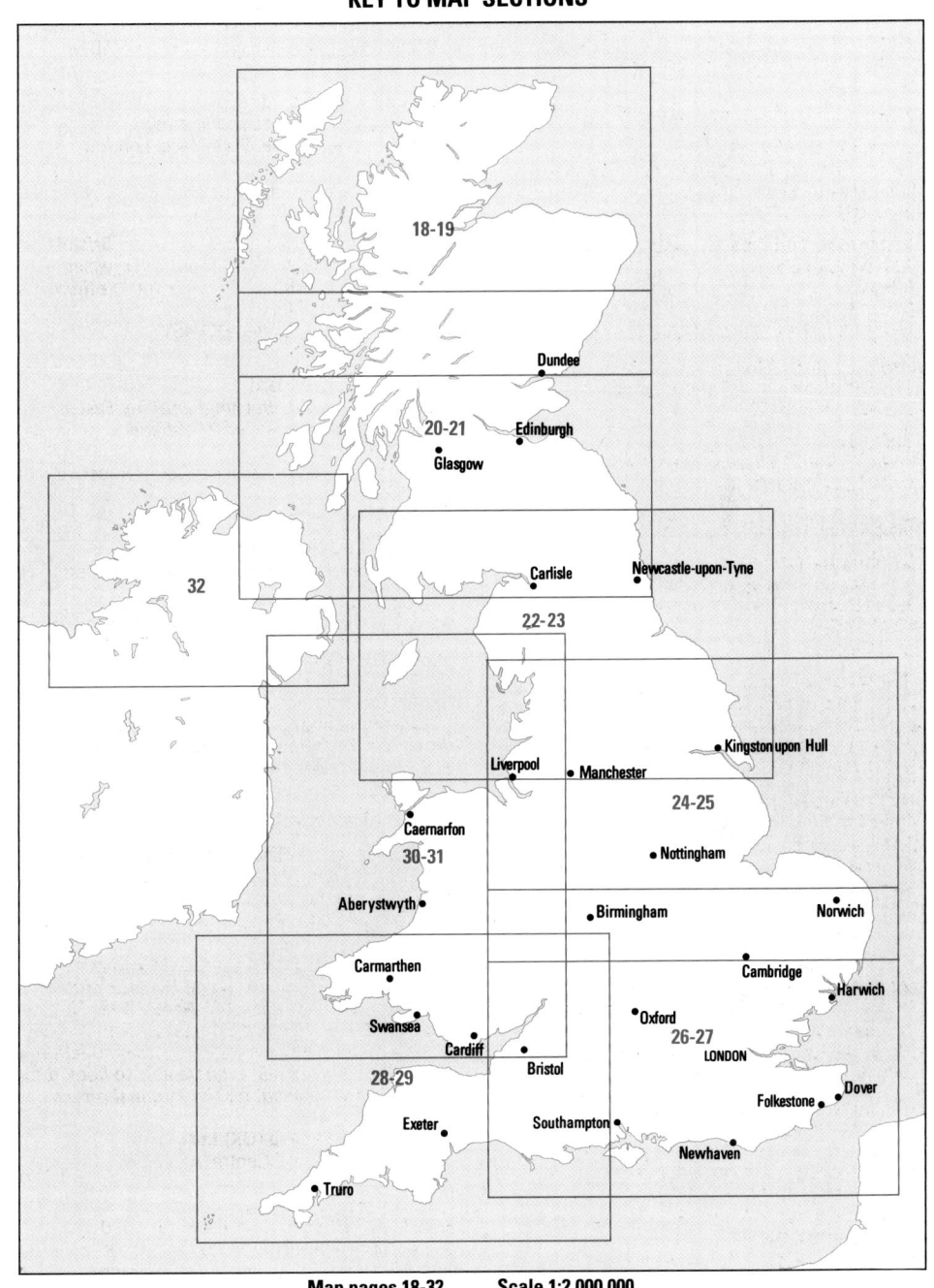

18-19

Dundee

20-21   Edinburgh
Glasgow

Carlisle   Newcastle-upon-Tyne

32   22-23

Kingston upon Hull

Liverpool   Manchester

24-25

Caernarfon

30-31   Nottingham

Aberystwyth   Birmingham   Norwich

Carmarthen   Cambridge

Harwich

Swansea   Oxford

Cardiff   26-27

Bristol   LONDON

28-29   Dover

Exeter   Southampton   Folkestone

Newhaven

Truro

Map pages 18-32   Scale 1:2 000 000

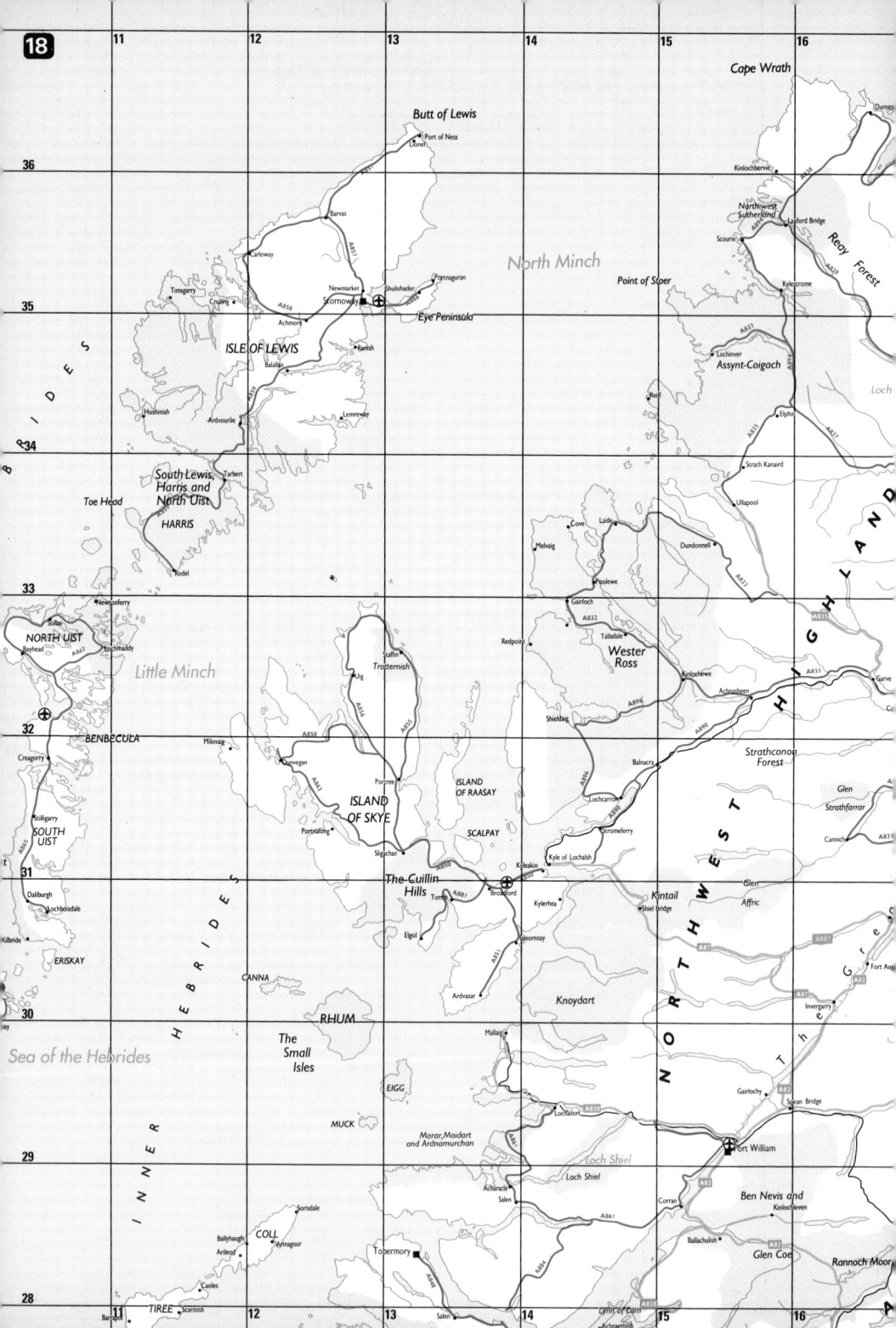

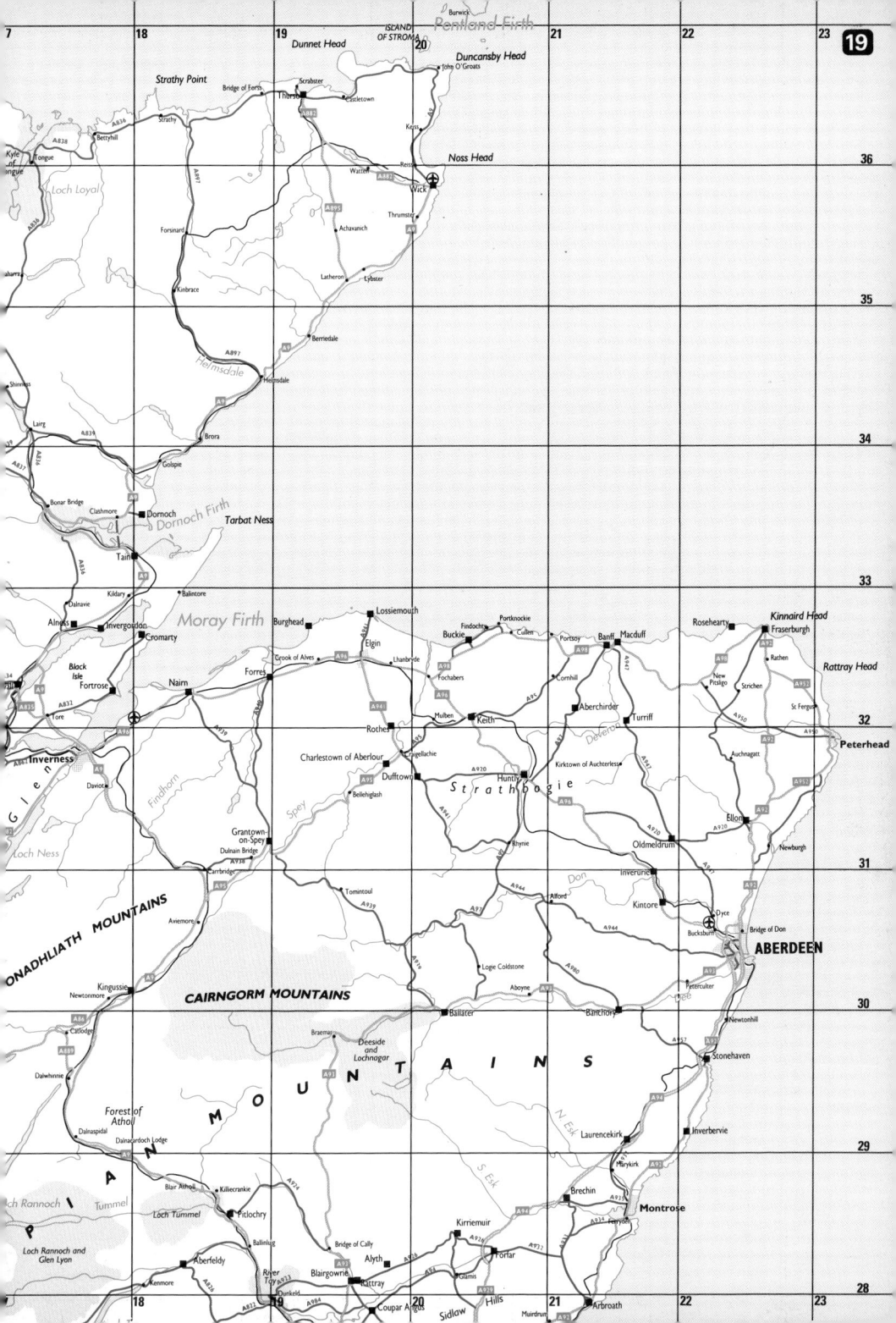

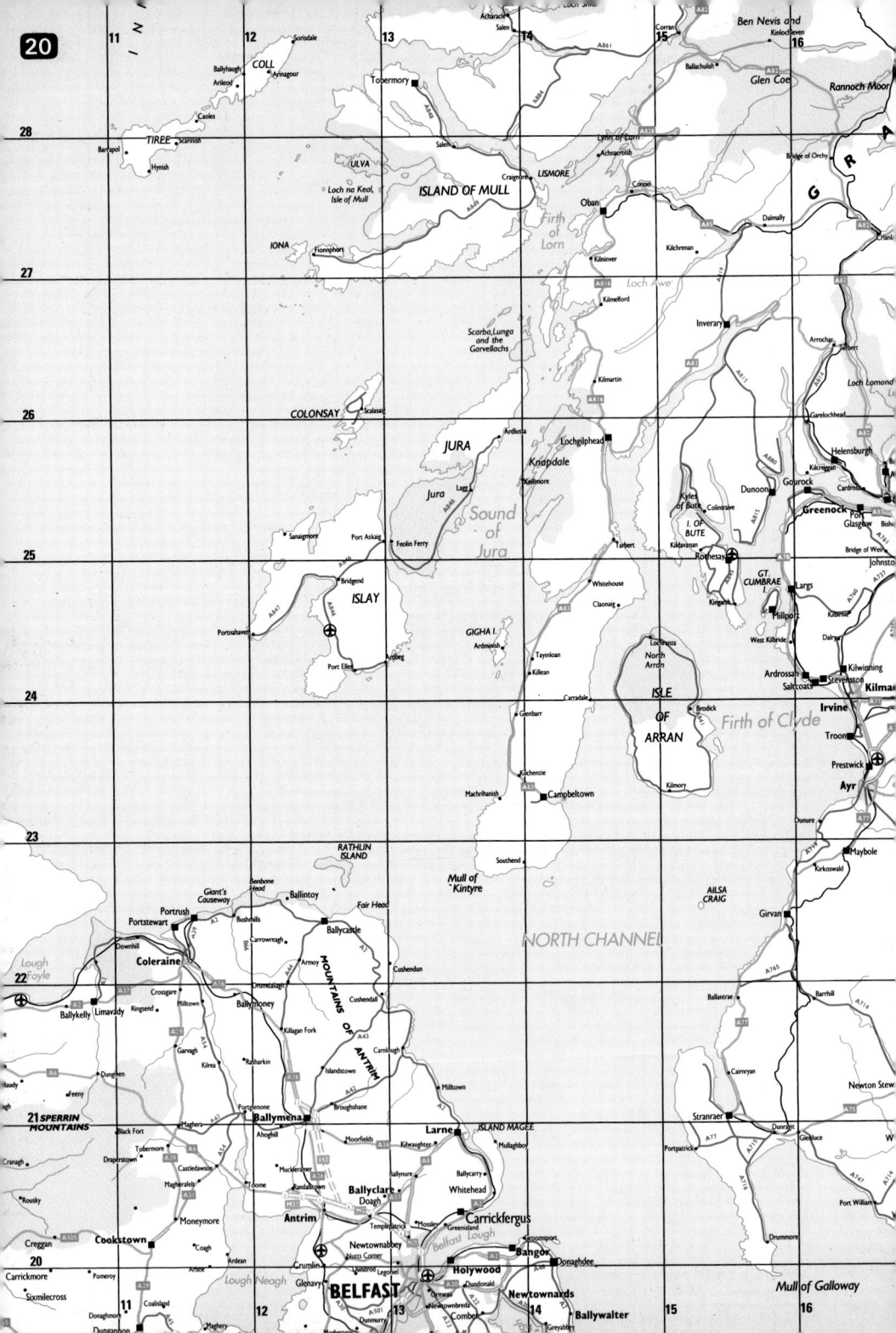

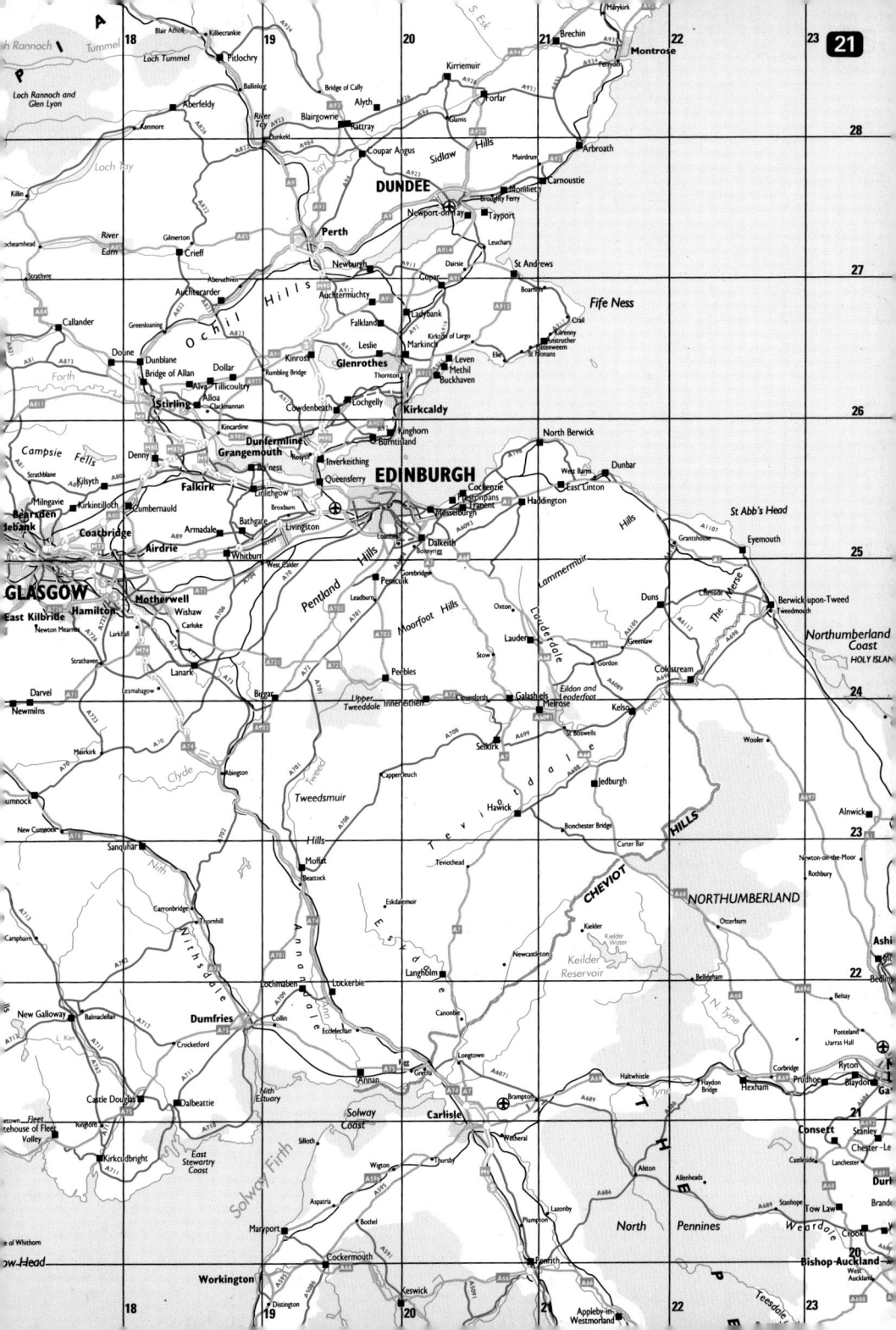

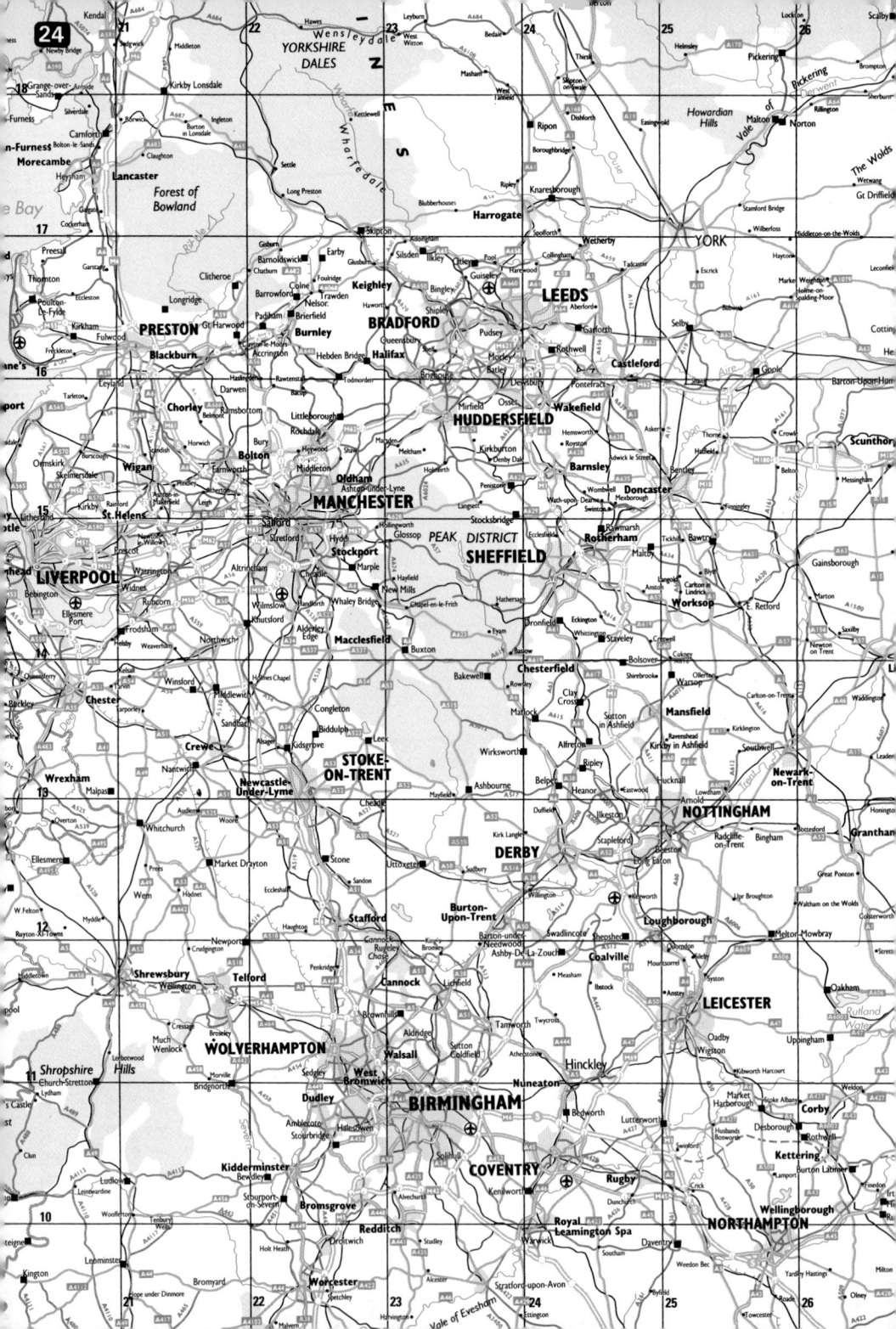

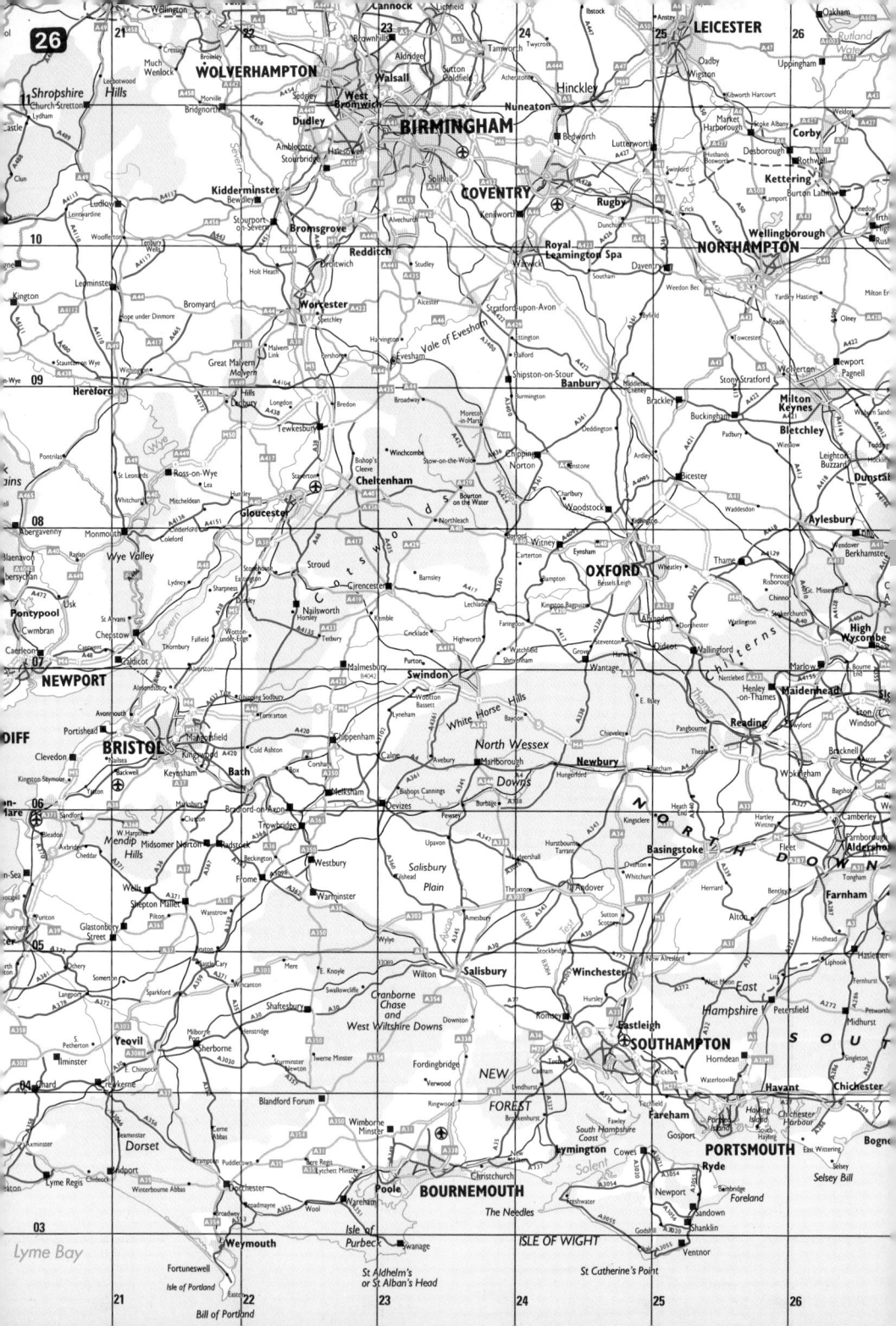

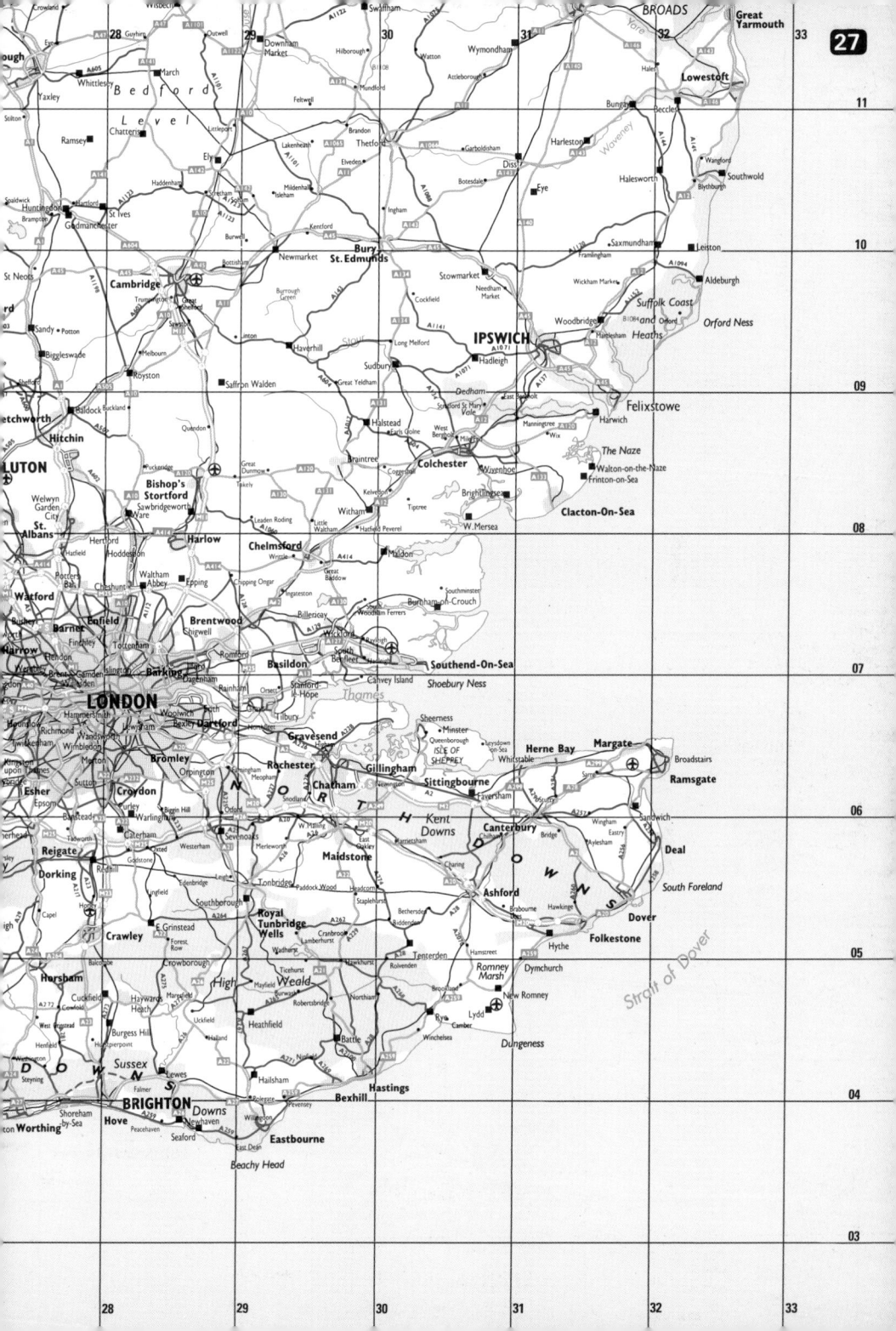

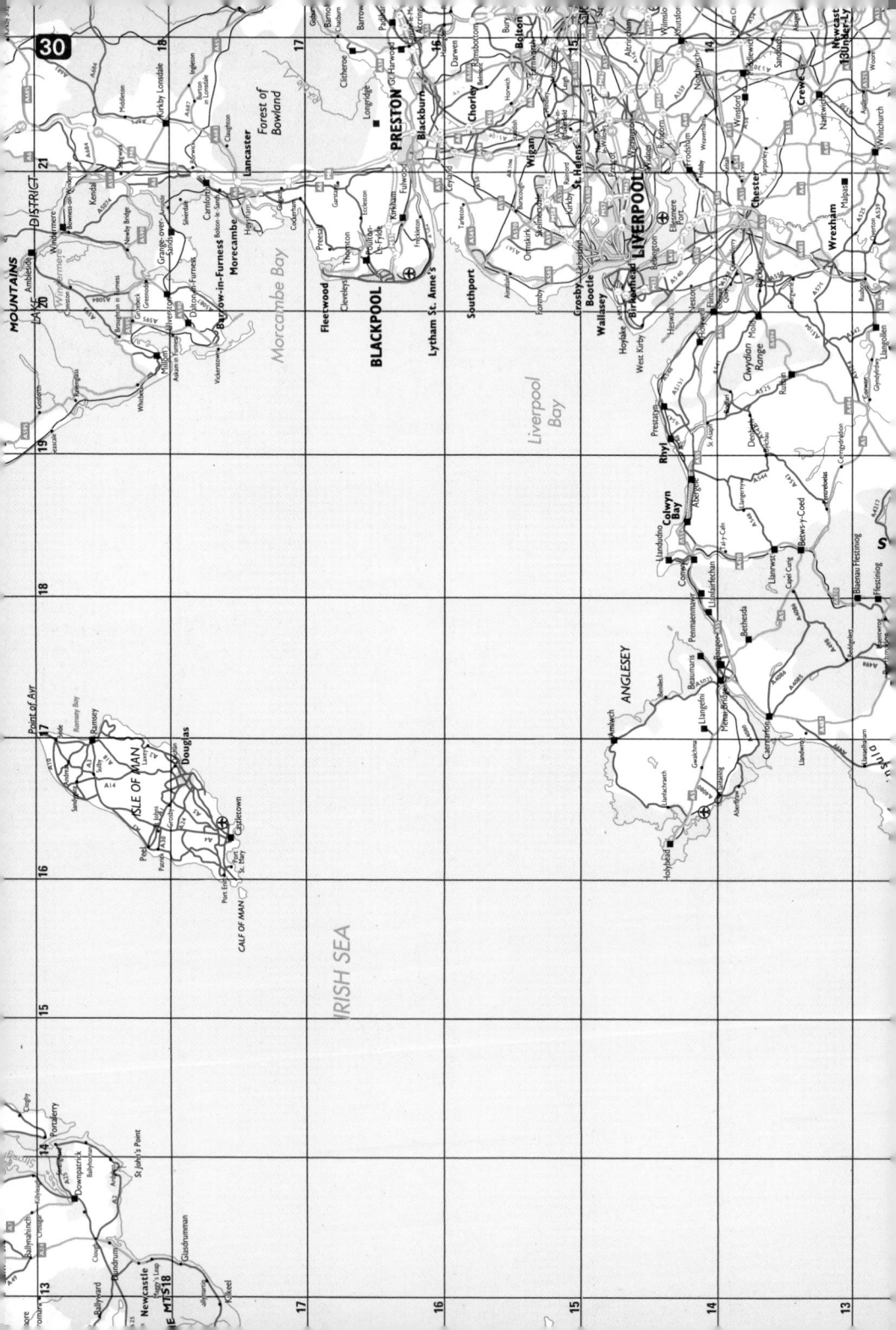

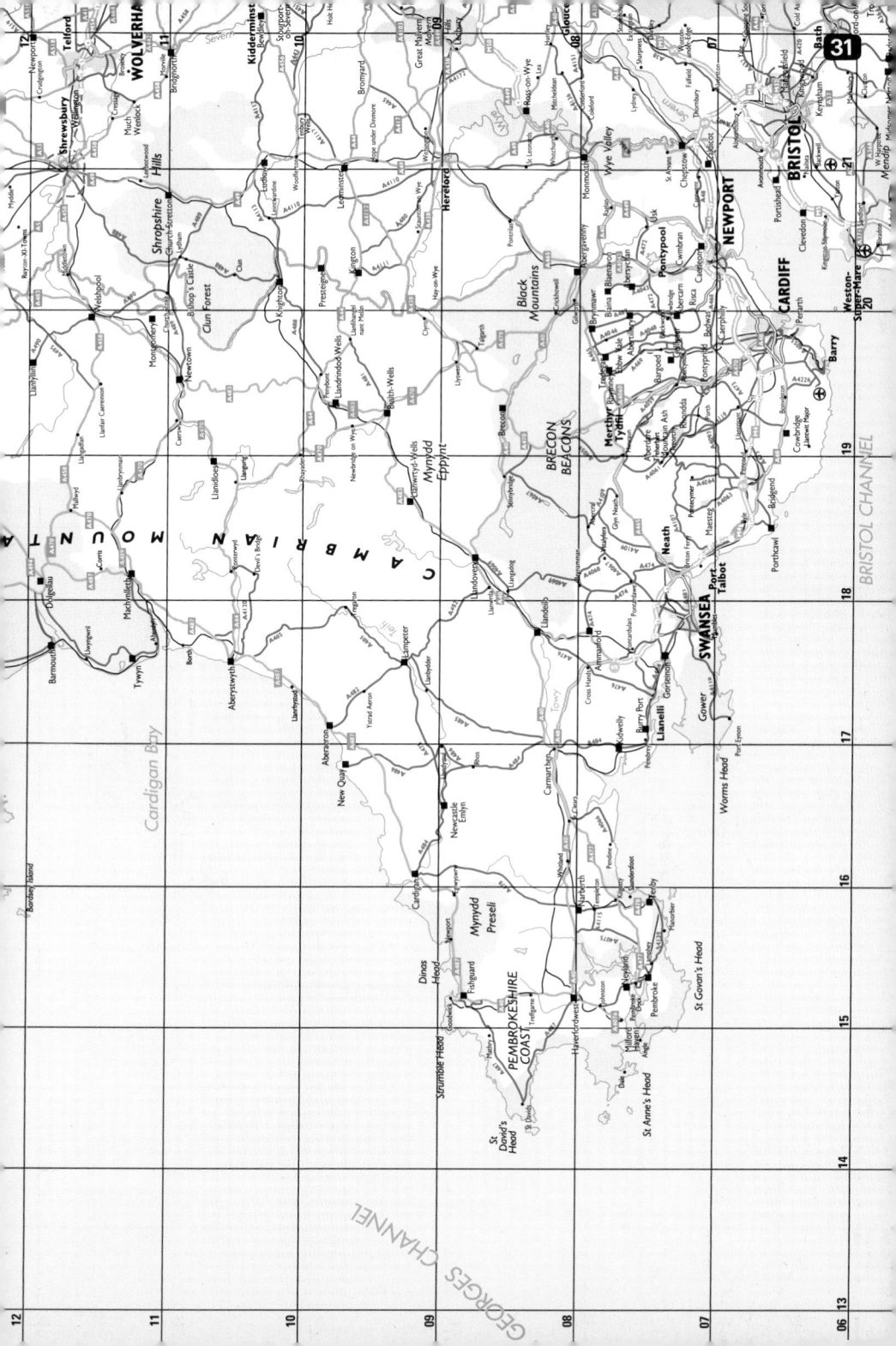

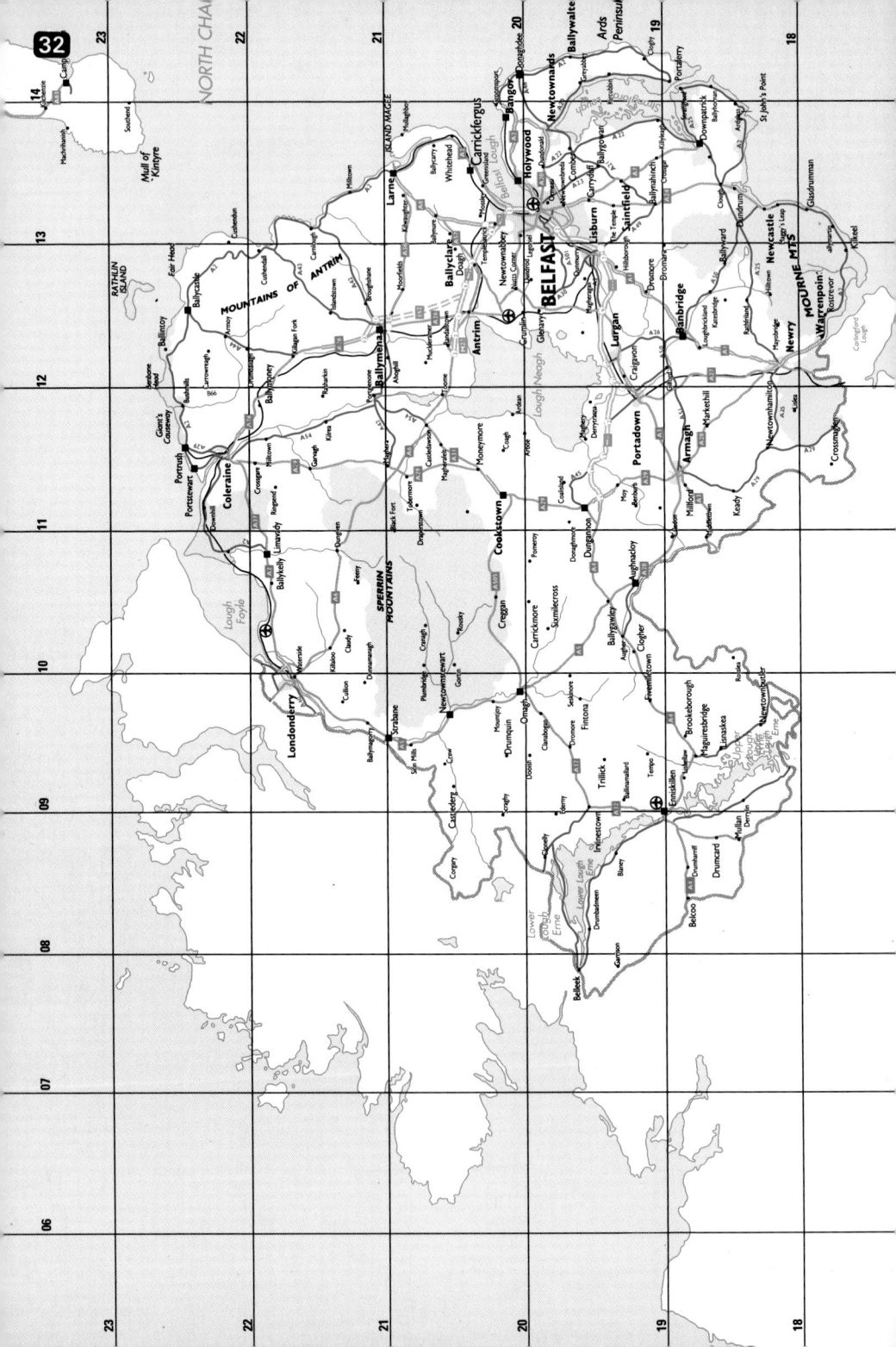

Highlands

Group Contacts: BB *Margaret Pottie* ☎/Fax 01667 462213
SC *Jessie Masheter* ☎ 01463 782423/782942

'Ceud mìle fàilte', – a hundred thousand welcomes – to the Highlands and Islands, the last great open space in Europe, a spectacular land mass and myriad islands covering nearly 15,000 square miles of unsurpassed scenic beauty. Mountains, glens, lochs, lonely sandy beaches and rugged unspoilt coastline.

Contrasting Highland landscapes provide an unrivalled backdrop for holiday activities. Enthusiasts of boating, fishing, golf, walking, birdwatching and geology are well catered for. In the land where deer and eagle roam free, wildlife lovers can also observe seals, ospreys and otters in their natural habitat. Old castles, battlefield monuments and folk museums testify to a past rich in history, culture and folklore. Land use ranges from small west coast crofts to larger hill sheep farms and to beef and grain producing units further east.

Easily accessible by road, rail and aeroplane from the south. You are assured of the clean air, peace and freedom and the traditional Highland welcome famed throughout the world. 'Haste ye back.'

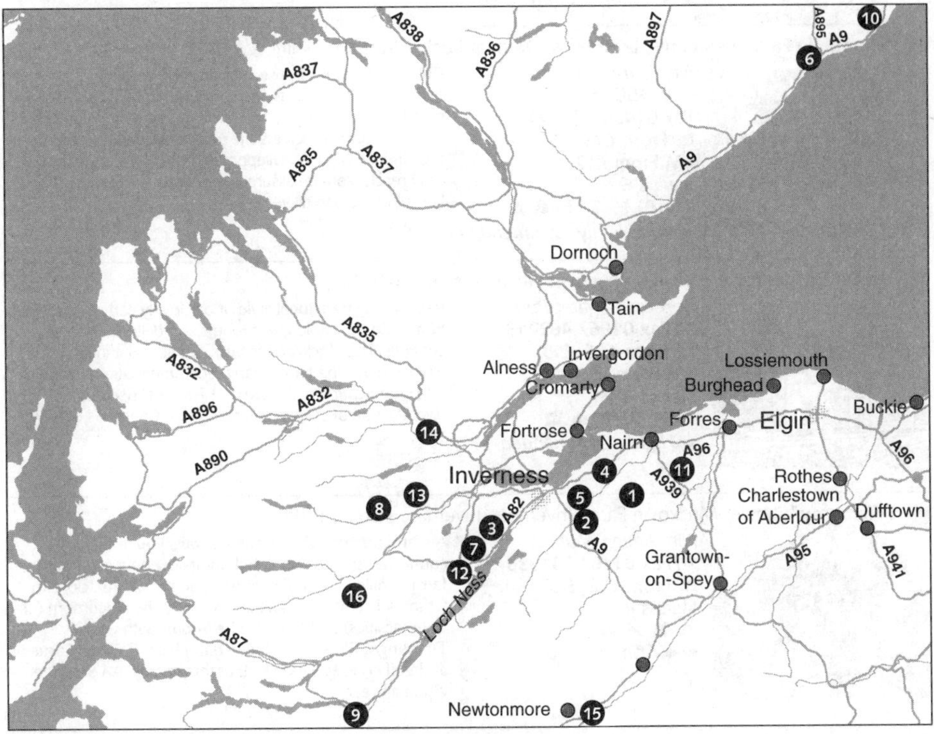

BED AND BREAKFAST

(and evening meal)

---

1 **Balaggan Farm,** Culloden Moor, By Inverness, Inverness-shire IV1 2EL

Mrs Phyllis Alexander
☎ 01463 790213
BB **From £16**
EM From £9
Sleeps 5
🛏 🐕 🛍 ☕ W

Listed *Commended*

A warm welcome awaits you on our small stock rearing farm set in peaceful surroundings. Good home cooking and baking is served. Log fires burn in lounge and dining room. 1 family and 1 twin bedroom, with electric blankets and tea/coffee-making facilities. Ideal for touring Highlands with Culloden battlefield and Cawdor Castle. Many places of interest close by. Open April–Nov.

---

2 **Daviot Mains Farm,** Daviot, Nr Inverness, Inverness-shire IV1 2ER

Margaret & Alex Hutcheson
☎ 01463 772215
Fax 01463 772099
BB **From £18–£23**
EM From £12
Sleeps 6
🛏(3) 🐕 ✂ £ 🛍 W
🌿🌿 *Highly Commended*

Comfortable early 19th century listed farmhouse in quiet situation near Inverness. Relax in the warm atmosphere of this friendly home where delicious meals are thoughtfully prepared for you (residents' license). Log fires in sitting and dining rooms. En suite/private facilities. The perfect base for exploring the Scottish Highlands. Selected by "Taste of Scotland", recommended by Elizabeth Gundrey's S.O.T.B.T. and *Which Guide*. Closed Christmas.

---

3 **Drumbuie Farm,** Drumbuie, Loch Ness, Drumnadrochit, Inverness-shire IV3 6XP

Mrs Caroline Urquhart
☎ 01456 450634
Fax 01456 450595
BB **From £16–£20**
EM From £12
Sleeps 6
🛏(10) ✂ 🕯 £ 🛍 W
🌿🌿🌿 *Highly Commended*

Custom-built farmhouse with en suite accomodation overlooking Loch Ness and sorrounding hills. Farm is mostly cattle including several Highland (hairy) cows and calves. Drumnadrochit is the perfect base when visiting the Highlands. Skye, Ullapool and the North all within easy reach. You are assured of a Scottish welcome at Drumbuie. Open all year.

---

4 **Easter Dalziel Farm,** Dalcross, Inverness, Inverness-shire IV1 2JL

Bob & Margaret Pottie
☎/Fax 01667 462213
BB **From £16–£19**
EM From £12
Sleeps 6
🛏 🐕 £ ✗ 🛍 W
🌿 *Highly Commended*

Relax in the traditional style of our lovely early Victorian home. Comfortable guest rooms and delicious home cooking. This stock/arable farm provides the ideal Highland touring base. Many recommendations including *The Good Guide to Britain* and *The Best Bed and Breakfast* guide. Open all year except Christmas & New Year.

---

5 **"Taransay",** Lower Muckovie Farm, Inverness, Inverness-shire IV1 2BB

Mrs Aileen Munro
☎/Fax 01463 231880
BB **From £18–£20**
Sleeps 4
🛏 🐕 ✂ 🛍

🌿🌿 *Commended*

A warm and friendly welcome awaits you at this comfortable, well-appointed bungalow on a quiet dairy farm. 2 miles south of Inverness, on the old A9, close to Drumossie Hotel. Magnificent views. 1 twin bedroom (en suite facilities) and 1 double bedroom, both with TV. TV lounge. Close to Culloden battlefield, Cawdor Castle and golf courses. Good restaurants nearby. AA Selected. Open all year.

Upper Latheron Farm, Latheron, Caithness KW5 6DT   **6**

Mrs Camilla Sinclair
☎ 01593 741224
🅱🅱 From £16–£17
Sleeps 6
♿ 🐕 ✄ 🛏 ♨ W
Listed *Highly Commended*

This attractive farm is idyllically situated with breathtaking views of the coastline. Excellent coastal or hill walks with abundant wildlife. See seals and puffins at John O'Groats, explore castles, ancient cairns, attend Highland gatherings, take day trip to Orkney Isles or just relax on farm. Frolicsome foals, pet lambs and Sarah, the Jersey cow always enjoy attention. AA recommended QQQ Open May–Sept.

SELF-CATERING

Achmony Holidays, Drumnadrochit, by Loch Ness IV3 6UX   **7**

Mrs Elizabeth Mackintosh
☎ 01456 450357
Fax 01456 450830
🆂🅲 From £190–£490
Sleeps 6
♿ ☕ 🛏 ♨ W
🌺🌺🌺🌺 *De Luxe*

Enjoy your holiday in an idyllic location above Loch Ness. Each 3 bedroomed chalet bungalow is situated to afford maximum privacy in over 40 acres of silver birch-studded hillside. Central for touring (car essential), Drumnadrochit has several hotels, restaurants, shops, exhibition centres, pony trekking, fishing and boat trips on Loch Ness. Open Mar–Nov.

Culligran Cottages, Glen Strathfarrar, Struy, Nr Beauly, Inverness-shire IV4 7JX   **8**

Frank & Juliet
Spencer-Nairn
☎/Fax 01463 761285
🆂🅲 From £99–£399
Sleeps 5/7
♿ 🐕 ☕ ♨ 🛏 W
🌺🌺🌺 *Commended to*
Highly Commended

A regular? You soon could be. So don't delay – send for a brochure! This is your opportunity to stay on a deer farm within the beautiful Strathfarrar Nature Reserve. Watch the wild deer from your window and feed the farm deer during a conducted tour. Choice of chalet or cottage. Bikes for hire. Salmon and trout fishing. Hotel and inn nearby. Open late Mar–mid Nov.

Easter Dalziel Farm, Dalcross, Inverness, Inverness-shire IV1 2JL   **4**

Bob & Margaret Pottie
☎/Fax 01667 462213
🆂🅲 From £120–£385
Sleeps 4/6
♿ 🐕 ⅏ 🛏 ✕ W
🌺🌺🌺 – 🌺🌺🌺🌺
Commended to Highly
Commended

Enjoy a relaxing holiday in our cosy, traditional stonebuilt cottages. Between Inverness and Nairn on our stock/ arable farm. A truly central location from which to explore the Highlands. The local area offers a wide range of activities to suit the sports-minded, tourer or walker alike. Look out for dolphins, badgers and buzzards, visit Cawdor, Culloden, Fort George and Loch Ness. Short breaks or long stays welcome all year. Brochure. Open all year.

Great Glen Holidays, Torlundy Farm, Torlundy, Fort Wlliam PH33 6SW   **9**

C Carver
☎ 01397 703015
Fax 01397 703304
🆂🅲 From £250–£395
Sleeps 4/5
♿ 🐕 🛏 🏹 ☕ ♨ ✕ W
🌺🌺🌺 *Commended*

For a great family holiday stay in our Scandinavian timber lodges situated in a quiet wooded site with spectacular views of Ben Nevis. There are 8 comfortable 2-bedroomed lodges with linen provided. Horse riding, trout fishing and farm walks. Ideal for touring the West Highlands. Open all year.

10   Greenhill Farmhouse, Mid-Clyth, Lybster, Caithness, Highland KW3 6BA

Mrs Camilla Sinclair
☎ 01593 741224
[SC] From £150–£375
Sleeps 6
Highly Commended

Relax in the romantic Highlands amidst tranquil surroundings and enjoy magnificent coastal scenery from your bedroom window. Beautifully renovated farmhouse with all mod cons offers high standard of comfort and cleanliness. For the energetic there is a wide range of outdoor activities. Enjoy a day trip to Orkney. Perfect centre for exploring the far north and discovering its exceptional attractions. Open all year.

---

11   Laikenbuie Holidays, Nairn, Moray Firth IV12 5QN

Thérèse Muskus
☎ 01667 454630
[SC] From £100–£436
Sleeps 6
Highly Commended

Watch roe deer and osprey among the abundant wildlife on tranquil organic croft (cows, sheep, hens) with beautiful outlook over trout loch amid natural birch woods. Large warm chalet (quality unbeaten) or residential caravan provide luxury accommodation. Excellent holiday centre, safe for children, low rainfall, plentiful sunshine, sandy beaches and dolphins. Near Loch Ness, Cairngorms, Cawdor Castle. Colour brochure. Open all year.

---

12   Larch Cottage, Borlum Farm, Drumnadrochit, Inverness, Inverness-shire IV3 6XN

Mrs Vanessa MacDonald-Haig
☎/Fax 01456 450358
[SC] From £185–£465
⚡ (by arrangement)
Commended

Borlum Farm is a working hill farm with its own BHS-approved riding centre. The self-catering cottage is spacious, comfortable, and tastefully furnished, with splendid views overlooking Loch Ness. Excellently equipped, including microwave cooker, hair dryer and even hot water bottle! Oil-fired central heating also available if required in colder periods. Open all year.

---

13   Mains of Aigas, By Beauly, Inverness-shire IV4 7AD

Mrs Jessie Masheter
☎/Fax 01463 782423
[SC] From £160–£420
Sleep 4/6
[W] **Guide dogs only**
Commended to Highly Commended

Absorb the peace and quiet of this beautiful, unspoilt area. Enjoy special guest rates on our own challenging 9-hole golf course, tour the Highland beauty spots, study the abundant wildlife or simply "stay at home", relax and unwind. Comfortable attractive courtyard house and self-contained apartments. Open Mar–Nov.

---

14   Scatwell Farm, Comrie, Contin, Strathpeffer, Ross-shire IV14 9EN

Margaret Cuthbert
☎/Fax 01997 466234
[SC] From £160–£280
Sleep 5/9
Approved to Commended

Two comfortable cottages in a quiet location in beautiful Strathconon. Ideal for fishing, hill walking, bird-watching and as a touring base yet only 25 miles north of Inverness. Come and see the Red deer, salmon, eagles and abundant wildlife. Electric heating, well equipped kitchens, TV's, cot available. Prices include linen, electricity on meter, laundry on site. Fishing arranged. Illustrated brochure on request. Open Apr–Oct.

---

15   Strone Cottage, c/o Lochbuie Croft, Newtonmore, Inverness-shire PH20 1BA

Mary Mackenzie
☎/Fax 01540 673504
[SC] From £180–£410
Sleeps 6
Commended

You'll be very welcome at our croft on the outskirts of our lovely Highland village. Cosy renovated cottage has open fire, double glazing and CH. Downstairs en suite bedroom, upstairs 2 bedrooms and bathroom with small drying area. Electricity & coal incl. Enjoy peace and scenery, visit local attractions or take part in varied activities. Central for touring. Edinburgh 2 hours, Loch Ness 1 hour, Aviemore 15 mins. Brochure/special offers. Open all year.
E mail: MMacKenzie@Sprite.co.uk

Tomich Holidays, Guisachan Farm, Tomich, by Beauly, Inverness-shire IV4 7LY   16

Mr & Mrs D J Fraser
☎ 01456 415332
Fax 01456 415499
SC From £150–£450
Sleeps 4–6

Our magnificent farm steading houses three luxury cottages and a heated indoor swimming pool. Other accommodation is in spacious chalets set in woodland and a Victorian dairy. All have central heating, hot water and electricity included in the price. Tomich, in the depths of the Highlands near Glen Affric, is an ideal base for walking, touring or just relaxing. Open all year.

☞ ♞ ← ⚮ £ W
♨ ♨ ♨ *Commended to Highly Commended*

FARM HOLIDAY BUREAU

Our Internet Address is
http://www.webscape.co.uk/farmaccom/

CONFIRM BOOKINGS

Disappointments can arise from misunderstandings over the telephone. Please write to confirm your booking.

FINDING YOUR ACCOMMODATION

FARM HOLIDAY BUREAU

The Group contacts at the beginning of each section can always help you find a vacancy in your chosen area.

Oban, Mull, Kintyre & Fort William

Group Contact: *Mrs Kathie Lambie* ☎ *01866 833339*

Settle into a slower pace of life, from Fort William in the lands of Lochaber down the Argyll coast to Oban on to Loch Awe and following its length on through to the Kintyre peninsula. Miss the hustle and bustle, hop across to Arran then on to the Ayrshire coast and home.

Fort William is an ideal holiday base on the mainland with its year round tourist facilities and ski resort. Take the coast road to Oban, the 'Gateway to the Isles', or the road through mighty Glen Coe with its haunting atmosphere. Enchantment awaits you in Argyll, stately homes, famous gardens, historic sites, castles, nature trails and sandy beaches. Follow Loch Awe, the longest freshwater loch in Scotland, through to mid Argyll and on to Kintyre. The charming traditional village of Carradale is a popular holiday destination. Holiday makers are welcomed by the friendly inhabitants of this unspoilt village which boasts a fine sandy beach over 5 miles long. A 9-hole golf course offers an interesting challenge if you can take your eyes off the scenery. In Campeltown there is a whisky distillery and a famous creamery where you can watch cheese being made. Why not leave your car at Tayinloan and hire a bike on Gigha, the ideal way to see the island. A warm highland welcome awaits you.

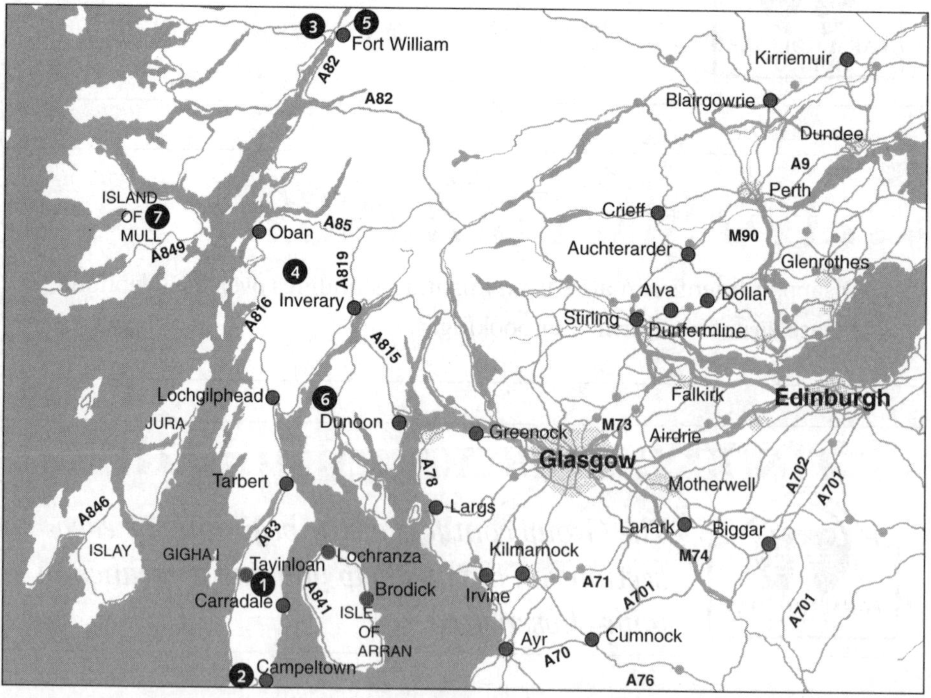

BED AND BREAKFAST

(and evening meal)

Mains Farm, Carradale, Campbeltown, Argyll PA28 6QG ①

Mrs Dorothy MacCormick
☎ **01583 431216**
🅱 **From £15.50**
EM from £7
Sleeps 6
🛏 ⛺
Listed *Commended*

Comfortable accommodation in traditional farmhouse five minutes' walk from mile-long safe beach, forest walks. Golf and river fishing. Scenic views of Isle of Arran over the Kilbrannon Sound and picturesque fishing harbour. Good home cooking and warm hospitality with coal fires and heating in rooms. Not suitable for disabled visitors. Open Apr–Oct.

Ormsary Farm, Southend, By Campbeltown, Argyll PA28 6RN ②

Mrs Inez Ronald
☎ **01586 830665**
🅱 **From £17–£19**
EM From £7
Sleeps 6
🛏 ⛺ 🧳 ⚓
🌺 🌺 *Commended*

Situated 10 miles south of Campbeltown close to the famous and beautiful Mull of Kintyre, Ormsary Farm is a small dairy and sheep farm. Comfortable accommodation, traditional cooking and home baking. Two en suite bedrooms, one double downstairs with washbasin. Championship golf course nearby, sandy beaches, fishing, birdwatching. Open May–Sept.

Strone Farm, By Banavie, Fort William PH33 7PB ③

Eileen Cameron
☎ **01397 712773**
🅱 **From £18–£25**
Sleeps 6
🛏(5) ✂ 🛁
🌺 🌺 *Commended*

A friendly welcome awaits you in our beautiful farmhouse which sits in a rural setting with magnificent panoramic views of Ben Nevis and Caledonian Canal. All double bedrooms tastefully decorated with en suite facilities and hostess tray. Large lounge with woodburning stove. Fresh food well presented. Open Feb–Sept.

Thistle-Doo, Kilchrenan, by Taynuilt, Oban, Argyll PA35 1HF ④

K Lambie
☎ **01866 833339**
🅱 **From £17–£21**
EM from £10
Sleeps 6
🛏 ✂ 🏕 ⚓
🌺 🌺 🌺 *Commended*

Awe-inspiring view of Loch Awe from our friendly family-run establishment. Ideal for all outdoor activities. Very peaceful and relaxing. 20 miles east of Oban, taking the B845 off the A85 at Taynuilt to the shore of Loch Awe. Open all year.

FARM HOLIDAY BUREAU

Please mention **Stay on a Farm** when booking

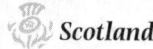

SELF-CATERING

⑤ Dalaraban, Upper Achintore, Fort Wlliam PH33 6JR

Eileen Cameron
☎ **01397 712773**
⑤ **From £250–£600**
Sleeps 8
🐕 💼

🏵🏵🏵🏵 *Commended*

Large, superior detached house comfortably accommodating 8. Set in superb rural location perched on a hill above Fort William in an unrivalled position with spectacular panoramic views. Three bedrooms upstairs, 1 on ground level, all with wash basin and electric blankets. Open fire starter pack, oil-fired CH. Electricity and linen included. Open all year.

---

⑥ Maymore, Glendaruel, By Dunoon Argyll PA22 3AE

Shona Mackellar
☎ **01369 820209**
⑤ **From £235–£480**
Sleeps 9
🐕 🐎

🏵🏵 *Approved*

This traditional family farmhouse overlooks glorious, peaceful Glendaruel in the heart of Cowal off the A886. Dunoon, Inverary, Kintyre ferry , Bute ferry, all within ½ hr. Super spot for a refreshing holiday. Touring, cruising, country pursuits. Three bedrooms upstairs and on ground level a second bathroom, two bedrooms. Open fire, cot, sunroom, walled garden, swing. Open Apr–Oct.

---

⑦ Torlochan, Gruline, Isle of Mull, Argyll PA71 6HR

Diana McFarlane
☎/Fax **01680 300380**
⑤ **From £205–£285**
Sleeps 4
🐕 🐎 ✂ 💼 🎾 🎇

🏵🏵🏵 – 🏵🏵🏵🏵
Commended to Highly Commended

Situated in 26 acres, Torlochan is surrounded by beautiful scenery in the centre of the Isle of Mull. Our working croft has 2 cottages with open fires and 2 log cabins, all with the 'comforts of home'. Also an old-fashioned tea room, unusual animals, children's play area and woodland walk. Open all year.

Grampian

Group Contact: *Rhona Cruickshank* ☎ *01464 841229*

The eagle soaring in the sky over a vastness of magnificent scenery sets the stage on this beautiful part of Scotland where the air is pure, time is of the essence, and the welcome is from the heart. On your travels relish the heather-clad mountains – a skiers' paradise in winter, the walkers and hill climber's paradise in summer, and home of the red deer. Sample the delights of the unspoilt north-east where farming and fishing go hand in hand. Follow the long winding rivers of the Spey and Dee renowned for salmon and trout and meander through the rich agricultural land famed for its quality stock and crops. Along the coastline are numerous, picturesque fishing villages and harbours, interspersed with quiet, attractive beaches. Attend the many agricultural shows and famous Highland Games held throughout the summer. Enhance your knowledge of the area by exploring Royal Deeside and the 'Trails' – choose from either the Castle, Whisky, Coastal or Victorian Heritage. If golf is your forte there are umpteen championship courses to try out. There are also numerous facilities for pony trekking, fishing, shooting and watersports to suit all standards.

Whatever your interest, there is ample to whet your appetite and give you a holiday to remember.

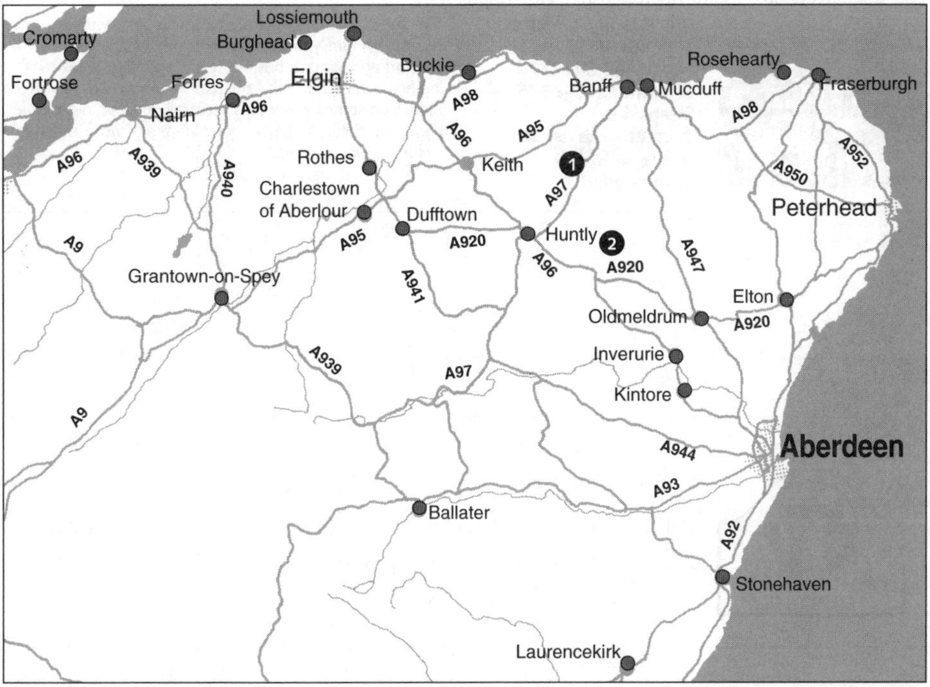

BED AND BREAKFAST

(and evening meal)

---

1 **The Bungalow,** Yonder Bognie, Forgue, By Huntly, Aberdeenshire AB54 6BR

Paula Ross
☎ **01466 730375**
BB **From £15–£18**
EM From £7.50
Sleeps 4
☙ ♞ ♨ ✂
❦ *Commended*

Comfortable accommodation near Huntly on castle and whisky trails. Central heating throughout, residents' lounge with colour TV. En suite bedrooms have electric blankets, colour TV, tea/coffee-making facilities and hairdryers. Food hygiene certificate held. French and Italian spoken. Warm welcome assured. Open all year.

SELF-CATERING

---

2 **Logie Newton,** Huntly, Aberdeenshire AB54 6BB

Mrs Rhona Cruickshank
☎ **01464 841229**
Fax 01464 841277
SC **From £200–£375**
Sleeps 4,6
♞ ☙ ♞ ⊞ ♨ ✗ Ⓦ
❦❦❦ *Highly Commended*

Two superior country cottages in castle and whisky country on family farm where warmth, cleanliness, comfort and Scottish hospitality are priorities. Relax by a log fire in winter or enjoy the panoramic view at dusk from Kirkhill on summer evenings. Centrally heated, dishwasher, play area, children's pony rides. Linen, electricity and logs included. Open all year.

Angus Tayside

Group Contact: *Mrs Deanna Lindsay* ☎/Fax 01307 462887

Whatever you seek in Scotland, you'll find in Angus, where the Braes of Angus meet the valley of Strathmore. From the glens with their gushing waterfalls to the numerous sandy beaches and bays along the east coast.

Visit Glamis Castle, former home of Queen Elizabeth the Queen Mother and birthplace of Princess Margaret, or Kirriemuir, birthplace of poet J.M. Barrie (Peter Pan). National Trust places of interest include the House of Dun (Adam), the Angus Folk Museum and many others.

Many sports are available, including hill-walking, birdwatching, riding, bowls, swimming, sailing and leisure centre sports. You can fish on the shores and banks of rivers and lochs, or hire a boat and fish the sea. Golf is Angus' most famous sport and can be enjoyed on a wide variety of courses: you can play a different course each day!

The Heritage Trail is a must for the visitor to our area, and Arbroath Abbey, Brechin Cathedral, Restenneth Priory and various Pictish standing stones and hill forts should be seen.

Angus is also an ideal touring base for a day visit to either Aberdeen, Dundee, Perth, St Andrews, Edinburgh or Balmoral. All Group hold Food Hygiene Certificates.

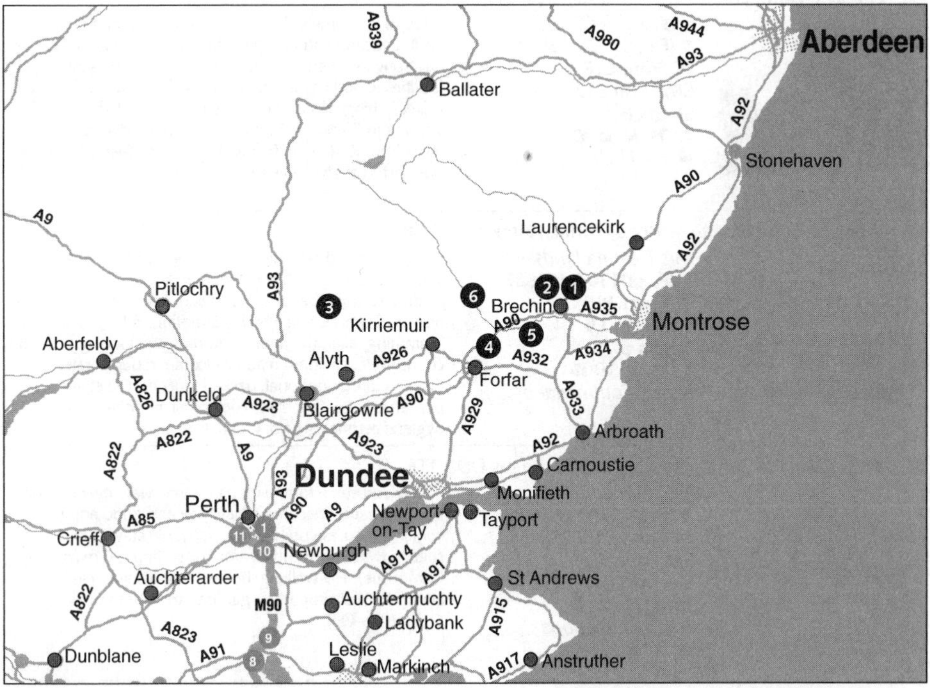

BED AND BREAKFAST

(and evening meal)

---

1 **Blibberhill Farm,** By Brechin, Angus, Tayside DD9 6TH

Mrs Wendy Stewart
☎/Fax 01307 830323
BB From £16
EM From £9
Sleeps 6
🐴 ⚰ Å ♨
🐝🐝 *Commended*

Peacefully situated near Glamis, 1 hour's drive from Royal Deeside and St Andrews, cental to many golf courses, fishing and hillwalking. Tastefully decorated and furnished en suite rooms with TV and tea/coffee facilities. Warm welcome assured. All home cooking, baking and preserves. Beautiful large garden. Many animals. Excellent children's facilities. Open all year excluding Christmas.

---

2 **Brathinch Farm,** by Brechin, Angus DD9 7QX

Rosemary Beatty
☎ 01356 648292
Fax 01356 648003
BB From £15–£20
Sleeps 6
🐴 ♨
🐝 *Commended*

18th century farmhouse on a family-run, working arable farm with a large garden. Situated off the B966 between Brechin and Edzell. Easy access to Angus glens, country walks, golf and other attractions. Open all year.

---

3 **Purgavie Farm,** Lintrathen, Kirriemuir DD8 5HZ

Mrs Moira Clark
☎/Fax 01575 560213
BB From £18–£20
EM From £12
Sleeps 6
🐴 🛏 Å ♨ W
🐝🐝🐝 *Highly Commended*

A warm welcome in homely accommodation on our farm set in peaceful countryside with excellent views. All rooms have private or en suite bathroom, TV and tea-making facilities. Good home cooking providing traditional Scottish fayre. Fishing on Lintrathen loch, pony trekking and hill-walking in Glen Isla. Glamis Castle 10 miles. Located 7 miles from Kirriemuir, follow the B951 to Glen Isla; farm signposted at roadside. Open all year.

---

4 **Wemyss Farm,** Montrose Road, Forfar, Angus DD8 2TB

Mrs Deanna Lindsay
☎/Fax 01307 462887
BB From £15
EM From £9
Sleeps 6
🐴 🐾 Å ♨ 🆒 W
Listed *Commended*

190-acre mixed farm situated on the B9113 with a wide variety of animals. Ideal for touring Angus Glens, St Andrews, Royal Deeside, Aberdeen, Edinburgh, east coast resorts. Glamis Castle nearby. Shooting, fishing, golf, swimming, all in the area. Bedrooms overlooking beautiful countryside. Children made welcome, reduced rates. Evening dinner optional, packed lunches. Quiet and peaceful, yet within easy reach of all amenities. Food hygiene certificate held. Open all year.

---

5 **West Mains of Turin,** Rescobie, Forfar, Angus DD8 2TE

Mrs Catherine Jolly
☎/Fax 01307 830229
BB From £15–£19
EM From £9
Sleeps 6
🐴 🛏 🐾 🎾 W
🐝🐝 *Commended*

Family-run stock farm with panoramic view over Rescobie Loch. A warm welcome awaits you and good home cooking ensures you have an enjoyable stay. Two en suite/private rooms. Ideal area for golfing (20 mins from Carnoustie). Hill walking, horse riding, fishing, castles, National Trust properties, gardens and our local glens. Open Mar–Oct.

Wood of Auldbar, Aberlemno, By Brechin, Angus, Tayside DD9 6SZ **6**

Jean Stewart
☎ 01307 830218
BB From £15
EM From £9.50
Sleeps 6
☷ ☗ ✄ Ⓦ
Listed *Commended*

Wood of Auldbar is a family farm of 187 acres with lovely farmhouse in first class condition. Very central for touring the Angus Glens, Royal Deeside, Balmoral, Glamis; many more castles within easy reach. Beaches, nature walks, birdwatching, fishing, golf, leisure facilities all near at hand. Standing stones and lovely churches. Excellent farmhouse cooking in award-winning farmhouse. Food hygiene certificate held. Tea facilities in all bedrooms. A warm welcome awaits you. Open all year.

SELF-CATERING

Purgavie Farm, Lintrathen, Kirriemuir DD8 5HZ **3**

Mrs Moira Clark
☎/Fax 01575 560213
SC From £200–£400
EM From £12
Sleeps 4/6
⚲ ☷ ☗ Å ⊕ ♨ Ⓦ
❀❀❀❀ *Commended to Highly Commended*

Escape the stress and relax in our Swedish log house or bungalow and enjoy the panoramic views of the lovely countryside. Explore the hills and see the widlife or fish in Lintrathen loch. Properties furnished to a high standard with dishwasher, shower, fridge freezer, washer dryer, payphone and microwave. Open fire in bungalow. Located 7 miles from Kirriemuir, follow B951 signposted at roadside. Open all year.

NO ANSWER?

Farmers are mostly out and about during the day.
Try to telephone before 9.30am or after 4pm.

FOLLOW THE COUNTRY CODE

Leave nothing but footprints,
Take nothing but photographs,
Kill nothing but time!

Scotland
Perthshire

Group Contacts: 📖 *Jo Andrew* ☎ *01350 724254*
           🆂🅲 *Nigel Bruges* ☎ *01350 724208/724241*

Perthshire lies in the very centre of Scotland. For centuries the area has been the crossroads of the nation, and today's modern road, rail and coach service networks maintain that tradition, making it the ideal base for your Scottish holiday.

Here you'll find an area of outstanding beauty, the grandeur of mountains and glens, home of the native deer and other wild animals and flowers, the glimmer of lochs, hunting ground of the rare Osprey, and the River Tay, Scotland's greatest river – a true Angler's paradise.

See Perthshire at work producing top quality glass, pottery, hand-knitted woollens, leather goods, hornware and of course 'the water of life'. In Perthshire four malt whisky distilleries invite visitors to see (and taste) this unique product.

Perthshire is famed for its agriculture from quality cattle and sheep, barley for whisky and other arable crops to field vegetables and soft fruit.

There's something for everyone here – historic castles, houses and gardens, the world's highest beech hedge, Europe's oldest living tree, Perth's ultra modern leisure pool, 25 golf courses, Perth and Pitlochry theatres and of course numerous highland nights and ceilidhs.

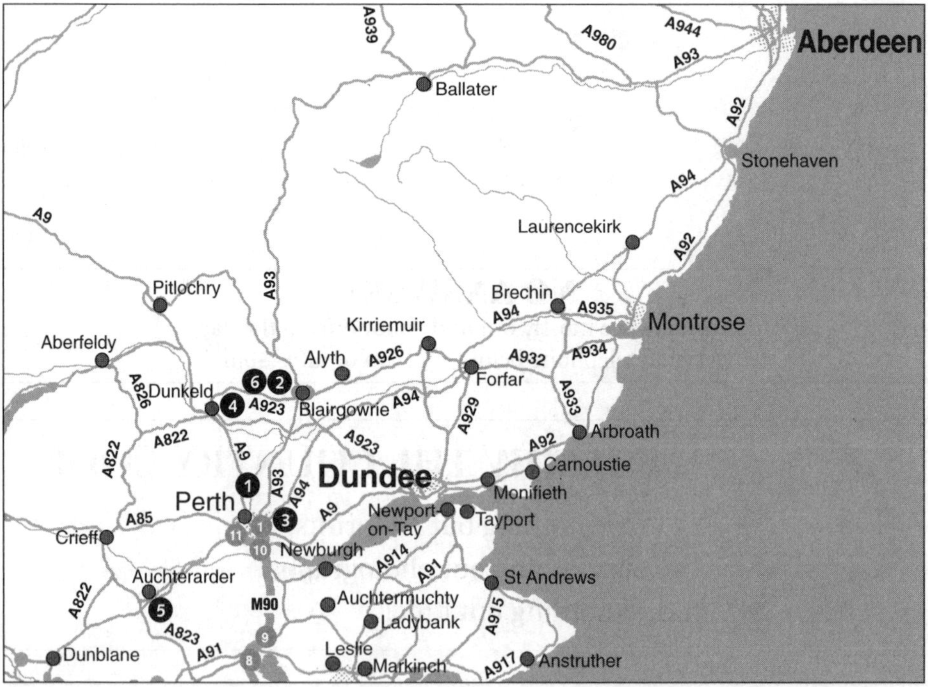

[Map of Perthshire and surrounding area showing locations including Aberdeen, Ballater, Stonehaven, Laurencekirk, Brechin, Montrose, Pitlochry, Aberfeldy, Dunkeld, Kirriemuir, Alyth, Blairgowrie, Forfar, Arbroath, Perth, Dundee, Crieff, Auchterarder, Dunblane, St Andrews, and road numbers.]

BED AND BREAKFAST

(and evening meal)

'Avonlea' at Pitmurthly, Redgorton, Nr. Luncarty, Perth PH1 3HX

Mrs Christine Smith
☎ 01738 828363
Fax 01738 828053
BB From £17–£20
Sleeps 5
⏰(9) ✂ 🖼
🌺🌺 *Highly Commended*

Quiet, comfortable farmhouse in ideal touring location set amidst lovely countryside yet only 5 minutes from historic Perth with its unique shops and excellent restaurants. Log fires and full CH. Working farm with plenty to watch. Golf, fishing, riding and swimming can be arranged. Warm welcome assured. Open all year except Dec & Jan.

Bankhead, Clunie, Blairgowrie, Perthshire PH10 6SG

Mrs H Wightman
☎/Fax 01250 884281
BB From £18–£20
EM From £8
Sleeps 5
⏰ 🐾 ✂ 🖼
🌺 *Commended*

A friendly and peaceful atmosphere awaits you on our family-run farm. Traditional farmhouse cooking using our own free range eggs and raspberries. Log fire, CH. Two ground floor bedrooms with electric blankets, tea/coffee facilities. Ideally situated for touring Perthshire and beyond. Enjoy birdwatching at Loch of Lowes, walking on hills above Dunkeld, fishing on local lochs. Glenshee ski slopes 40 mins. Open Jan–Nov.

Blackcraigs Farm, Scone, Perthshire PH2 7PJ

Irene Millar
☎/Fax 01821 640254
BB From £16–£20
Sleeps 6
⏰ 🐾 ✂ 🖼
🌺🌺 *Commended*

18th century farmhouse set in a well maintained garden where a warm welcome awaits you. Relax and enjoy the quiet, peaceful surroundings. Comfortable bedrooms all with colour TV and tea/coffee-making facilities. Elegant residents' lounge with an open fire. The Fair City of Perth has lots of charm and many amenities and is only 4 miles away. Golf and fishing nearby. Ideally situated for a quiet holiday. Open all year.

Letter Farm, Loch of Lowes, By Dunkeld, Perthshire PH8 0HH

Jo Andrew
☎/Fax 01350 724254
BB From £20–£27
Sleeps 6
⏰ 🐾 ✂ 🎄 🖼
🌺🌺 *Highly Commended*

Enjoy our recently renovated farmhouse, kingsize beds in en suite rooms, log fire in guest lounge and good home baking. Our family-run stock farm nestles next to the Loch of Lowes Wildlife Reserve, home to ospreys, otters and others. It exudes peace and tranquillity – come see for yourselves, you'll be warmly welcomed. Closed Christmas, New Year and April.

> Although the majority of farms will accept *'Stay on a Farm'* Gift Tokens, please check when booking to avoid disappointment.

SELF-CATERING

---

⑤ Milton of Duchally Cottage, Millhill Farm, Auchterarder PH3 1PQ

Jennifer Davidson
☎ 01764 662227
Fax 01764 664033
🆂 From £200–£450
Sleeps 4 + cot
🐶 🛉 ⚲ ▄
🌼🌼🌼🌼 *Highly Commended*

Very comfortable, well equipped, two bedroomed detached cottage. Tumble drier, auto washing machine, coffee maker, colour TV, living room with open fire. Cot, high chair, play pen, stairgates available. Fenced garden with furniture. Ideal for golfing and touring central Scotland. Three miles from shops. If you like peace and quiet this is the cottage for you. Open Apr–Oct.

---

⑥ Wester Riechip, Laighwood, Butterstone, Dunkeld, Perthshire PH8 0HB

W & WI Bruges
☎ 01350 724241/724208
🆂 From £352–£545
Sleeps 8
🐶 ☕ ▄ ✄ 🅦
🌼🌼🌼🌼 *De Luxe*

Wester Riechip has been constructed from the west wing of a 19th century shooting lodge to create a luxurious detached holiday house with superb modern facilities. Comfortably accommodates 8. Spectacular views over surrounding hills and lochs. An ideal base for touring, golfing and birdwatching. Shooting and fishing available on our family-run hill farm. Open all year.

CONFIRM BOOKINGS

Disappointments can arise from misunderstandings over the telephone.
Please write to confirm your booking.

FINDING YOUR ACCOMMODATION

FARM HOLIDAY BUREAU

The Group contacts at the beginning of each section can always help you find a vacancy in your chosen area.

Kingdom of Fife

Group Contact: *Mrs Kathleen Baird* ☎ *01337 840218*

The Kingdom of Fife, a Kingdom shaped by it's coastline has miles of clean sandy beaches and quaint fishing villages. Visit the Fisheries Museum at Ansthruther and the Sea Life Centre in St Andrews where you can watch the seals being fed. There are country parks with something for all the family and a wealth of delightful and fascinating museums which includes the Ceres Folk Museum and the Secret Bunker.

For those who are interested in history there is an abundance of places to visit. Dunfrermline Abbey, Falkland with its Royal Palace, Kellie Castle near Pittenweem, and St Andrews, The Scottish Deer Centre, near Cupar, and the Ostrich Centre are well worth a visit. St Andrews the home of golf has many fine courses including the Old Course, venue of the British Open Golf.

Fife is blessed with a sunny climate, a wide range of holiday activities can be found for the energetic members of the family which includes gliding, sailing, golf, cycling, birdwatching, walking and sightseeing.

Fife is easily reached by road and rail and makes an ideal touring base for visiting Dundee, Edinburgh and Perth. Come and enjoy the hospitality of the farming families in Fife.

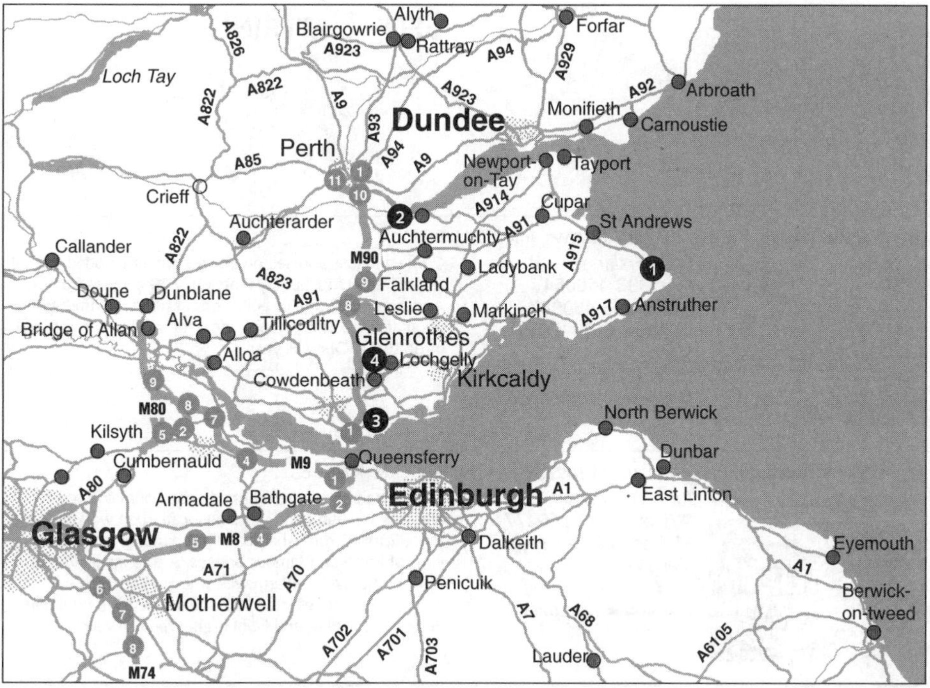

BED AND BREAKFAST

(and evening meal)

Cambo House, Kingsbarns, St Andrews, Fife KY16 8QD

Peter Erskine
☎ 01333 450054
Fax 01333 450987
BB From £35–£45
EM From £25
Sleeps 6

Highly Commended

Come and lose yourself in a glorious four-poster bed in our magnificent Victorian family home hardly touched by time, set in parkland and woods that meander down to an unspoilt coastline with a fine sweeping beach. Only 10 minutes from St. Andrews. Open all year except Christmas and New Year.

Easter Clunie Farmhouse, Easter Clunie, Newburgh, Fife KY14 6EJ

Mrs Kathleen Baird
☎ 01337 840218
BB From £16–£20
Sleeps 6

Commended

David and Kathleen Baird warmly welcome you to their 18th century centrally heated home on a working farm. Comfortable bedrooms with en suite or private facilities. Home baking and tea on arrival. Relax in walled garden, enjoy panoramic views of the River Tay. Surrounding countryside provides a wealth of scenic walks. Ideal touring base for Fife and Perthshire. Situated on A913. Open Mar–Nov.

SELF-CATERING

Cambo House, Kingsbarns, St Andrews, Fife KY16 8QD

Peter Erskine
☎ 01333 450054
Fax 01333 450987
SC From £190–£625
Sleeps 2/8

Commended

Come and lose yourself on an enchanting wooded coastal estate hardly touched by time. Only 10 minutes from St Andrews, the home of golf. Cottages and apartments in a magnificent country house. Ideal for families and groups of up to 32. Open all year.

Parkend Cottage, Parkend Farm, Crossgates, Cowdenbeath KY4 8EX

June Weatherup
☎/Fax 01383 860277
SC From £225–£350
Sleeps 6

De Luxe

Luxury traditionally refurbished 3-bedroom cottage enjoying beautiful and peaceful location on working dairy farm, 2 miles from Aberdour, with panoramic views to Firth of Forth and famous bridges. A true family 'home from home' with a warm welcome assured. Fully equipped to highest standard. Ideal base for touring Fife, Perthshire, Stirling and Edinburgh. Open all year.

Rose Cottage, Lumphinnans Farm, Cowdenbeath, Fife KY4 8HN

Isobel Wilson
☎/Fax 01592 780279
SC From £175–£300
Sleeps 6
☞ W
🌼🌼🌼🌼 *Commended*

Come and feed the lambs and see the baby calves in Spring, walk to the woods and fields with wild flowers in Summer, have a picnic in the harvest field in Autumn and feed the cows in Winter, then relax in front of the coal fire. Rose Cottage is 50 yds from the farmhouse. Open all year.

Heart of Scotland

Group Contact: *Mrs Elsie Hunter* ☎ *01236 830243*

Here at the very crossroads of Scotland, the Highlands meet the Lowlands against a scenic backcloth of mountains, shimmering lochs and glens. Cruise Loch Lomond, explore the Trossachs. Discover what so inspired Liam Neeson, star of Hollywood's 'Rob Roy' to declare: 'It's wonderful to stand there and know that these hills and mountains haven't changed in millennia – that Rob Roy and his clan actually trudged these hills, would have seen those views and marvelled at those sunsets'.

This, a land for all seasons, boasts an astonishing treasure trove of places to visit, indoors and out. Equally enticing is a wealth of local events and entertainments, traditional and modern. Lots of outdoor pursuits cater for all tastes. 'Look aboot ye.' Edinburgh, Glasgow, Perth, Linlithgow, with their rich history and present day attractions are just a short drive away. Or retreat to the more remote Campsie Fells or Ochil Hills, a walker's paradise.

Don't miss Royal Stirling, close to the battle site where William Wallace led his army to glorious victory. Recall Mel Gibson, star of the epic 'Braveheart', and how he enthused over Stirling? 'I've never had such a welcome. I've never seen anything like it'. You too can savour true hospitality in the Heart of Scotland. There's no better place to reach out and to explore the full magnificent diversity of Scotland's scenery, history and culture with the bonus of good food and comfortable farm accommodation. Motorway access is easy. Excellent rail and air links too.

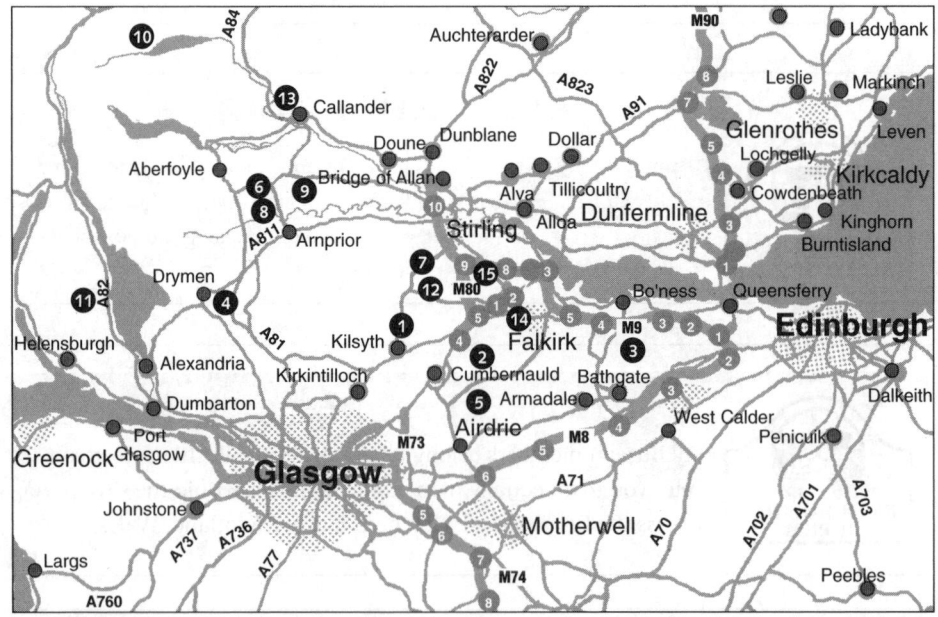

BED AND BREAKFAST

(and evening meal)

Allanfauld Farm, Kilsyth, Glasgow G65 9DF   ❶

Libby MacGregor
☎/Fax 01236 822155
[BB] **From £16**
Sleeps 4
🛏 🐕 ⅍ 💼
Listed *Commended*

A working family farm situated close to the town of Kilsyth at the foot of the Kilsyth Hills, a great base to explore central Scotland. Located near A803 with easy access to M8 and M9. Golf, fishing, hill walking and a swimming pool are all within half a mile. Glasgow, Stirling 20 minutes. 1 twin/family room, 1 single room, both with TV and tea/coffee facilities. Open all year.

Bandominie Farm, Walton Road, Castlecary, Bonnybridge FK4 2HP   ❷

Jean Forrester
☎ 01324 840284
[BB] **From £15–£16.50**
Sleeps 5
🛏 🐕 ⅍ 💼 Ⓦ
Listed *Commended*

A working farm located 2 miles from the A80 at Castlecary (B816). Easy access from Glasgow and Edinburgh. Lovely view with a homely atmosphere. Central heating, TV lounge. Ample parking. Open all year except Christmas.

Belsyde Farm, Lanark Road, Linlithgow, West Lothian EH49 6QE   ❸

Mrs Nan Hay
☎/Fax 01506 842098
[BB] **From £16–£25**
Sleeps 6
🛏 🐕 ⅍ Ⓔ 💼 ⅄ Ⓦ
🚣 *Commended*

An 18th century farmhouse located in large, secluded gardens with panoramic views over the Forth estuary. Golfing and fishing available locally. All bedrooms have washbasin (hot & cold), tea/coffee-making facilities, colour TV, central heating, 1 bedroom en suite. AA listed. Located close to M8, M9 and M90 and to Edinburgh airport. Follow A706 south-west from Linlithgow (1½ miles); first entrance on left after crossing Union Canal. Open all year except Christmas.

Easter Drumquhassle Farm, Drymen, By Loch Lomond, Stirlingshire G63 0DN   ❹

Mrs Julia Cross
☎ 01360 660893
Mobile 0410 523090
[BB] **From £15–£20**
EM From £9.50
Sleeps 8
🛏 🐕 ⅍ ⅄ 💼 ⚒ 🐾
🚣 *Commended*

Early 19th century farmhouse in quiet, rural setting with beautiful, panoramic views. Excellent home cooking, produce from our own garden. Lovely rooms with en suite facilities, colour TV, radio, tea tray. An ideal base for walking (on West Highland Way) and touring Loch Lomond and Central Scotland. Glasgow 40 minutes. Open all year.

Easter Glentore Farm, Slamannan Road, Greengairs, Airdrie, Lanarkshire ML6 7TJ   ❺

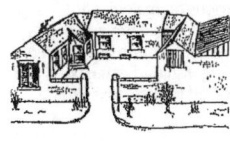

Elsie Hunter
☎/Fax 01236 830243
Mobile 0370 746950
[BB] **From £18**
Sleeps 6
🛏 ⅍ Ⓔ 💼 Ⓦ
🚣🚣 *Highly Commended*

Enjoy real Scottish hospitality in our comfortable 18th century ground floor farmhouse in beautiful countryside midway between Glasgow and Stirling on B803 (2 miles Greengairs, 30 miles Edinburgh). Quality accommodation, en suite available, tea/coffee, homebaking, alarms, guests' bathroom, lounge with panoramic views, warm friendly atmosphere. Best B&B award winner. 10 mins' drive Glasgow/Edinburgh rail line. Closed Christmas & New Year.

6 **Inchie Farm,** Port of Menteith, Stirling FK8 3JZ

Mrs Norma Erskine
☎ 01877 385233
BB From £15–£16
EM From £10
Sleeps 5
Commended

Family farm on the shores of Lake of Menteith where ospreys nest between April and Sept. Featured in 'Wish You Were Here' TV programme. Comfortable twin/family rooms both with washbasins and tea-making facilities, also guests' own bathroom and lounge with colour TV. Central heating throughout. Ideal for trout fishing or hill walking in nearby Trossachs. Open Mar–Oct.

---

7 **Lochend Farm,** Carronbridge, Denny, Stirlingshire FK6 5JJ

Jean Morton
☎ 01324 822778
BB From £16.50
Sleeps 4
(3)
Highly Commended

Peace, panoramic view and good wholesome food. Delightfully situated overlooking Loch Coulter in unspoiled countryside, yet only 5 miles from M9/M80 (jct 9). A perfect base for exploring this beautiful part of Scotland. Farmhouse centrally heated, traditionally furnished. 2 double bedrooms with washbasin, radio, tea-making facilities; also guests' own bathroom, dining room and lounge with colour TV. Selected by *'Which' Good Bed & Breakfast Guide.* Open Mar till Oct or by arrangement.

---

8 **Lochend Farm,** Port of Menteith, Stirling FK8 3JZ

Mrs Rhona Millar
☎ 01877 385235
BB From £18–£20
EM From £10
Sleeps 4
Commended

Enjoy a peaceful stay at Lochend, a mixed arable stock farm next to Scotland's only Lake in the heart of the Trossachs. Farmhouse dates back to 1726 being the former dower house of the estate. Spacious accommodation with en suite bedrooms. A warm friendly atmosphere and good home cooking await. Open April–Oct.

---

9 **Lower Tarr Farm,** Ruskie, Port of Menteith, Stirling FK8 3LG

Mrs Effie Bain
☎/Fax 01786 850202
BB From £18
EM From £10
Sleeps 6 + cot
Commended

A mixed arable farm with clear panoramic views, peaceful situation and pretty garden, with Ruskie burn running past. There are cattle, sheep and hens to be seen, plus lots of interesting wildlife. Good home cooking and baking using fresh local produce where possible. Central for touring the Trossachs, Loch Lomond, Stirling and Edinburgh. En suite room. Open Feb–Nov.

---

10 **Monachyle Mhor,** Balquhidder, Lochearnhead, Perthshire FK19 8PQ

Robert, Jean & Tom Lewis
☎ 01877 384622
Fax 01877 384305
BB From £32.50–£40
EM From £21–£25
Sleeps 10
Commended

Monachyle Mhor is an award winning 18th century hotel located in its own 2000 acre estate. All rooms are en suite and have magnificent views over Lochs Voil and Doine. The hotel is delightfully furnished with family antiques and country fabrics. Fully licensed restaurant serving interesting dishes including game and herbs from our own estate. Taste of Scotland and AA 2 stars, 2 rosettes, private fishing and stalking to guests. Closed mid–end Jan.

---

11 **Shantron Farm,** Luss, Alexandria, Dumbartonshire G83 8RH

Anne M Lennox
☎/Fax 01389 850231
Mobile 0468 378400
BB From £18–£25
Sleeps 11
Commended

Enjoy a relaxing break in a spacious bungalow with outstanding views of Loch Lomond. The farm is Morag's croft in 'High Road' and other scenes. Four miles south of Luss. Ideal for touring, hillwalking, fishing, watersports and golf on the new Loch Lomond Golf Course. En suite available. Open Mar–Nov.
E mail: rjlennox@shantron.u-net.com

The Topps Farm, Fintry Road, Denny, Stirlingshire FK6 5JF ⑫

Mrs Jennifer Steel
☎ 01324 822471
Fax 01324 823099
🅱🅱 From £19–£32
EM From £16
Sleeps 14
Commended

A modern farmhouse guesthouse in a beautiful hillside location with stunning, panoramic views. Family, double or twin-bedded rooms available, all en suite with tea/coffee, shortbread, TV, radio, telephone. Food a speciality ("Taste of Scotland" listed). Restaurant open to non-residents. A la carte menu only. Easy access to all major tourist attractions. Your enjoyment is our aim and pleasure! Open all year.

Trean Farm, Leny Feus, Callander, Perthshire FK17 8AS ⑬

Janette Donald
☎/Fax 01877 331160
🅱🅱 From £17–£20
Sleeps 6
Commended

A working farm situated in open parkland beside Callander with a 15 minute walk to shops. Outstanding views of Ben Ledi. An ideal base for touring and hill walking. 2 en suite rooms with TV and 1 with washbasin. Tea/coffee facilities. Residents' lounge. Open May–Oct.

Wester Carmuirs Farm, Larbert, By Falkirk, Stirlingshire FK5 3NW ⑭

Mrs Sheila Taylor
☎ 01324 812459
🅱🅱 From £18
Sleeps 6
Commended

Relax and enjoy friendly hospitality and good food in our comfortable home on mixed farm on A803 near Falkirk (M9/A80). Comfortable twin/double/family rooms all with washbasins and tea/coffee. Guests' own bathroom, shower room, dining room and TV room with log fire. Ideal centre to visit local attractions, eg. Mariner Centre with swimming pool; also Trossachs, Loch Lomond, Stirling, Glasgow and Edinburgh. Open Jan–Oct.

West Plean, Denny Road, Stirling FK7 8HA ⑮

Mrs Moira Johnston
☎ 01786 812208
🅱🅱 From £22
Sleeps 6
Commended

Enjoy warm Scottish farming hospitality in a historic setting, with sweeping lawns, walled garden, extensive woodland walks, surrounded by our mixed farm. We offer quality food, spacious comfort, bedrooms en suite, hot drink facilities and attentive hosts. Riding and fishing can be arranged locally. Located on the A872 Denny road, 2 minutes from M9/M80 (jct9). Open Feb–Nov.

SELF-CATERING

Shemore Farm Cottage, Shantron Farm, Luss, Alexandria, Dumbartonshire G83 8RH ⑪

Mrs Anne M Lennox
☎/Fax 01389 850231
Mobile 0468 378400
🆂🅲 From £120–£300
Sleeps 6
Commended

Regulars often return to this traditional stone cottage attractively situated on a hill sheep farm, 300 ft above Loch Lomond, over which the cottage has magnificent views. The farm has often been filmed for 'High Road' TV series. Four miles south of picturesque village of Luss. Edinburgh, Oban, Fort William, Ayr – 1½ hours. Ideal for hillwalking, fishing, watersports. Children love to feed lambs. Short breaks available. Open all year.
E mail: rjlennox@shantron.u-net.com

Around Edinburgh

Group Contact: *Mrs Geraldine Hamilton* ☎ *01501 785205*

Edinburgh generates excitement. Visual drama, an unmistakably dramatic skyline, historic buildings, elegant architecture, a guardian castle... these are the images you will keep from your visit to Edinburgh, the most beautiful city in Britain.

Perfectly complementing Edinburgh is Glasgow, just 30 miles away and renowned for a fascinating array of art museums and galleries and for the warmth of its people.

In between there's so much to discover around Edinburgh in Mid and West Lothian, each with their own tales of romance and history. Survey a panorama of Scotland's past from the Stone Age Fort on Cairnpapple's summit. Admire the splendour of Linlithgow Palace, birthplace of Mary Queen of Scots and home to the Stuart Kings. Or who could resist the grandeur of Hopetoun House, a classical Adam masterpiece? Or Rosslyn Chapel's gothic intimate lush interior with amazing carvings and images?

Here, too, you can explore the rolling landscape and rocky shores which inspired the authors of Ivanhoe and Treasure Island. And close to Edinburgh the sweep of the Pentlands create the perfect setting for exhilarating walks, or even a downhill ski. Cruise the canals. Go fishing. Treat the children to Dalkeith's tree-top Adventure Park or sail under the magnificent Forth Bridge to lovely Inchcolm Island where there are seals to see and an abbey to explore. Close by is awe-inspiring Deep Sea World.

And within an hour's drive are Stirling, Braveheart and Rob Roy Country where lofty crags cast their reflections into sparkling lochs bordered by leafy forests in the Trossachs. Such a contrast to cosmopolitan, cultured Edinburgh and yet so close.

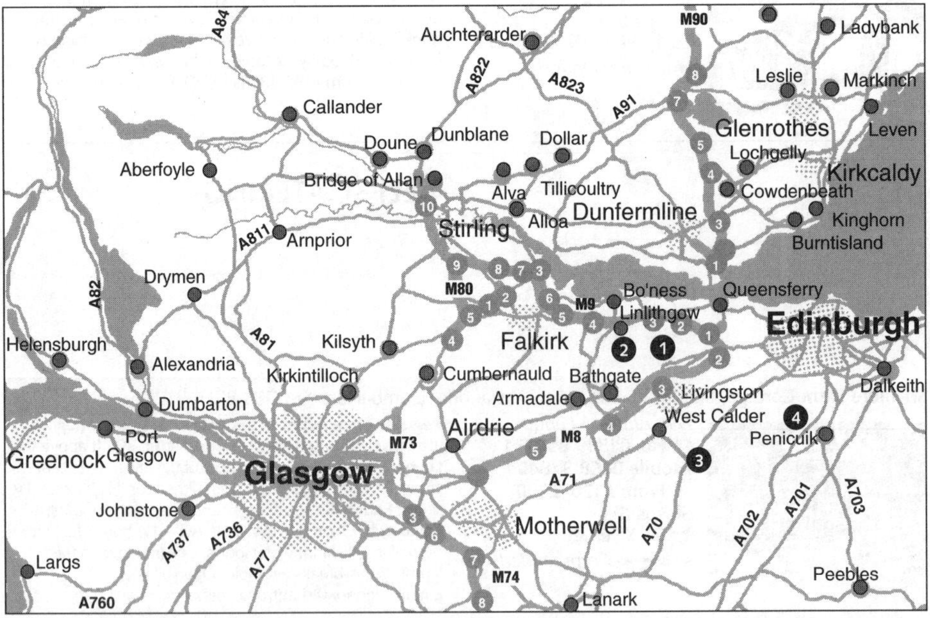

BED AND BREAKFAST

(and evening meal)

Bankhead Farm, Dechmont, Broxburn, West Lothian EH52 6NB

Heather Warnock
☎/Fax 01506 811209
BB From £20–£25
Sleeps 5
🛏 🐂 ⅍ ▲ W
🐝 *Commended*

This livestock farm in the Bathgate Hills has three modern en suite bedrooms and private kitchen. Panoramic views of Edinburgh, West Lothian and over the Forth to Fife belie the fact that we are close to three historic towns, and only 20 minutes from Scotland's capital city.

Belsyde Farm, Lanark Road, Linlithgow, West Lothian EH49 6QE

Mrs Nan Hay
☎/Fax 01506 842098
BB From £16–£25
Sleeps 6
🛏 🐂 ⅍ 🖼 ▲ 人 W
🐝🐝 *Commended*

An 18th century farmhouse located in large, secluded gardens with panoramic views over the Forth estuary. Golfing and fishing available locally. All bedrooms have washbasin (hot & cold), tea/coffee-making facilities, colour TV, central heating, 1 bedroom en suite. AA listed. Located close to M8, M9 and M90 and to Edinburgh airport. Follow A706 south-west from Linlithgow (1½ miles); first entrance on left after crossing Union Canal. Open all year except Christmas.

SELF-CATERING

Crosswoodhill Farm, By West Calder, West Lothian EH55 8LP

Mrs Geraldine Hamilton
☎ 01501 785205
Fax 01501 785308
SC From £220–£440
Sleeps 5/6
🛏 🐂 ▲ W
🐝🐝🐝🐝 – 🐝🐝🐝🐝🐝
Commended to Highly Commended

Imagine the best of both worlds....historic Edinburgh just ½ hour by car....rural tranquillity on our hill livestock farm with 1700 acres to roam. Perfectly placed for exploring the Borders, Fife, Glasgow, Rob Roy and Braveheart Country. Choose between a gem of a cottage on the Pentland Hills or, nearby, a self-contained wing of our handsome 18th century farmhouse. Both thoughtfully equipped. Cosy peat fires, relaxing atmosphere. CH. Own phone. Car essential. Brochure. Open all year.

Eastside Farm, Penicuik, Midlothian EH26 9LN

Susan Cowan
☎/Fax 01968 677842
SC From £150–£250
Sleeps 4
🛏 ▲ 🕺
🐝🐝🐝 *Commended*

Relax in this beautifully converted 18th century farmsteading located on a working family sheep farm in the scenic Pentland Hills Regional Park. Historic Edinburgh is only an eight mile drive away while New Lanark and the Border towns are a few miles further. Horseriding, fishing and golf nearby. Open all year.

Edinburgh's Coast & Country – East Lothian

Group Contact: *Barbara Williams* ☎ *01620 810491*

The beautiful, unspoilt countryside of East Lothian unfolds from Edinburgh's eastern edge along the Firth of Forth. Nestling under the heather-covered Lammermuir hills are many historic towns and picturesque villages – the county town of Haddington is one of the best preserved traditional market burghs in Scotland.

The area combines an extraordinary blend of scenery, antiquity and culture, with ancient castles, fine country houses, fascinating museums, National Trust properties, sports and leisure centres, and our own working Lowland whisky distillery, Glenkinchie. The choice of outdoor pursuits is endless – 40 miles of sandy beaches, the famous Bass Rock seabird and seal sanctuary, several country parks, racing at Musselburgh, as well as hill walking, pony trekking, fishing and the ubiquitous golf! East Lothian boasts 14 courses including the championship course at Muirfield.

There are numerous pubs, restaurants and bistros to suit all palates and purses. We look forward to seeing you.

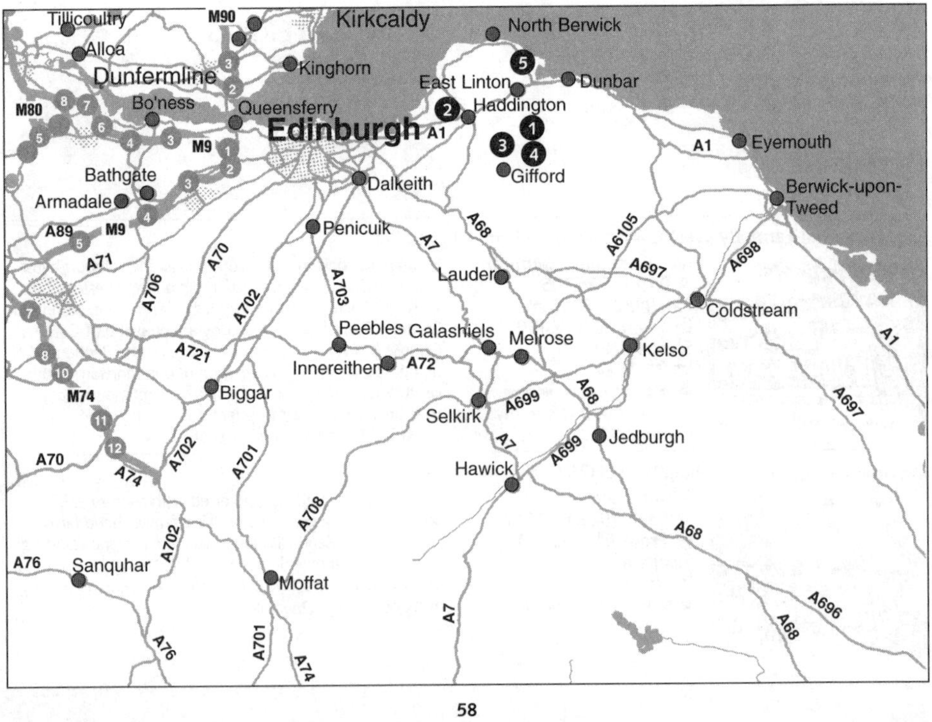

BED AND BREAKFAST

(and evening meal)

Carfrae Farmhouse, Carfrae, Haddington, East Lothian EH41 4LP ①

Mrs Dorothy Gibson
☎ 01620 830242
Fax 01620 830320
BB From £18.50–£25
Sleeps 6
🐕 ✄ 🧳 🎣 ⚲
🏵🏵 *Highly Commended*

Set on 800-acre mixed farm, beautifully furnished farmhouse overlooking walled garden with uninterrupted views of the Lammermuir Hills. Close to many golf courses, own fishing loch. Edinburgh 35 minutes. Open May–Oct.

Coates Farm, Longniddry, East Lothian EH32 0PL ②

Zoë Peace
☎/Fax 01620 822131
BB From £22.50
Sleeps 4
✗ ✄ 🧳
🏵🏵 *Highly Commended*

Spacious Georgian farmhouse tastefully decorated and furnished throughout. Ideally situated for exploring countryside, coastline or visiting Edinburgh. Train station nearby. Comfortable bedrooms with private facilities. Separate lounge and dining room for guests. Large, well tended, interesting garden. Excellent local pubs and restaurants. Coates is 1¾ miles from the A1. Open May–Sept.

Eaglescairnie Mains, Gifford, Haddington, East Lothian EH41 4HN ③

Mrs Barbara Williams
☎/Fax 01620 810491
BB From £18
Sleeps 6
🐕 🐎 🧳 ✗ 🅆
🏵🏵 *Commended*

Join us at Eaglescairnie Mains, a beautifully furnished Georgian house on our 350-acre arable/sheep farm which recently won a National Conservation Award. Near A1, ideal for the coast, golf courses, the Borders or Edinburgh. Double, twin and single rooms – some en suite, full CH, basins, tea/coffee trays. Conservatory, tennis court and games room. Open all year (closed Christmas and New Year).

Rowan Park, Longnewton Farm, Gifford, East Lothian EH41 4JW ④

Mrs Margaret Whiteford
☎ 01620 810327
BB From £18
Sleeps 6
🐕(7) ✗ ✗ 🧳
Listed *Highly Commended*

Our family farm of 450 acres consists of cattle, cereals and ponies. Situated at the foot of the Lammermuir Hills, with magnificent views to the Forth. Only 30 minutes from Edinburgh and near to the Border Country with its stately homes. Golf, fishing, tennis, swimming and pony trekking nearby. Furnished to a high standard, CH, guests' lounge, dining room and ground floor bedrooms, also welcome tray. A warm welcome awaits you. Open Mar–Nov.

Whitekirk Mains, Whitekirk, North Berwick, East Lothian EH42 1XS ⑤

Mrs J Tuer
☎ 01620 870245/870300
Fax 01620 870330
BB From £20–£25
Sleeps 6
🐕 £ 🧳
🏵🏵 *Highly Commended*

Spacious Georgian farmhouse on a 600-acre mixed farm at the edge of a historic village. Large en suite rooms with tea/coffee facilities and colour TV. Oak panelled dining/drawing rooms, log fires, superb views. Country and beach walks. 20 miles Edinburgh/Lammermuir Hills. Adjoining our new Whitekirk Golf Course and club house, restaurant/bar. Open Mar–Oct.

Scottish Borders

Group Contact: *Ann Prentice* ☎ *01361 882811*

Between Edinburgh and the North of England, the softly rolling landscape and richly historic past of the Scottish Borders makes it an uniquely inviting place to explore. In a tranquil land that once bore witness to raids and battles, you'll travel quiet roads through rolling farmlands to discover bustling towns and tiny hamlets, friendly local communities each with a distinctive character.

There are historic houses and gardens of all periods throughout the area, from Abbotsford, beloved home of Scott, to Mellerstain the finest complete Adam House in Scotland. These and others have superb gardens just waiting to be discovered. The ruins of the great abbeys of Kelso, Jedburgh, Melrose and Dryburgh stand testament to more troubled times.

The sun dappled River Tweed, the majestic Eildon hills, the broad sweep of the Merse, everyone has their favourite view. The beautiful landscape provides a breathtaking setting for all your favourite outdoor pursuits and unmissable opportunities to try something new.

Come and discover the beautiful Scottish Borders.

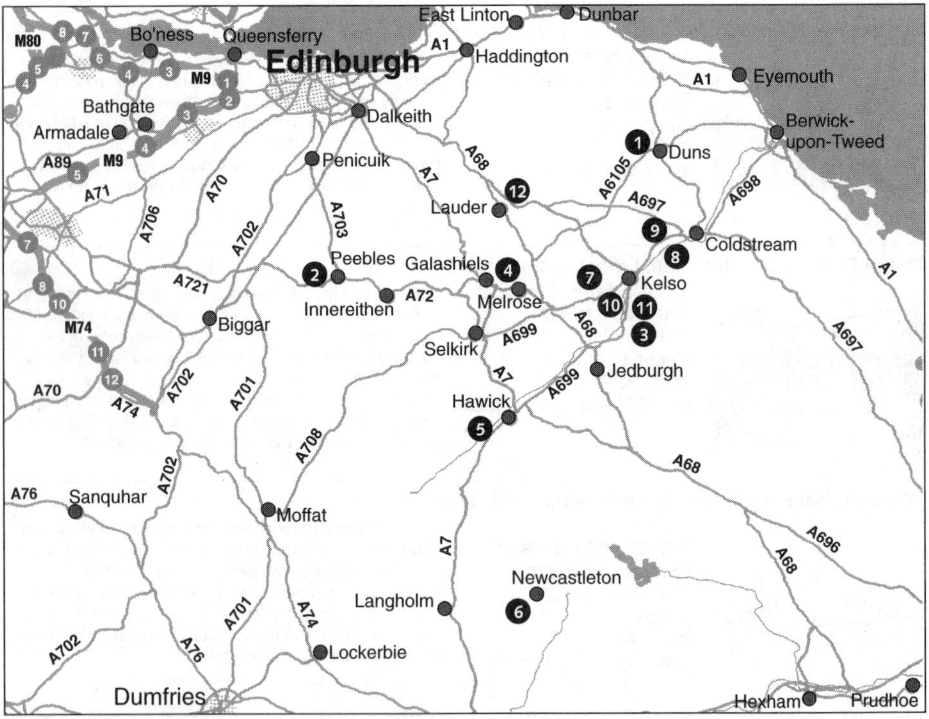

BED AND BREAKFAST

(and evening meal)

Cockburn Mill, Duns, Berwickshire TD11 3TL ①

Mrs A M Prentice
☎ 01361 882811
⬛ From £18–£20
EM £13
Sleeps 4
🐴 ⅄ 🐾 ▪
👄👄 Commended

Riverside farmhouse offering 2 luxurious twin en suite bedrooms with electric blankets and tea/coffee-making facilities. Within sight and sound of River Whiteadder. Home baking and farm produce. Water from hillside spring. Trout fishing included. Abundant plant and bird life. Ideal for hill-walking, birdwatching, cycling or just relaxing. Hens, ducks, donkeys and pet lambs. Brochure and colour photo available. Open Mar–Nov.

Lyne Farm, Peebles EH45 8NR ②

Mrs Arran Waddell
☎ 01721 740255
⬛ From £16–£18
Sleeps 6
🐴(5) 🐓 ▪ 🎋 🐾 �CW
Listed Commended

Spacious Georgian farmhouse situated on 1300 acre arable/stock farm with outstanding panoramic views. Tastefully decorated rooms, tea/coffee-making facilities. Walled garden. Hillwalking and picnic areas to enjoy. Excellent pubs and restaurants in picturesque town of Peebles. Ideal base for castles, historic houses, museums and outdoor pursuits. A warm welcome awaits you. Peebles 4 miles, Edinburgh 20 miles. Open March–Nov.

Morebattle Tofts, Kelso, Roxburghshire TD5 8AD ③

Mrs Debbie Playfair
☎ 01573 440364
Fax 01573 420750
⬛ From £17–£18
EM from £11
Sleeps 6
🐴 🐓 ▪ 🐾 ⅍ �CW
👄👄 Commended

Large, elegant 18th century farmhouse set in 3 acres of garden beside the River Kale. Area of Outstanding Natural Beauty, ideal for touring, walking, fishing, golf. Beautifully appointed rooms, 2 double rooms en suite, twin room with private bathroom. Tea and coffee-making facilities. Tennis court, croquet lawn. Brochure available. Open Mar–Oct.

Overlangshaw Farm, Langshaw, Galashiels, Selkirkshire TD1 2PE ④

Sheila Bergius
☎ 01896 860244
⬛ From £18–£20
Sleeps 6
🐴 🐓 ⅄ ⅀
👄 Commended

Our beautifully situated rambling farmhouse extends a warm welcome and provides delicious food from the kitchen. Near Galashiels and Melrose, Edinburgh 34 miles. The specially large family bedroom has a dressing room and private bathroom. Very attractive double room with en suite shower room. Cot available. Our farm has dairy and beef cows, Scottish Mule and Blackface Ewes. Southern Upland Way nearby. Open all year.

Wiltonburn Farm, Hawick, Roxburghshire TD9 7LL ⑤

Mrs Sheila Shell
☎ 01450 372414
Mobile 0374 192551
⬛ From £17–£18
EM From £10
Sleeps 6
🐴 🐓 ⅄ 🖼 🎋 ▪ ⅀
Listed Commended

You will be warmly welcomed and cared for as you unwind on our friendly, working mixed farm. Enjoy our rolling green hills and idyllic valley, 2 miles from Hawick, the centre of Scottish textiles. Your base for walking, riding, fishing, golf, castles and stately homes. Log fires, cosy rooms and our showroom containing designer cashmere knitwear, paintings, jewellery and small gifts will make your stay more pleasurable. Closed Christmas.

SELF-CATERING

---

6 **Bailey Mill,** Bailey, Newcastleton, Roxburghshire TD9 0TR

Pamela Copeland
☎/Fax 016977 48617
🆂🅲 From £78–£448
EM From £8
Sleeps 2/9
🏃 🛏 🐎 🍴 🎠 🐴 ♨
Applied

Surrounded by wildlife in unspoiled countryside and forests. This Scottish border area is ideal for walking and touring. Our home from home accommodation offers on-site sauna, solarium, jacuzzi, steam shower, games room and bar. Baby sitting and meal service. Also trekking centre and outdoor riding school. (Full board riding holidays available.) Brochure. Open all year.

---

1 **The Cottage,** Cockburn Mill, Duns, Berwickshire TD11 3TL

Ann Prentice
☎ 01361 882811
🆂🅲 From £130–£260
Sleeps 4/5 + cot
🛏 🐎 🍴 ♨
🌺 🌺 🌺 *Commended*

Stone-built cottage within sight and sound of River Whiteadder. Children welcome. Barbecue, colour TV. Overnight storage heating included. Trout fishing included. Water from hillside spring. Abundant plant and bird life. Chicks, donkeys, ducklings and pet lambs. Coast, beaches, Edinburgh, Border keeps and abbeys within easy reach on quiet roads. Pets by arrangement only. Brochure and colour photo available. Open all year.

---

7 **Craggs Cottage,** Cliftonhill Farm, Kelso, Roxburghshire TD5 7QE

Archie & Maggie Stewart
☎ 01573 225028
Fax 01573 226416
🆂🅲 From £75–£350
Sleeps 6/7
🛏 🍴 🐴 🎠 ♨ 🐾
🌺 🌺 🌺 *Commended*

A terraced sandstone cottage, lovingly restored, maintaining its character and charm. One double room – large and luxurious, 1 bedroom with 3 single beds and 1 with bunks. Large comfortable kitchen with Rayburn and electric cookers. CH. Sitting room with log fire and colour TV and video. Enclosed colourful garden, garden furniture. Delightful restaurant 3 miles. Coast 18 miles, Edinburgh 35 miles. Short breaks and special winter break offer. Open all year.

---

8 **Kerchesters,** Kelso, Roxburghshire TD5 8HR

Mrs M Clark
☎ 01573 224321
Fax 01573 226609
🆂🅲 From £120–£320
Sleeps 5/7
🛏 🐎 ♨ 🐾 🖵
🌺 🌺 🌺 🌺 *Commended*

Cockerlaw and Todrig cottages are warm, welcoming terraced cottages on a working farm. Relax in front of an open fire in well equipped surroundings. Shower, colour TV. Three miles east of Kelso. Well placed for touring Borders and Northumbria. Edinburgh 1 hour, beach 30 minutes. Golf, swimming, good walking locally. Linen included. Brochure on request. Open all year.

---

9 **Lochton Farm Cottages,** Lochton, Coldstream, Berwickshire TD12 4NH

Mrs Rosalind Aitchison
☎ 01890 830205
Fax 01890 830210
🆂🅲 From £200–£350
Sleeps 6
🛏 🍴 ♨ 🖵
🌺 🌺 🌺 – 🌺 🌺 🌺
Commended to Highly Commended

A warm welcome awaits you at Rowan Tree Cottage. Enjoy all year round comfort, lounge with wood-burning stove, CH, dining/kitchen/utility area, downstairs cloakroom, 3 charming bedrooms, bath/power shower. Relax in tranquil surroundings on our sheep/ arable farm beside the River Tweed. Sunny patio. Lovely views, walks, trout fishing. Kelso 4 miles, Edinburgh 1 hour. Short breaks. Open all year.

Roxburgh Newtown Farm, Kelso, Roxburghshire TD5 8NN   10

Mrs Pauline Twemlow
☎/Fax 01573 450250
[SC] From £120–£300
Sleeps 2–6
🐕 🛏 ♿ Ⓦ
❀ ❀ ❀ *Commended*

In a picturesque rural location 5 miles west of Kelso, Swallow and Jimmy's Cottages have been modernised and offer spacious, comfortably furnished accommodation. Jimmy's sleeps 6 and Swallow 2/4. Colour TV, microwave, dishwasher, central heating, electricity and linen included. Large play area. Ample parking. Open all year.

Steading Cottage, Sunlawshill, Kelso, Roxburghshire TD5 8LB   11

Louise Stewart
☎ 01573 450272
[SC] From £180–£250
Sleeps 5
🐕 🛏 ♿ ✂
❀ ❀ ❀ *Commended*

Built in 1851, this two-bedroomed stone cottage has been newly refurbished. Its fully equipped stone floored kitchen has washing machine, tumble drier and microwave. There is an open fire and storage heaters. Outside is a fenced-off area with patio and picnic table. Pets welcome. Open all year.

Thirlestane Farm Cottages, Thirlestane, Lauder, Berwickshire TD2 6SF   12

Mrs Caroline Barr
☎ 01578 722216
[SC] From £180–£300
Sleeps 6
🐕 🛏 ☂
❀ ❀ ❀ ❀ *Commended*

Renovated to retain their original charm and character, these cottages each provide 3 bedrooms (to sleep 6), large sitting room with open fire and panoramic view, pine kitchen/dining area. Rent includes bedlinen and fuel. Ideal for touring, walking, fishing, riding, easy access to all border towns, only 28 miles from Edinburgh. Pets by arrangement. Open all year.

Biggar & Clyde Valley

Group Contact: *Mrs Margaret Kirby* ☎ *01899 810338*

The Romans were the first to cultivate 'Y Strad Cluyd' – the warm valley – where even today the Clyde Valley's many garden centres show the area to be one of Scotland's most fertile. In all, the valley boasts 23 golf courses, including Scotland's highest at 1,400ft in the Lowther Hills at Leadhills, and where gold and lead mines first worked by the Romans have been restored and serve as a unique museum to the industry.

Then 'Follow the Wallace' through Biggar, with its wide, sweeping main street, its four museums, and home to the internationally-famous Purves Puppets. It was here, in 1297, that Scottish patriot William Wallace, disguised as a beggar, hid from the English troops. Moving on to Lanark, pass Tinto Hill, Clyde Valley's highest point at 2320ft, and topped by a large Bronze Age cairn where Druids once held fertility rites. A most rewarding view for the very fit! Nestling in a gorge by the famous 'Falls of Clyde' is the cotton mill village of New Lanark, built in the 18th century, but now a living museum with working spinning looms, visitors' centre and magical history tour.

The Clyde Valley is steeped in history, from Blantre's David Livingstone Centre, which traces the explorer's journeys through Africa, to Chatelherault Country Park, a William Adam 18th century hunting lodge of the Dukes of Hamilton.

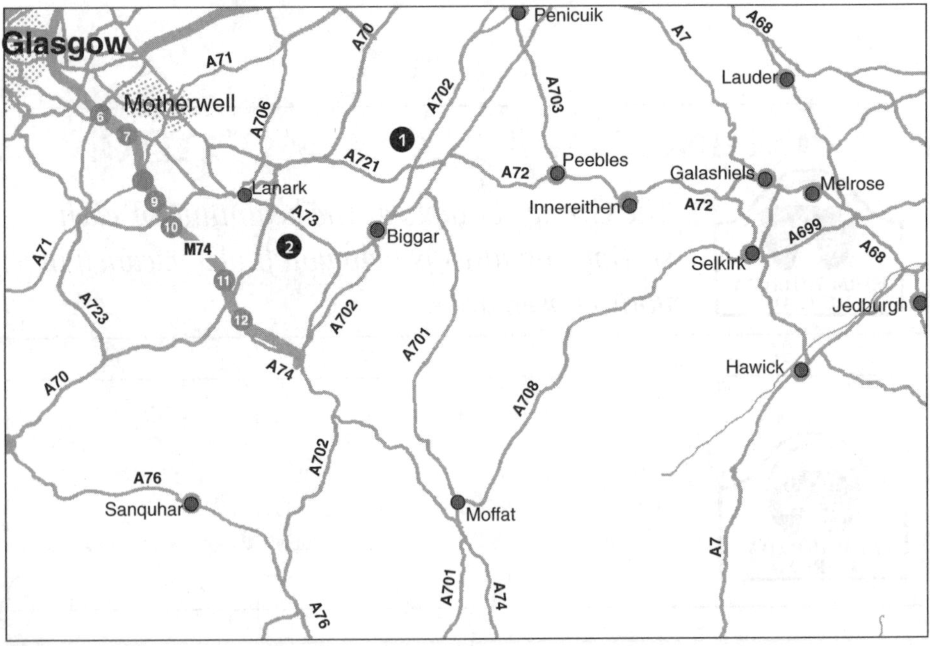

BED AND BREAKFAST

(and evening meal)

Walston Mansion Farmhouse, Walston, Carnwath, Lanark ML11 8NF ①

Mrs Margaret Kirby
☎/Fax 01899 810338
BB £14–£16
EM From £7.50
Sleeps 6
🛏 🐓 ♿ 🅦
♨ ♨ ♨ *Commended*

A very pleasant family home situated 5 miles from Biggar. A friendly and relaxed atmosphere; children most welcome. Good home cooking with home-produced meat, eggs and organic vegetables. Two en suite rooms, guests' lounge with log fire, TV/video and children's games. An ideal base for touring Strathclyde, Lothian and the Borders; Lanark, Edinburgh and Glasgow only a short drive away. Open all year.

SELF-CATERING

Carmichael Country Cottages, Estate Office, Westmains, Carmichael, Biggar, Lanarkshire ML12 6PG ②

Richard Carmichael of Carmichael
☎ 01899 308336
Fax 01899 308481
SC From £160–£450
EM From £7.50
Sleeps 2/7
🛏 🐓 ♿ 🧍🚶 ☚ ☂ ♨ 🅦
♨♨♨ – ♨♨♨♨♨ *Commended*
to Highly Commended

Fifteen 200-year-old stone cottages nestle among the woods and fields of our 700-year-old family estate. Enjoy our private tennis court and fishing loch. We guarantee comfort, warmth and a friendly welcome in an accessible, unique rural and historic time capsule. We farm deer, cattle and sheep and sell meats and tartan – Carmichael, of course. Breakfast and evening meal available. Visitor centre. Open all year. E mail: chiefcarm@aol.com. Web site: http://www.carmichael.co.uk/cottages

---

NO ANSWER?

Farmers are mostly out and about during the day.
Try to telephone before 9.30am or after 4pm.

FOLLOW THE COUNTRY CODE

Leave nothing but footprints,
Take nothing but photographs,
Kill nothing but time!

Ayrshire & Arran

Group Contact: *Jessie Bone* ☎/*Fax 01563 820567*

Wherever you travel in Ayrshire, you experience a sense of other ages, other lives. There are many facets to the past of Ayrshire. Well designed museums and visitor centres bring you face to face with them all. Walk along the sandy beaches and glance upwards at ancient castles which line the Ayrshire coast. Imagine what it must have been like to live in Turnberry Castle when Robert The Bruce was born, or look up at the vastness of Culzean Castle. A visit to Culzean Country park and gardens is a must for every visitor to Ayrshire. Ayr boasts theatres, swimming pool, restaurants, golf courses, children's play area, and a large modern shopping centre. A visit to Burn's Cottage, the birth place of Scotland's national poet, and the Burns experience in Alloway is time well spent. Away from the coast are small sleepy villages where good food and refreshment can be had in relaxed surroundings. For the sports enthusiast there are golf courses to suit the beginner or the world professional, horse riding, pony trekking, hill-walking, river fishing for salmon or trout, sea angling or bowling.

From Ardrossan in the north take the ferry to the mystical Island of Arran and visit Brodick Castle and gardens. The more energetic can take the path from the castle garden to the top of Goats Fell, Arran's tallest mountain, and experience the view over south west Scotland and Ireland. Arran is Scotland in miniature with rugged mountains in the north, sloping to the green pasture in the south. The quiet sandy beaches are a bird watcher's paradise.

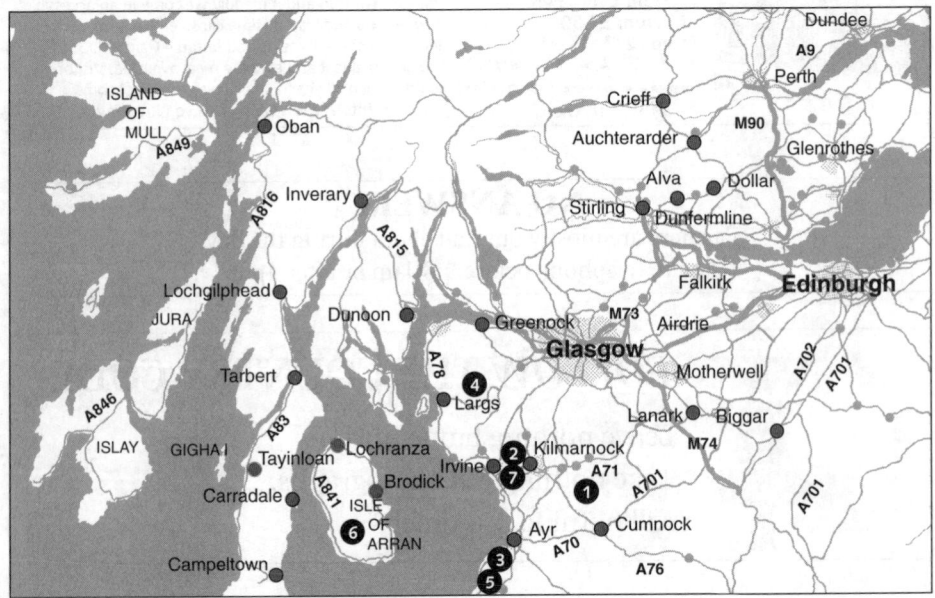

BED AND BREAKFAST

(and evening meal)

Auchencloigh Farm, Galston, Ayrshire KA4 8NP

Mrs Jessie Bone
☎/Fax 01563 820567
From £16
Sleeps 6
Listed *Commended*

Auchencloigh is a 250-acre beef and sheep farm in central Ayrshire situated on B7037. The tranquil setting of this 18th century spacious farmhouse, set in mature gardens, offers guests old and new a warm and relaxing atmosphere after a day spent visiting the many attractions in Ayrshire. Please send for brochure. AA recommended QQQ. Open all year except Christmas and New Year.

Aulton Farmhouse, Aulton Farm, Kilmaurs KA3 2PQ

Ena Hawkshaw
☎ 01563 538208
From £16
Sleeps 6
Listed *Commended*

Aulton is a beef farm situated in a quiet country location, ideal for touring, golfing, fishing and relaxing. Recently renovated to a very good standard with modern decor. All bedrooms have TV and tea/coffee-making facilities. A warm welcome awaits you with good home cooking. AA QQQ recommended. Open all year.

Dunduff Farm, Dunure, Ayr KA7 4LH

Agnes Gemmell
☎ 01292 500225
Fax 01292 500222
From £20–£25
Sleeps 6
Highly Commended

Dunduff Farm is a 650-acre beef and sheep farm overlooking the Firth of Clyde to the Holy Isle and Arran. Culzean Castle, Burns Cottage, Turnberry and many more are nearby. All rooms have en suite facilities or private bathroom and sea view. So come and enjoy the ambience of the Ayrshire coastline where a cheerful, warmhearted welcome awaits you. AA Selected QQQQ. Open Feb–Nov.

East Lochhead, Largs Road, Lochwinnoch PA12 4DX

Janet Anderson
☎/Fax 01505 842610
From £25–£30
Sleeps 2–6
Highly Commended

East Lochhead is a 100 year old farmhouse standing in 2 acres of beautiful landscaped gardens. Both bedrooms, one of which is on the ground floor, have magnificent views over over Barr Loch and the Renfrewshire hills. The Irvine/Paisley cycle track passes close to the house. Janet would be delighted to cook you an evening meal by prior arrangement. AA Premier Selected QQQQQ. Open all year. E mail: Winnoch@aol.Com

Fisherton Farm, Dunure, Ayr KA7 4LF

Mrs Lesley Wilcox
☎/Fax 01292 500223
From £17.50–£20
Sleeps 4–6
Commended

Delightful traditional Scottish farmhouse in coastal location on working farm. Convenient for Turnberry, Troon and many golf courses, also agate picking, fishing, walking, touring Burns Country and Culzean Castle. Ground floor en suite bedrooms with tea/coffee-making facilities. TV lounge. Open Mar–Nov.

6 **Glen Cloy Farmhouse,** Brodick, Isle of Arran KA27 8DA

Mark and Vicki Padfield
☎ **01770 302351**
🅱🅱 **From £20–£25**
EM From £13.50
Sleeps 9
♿ 🐾 ⊞ ♨
♨♨ *Commended*

Glen Cloy farmhouse is a century-old farmhouse set in a quiet glen just outside Brodick. The house is surrounded by a mixed farm and offers warm, cosy rooms and excellent cooking using homegrown produce. A log fire burns cheerily in the drawing room. Taste of Scotland selected member. Close to golf, pony trekking, castle and mountains. Open Mar–Nov.

7 **Muirhouse Farm,** Gatehead, Kilmarnock KA2 0BT

Mrs Martha S Love
☎ **01563 523975**
🅱🅱 **From £16**
Sleeps 6
♿ 🐾 ♨ 🆆
♨♨ *Commended*

A warm welcome is assured on our family-run dairy farm. In our traditional stone-built farmhouse all rooms have private or en suite bathrooms, TV and tea-making facilities. Near to Troon, we are ideally situated for golfers. Easy access to Glasgow also Arran ferry. Choice of excellent eating places nearby. Open all year.

SELF-CATERING

3 **Bothy Cottage,** Dunduff Farm, Dunure, Ayr KA7 4LH

Agnes Gemmell
☎ **01292 500225**
Fax 01292 500222
🆂🅲 **From £190–£225**
Sleeps 6
♿ 🐾 ✂ ⊞ ♨🐾☂🌤🆆
♨♨♨ *Commended*

Bothy Cottage is situated five miles south of Ayr at the coastal village of Dunure on a working farm. Overlooking Firth of Clyde to Arran. It has two double rooms, one is en suite, lounge and kitchen. Ideal for Culzean Castle and Parks, Burns Cottage, Galloway Forest, Farm Parks and many more. Capture this country coastal farm atmosphere at its best. Open Feb–Nov.

4 **East Lochhead,** Largs Road, Lochwinnoch PA12 4DX

Janet Anderson
☎/Fax **01505 842610**
🆂🅲 **From £150–£400**
EM From £16
Sleeps 2–5
♿ 🐾 ⊞ ♨ 🆆
Applied

Three cosy comfortable cottages newly converted from our old byres. Furnished and equipped to a high standard. Beautiful views over Barr Loch and the Renfrewshire hills. Linen is included and home cooking is available. The Paisley/Irvine cycle track passes close to the house. Convenient base for touring Glasgow, Ayrshire, Trossachs and Loch Lomond. Open all year.
E mail: Winnoch@aol.Com

LET THE TELEPHONE RING!

Some farmhouses are big places. Let the telephone ring
long enough to give the owner time to answer it.

South West Scotland

Group Contact: *Mrs Vera Dunlop ☎/Fax 01465 861220*

You will find plenty of space on our quiet roads and wide rolling countryside. With lush farmlands and miles of beautiful coastline the scenery is enhanced by golden sunsets.

Thanks to our mild climate, many subtropical plants bloom around Port Logan (just one of the many gardens in the area). South-West Scotland is a golfer's paradise, with courses wherever you go, both links and inland.

Fishermen will find plenty of opportunities for river, loch and sea fishing, while the hill climber or gentle walker may even be lucky enough to see the golden eagle, an inhabitant of the area for many years.

The area is also rich in historical and Christian heritage. A visit to the archaeological dig at Whithorn, where St Ninian founded the first Christian church, is a must.

Nearby, Culzean Castle with its famous Adam ceilings and superb furnishings is just one of the many castles to be explored in the area. Only the most discerning visitors choose this area of Scotland, and they are always amply rewarded.

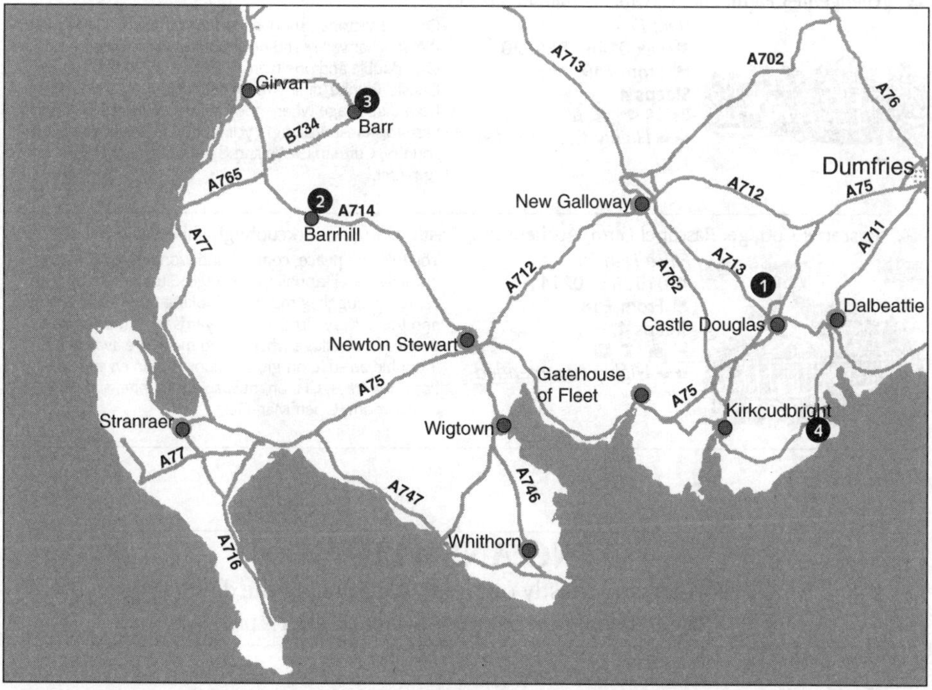

BED AND BREAKFAST

(and evening meal)

1 Airds Farm, Crossmichael, Castle Douglas, Kirkcudbrightshire DG7 3BG

Tricia Keith
☎ 01556 670418
BB **From £15–£18**
Sleeps 10
🐴 🐶 ✂ 🎄 🎣 W
🌺🌺 *Commended*

Airds farmhouse overlooks lovely Loch Ken, 4 miles from Castle Douglas on the A713. All bedrooms tastefully decorated, heated, with wash handbasins, colour TV and tea and coffee facilities. Family and twin rooms are en suite. Private lounge with colour TV. Fire certificate held. Non-Smoking only. Pleasant walks within grounds. A warm welcome and comfortable stay are assured. Open all year.

2 Blair Farm, Barrhill, Girvan, Ayrshire KA26 0RD

Mrs Elizabeth Hughes
☎ 01465 821247
BB **From £16–£18.50**
EM From £8.50
Sleeps 6
🐴 🐶 ☕ 🎣 W
🌺🌺 *Highly Commended*

We warmly invite you to enjoy peace, comfort and good home cooking at Blair, situated 1 mile south of Barrhill on A714, close to Galloway Forest Park. Spacious accommodation, tastefully furnished and decorated throughout. One double en suite, 1 double and 1 twin with washbasin, electric blankets and tea/coffee facilities. Visitors' lounge, central heating, log fires, TV etc. Fishing available. Brochure. Open Easter–Oct.

3 Glengennet Farm, Barr, Girvan, Ayrshire KA26 9TY

Vera Dunlop
☎/Fax 01465 861220
BB **From £19**
Sleeps 4
🐴 ✂ ☕ 🎣 W
🌺🌺 *Highly Commended*

Original Victorian shooting lodge with lovely views over the Stinchar valley and neighbouring Galloway Forest Park. One double and one twin, both en-suite with tea trays. Guests' lounge/dining room with colour TV. Two miles from Barr village where good meals are available. Good base for forest walking/ cycling, golf, Ayrshire coast, Burns country, Culzean Castle and Glentrool National Park. Open Apr–Oct.

4 Rascarrel Cottage, Rascarrel Farm, Auchencairn, Castle Douglas, Kirkcudbrightshire DG7 1RJ

Ellice Hendry
☎ 01556 640214
BB **From £18**
Sleeps 4
✂ 🎣 🎄 W
🌺🌺 *Highly Commended*

You will find peace, comfort and wonderful views at our attractive, well-appointed cottage. Situated on an 18th century smuggling route overlooking our 400 acre farm and the Solway Firth, it is 500 yards from the sea and 2 miles from village where good meals are available. 1 double en suite on ground floor, 1 twin en suite on first floor. Tea trays, CH, bright spacious lounge, sunroom/dining room. Open Mar–Oct.

NO ANSWER?

Farmers are mostly out and about during the day.
Try to telephone before 9.30am or after 4pm.

SELF-CATERING

Upper Barr Farm, Glengennet, Barr, Girvan, Ayrshire KA26 9TY   (3)

Vera Dunlop
☎/Fax 01465 861220
[SC] From £140–£495
Sleeps 6/8 + cot
🛏 🐴 🎣 🐕 [W]
🌸🌸🌸 *Commended*

Choose between detached period black and white farmhouse, recently modernised to provide centrally heated accommodation for 8 in 4 bedrooms (one en suite) or farmhouse wing sleeps 6 (one ground floor bedroom and bathroom). On working hill farm in peaceful Stinchar Valley, lovely views to Galloway Forest Park. Short breaks offseason, brochure. Open all year.

FINDING YOUR ACCOMMODATION

FARM HOLIDAY BUREAU

The Group contacts at the beginning of each section can always help you find a vacancy in your chosen area.

THE 1000+ BUREAU MEMBERS OFFER A UNIQUE LINK TO CUSTOMERS ACROSS THE UK

FARM HOLIDAY BUREAU

All Bureau members belong to a local Group. Each member can refer you to an equally high quality member within the Group... or across the UK: England, Northern Ireland, Scotland, Wales.

Dumfriesshire

Group Contact: *Mrs Kate Miller ☎/Fax 01683 300320*

A peaceful, undiscovered, easily accessible part of south-west Scotland. Take time to explore the countryside and sample the tranquility.

From the beaches of the Solway coast to the rugged Moffat Hills, with the spectacular 'Grey Mare's Tail' and the striking 'Devil's Beef Tub', here is a variety of scenery unmatched in Britain. Quiet lanes winding through lush green countryside, busy small towns with a variety of interesting shops, numerous challenging golf courses, excellent fishing and much, much more. The county town of Dumfries contains the excellent Robert Burns Centre which documents the many links Scotland's foremost poet has with the area. Moffat is a most attractive town with tennis courts, bowling green, woollen mill and many craft shops. Lockerbie, with its bustling cattle market, is well worth a visit. So, whether you enjoy birdwatching or hill walking, swimming or horseriding, sailing or just relaxing with friendly people, you will find everything you want in Dumfriesshire.

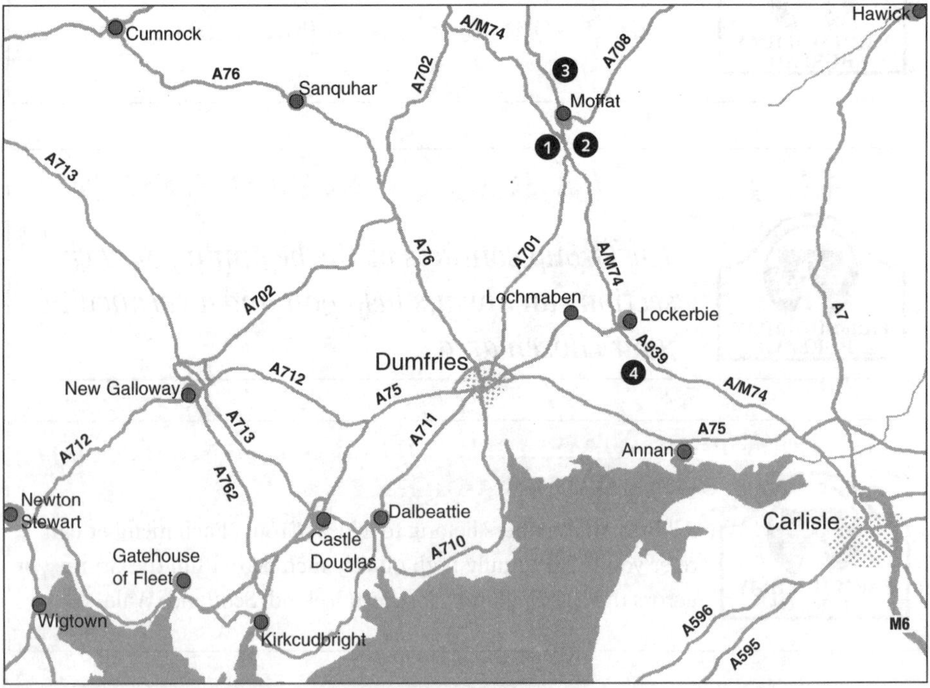

BED AND BREAKFAST

(and evening meal)

Broomlands Farm, Beattock, Moffat, Dumfriesshire DG10 9PQ

Kate Miller
☎/Fax 01683 300320
[BB] **From £18–£20**
Sleeps 5
⌕(12) ✄ ♙ ♫ ← ✿ W
♨♨ *Highly Commended*

A lovely comfortable farmhouse situated in the Annandale Valley only 2 miles from Moffat, a wonderful area to tour, walk, play golf, etc. High standard accommodation offering double, twin and single rooms, all with beautiful en suite facilities, colour TV, tea/coffee-making facilities. Delicious farmhouse breakfast. Personal attention. Safe private parking. Convenient for A/M74. Brochure available. Open Mar–Oct.

Coxhill Farm, Old Carlisle Road, Moffat, Dumfriesshire DG10 9QN

Mrs Sandra Long
☎ 01683 220471
[BB] **From £17**
Sleeps 6
⌕ ✄ ♙
♨♨ *Commended*

A very attractive farmhouse in 70 acres of unspoilt countryside with outstanding views, beautiful rose gardens and ample parking. 2 double, 1twin bedrooms, all with washbasins, tea/coffee-making facilities and central heating. Situated 1 mile south of the charming town of Moffat, and 1½ miles from Southern Upland Way. Excellent base for golf, tennis, fishing and touring SW Scotland. Open Mar–Oct.

Ericstane, Moffat, Dumfriesshire DG10 9LT

Robert Jackson
☎ 01683 220127
[BB] **From £18–£23**
Sleeps 4
⌕ ♈ ♙ ♫
♨♨ *Commended*

Ericstane offers peace and quiet in attractive surroundings on a working hill farm 4 miles from Moffat. Period farmhouse with twin and double-bedded rooms with en suite facilities, TV, tea/coffee-making facilities. Central heating. In *Staying Off the Beaten Track* and *The Which Good Bed and Breakfast Guide*. Open all year.

SELF-CATERING

Kirkwood Cottages, Kirkwood, Dalton, Lockerbie DG11 1DH

Anthony Steel
☎ 01576 510200
Fax 01576 510363
[SC] **From £119–£380**
Sleeps 3–6
⌕ ♈ ♙ ← ✿ ♫ W
♨♨♨ – ♨♨♨♨
Approved to Commended

In idyllic countryside of rolling hills, lush pastures and wooded valleys, Kirkwood Farm is 4 miles south of Lockerbie, close to London – Glasgow motorway, yet beautifully unspoilt. The farm has salmon, sea trout and trout fishing on the River Annan, and 150 acres of woods, and has had self-catering cottages for 25 years. Open all year.

Hadrian's Wall, North Cumbria & The Borders

Group Contact: *Mrs Elizabeth Woodmass* ☎ *016977 47285*

Discover the Border Country, a wild wonderland of moors, tarns and loughs, wooded river valleys and rich pastureland. Wildlife abounds with peace and quiet for all who seek it. This is an exciting area for the heritage enthusiast with Roman sites and the world famous Hadrian's Wall, Lanercost Priory, Hexham Abbey, Carlisle, and Hermitage Castle. The historic city of Carlisle with its gem of a cathedral has an excellent Lanes shopping centre of large and small shops.

Whether walking, golfing, fishing, birdwatching or gently touring our quiet roads you will find this area has so much to offer – lots of country inns, market towns, woollen and tweed mills, local craft and agricultural shows and, most important of all, friendly people. Kielder Water is on our doorstep offering many water activities, birdwatching and magnificent forest surroundings. Once you have enjoyed the peace, freedom and our North Country hospitality, you will most certainly wish to return to this unspoilt area.

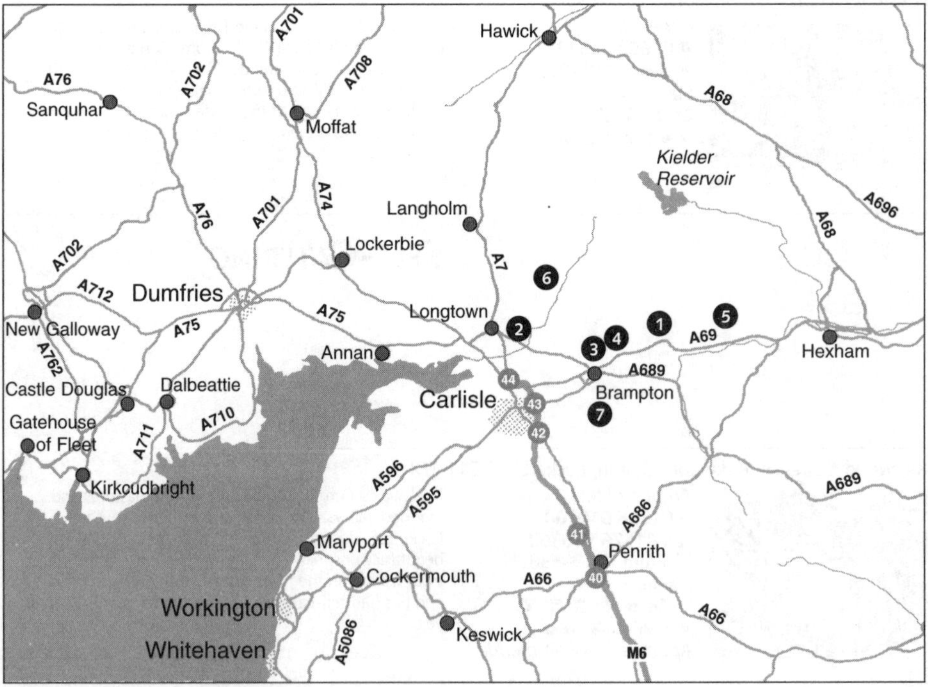

BED AND BREAKFAST

(and evening meal)

Howard House Farm, Gilsland, Carlisle, Cumbria CA6 7AN

Elizabeth Woodmass
☎ 016977 47285
▥ From £18–£21
EM From £9.50
Sleeps 6
☺(5) 🐴 🐈 ♿ 🛪 ⊚
🐾 🐾 *Highly Commended*

A warm welcome and comfortable accommodation await you on beef/sheep farm. Situated on an elevated site enjoying magnificent views over 2 counties in the heart of Roman wall country. Guests lounge, colour TV, tea/coffee-making facilities. Dinner by arrangement or bar meals nearby. Discount on 3 night stay. Open all year, except Christmas.

New Pallyards, Hethersgill, Carlisle, Cumbria CA6 6HZ

Mrs Georgina Elwen
☎/Fax 01228 577308
▥ From £19–£21
EM From £13
Sleeps 6
☺ 🐴 ⊞ 🛪 🐈 🛪 ♿ ⊚
🐾 🐾 🐾 *Commended*

Friendly hospitality, warmth and comfort await you in this modernised 18th century farmhouse. Situated in the peaceful countryside, surrounded by nature yet easily accessible from M6, A7, M74. All bedrooms en suite, tea/coffee facilities, disabled people welcome. A wide range of leisure and recreational activities are within a few minutes' drive from the farm. National Gold Award winner. Open all year.

Town Head Farm, Walton, Brampton, Cumbria CA8 2DJ

Mrs Una Armstrong
☎ 016977 2730
▥ From £14–£15
EM From £9
Sleeps 4
☺ ✂ 🛪 ♿
Listed *Commended*

Relax in the friendly atmosphere of our dairy/sheep farm. Our cosy farmhouse overlooks the village green with play area and small nature trail. Scenic views of Pennines and Lakeland Hills. Ideal base for walking/touring. Near Hadrian's Wall, Lakes, Scottish Borders and Northumbria. 10 miles M6 jct43. Bar meals at local pub (400 yds). Special breaks. Open all year except Christmas and New Year.

Walton High Rigg, Walton, Brampton, Cumbria CA8 2AZ

Margaret Mounsey
☎ 016977 2117
▥ From £16
EM From £9
Sleeps 4
☺ ✂ 🐈 🛪 🐾 ♿ ⊚
🐾 *Commended*

Working dairy/sheep farm with attractive 18th century listed farmhouse near Walton and Roman Wall. Friendly welcome, excellent home cooking, panoramic views of the Lakes and Pennines. Convenient also for Northumbria and Scottish Borders. Patio, children's play area. Follow the farm trail to the waterfall, help feed the animals or relax in the garden. Good parking. Golf courses and riding nearby. Closed Christmas and New Year.

NO ANSWER?

Farmers are mostly out and about during the day.
Try to telephone before 9.30am or after 4pm.

SELF-CATERING

---

5 **Ald White Craig Farm Cottages,** Nr.Hadrian's Wall, Haltwhistle, Northumberland NE49 9NW

Isobel Laidlow
☎/Fax 01434 320565
SC From £115–£400
Sleeps 2/8 + cot
🛏 🐕 ⌂ 💼 ◉
🍴 🍴 🍴 🍴 *Highly Commended*

Warm and comfortable, these farm cottages offer you award-winning accommodation. Nearby are country inns, restaurants and varied attractions including Hadrian's Wall with its stunning scenery and peaceful moorland. On the edge of Northumberland National Park overlooking North Pennine Fells. Open all year.

---

6 **Bailey Mill,** Bailey, Newcastleton, Roxburghshire TD9 0TR

Pamela Copeland
☎/Fax 016977 48617
SC From £78–£448
EM From £8
Sleeps 2/9
↑ 🛏 🐕 ⌂ 💺 🏇 💼 ◉
🍴 🍴 🍴 *Commended*

A warm welcome awaits you from Pam and Ian on this small farm holiday complex nestling on the Roxburgh/Cumbria border. The superior self-contained courtyard apartments include heating (oil), electricity and linen in rent. Full board riding holidays. On-site sauna, solarium, multi-gym, games room, laundry, farm kitchen service and horse riding. Baby sitting service. Brochure. Open all year.

---

2 **Burn and Meadow View,** New Pallyards, Hethersgill, Carlisle, Cumbria CA6 6HZ

Georgina Elwen
☎/Fax 01228 577308
SC From £80–£380
Sleeps 5/8
🛏 🐕 ⌂ 🏇 🐕 💺 💼 ◉
🍴 🍴 🍴 – 🍴 🍴 🍴 🍴
Commended

Set amidst beautiful countryside close to the Scottish Borders, our fully centrally heated cottages offer a high standard of accommodation with all modern-day facilities. A wide range of leisure and recreational activities are within a few minutes' drive from the farm. Our on-site games and dining room will make your stay more enjoyable. Open all year.

---

7 **Long Byres,** Talkin Head Farm, Talkin, Brampton, Cumbria CA8 1LT

Mrs Harriet Sykes
☎ 016977 3435
Fax 016977 2228
SC From £95–£275
Sleeps 2–5
🛏 🐕 ⌂ 🐈 💼 ◉
🍴 🍴 – 🍴 🍴 🍴 🍴
Commended

Seven specially designed, fully equipped, warm holiday cottages on North Pennine hill farm. Freshly home-cooked meal service. Enjoy walking (access direct to fells); cycling (green and quiet roads); bird watching (RSPB reserve next door); touring centre for Scottish Borders, Hadrian's Wall, Lake District. Golf, boating, fishing and good pubs close by. Open all year. E mail: harriet@talkinhead.demon.co.uk

---

Although the majority of farms will accept '*Stay on a Farm*' Gift Tokens, please check when booking to avoid disappointment.

Carlisle's Border Country

Group Contact: *Jane Lawson* ☎ *01228 577214*

The country to the north east of Carlisle is one of the last truly peaceful places in England. Here in the Debateable Land where the Border Reivers once rode; your only debate today will be which of the many beautiful and historic places will you visit. Will it be Carlisle with its cathedral, castle, city walls, pedestrianised shopping centre and award winning museum, the Tullie House; or the north to Scotland and wild Liddesdale, Hermitage Castle and the Border Abbeys and historic houses; or the west and the Solway coast and its world renowned birdlife; or will you just walk or cycle on the peaceful tracks of the Border Forest Park basking in tranquility, perhaps catching sight of a deer?

Easily accessible from the M6, M74 and A7, this area is ideal for a stopover for Scotland and Northern Ireland is within easy distance of the Lake District, Hadrian's Wall, Northumberland and Kielder Water, and the Eden Valley: whilst only a step from romantic Gretna Green. A haven of peace with enough to keep you involved for many more holidays because once you have been welcomed for the first time in one of Carlisle's Border Country farms you will certainly want to come back ...

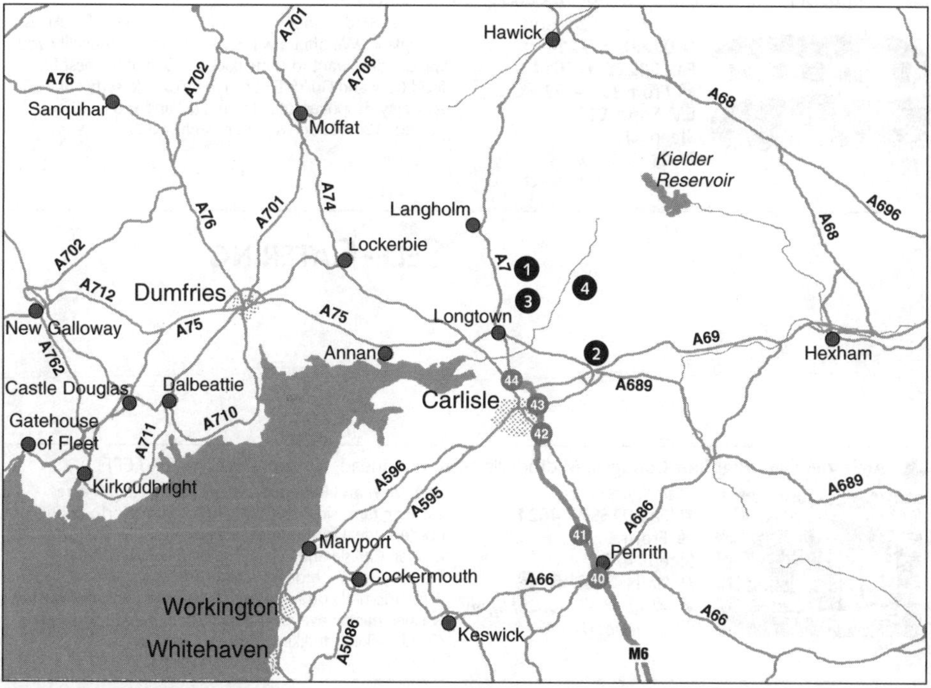

BED AND BREAKFAST

(and evening meal)

1 **Bessiestown Farm,** Catlowdy, Longtown, Carlisle, Cumbria CA6 5QP

Margaret Sisson
☎/Fax 01228 577219
BB From £21–£23
EM From £11
Sleeps 8
⛲ ✗ ⊞ ♨ ◎
♨ ♨ ♨
Highly Commended

An award-winning farm guesthouse overlooking Scottish Borders. Friendly, relaxing atmosphere assured. Warm, pretty en suite bedrooms with colour TV, radio and tea/coffee. Delicious home cooking using traditional recipes. Residential drinks licence. Indoor heated swimming pool (May–Sept). AA QQQQQ Premier Selected. Stop off Scotland and Northern Ireland. M6 J44, A7 to Longtown, then follow signs to Catlowdy. Open all year.

2 **Cracrop Farm,** Kirkcambeck, Brampton, Cumbria CA8 2BW

Marjorie Stobart
☎ 016977 48245
Fax 016977 48333
BB From £25
EM From £17
Sleeps 6
⛲(12) 🐾 ⊞ ✗ ⬥ ⚒ ♨
♨ ♨ *Highly Commended*

Looking for somewhere special? Then try our superbly appointed large (1847) farmhouse. Set in peaceful countryside with super views, excellent for birdwatching and walking. Spacious en suite bedrooms, hostess tray, colour TV, fresh flowers. Relax in spa bath or sauna. Games room. Near Roman Wall, Borders, 1 mile from B6318. Excellent pubs nearby. AA selected QQQQ. Every effort has been made to ensure a memorable stay.

3 **Craigburn Farm,** Catlowdy, Longtown, Carlisle, Cumbria CA6 5QP

Jane & Jack Lawson
☎ 01228 577214
Fax 01228 577014
BB From £21–£22
EM From £12
Sleeps 12
⛲ 🐾 ⚒ ⊞ ♨ ◎
♨ ♨ ♨ *Commended*

Carlisle's Border Country, one of the most peaceful places in England. We offer a warm welcome and hospitality you will certainly want to come back to. One of the best for food (City and Guilds Distinction held) – desserts our speciality. Stopover to and from Scotland and Northern Ireland. 'We look forward to meeting you'.

SELF-CATERING

4 **Arch View and Riggfoot Cottages,** Midtodhills farm, Roadhead, Carlisle, Cumbria CA6 6PF

Jean James
☎/Fax 016977 48213
SC From £130
Sleeps 4/8
♿ ⛲ 🐾 ⊞ ⚑ ♨ ◎
♟ ♟ ♟ ♟ ♟ *Up to Highly Commended*

Arch View and Riggfoot Cottages are on a 320-acre working farm close to Cumbria/Scotland/Northumbria/borders. Ideal for touring Hadrian's Wall, Gretna Green, Kielder, Carlisle and Lakes. The barn conversion has 5 bedrooms, 2 bathrooms, kitchen/diner, lounge. P.O.A. The 2-bedroomed cottages have four-poster beds, dishwasher, washer, microwave, payphone, video, garden, barbecue. Good walking, trekking, fishing. Open all year.

Bessiestown Farm, Catlowdy, Longtown, Carlisle, Cumbria CA6 5QP — ①

Margaret Sisson
☎/Fax 01228 577219
⌗ From £100–£350
Sleeps 4–6
EM From £11
❄ ⌂ ♨ ◉
♫ ♫ ♫ *Commended*

Three tastefully converted two bedroomed courtyard cottages enjoying extensive views over Border country. Well furnished, spacious, warm and welcoming. Swim in the pool, meander through the meadows, picnic by the stream, dine in the main house – simply unwind. Indoor heated swimming pool (mid May–mid Sept). Special winter breaks. Phone for colour brochure. Open all year.

CONFIRM BOOKINGS

Disappointments can arise from misunderstandings over the telephone. Please write to confirm your booking.

FINDING YOUR ACCOMMODATION

FARM HOLIDAY BUREAU

The Group contacts at the beginning of each section can always help you find a vacancy in your chosen area.

STAY ON A FARM GIFT TOKENS

FARM HOLIDAY BUREAU

If you have enjoyed your Stay on a Farm, why not treat your friends and relatives to *Stay on a Farm* gift tokens? Available from the Bureau office, telephone 01203 696909, they can be redeemed against accommodation booked on the majority of our farms

North Northumberland

Group Contact: *Mrs Susan Aynsley* ☎ 01665 570257

North Northumberland is an area of great beauty still little known to many people. There are miles of heritage coastline dotted with castles such as Lindisfarne, Bamburgh and Dunstanburgh and further inland a wealth of historic homes including Alnwick Castle and Cragside. Holy Island (Lindisfarne) is accessible by car at low tide and boats run daily in the summer months to the Farne Islands, famous for their colonies of seals and seabirds.

The Northumberland National Park offers wonderful opportunities for those wishing to walk and explore in peace and solitude. Berwick-upon-Tweed and Alnwick are two busy country towns which still have weekly street markets. Scotland's capital city, Edinburgh to the north and Newcastle with its much acclaimed Metro Shopping Centre to the south are within easy reach by car, train or bus.

Our group offers a wide variety of holiday accommodation of a high standard based on working farms in this unspoilt corner of England's most northerly county.

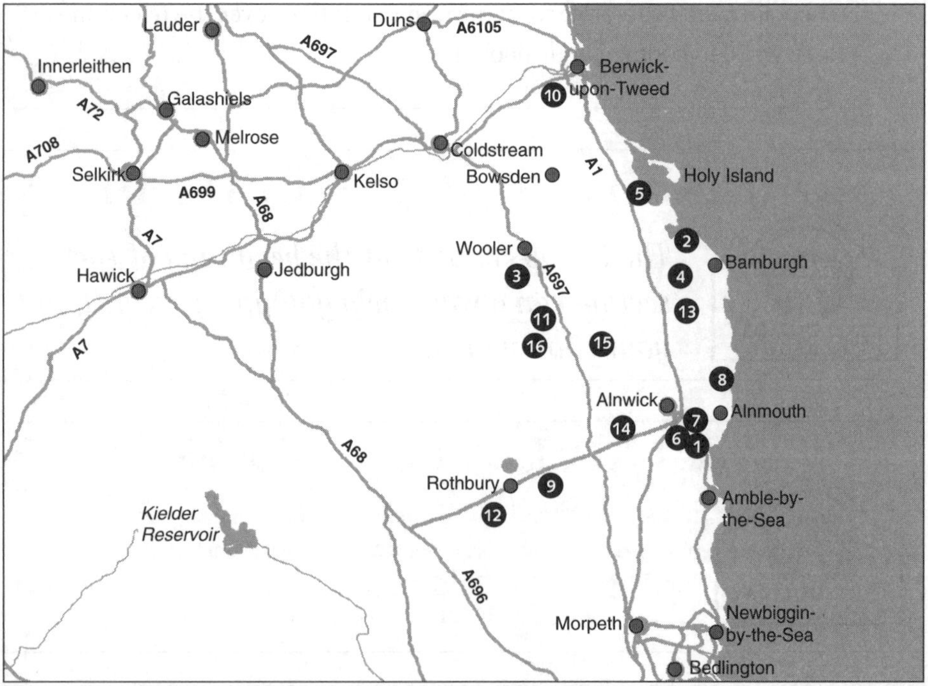

BED AND BREAKFAST
(and evening meal)

Bilton Barns, Alnmouth, Alnwick, Northumberland NE66 2TB

Dorothy Jackson
☎ 01665 830427
Fax 01665 830063
BB From £19.50–£22
EM From £11.50
Sleeps 6
🐕 ⛄ 🏕
♨ ♨ *Highly Commended*

Spacious farmhouse in lovely countryside with magnificent views over Alnmouth and Warkworth bays. Many splendid walks, beaches and castles nearby. Full central heating, guests' lounge and dining room. All with en suite bedrooms, TV and tea/coffee-making facilities. Brian is pleased to take interested guests on a farm walk. Recommended in *Best Bed and Breakfast in the World* and *Which? Good B&B Guide*. Open Easter–mid Oct.

Burton Hall, Bamburgh, Northumberland NE69 7AR

Eve Humphreys
☎ 01668 214213/214458
Fax 01668 214538
BB From £19–£30
Sleeps 16
🐕(4) ⛄ 🐴 🏕 🎠 🎾 ◎
Listed *Commended*

A traditional farmhouse offering a friendly atmosphere with a high standard of service only 1½ miles from Bamburgh Castle. All bedrooms are spacious with tea/coffee facilities, en suites with colour TV. Ground floor bedrooms available as well as an elegant residents' lounge and dining room where delicious breakfasts are served. Open all year.

Earle Hill Head Farm, Wooler, Northumberland NE71 6RH

Sylvia Armstrong
☎/Fax 01668 281243
BB From £20
Sleeps 5
🐕(7) 🏕 ⛄ 🏕
Listed *Highly Commended*

Earle Hill Farm is 2 miles from Wooler at the foot of the Cheviot Hills. We have a 4,000-acre stock farm in the National Park. Lovely walks and a warm welcome will await you in our comfortable farmhouse. Wooler is a perfect centre for the coast, castles and Scottish Borders. Household and Farming Museum. Local nature trails and conducted tours. Open all year.

Elford Farmhouse, Elford, Seahouses, Northumberland NE68 7UT

Mrs M Robinson
☎/Fax 01665 720244
BB From £17–£18
Sleeps 6
🐕(12) 🏕 🎠
Listed *Highly Commended*

An old stone farmhouse of great character on an arable farm near the villages of Bamburgh and Seahouses, 1½ miles from the sea. Nearby are beautiful beaches, castles, golf, riding and boat trips to the Farnes and Holy Island. Good local restaurants. Comfortable bedrooms with central heating, colour TV, hair dryers and tea/coffee facilities. Elegant dining room. Some use of outdoor heated swimming pool and lawn tennis court in summer. Open Mar–Oct.

Fenham-le-Moor Farmhouse, Belford, Northumberland NE70 7PN

Mrs K Burn
☎ 01668 213247
BB From £18–£22
Sleeps 3
🐕(12) ✂ 🏕 ◎
♨ ♨ *Highly Commended*

A comfortable stone-built farmhouse in a peaceful situation with magnificent views overlooking farmland and the bay of Lindisfarne Nature Reserve. An area of outstanding natural beauty and excellent centre for birdwatching, golf, good beaches and visiting many castles. One twin room en suite. Open Easter–Oct.

6 **Hawkhill Farmhouse,** Hawkhill, Lesbury, Alnwick, Northumberland NE66 3PG

Mrs Margery Vickers
☎/Fax 01665 830380
[BB] From £20–£28
Sleeps 6
⌕(12) ♿
☙ ☙ *Commended*

Large traditional farmhouse set in extensive, secluded grounds with magnificent views of the Aln valley and surrounding countryside. Midway Alnwick/Alnmouth, ideal for good beaches, castles and places of interest. One double and 2 twin rooms, all en suite with TV, tea/coffee. Very spacious guests' sitting room and dining room. Full CH and private parking. Open Easter–Oct.

7 **Hipsburn Farm,** Lesbury, Alnmouth, Northumberland NE66 3PY

Hilda Tulip
☎ 01665 830206
[BB] From £18–£22
Sleeps 6
⌕(12) ✂
☙ *Highly Commended*

A spacious farmhouse situated ½ mile from Alnmouth, overlooking the Aln estuary. Rooms comfortably furnished, one double en suite, one twin en suite and one double with private bathroom. TV, tea/coffee-making facilities in all bedrooms. All rooms are centrally heated, dining room – lounge. Ideal area for golfers, walkers and birdwatchers. Private parking. Open Easter–Oct.

8 **Howick Scar Farm,** Craster, Alnwick, Northumberland NE66 3SU

Mrs Celia Curry
☎ 01665 576665
[BB] From £15
Sleeps 4
⌕(5) ♞ ♿
Listed *Commended*

Comfortable farmhouse accommodation on mixed farm situated on the coast between the villages of Craster and Howick. Ideal base for walking or exploring the coast, moors and historic castles. Guests have their own television lounge/dining room, double bedrooms with washbasins and full central heating. Open May–Nov.

9 **The Lee Farm,** nr Rothbury, Longframlington, Morpeth, Northumberland NE65 8JQ

Mrs Susan Aynsley
☎ 01665 570257
[BB] From £16–£20
Sleeps 5
⌕ ♞ ♿ ♞
☙ *Highly Commended*

Large traditional farmhouse on 1,200 acre farm. Comfortable bedrooms with tea/coffee-making facilities and washbasins, one en suite. Guests' lounge with log fire and dining room. Central heating throughout. Excellent central location for walking or exploring Northumberland's many attractions. Fishing, riding and golf available nearby. Open Mar–Nov.

10 **Middle Ord Manor House,** Middle Ord Farm, Berwick-on-Tweed TD15 2XQ

Joan Gray
☎ 01289 306323
Fax 01289 308423
[BB] From £25
Sleeps 6
✂ ♿ ♞ ♞ ◉
☙ ☙ *De Luxe*

Feeling stressed, want to unwind, or are you just wanting to indulge yourself? Either way, why not visit our elegant home and experience the warmth and quality of gracious living in a secluded, tranquil setting. Relax in our spacious en suite rooms (four poster if desired). Holder of Pride of Northumbria Best B&B and England for Excellence Awards. Sorry no children or pets. Open Easter–Oct.

11 **Northfield Farm,** Glanton, Alnwick, Northumberland NE66 4AG

Jackie Stothard
☎ 01665 578203
[BB] From £17.50–£20
Sleeps 6
⌕ ♿ ♞
Listed *Highly Commended*

Traditional farmhouse in secluded location with stunning views on a smallholding with a variety of livestock. Ideal centre for exploring Northumberland and the Borders. Bedrooms are spacious and comfortable with tea/coffee-making facilities. Twin and double rooms with basins. Ground floor bedroom with private WC. Central heating throughout. Children's play area. Open Apr–Oct.

Tosson Tower Farm, Great Tosson, Rothbury, Morpeth, Northumberland NE65 7NW   12

Mrs Ann Foggin
☎ **01669 620228**
▦ **From £18.50–£20**
Sleeps 6
🐕 🐴 💼 ← 🌲
🏵 🏵 *Highly Commended*

Breathtaking views over Coquet Valley and Cheviots combined with traditional farmhouse comforts in this former coaching inn nestling in peaceful hamlet. Border history starts on doorstep with ruined 15th century Tosson Pele Tower. Surrounding hills and forests provide invigorating challenges for serious walkers or a peaceful return to nature for ramblers. Private fishing. Cosy en suite bedrooms, hairdryers, electric blankets, beverages at anytime. CH, real log fires. Closed Christmas only.

SELF-CATERING

Bilton Barns Cottage, Bilton Barns, Alnmouth, Alnwick, Northumberland NE66 2TB   1

Mrs Dorothy Jackson
☎ **01665 830427**
Fax 01665 830063
🆂🅲 **From £100–£360**
Sleeps 7
🐕 🐴
🔑 🔑 🔑 🔑 *Highly Commended*

Ideally situated for exploring the beautiful Northumbrian coastline with its castles and magnificent walks. Our farm cottage has been recently modernised to a very high standard with a new and fully equipped kitchen, central heating and an open fire with fuel provided. Bed linen is also included in rental. Open all year.

Doxford Newhouses, Doxford Farm, Chathill, Northumberland NE67 5DY   13

Sarah Shell
☎/Fax **01665 579348**
🆂🅲 **From £225–£425**
Sleeps 4
🐕 🐴 📺 💼 ← 🌲
🔑 🔑 🔑 🔑 *Highly Commended*

A delightful 17th century stone cottage with well maintained garden ideally situated midway between the Cheviot foothills and the heritage coastline. Tastefully modernised, the open beams have been retained and a woodburning stove installed in the huge stone fireplace. The cottage is very comfortable and well furnished, heated and equipped to a high standard. All fuel power and bed linen provided. Pets are welcome. Open all year.

East Burton Farm Holiday Cottages, East Burton, Bamburgh, Northumberland NE69 7AR   2

Eve Humphreys
☎ **01668 214213/214458**
Fax 01668 214538
🆂🅲 **From £200–£450**
Sleeps 4–6
🐕 🐴 📺 💼 🌲 ⚡ ◉
🔑 🔑 🔑 🔑 *Up to Highly Commended*

Six comfortable cottages on a working farm 1½ miles from Bamburgh, all well equipped and furnished. Heat, light, sheets and towels included in rent. Ideal base for birdwatching, golf, sightseeing or relaxing. Open all year.

Firwood Bungalow and Humphreys House, Earle Hill Head Farm, Wooler, Northumberland NE71 6RH   3

S E Armstrong
☎/Fax **01668 281243**
🆂🅲 **From £180–£550**
Sleeps 6–11
🐕 🐴 💼 ← 🌲
🔑 🔑 🔑 🔑 – 🔑 🔑 🔑 🔑
Up to Highly Commended

Firwood and Humphreys, a choice of two beautiful homes offering a unique and private situation. Standing in 1.5 acres of well maintained gardens on 4,000 acre farm within the National Park at the foot of the Cheviots. Ideal throughout the year. Every comfort, open fires, central heating. Open all year.

14 **Garden Cottage,** Lumbylaw Farm, Edlingham, Alnwick, Northumberland NE66 2BW

Mrs Sally Lee
☎/Fax 01665 574277
sc From £125–£254
Sleeps 2
⚄ ☗ ⚇
⚘ ⚘ ⚘ *Highly Commended*

The cottage is situated in beautiful valley with extensive hill views, rich in wildlife with a 13th century castle ruin and a Victorian viaduct providing easy walking along the disused railway line. Centrally heated, prettily decorated, furnished and equipped to a high standard. Own garden. All power, bedlinen, towels included in rent. Sorry no pets or smokers. Open all year.

12 **Keepers Cottages,** Tosson Tower Farm, Great Tosson, Rothbury, Northumberland NE65 7NW

Mrs Ann Foggin
☎ 01669 620228
sc From £135–£450
Sleeps 4–6
⚄ ⚇ ⚅ ⚆ – ⚘ ⚘ ⚘ ⚘
Up to Highly Commended

Four delightful cottages situated in the Coquet Valley enjoying panoramic views of the Cheviot Hills. Cosy, comfortable, centrally heated, well equipped and all with enclosed gardens. Set in National Park with many forest and moorland walks clearly marked. Private fishing. 2 miles from Rothbury and the NT property of Cragside. Very central for touring all Northumberland. Bedlinen provided. Log fires during winter. Open all year.

14 **Lumbylaw Cottage,** Lumbylaw Farm, Edlingham, Alnwick, Northumberland NE66 2BW

Mrs Sally Lee
☎/Fax 01665 574277
sc From £170–£418
Sleeps 6 + cot
⚄ ⚇ ☗ ⚇
⚘ ⚘ ⚘ ⚘ *Highly Commended*

The cottage is situated in beautiful valley with extensive hill views, rich in wildlife with a 13th century castle ruin and a Victorian viaduct providing easy walking along the disused railway line. Centrally heated, prettily decorated, furnished and equipped to a high standard. Own garden. All power, bedlinen, towels included in rent. Sorry no pets or smokers. Open all year.

15 **Nos. 2 and 3 Cottages,** Titlington Hall Farm, Alnwick, Northumberland NE66 2EB

Mrs Vera Purvis
☎/Fax 01665 578253
sc From £165–£295
Sleep 4–6
⚄ ⚇ ⚇
⚘ ⚘ ⚘ ⚘ *Commended*

Two lovely country cottages available for holiday lets all year round. They are situated in a beautiful area with many interesting places close by. Facilities include central heating, TV, fridge, washing machine, microwave, tumble dryer and all linen. Children and pets welcome. Can sleep families of up to 10. Open all year.

16 **Shepherd's Cottage,** Ingram Farm, Powburn, Alnwick, Northumberland NE66 4LT

Sarah Wilson
☎/Fax 01665 578243
sc From £220–£400
Sleeps 7
⚄ ⚇ ⚅ ⚇ ⚇ ⚇
⚘ ⚘ ⚘ ⚘ *Commended*

On a working family farm in the beautiful Breamish Valley, the cottage has superb scenery on the doorstep. Explore the unspoilt Cheviot Hills or the coast and castles. Most mod cons are provided and there are no extras – fuel, linen and towels all included. Central heating from open fire. Night storage heating. Open all year except Christmas and New Year.

LET THE TELEPHONE RING!

Some farmhouses are big places. Let the telephone ring
long enough to give the owner time to answer it.

Northumberland South

Group Contact: *Mrs Susan Dart* ☎ *01434 673240*

All of our members live within easy distance to the mass of Roman sites connected with Hadrian's Wall in its beautiful open countryside, where you can feel 'on top of the world'. Apart from the wide open spaces where nature rules its way, there are many historic and rural attractions notably the National Trust Properties of Wallington Hall and Cragside, the first house to be powered by electricity, the market town of Hexham with its abbey that was a cathedral from 600–800, Beamish Open Air Museum depicting life in the area as of 1913, and the Keilder Forest and reservoir with all its outdoor pursuits. Then of course there are the excellent shopping facilities of the Metro Centre and Newcastle as well as the out of town shopping in Hexham, Corbridge and Morpeth. Enough to keep you happy for at least a week!

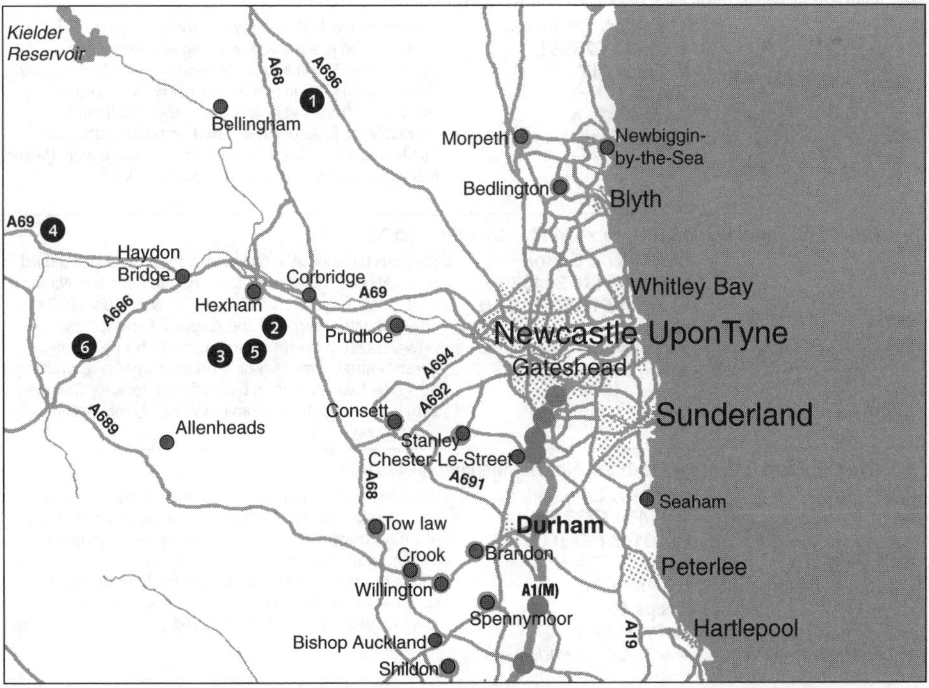

Kielder Reservoir

A68 · A696

Bellingham ● **1**

Morpeth ●
Newbiggin-by-the-Sea

Bedlington ●
Blyth

A69 ● **4**

Haydon Bridge ●
Corbridge ● A69
Whitley Bay

A686
Hexham ●
2
Prudhoe ●
Newcastle UponTyne

6
3 **5**
A694
Gateshead

A692
Sunderland

A689
Allenheads ●
Consett ●
A692

Stanley ●
Chester-Le-Street ●
A691
Seaham ●

A68
Tow law ●
Durham

Crook ●
Brandon ●
Peterlee

Willington ●
A1(M)
Spennymoor ●
A19
Hartlepool

Bishop Auckland ●
Shildon ●

BED AND BREAKFAST

(and evening meal)

---

1 Cornhills, Kirkwhelpington, Northumberland NE19 2RE

Lorna Thornton
☎ 01830 540232
BB **From £17.50**
Sleeps 6
Listed *Highly Commended*

A large Victorian farmhouse complete with mosaic tiled hall, spacious beautifully decorated and furnished bedrooms (one en suite), all with outstanding views. Our stock farm is in the centre of Northumberland, ideal for visiting Cragside, Wallington and Belsay Hall. Recommended by the *Which* report *The Good Bed & Breakfast* guide. Newcastle 30 minutes away, 1 mile from the A696. Closed April.

---

2 Flothers Farm, Slaley, Hexham, Northumberland NE47 0BJ

Susan Dart
☎ 01434 673240/673587
BB **From £17.50–£20**
Sleeps 5
Commended

We are a typical Northumbrian dairy farm, set in beautiful countryside. Accommodation in self-contained area. Full central heating, all rooms en suite, tea/coffee and colour TV. Country pubs within walking distance. Excellent breakfasts provided. Open all year except Christmas.

---

3 Gairshield Farm, Whitley Chapel, Hexham, Northumberland NE47 0HS

Mrs Hilary Kristensen
☎ 01434 673562
BB **From £17**
Sleeps 3
(6)
Listed *Highly Commended*

A comfortable 17th century farmhouse on a quiet hill farm (1,000 ft above sea level), with superb views over open countryside. 20 mins south of Hexham. Ideal for exploring this beautiful historic region. Perfect walking and horse-riding area; horses very welcome. Relaxed, friendly atmosphere. Tastefully decorated with large attractive family bedroom. Guests' dining room/lounge with TV and tea/coffee-making facilities. Open Apr–Oct.

---

4 Gibbs Hill Farm, Bardon Mill, Hexham, Northumberland NE47 7AP

Mrs Valerie Gibson
☎/Fax 01434 344030
BB **From £17.50–£19.50**
Sleeps 4
(12)
Commended

Spacious farmhouse accommodation of highest standard on traditional 700-acre hill farm/nature reserve in National Park. Beautifully fuirnished rooms, 1 twin, 1 double (both en suite) with tea/coffee and colour TV and spectacular views. Excellent breakfasts in huge farmhouse kitchen, guests' lounge. Private fishing on own small lake, walking, riding, birdwatching from bird hide overlooking Greenlee Lough. Five minutes to Roman Wall and main Roman sites. Open Apr–Oct.

---

5 Rye Hill Farm, Slaley, Nr Hexham, Northumberland NE47 0AH

Elizabeth Courage
☎ 01434 673259
Fax 01434 673608
BB **From £20–£24**
EM **From £12**
Sleeps 15
Commended

We are a small family-run livestock farm set in beautiful countryside with 360-degree panoramic views. We have recently converted some of the old byres into superb modern guest accommodation. We aim for high standards with a homely atmosphere. Good, fresh, homemade cooking. All rooms are en suite and have large bath towels. Well mannered children and pets welcome. Open all year.

Struthers Farm, Catton, Allendale, Hexham, Northumberland NE47 9LP   6

Mrs Ruby Keenleyside
☎ 01434 683580
BB From £17.50–£20
EM From £9.50
Sleeps 5
🐴 🐕 🎪 ⚓
🐛 🐛 *Commended*

A small working livestock farm situated in a designated area of natural beauty. Quiet country walks, ample safe parking. Children and pets by arrangement. We offer spacious double/twin en suite rooms, Guests' lounge/dining/TV room. Fresh home cooking. Come and enjoy our countryside. Open all year.

Self-Catering

Gibbs Hill Farm Cottages, Bardon Mill, Hexham, Northumberland NE47 7AP   4

Mrs Valerie Gibson
☎/Fax 01434 344030
SC From £100–£390
Sleep 2–5 + cot
🐴 🐕 ⅋ ⚓ ☕ 🎪 🌾
🏠 🏠 🏠 🏠 *Up to De Luxe*

Superb stone cottages on 700-acre traditional hill farm nature reserve in National Park. Central heating, log fires. Outstanding views, walking, riding, trout fishing in own small lake. Birdwatching from bird hide. 5 minutes to Roman Wall and main Roman forts. Centrally placed for north east coast, Tynedale and Lakes. Brochure available. Short breaks. Open all year.

The Herdsman Cottage, Cornhills, Kirkwhelpington, Northumberland NE19 2RE   1

Lorna Thornton
☎ 01830 540232
SC From £180–£320
Sleeps 5
🐴 ⅋ 🎪
🏠 🏠 🏠 🏠 *Commended*

A beamed 19th century farm cottage, provides comfortable accommodation for 5 people (double, twin, single). The fully fitted kitchen is equipped with fridge, microwave, washing machine, night storage heaters, open fire. All fuel included in price. Bed linen provided. Enjoy the peace on our stock farm, in the centre of Northumberland. Open all year.

Durham & Its Dales

Group Contact: *Mrs Judith Stephenson* ☎ *01388 527285*

County Durham's fascinating blend of Christian, Social and Industrial heritage, combined with some of England's most unspoilt countryside, makes it an area where there's plenty to do and see.

The historic city of Durham, its cathedral and castle dominating the winding streets of the old town; the Open Air Museum at Beamish where you can experience life at the turn the century; the reconstructed Killhope lead mine high up in Weardale with the opportunity to explore underground; the largest waterfall in England at High Force in Teesdale; impressive castles and fortified farmhouses; the Josephine and John Bowes Museum's collections of 18th century furniture, paintings and ceramics; the breathtaking scenery of high, wild fells and wooded valleys of 'England's last wilderness' – are only a few of many attractions.

You are also within reach of the activities of our vibrant urban areas, the theatres, cinemas, concerts, galleries, pubs, clubs and restaurants of Tyneside and Teeside; and the Metro Centre at Gateshead is one of Europe's largest shopping and leisure complexes.

There is something for everyone, and you will find a warm North Country welcome wherever you go.

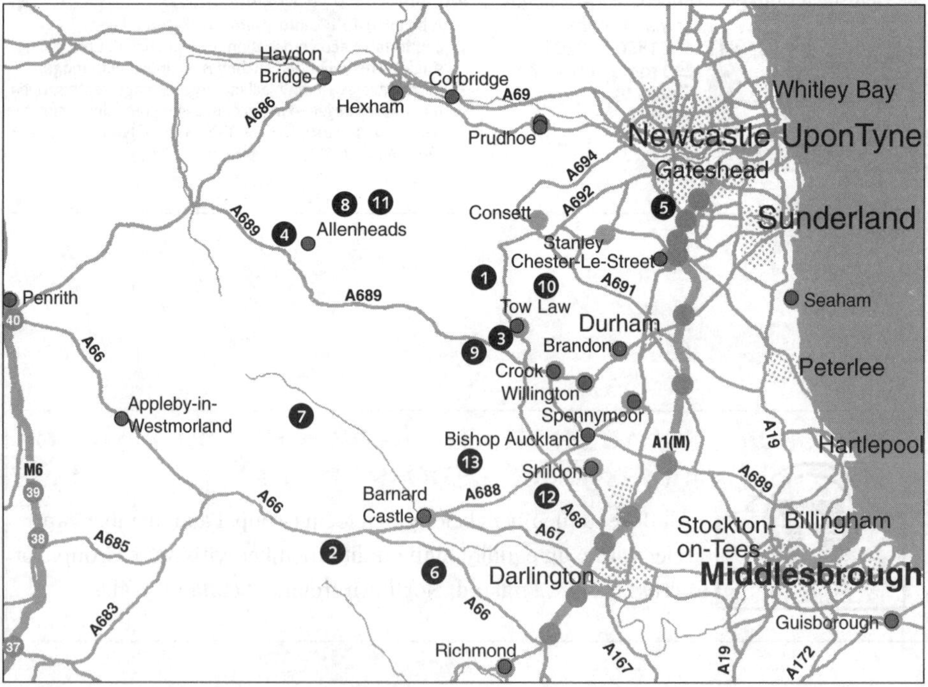

BED AND BREAKFAST

(and evening meal)

Bee Cottage Farm, Castleside, Consett, Co Durham DH8 9HW ①

Liz Lawson
☎ 01207 508224
🅱 From £22
EM £13.50
Sleeps 30
🛏🐓✂🔥♨ ⊛
🐾 *Highly Commended*

A working farm in lovely surroundings with unspoilt views, situated 1½ miles west A68 between Tow Law and Castleside. Tea room open daily. Quiet country walks. Fire certificate. No smoking in farmhouse. Ideally located for Beamish Museum, Metro Centre, Durham Cathedral or a break on a journey between England and Scotland. You will be made most welcome. Open all year.

East Mellwaters Farm, Bowes, Barnard Castle, Co Durham DL12 9RH ②

Patricia Milner
☎/Fax 01833 628269
🅱 From £18–£20
EM From £10
Sleeps 12
🛏🐓✂♨🏹🎣 ⊛🔥♨
⊛
🐾🐾 *Commended*

Come and meet Dolly, our highland cow, watch the dippers and golden plovers or glimpse badgers. Learn about the Bronze Age on our waymarked walks. Fish for brown trout, we'll show you the best pools. Visit Beamish, Bowes Museum, ancient castles, market towns or the Metro Centre for shopping (Christmas?). Then relax with a cup of tea, log fire and delicious food in best farmhouse tradition. Holidays and special break rates. Open mid Jan–mid Dec.

Greenwell Farm, Nr Wolsingham, Tow Law, Bishop Auckland, Co Durham DL13 4PH ③

Mike & Linda Vickers
☎ 01388 527248
Fax 01388 526735
🅱 From £20–£22.50
EM From £12.50
Sleeps 12
🛏✂🐓🔥♨ ⊛
🐾🐾 *Commended*

There is something special about Greenwell Farm and its 300 year-old stone barn, now converted into accommodation. That speciality is homeliness, the unique atmosphere that our visitors come for. We offer warmth and comfort with blend of pine and dark oak antique furniture. High quality food using home produced, naturally reared meat and vegetables where possible. Enjoy our working mixed farm with nature trails and beautiful countryside. Closed Christmas and New Year.

Lands Farm, Westgate-in-Weardale, Co Durham DL13 1SN ④

Mrs Barbara Reed
☎ 01388 517210
🅱 From £20–£25
Sleeps 5
🛏🔥♨
🐾🐾 *Highly Commended*

A friendly welcome awaits you on our 280-acre beef and sheep farm peacefully situated in beautiful Weardale. All bedrooms have luxury en suite facilities, TV and tea/coffee. Conveniently located for Durham City, Beamish Museum, Hadrian's Wall, High Force and walking in the North Pennines. Open Mar–Nov.

Low Urpeth Farm, Ouston, Chester Le Street, Co Durham DH2 1BD ⑤

Hilary Johnson
☎ 0191 410 2901
Fax 0191 410 0081
🅱 From £20–£25
Sleeps 6
🛏(12)✂🔥♨ ⊛
Listed *Highly Commended*

Traditional farmhouse accommodation in spacious and comfortably furnished rooms with TV/beverage facilities, one double with washbasin, 2 twin en suite. Within easy reach of Beamish Open Air Museum, Durham and castles and coast of Northumberland. Directions – leave A1(M) at Chester Le Street, follow A693, at 2nd roundabout fork right to Ouston, down hill, over roundabout, turn left at 'Trees Please' sign. Closed Christmas and New Year.

6   **Wilson House,** Barningham, Richmond, North Yorkshire DL11 7EB

Mrs Helen Lowes
☎ 01833 621218
🅱🅱 From £16–£20
EM From £10
Sleeps 6

😺 ✕ ⅄ ⚘ 🖻

😺😺 *Commended*

Relax and unwind in a traditional country retreat. Set amidst magnificent scenery, Wilson House offers a high standard of accommodation, a relaxing atmosphere and friendly welcome. (FHG Diploma 1997.) Tour the Dales by car or take one of the many beautiful walks then return to the open fire and smell of home cooking. Varied menus using fresh local/home produce and tailored to your tastes. Open Mar–Nov.

---

7   **Wythes Hill Farm,** Lunedale, Middleton-in-Teesdale, Co Durham DL12 0NX

Mrs June Dent
☎ 01833 640349
🅱🅱 From £17–£17.50
EM From £9
Sleeps 5

😺 ⚘

😺 *Commended*

Wythes Hill is a working stock-rearing farm with panoramic views from all rooms. Situated on the Pennine Way route with many picturesque walks in Teesdale. Visit the Bowes Museum, Raby Castle and High Force Waterfall. Good plain cooking. One family room with H&C, one twin en suite. All rooms with tea/coffee-making facilities. Lounge with coal fire. Open Mar–Oct.

SELF-CATERING

8   **Bail Hill,** Allenshields, Blanchland, Consett, Co Durham DH8 9PP

Jennifer Graham
☎ 01434 675274
🆂🅲 From £120–£220
Sleeps 5

😺 ⊞ ⚘ 🖻

🐾 🐾 🐾 *Commended*

Centrally heated, 2-bedroomed farmhouse with breathtaking views to Derwent Reservoir near Blanchland. Enjoy the peaceful surroundings of a typical hill farm or use as a central location for Tynedale, Durham and N E Coast. Blanchland is one of the most picturesque of Northumbrian historic villages with Abbey, pub and post office. Open fire and well-equipped kitchen. Enclosed garden and parking outside the house. Open all year.

---

9   **Bradley Burn Holiday Cottages,** Wolsingham, Weardale, Co Durham DL13 3JH

Mrs Judith Stephenson
☎/Fax 01388 527285
🆂🅲 From £130–£320
Sleeps 2–6

🚶 😺 🦃 ⚘ 🍽 ⚘ 🖻 ◉
🐾 🐾 🐾 – 🐾 🐾 🐾 🐾

Up to Highly Commended

Explore our fields and woods, observe modern farming, watch for owls and herons. Stay in one of four comfortable, well equipped cottages adjoining the farmhouse at Bradley Burn, at the gateway to Weardale and the North Pennines. Excellent sightseeing and walking base, or just unwind. Granary Cottage is ideal for families, Stable and Harvest Cottages perfect for couples. Our brochure has full details. Short breaks available. Open all year.

---

10   **Browney Cottage,** c/o Hall Hill Farm, Lanchester, Durham DH7 0TA

Mrs Pat Gibson
☎/Fax 01388 730300
🆂🅲 From £150–£230
Sleeps 4

😺 ⚘ 🖻 ◉

🐾 🐾 🐾 🐾 *Up to Commended*

Browney Cottages are one mile from our family-run open farm. During your stay visitors can bottle feed the lambs, see fluffy chicks and lots more. Both cottages have 1 double and 1 twin. Newly refurbished kitchen with fridge/freezer, microwave, washer and tumble dryer. Bedlinen included. Open all year except Christmas.

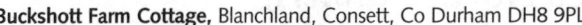

Buckshott Farm Cottage, Blanchland, Consett, Co Durham DH8 9PL **11**

Lorraine Bainbridge
☎ 01434 675227
⑤ From £120–£235
Sleeps 6
🎿 🐕 ♨
🔑 🔑 🔑 *Commended*

Attractive 2-bedroom cottage which adjoins the farmhouse and overlooks the beautiful Derwent Valley. Central heating, fitted kitchen, private garden, ample parking. Blanchlands historic village has a shop, post office, pub and a 12th century abbey. Hexham, Durham, Beamish Open Air Museum, Gateshead Metro Centre and the Northumberland coast are all within an easy day's outing. Open Apr–Oct.

Greenwell Hill Stables & Byre, c/o Greenwell Farm, Nr Wolsingham, Tow Law, Co Durham DL13 4PH **3**

Linda Vickers
☎ 01388 527248
Fax 01388 526735
⑤ From £160–£365
Sleeps 2/7
🎿 🐕 ♨ ♿ ◎
🔑 🔑 🔑 🔑 *Up to Highly Commended*

Enjoy a relaxing stay in one of two quality cottages. This is a traditional farm in peaceful countryside. Marvellous views, pleasant walks and our own nature trail with conservation area. The larger cottage has a four poster bed, dishwasher and en suite bedrooms. Both are well equipped with gas central heating, double glazing, natural beams, pine furniture, fitted carpets, comfy chintzy suites and woodburing stoves. Evening meals available. Open all year.

High House Farm Cottages, High House Farm, Houghton Le Side, Darlington DL2 2UU **12**

Harry & Peggy Wood
☎ 01388 834879
⑤ From £120–£340
Sleeps 2–6
🎿 🐕 ♨ ♿
🔑 🔑 🔑 🔑 *Highly Commended*

Gateway to Northumbria with panoramic views across Teesdale to North Yorks Moors. Near A1(M), A68 scenic route and Dere Street Roman Road. Home of 'Fairisle' Shetland sheep and 'Aymara' alpacas. Smithy, Granary and Coach House conversions, sensitively combining four-poster, beams and log burning stove with night storage heaters, power showers, TVs and other modern amenities. Open all year.

Katie's Cottage, c/o Low Urpeth Farm, Ouston, Chester Le Street, Co.Durham DH2 1BD **5**

Hilary Johnson
☎ 0191 410 2901
Fax 0191 410 0081
⑤ From £210–£275
Sleeps 4
🎿 ✂ ♿ ♨ ◎
🔑 🔑 🔑 🔑 🔑

Highly Commended

Relax in our newly converted stone cottage, tastefully furnished. Two en suite bedrooms, cosy living area with timber beams. Excellent base for Durham, Beamish Museum and easy access to Northumberland and Hadrian's Wall. Open all year.

North Wythes Hill, Wythes Hill Farm, Lunedale, Middleton-in-Teesdale, Co Durham DL12 0NX **7**

Mrs June Dent
☎ 01833 640349
⑤ From £160–£325
Sleeps 6/7
🎿 🐕 ♨
🔑 🔑 🔑 🔑 *Commended*

Cosy, three bedroomed cottage with full central heating. Peaceful situation on a working hill farm where children can feed pet lambs (in season), ducks and see plenty of wildlife. Actually on Pennine Way route. Circular walks from the door. Large garden. Prices include bedlinen and towels. Open all year.

Stonecroft, Low Lands Farm, Low Lands, Cockfield, Bishop Auckland DL13 5AW **13**

Mr K & Mrs A Tallentire
☎ 01388 718251
⑤ From £120–£250
Sleeps 4 + cot
🎿 🐕 ♨ ♿
🔑 🔑 🔑 🔑

Highly Commended

Charming old farmworker's cottage recently renovated and decorated to retain its traditional style and character. On the borders of wonderfully unspoilt Teesdale, Weardale and Durham Dales. Set in an area full of historic towns and sights. Ideally suited for walkers, families and professionals wanting a quiet restful break. Open all year.

Cleveland & North Yorkshire Borders

Group Contact: *Mrs June Dent* ☎ *01833 640349*

Cleveland & North Yorkshire is an Area of Outstanding Natural Beauty bordering the north-western edges of the North Yorkshire Moors, the largest expanse of heather moorland in England, familiar from the television series 'Heartbeat'. The name Cleveland comes from the Norse word 'Klifland' meaning land of cliffs and the picturesque Cleveland hills offer many good walks with spectacular views. The area gives its name to the 'Cleveland Way', the long distance walk from Helmsley to Filey, and also to the local breed of horse, the 'Cleveland Bay'.

Tucked beneath the northern edge of the moors lies Great Ayton where the famous explorer Captain Cook was educated and the 50ft monument on Easby Moor can be seen from miles around.

When staying on a farm in this area, tourists have access not only to the beauty of the moors and Yorkshire Dales but also to Teesside with its industry and commerce. Businessmen will be offered the warmth of Yorkshire hospitality within easy reach of Middlesbrough and Stockton.

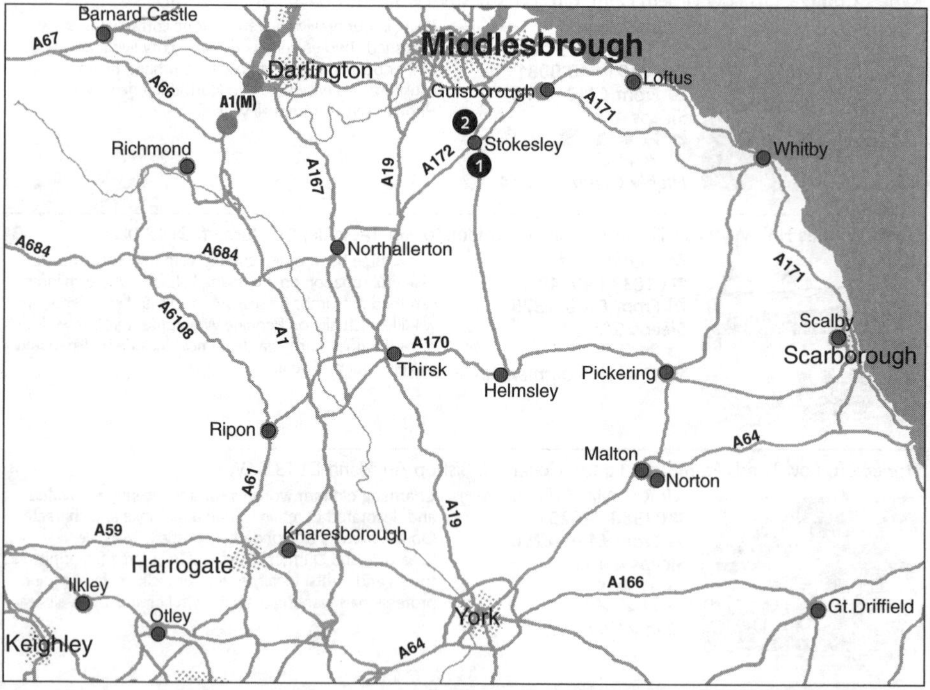

BED AND BREAKFAST

(and evening meal)

Dromonby Hall Farm, Busby Lane, Kirkby-in-Cleveland, Stokesley, Middlesbrough TS9 7AP

Mrs Patricia Weighell
☎/Fax 01642 712312
🆎 From £16–£18.50
Sleeps 6
🐕(2) 🐴 ⊁ ♨ 🎣 🏕 ⚽
💐 *Commended*

Modern farmhouse on 170-acre working farm with superb views of Cleveland Hills. Ideal for walking or touring by car. Easy access from A19 and B1257, 8 miles south of Middlesbrough. ½ hr drive from coast and from Teesside. A warm welcome and good food. Horse riding available locally. Enjoy the peace and beautiful surroundings. Open all year.

Harker Hill Farm, Harker Hill, Seamer, Stokesley, Nr Middlesbrough, North Yorkshire TS9 5NF

Pam & John Fanthorpe
☎/Fax 01642 710431
🆎 From £17
EM From £7.50
Sleeps 6
🐕 🐴 ⊁ 🏕 ♨
Listed *Commended*

Harker Hill is a two hundred year old farm offering warmth and comfort. The cosy accommodation includes full central heating, log fires, lounge and television. Home cooked food is served at times to suit you so businessmen visiting Teesside can enjoy early cooked breakfasts and late evening meals. Open all year except Christmas.

FOLLOW THE COUNTRY CODE

Leave nothing but footprints,
Take nothing but photographs,
Kill nothing but time!

North Pennines

Group Contact: *Pat Dent* ☎ *01434 381383*

The North Pennines – Area of Outstanding Natural Beauty – is truly 'England's Last Wilderness'.

The upland moors and valleys of Cumbria, Durham and Northumberland are encompassed by this area of remote moorland, famed for wild flowers and birds.

Three famous rivers rise here, the Tyne, the Tees and the Wear, fast-flowing streams growing to mighty torrents. In Teesdale, High Force shows the power of the water as does the river Wear harnessed by the lead miners at Killhope Wheel.

Landscapes have been formed by generations of hill farmers, a patchwork separated by stone walls and grazed by sheep and cattle, with heather moors and, from long ago, the remains of Roman occupation.

This area is criss-crossed with footpaths, the most well known being the Pennine Way, but there is something for everyone, from the gentle stroll to the energetic journey to the top of Cross Fell at 2,930 ft. The scenery is varied, with many panoramic views and a different scene around every corner.

Alston with its narrow cobbled street and market cross nestles amongst these hills, as do Allendale town where New Year is celebrated with a procession of blazing tar barrels. St John's Chapel, host to one of the many agricultural shows held in this area. Stanhope boasts a fossilised tree. Nearby are the market towns of Barnard Castle, Appleby, Hexham and Penrith.

Easily accessible, yet far from the hustle and bustle of modern life, this area is excellent for touring, but most people find that once here, they do not want to leave.

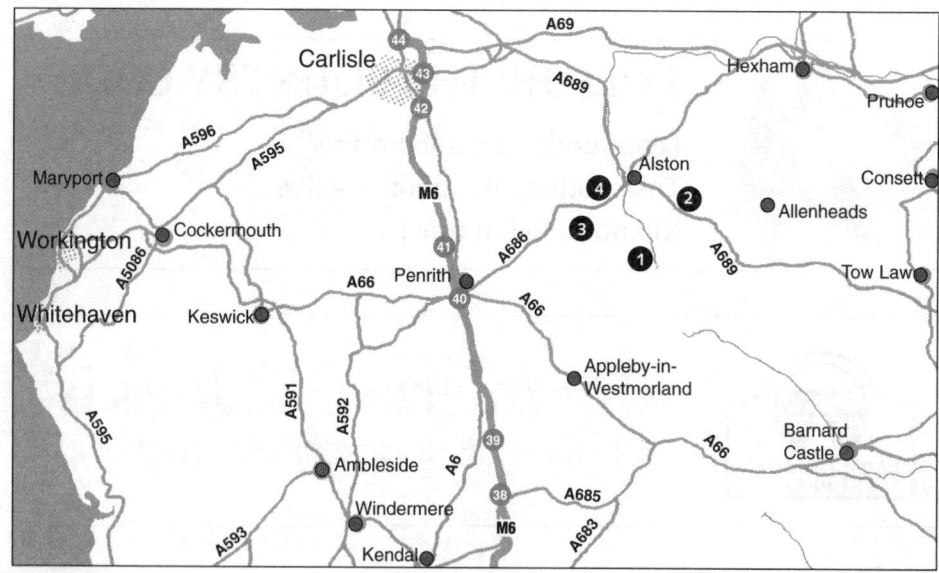

BED AND BREAKFAST

(and evening meal)

Crossgill Farm, Garrigill, Alston, Cumbria CA9 3HE (1)

Mrs Pat Dent
☎ 01434 381383
🅱 From £16–£19
EM £10
Sleeps 6
🐕 ✂ ☂ 🌳 ◎
🌺 🌺 *Highly Commended*

A large, family-run hill farm where visitors are welcome to wander. A warm welcome awaits you at our warm, tastefully furnished home, formerly a shooting lodge. One double and one family en suite, single with handbasin. Tea trays, central heating, electric blankets. All good home cooking including our own bread. Closed Christmas & April for lambing.

Low Cornriggs Farm, Cowshill-in-Weardale, Bishop Auckland, Co Durham DL13 1AQ (2)

Mrs Janet Ellis
☎/Fax 01388 537600
🅱 From £18–£18.50
EM From £10
Sleeps 6
🐕 🐎 🐖 🌳 ♿

🌺 🌺 🌺 *Commended*

Low Cornriggs has wonderful views over the High Pennines. Luxury 200-year-old farmhouse with antiques, en suite rooms, electric blankets, tea trays. Log fires, stone floors, beams, pine doors, full CH. Take breakfast in large conservatory, enjoy wonderful home-cooked food in licensed dining room. TV lounge. We are an Approved British Riding School offering lessons, treks, riding holidays. Good walking, Green Tourism Award Winner. Open all year.

SELF-CATERING

Ghyll Burn Cottage, Hartside Nursery Garden, Nr Alston, Cumbria CA9 3BL (3)

Mrs Susan Huntley
☎ 01434 381372/381428
Fax 01434 381372
🆂🅲 From £155–£350
Sleeps 4/6 + cot
🐕 🐖 ♿ 🌳 🐾 ♿ ◎
🐾 🐾 🐾 *Commended*

Recently renovated farm buildings dating back to 1630 offer spacious and comfortable accommodation for 4/6 people. Kitchen/diner, large lounge with oak beams and wood burning stove on first floor. Attractive twin and double bedrooms, bathroom, are downstairs. Full gas central heating. The cottage is set in a secluded valley with small nursery garden. Ideal for bird wildlife and gardening enthusiasts. Open all year.

Grey Croft, The Raise, Alston, c/o Crossgill Farm, Garrigill, Alston, Cumbria CA9 3HE (4)

Mrs Pat Dent
☎ 01434 381383
🆂🅲 From £170–£340
Sleeps 2–6
🚶 🐕 🐎 ✂ ♿ ◎
🐾 🐾 🐾 🐾 🐾 *Highly Commended*

Luxury bungalow with open views south towards Crossfell on the fringe of The Raise hamlet, one mile from Alston. Fully equipped and furnished to a very high standard. Two bedrooms with double and single beds, linen provided. Fitted kitchen, dishwasher, microwave, washer/dryer. Gas CH, open fire, TV, telephone. Open all year.

Eden Valley & North Pennines

Group Contacts: BB *Ruth Tuer ☎/Fax 01931 715205*
SC *Anne Ivinson ☎ 016974 76230(24hr answerphone/Fax 76523)*

The River Eden rises in Mallerstang, an isolated corner of the old County of Westmorland, and, rushing through the alpine flowers of the still untamed North Pennines, gradually descends, gathering strength from its many tributaries, until it reaches Appleby, a sleepy market town straddling the Eden. The broad tree lined street linking the Castle and the Church make it one of the loveliest towns in the valley. For two weeks every year Appleby awakes from its slumber to host the largest gipsy gathering and horse fair in the country, a sight not to be missed!

On to the attractive town of Penrith, Gateway to the Lakes, a focus for travellers since Roman times the Eden meanders through picturesque villages built of local red sandstone until it reaches the historic City of Carlisle and the Solway Plain. This area is truly a 'Garden of Eden' with its lush vegetation and wide variety of wildlife. The visitor can enjoy a variety of walks, climbing Cross Fell or Wild Boar Fell in the Pennines or take an easier route along one of the many woodland and riverside footpaths signposted through the area.

For the less energetic there are tours around historic houses and sites travelling on the local minibus, the Fellrunner and last but by no means least, the famous Carlisle to Settle railway runs right through Eden with stations at Armathwaite, Lazonby, Langwathby and Appleby: what better way to enjoy the magnificent scenery of the Eden Valley and the North Pennines?

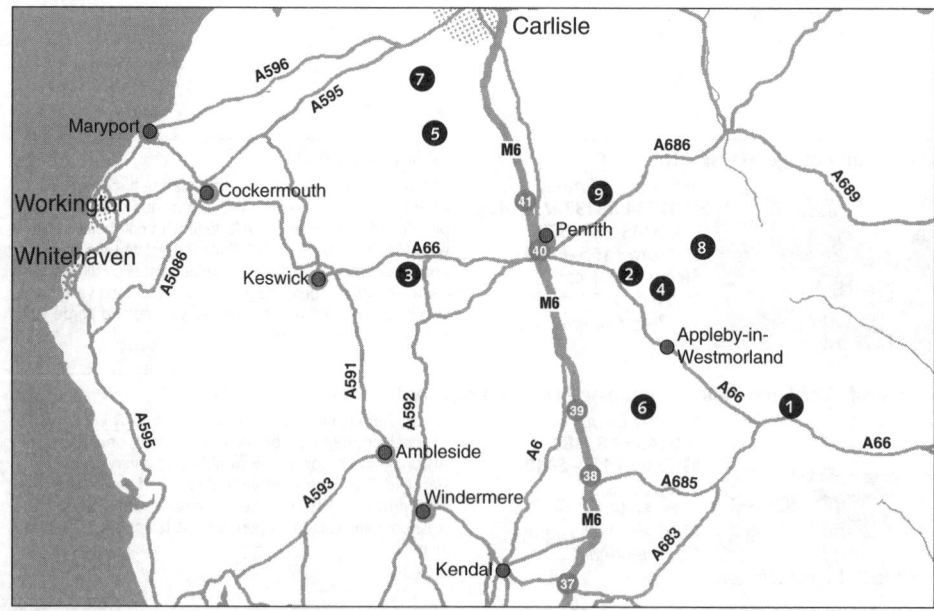

BED AND BREAKFAST

(and evening meal)

Augill House Farm, Brough-under-Stainmore, Kirkby Stephen, Cumbria CA17 4DX

Jeanette Atkinson
☎ 017683 41305
BB From £20–£22
EM From £10
Sleeps 6
☺(12) ✄ ✗ ▜ ☂ ⊛
✿ *Highly Commended*

Enjoy good food and hospitality at this much recommended farmhouse in the Upper Eden Valley. En suite bedrooms with colour TV and hospitaility tray. Ideal for visiting the Lakes, Dales and North Pennines. Breakfast and dinner served in our lovely conservatory overlooking the garden. RAC Highly Acclaimed. AA QQQQ Selected. Open Apr–Nov.

Bridge End Farm, Kirkby Thore, Penrith, Cumbria CA10 1UZ

Mrs Yvonne Dent
☎ 01768 361362
BB From £20–£22
EM From £9
Sleeps 6
☺ ✗ ✄ ✿ ▜
✿✿ *Highly Commended*

Relax in 18th century farmhouse on a dairy farm in the Eden Valley near Appleby. Lovely, spacious, antique-furnished en suite rooms featuring patchwork quilts. Delicious homemade breakfast and dinner served in dining room. All food is freshly prepared and you will never forget Yvonne's sticky toffee pudding. Finish with a a stroll along the River Eden. Open all year except Christmas.

Park House Farm, Dalemain, Penrith, Cumbria CA11 0HB

Mrs Mary Milburn
☎ 017684 86212
BB From £17–£19
Sleeps 6
☺ ☂ ▜ ⊛
✿✿ *Commended*

Peace and tranquillity in our valley – you can relax and enjoy stunning views of Lakeland fells. 3 miles from Lake Ullswater or M6 (J40) on A592 entering via Dalemain Mansion (historic house) ignoring the 'no cars' sign. Cumbrian hospitality assured, home baking and generous breakfast. Evening meals available locally. 2 family bedrooms (1 en suite), electric blanket, heater, tea/coffee facilities. Bathroom and shower room. TV lounge with open fire. Open Apr–Oct.

Slakes Farm, Milburn, Appleby in Westmorland, Cumbria CA16 6DP

Mrs C Braithwaite
☎ 017683 61385
BB From £15
EM from £8.50
Sleeps 6
☺ ✗
Listed *Commended*

Slakes Farm was built in 1734 and is situated between the villages of Milburn and Knock 6 miles from Appleby. The farm is approx 40 acres rearing cattle and sheep. It makes an ideal base for walking and touring, returning to good farmhouse cooking using fresh local produce. Open Easter–Oct.

Streethead Farm, Ivegill, Carlisle, Cumbria CA4 0NG

Mrs J Wilson
☎ 016974 73327
BB From £17.50–£20
Sleeps 4
☺(7) ✗ ▜
✿✿ *Commended*

Roman soldiers used to stay here en route from Lakes to Scotland. Nowadays both are 20 minutes' drive. Relax and enjoy guests' lounge with woodburnrer, choice of breakfasts in character dining room. Two bedrooms (one en suite). Many extra comforts. Meals are available locally. Recommended by *Which Good Bed and Breakfast Guide.* Brochure.

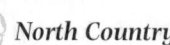
SELF-CATERING

6 Chestnuts, Meaburn Hill Farm, Maulds Meaburn, Penrith, Cumbria CA10 3HN

Ruth Tuer
☎/Fax 01931 715205
sc From £160–£350
Sleeps 4 + cot
🐕 🍽 🎿 🏛 ✾ 🎣 ⊛
🔑 🔑 🔑 🔑 🔑 *Highly Commended*

Lovely cottage converted from traditional Cumbrian long barn, with unsurpassed views of tranquil Lyvennet Valley and village green. Enjoy a peaceful break in this bright, cheerful cottage, mainly on one floor, with excellent standards of facilities, furnishing and decoration. Full oil CH. Small conservatory and garden area, patio, barbecue, parking. Linen and heating included. Short breaks. Open all year.

---

7 Green View Lodges & Well Cottage, Green View, Welton, Nr Dalston, Carlisle, Cumbria CA5 7ES

Anne Ivinson
☎ 016974 76230
Fax 016974 76523
sc From £150–£485
Sleeps 2/7
🕴 🐕 🎣 🐎 ✾ 🏛 ⊛
🔑 🔑 🔑 🔑 – 🔑 🔑 🔑 🔑
Highly Commended

Superb Scandinavian lodges in peaceful garden setting. 17th century oak-beamed cottages oozing character, 1 with open fire and 2nd WC. Also for non-smokers only, a tastefully converted Wesleyan chapel (regret no pets). Own gardens. In tiny, picturesque hamlet with unspoilt views to Caldbeck Fells 3 miles. Every home comfort provided for a relaxing country holiday. CH, telephones. ½ hr's drive from Keswick, Lake Ullswater, Gretna Green. Open all year.

---

8 Skirwith Hall Cottage, Skirwith Hall, Skirwith, Penrith, Cumbria CA10 1RH

Mrs Laura Wilson
☎/Fax 01768 88241
sc From £160–£350
Sleeps 4–8
🐕 🐎 🏛 ⊛
🔑 🔑 🔑 🔑 *Commended*

Georgian farmhouse wing overlooking large landscaped garden and stream on 400-acre mixed dairy farm. Exposed beams and open fire in lounge, CH, electric and Rayburn cookers. Two double rooms and one with twin beds and bunks. Cot and high chair. Ideal for Lakes, North Pennines or Borders, or simply relaxing in peaceful idyllic rural surroundings. Well behaved children and dogs welcome. Brochure. Short breaks in low season. Open all year.

---

8 Smithy Cottage, c/o Skirwith Hall, Skirwith, Penrith, Cumbria CA10 1RH

Mrs Laura Wilson
☎/Fax 01768 88241
sc From £125–£260
Sleeps 2–4
🐕 🐎 🏛 ⊛
🔑 🔑 🔑 🔑 *Commended*

Originally the home of the village blacksmith. Situated on the outskirts of an unspoilt village in the shadow of Crossfell. Tastefully and comfortably furnished with 1 twin and 1 double room. Nightstore heaters and open fires in sitting and dining rooms. Colour TV, telephone, cot, high chair. Private garden by stream. Good pubs, Carlisle–Settle railway, golf, riding, fishing nearby. Ideal for walking or touring Lakes, Pennine Dales or Borders. Open all year.

---

9 West View Cottages, West View Farm, Winskill, Penrith, Cumbria CA10 1PD

Alan and Susan Grave
☎ 01768 881356
sc From £160–£350
Sleeps 2–6
🐕 🐎 🎿 🖼 🏛
🔑 🔑 🔑 🔑 *Commended*

A roomy cottage and 2 barn conversions on a mixed working farm. All units have central heating, TV, modern kitchen, washing facilities, and linen provided. Ideally situated for touring and within easy reach of the lakes, North Pennines and Scotland. Local facilities include children's play area, open air swimming pool, walking. Sleeps 2/4/5. Short breaks available in low season. Brochure sent on request. Open all year.

Central Lakeland

Group Contact: *Margaret Harryman* ☎ *017687 78544*

Stay on a farm in the heart of Cumbria and enjoy the peace and quiet of our valleys. Central Lakeland, with its mountains, lakes and woods is well-known and loved.

For over 200 years travellers have come to this most beautiful corner of England to walk the fells and wander the by-ways. Wonderful at any time of year, certainly in the spring, definitely in the autumn, this is the ideal base for touring.

The Keswick area offers the Pencil Museum, home of the first pencil; the Druid's Stone Circle; Lingholm Gardens; Mirehouse, built 1666, and the 10th century Church of St Bega nearby; or England's only mountain forest park at Whinlatter.

In Grasmere, there are Heaton Coopers Studio and 'Dove Cottage', William Wordsworth's home, now an award winning museum. Ambleside has Hayes marvellous garden centre. See the Beatrix Potter exhibition at Bowness, gallery at Hawkshead or her home 'Hill Top', at Near Sawrey.

Attend local shows, see local crafts, Cumberland wrestling, fell running and hound trailing.

We warmly welcome you to our homely, comfortable and traditional farmhouses.

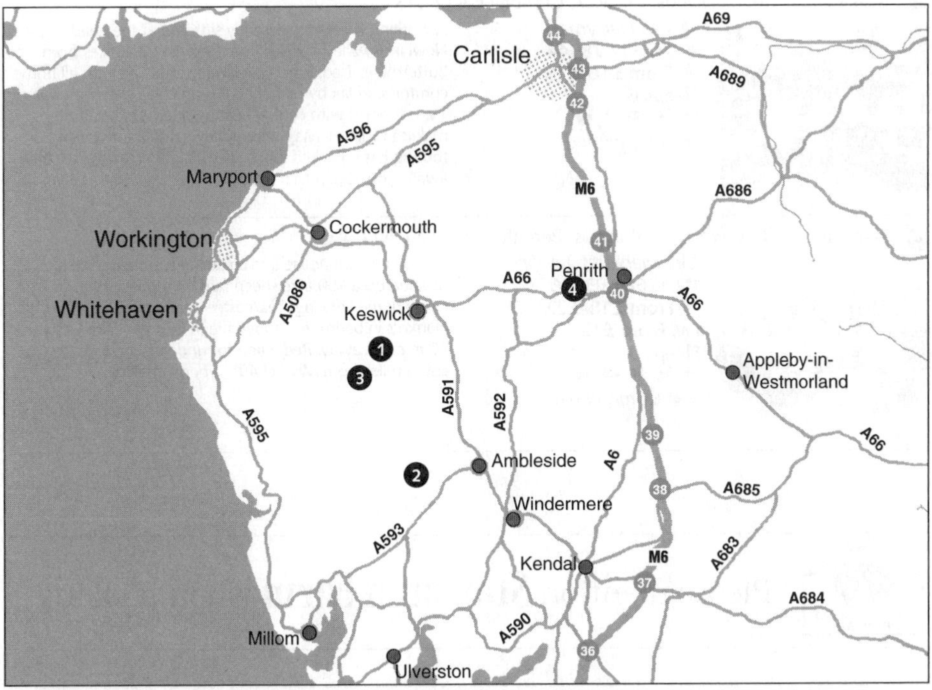

BED AND BREAKFAST

(and evening meal)

---

1 **Birkrigg Farm,** Newlands, Keswick, Cumbria CA12 5TS

M M Beaty
☎ 017687 78278
🅱🅱 From £15–£18
Sleeps 12
🛇 ⅍ 🛪 🛋
Listed *Approved*

Birkrigg is a dairy and sheep farm very pleasantly situated with excellent outlook in the peaceful Newlands Valley, 5 miles from Keswick. Surrounded by mountains, this is an ideal place to walk and climb. Central for touring. Clean, comfortable accommodation. The breakfasts are good too! Meals available at inns nearby. Packed lunches provided. Open Mar–Nov.

---

2 **Fell Foot Farm,** Little Langdale, Ambleside, Cumbria LA22 9PE

Mrs S Harryman
☎ 015394 37294
🅱🅱 From £17
EM From £10.50
Sleeps 6
🛇(10) 🛪 🛋 ⌖ 🛆 ⊚
Listed *Commended*

Nestling at the foot of the famous Wrynose Pass, this 17th century farmhouse was once a coaching Inn. Owned by the National Trust, it contains fine oak beams and panelling. The house offers warm, comfortable accommodation with beautiful views and excellent home cooking. Three rooms, 1 en suite, tea/coffee-making facilities. Open Easter–Nov.

---

3 **Keskadale Farm,** Newlands, Keswick, Cumbria CA12 5TS

Mrs M Harryman
☎ 017687 78544
🅱🅱 From £16–£18
Sleeps 6
🛇 ⅍ 📺 ⌖ 🛋
🐝 *Commended*

A working hill farm pleasantly situated at the head of the Newlands Valley, 6 miles from Keswick, 2½ miles from Buttermere. Traditional Lakeland farmhouse with all home comforts. Relax by real open fire on chilly evenings, colour TV. All rooms with central heating, H&C, tea/coffee-making facilities. Magnificent views. Ideal for walking or touring base. Packed lunches available. A warm welcome awaits you. Open Mar–Dec.

---

4 **Tymparon Hall,** Newbiggin, Stainton, Penrith, Cumbria CA11 0HS

Mrs Margaret Taylor
☎ 017684 83236
🅱🅱 From £18–£22
EM From £12
Sleeps 9
🛇 🛪 ⅍ 📺 🛋
🐝🐝 *Commended*

A spacious farmhouse and colourful summer garden situated on a 150 acre sheep farm in a peaceful rural area. Good home cooking. Tea/coffee-making facilities, electric blankets in bedrooms. Open fire in lounge. Lake Ullswater 10 minutes away. Reduction for under 12s; no charge for cot. 4 miles from M6 (jct.40). Open Feb–Nov.

FARM HOLIDAY BUREAU

Please mention **Stay on a Farm** when booking

West Lakeland

Group Contact: *Mrs Carolyn Heslop* ☎ *01900 824222*

Our hospitality and the warmth of our welcome are renowned. If it is home comforts and peace and tranquillity you are after, then this is the place for you.

To most people the Lakes begin and end at Windermere but just venture a little further and you will discover a whole new experience. See the Border City of Carlisle with its chequered history of Romans, Picts and Scots, or the wild, untamed fells of Wasdale. View the hunting grounds of John Peel at Caldbeck, walk around Cockermouth, home of John Dalton, Fletcher Christian and William Wordsworth. Visit Whitehaven, the site of the last invasion of Britain by John Paul Jones, founder of the American Navy. Take the whole family for a ride on 'laal ratty', the miniature steam railway at Ravenglass. Trace the footsteps of the 'Maid of Buttermere' with the help of Melvyn Bragg, son of Wigton, or take the road to the future and spend a day at the British Nuclear Fuels Exhibition Centre at Sellafield. The energetic may like to discover the secrets of our lakes – Ennerdale, Crummock and Buttermere – and enjoy walking, boating, sea, river or lake fishing.

We are the ideal base for touring anywhere in Cumbria – then it's home to the relaxing atmosphere of your friendly farmhouse hosts.

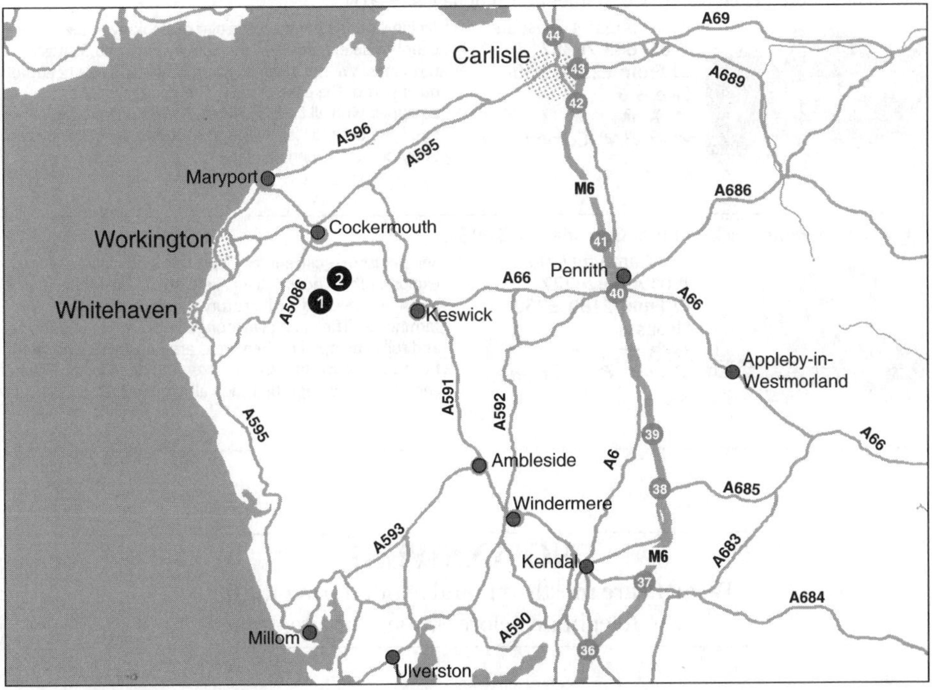

BED AND BREAKFAST

(and evening meal)

---

1 **Stanger Farm,** Cockermouth, Cumbria CA13 9TS

Mrs Carolyn Heslop
☎ **01900 824222**
BB **From £16.50**
Sleeps 4
ॐ ☜ ☘ ☔ ▦
🐝 *Commended*

With breathtaking fell views, yet only 2 miles from the lovely market town of Cockermouth, Stanger Farm lies peacefully beside the River Cocker in the beautiful Lorton Valley. Comfortable lounge and dining room with log fires, spacious bedrooms with tea-making facilities, a traditional farmhouse breakfast and good old-fashioned hospitality all await you. Open all year except Christmas and New Year.

SELF-CATERING

---

2 **Jenkin Cottage,** Embleton, Cockermouth, Cumbria CA13 9TN

Mrs Margaret Teasdale
☎ **017687 76387**
SC **From £230–£350**
Sleeps 6
ॐ ☔ ▦
🔑 🔑 🔑 🔑 *Commended*

Jenkin Cottage has a spectacular outlook over open countryside extending to the Solway Firth and Scottish Lowlands. We are a working family hill farm in a beautiful quiet part of the Lake District. The cottage is fully equipped with all fuel, bed linen, towels provided. Open fire. Ideal base for fell walking or touring the Lakes by car. Sorry no pets. Open all year.

---

1 **Stanger Farm,** Cockermouth, Cumbria CA13 9TS

Mrs Carolyn Heslop
☎ **01900 824222**
SC **From £180–£350**
Sleeps 4
ॐ ☀ ☜ ☔ ▦
🔑 🔑 🔑 🔑 *Commended*

Set amidst magnificent fell views this is an ideal base for exploring the whole of the Lake District. The Stable is a recently converted 17th century barn adjoining the farmhouse. The open plan lounge with log fire and dining and fully equipped kitchen areas are "upstairs" to benefit from view across the River Cocker and open fields. Fishing, central heating, logs, bed linen all included. Open all year.

NO ANSWER?

Farmers are mostly out and about during the day.
Try to telephone before 9.30am or after 4pm.

South Lakeland

Group Contact: *Mrs Olive Simpson* ☎ *01539 823682*

Find true country hospitality on a farm in this most beautiful corner of England. South Lakeland centres on the town of Kendal, which, in time, has developed into the focal point of the local community and the 'southern gateway' to the Lake District.

There's plenty to do – you can visit the award-winning Abbot Hall art gallery and Museums of Lakeland Life and Industry and Natural History and Archeology – or even the 'K' Village! There are also many National Trust properties and, especially for the children, the new Beatrix Potter exhibition!

If you're feeling active, Windermere and Bowness – where you can stroll by the lakeside, take a cruise on the 'Teal' or 'Swan', or ride on the steam train to Haverthwaite – are only a few minutes drive away. The fell walking is great too – whether in the valleys of Longsleddale or Kentmere, or on Scout Scar.

The seasons come and go in South Lakeland. Springtime here is a photographer's delight, with rhododendrons, azaleas, and daffodils – so immortalised by Wordsworth – while new-born lambs frolic in the pastures. Yet in autumn, the rich golds of the bracken and leaves contrast with the blue sky – a sightseer's delight.

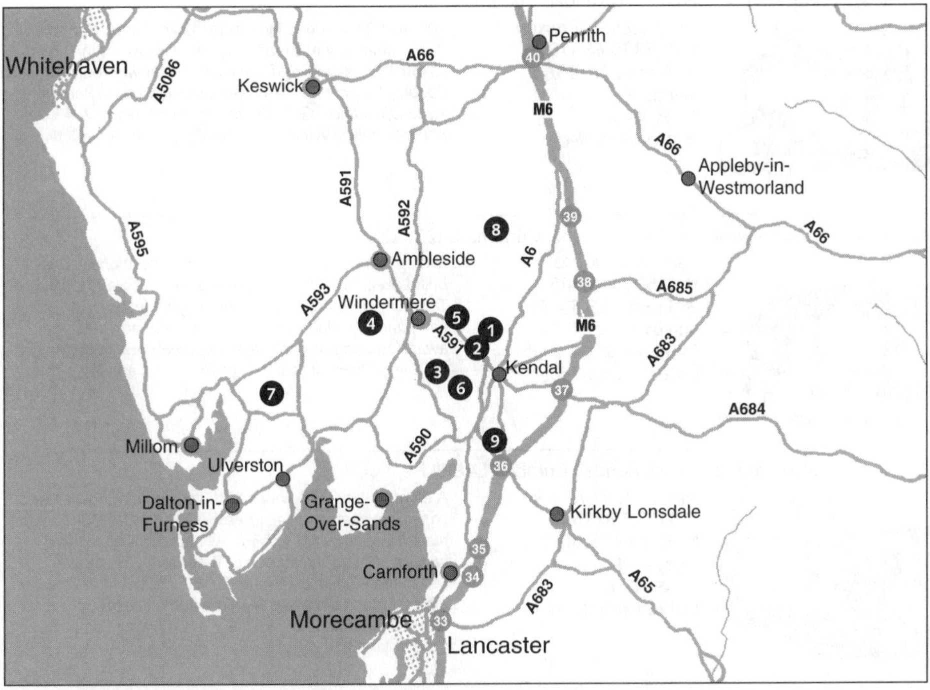

Whitehaven
A5086
Keswick
A66
Penrith
40
M6
A66
Appleby-in-Westmorland
A591
A592
A66
A595
8
A6
A66
Ambleside
39
A593
Windermere
4
5
1
38
A685
A591
2
M6
3
6
Kendal
A683
7
37
A684
Millom
A590
9
Ulverston
36
Dalton-in-Furness
Grange-Over-Sands
Kirkby Lonsdale
Carnforth
35
34
A683
A65
Morecambe
33
Lancaster

BED AND BREAKFAST

(and evening meal)

---

1 **Garnett House Farm,** Burneside, Kendal, Cumbria LA9 5SF

Mrs Sylvia Beaty
☎ 01539 724542
🅱🅱 From £16–£20
EM From £8.50
Sleeps 10
🐾 🏕 🛍 ◎
👑 👑 *Commended*

AA/RAC acclaimed 15th century farmhouse, just ½ mile from A591 Windermere Road, village inn, shops and public transport. Bedrooms have colour TV, washbasins and tea-making facilities en suites available. Oak panelled lounge, dining room with choice of breakfast and 5 course dinners. Lovely views of our countryside and close to Windermere. Good parking. Nov–end Mar 3 night breaks £48, en suite £53. Closed Christmas and New Year.

---

2 **Gateside Farm,** Windermere Road, Kendal, Cumbria LA9 5SE

Mrs June Ellis
☎ 01539 722036
🅱🅱 From £17–£20
EM £8.50
Sleeps 10
🐾 🐕 🛍 🏕 ◎
Listed *Commended*

AA/RAC acclaimed. Traditional Lakeland working farm, 2 miles north of Kendal on A591. Easily accessible from M6 (jct36). Ideal for touring Lakes and Yorkshire Dales. 16th century farmhouse, all bedrooms have colour TV, tea/coffee facilities, most en suite. Short or weekly stays welcome. Good home cooked breakfasts and evening meals. Lovely walks from the farm with maps provided. Golf and fishing 2 miles. Open all year.

---

3 **High Gregg Hall,** Underbarrow, Kendal, Cumbria LA8 8BL

Mrs Ciceley Simpson
☎ 015395 68318
🅱🅱 From £14–£16
Sleeps 4
🐾 🐕 🛍 🏕
👑 *Commended*

100-acre dairy/sheep farm in the Lake District National Park within easy reach of M6 jct36. Guests' sitting room, colour TV, tea-making facilities. Bath/shower room. 1 double, 1 twin with washbasins, shaver points. Pub within walking distance. Golf, swimming, horse riding 2–4 miles, Kendal 4 miles, Windermere 6 miles. Open Apr–Oct.

---

4 **Howe Farm,** Hawkshead, Nr Amblesde, Cumbria LA22 0QB

Lisa Woodhouse
☎ 015394 36345
🅱🅱 From £15.50–£17
Sleeps 6
🐾 ✂ 🛍 🏕
Listed *Commended*

Dating back to 1698, Howe Farm is a traditional stone-built Lakeland farmhouse overlooking Esthwaite Lake. Tastefully decorated with many original features including oak panelling, staircase and log fires. A warm welcome awaits and an excellent breakfast greets you in the morning. Open all year except Christmas and New Year.

---

5 **Stock Bridge Farm,** Staveley, Kendal, Cumbria LA8 9LP

Mrs Betty Fishwick
☎ 01539 821580
🅱🅱 From £15.50–£16
Sleeps 11
🐾 🐕 🏕 🛍
Listed *Commended*

A comfortable, modernised 17th century farmhouse on edge of bypassed village just off A591 Kendal–Windermere road, 15 minutes M6 (jct 36). All bedrooms have fitted washbasins and shaver points. Bathroom with shower. Separate WC. Fire certificate. Full central heating. Separate tables, English breakfast, bedtime drink. Friendly, personal service. Good parking facilities. On Dalesway Footpath. Open Mar–Oct.

Tranthwaite Hall, Underbarrow, Nr Kendal, Cumbria LA8 8HG   6

Mrs D Swindlehurst
☎ 015395 68285
BB From £19–£20
Sleeps 4
🐄 ⅍ ☕ 🍴 🍷 ⚕
🌸 🌸 Commended

Magnificent old farmhouse dating back to 11th century. Beautiful oak beams, doors and rare antique fire range. Tastefully modernised with full CH, pretty en suite bedrooms with tea/coffee, radio and hairdrier. Colour TV lounge, separate dining room. This dairy/sheep farm is set in a small, picturesque village between Kendal and Windermere. Walking, golf, pony trekking. Many good pubs and inns nearby. SAE for brochure. Open all year except Christmas.

SELF-CATERING

Birchbank Cottage, Birchbank, Blawith, Ulverston, Cumbria LA12 8EW   7

Mrs Linda Nicholson
☎ 01229 885277
SC From £125–£260
Sleeps 4+ cot
🐄 🐓 👤 ✈ 🍷 ⚕ ◎
🏡 🏡 🏡 🏡 Commended

Relax and unwind in this comfortable beamed cottage on a Lakeland sheep farm only 5 miles from Coniston Water. Enjoy marvellous views of the Duddon estuary and Coniston Old Man while walking on the fells around the farm. One double, 1 twin, linen and electricity included. Short breaks in low season. Open all year.

High Swinklebank Farm, Longsleddale, Nr Kendal, Cumbria LA8 9BD   8

Mrs Olive Simpson
☎ 01539 823682
SC From £100–£200
Sleeps 4
🐄 🐓 ⚕
🏡 🏡 🏡 Commended

High Swinklebank is near the head of the beautiful Longsleddale Valley with lovely views and walking. A recent conversion which is well appointed includes fitted carpets throughout. Comprising lounge with electric fire, bed settee, TV, lovely kitchen, shower room, 2 bedrooms – double and bunk. Children welcome. Linen provided. Weekends available. Cleanliness and personal attention assured. Open all year.

Preston Patrick Hall Cottage, Preston Patrick Hall, Crooklands, Milnthorpe, Cumbria LA7 7NY   9

Stephen & Jennifer Armitage
☎/Fax 015395 67200
SC From £105–£305
Sleeps 2/6
🐄 ☕ ⚕
🏡 🏡 🏡 Commended

Green fields with sheep and cows will be your first sight as you open your bedroom curtains. Our cottage is a self-contained, fully equipped wing of a magnificent medieval manor house. You may spend your time walking the quiet lanes, swimming in our pool or perhaps take advantage of the easy access to the Lakes, Dales and Morecambe Bay. Brochure available. Open all year.

Although the majority of farms will accept 'Stay on a Farm' Gift Tokens, please check when booking to avoid disappointment.

Isle of Man

Group Contacts: 🆒 *Elaine Taggart 01624 822250 or Jean Jackson 01624 801871*

The Isle of Man is in the centre of the British Isles surrounded by the Irish Sea, exactly halfway between John O' Groats and Lands End.

The 100 miles of coastline varies from rocky cliffs looking down on to clear sparkling sea, to the sandy beaches and shingle ridges. The contrast of inland scenery is equally varied, from wooded glens, through the patchwork of small fields, to open moorland and mountain.

The island has retained a rich transport system from the Victorian times, offering steam trains to seaside villages, an electric tram up the highest mountain, and horse trams along Douglas sea front. A visit to the island wouldn't be complete without a trip to the largest working waterwheel in Europe at Laxey, and the castles of Peel and Castletown. We have our own language, currency and culture but still give a big welcome to all our visitors. Only 35 minutes from Liverpool Airport or sail from Heysham or Liverpool.

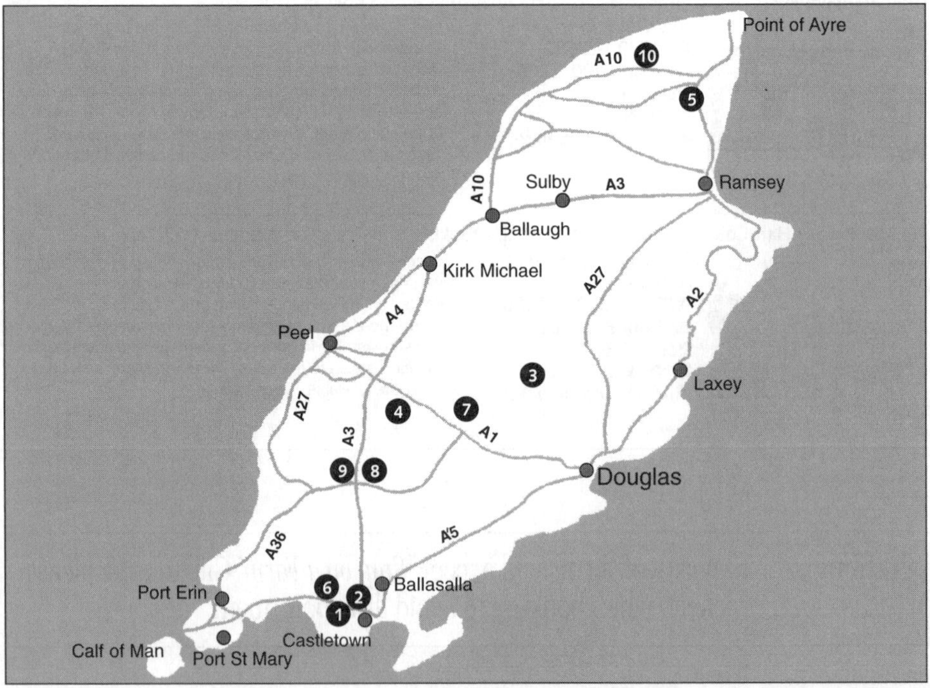

Point of Ayre

A10 **10**

5

A10

Sulby   A3   Ramsey

Ballaugh

Kirk Michael

A27

A2

Peel

A4

3   Laxey

A27

4   **7**

A3   A1

9 **8**

Douglas

A36

A5

Port Erin

6 **2**   Ballasalla

1

Calf of Man   Port St Mary   Castletown

BED AND BREAKFAST

(and evening meal)

Ballamaddrell Farm, Ballamaddrell Road, Ballabeg, Nr Castleton, Isle of Man IM9 4HD   **1**

Mrs E A Comish
☎ **01624 822654**
🅱 **From £17–£18**
EM From £12
Sleeps 3
🐴 ✂ 🗄 🎋
Listed *Commended*

Family-run working sheep and cattle farm situated in the south of the island with panoramic views. Tranquil base from which to explore the island. Sea fishing, scuba diving, golf, golf, walking; activities to name but a few, in this rich Celtic heritage. Dinner if required, lunchtime hampers, brochure on request. Good food and warm welcome await. Open Mar–Oct.

Ballavell Farm, Ballasalla, Isle of Man IM9 3DP   **2**

Mrs H E Duggen
☎ **01624 824306**
🅱 **From £16.50**
EM From £7
Sleeps 6
🐴 🐕 ✂ 🗄
🐝 *Commended*

Family-run dairy farm in a tranquil setting with lovely views of the south of the island. The traditional Manx farmhouse has been refurbished and has central heating throughout. Bedrooms are fully equipped for a luxurious stay and there is a large sunny garden to relax in. Open May–Oct.

Booilshuggel Farm, East Baldwin, Braddan, Douglas, Isle of Man IM4 5ER   **3**

Mrs Margaret Caley
☎ **01624 851235**
🅱 **From £16**
Sleeps 4
🐴(5) ✂ 🎋 🗄
🐝 *Highly Commended*

A warm welcome awaits you on our family-run beef and sheep farm situated 5 miles from Douglas. Beautiful picturesque scenery and delightful country walks. Relax in our comfortable, modern, centrally heated farmhouse. Friendly atmosphere and good home cooking. Central location to explore the island's natural beauty steeped in history, culture and traditions. Open Mar–Nov.

Kerrowgarrow Farm, Greeba, Douglas, Isle of Man IM4 3LQ   **4**

Mrs Jean Jackson
☎ **01624 801871**
🅱 **From £16**
Sleeps 5
🐴 🐕 ✂ 🗄 🎋
🐝 *Commended*

Kerrowgarrow offers you a homely atmosphere and an ideal base from which to explore the whole island by foot, bike or car. TV, tea-making facilities and CH in all rooms. Cows, chickens and Manx cat. Walks arranged for naturalists. Good pub food and restaurant in St Johns 1 mile. Open Mar–Nov.

LET THE TELEPHONE RING!

Some farmhouses are big places. Let the telephone ring
long enough to give the owner time to answer it.

SELF-CATERING

---

5 **Ballachrink Bungalow,** Ballachrink Farm, Bride, Isle of Man IM7 4AP

Mrs Val Teare
☎/Fax 01624 880364
SC From £175–£240
Sleeps 4
🐴 💼 ⊚
🔑 🔑 🔑 🔑 *Commended*

Situated in the north of the island, enjoying magnificent views of the Manx countryside, our bungalow offers you a comfortable base from which to explore the island. Well equipped with towels and linen provided. Just the place to get away from it all and relax. Open all year.

---

6 **Balladuke Farmhouse,** Ballabeg Arbory, Isle of Man IM9 4HD

Mrs Elaine Taggart
☎/Fax 01624 822250
SC From £300–£450
Sleeps 6 + cot
🐴 💼 🕷
🔑 🔑 🔑 🔑 *Highly Commended*

Lovely Manx stone four-bedroomed farmhouse situated on small working farm. Refurbished and equipped to a very high standard, ideal family accommodation, suitable for small children. Magnificent sea and country views over the south of the island. Half a mile from village and shop. No meters or hidden extras. Full colour brochure on request. Open all year.
E mail: e.taggart@advsys.co.uk

---

7 **Cronk-Dhoo Farm Cottages,** Cronk-Dhoo Farm, Greeba IM4 2DX

Ms Lin Kermode
☎ 01624 851327
SC From £95–£375
Sleeps 4
🐴 🕷 🐕 🕷
🔑 🔑 🔑 🔑 *Commended – Highly Commended*

Lovely farmhouse and converted barn with southerly aspect over the central valley. Refurbished to a high standard, fully equipped with colour TV, satellite, microwave, CH. Towels and linen provided. Private garden, barbecue area, plenty of parking. 100 meters main bus route, near craft centre, pubs and restaurants. Ideal base for keen conservationists. Open all year.

---

8 **Kionslieu Farm Cottages,** Higher Foxdale, Isle of Man IM4 3HB

Mrs Fiona Barker
☎/Fax 01624 801349
SC From £200–£550
Sleeps 2–6
🐴 🕷 💼
🔑 🔑 🔑 🔑 *Highly Commended*

Beautiful farm cottages on a traditional sunny courtyard. Fully equipped and furnished to highest standards. Centrally situated in peaceful Foxdale countryside, 10 min walk village shop and inn and 10/15 min drive Douglas, Castletown and Peel. Friendly animals, play area, laundry, payphone and delightful rural views make Kionslieu your ideal holiday home. Open all year.

---

9 **Little Cresta,** Lower Gleneedale, St Johns, Douglas, Isle of Man IM4 3BF

Mrs G C Osborne
☎ 01624 801237
SC From £110–£250
Sleeps 2
🐴 🕷 💼 🕷 🌾
🔑 🔑 🔑 *Commended*

Recently renovated, this delightful cottage stands adjacent to owners' smallholding and enjoys superb views across surrounding countryside. Featuring a slate fireplace in the lounge, a fitted kitchen and shower, the cottage retains much original character with exposed beams. Excellent area for walking and a good general base from which to explore the whole island. Short drive to beautiful beach at Peel. Open Mar–Oct.

Smeale Cottage, Andreas, Isle of Man IM7 3EB   ⑩

Beth and Steve Martin
☎ **01624 880888**
Fax 01624 880955
sc **From £200–£280**
Sleeps 5 + cot
🛏 ♿
🐾 🐾 🐾 *Highly Commended*

Treat yourselves to a memorable Manx holiday in our comfortable, well appointed, semi-detached farm cottage surrounded by the family-run sheep farm. Enjoy the wonderful views and spacious, private garden. Children very welcome. Fully equipped with CH, washing machine, linen, etc. Ample parking. Perfect base for exploring our beautiful island. All-inclusive price. Brochure available. Open all year.

Soalt Veg, Kerrowgarrow Farm, Greeba, Douglas, Isle of Man IM4 3LQ   ④

Mrs Jean Jackson
☎ **01624 801871**
sc **From £250–£400**
Sleeps 6
🛏 🐕 ✂ ♿ ☂
🐾 🐾 🐾 🐾 *Highly Commended*

Traditional Manx stone barn carefully converted to provide comfortable centrally heated accommodation, whilst retaining all the character of country living. Ideally situated for exploring the whole island. Enclosed garden, children's games, TV, washing machine, tumble dryer, microwave and all linen provided. Open all year.

FARM HOLIDAY BUREAU

Our Internet Address is
http://www.webscape.co.uk/farmaccom/

CONFIRM BOOKINGS

Disappointments can arise from misunderstandings over the telephone. Please write to confirm your booking.

STAY ON A FARM GIFT TOKENS

FARM HOLIDAY BUREAU

If you have enjoyed your Stay on a Farm, why not treat your friends and relatives to *Stay on a Farm* gift tokens? Available from the Bureau office, telephone 01203 696909, they can be redeemed against accommodation booked on the majority of our farms

Yorkshire Dales & Brontë Country

Group Contact: *Anne Pearson* ☎ *01756 791579*

Mention the Yorkshire Dales and you immediately picture a vista of lush green valleys, dry stone walls and fields dotted with stone barns, clear tumbling streams, quaint villages and warm friendly people. 'Brontë Country' conjures up many images of wind-swept moors, heather, romance, deep valleys and the home of woollen mills and industrial heritage. Visit any of our farms and all this is at hand.

This beautiful region extends from Buckden and Settle in the north to Bradford in the south. In between there is something for everyone. The dales and the moors are criss-crossed with walks and footpaths suitable for all abilities. For history and heritage visit Haworth and the Brontë Parsonage, Bolton Abbey, Skipton Castle and the Bradford Industrial Museum.

Mill shops, markets and inexpensive shopping are a feature of our region, unsurpassed anywhere.

Bring back childhood memories with a ride on a steam train on either the Yorkshire Dales Railway or the Keighley and Worth Valley Steam Railway. Time it right and it may be Thomas the Tank Engine pulling the train!

Whatever your interests you can be sure you will be made most welcome in our warm, comfortable accommodation.

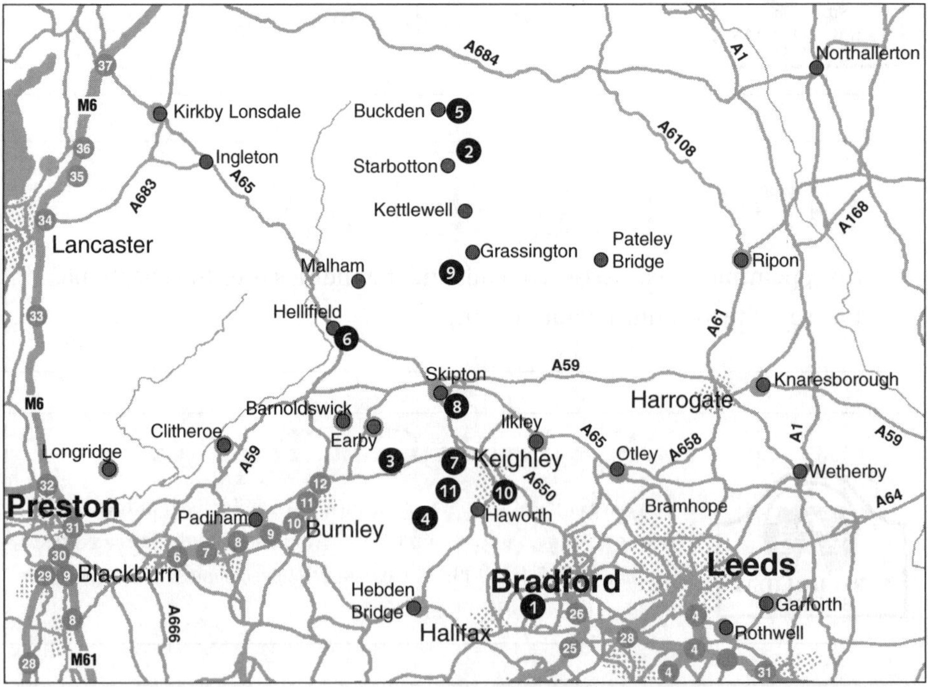

BED AND BREAKFAST

(and evening meal)

Brow Top Farm, Baldwin Lane, Clayton, Bradford, West Yorkshire BD14 6PS **❶**

Margaret Priestley
☎ **01274 882178**
🆎 **From £17.50–£20**
Sleeps 4
🐴 ▪ ◉
👑👑 *Highly Commended*

Visitors are most welcome to our family dairy and beef farm. The farmhouse has recently been modernised to a very high standard with central heating throughout. 1 double, 1 twin and 1 family room all with private bathroom, colour TV and tea/coffee-making facilities. Conveniently situated for visiting the Dales and Brontë Country. Plenty of good eating places in the area. Open all year (closed Christmas).

Bushey Lodge Farm, Starbotton, Skipton, North Yorkshire BD23 5HY **❷**

Rosie Lister
☎ **01756 760424**
🆎 **From £20**
Sleeps 4
🐿(10) 🐾 ⅍ 🐕 🎋 ⬿ ◉
👑👑 *Highly Commended*

Traditional Dales farmhouse in quiet position in Upper Wharfedale village, with extensive views along the valley, much of which is owned and protected by the National Trust. Superb walking and sightseeing area. Local inns provide excellent evening meals. Each bedroom has en suite bathroom, TV, and tea/coffee-making facilities. Open all year except Christmas.

Far Laithe Farm, Laycock, Keighley, West Yorkshire BD22 0PU **❸**

Sylvia Lee
☎ **01535 661993**
🆎 **From £17.50–£19.50**
EM From £12
Sleeps 4
🐿(12) 🐾 ▪
👑👑 *Highly Commended*

Traditional Yorkshire farm close to Haworth, Skipton and the Dales, set in the heart of open countryside . Tea-making facilities and colour TV in all bedrooms. Luxury en suite facilities. Enjoy dinner in our licensed oak-furnished dining room. We pride ourselves on the quality of our food and hospitality and look forward to welcoming you to our home. Open all year.

Hole Farm, Dimples Lane, Haworth, Bradford, West Yorkshire BD22 8QT **❹**

Janet Milner
☎/Fax **01535 644755**
🆎 **From £19.50–£24.99**
Sleeps 4
🐿(12) ⅍ 🎋 ▪ ◉
👑👑 *Highly Commended*

17th century farmhouse, on 8 acre small holding 5 minutes walk from Brontë Parsonage and 2 minutes from the moors. One twin and one double en suite rooms, central heating, colour TV; tea.coffee-making facilities. Full English breakfast. Have your breakfast watching the peacocks on the lawn. Open all year.

Redmire Farm, Buckden, Nr Skipton, North Yorkshire BD23 5JD **❺**

Mrs Julia Horner
☎ **01756 760253**
🆎 **From £18–£20**
EM From £10
Sleeps 6
🐿(6) 🐾 ⅍ ▪ ⬿ 🎋 ◉
👑👑 *Highly Commended*

Family-run, traditional working hill farm set in heart of Yorkshire Dales. 1,600 acres of stunning woodland, moorland and farmed parkland bound by 2½ mile stretch of the River Wharfe. Our farmhouse was formerly a shooting lodge, now sympathetically restored and very comfortably refurbished, with 2 double and 1 twin rooms, all en suite. A welcoming family providing an excellent table of mainly home-reared and locally produced food. Open all year.

6 **Wenningber Farm,** Hellifield, Nr Skipton, North Yorkshire BD23 4JR

Mrs Barbara Phillip
☎ **01729 850856**
🅱 **From £18–£20**
Sleeps 4
⛄🐎⚡🏕🐕🏕🐾🐾 ⓖ
🕊 *Highly Commended*

Wenningber Farm is a charming 16th century farmhouse just 4 miles from Malham in the heart of the Yorkshire Dales. Furnished to a very high standard with oak beams and inglenook fireplace. Full central heating, H&C in both rooms, tea and coffee-making facilities. Warm welcome assured. Open all year except Christmas.

SELF-CATERING

7 **Bottoms Farm Cottages,** Bottoms Farm, Laycock, nr Keighley, West Yorkshire BD22 0QD

Mrs J Parr
☎ **01535 607720**
🆂🅲 **From £140–£270**
Sleep 2/4
🐎🏕📷 ⓖ
🐾 🐾 🐾 🐾 *Highly Commended*

Bottoms Farm is a rural 35-acre sheep farm situated on the south side of a beautiful valley with spectacular views. Howarth 4 miles, Skipton 7 miles. These luxury cottages have been recently converted to the highest standard from 200 years mistal/barn. Fully equipped. Heating and linen included. Sorry no pets. Open all year.

8 **Cawder Hall Cottages,** c/o Cawder Hall, Cawder Lane, Skipton, North Yorkshire BD23 2QQ

Anne Pearson
☎ **01756 791579**
Fax **01756 797036**
🆂🅲 **From £120–£340**
Sleeps 2/6
🧍🐕🎠📷🏕🎾 ⓖ
🐾 🐾 🐾 – 🐾 🐾 🐾 🐾
Up to Highly Commended

Enjoy the peace and quiet of our warm, welcoming cottages which, while being surrounded by fields of animals are only 1 mile from Skipton with its thriving street market, medieval castle and church. Each cottage is well equipped (colour TV, video, microwave) and is suitable for disabled guests. There is a lawned garden, barbecue, phone, laundry room and children's play area. Linen, gas and electricity included as are cots and high chairs. Open all year.

4 **Heather & Bilberry Cottages,** Hole Farm, Dimples Lane, Haworth, Bradford, West Yorkshire BD22 8QT

Mrs Janet Milner
☎/Fax **01535 644755**
🆂🅲 **From £200–£550**
Sleeps 4/8 + cot
🐎🎠🏕 ⓖ
🐾 🐾 🐾 🐾 *Highly Commended*

The old barn has been carefully converted to make two cottages with most bedrooms en suite. We are a small working farm, the sort that appears in children's Ladybird books. Gloria the sow, Gilbert the turkey, foals and calves. Ideal for children. A short walk to the village to see the Brontë Museum or a walk on the moors 2 minutes from our door. Sorry no pets. Open all year.

9 **Maypole Cottage,** Blackburn House Farm, Thorpe, Skipton, North Yorkshire BD23 6BJ

Liz Gamble
☎ **01756 720609**
🆂🅲 **From £190–£320**
Sleeps 4
🐎🎠📷 ⓖ
🐾 🐾 🐾 🐾 *Highly Commended*

An 18th century stable converted to a particularly high standard in the tiny hamlet of Thorpe near Burnsall. This well equipped cottage has full central heating, exposed beams and stonework open fire. Colour TV, microwave, washer/dryer. Bathroom with shower. Linen provided. Large walled garden, ample parking. Open all year.

Meadow & Field Cottages, The Coach House, Spring Head, Tim Lane, Haworth, West Yorks BD22 7RX

David and Hilary Freeman
☎ **01535 644140**
🆂 **From £120–£260**
Sleeps 2/4
🛏 🐴 👶 ♨ 🍴 🅿
🐾 🐾 🐾 🐾 *Highly Commended*

A warm Yorkshire welcome is assured at our two cosy cottages, converted from a 200-year-old barn, ½ mile from the Brontë sisters' Haworth and within easy reach of the Yorkshire Dales. We pride ourselves on our high standard of cleanliness and comfort. Each cottage has full CH, with colour TV, cooker, fridge, microwave, washer, dryer. Gas, electricity, linen and towels, cot, highchair inclusive. Pets by arrangement. Open all year.

Westfield Farm Cottages, c/o Westfield Farm, Tim Lane, Haworth, West Yorkshire BD22 7SA

Clare Pickles
☎ **01535 644568**
Fax **01535 646686**
🆂 **From £140–£390**
Sleeps 2/6
🚶 🛏 🐴 👶 🅿 🍴 🐕 🅿
🐾 🐾 🐾 – 🐾 🐾 🐾 🐾
Highly Commended

Delightful, quality accommodation surrounded by 100 acres of grazing farmland and overlooking Brontë Parsonage and Haworth Parish Church. Farm trail and safe river for fishing and play. Farmhouse sleeps 6, cottages sleep 2 to 4. Cottage for 2 disabled guests. Safe, quiet, south-facing position. Colour TV, automatic washer, microwave in each. Dogs by arrangement. Open all year.

FINDING YOUR ACCOMMODATION

The Group contacts at the beginning of each section can always help you find a vacancy in your chosen area.

THE 1000+ BUREAU MEMBERS OFFER A UNIQUE LINK TO CUSTOMERS ACROSS THE UK

All Bureau members belong to a local Group. Each member can refer you to an equally high quality member within the Group... or across the UK: England, Northern Ireland, Scotland, Wales.

CONFIRM BOOKINGS

Disappointments can arise from misunderstandings over the telephone. Please write to confirm your booking.

Harrogate & Nidderdale

Group Contacts: *Christine Ryder* ☎ *01943 880354*
Sheila Smith ☎ *01423 771040*

Harrogate has a reputation as one of the most attractive towns in Britain, with acres of immaculate parks and gardens, shops and elegant architecture.

Nidderdale has captured the attention of many by means of films, television, literary works and the personalities of their people.

Imagination becomes reality where sheep and cattle safely graze amongst the seemingly endless green fields divided by dry stone walls. The gentle rise and fall of hills and vales, sparkling streams and rushing rivers interplay with wide expanses of moorland and reservoirs. Picturesque towns, villages and traditional country pubs abound amidst a rarefied atmosphere of peace and tranquillity. A designated Area of Outstanding Natural Beauty.

Ideally situated for visiting York, Skipton, The Yorkshire Dales, Herriot Country, Emmerdale, Fountains Abbey, Brimham Rocks (Natural Rock Sculptures), Stump Cross Caverns (Show Caves), Ripley Castle, Lightwater Valley Theme Park and Factory Shops.

Come Spring, Summer, Autumn and Winter the welcome and warmth remains the same.

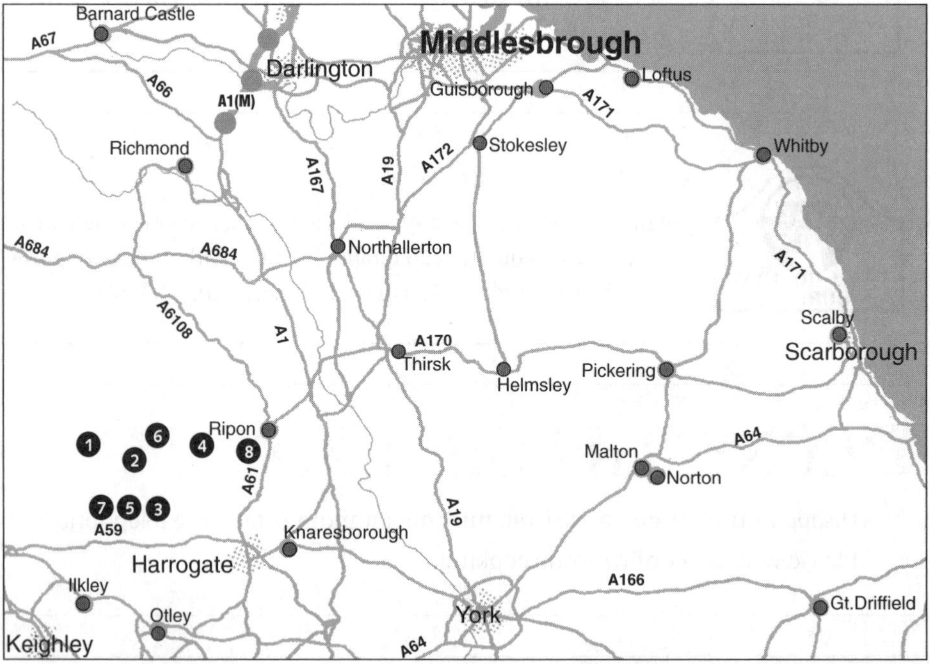

Barnard Castle
A67
A66
Darlington
A1(M)
Middlesbrough
Guisborough
Loftus
A171
Richmond
A167
A19
A172
Stokesley
Whitby
A684
A684
Northallerton
A171
A6108
A1
Scalby
A170
Thirsk
Helmsley
Pickering
Scarborough
❶ ❻ ❹ Ripon
❷ ❽
❼❺❸
A59
A61
Malton
A64
Norton
A19
Knaresborough
Harrogate
A166
Ilkley
A64
Otley
York
Gt.Driffield
Keighley
A64

BED AND BREAKFAST
(and evening meal)

Bewerley Hall Farm, Bewerley, Pateley Bridge, Nr Harrogate, North Yorkshire HG3 5JA ①

Mrs Eileen Bulmer
☎ 01423 711636
▣ From £16–£21
EM £12
Sleeps 12
🛏(8) ✄ ☂ ▪
♨ ♨ ♨ *Commended*

Bewerley Hall is a working farm situated in 87 acres in a secluded position near the Rivèr Nidd. ¾ mile Pateley Bridge. Grade II listed farmhouse offers luxurious accommodation with lovely homely atmosphere in peaceful surroundings. Full central heating. Guests' drawing room and TV lounge. Licensed. Good home cooking. Free fishing to guests. Horse riding nearby. Open Feb–Nov.

Clough House Farm, Summerbridge, Harrogate, North Yorkshire HG3 4JR ②

Mrs Brenda Walmsley
☎/Fax 01423 780823
▣ From £22.50–£45
EM From £10
Sleeps 14
🛏 ☂ ▪ ◉
♨ ♨ *Commended*

17th century farmhouse/attached farm building converted into 8 delightful en suite bedrooms (three ground floor) tastefully decorated with CH and tea/coffee-making facilities. Peaceful position with far-reaching views. Private guests' sitting and dining room. Private horse riding lessons or hack around beautiful countryside. Featured in the *Which? Good Bed and Breakfast Guide* and recommended by the *Good Bed and Breakfast Guide*. Open all year.

Graystone View Farm, Graystone Plain Lane, Hampsthwaite, Harrogate, North Yorkshire HG3 2LY ③

Gloria Metcalfe
☎ 01423 770324
Fax 01423 772536
▣ From £18–£25
Sleeps 6
🛏 ⚡ ▪ ☂ ◉
♨ ♨ *Commended*

18th century farmhouse in tranquil setting with comfortable rooms to come back to after a lovely day seeing the wonderful sights that Yorkshire has to offer. Bedrooms have tea/coffee-making facilities. We are a family run farm set in 100 acres and located ¼ mile from the A59 west of Harrogate. Open all year except Christmas and New Year.

Hatton House Farm, Colber Lane, Bishop Thornton, Nr Harrogate, North Yorkshire HG3 3JA ④

Mrs Joyce Kellett
☎ 01423 770315
▣ From £17.50–£25
EM £12
Sleeps 6
🛏(10) ✄ ☂ ▪ ◉
Listed *Highly Commended*

Farmhouse accommodation at its best on a dairy mixed farm in Nidderdale, close to Harrogate. Quiet and peaceful area. Emphasis on home cooking, beautifully presented. Wash basins, tea-making facilities in all rooms. Luxury bathroom. Separate tables in dining room, large comfortable lounge. Safe parking no problem. Open all year.

Knabbs Ash, Skipton Road, Felliscliffe, Nr Harrogate, North Yorkshire HG3 2LT ⑤

Sheila Smith
☎ 01423 771040
Fax 01423 771515
▣ From £21–£25
Sleeps 6
🛏(10) ✄ ✗ ▪ ◉
♨ ♨ *Highly Commended*

White Rose Award-winning B&B. Recommended by *Which? Good Bed and Breakfast Guide*. Smallholding 6 miles west of Harrogate set back off the A59 in a tranquil position with delightful views over the countryside. En suite rooms enhanced by quality furnishings, colour TV, hair dryer, tea/coffee-making facilities, CH. Private guest sitting and dining room with separate tables. Ideal area for walking and touring. Good local inns. Open all year except Christmas.

---

6   **North Pasture Farm,** Brimham Rocks, Summerbridge, Harrogate, North Yorkshire HG3 4DW

Eileen Payne
☎ 01423 711470
BB £21
EM from £12
Sleeps 4
✂ ⚒ 🖤 ⓖ
♚♚♚ *Highly Commended*

North Pasture Farm, a 14th century listed farmhouse, beamed and mullioned and oozing with character, awaits discerning guests. Warm and cosy with central heating throughout, together with en suite bedrooms and separate dining room and separate TV lounge. Peaceful and quiet, sheltered by Brimham Rocks. Within easy reach of Harrogate, Ripon, Skipton, York and Fountains Abbey. Open Mar–Nov.

7   **Scaife Hall Farm,** Blubberhouses, Otley, West Yorkshire LS21 2PL

Christine Ryder
☎ 01943 880354
BB From £20
Sleeps 6
🐎✂⚒🖤ⓖ
♚♚ *Highly Commended*

Scaife Hall is a working farm set in picturesque countryside, halfway between Harrogate and Skipton. Comfortable accommodation in two double bedrooms and one twin bedded room, each tastefully decorated with en suite facilities, central heating, beverage tray. Sitting room with blazing log fires on chilly winter nights. Local inns provide excellent meals. Open all year except Christmas and New Year.

SELF-CATERING

2   **Clough House Farm,** Summerbridge, Harrogate, North Yorkshire HG3 4JR

Mrs Brenda Walmsley
☎/Fax 01423 780823
SC From £125–£300
EM from £10
5 cottages + flat
🐎🐾ⓖ
🐾 *Commended*

Clough House Farm offers five delightful small stone cottages and one 2-bedroom flat. Tastefully decorated, fully equipped, heating and linen included. Breakfast and evening meals also available. Village of Summerbridge 5-minute walk. Brimham Rocks and Fountains Abbey close by. Featured in the *Which? Good Bed and Breakfast Guide* and recommended by the *Good Bed and Breakfast Guide.* Open all year.

8   **Dukes Place,** Fountains Abbey Road, Bishop Thornton, Harrogate, North Yorkshire HG3 3JY

Jaki Moorhouse
☎ 01765 620229
Fax 01765 620454
SC From £150–£300
Sleeps 2–6
🐎🐕🖤⚒🐾✿ⓖ
🐾🐾🐾 *Up to Highly Commended*

Situated in the heart of Nidderdale yet close to Harrogate, Dukes Place is a well-maintained property comprising the owners' 18th century farmhouse and cottage-style apartments developed from the original farm buildings. Working stables from which riding can be arranged. Pets welcome. Open all year.

LET THE TELEPHONE RING!
Some farmhouses are big places. Let the telephone ring
long enough to give the owner time to answer it.

Herriot's Yorkshire Moors and Dales

Group Contacts: 📖 *Mrs Mary Pearson* ☎ *01609 772311*
🆂🅲 *Lady Mary Furness* ☎ *01609 748614*

Take a trip around North Yorkshire and sample for yourself the delights of this area as portrayed in James Herriot's 'All Creatures Great and Small', and TV's 'Heartbeat'.

Start with the ancient city of York and wander through narrow streets to the Minster, ride up-river to the Bishop's Palace or visit the Railway Museum and Jorvik Centre. Or drive from Helmsley, over Sutton Bank – a favourite for hang gliders – to the market town of Thirsk where James Herriot's veterinary practice still flourishes. Take a day out for all the family at the Lightwater Valley theme park, or maybe you prefer the peace and tranquillity of the romantic abbeys, stately homes, gardens and deerparks found here.

In Wensleydale, home of the famous cheese, you can fish or picnic by the waterfalls and enjoy real ale in friendly village pubs.

Walkers can follow the Pennine Way past the Buttertubs, through panoramic Swaledale where shepherd and sheepdog work the hills, to the cobbled streets and Norman castle of Richmond, towering over the river below.

Whatever the weather, whatever your interest, you are spoilt for choice. There is something for everyone in North Yorkshire

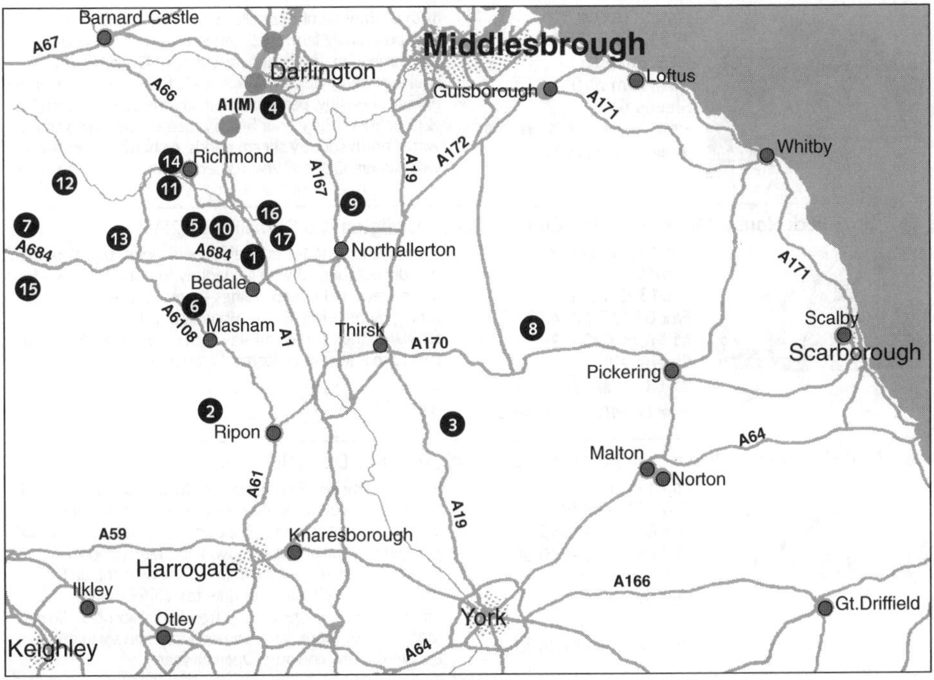

BED AND BREAKFAST

(and evening meal)

---

1 Ainderby Myers Farm, Nr Hackforth, Bedale, North Yorkshire DL8 1PF

Mrs Valerie Anderson
☎ 01609 748668
☎/Fax 01609 748424
BB **From £16–£18**
EM From £10
Sleeps 6
♿ ✂ ☂ ♨ ✗ ⊛
🏵 *Commended*

Historical manor house set amidst moors and dales with origins going back to the 10th century. Terrific atmosphere. Once farmed by the monks of Jervaulx Abbey. Sheep, crops, pastures and a stream. Walk the fields and discover the wildlife. Visit castles and abbeys. Excellent base for walkers. Pony trekking and fishing by arrangement. Traditional Yorkshire breakfasts. Picnic facilities. Open all year.

---

2 Bay Tree Farm, Aldfield, Nr Fountains Abbey, Ripon, North Yorkshire HG4 3BE

Valerie Leeming
☎/Fax 01765 620394
BB **From £20–£25**
EM From £11.50
Sleeps 12
♿ 🐴 ✂ ⊞ ✗ ♨ ⊛
🏵🏵🏵
Highly Commended

As featured in *Which* B&B, this 17th century converted stone hay barn combines character with comfort in quiet hamlet. Beautiful Fountains Abbey, ½ mile. York, Harrogate and Dales all in easy reach. Lovely circular walks from our door returning to open fires and super cooking (HE trained). All rooms en suite, CH, beverages, TV. Kettle always on the boil. Ideal for 'get togethers' or just a peaceful few days. Colour brochure. Open all year.

---

3 Carr House Farm, Shallowdale, Ampleforth, York, North Yorkshire YO6 4ED

Anna Lupton
☎ 01347 868526
BB **From £15**
EM From £10
Sleeps 6
♿(7) ✂ Å ⊕ ♨ ⊛
🏵🏵 *Commended*

16th century farmhouse filled with memorabilia. Part of 400-acre family farm for 5 generations. Internationally recommended, 'fresh air fiend's dream! Good food, walking, warm welcome'. Romantic four-poster bedroom en suite. Relaxing, peaceful, informal – 'heartbeat country'. ½ hour York. Make your holiday memorable – own spring water, north country sheep, ponds, orchards, green fields, wild flowers. Open all year (closed Christmas and New Year).

---

4 Clow-Beck House, Monk End Farm, Croft-on-Tees, Darlington, Co Durham DL2 2SW

Heather & David Armstrong
☎ 01325 721075
Fax 01325 720419
BB **From £25–£35**
Sleeps 22
♿ ⊞ ☕ ⊛
🏵🏵 *Highly Commended*

If you are looking for fresh air, superb views, true Yorkdhire friendliness coupled with luxuriously furnished rooms – four-poster beds and tented ceilings – a place to relax perhaps fishing by the River Tees or walking through 90 acres of farmland, then come and stay with us. Breakfast is a feast. Everyone is always welcome. Open all year.

---

5 Elmfield Country House, Arrathorne, Bedale, North Yorkshire DL8 1NE

Edith & Jim Lillie
☎ 01677 450558
Fax 01677 450557
BB **From £21–£30.50**
EM From £11.50
Sleeps 20
♿ ⊛ ⊞ ⊛
🏵🏵🏵 *Commended*

Situated between Richmond and Bedale. Superb views of surrounding countryside, relaxed friendly atmosphere in luxurious country house. 9 spacious bedrooms (all en suite) including a four-poster bed, twin and family rooms. 2 bedrooms equipped for disabled. All with colour TV (satellite channel), radio, phone, tea/coffee-making facilities, CH. Lounge and bar (residential licence), dining room, games room, large conservatory and solarium. Excellent home cooking. Open all year.

Haregill Lodge, Ellingstring, Masham, Ripon, North Yorkshire HG4 4PW

Mrs Rachel Greensit
☎ 01677 460272
[BB] From £18–£19
EM From £10
Sleeps 6
🐕 🐎 🎣 ⓦ
🍴 🍴 *Commended*

Wanting a peaceful break? Then come and join us in our 18th century farmhouse set on a mixed farm. Secluded garden with play area overlooking Hambleton Hills, Vale of York. Ideal for Dales, moors and Herriot Country. Two rooms en suite and one with private facility, TV/radio, tea/coffee. Log fire, CH, satellite TV lounge, games room. Excellent home cooking with supper tray. Fishing and trekking nearby. Warm welcome. Closed Christmas.

High Force Farm, Bainbridge, Leyburn, North Yorkshire DL8 3DL

Margaret Iveson
☎ 01969 650379
[BB] From £15–£18
Sleeps 6
🐕(4) ✂ 🎣 ⓦ
🍴 *Commended*

Working hill farm used in James Herriot TV programme. Ideal centre for exploring the Dales offering guests a warm welcome in a relaxed atmosphere. A non-smoking establishment. Open Jan–Nov.

Laskill Farm, Hawnby, Nr Helmsley, North Yorkshire YO6 5NB

Sue Smith
☎ 01439 798268
[BB] From £20.50–£23.50
EM From £11
Sleeps 8
🐕 🐎 🏇 ⛱ ☕ ☂ 🎣 ⓦ
🍴 🍴 *Commended*

Amidst beautiful North Yorkshire Moors, in heart of James Herriot and Heartbeat Country. Attractive farmhouse with own lake/large walled garden. Own natural spring water. High standard of food and comfort. Rooms have en suite/private facilities, colour TV, beverage tray. Ideal for nearby places of interest and scenic beauty, or simply enjoy tranquil surroundings. Open all year except Christmas Day.

Lovesome Hill Farm, Lovesome Hill, Northallerton, North Yorkshire DL6 2PB

Mrs Mary Pearson
☎ 01609 772311
[BB] From £19–£25
EM From £11
Sleeps 9
🏇 🐕 🏇 ⛱ 🎣 ⓦ
🍴 🍴 *Commended*

19th century farmhouse on working farm 4 miles north of Northallerton on A167 with lovely views of Hambleton Hills. On arrival enjoy tea and homemade biscuits. Our tastefully converted granary adjoins house with spacious, well furnished en suite rooms (two on ground floor). CLA commendation for conversion. Central for exploring Dales, Moors, Durham and York. A warm welcome and delicious homemade meals await you. You'll love it.

Mill Close Farm, Patrick Brompton, Bedale, North Yorkshire DL8 1JY

Mrs Patricia Knox
☎ 01677 450257
Fax 01677 450585
[BB] From £17–£20
Sleeps 4
🐕 🐎 🎣 🎾 ⓦ
🍴 🍴 *Highly Commended*

17th century working farm surrounded by beautiful rolling countryside at foothills of Yorkshire Dales. 2 miles from A1. Charming bedrooms. Guests' private bathrooms, dining and sitting room with log fires. Highland cattle, sheep, calves, pony, wild flowers and woodland. A relaxing, peaceful atmosphere. Romantic walled garden with pond and summerhouse. Sumptuous breakfasts in our conservatory dining room. Colour brochure. Open Mar–Nov.

Mount Pleasant Farm, Whashton, Richmond, North Yorkshire DL11 7JP

Alison Pittaway
☎ 01748 822784
[BB] From £20–£22
EM From £10
Sleeps 12
🏇 🐕 🐎 ☂ 🎣 🎾 ⓦ
🍴 🍴 *Commended*

A very warm welcome to our comfortable farmhouse set in beautiful, peaceful countryside with lovely views. Three miles from Richmond and ideally situated for exploring the North Yorkshire Dales. Renovated farm buildings offer cosy cottage-style en suite rooms, each with own front door, colour TV and beverage tray. All home cooking using fresh local produce. Table licence and friendly atmosphere. This really is a pleasant place to stay for your special holiday or short break. Open all year except Christmas.

12 Oxnop Hall, Low Oxnop, Gunnerside, Richmond, North Yorkshire DL11 6JJ

Annie Porter
☎ **01748 886253**
BB **From £23**
EM From £14
Sleeps 11
☺(5) ⚊ ✂ ▪ ⊚
☙ ☙ ☙ *Commended*

Stay with us on our working hill farm with beef cattle and Swaledale sheep. Oxnop Hall is of historical interest and has recently been extended with all en suite rooms. Ideal walking and touring. We are in the Yorkshire Dales National Park, Herriot Country, an Environmentally Sensitive Area which is renowned for its stone walls, barns and flora. Good farmhouse food. Tea/coffee-making facilities. Open all year except Christmas.

13 Walburn Hall, Downholme, Richmond, North Yorkshire DL11 6AF

Diana Greenwood
☎/Fax **01748 822152**
BB **From £22–£24**
Sleeps 5
☺ ✂ ▪ ⊚
☙ ☙ *Highly Commended*

Walburn Hall is one of the few remaining working farms with a fortified farmhouse, an enclosed cobbled courtyard and terraced garden. For guests' comfort there is a separate lounge and dining room with beamed ceilings, stone fireplaces and log fires (when required). Centrally heated. Double/twin or family rooms (en suite) with tea/coffee-making facilities. Ideally situated between Richmond and Leyburn for exploring the Dales. Open Mar–Nov.

14 Whashton Springs Farm, Richmond, North Yorkshire DL11 7JS

Fairlie Turnbull
☎ **01748 822884**
Fax 01748 826285
BB **From £21**
Sleeps 16
☺(5) ▪ ⚊ ⊚
☙ ☙ *Highly Commended*

400-acre beef/sheep, family working farm in heart of Herriot Country. Delightful Georgian farmhouse, featured on 'Wish You Were Here', 1988 AA 'Farmhouse of the North' Award, unusual bay windows, overlooking lawns sloping to a sparkling stream. Real Yorkshire breakfast. Home cooking using local produce. All 8 bedrooms have en suite baths/showers, TV, phone. One 4-poster bedroom. Historic Richmond 3 miles away. Open all year (closed Christmas & New Year).

SELF-CATERING

15 Clematis & Well Cottage, c/o Mile House Farm, Hawes, Wensleydale, North Yorkshire DL8 3PT

Anne Fawcett
☎ **01969 667481**
SC **From £150–£375**
Sleeps 4/8
☺ ⚊ ⊲ ☙ ▪ ⊚
⚲ ⚲ ⚲ ⚲
Highly Commended

Two lovely old Dales stone cottages of character with open fires, exposed beams and Laura Ashley prints. Both cottages are peacefully situated with spectacular views over Wensleydale. Fully renovated to a high standard, these cottages provide charming, spacious accommodation with lovely, old fashioned walled gardens. Free trout fishing on farm. Private parking. Open all year.

14 The Coach House, Whashton Springs Farm, Richmond, North Yorkshire DL11 7LS

Fairlie Turnbull
☎ **01748 822884**
Fax 01748 826285
SC **From £150–£260**
Sleeps 4–5
☺ ▪ ⊚
⚲ ⚲ ⚲ ⚲
Highly Commended

The Coach House offers luxury accommodation on our 400-acre working family farm near Richmond, gateway to the Dales. This warm spacious house sleeps 4–5 in double and twin bedrooms. Beamed lounge and well equipped kitchen with washer, freezer, microwave, etc. Heating and bed linen included in tariff. Good local hospitality. Open all year.

Duftons House, Low Oxnop, Gunnerside, Richmond, North Yorkshire DL11 6JJ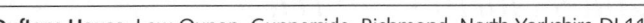

Annie Porter
☎ **01748 886253**
🆂🅲 **From £275–£475**
Sleeps 7
🛏 ✗ 🔋 🎇 ⊚
🔑 🔑 🔑 🔑 *Commended*

Come and relax in peace and comfort in our cottage on family-run farm in Upper Swaledale renowned for its walls, barns and wild flowers. 1 twin and 1 double room with washbasin, 1 family en suite. Cot available. Sitting room with open fire and colour TV, modern kitchen, CH. Bedlinen, towels, electricity and fuel included. Regret no pets, no smoking. Open all year.

Mount Pleasant Farm, Whashton, Richmond, North Yorkshire DL11 7JP

Alison Pittaway
☎ **01748 822784**
🆂🅲 **From £120–£280**
Sleeps 8
🛏 🐕 🎇 🔋 🐾 ⊚
Applied

Enjoy a break in one of our two newly converted cottages, set in lovely peaceful countryside with superb views. Three miles from Richmond and ideally situated for touring the North Yorkshire Dales. Each cottage comprises 1 double and 1 twin bedroom, lounge with dining area, fully equipped kitchen, shower room, colour TV, CH. Electricity, linen and heating included. Good local hospitality. Open all year.

Stanhow Farm Bungalow, c/o Stanhow Farm, Great Langton, Northallerton, North Yorks DL7 0TJ

Lady Mary Furness
☎ **01609 748614**
Mobile 0378 417625
🆂🅲 **From £180–£340**
Sleeps 6
🛏 🐕 🎇 🔋 ⊚
🔑 🔑 🔑 🔑 *Commended*

Peacefully situated on a 230-acre family farm, a cosy spacious bungalow with private garden and parking. Heating, CTV, open fire. Fully equipped kitchen, washer, fridge/freezer, microwave, etc. Three bedrooms (bed linen included). Lovely views of Swaledale and Herriot Country. Close to Richmond, Northallerton, Thirsk and historic cities. Good local hospitality and recreations. A warm welcome assured. Open all year.

Trip's Cottage, Bay Tree Farm, Aldfield, Nr Fountains Abbey, Ripon, North Yorkshire HG4 3BE

Valerie Leeming
☎/Fax **01765 620394**
🆂🅲 **From £135–£200**
Sleeps 2
🐕 🖼 🔋 ⊚
🔑 🔑 🔑 *Commended*

Converted stable which sleeps 2, shown to the left of the farmhouse. Fine panoramic views over Fountains Abbey. Tasteful conversion consists of lobby, shower, toilet, fitted kitchen (microwave/electric cooker), lounge/ diner (with colour TV). Double bedroom, bed linen and storage heaters included in the rent. Pay–phone available. Shops at Ripon (3 miles), eating 2 miles. Private parking and gardens. Ideal for touring Dales, Moors and York. Local walks. Open all year.

Wren Cottage, c/o Street House Farm, Little Holtby, Northallerton, North Yorkshire DL7 9LN

Mrs Jennifer Pybus
☎ **01609 748622**
🆂🅲 **From £110–£235**
Sleeps 4
🛏 🐕 🔋 ⊚
🔑 🔑 🔑 *Commended*

This cosy cottage in Kirkby Fleetham overlooks the village green, with pub serving food and shop/PO nearby. Ideal centre for exploring Yorkshire Dales and North Yorkshire Moors and within easy reach of York and Durham. The cottage with its traditional oak beams and open fire in the lounge has a fully equipped kitchen with electric cooker and microwave. Also night storage heaters and telephone. Electricity included. Open all year.

Please mention Stay on a Farm when booking

Ryedale, North Yorkshire

Group Contacts: 🆃 *Brenda Johnson* ☎ *01439 798278*
             🆂 *Mrs Sally Robinson* ☎ *01439 798221*

Upper Ryedale is an area of outstanding beauty with wild open moors and pleasant valley floors. There is plenty to entertain the visitors in this captivating area.

For the energetic, miles and miles of footpaths like the Cleveland Way and the Lyke Wake Walk, or study the wealth of flora and fauna as you discover the countryside.

Literary pilgrimages can be made to Thirsk where James Herriot had his practice, and to Goathland where the Heartbeat series is based.

Perhaps you are more interested in the historical aspect of Ryedale. We have many stately homes like Castle Howard and Duncombe Park. The walled city of York is within an hour by car. Local museums include the Ryedale Folk Museum at picturesque Hutton-le-Hole, and Eden Camp at Malton. Famous ruins include Rievaulx and Byland Abbeys amongst others.

Children are well catered for with the seaside towns of Scarborough, Whitby and quaint Robin Hoods Bay within easy reach. Flamingoland Pleasure Park is close by.

If you plan to just relax then drive into the many pretty villages like Kilburn with its White Horse on the hillside, take a trip on the North Yorkshire Moors Steam Railway from Pickering, or maybe just take a picnic out onto the Moors and enjoy the beautiful surroundings.

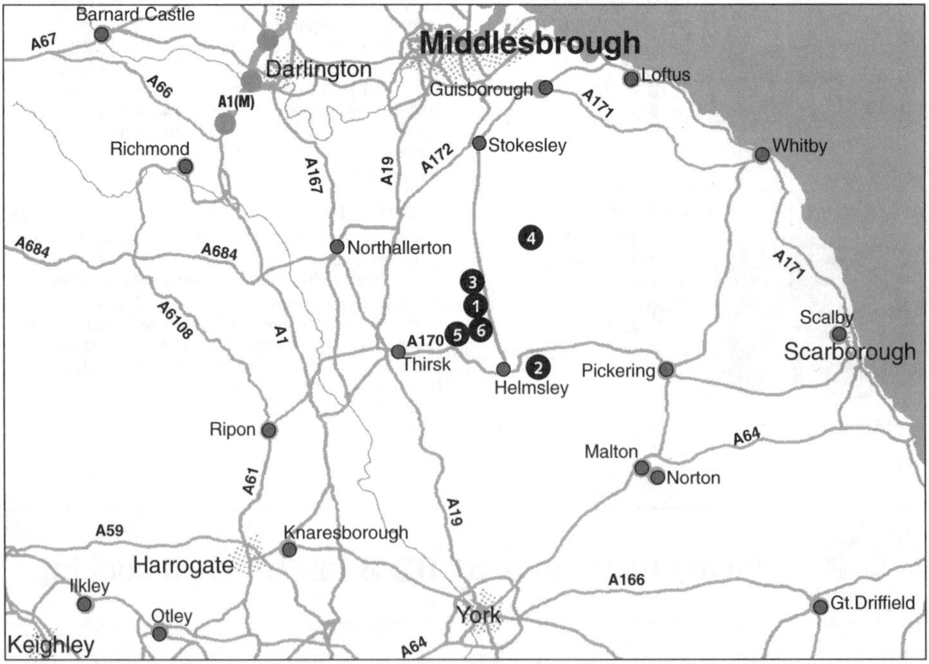

BED AND BREAKFAST
(and evening meal)

Barn Close Farm, Rievaulx, Helmsley, North Yorkshire YO6 5HL

Joan Milburn
☎ 01439 798321
[BB] From £20–£22
EM From £12
Sleeps 5
🔥 🐴 🐤 🛶 🎋 🍖
♨ ♨ ♨ *Commended*

Comfortable, relaxed atmosphere at Barn Close Farm set in an idyllic wooded valley of outstanding beauty close to Rievaulx Abbey and Old Byland. Farmhouse cooking recommended by the Daily Telegraph. Speciality home baked bread. Riding, walking from farmyard. Central for touring countryside, 1 hour from York or coast. 1 en suite, 1 family with private bathroom, tea/coffee-making facilities. Open all year.

Beech Tree House Farm, South Holme, Slingsby, York YO6 7BA

Mrs Carol Farnell
☎ 01653 628257
[BB] £16
EM £8
Sleeps 10
🔥 🍖 🐤 🛶 🎋 ⊚
Listed *Approved*

Large Victorian farmhouse on 260-acre arable farm with sheep, pigs, poultry. In peaceful valley ¼ mile inland, close to Castle Howard, central for York, moors, dales, coast and Flamingoland. 1 family, 2 doubles, 1 twin room, 3 guest bathrooms. Lounge with log fire, TV. Snooker/games room. Large garden with safe play area, toys and cycles available. Children welcome at reduced rates. Babysitting. Open all year except Christmas.

Easterside Farm, Hawnby, Helmsley, North Yorkshire YO6 5QT

Mrs Sarah Wood
☎ 01439 798277
[BB] From £18–£20
EM From £10
Sleeps 12
🔥 🎋 🐾 ⊚
♨ ♨ *Commended*

A large 18th century Grade II listed farmhouse, nestling on Easterside Hill and enjoying panoramic views. Ideal base for walking, touring, the coast and the city of York. Enjoy good food and a warm welcome in comfortable surroundings. All rooms have en suite facilities. Open all year (closed Christmas).

Hill End Farm, Chop Gate, Bilsdale, North Yorkshire TS9 7JR

Brenda Johnson
☎ 01439 798278
[BB] From £20–£22
Sleeps 5
🔥 🐴 🎋 🍖
♨ ♨ *Commended*

Recommended by the *Which? Good Bed & Breakfast Guide*. Hill End Farm has beautiful views down the valley of Bilsdale which is midway between the market towns of Helmsley and Stokesley. Two en suite bedrooms with tea/coffee-making facilities. Comfortable lounge for our guests to relax in. Open Mar–Nov.

Mount Grace Farm, Cold Kirby, Thirsk, North Yorkshire YO7 2HL

Joyce Ashbridge
☎ 01845 597389
[BB] From £20–£23
EM From £12
Sleeps 6
🔥(12) ⅍ 🍖 ⊚
♨ ♨ *Highly Commended*

A warm welcome awaits you on working farm surrounded by beautiful open countryside with magnificent views. Ideal location for touring, or exploring the many walks in the area. Luxury en suite bedrooms with tea/coffee facilities. Spacious guests' lounge with colour TV. Garden. Enjoy delicious, generous helpings of farmhouse fayre cooked in our Aga. Weekly rates. Open all year except Christmas.

6 **Valley View Farm,** Old Byland, Helmsley, York, North Yorkshire YO6 5LG

Sally Robinson
☎/Fax 01439 798221
BB From £25–£28
EM From £13.50
Sleeps 10
♨ ♞ ⊞ ♟ ♒ ♣
♥ ♥ *Highly Commended*

Enjoy the delights of traditional Yorkshire hospitality, hearty country breakfasts and delicious farmhouse fayre. Relax in the beautiful countryside of the North York Moors National Park or see the many places of interest and visit historic towns. Rooms are tastefully furnished and en suite. Guests' lounge with open fire. Licensed. Way marked walks from the farmyard. Open all year.

SELF-CATERING

6 **Valley View Farm,** Old Byland, Helmsley, York, North Yorkshire YO6 5LG

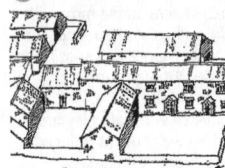

Sally Robinson
☎/Fax 01439 798221
SC From £120–£450
Sleeps 2–6
♨ ♞ ⊞ ♟ ♒ ♣
♘ ♘ ♘ ♘ *Highly Commended*

A beef, sheep and pig farm set on the edge of small village. Newly converted barn furnished with traditional farm theme. The cottages have TV, video, dishwasher, washer/dryer, open fires, CH. All bedrooms are en suite, beds double or twin. Delicious farmhouse meals available (see B&B listing). Phone for colour brochure. Open all year.

STAY ON A FARM GIFT TOKENS

FARM HOLIDAY BUREAU

If you have enjoyed your Stay on a Farm, why not treat your friends and relatives to *Stay on a Farm* gift tokens? Available from the Bureau office, telephone 01203 696909, they can be redeemed against accommodation booked on the majority of our farms

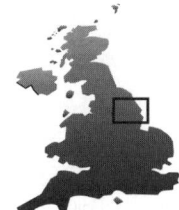

Yorkshire Moors, National Park and Coast

Group Contact: *Mrs Anne Barrett* ☎ *01751 473131*

When you come to stay with us on our farms you have the opportunity to visit the seaside and enjoy the countryside inland as well.

The coast offers sandy beaches, secret caves, pretty fishing villages and 30 miles of Heritage Coast with bird sanctuaries and wildlife. The resorts of Scarborough, Whitby and Bridlington offer lively entertainment in the evenings for all tastes.

There are over 1,000 miles of public footpaths and bridleways in the area and recognised walks like the White Rose Walk, the Cleveland Way and the Lyke Wake Walk. Or perhaps pony trekking through the National Park appeals to you. The North Yorkshire Moors steam railway provides superb nostalgia for railway enthusiasts and spectacular scenery for all who travel on it between Grosmont and Pickering.

Those interested in historic heritage will find much to enjoy. At Pickering the parish church is famous for its unique 15th-century wall painting of St George and the Dragon. Whitby and Rievaulx Abbeys are examples of the magnificent religious architecture of the area. Ancient castles can also be explored at Helmsley, Pickering and Scarborough.

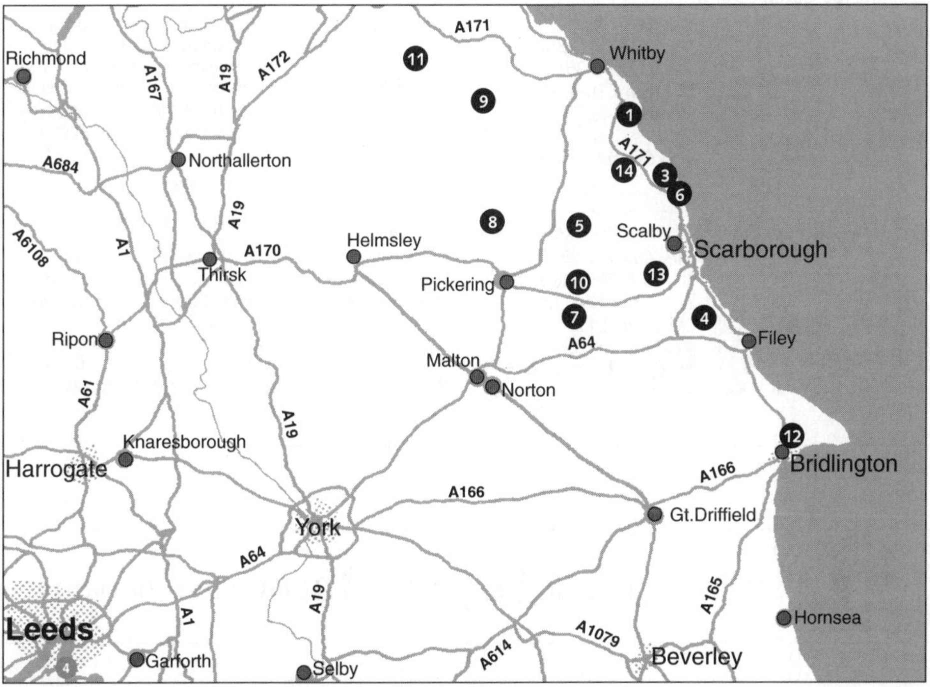

Richmond
A171
A19
A172
A167
11
Whitby
9
A684
Northallerton
1
A19
A171
14
3
6
A6108
A1
A170
Helmsley
8
5
Scalby
Scarborough
Thirsk
Pickering
10
13
Ripon
7
A64
4
Filey
Malton
Norton
A61
A19
Knaresborough
12
Harrogate
A166
Bridlington
A166
York
Gt.Driffield
A64
A19
A165
A1
Hornsea
Leeds
A614
A1079
Garforth
Selby
Beverley

BED AND BREAKFAST

(and evening meal)

---

(1) Croft Farm, Church Lane, Fylingthorpe, Whitby, North Yorkshire YO22 4PW

Pauline Featherstone
☎ 01947 880231
[BB] From £17.50–£21.50
Sleeps 6
⌂(5) ✂ ♨ ♞ ◉
Listed *Highly Commended*

18th century farmhouse in lawned garden on small working farm overlooking Robin Hood's Bay. Tastefully furnished in the 'olde worlde' charm with open beams, staircase and fireplaces. Rooms with washbasins (1 en suite) all with tea-making facilities and panoramic views of the sea, moors and country-side. Guests' lounge, bathroom. Ideal base for coastal resorts, walking and touring the beauty spots of North Yorkshire. Our speciality is a good hearty breakfast. Open Easter–mid-Oct.

---

(3) Island Farm, Staintondale, Scarborough, North Yorkshire YO13 0EB

Mary Clarke
☎ 01723 870249
[BB] From £17–£20
Sleeps 6
⌂ ✂ ♞ ♨ ♞ ◉
♨ ♨ *Commended*

Relax in our spacious and comfortable farmhouse and garden. All bedrooms have en suite facilities. Being close to coast and in open countryside, it is ideal for walking or visiting many places of interest. Visitors appreciate our large games room with toys, full size snooker table and tennis court. Brochure on request. Open Easter–Nov.

---

(4) Killerby Cottage Farm, Killerby Lane, Cayton, Scarborough, North Yorkshire YO11 3TP

Valerie Green
☎ 01723 581236
Fax 01723 585465
[BB] From £16–£20
Sleeps 6
[£] ♨
♨ ♨ *Commended*

Simon and Val Green welcome you to Killerby Cottage Farm in the pleasant countryside between Scarborough and Filey. The farmhouse has many charming features and our double, twin bedded and en suite rooms are tastefully decorated. Guests' lounge with log fires, sun room, lovely garden, good food – all for you to enjoy. Open all year.

---

(5) Newgate Foot Farm, Saltersgate, Pickering, North Yorkshire YO18 7NR

Mrs Alison Johnson
☎/Fax 01751 460215
[BB] From £17–£22
EM From £11
Sleeps 5
⌂(5) [£] Å ⇐ ♞ ♨ ✗ ◉
♨ ♨ *Highly Commended*

Just 1 mile off the A169, but in a world of its own in the middle of the moors with no neighbours in sight! Enjoy walking on the moors, through the forest, or trout fishing in our own lake. See the ewes and lambs and thorough-bred mares and foals. Whitby 14 miles, York 35 miles, "Aidensfield" 6 miles. One en suite bedroom, 1 twin/3 bedded, 1 single. Open all year except Christmas.

Please mention **Stay on a Farm** when booking

Plane Tree Cottage Farm, Staintondale, Scarborough, North Yorkshire YO13 0EY

Mrs Marjorie Edmondson
☎ 01723 870796
ⒷⒷ From £16
EM From £10
Sleeps 4
⚭ ♨ ♞ ◉

Listed *Approved*

This 60-acre mixed farm is situated off the beaten track, between Scarborough and Whitby. We have rare breeds of sheep, pigs and free range hens. Also a very friendly cat called 'Danny'. This small, homely cottage has character with its beams and low ceilings, and beautiful open views. Good wholesome home cooking. Open March–Nov.

Rains Farm, Allerston, Pickering, North Yorkshire YO18 7PQ

Jean or Lorraine Allanson
☎/Fax 01723 859333
ⒷⒷ From £19–£23
EM From £14
Sleeps 11
⚭ ⊞ ♨ ♔ ◉

♕♕ *Commended*

Rains Farm nestles very peacefully in beautiful grounds amidst Ryedale's pastoral countryside. Relax and enjoy our unique Yorkshire hospitality, hearty breakfasts and mouthwatering farmhouse fayre. Double/twin/single en suite rooms (one on ground floor), all tastefully furnished and decorated. Private parking. Warm farmhouse and a warm welcome awaits you. Open all year except Christmas.

Seavy Slack, Stape, Pickering, North Yorkshire YO18 8HZ

Anne Barrett
☎ 01751 473131
ⒷⒷ From £15–£17
EM From £12
Sleeps 6
♿ ♞ ♨ ♔ ◉

Listed *Approved*

Relax and enjoy good food and a very warm welcome on our 160-acre stock and arable farm situated on the edge of the North Yorkshire Moors. Pickering 7 miles, Whitby, Scarborough and York within easy reach. One double, one family room both with tea-making facilities. Guests' lounge/dining room with colour TV. Open all year except Christmas and New Year.

Stonebeck Gate Farm, Little Fryup, Danby, Whitby, North Yorkshire YO21 2NS

Jill Kelly
☎/Fax 01287 660363
ⒷⒷ From £15
EM From £10
Sleeps 6
♿ ⚭ ♞ ♨ ♔

Applied

Jill and Andrew Kelly welcome you to Little Fryup in the heart of the North Yorkshire Moors National Park. We offer you a comfortable base for your holiday, with guests' own bathroom, dining room and lounge (with satellite TV). Bedrooms are spacious with fine views. Evening meal by prior arrangement.

Studley House, 67, Main Street, Ebberston, Scarborough, North Yorkshire YO13 9NR

Ernie & Jane Hodgson
☎ 01723 859285
ⒷⒷ From £18–£20
Sleeps 6
♿(8) ⚭ ⊞ ☎ Å ♨ ♔ ◉

♕♕ *Commended*

Studley House is situated in a pretty village with much charm and character. Enjoy an excellent Yorkshire breakfast then take a leisurely stroll by the stream. All bedrooms are en suite with hospitality trays, colour TV, own keys. CH throughout. We are central for moors, coast, pretty villages and historic York. A friendly welcome awaits. Open all year except Christmas.

Although the majority of farms will accept 'Stay on a Farm' Gift Tokens, please check when booking to avoid disappointment.

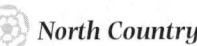
SELF-CATERING

⑪ Blackmires Farm, Danby Head, Danby, Whitby, North Yorkshire YO21 2NN

Gillian & Lewis Rhys
☎ **01287 660352**
ᔆᴄ **From £150–£350**
Sleeps 6
♨ 🐕 ☂ 🎪 ◎
🔑 🔑 🔑 🔑 *Commended*

Stone cottage for six. Two bedrooms and bathroom on ground floor, twin bedroom upstairs. Garden, swing and sandpit. Quiet situation adjacent to moors in an area of outstanding natural beauty. Our small working farm is in Danby Dale, 3 miles from Danby, Castleton and the North York Moors National Park Information Centre. Open all year.

① Croft Farm Cottage, Croft Farm, Church Lane, Fylingthorpe, Whitby, North Yorkshire YO22 4PW

Pauline Featherstone
☎ **01947 880231**
ᔆᴄ **From £140–£270**
Sleeps 4
♨ ☂ 🎪 ◎
🔑 🔑 🔑 *Commended*

Forget the pressures of everyday living! Come and relax in the cottage attached to our 18th century farmhouse on a working farm, offering spectacular views, home comforts, peace and tranquillity. Overlooking Robin Hood's Bay, within easy reach of coastal resorts, Moors Railway and termination of well-known walks. 2 bedrooms, 1 double and 1 with built-in bunk beds. Fully equipped including linen. Colour TV and sun lounge. Open all year.

⑫ Field House, Jewison Lane, Sewerby, Bridlington, East Yorkshire YO16 5YG

Angela Foster
☎ **01262 674932**
Fax 01262 608688
ᔆᴄ **From £250–£375**
Sleeps 6 + cot
♨ ☂ 🎾
🔑 🔑 🔑 🔑
Highly Commended

Our highly rated farmhouse with walled garden, tennis court and croquet lawn is an excellent base from which to explore a spectacular coastline or, within an hour's drive, some of Yorkshire's finest features. Sample life on a large dairy/arable farm. Children especially welcome. Open all year.

⑦ Rains Farm, Allerston, Pickering, North Yorkshire YO18 7PQ

Jean or Lorraine Allanson
☎ **/Fax 01723 859333**
ᔆᴄ **From £140–£395**
Sleeps 2/6
♨ ✂ 🐈 🖼 ☂ 🎾 ◎
🔑 🔑 🔑 – 🔑 🔑 🔑 🔑
Highly Commended

Five warm and comfortable newly converted barns. Very peaceful, magnificent views. Relax, unwind and ease away the pressures of life in this idyllic rural retreat. Gaze on the ponies grazing in the paddocks. Furnished, decorated and equipped for luxury living. We are centrally situated for many attractions. Safe parking. Colour brochure. Open all year.

Please mention **Stay on a Farm** when booking

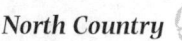
CAMPING AND CARAVANNING

Low Yedmandale Farm, West Ayton, Scarborough, North Yorkshire YO13 9JZ

Mrs C M Cussons
☎ **01723 863193**
SC **From £130–£200**
Sleeps 8
🐎 🐕 🚐 🛉 ⛺
Tourist Board Inspected

The caravan is located at Low Yedmandale Farm in its own plot in font of the farmstead. The dairy farm is set in a south-facing valley in the North York Moors National Park, 1 mile from West Ayton. Close to Forge Valley, the North York Moors and the coastal resorts of Scarborough, Whitby and Filey and Flamingo Land Pleasure Park. Open Apr–Oct.

Pond Farm, Fylingdales, Whitby, North Yorkshire YO22 4QJ

Grace Cromack
☎ **01947 880441**
SC **From £120–£200**
Sleeps 6
🐎 🐕 🚐 🛉 ⛺ ◉
Tourist Board Inspected

We offer one 6-berth caravan, situated on 400-acre mixed stock farm edging the North Yorkshire Moors and near to Robin Hood's Bay. It is situated in a walled garden with open views and has all mains services including shower, toilet. TV, fridge, double and bunk-bedded rooms. Ideal for visiting historic towns, coastal resorts. Forest and moorland walks, pony trekking and clay pigeon shooting nearby. Short breaks out of season. Open Apr–Nov.

FARM HOLIDAY BUREAU

Our Internet Address is
http://www.webscape.co.uk/farmaccom/

FARM HOLIDAY BUREAU

FINDING YOUR ACCOMMODATION

The Group contacts at the beginning of each section can always help you find a vacancy in your chosen area.

Vale of York and the Wolds

Group Contact: *Mrs Helen Middleton* ☎ *01757 228775*

When you come to stay with us on our farms you are within easy reach of Yorkshire's capital city with its beautiful Minster and a wealth of history; visit the Railway Museum and Jorvik Centre. Whilst in the area see Castle Howard where 'Brideshead Revisited' was filmed and the abbeys of Rievaulx, Byland and Selby.

The area is rich in market towns: Driffield, the capital of the Wolds where reputedly King Alfred is buried, and Beverley, described as the most perfect of county towns with its cobbled streets and 'bars' or town gates. Beverley Minster is one of the finest churches. Explore the many country houses all rich in history and full of beautiful furniture.

Hull is a major port where sailing ships have given way to modern ferries and some of its docks to a yacht marina.

Horse racing takes place at York, Beverley, Ripon and Thirsk, all providing an exciting day out.

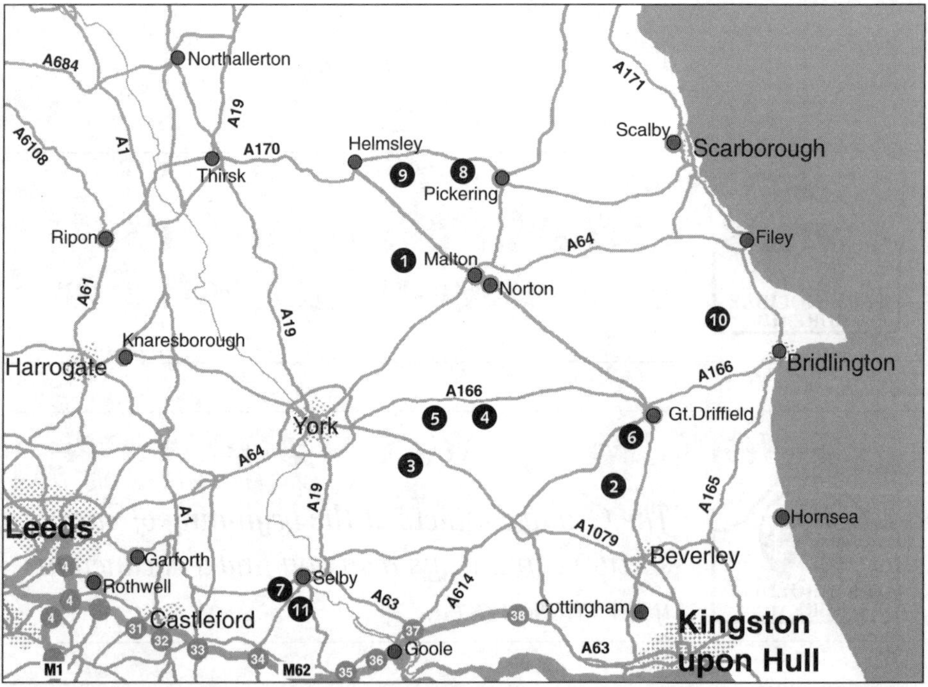

A684 — Northallerton — A19 — A170 — Helmsley — A171 — Scalby — Scarborough — Thirsk — **9** — **8** Pickering — A6108 — A1 — Ripon — A61 — A64 — **1** Malton — Norton — Filey — Kharesborough — A19 — **10** — Harrogate — Bridlington — A166 — A166 — York — A166 — **5** **4** — Gt.Driffield — A165 — **3** — **6** — Leeds — A1 — A19 — **2** — Hornsea — Garforth — A1079 — Beverley — Rothwell — **7** Selby — A63 — A614 — Cottingham — **Kingston upon Hull** — Castleford — **11** — A63 — Goole — M1 — M62

BED AND BREAKFAST
(and evening meal)

Church Farm, Scackleton, York, North Yorkshire YO6 4NB ①

Mrs Cynthia Firby
☎/Fax 01653 628403
[BB] **From £17–£19**
EM From £10
Sleeps 6
🐴 ⅟ 🐓 🖥 ⅍
Listed *Highly Commended*

A spacious, comfortable stone farmhouse on our sheep and arable farm in a quiet hamlet in the Howardian Hills designated Area of Outstanding Natural Beauty. 1 double en suite, 1 family en suite. Tea/coffee-making facilities in all bedrooms. Central heating, good home cooking, wonderful views. Ideal base for walking or visiting York, the moors and coast. Open Mar–Nov.

Clematis House, 1 Eastgate, Lund, Nr Driffield, East Yorkshire YO25 9TQ ②

Mrs Gill Lamb
☎/Fax 01377 217204
[BB] **From £17.50–£19.50**
Sleeps 4/5
🐴 ⅟ 🖥 ◉
🐛 *Commended*

Family-run 389-acre arable and livestock farm in pretty rural village. Farmhouse with character, spacious yet cosy. En suite rooms with TV and tea/coffee-making facilities. Lounge with log fire. Secluded south-facing walled garden and off-road parking. Ideal for visiting York, Hull, Beverley, the coast and North Yorkshire Moors. Open all year except Christmas.

Cuckoo Nest Farm, Wilberfoss, York YO4 5NL ③

Joan Liversidge
☎ 01759 380365
[BB] **From £18**
Sleeps 6
🐴 🐓 🖥 ◉
🐛 🐛 *Commended*

Situated 7 miles east of York off A1079 Hull road, 200-year-old traditional red-brick farmhouse on cattle/dairy/arable farm. Oak-beamed rooms, pleasant sitting room and separate dining room. One en suite bedroom; one double and one twin, both H&C. Good country pubs nearby. Easy drive to coast, dales and moors. A warm welcome awaits you here. Open all year.

High Belthorpe, Bishop Wilton, Nr. York, Humberside YO4 1SB ④

Meg Abu Hamdan
☎ 01759 368238
Mobile 0973 938528
[BB] **From £17.65**
Sleeps 6
🐴 🐓 🏕 ⟲ ⅍ 🖥
🐛 *Commended*

Set on an ancient moated site in the Yorkshire Wolds, this large Victorian farmhouse has spacious bedrooms with uninterrupted panoramic views. The centre of a working livery yard, the house has own private fishing lake and access to fabulous country walks. Croquet, small snooker table available. York 12 miles, coast 20 miles. Open all year.

High Catton Grange, High Catton, near Stamford Bridge, York YO4 1EP ⑤

Sheila Foster
☎ 01759 371374
[BB] **From £16.50**
Sleeps 6
🐴 🐓 🖥 ⅍ ◉
🐛 🐛 *Commended*

Only 8 miles east of York, High Catton Grange is a 300-acre mixed farm with comfortable 18th century farmhouse. Friendly, relaxed atmosphere and attractive bedrooms, 2 with washbasin, 1 en suite, guest bathroom, central heating, tea/coffee-making facilities. Within 2 miles, local country inns providing excellent meals. Ample private parking. Open all year except Christmas and New Year.

---

6   **Kelleythorpe Farm,** Kelleythorpe, Great Driffield, East Yorkshire YO25 9DW

Mrs Tiffy Hopper
☎ 01377 252297
🅱🅱 From £15–£20
EM £10
Sleeps 6
ㅎ 🕇 🐕 ♨ 🎾 ⊚
Listed *Commended*

Imagine peacocks strutting, ducks swimming and trout rising. Enjoy tea on the sun terrace overlooking a crystal clear shallow river, the friendly atmosphere of our lovely Georgian farmhouse with its mellow antique furniture, pretty chintz and new bathrooms, 1 en suite, is sure to captivate you. Delicious country cooking. Children very welcome. Ideally placed for touring. Open all year (closed Christmas & New Year).

7   **Lund Farm,** Gateforth, Selby, North Yorkshire YO8 9LE

Chris & Helen Middleton
☎ 01757 228775
Fax 01757 228004
🅱🅱 From £18–£25
EM From £7
Sleeps 6
ㅎ 🗲 🏃 ♨ ⌣ ♨ 🎾
🐝 *Highly Commended*

Convenient for York and the Dales, our peaceful 18th century farmhouse has 2 en suite rooms, pine beams and log fires. Children most welcome; 200-acre farm with lambs, eggs to collect, Shetland pony, bicycles, baby listening and nursery teas. Evening meals on request. Lambing breaks Dec–Mar. Business visitors welcome too; phone and fax available. Open all year.

8   **Sinnington Manor,** Sinnington, York YO6 6SN

Mrs J M Wilson
☎ 01751 433296
🅱🅱 From £20–£25
Sleeps 5
ㅎ(3) 🗲 🕇 ♨ 🎾 🎾
🐝 *Highly Commended*

Welcome to our Georgian manor house, recently restored into a warm and comfortable family home, but still retaining its original charm and elegance. Relax outside in beautiful gardens or walk in 275 acres with conservation areas, woodland and beck. Farm animals include suckler cows, longhorns and a stud of coloured horses. Peaceful countryside, yet close to moors, coast, York, etc. Children, dogs and horses welcome. Open Mar–Sept.

9   **Sunley Court,** Nunnington, York, North Yorkshire YO6 5XQ

Mrs Joan Brown
☎ 01439 748233
🅱🅱 From £15
EM £10
Sleeps 6
ㅎ 🕇 ♨ ⊚
🐝🐝 *Commended*

Sunley Court is a comfortable modern farmhouse with open views in a quiet secluded area. The farm is arable with sheep and horses. All bedrooms have tea/coffee-making facilities, washbasins, electric blankets, 2 have shower/toilet en suite, 2 single bedrooms. Good home cooking. Central for York, moors and coast. Open all year except Christmas.

10   **The Wold Cottage,** Wold Newton, Driffield YO25 0HL

Mrs Katrina Gray
☎/Fax 01262 470696
🅱🅱 From £19
EM From £10
Sleeps 4
ㅎ 🗲 🏃 ♨ ♨ 🎾 ⊚
🐝🐝 *Highly Commended*

Georgian farmhouse set in own grounds overlooking new and mature woodlands and continuous wold land. Come and relax and forget the pressures of everyday life. Stroll around our field margins and observe the wildlife and history. All rooms are en suite with tea/coffee-making facilities. Lambing breaks Jan–Mar. Open all year.

LET THE TELEPHONE RING!

Some farmhouses are big places. Let the telephone ring
long enough to give the owner time to answer it.

SELF-CATERING

The Cottage, High Catton Grange, High Catton, near Stamford Bridge, York YO4 1EP   **5**

Sheila Foster
☎ **01759 371374**
⌗ **From £150–£280**
Sleeps 4–6
☱ ☃ ♞ ♨ ☀ ⊚
♟ ♟ ♟ ♟ *Commended*

This former gig shed and stable has been converted to a high standard yet retains many original features. Comfortable and tastefully furnished with colour TV, automatic washer/dryer, fridge, microwave, storage heaters,etc. Patio doors onto large private patio and garden furniture. Glorious views across green meadows. Working farm in peaceful, rural setting, ideally situated for York or touring. Linen/fuel included. Open all year.

1 & 2 Dove Cottages, Primrose Hill Farm, c/o Staynor Hall, Selby, North Yorkshire YO8 8EE   **11**

Jenny Webster
☎ **01757 708931**
Fax **01757 704386**
⌗ **From £145–£350**
Sleep up to 5
☱ ✄ ♨ ♔
♟ ♟ ♟ *Highly Commended*

Our restored 19th century farm cottages on a mixed farm are well equipped with central heating, open log fires and fitted kitchens. Dove cottages offer a quiet retreat in comfortable accommodation. Set in peaceful surroundings with open views only 20 minutes south of historic York. Linen included as are cots and high chair. Open all year.

Lund Farm Cottage, Lund Farm, Gateforth, Selby, North Yorkshire YO8 9LE   **7**

Chris & Helen Middleton
☎ **01757 228775**
Fax **01757 228004**
⌗ **From £180–£350**
EM **From £7**
Sleeps 6
☱ ✄ Å ♘ ♔ ♥ ♨ ☀
♟ ♟ ♟ *Highly Commended*

Convenient for York and the Dales, our 18th century farmyard cottage has beams, fireside range, safe patio and lawn, and friendly owners next door. Children most welcome. 200-acre farm with lambs, eggs to collect, Shetland pony, and bicycles. Evening meals available. Lambing breaks Dec–Mar. Prices fully inclusive. Open all year.

STAY ON A FARM GIFT TOKENS

FARM HOLIDAY BUREAU

If you have enjoyed your Stay on a Farm, why not treat your friends and relatives to *Stay on a Farm* gift tokens? Available from the Bureau office, telephone 01203 696909, they can be redeemed against accommodation booked on the majority of our farms

---

Although the majority of farms will accept 'Stay on a Farm' Gift Tokens, please check when booking to avoid disappointment.

South and West Yorkshire

Group Contact: *Mrs Marie Gill* ☎ *01924 848339*

We extend a warm welcome to you to visit the gently rolling countryside of South and West Yorkshire.

On the edge of the Peak District National Park is the small town of Holmfirth 'Last of the Summer Wine Country'. Surrounded by hills and moors, it is perfect for walkers who like to try the Kirklees Way which is a circular walk of 75 miles.

The open air markets of Dewsbury, Leeds and Barnsley are very popular and the area abounds with mill shops. Beside the M1 is Meadowhall Shopping Mall which has 200 shops under one roof.

Within easy access are the Yorkshire Sculpture Park, the Yorkshire Mining Museum and Kirklees Light Steam Railway.

Why not visit Sheffield with its parks and gardens or Leeds with the Henry Moore Gallery or Wakefield's Chantry Chapel?

For water sports enthusiasts there are three water parks in the area.

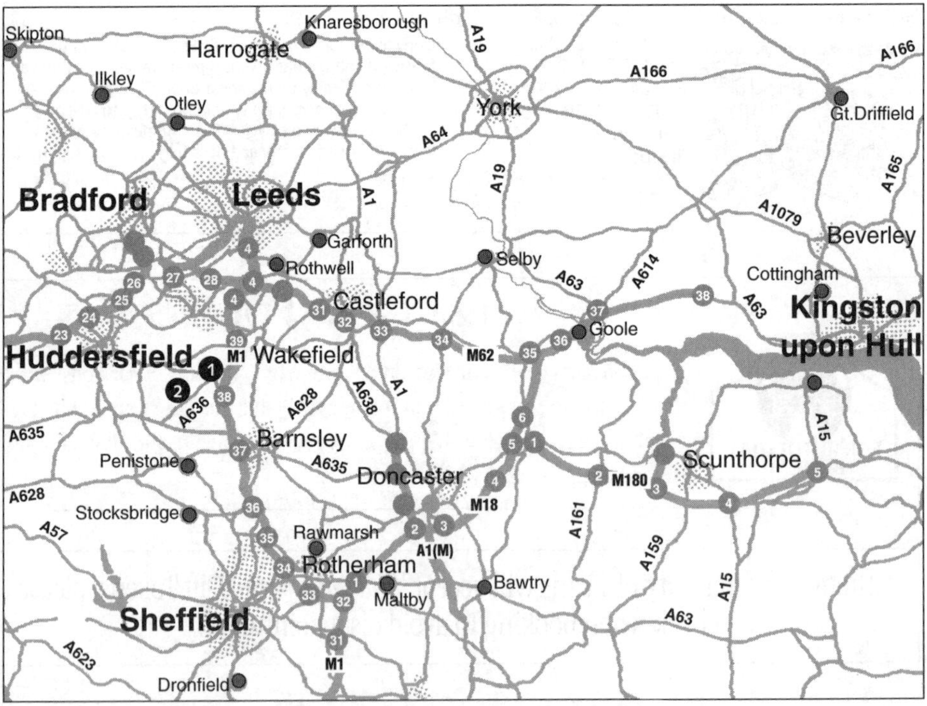

Bed and Breakfast

(and evening meal)

Birch Laithes Farm, Bretton Lane, Bretton, Wakefield, West Yorkshire WF4 4LF

Pat Hoyland
☎ 01924 252129
From £17–£19
Sleeps 6
🐕 ♞ ♨ ♠
❦ *Commended*

A mixed working farm with 18th century house. Comfortable bedrooms, tea/coffee-making facilities, TV, separate dining room and TV lounge, central heating. Ideally situated for Yorkshire towns and countryside, Yorkshire Sculpture Park nearby. 1½ mile J38/39 M1. Open all year.

White Cross Farm, Ash Lane, Emley, Nr Huddersfield, West Yorkshire HD8 9QU

Marie Gill
☎ 01924 848339
From £16–£18
Sleeps 5
🐕 ♞ ♠ ♟ ◉
Listed *Approved*

Mixed working farm with listed farmhouse. Some buildings date from 12th century when monks from Byland Abbey lived here and dug for iron ore and kept sheep. Set in rolling Pennine countryside. Tea/coffee-making facilities, TV, central heating in all bedrooms. Close to Yorkshire Mining Museum, Yorkshire Sculpture Park and Holmfirth (Last of Summer Wine country). 3 miles from M1 (jct. 38/39). Open all year (closed Christmas).

FARM HOLIDAY BUREAU

Our Internet Address is
http://www.webscape.co.uk/farmaccom/

FARM HOLIDAY BUREAU

FINDING YOUR ACCOMMODATION

The Group contacts at the beginning of each section can always help you find a vacancy in your chosen area.

Vale of Lune, Morecambe Bay to Pennine Way

Group Contact: *Mrs Gillian Burrow* ☎ *015242 71446*

Rising in the hills of Cumbria, the Lune flows through richly pastoral countryside. One of its first ports of call is Kirkby Lonsdale, an attractive market town with its 13th century church and Devils Bridge. To the south east lies the busy moorland market town of High Bentham with its Wednesday cattle market and Ingleton, famous for its show caves and spectacular waterfall glens. To the north west lie the unique Limestone Crags of Arnside and Silverdale with its many splendid coastal walks, together with the RSPB bird sanctuary at Leighton Moss and for railway enthusiasts 'Steam Town' at Carnforth will take you back in time. The Lune then flows down to the Roman city of Lancaster with its castle and museums including the Maritime Museum, Museum of Childhood and the Judges Lodgings. At the end of the Lune Valley lies Morecambe Bay.

The River Wyre starts its journey to the sea high in the fells of the ancient hunting Forest of Bowland and flows down through unspoilt villages such as Marshaw, Abbeystead and Dolphinholme to the market town of Garstang. Beacon Fell Country Park is nearby and well worth a visit. The River Lune and the Wyre offer plenty of opportunities for coarse fishing.

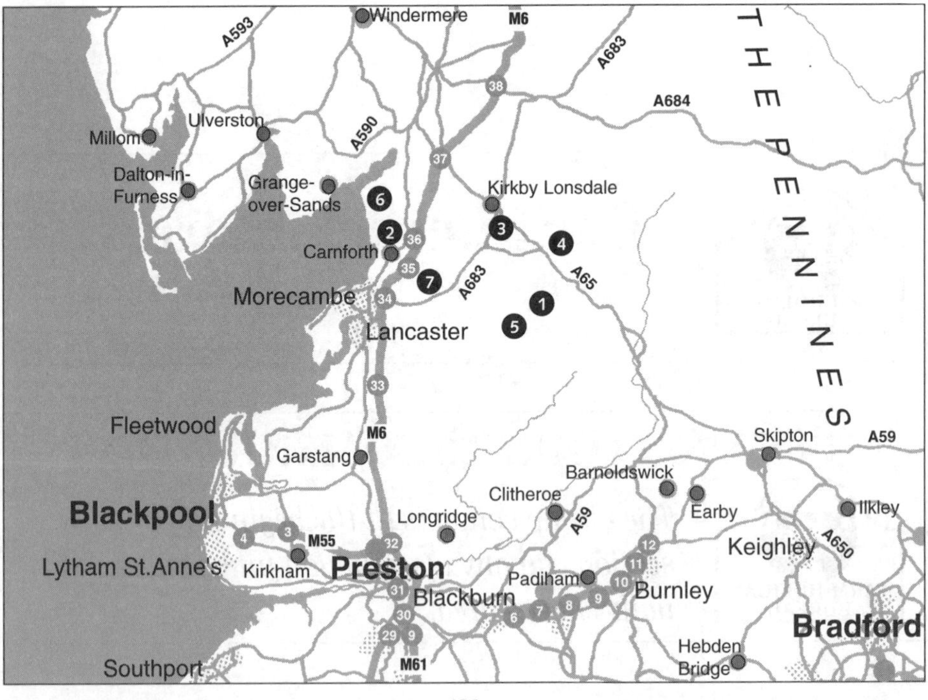

BED AND BREAKFAST

(and evening meal)

Fowgill Park Farm, High Bentham, Nr Lancaster, North Yorkshire LA2 7AH

Shirley Metcalfe
☎ 015242 61630
🅱 From £15–£17
EM From £8. 50
Sleeps 6
🛇 🏂 ⅍ 🛍 ⊚
👄 👄 *Commended*

Fowgill is a stock rearing farm, ideal for those who wish to stay where it is quiet. Guests enjoy panoramic views of the Dales and Fells. A good centre for visiting the Lakes, Dales, coast, waterfalls and caves. Beamed bedrooms have washbasins, shaver points and tea/coffee-making facilities; two bedrooms en suite. Comfortable beamed lounge with television. Separate dining room. Bedtime drink included. Open Mar–Nov.

Galley Hall Farm, Shore Road, Carnforth, Lancashire LA5 9HZ

Vera Casson
☎ 01524 732544
🅱 From £15–£16
EM From £9
Sleeps 5
🛇 🏂 ⅍ 🚗
Listed *Commended*

Galley Hall is situated on the coast within easy reach of the Lake District, the Dales and historic Lancaster. We offer a warm and friendly welcome to all at our working farm and 17th century farmhouse with views of Lakeland hills and Morecombe Bay. Share the comforts of our large lounge with TV and log fires. Bedrooms have washbasins, tea-making facilities and TV on request. 5 minutes from M6 J35. Open Jan–Nov.

Garghyll Dyke, Cowan Bridge, Kirkby Lonsdale, Cumbria LA6 2HT

Mrs Gillian Burrow
☎ 015242 71446
🅱 From £16–£18
Sleeps 4
🛇 🏂 ⅍ 🛍 ⊚
Applied

We offer a warm, friendly welcome with super breakfasts in our comfortable ivy-clad farmhouse where guests can feel at home. A working dairy farm 3 miles from Kirkby Lonsdale, an ideal base to explore coast, Lakes and Dales. Double and twin room tastefully furnished, each with washbasins and tea/coffee facilities. Country pubs and excellent eating places nearby. Reductions for children. Open Mar–Oct.

Gatehouse Farm, Far Westhouse, Ingleton, Carnforth, Lancashire LA6 3NR

Nancy Lund
☎ 015242 41458/41307
🅱 From £16–£18
EM From £9
Sleeps 6
🛇 🏂 ⅍ 🛍 ⏎ ⊚
👄 👄 *Commended*

Bryan and Nancy welcome you to our dairy and sheep farm built in 1740, rooms with old oak beams in elevated position enjoying panoramic views over open countryside in the YORKSHIRE DALES NATIONAL PARK. Guests dining room, and lounge with colour TV. Bedroom with private facilities and tea trays. Welcome drink on arrival. 15 miles exit 34 M6, 1½ miles west of Ingleton just off A65. Open all year (closed Christmas and New Year).

Lane House Farm, High Bentham, Lancaster, North Yorkshire LA2 7DJ

Betty Clapham
☎ 015242 61479
🅱 From £16–£18
Sleeps 6
🛇 🏂 🚗 ⅍ 🏕 🛍 ⊚
👄 👄 *Commended*

Enjoy a relaxing break at our 17th century beamed farmhouse, within ½ mile of the Forest of Bowland, with beautiful views of the Yorkshire Dales. 1 mile from the market town of High Bentham, ½ hour from M6. Ideal for caves, waterfalls, touring the Lakes. Bedrooms have washbasins and tea-making trays. En suite facilities. Guests' lounge with colour TV. Separate dining room. Open Mar–Nov.

SELF-CATERING

⑥ Brackenthwaite Cottages, Brackenthwaite Farm, Yealand Redmayne, Carnforth, LA5 9TE

Susan Clarke
☎ 015395 63276
🆂 From £95–£325
Sleeps 4/6
🐴 🎣 👤 🐴 ♨ 🏠
🐾 🐾 🐾 – 🐾 🐾 🐾 🐾 🐾
Commended

Relax comfortably in one of our three cottages. Walk our nature trail or through nearby nature reserves in AONB. Children can play on the adventure playground and feed the animals. Keepers Cottage has all rooms on a single level, the Old Stables have beams and exposed limestone. Laundry room available. Short lets Nov–Easter. Open all year.

⑦ Garden Cottage, High Snab, Gressingham, Lancaster LA2 8LS

Mrs Margaret Burrow
☎ 015242 21347
🆂 From £180–£260
Sleeps 4 + cot
🐴 🏠
🐾 🐾 🐾 *Commended*

Garden cottage, with its own private drive and garden, adjoins our farmhouse on a working dairy and sheep farm in a quiet location. Ideal for touring lakes, dales and coast. Winner of Lancashire Farm Landscape Trophy and NWTB 'Place to stay 93'. Well equipped kitchen/oak beamed lounge. Two bedrooms, 1 double, 1 twin, snooker table, bathroom with shower. CH from farmhouse, cot/high chair available. Electric and linen included. 5 miles M6 J35. Brochure. Open Mar–Nov.

STAY ON A FARM GIFT TOKENS

FARM HOLIDAY BUREAU

If you have enjoyed your Stay on a Farm, why not treat your friends and relatives to *Stay on a Farm* gift tokens? Available from the Bureau office, telephone 01203 696909, they can be redeemed against accommodation booked on the majority of our farms

THE 1000+ BUREAU MEMBERS OFFER A UNIQUE LINK TO CUSTOMERS ACROSS THE UK

FARM HOLIDAY BUREAU

All Bureau members belong to a local Group. Each member can refer you to an equally high quality member within the Group... or across the UK: England, Northern Ireland, Scotland, Wales.

Lancashire Coast & Country

Group Contact: *Mrs Maureen Smith* ☎ *01253 882537*

Contrasting scenery beckons you to Lancashire Coast and Country. The bracing coastline changes from wide sandy beaches to pebble beaches and from sand dunes to estuary marshes. There is Blackpool with its hustle and bustle and famous illuminations, and Southport which is noted for its elegant shops and arcades. Both seaside resorts have excellent theatres and restaurants and night-life.

Inland from the coast, the acres of rich farmland are dotted with unspoilt villages and small market towns like Poulton-le Fylde, with its ancient stocks and Norman church, and Ormskirk, whose street market was first chartered in the 13th century.

The Wildfowl Trust Centre at Martin Mere and the National Nature Reserve at Lytham St Annes offer sanctuary for wildlife. Energetic walkers and explorers will be attracted to the Forest of Bowland and Bleasdale Fells, whilst those preferring a gentle stroll will head for the banks of the canals or Rivers Douglas, Ribble or Wyre.

A visit to the Lancashire coast offers the peace and tranquillity of the countryside or all the fun of the fair – whichever you chose, a warm Northern welcome awaits you.

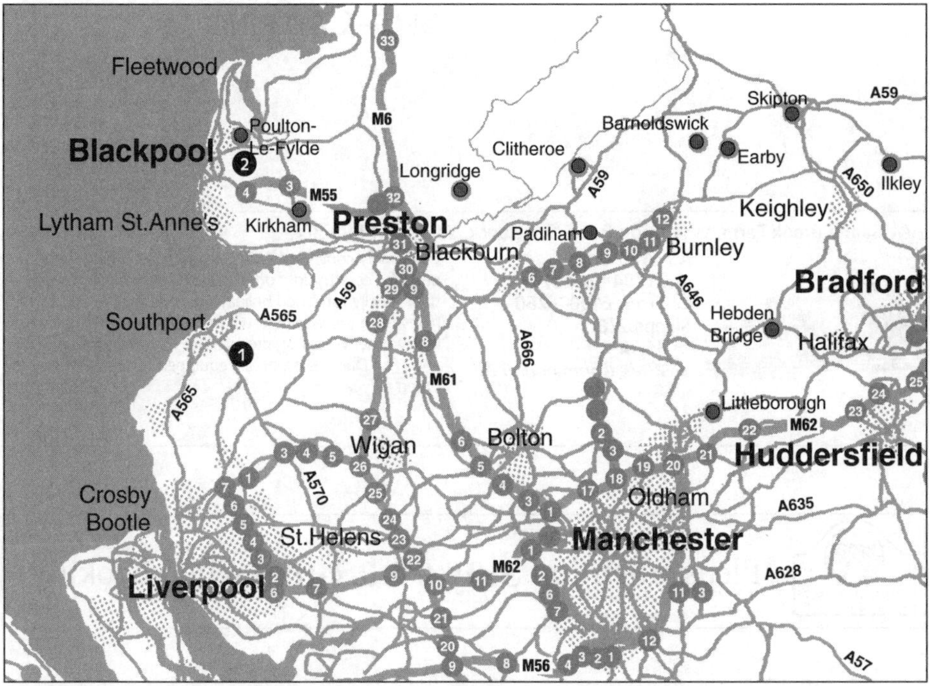

BED AND BREAKFAST

(and evening meal)

---

① Sandy Brook Farm, Wyke Cop Road, Scarisbrick, Southport, Lancashire PR8 5LR

Mrs W E Core
☎ 01704 880337
BB From £16.50
Sleeps 15
♿ 🐾 ♨
💐 💐 *Commended*

This small, comfortable arable farm is situated in the rural area of Scarisbrick, midway between the seaside town of Southport and the ancient town of Ormskirk. A570 ½ mile. The converted farm buildings are attractively furnished, and all bedrooms have en suite facilities, colour TV and tea/coffee facilities. Silver winners NWTB Place to Stay, 'Commended' award Holiday Care Service. Open all year except Christmas.

---

② Todderstaffe Hall Farm, off Fairfield Road, Singleton, Poulton-le-Fylde, Lancashire FY6 8LF

Mrs Maureen Smith
☎/Fax 01253 882537
BB From £18
Sleeps 4
🐎 ✂ 🍴 ♨ ♨
💐 *Commended*

A friendly welcome awaits you at our 260-acre arable farm situated 4 miles from the attractions of Blackpool in a peaceful corner of the Fylde and within easy reach of Lake District. Oak beams and open fires maintain the charm of the old farmhouse but modern comforts, like central heating have been added. One twin/family room with en suite bathroom, colour TV, and tea making facilities. Open Jan–Nov.

SELF-CATERING

---

① Sandy Brook Farm, Wyke Cop Road, Scarisbrick, Southport PR8 5LR

Mr W H Core
☎ 01704 880337
SC From £100–£260
Sleeps 2/6
🐎 ✂ ♨
🪑 🪑 🪑 *Commended*

Our newly converted 18th century barn, which stands in peaceful countryside, offers five superbly equipped and traditionally furnished holiday apartments. We are 3½ miles from the seaside town of Southport and close to many other places of interest. The apartments sleep 2/6 and 'The Dairy' is especially equipped for disabled guests. Open all year.

FARM HOLIDAY BUREAU

Please mention **Stay on a Farm** when booking

Lancashire Pennines

Group Contact: *Mrs Carole Mitson* ☎ *01282 865301*

The Forest of Bowland, the largest area of unspoilt countryside in Lancashire, 1,827ft high Pendle Hill and the Pennines afford the visitor a chance to appreciate Lancashire at its most beautiful. Complementing such countryside are towns and villages, all with their own individual character: Clitheroe with its castle and museum; Whalley with its Cistercian Abbey (founded in 1296) and Georgian and Tudor houses; the old market towns of Colne, Skipton and Ribchester, with its Roman Museum; Barley, at the foot of Pendle Hill, with its connections with the Witch Trials of 1612; and Slaidburn, the gateway to the Forest of Bowland, once a royal hunting ground.

There is something here to suit all tastes. For example, places of historic interest, such as Browsholme Hall, the home of the Parker family, which houses a display of 13th century domestic articles, can be contrasted with the new Preston Guild Hall with facilities for many social, cultural and educational activities. If you prefer a quiet, more sedate pace, you can enjoy one of the several country parks and picnic areas, such as Beacon Fell, Spring Wood, Barley or Wycoller. A holiday in the farms of the Lancashire Pennines will also leave you within easy reach of the Yorkshire Dales, the Lake District, Haworth and Brontë Country. The area is also famous for its large variety of mill shops, popular with tourists hunting real bargains.

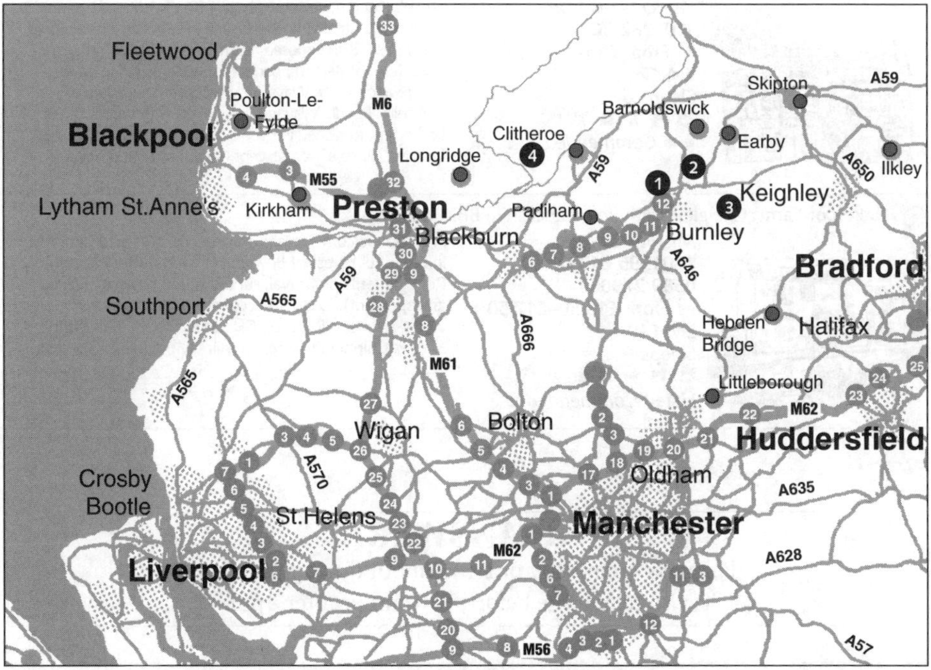

BED AND BREAKFAST

(and evening meal)

① Blakey Hall Farm, Red Lane, Colne, Lancashire BB8 9TD

Mrs R Boothman
☎ 01282 863121
🅱 From £18–£22
EM From £7.50
Sleeps 6
👜 ✂ 🐾 ⛺ ♨
Listed *Commended*

Delightful old Grade II listed working dairy farm. Oliver Cromwell is reputed to have stayed here. Ideally situated to provide the holidaymaker with a good base to visit the Yorkshire Dales/Brontë Country and Lake District. Full English breakfast. Comfortable accommodation, guests' own TV lounge. 3 bedrooms, 1 en suite, tea/coffee facilities. Open all year.

② Higher Wanless Farm, Red Lane, Colne, Lancashire BB8 7JP

Carole Mitson
☎ 01282 865301
🅱 From £18–£22
EM From £11
Sleeps 4
👜(3) 🧍 ♨ ☞ ⛺ ✾
🐛 🐛 *Highly Commended*

Ideally situated for visiting 'Pendle Witch' country, Haworth or Yorkshire Dales – the farm nestles peacefully alongside the Leeds/Liverpool Canal. Shire horses and sheep are reared on the farm, where the warmest of welcomes awaits you. Spacious and luxurious bedrooms (1 en suite) offer every comfort for our guests. Several country inns nearby offering wide range of meal facilities. AA selected establishment. Open mid Jan–Nov.

③ Parson Lee Farm, Wycoller, Colne, Lancashire BB8 8SU

Patricia Hodgson
☎ 01282 864747
🅱 From £15–£17
EM £7
Sleeps 6
👜 🐓 ⛺ ♨ ☞ ✾ ◉
🐛 🐛 *Commended*

There's a warm welcome at our 110-acre sheep farm on the edge of beautiful Wycoller Country Park. The 250-year old farmhouse, with exposed beams and mullion windows, is peacefully located and perfect for walking, being on the Brontë and Pendle Ways. Easy access to Lancashire or Yorkshire. Pendle Way walking breaks with transport. En suite bedrooms, furnished in country style, have tea/coffee-making facilities. Open all year except Christmas & New Year.

④ Rakefoot Farm, Chaigley, Clitheroe, Lancashire BB7 3LY

Mrs Pat Gifford
☎ 01995 61332
0589 279063
🅱 From £13.50–£17.50
EM £10
Sleeps 6
👜 🐓 🐕 ⛺ ♨ ✾ ◉
Listed *Commended*

A warm welcome awaits on peaceful 100-acre family farm in beautiful Forest of Bowland in 17th century farmhouse. Refreshments on arrival, superb home cooking (EM by arrangement). Excellent accommodation, panoramic views. Laundry, log fires, CH, games room, babysitting. 3 miles Chipping village, 12 miles M6 J31/32. Open all year.

NO ANSWER?

Farmers are mostly out and about during the day.
Try to telephone before 9.30am or after 4pm.

SELF-CATERING

Rakefoot Barn, Chaigley, Clitheroe, Lancashire BB7 3LY ④

Mrs Pat Gifford
☎ **01995 61332**
0589 279063
SC **From £85–£378**
Sleeps 2–8
🦢 🐕 🚶 ♨ 🎱 ⛷ ◎
🌳 🌳 🌳 🌳 🌳 *Highly Commended*

A warm welcome awaits on peaceful 100-acre family farm in Forest of Bowland. Traditional stone barn conversion, original features, superbly furnished. Fully fitted kitchens, CH, woodburners, en suite bedrooms (some ground floor). Meals service, laundry, games room, play areas, patios, gardens, panoramic views. Babysitting. 3 miles Chipping village, 12 miles M6 J31/32. 3 properties can be internally interlinked to sleep 16. Open all year.

CONFIRM BOOKINGS

Disappointments can arise from misunderstandings over the telephone. Please write to confirm your booking.

STAY ON A FARM GIFT TOKENS

If you have enjoyed your Stay on a Farm, why not treat your friends and relatives to *Stay on a Farm* gift tokens? Available from the Bureau office, telephone 01203 696909, they can be redeemed against accommodation booked on the majority of our farms

THE 1000+ BUREAU MEMBERS OFFER A UNIQUE LINK TO CUSTOMERS ACROSS THE UK

All Bureau members belong to a local Group. Each member can refer you to an equally high quality member within the Group... or across the UK: England, Northern Ireland, Scotland, Wales.

South Pennines

Group Contacts: *Mrs Charlotte Walsh* ☎ *0161 3684610*
Mrs Jean Mayall ☎ *01457 873040*

A warm and friendly welcome awaits visitors to this beautiful and dramatic countryside, still remarkably untouched by tourism. Holiday-makers will find unusual and interesting places to visit close by, with Blackpool, York and the Peak District less than an hour away. The Lake District and the North Yorkshire Moors are an easy two hours, whilst businessmen are well placed for work in Manchester, Liverpool, Leeds and Bradford and close to Manchester Airport and Intercity rail.

Walkers on the Pennine Way will experience stark moorland scenery blending with attractive valley towns like Delph, Uppermill, Marsden and Hebden Bridge and there are equally interesting routes over Blackstone Edge with the Roman Road, the Rossendale Way, the Calderdale Way and the Colne Valley Circular. There are canal trips at Uppermill, Sowerby Bridge and Littleborough, and water sports at Hollingworth Lake and Scammanden Dam, where flocks of wild fowl can be seen. The South Pennine textile heritage is magnificently illustrated in the Colne Valley Museum, Golcar, the Helmshore Museum at Haslingden, and the Saddleworth Museum at Uppermill. Craft centres and mill shops abound and traditional handweaving, clog and slipper making and dyeing and printing can be studied here.

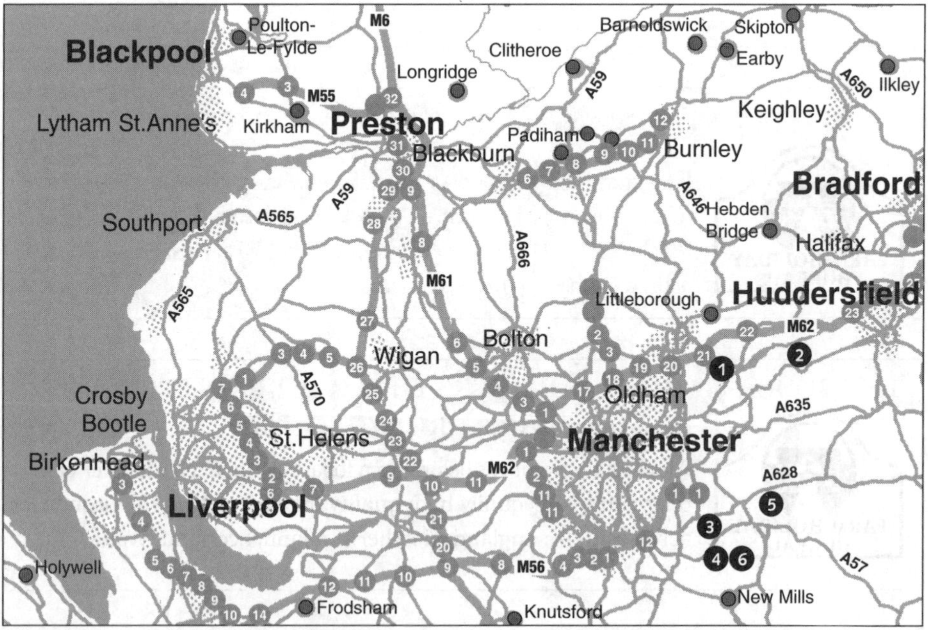

BED AND BREAKFAST

(and evening meal)

Boothstead Farm, Rochdale Road, Denshaw, Oldham, Greater Manchester OL3 5UE   **1**

Mrs Norma Hall
☎ **01457 878622**
BB **From £18–£20**
Sleeps 4
🐴 ⅄ 🛍 🐕 🌣
Listed *Commended*

An 18th century hill farm catering for people in the area on business or taking a relaxing break. Ideally situated within 3½ miles of M62 Junctions 21 and 22 (A640). Cosy lounge with open fire, TV, tea/coffee-making facilities, wash basins in rooms. Good base for touring neighbouring counties and beauty spots. Close to Saddleworth leisure amenities, ie. golf, swimming, walking, sailing. Open 2 Jan–22 Dec.

Globe Farm, Huddersfield Road, Standedge, Delph, Nr Oldham, Greater Manchester OL3 5LU   **2**

Jean Mayall
☎/Fax **01457 873040**
BB **From £20**
Sleeps 17
🐴 ⊞ 🛆 🐕 🛍
🌼 🌼 🌼 *Commended*

Overlooking the picturesque valleys of Saddleworth but within easy reach of M62 junction 22, Manchester Airport, Yorkshire Dales and Peak District. Only ¼ mile from Pennine Way. All rooms en suite. Evening meal can be provided if required. Colour TV, CH, drying room, tea/coffee-making facilities. Good home cooking and real northern hospitality. Open all year (closed Christmas & New Year).

Needhams Farm, Uplands Road, Werneth Low, Gee Cross, near Hyde, Cheshire SK14 3AQ   **3**

Mrs Charlotte Walsh
☎ **0161 368 4610**
Fax **0161 367 9106**
BB **From £18–£20**
EM **From £7**
Sleeps 15
🐴 🐴 ⊞ 🛆 🌣 🛍 ◎
🌼 🌼 🌼 *Commended*

Farmhouse accommodation dating back to the 16th century, offering 5 en suite rooms. Evening meals available each evening. Residential licence. Surrounded by lovely views. Ideal for Manchester Airport and city centre. Courtesy service from airport and Piccadilly station for a small charge. Six bedrooms in all. Open all year.

Shire Cottage Farmhouse, Benches Lane, Marple Bridge, Stockport, Cheshire SK6 5RY   **4**

Monica Sidebottom
☎ **01457 866536**
BB **From £19–£24**
Sleeps 6
🐴 🐴 🌣 🛍
🌼 🌼 *Commended*

Real home from home accommodation in peaceful location. Magnificent views overlooking Etheroe Country Park. Convenient for Manchester Airport, city centre, Peak District, stately homes and numerous places of interest. Ground floor bedrooms and bathroom. All rooms have vanity units/shaver points/tea-making facilities/TV. Family room has own shower and toilet. Bathroom has shower and bidet. Early breakfast for businessmen and travellers. Open all year.

White House Farm, Padfield, Nr Glossop, Derbyshire SK14 7ET   **5**

Mrs S Wynne
☎ **01457 854695**
BB **From £15–£18**
EM **From £8**
Sleeps 6
🐴 🐴 🛍 🌣 🛍
Listed *Commended*

Comfortable farmhouse on mixed farm overlooking the Woodhead Valley. Ideal for walking holidays and the Peak District yet only ½ hour from Manchester and airport. One double room with vanity unit, two twin rooms (one with vanity unit). All have tea-making facilities, TV. Two bathrooms with shower. Open all year.

SELF-CATERING

6 **Lake View,** Ernocroft Farm, Marple Bridge, Stockport, Cheshire SK6 5NT

Monica Sidebottom
☎ 01457 866536
SC From £275–£320
Sleeps 6 + cot
🛏 ⚜ 💼
🐾 🐾 🐾 *Commended*

A new, self-catering farm bungalow, 2 miles Marple Bridge, 4 miles Glossop. Overlooking Etherow Country Park. Ideal base for exploring Peak District, Marple locks and waterways, country parks and stately homes. Peaceful location. Accommodates 6 with all mod cons. TV. Cot available. Open all year.

FARM HOLIDAY BUREAU

Our Internet Address is
http://www.webscape.co.uk/farmaccom/

FINDING YOUR ACCOMMODATION

FARM HOLIDAY BUREAU

The Group contacts at the beginning of each section can always help you find a vacancy in your chosen area.

FOLLOW THE COUNTRY CODE

Leave nothing but footprints,
Take nothing but photographs,
Kill nothing but time!

Cheshire

Group Contact: *Mrs Hilary Bennion* ☎ *01270 811324*

Cheshire is one of England's undiscovered counties. Renowned for lovely black and white architecture and its superb cheese, it is a county of contrasts. From the majesty of the Peak District across the Cheshire Plain to the Dee estuary, from North Wales to Manchester, from the Shropshire Hills to Liverpool, Cheshire has something for everyone. The county has a rich history, well-documented for visitors, with Roman remains in Chester, Elizabethan towns like Nantwich, fine castles and country mansions and museums about the industrial revolution such as Salt Museum at Northwich or Paradise Silk Mill at Macclesfield.

Cheshire offers many peaceful country pursuits: there are canals, wonderful walking (from the Sandstone Trail to shorter farm walks), cycling and fishing. The county has many charming villages and towns, fine old churches, numerous antique shops. There are beautiful gardens in Cheshire – country house, botanical and municipal – plus two of Europe's largest garden centres, Bridgemere Garden World and Stapley Water Gardens.

Chester, the county town, is one of Britain's top tourist destinations. Situated on the River Dee with a splendid cathedral and unique Rows, it offers sophisticated shopping facilities as well as a fine heritage.

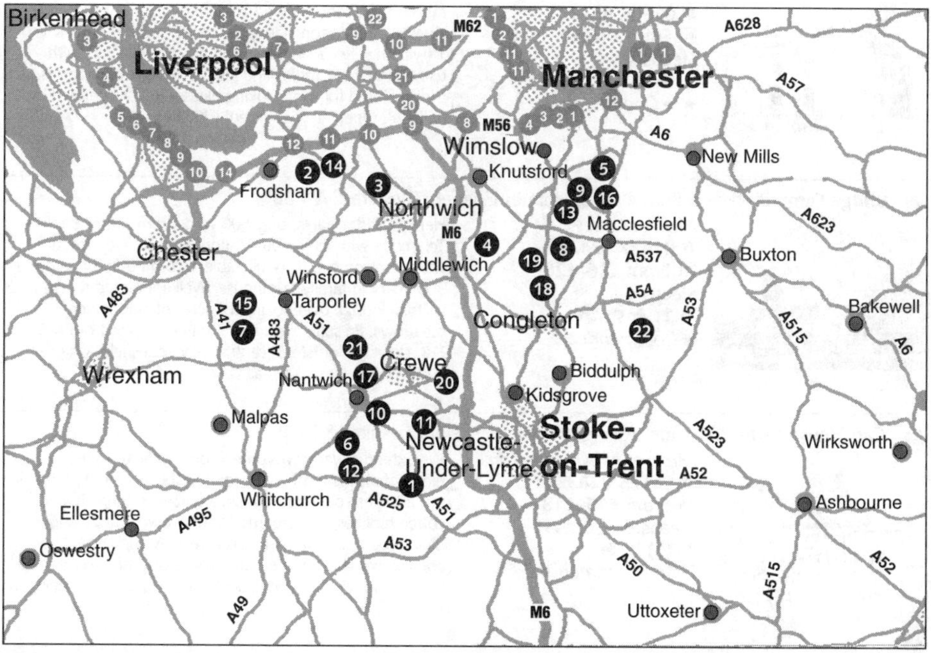

BED AND BREAKFAST

(and evening meal)

---

1 Adderley Green Farm, Heighley Castle Lane, Betley, Nr Crewe, Cheshire CW3 9BA

Mrs Sheila Berrisford
☎ **01270 820203**
Fax 01270 820542
BB **From £16–£20**
Sleeps 6
🐕 ♀ ⛺ 🛝 🅿 ◉
♥ *Highly Commended*

Relax in our lovely Georgian farmhouse on a 250-acre dairy farm set in large garden along a pretty country lane near an old ruined castle. Full CH. Colour TV, radio, washbasin and tea tray in all bedrooms. En suites available, draped and 4-poster beds. Beautifully decorated in the Laura Ashley style, separate tables in dining room. Ideally situated for Stapeley Water Gardens, Alton Towers and Chester. Near Keele University and Potteries, 10 mins M6 J16. Open all year except Christmas and New Year.

---

2 Ash House Farm, Chapel Lane, Acton Bridge, Northwich, Cheshire CW8 3QS

Mrs Sue Schofield
☎ **01606 852717**
BB **From £18–£20**
Sleeps 5
🐕 ♀ ⛺ 🅿 ◉
Listed *Commended*

A warm welcome awaits you at Ash House Farm, a mixed working farm in the heart of Cheshire in peaceful, scenic surroundings. Relax in our lovely Georgian farmhouse which is full of traditional architectural features. Guests' TV lounge and dining room with log fire. Tea/coffee facilities in bedrooms. Very rural, excellent for country walks yet only short distance from M56 J10. Secure parking. Open all year.

---

3 Beechwood House, 206 Wallerscote Road, Weaverham, Northwich, Cheshire CW8 3LZ

Janet Kuypers
☎ **01606 852123**
BB **From £16.50**
Sleeps 4
✂ 🅿
♥ ♥ *Commended*

Peaceful, comfortable 1830s farmhouse and small stock farm 1 mile from Weaverham in easy reach of M56, M6. Guests' dining room/lounge with TV and hot drinks. 1 twin en suite, 2 single bedrooms with H&C; all with tea/coffee trays, radios and individual control radiators. Diets catered for. No smoking please. Recommended by 'Which'. Open all year except Christmas.

---

4 Bridge Farm, Blackden, Bridge Lane, Holmes Chapel, Cheshire CW4 8BX

Mrs A Massey
☎ **01477 571202**
BB **From £16–£20**
Sleeps 6
🐕 ♀ 🛝 ♥ ◉
♥ *Commended*

Here at Bridge Farm, only 500 yards from Jodrell Bank Telescope with its famous Visitors' Centre, we offer a warm welcome and comfortable accommodation in our 300 year old family farmhouse. Well appointed rooms and visitors' lounge overlooking 12 acres of wildflower meadows. En suite available. Situated 3 miles from M6 J18, close to Knutsford, central to Macclesfield, Chester and the Potteries. Open all year.

---

5 Carr House Farm, Mill Lane, Adlington, Macclesfield, Cheshire SK10 4LG

Mrs Isobel Worthington
☎ **01625 828337**
BB **From £15–£18**
Sleeps 5
🐕 (5) ✂ 🅿
Listed *Commended*

We extend a warm welcome to our cattle and sheep rearing farm, and offer you comfortable accommodation in our 200 year-old farmhouse in a garden setting. Tea and coffee facilities in bedrooms. Visitors' own lounge and dining room. Adlington Hall one mile, Manchester Airport approx six miles. Situated four miles north of Macclesfield just off the A523. Open Feb–Oct, but closed for lambing in April.

Coole Hall Farm, Hankelow, Nantwich, Cheshire CW3 0JD ⑥

Carolyn Goodwin
☎ **01270 811232**
🅱 **From £15–£20**
Sleeps 3
🐎 ⅄ 🛏 🚲 🛢 ☕ ☂
🌺 🌺 *Commended*

Get away from the rat race and enjoy staying with a young Christian family. We are off the beaten track which offers scenic views across our 'green and pleasant land'. We promise you a relaxing stay which you will want to experience again. Open all year.

Ford Farm, Newton Lane, Tattenhall, Chester, Cheshire CH3 9NE ⑦

Audrey Charmley
☎ **01829 770307**
🅱 **£15**
Sleeps 6
🐎 🐴 ☂ 🛢
Listed *Commended*

A friendly welcome to our dairy farm set in beautiful countryside with views of Beeston and Peckforton Castles. Close to ice cream farm and Cheshire workshops and many tourist attractions. Chester 7 miles, Oulton Park 8 miles. Guests' own lounge and dining room with TV. Two double rooms and one twin, tea/coffee-making facilities, bathroom with shower. Open all year.

Golden Cross Farm, Siddington, Nr Macclesfield, Cheshire SK11 9JP ⑧

Hazel Rush
☎ **01260 224358**
🅱 **From £16–£20**
Sleeps 6
⅄ 🐎 🛢 ☂ ◎
🌺 🌺 *Commended*

Small organic farm, 100 yards from the A34 on the B5392 in picturesque surroundings. Central for Macclesfield, Congleton, Holmes Chapel and Alderley Edge. Places of local interest include Capesthorne Hall, Gawsworth Hall, Tatton Hall, Styal Mill and Nether Alderley Mill. 2 double rooms, 2 single rooms, all with washbasins and tea/coffee-making facilities. Central heating, guests' lounge, colour TV. Open all year (closed Christmas & New Year).

Goose Green Farm, Oak Road, Mottram St Andrew, Nr Macclesfield, Cheshire SK10 4RA ⑨

Dyllis Hatch
☎ **01625 828814**
🅱 **From £18–£20**
Sleeps 6
🐎(6) ⅄ ☕ ☂ 🛢 ◎
🌺 🌺 *Commended*

Welcome to our beef farm set in beautiful countryside with panoramic views. Just off A538 between Wilmslow and Prestbury, in easy reach of M6, M56 and Manchester Airport. Own fishing, horse riding nearby. Comfortable, homely with log fire in guests' lounge. Separate dining room. Pay phone. Double en suite, twin and single rooms, all with washbasin, TV, CH and tea/coffee-making facilities. Open all year (closed Christmas).

Henhull Hall, Welshmans Lane, Nantwich, Cheshire CW5 6AD ⑩

Joyce Percival
☎ **01270 624158**
🅱 **From £20–£25**
Sleeps 5
🐎 🛢 ◎
🌺 🌺 *Highly Commended*

Welcome to our spacious farmhouse,
View the garden, duckpond, cows,
Walk to Nantwich, drive to Chester,
Along the canalside you may wander.
Beds and bathrooms are luxurious
Wait no longer, come and join us.

Lea Farm, Wrinehill Road, Wybunbury, Nantwich, Cheshire CW5 7NS ⑪

Allen & Jean Callwood
☎/Fax **01270 841429**
🅱 **From £15**
EM From £10
Sleeps 6
🐴 🐎 ☕ ☂ 🛢 ◎
🌺 🌺 *Commended*

A charming farmhouse set in landscaped gardens where peacocks roam a pedigree dairy farm. Spacious, attractive bedrooms with washbasins, TV and tea/coffee-making facilities, two en suite. Luxurious lounge with open log fire, with dining room overlooking garden. Snooker, pool table, fishing available. Near to Stapeley Water Gardens and Bridgemere Garden World. M6 J16, Chester and Alton Towers. Open all year (closed Christmas & New Year).

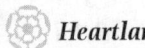
12 Little Heath Farm, Audlem, Nantwich, Crewe, Cheshire CW3 0HE

Hilary Bennion
☎/Fax 01270 811324
BB From £15–£20
EM From £8.50
Sleeps 6
♿ ⛌ ⅄ ⚘ ▪ ◉
Commended

17th century farmhouse on a working dairy farm on the A529, 6 miles from Nantwich in lovely canalside village with shops, pubs, church and village trails. Large, warm bedrooms with all facilities. Beamed lounge and dining room traditionally furnished. Ideal for Chester, Shrewsbury (Ironbridge) and Potteries. We are close to Bridgemere Garden World and Stapeley Water Gardens. We look forward to meeting you! Closed Christmas.

13 Lower Harebarrow Farm, Over Alderley, Macclesfield, Cheshire SK10 4SW

Mrs Beryl Leggott
☎ 01625 829882
BB From £15–£16
Sleeps 5
♿ ⛌ ▪
Commended

Comfortable farmhouse within easy reach of many Cheshire beauty spots, stately homes and the Derbyshire hills. Situated on the B5087 midway between Alderley Edge and Macclesfield. Near M6, M56 and Manchester Airport. One double, one twin and one single bedroom all with HC. Open all year.

14 Manor Farm, Cliff Road, Acton Bridge, Northwich, Cheshire CW8 3QP

Mrs T H Campbell
☎/Fax 01606 853181
BB From £20–£27
Sleeps 5
♿ ⛌ ⅄ ⅄ ⚘ ▪ ♨ ⚲
◉
Highly Commended

Set in secluded location down private drive with fields and walks beside the River Weaver. Convenient for M6, M56 (J10), Chester, Northwich and Merseyside. We give a warm welcome to our quiet country house. Comfortable bedrooms, each with private/en suite facilities. Tea/coffee, hairdrier, trouser press, drying, own TV lounge and peaceful garden. English breakfast served in elegant oak-furnished dining room. Safe car park. Open all year.

15 Newton Hall, Tattenhall, Chester, Cheshire CH3 9AY

Mrs Anne Arden
☎ 01829 770153
Fax 01829 770655
BB From £20–£25
Sleeps 5
♿ ⛌ ⅄ ♨
Highly Commended

Part 16th century oak-beamed farmhouse set in large well kept grounds, with fine views of historic Beeston and Peckforton Castles and close to the Sandstone Trail. Six miles south of Chester off A41 and ideal for Welsh Hills. Rooms are en suite or have adjacent bathroom. TV in bedrooms. Guests' own sitting room. Full central heating.

16 Oldhams Hollow Farm, Manchester Road, Tytherington, Macclesfield, Cheshire SK10 2JW

Brenda Buxton
☎/Fax 01625 424128
BB From £18.50
EM From £9.50
Sleeps 6
♿ ⛌ ⅄ ▪ ◉
Listed Commended

Welcome to Oldhams Hollow – a 16th century listed farmhouse one mile north of Macclesfield, close to the peaks and plains of Cheshire. Snug, warm and restful with oak beams, large lounge, open fire, spacious dining room, central heating. Comfortable bedrooms with colour TV, washbasins, tea/coffee-making facilities, electric blankets.

17 Poole Bank Farm, Wettenhall Road, Poole, Nantwich, Cheshire CW5 6AL

Caroline Hocknell
☎ 01270 625169
BB From £15–£19
Sleeps 6
♿ ⅄ ⚘ ▪ ♨
Commended

A charming 17th century timbered farmhouse on 260-acre dairy farm set in quiet countryside 2 miles from the historic town of Nantwich. Ideal base for discovering the beautiful Cheshire countryside. Central for Chester and the Potteries. Comfortable and attractive rooms, all with period furnishings. TV and tea/coffee making facilities. A warm welcome and an excellent breakfast are assured. Open all year.

Sandhole Farm, Hulme Walfield, Congleton, Cheshire CW12 2JH [18]

Veronica Worth
☎ **01260 224419**
Fax 01260 224766
BB **From £23.50–£37**
Sleeps 36
🚶 🐎 🐕 ⊞ 🛍 ⊚
❦ ❦ *Highly Commended*

The comfortable traditional farmhouse and delightful converted stable block are situated 2 miles north of Congleton on A34, 15 mins from M6 and 30 mins from Manchester airport. Most of our rooms have modern en suite facilities and all have the usual extras, including hairdryer, remote control teletext TV plus trouser press and direct dial telephone. Large comfortable lounge, separate newly built conservatory/dining room. Cheshire Tourism Award Winner. Now approved for Civil Marriages. Open all year.

Sandpit Farm, Messuage Lane, Marton, Macclesfield, Cheshire SK11 9HS [19]

Mrs I H Kennerley
☎ **01260 224254**
BB **From £16–£20**
Sleeps 6
🐎(3) 🐓 ⅓ 🛍 ☕ 🎋
❦ ❦ *Commended*

A friendly welcome to our 300 year old farmhouse surrounded by 100 acres of grassland. Traditional farmhouse with oak timber features and heated throughout. Separate dining room and TV lounge. H&C in T/S, en suite facilities in double and twin, all with tea/coffee and TV. Excellent touring centre for Peak District, Potteries, Chester. Manchester Airport 14 miles, NT properties, stately homes and Jodrell Bank Science Centre nearby. Closed Christmas.

Snape Farm, Snape Lane, Weston, Nr Crewe, Cheshire CW2 5NB [20]

Mrs Jean Williamson
☎/Fax 01270 820208
BB **From £15–£20**
EM From £8
Sleeps 6
🐎 🐓 ☕ 🛍 ⊚
❦ ❦ *Commended*

Enjoy a warm welcome to our centrally heated farmhouse on a 150-acre beef/arable farm set in rolling countryside. 3 miles from Crewe. A good centre for visiting Nantwich, Chester or the Potteries. Guests' lounge and snooker room. 1 twin (en suite), 1 twin, 1 double room, each with colour TV and tea/coffee-making facilities. 4 miles from M6 (J 16). Open all year except Christmas.

Stoke Grange Farm, Chester Road, Nantwich, Cheshire CW5 6BT [21]

Georgina West
☎/Fax 01270 625525
BB **From £17.50–£25**
Sleeps 6
🐎 🛍 ☕ 🎋 ⊚
❦ ❦ *Commended*

In a picturesque setting, an attractive canalside farmhouse, with large car park and beautiful garden. Spacious en suite bedrooms with colour TV and hot drink facilities. Comfortable guest lounge with TV, dining room with log fire. Honeymoon suite with four-poster bed. Warm welcome and excellent breakfast. Vegetarians catered for. Past Cheshire Tourism Development Award winner. Short walk to pub and village. Open all year.

SELF-CATERING

Stoke Grange Mews, Stoke Grange Farm, Chester Road, Nantwich, Cheshire CW5 6BT [21]

Georgina West
☎/Fax 01270 625525
SC **From £150–£350**
Sleeps 2–6 + cot
🐎 ☕ 🎋 🛍 ⊚
🐾 🐾 🐾 *Highly Commended*

Holiday home created from a fine old barn near the owner's canalside farmhouse and dairy farm in lush heritage rich countryside 15 miles south Chester. Each has exposed beams, quality furniture, and offers fully equipped accommodation. Linen and towels provided. Small rear patio, large shared garden with canal access. Children's play area and farm pets corner. Barbeque area. Past Cheshire Tourism Development Award winner. Open all year.

22 **Wood Cottage,** Wood Cottage Farm, Wincle, Macclesfield, Cheshire SK11 OQG

Susan Hughes
☎ **01260 227641**
🆂🅲 **From £150–£300**
Sleeps 4 + cot
🐴 ⛺ 🚽
🍃 🍃 🍃 🍃 *Highly Commended*

A fine old stone barn tastefully restored and retaining many original features. Two pretty bedrooms, 1 twin, 1 double with vanity units. Lounge/dining room, well equipped kitchen, gas central heating, private patio, ample parking. In Peak District National Park with panoramic views. The Gritstone Path, fishing, clay pigeon shooting, riding and trout farm nearby. Open all year.

STAY ON A FARM GIFT TOKENS

If you have enjoyed your Stay on a Farm, why not treat your friends and relatives to *Stay on a Farm* gift tokens? Available from the Bureau office, telephone 01203 696909, they can be redeemed against accommodation booked on the majority of our farms

---

THE 1000+ BUREAU MEMBERS OFFER A UNIQUE LINK TO CUSTOMERS ACROSS THE UK

All Bureau members belong to a local Group. Each member can refer you to an equally high quality member within the Group... or across the UK: England, Northern Ireland, Scotland, Wales.

CONFIRM BOOKINGS

Disappointments can arise from misunderstandings over the telephone. Please write to confirm your booking.

Staffordshire

Group Contacts: 🅱🅱 *Mrs Christine Shaw* ☎ *01538 702830*
🆂🅲 *Mr John Myatt* ☎ *01889 504269*

The varied landscape of Staffordshire ranges from that of the Peak District National Park through the moorlands in the north to the fertile valleys of the Trent and its tributaries in the south. In the heart of the county is the extensive Cannock Chase, an area of outstanding natural beauty which offers scope for varied leisure pursuits.

A popular target for visitors to the county are its two leisure parks: Alton Towers, with its exciting rides, is the premier leisure park in the country, while Drayton Manor Park offers an open-plan zoological garden, lakes and an amusement park.

In the county town of Stafford the impressive timber-framed Ancient High House has to be seen. Tamworth, with its Norman Castle, was once the capital of the ancient kingdom of Mercia, while Burton on Trent is famous as the home of the brewing industry. Of particular attraction is the cathedral city of Lichfield, birthplace of Dr Samuel Johnson and host to international music and folk festivals. But of equal antiquity is the town of Tutbury with its fine castle and its glass making tradition.

Many visitors seek out the potteries and visitor centres which offer the chance to see craftsmen at work and perhaps to make purchases at the factory shops.

Whatever your particular interest you can be sure of a warm welcome in Staffordshire!

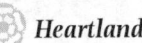

BED AND BREAKFAST

(and evening meal)

(1) Ribden Farm, Nr Oakamoor, Stoke-on-Trent, Staffordshire ST10 3BW

Christine Shaw
☎/Fax **01538 702830**
🅱 **From £20–£24**
Sleeps 11
🐕 🍴 ⬛ 💼 🎪
🌷🌷 *Highly Commended*

Ribden Farm is an 18th Century farmhouse c1748 which is situated 1,000 ft high in the Weaver Hills yet is only 5 minutes from Alton Towers. Plenty of underused footpaths. Local inns. All rooms en suite with colour TV, coffee/tea-making facilities. Separate TV lounge and dining room. Secure off road parking. RAC Highly Acclaimed. AA QQQQ selected. Open all year.

SELF-CATERING

(2) Priory Farm Fishing House, c/o Priory Farm, Blithbury, Rugeley, Staffordshire WS15 3JA

Mr John Myatt
☎ **01889 504269**
🆂🅲 **From £75–£120**
Sleeps 4
🐕 🏠 💼 💺 🎪
🔑 🔑 *Approved*

Converted 18th century fishing house overlooking River Blithe, offering unique accommodation for up to 4 persons on secluded dairy farm. Ideal for lovers of the countryside and wildlife. Convenient for Abbots Bromley, Lichfield, Cannock Chase, Alton Towers and the Peak District. Comfortable, tastefully furnished accommodation includes large bed-sitting room with colour TV, modern kitchen and shower room. Brochure on request. Open all year.

Although the majority of farms will accept '*Stay on a Farm*' Gift Tokens, please check when booking to avoid disappointment.

Please mention **Stay on a Farm** when booking

Peak District

Group Contact: *Joy Lomas* ☎ *01629 540250*

Britain's first National Park offers variety and spectacular scenery, from the exhilaration of the wide, windswept moorlands in the north to the softer south where the Manifold and Dove rivers run parallel through water meadows, woodlands and rocky gorges.

As well as some of the best walking in the country, the Peak District offers numerous stately homes such as Chatsworth, Haddon and Hardwick, as well as the thrills of Alton Towers and Water World, and Water Sports at Carsington Water.

Find a bargain in the Potteries seconds shops and at Gladstone Pottery Museum go back in time amongst the bottle kilns. Wedgwood shows a complete contrast by demonstrating modern production of fine china.

Leek and Bakewell markets transform sleepy country towns when farmers from miles around descend on them. At Matlock cable cars glide majestically across an awe-inspiring gorge to the Heights of Abraham. Castleton is famous for its show caves and Blue John stone. So, whether having afternoon tea at a stately home, admiring the Well Dressings or picnicking amongst the heather, you can be sure that the Peak District has something for you.

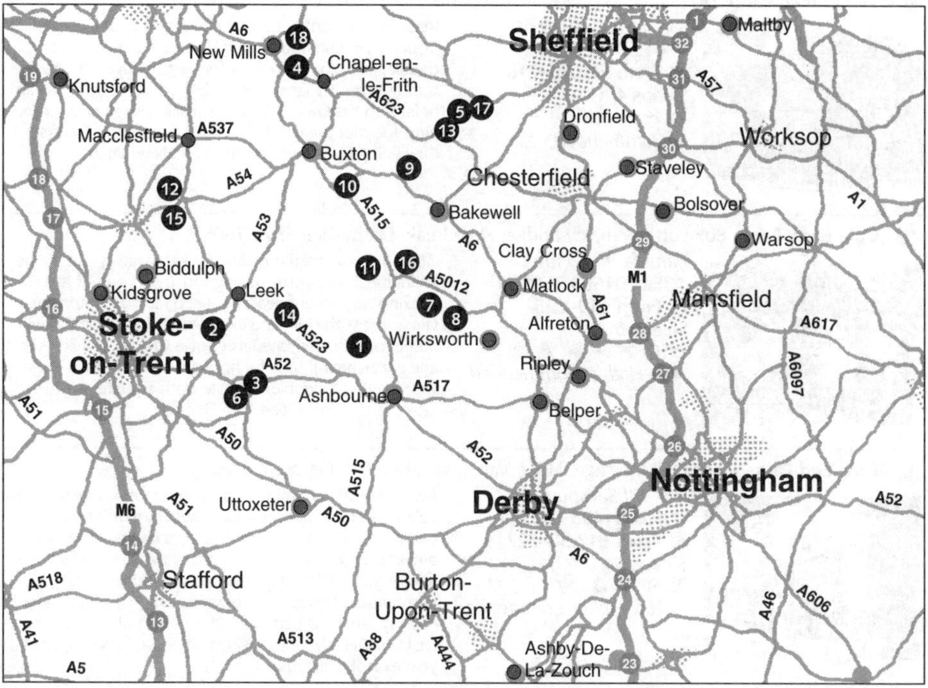

BED AND BREAKFAST

(and evening meal)

---

1 **Beechenhill Farm,** Ilam, Ashbourne, Derbyshire DE6 2BD

Sue Prince
☎/Fax 01335 310274
BB From £19–£25
Sleeps 5
🐕 ⅍ 💼 ⬤
♚♚ *Highly Commended*

Wake up to wonderful views over a country garden, grazing cows and sheep, Florence the goat, walkable hills and explorable valleys, at our warm old farmhouse near Dovedale. We've two delightful rooms; 1 family and 1 double, both en suite, own lounge, all beautifully decorated by artist Sue! Fruit, yoghurts and famous Beechenhill porridge feature as well as carefully cooked farmhouse breakfasts. Open Feb–Nov.

---

2 **Brook House Farm,** Cheddleton, Leek, Staffordshire ST13 7DF

Elizabeth Winterton
☎ 01538 360296
BB From £16–£19
EM From £10
Sleeps 10
🐕 ⅍ ⟵ ♦ 💼 ⬤
♚♚ *Commended*

A dairy farm in a picturesque and peaceful valley. Central for Peak District, Potteries, Churnet Valley steam railway, Cauldron Canal, Coombes Valley RSPB Reserve and Alton Towers. 3 spacious rooms in a tastefully converted cowshed and 2 in the farmhouse, all en suite with tea/coffee -makers and colour TV. Dine in our attractive conservatory with magnificent country views. Open all year.

---

3 **The Church Farm,** Holt Lane, Kingsley, Stoke on Trent, Staffordshire ST10 2BA

Mrs Jane Clowes
☎ 01538 754759
BB From £15.50–£18
Sleeps 4
🐕 ⅍ 💼 ⬤
♚ *Commended*

Relax in traditionally furnished rooms with oak beams. Country pine bedrooms with Victorian brass and iron double, and pine bunk beds forming family suite. Wander through country lanes, footpaths, lush meadows, orchard, or laze on the lawn. Watch the milking, feed hens, collect eggs for your breakfast. Five miles from Alton Towers. Open all year except Christmas and New Year.

---

4 **Cote Bank Farm,** Buxworth, Whaley Bridge, High Peak, Derbyshire SK23 7NP

Pamela Broadhurst
☎/Fax 01663 750566
BB From £19–£25
Sleeps 5
🐕(6) 🕎 ⅍ 💼 ⚘ ⬤
♚♚ *Highly Commended*

Good old fashioned hospitality, a kettle always on the boil and a breakfast worth waking for! Treat yourself to a relaxing stay on our peaceful sheep farm with stunning views across the hills and excellent walks. A home from home for business travellers (1 mile Chinley, 3 miles A6) and a welcoming base for holidaymakers. Guest lounge with log fire; 1 double, 1 family, both en suite, with TV, radio, tea/coffee. Open Mar–Dec.

---

5 **Lane End Farm,** Abney, Hathersage, Hope Valley, via Sheffield, Derbyshire S32 1AH

Mrs Jill Salisbury
☎/Fax 01433 650371
BB From £17.50–£27
Sleeps 6
🐕 🛏 🎋 💼 ⬤
Listed Highly Commended

Award-winning farmhouse on sheep farm above the Hope Valley. Wake up to unrivalled views from delightful bedrooms. Start the day with a large traditional English breakfast, then take to footpaths or explore the farm nature trail. Whether for pleasure or business, the farmhouse offers superb accommodation. Antiques and country fabrics. 3 bedrooms (1 en suite) all with tea/coffee facilities. CH. TV lounge. Own horse welcome. Open all year except Christmas.

Ley Fields Farm, Leek Road, Cheadle, Stoke-on-Trent, Staffordshire ST10 2EF 6

Mrs Kathryn Clowes
☎ **01538 752875**
🅱 **From £17–£19**
EM From £9.50
Sleeps 6
♿ ⅓ ♨ 🚗 ☂ ⊚
🌑🌑 *Commended*

Listed Georgian farmhouse amidst beautiful countryside with local walks offering abundant wildlife. Convenient for Alton Towers, Pottery museums and Peak District. Spacious, traditionally furnished accommodation includes guests' lounge and dining room. Luxury bedrooms with hot drink facilities, family suite, family en suite, double en suite. CH. Excellent home cooking and a warm welcome to our family home. Open Jan–Nov.

Lydgate Farm, Aldwark, Grange Mill, Matlock, Derbyshire DE4 4HW 7

Joy Lomas
☎ **01629 540250**
🅱 **From £18–£22**
Sleeps 6
♿ ♨ 🚗 ☂ ⊚
🌑 *Commended*

A warm welcome and good food await you in our 17th century house on a 300-acre dairy and sheep farm. Lydgate is ideally situated for visiting Chatsworth, Haddon Hall and all Derbyshire has to offer. Central heating and hot drink facilities in all rooms, private bathroom available. Guests' own dining room and sitting room. Open Jan–Nov.

Middlehills Farm, Grange Mill, Matlock, Derbyshire DE4 4HY 8

Mrs Linda Lomas
☎/Fax **01629 650368**
🅱 **From £18**
Sleeps 6
♿ 🐎 ☂ 🚗 ♨ ⊚
🌑🌑 *Commended*

Escape the rat race – taste the fresh air, absorb the peace, feast your eyes on the beautiful scenery and magnificent views that surround our small working farm 5 miles west of Matlock on the A5012. Large walled garden, two en suite family rooms, one en suite twin, all with tea/coffee facilities. Comfortable lounge with TV and pool table.

The Old Bake & Brewhouse, Blackwell Hall, Blackwell in the Peak, Taddington, nr Buxton, Derbys SK17 9TQ 9

Mrs Christine Gregory
☎ **01298 85271**
🅱 **From £17–£20**
Sleeps 4
♿ ⅓ ☂ 🚗 ♨ ☂ ⊚
🌑 *Commended*

Early 18th century friendly, much loved farmhouse set in peaceful mature garden. Footpath to Cheedale and Monsal Dale from our door. A warm welcome awaits you to our dairy, sheep and cereal farm. Private lounge, dining room, conservatory furnished with antiques. Delicious breakfasts to your requirements. Double with private bath/shower room, separate WC, twin en suite, both with colour TV, hospitality trays, CH. Open all year.

Shallow Grange, Chelmorton, nr Buxton, Derbyshire SK17 9SG 10

Christine Holland
☎ **01298 23578**
Fax **01298 78242**
🅱 **From £22–£30**
Sleeps 6
♿ ☂ 🚗 ♨ ☂ ⊚
🌑🌑 *Highly Commended*

Spectacular views, wide open spaces and a piece of rural England all await you at Shallow Grange. Luxury accommodation includes all rooms en suite, colour TVs, etc. This working dairy farm has numerous unspoilt walks whilst Chatsworth, Buxton and Bakewell are all within a short drive. We also have 20-pitch caravan site. Open all year.

Wolfscote Grange Farm, Hartington, Nr Buxton, Derbyshire SK17 0AX 11

Jane Gibbs
☎ **01298 84342**
🅱 **From £18–£20**
Sleeps 5
♿ ♨ ☂ ⊚
Applied

Find an ideal 'country hideaway' on our secluded hill farm with beautiful views over the Dove Valley. Along a stone-walled road from picturesque Hartington village. Feel at home in our ancient 15th century farmhouse with all its character, original oak beams, mullion windows, spiral staircase. Spacious guests' lounge, 2 pretty bedrooms, 1 family, 1 double en suite, tea/coffee facilities. Breakfast, then explore the many footpaths leading to hidden Dales below. Open Mar–Nov.

12 **Yew Tree Farm,** North Rode, Congleton, Cheshire CW12 2PF

Mrs Sheila Kidd
☎ **01260 223569**
BB **From £18**
EM **From £10**
Sleeps 6
Listed *Commended*

Discover an oasis of freedom, relaxation, wooded walks and beautiful views. Meet a whole variety of pets and farm animals on this friendly working farm. Your comfort is our priority. Good food is a speciality. Generous, scrummy breakfasts and traditional evening meals. A true taste of the countryside – just for you!

SELF-CATERING

5 **Archway Cottage,** Lane End Farm, Abney, Hathersage, Hope Valley, via Sheffield, Derbys S32 1AH

Jill Salisbury
☎/Fax 01433 650371
SC **From £150–£260**
Sleeps 2/4
🐶🐱 🐦 📺 ⛺ ⊙
🐾 🐾 🐾 *Commended*

Beams, pine furniture, lovely decor make our well-equipped cottage a must for the discerning visitor to the Peak District. Tucked away on our working hill farm in a small hamlet. Superb views, many fabulous walks. Ideally situated for all Derbyshire attractions. 1 double bedroom, sofa bed in lounge. Linen, electricity included. No pets. Own horse welcome. Open all year.

1 **Beechenhill Cottage & The Cottage by the Pond,** Beechenhill Farm, Ilam, Ashbourne, Derbys, DE6 2BD

Mrs Sue Prince
☎/Fax 01335 310274
SC **From £90–£430**
Sleeps 2–6
♿🐶 📺 ⊙
🐾 🐾 🐾 – 🐾 🐾 🐾
Highly Commended

Beechenhill Cottage, tiny and warm in pretty walled garden, a secluded holiday just for two.
The Cottage by the Pond, award-winning cottage, for all including wheelchair users. Sleeps six in three bedrooms, two bathrooms. Both cottages have real fires and beautiful decoration by artist Sue! Meet Florence the goat, Scrabble, Boggle and Meg! Open all year.

7 **Chapelgate Cottage,** c/o Lydgate Farm, Aldwark, Grange Mill, Matlock, Derbyshire DE4 4HW

Joy Lomas
☎ 01629 540250
SC **From £200–£270**
Sleeps 5 + cot
🐶🐱 📺 ⛺ ⊙
🐾 🐾 🐾 🐾 *Highly*
Commended

Beautiful oak beamed, stone mullioned cottage with lovely views and garden, set in the peaceful hamlet of Aldwark. Well appointed open plan kitchen/living area with log fire and colour TV. Two bedrooms and bathroom/shower room. The cottage is centrally heated, double glazed and fully carpeted throughout. Towels, fresh linen and electricity are included. Chapelgate Cottage will give you a wonderful holiday in the heart of the Peak District. Open all year.

4 **Cote Bank Farm Cottages,** Buxworth, Whaley Bridge, High Peak, Derbyshire SK23 7NP

Pamela Broadhurst
☎/Fax 01663 750566
SC **From £180–£450**
Sleeps 2/6 +cot
🐶🐦 📺 🐎 ⊙
🐾 🐾 🐾 🐾 *Highly*
Commended

Two warm, welcoming cottages on peaceful sheep farm with magnificent views and excellent walks. Chinley 1 mile, Buxton 7 miles. Children can feed the hens with farmer Nic and see happy animals reared naturally. Each cottage has 3 bedrooms (double, twin, bunks), lounge with logfire, TV and video, dining room, modern kitchen, full CH. 'Amongst the best farm cottages we know' – *Good Holiday Cottage Guide 1996*. Short breaks Nov–March. Open all year.

Cruck Cottage, Wolfscote Grange Farm, Hartington, Nr Buxton, Derbyshire SK17 0AX

Jane Gibbs
☎ 01298 84342
From £140–£290
Sleeps 4 + cot

Up to Highly Commended

This fine old 15th century cottage is an ideal country hideaway, completely on its own overlooking Wolfscote and Berrisford Dales. No neighbours, only cows and sheep! Cosy and warm with massive beamed interior, galley, double plus one twin bedroom. Walled garden, many footpaths to explore that lead from the cottage to the limestone Dales below. Fully equipped, linen inclusive. Ring for details. Open all year.

The Hayloft, Stanley House Farm, Great Hucklow, Derbyshire SK17 8RL

Margot Darley
☎ 01298 871044
From £100–£270
Sleeps 4

Highly Commended

Enjoy a relaxing holiday in peaceful surroundings in our stone barn conversion which offers excellent accommodation for four people. Spacious beamed sitting room with log fire and colour TV. Quality fitted kitchen/dining room, modern bathroom/WC. The Hayloft offers an ideal centre for exploring the Peak District. All linen, towels and fuel included in price. Open all year.

Honeysuckle, Jasmine & Clematis Cottages, Middlehills Farm, Grange Mill, Matlock, Derbys DE4 4HY

Linda Lomas
☎/Fax 01629 650368
From £140–£400
Sleeps 5/8

Commended

Take a break from the treadmill of life. Relax on the patio beneath the sweetly scented honeysuckle and jasmine. Enjoy the peace and tranquillity at our recently converted cottages. Full of character – beams, parquet floors, rustic rose arches, yet equipped with all modern conveniences – double glazing, CH, living flame fire. Clematis Cottage, available for 1998, one level especially designed for the less able. Open all year.

Lower Berkhamsytch Farm, Bottom House, Nr Leek, Staffordshire ST13 7QP

Edith & Alwyn Mycock
☎ 01538 308213
From £110–£210
Sleeps 2/6 + cot

Approved

Two delightful self-contained flats on stock rearing farm each with own private entrance and within walking distance of 2 pubs serving meals. Lounge/diner with colour TV and double bed-settee. Well equipped kitchen area, 1 double bedroom, 1 twin, shower room with toilet and washbasin. Ideal for Alton Towers, Potteries, Peak District and moorland beauty spots. Electricity, heating, linen included. Laundry room. Short breaks early and late season. Open all year.

The Old Byre, Pye Ash Farm, Leek Road, Bosley, Macclesfield, Cheshire CW12 3QD

Dorothy Gilman
☎ 01260 273650
Fax 01260 297115
From £200–£400
Sleeps 8 + cot

Commended

The Old Byre is especially designed so two families may holiday together. Cows, sheep, hens, ducks, etc make this a country paradise. Roomy enough to dine together, or good pub food is ½ mile walk away. The Peak District, Staffordshire Moorlands, Alton Towers, National Trust properties all easily reached.

Old House Farm Cottage, Old House Farm, Newhaven, Hartington, Buxton, Derbyshire SK17 0DY

Sue Flower
☎ 01629 636268
From £170–£320
Sleeps 6 + cot

Commended

Explore 'Peak Practice' Country from our warm well appointed cottage. Stay on a real working dairy/sheep farm where a high standard is maintained. Lambing time a must in April. We run a busy family farm, still having time to answer your questions and delighted to let you watch our farm activities. Off road cycling trails lead from our farm. Short breaks Nov–Mar. Brochure. Open all year.

17   **Shatton Hall Farm Cottages,** Bamford, Hope Valley, nr Sheffield, Derbyshire S33 0BG

Angela Kellie
☎ 01433 620635
Fax 01433 620689
⑤ℂ From £175–£325
Sleeps 4/6 + cot
🛏 🐓 ⛱ 💼 ◎
🐾 🐾 🐾 🐾 Up to Highly Commended

Our comfortable, well equipped cottages are stone barn conversions around the Elizabethan farmstead in a peaceful setting. Streamside and woodland walks. Fishing, riding, cycle hire nearby. Each cottage has terrace/garden. Ample car parking. Open plan living room, open fires, CH, colour TV, well equipped kitchen. 2 double bedrooms, linen included. Put-u-up and cot available. Laundry facilities. Hard tennis court. Open all year.

18   **Shaw Farm,** Shaw Marsh, New Mills, High Peak, Derbyshire SK22 4QE

Mrs Nicky Burgess
☎ 0161 427 1841
⑤ℂ From £170–£320
Sleeps 8
🛏 🐓 🐄 💼 ⛱ ◎
🐾 🐾 🐾 Commended

Views and cows, walks to suit, a picnic in the wood. Come to us we have it all, a real farm delight. Three bedroomed cottage, price reduced if family room not required. Full CH, south-facing garden with patio, children's play area. Pub with grub 5 mins' walk. Short breaks. Open all year.

FINDING YOUR ACCOMMODATION

FARM HOLIDAY BUREAU

The Group contacts at the beginning of each section can always help you find a vacancy in your chosen area.

THE 1000+ BUREAU MEMBERS OFFER A UNIQUE LINK TO CUSTOMERS ACROSS THE UK

FARM HOLIDAY BUREAU

All Bureau members belong to a local Group. Each member can refer you to an equally high quality member within the Group... or across the UK: England, Northern Ireland, Scotland, Wales.

Derbyshire Dales & Dovedale

Group Contacts: BB *Sylvia Foster* ☎ *01335 360346*
SC *Linda Adams* ☎ *01335 360352*

Discover the wealth of delights which makes this county of character and contrast the ideal choice for your short, or long, break destination. From the mellow lowlands of the south to the rugged peaks of the north – from picturesque villages to busy market towns – from historic houses and museums to the excitement of Alton Towers and the American Adventure – a warm and friendly welcome awaits you in every corner.

The countryside around the delightful old market town of Ashbourne, at the southern end of the Pennine Range in Derbyshire, is among the most beautiful in the whole of England. The spectacular scenery of Dovedale and the Manifold Valley, the rolling uplands with their scattered copses and stone walls and isolated traditional farmsteads are well known. Less dramatic but no less rewarding is the tranquil beauty of the unspoilt countryside and villages of the area.

Ashbourne itself is a small, historic country town of distinction, with shops, hotels, restaurants– its speciality Ashbourne gingerbread – a delight not to be missed!

Numerous footpaths provide ideal conditions for walking and there are ample facilities for pony trekking, cycle hire and fishing. Within easy access are many places of interest, great country mansions, the National Tramway Museum, Heritage Centres, Factory Shops, the Heights of Abraham and many more attractions for you to enjoy.

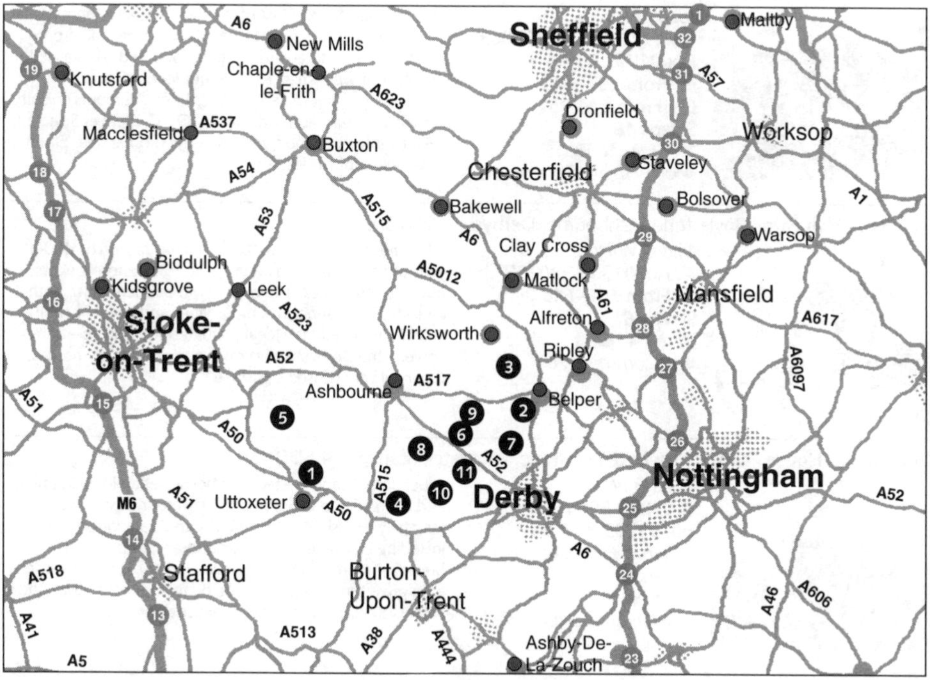

BED AND BREAKFAST

(and evening meal)

1 **The Beeches Farmhouse,** Waldley, Doveridge, Nr Ashbourne, Derbyshire DE6 5LR

Barbara Tunnicliffe
☎ **01889 590288**
Fax **01889 590559**
🅱 From £26–£39.50
EM From £12
🕭 ⌨ ♿ ⊚
🏵 🏵 *Highly Commended*

Winners of top national award for farm based catering. Enjoy dining in our oak beamed licensed restaurant – after exploring the Derbyshire countryside or the thrills of Alton Towers. Ten rooms including excellent en suite family rooms which retain the character of our 18th century farmhouse. Children love feeding the animals on our working dairy farm. A warm welcome awaits you. Open all year except Christnmas (open New Year).

---

2 **Chevin Green Farm,** Chevin Road, Belper, Derbyshire DE56 2UN

Carl & Joan Postles
☎ **01773 822328**
🅱 From £15–£21
Sleeps 14
🕭 🍴 ♿ 🛉 ⊚
🏵 *Commended*

Relax in peaceful picturesque countryside. Our extended and refurbished beamed farmhouse offers single, twin, double and family en suite rooms. Enjoy generous breakfasts. Guests own lounge and dining room. Within easy reach of Dales, Peak District, stately homes (6) and Alton Towers. Pleasant walks, riding and golf nearby. Reductions for children sharing and weekly terms. Open all year except Christmas.

---

3 **Dannah Farm Country Guest House,** Bowmans Lane, Shottle, Belper, Derbyshire DE56 2DR

Joan Slack
☎ **01773 550273/550630**
Fax **01773 550590**
🅱 From £32–£45
EM From £16.95
Sleeps 18
🕭 ⌨ ♿ 🛉 🛉 ⊚
🏵 🏵 *Highly Commended*

Winners Bed & Breakfast of the Year '94, also top national award for farm catering. Hopefully we have it all, from pot-bellied pigs to award-winning food and, above all, the warmest of welcomes! Relax in our lovely Georgian farmhouse on our mixed working farm. All rooms en suite. Colour TVs, fully licensed. AA QQQQQ Premier Selected, RAC Highly Acclaimed. Johansens recommended. Open all year except Christmas.

---

4 **Lees Hall Farm,** Boylestone, Ashbourne, Derbyshire DE6 5AA

Mavis Wilson
☎/Fax **01335 330259**
🅱 From £16–£18
Sleeps 6
🕭 ♿ 🅰 📺 🛉 🛉
🏵 *Commended*

Welcome to Lees Hall, a 100-acre beef farm. The 400-year-old house is set in an unspoilt, rural landscape amid quiet country lanes. 1 family, 1 twin bedded room, both en suite. Tea/coffee-making facilities and central heating. Full English breakfast. Ideally situated for visits to Alton Towers, the Derbyshire Dales and several stately homes. Open all year (closed Christmas).

---

5 **Manor House Farm,** Prestwood, Denstone, Uttoxeter, Staffs ST14 5DD

Chris Ball
☎ **01889 590415**
Fax **01335 342198**
🅱 From £18–£24
Sleeps 6
🕭 🐀 🛉
🏵 🏵 *Highly Commended*

A beautiful Grade II listed farmhouse set amid rolling hills and rivers. Three bedrooms, all with four-poster beds, tastefully furnished with antiques and traditional features including oak-beamed ceilings and an oak panelled breakfast room. Guests may relax in the extensive gardens with grass tennis court and Victorian summer house. Alton Towers 3 miles. Open all year except Christmas.

Mercaston Hall, Mercaston, Brailsford, Ashbourne, Derbyshire DE6 3BL ⑥

Angus & Vicki Haddon
☎ **01335 360263**
BB **From £18–£20**
Sleeps 6
☙(8) 🐾 🛏 🌋 🛁 ⚙ ⊛
⚘⚘ *Commended*

Timber-framed, historic, listed building in a quiet countryside location. Situated off the A52 halfway between Derby and Ashbourne. An ideal centre for visits to the Peak District, many tourist attractions and the commercial towns and cities of the Midlands. Kedleston Hall (NT) 1 mile. Hard tennis court. Open all year except Christmas.

Park View Farm, Weston Underwood, Ashbourne, Derbyshire DE6 4PA ⑦

Mrs Linda Adams
☎ **01335 360352**
BB **From £20–£25**
Sleeps 6
☙(6) ✂ 🛁 🌋 ⊛
⚘⚘ *Highly Commended*

Enjoy country house hospitality in our elegant farmhouse set in large gardens with lovely views overlooking the National Trust's magnificent Kedleston Park, hence the farm's name. Double en suite rooms with antique four-poster beds, twin with handbasin and bathroom. Drinks facilities. Guests' sitting room and delightful dining room. Superb English breakfasts. Country pubs and restaurants close by. AA QQQQQ Premier Selected.

Shirley Hall, Shirley, Ashbourne, Derbyshire DE6 3AS ⑧

Mrs Sylvia Foster
☎ **01335 360346**
BB **From £18–£22**
Sleeps 6
☙(6) ✂ 🐾 🌋 🛁 ⊛
⚘⚘ *Highly Commended*

Enjoy the tranquillity of our lovely old, part moated, timbered farmhouse, surrounded by large lawned garden and rolling dairy/arable farm just 4 miles from Ashbourne. Our English breakfasts are renowned. Village pub within walking distance for excellent evening meals. Free coarse fishing. Woodland walks. 2 double bedrooms en suite. 1 twin with handbasin and guest's bathroom. All with CH, TV and drinks facilities. Guests' sitting room. Open all year.

Yeldersley Old Hall Farm, Yeldersley Lane, Bradley, Ashbourne, Derbyshire DE6 1PH ⑨

Mrs Janet Hinds
☎ **01335 344504**
BB **From £18–£20**
Sleeps 6
☙ ✂ 🛁 🌋 ⊛
Listed *Commended*

Yeldersley Old Hall Farm is a family-run dairy farm of 112 acres. The Grade II listed farmhouse is situated in pleasant and quiet rural surroundings just 3 miles from the market town of Ashbourne and within easy reach of Dovedale, Alton Towers, Matlock and many stately homes. Farmhouse breakfast provided. Lounge with log fire. En suite rooms available. Non-smokers only please. Open Mar–Nov.

SELF-CATERING

Briar, Bluebell & Primrose Cottages,
c/o Yeldersley Old Hall Farm, Yeldersley Lane, Bradley, Ashbourne, Derbyshire DE6 1PH ⑨

Mrs Janet Hinds
☎ **01335 344504**
SC **From £130–£300**
Sleep 5/6
☙ 🛁 🌋 ⊛
🏠 🏠 🏠 *Commended*

Situated on a working family dairy farm in rural surroundings, our Grade II listed barn has been converted into 3 self-catering cottages. Two accommodate 5 people (maximum), one 6 people. Each has three bedrooms with bathroom containing bath and shower, fitted kitchen, colour TV. Ample parking area. Ideal spot for touring Derbyshire. Ashbourne 3 miles. Short breaks. Open all year.

2 **Chevin Green Farm,** Chevin Road, Belper, Derbyshire DE56 2UN

Carl & Joan Postles
☎ 01773 822328
[SC] From £90–£295
Sleeps 4/6

Commended

Enjoy a holiday in one of our four attractive cottages of character overlooking picturesque countryside. The cottages with original beams are fully equipped to a high standard. Lounge, fully fitted kitchen, bathroom, 2 or 3 bedrooms, one is specially adapted for the disabled. Ideally situated for all places of interest, Alton Towers, Dales, Peak District and 6 stately homes. Open all year.

---

10 **The Chop House,** Windle Hill Farm, Sutton-on-the-Hill, Ashbourne, Derbyshire DE6 5JH

K E & J Lennard
☎/Fax 01283 732377
[SC] From £130–£350
Sleeps 6

Commended

The Chop House was originally built in 1858 as the farm corn shed. It has been carefully converted to offer cosy, well-equipped family accommodation on our small working farm. Centrally heated, fully insulated, ideal for winter or summer lets. 3 twin bedrooms, kitchen/dining room, separate living room. Sheltered garden. Set amidst tranquil countryside south of Ashbourne. Open all year.

---

11 **Culland Mount Farm,** Brailsford, Ashbourne, Derbyshire DE6 3BW

Carol Phillips
☎ 01335 360313
[SC] From £150–£320
Sleeps 4/6

Commended

Come and enjoy a relaxing holiday in our magnificent Victorian farmhouse with splendid views of rolling countryside. Whilst retaining many original features (marble fire grate), the house is divided making a luxurious holiday home – equally attractive to holiday makers and business people. Signposted walks all around and we welcome visitors to walk around the farm to see the cows and calves.

---

8 **Hall Farm Bungalow,**
New House Farm &
The Saddlery,   c/o Shirley Hall, Shirley, Ashbourne, Derbyshire DE6 3AS

Mrs Sylvia Foster
☎ 01335 360346
[SC] From £130–£360
Sleeps 4/8

Up to Commended

Relax in one of our superb properties at separate locations in unspoilt countryside 4 miles from Ashbourne. Bungalow near Shirley village has 3 bedrooms, large garden, lovely views. Peacefully situated 18th century farmhouse at Mercaston has 4 bedrooms. The Saddlery is a listed self-contained 1st floor barn conversion (family bedroom) on our farm. All very comfortable and well appointed. Private coarse fishing. Open all year.

---

7 **Honeysuckle & Brook Cottages,** c/o Park View Farm, Weston Underwood, Ashbourne, Derbys DE6 4PA

Mrs Linda Adams
☎ 01335 360352
[SC] From £100–£380
Sleeps 4/6 + cot

Commended

Honeysuckle is a truly delightful country cottage set in its own secluded garden with wonderful views over the Derbyshire countryside. Full of character and charm, furnished to a very high standard, with beamed sitting room, antique furnishings and pretty four poster bed. Accommodation for 6 persons in 3 bedrooms. Brook is a welcoming village cottage with 2 bedrooms (double and twin). Short breaks. Open all year.

---

5 **Keepers Cottage,** Manor House Farm, Prestwood, Denstone, Uttoxeter, Staffordshire ST14 5DD

Chris Ball
☎ 01889 590415
Fax 01335 342198
[SC] From £100–£370
Sleeps 4

Commended

Beautifully converted stone cottage in the grounds of an historic Jacobean farmhouse. The cottage dates from around 1700 and has retained many original features including a four-poster, exposed stone walls and oak beams. Set in its own private garden, Keepers Cottage offers a delightful retreat for the discerning holidaymaker. Open all year.

Sherwood Forest/ Nottinghamshire

Group Contacts: BB *Fernie Palmer* ☎ *01623 842666*
SC *Janet Carr* ☎ *01623 861088*

Sherwood Forest is much smaller than it used to be, but near Edwinstowe you can still find Robin Hood, at the Sherwood Forest Visitor Centre where his story is told in a walk-through exhibition. There are also films, guided forest walks and other activities. Edwinstowe church is where Robin Hood is said to have married Maid Marion.

Worksop is a pleasant market town with a fine priory and 14th-century gatehouse. Retford has a small museum and some interesting Georgian buildings around its market square. The open-air markets at Newark and Mansfield are popular with visitors and each town has its local museums. Newark's parish church has a fine spire and interesting treasury but the nearby Minster at Southwell is on a larger scale even though Southwell, home of the Bramley apple, is hardly more than a village.

In Nottingham, Robin Hood's statue stands outside the castle which houses the city's fine arts museum, and there's a small Robin Hood exhibition at the gatehouse. At the foot of Castle Rock, beside the ancient Trip to Jerusalem Inn, is the Brewhouse Yard Museum illustrating the city's social history, while nearby the Canal Museum and the Museum of Costume and Textile show other aspects of the city's heritage. The Lace Centre, in an attractive timbered building, shows off a range of Nottingham's finest work, which you can buy as a souvenir.

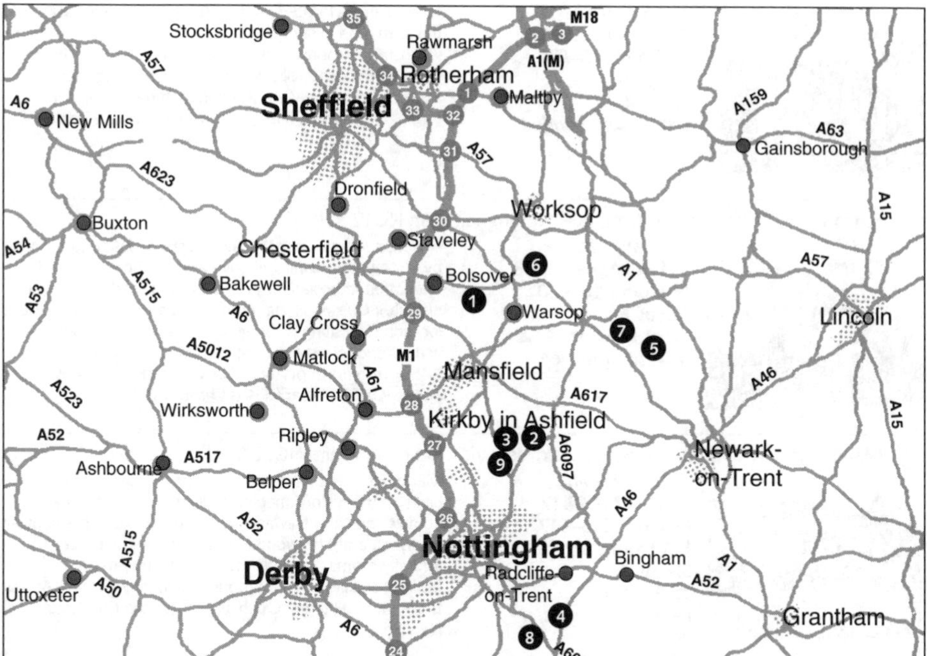

BED AND BREAKFAST

(and evening meal)

---

① Blue Barn Farm, Langwith, Mansfield, Nottinghamshire NG20 9JD

June Ibbotson
☎/Fax 01623 742248
🛏 From £17–£22
Sleeps 6
🐎 ♘ ♨ 🛁 ◉
👄👄 *Commended*

Welcome to our family-run 450-acre farm in peaceful surroundings on the edge of Sherwood Forest in Robin Hood country, 5 miles from M1 (J30) off A616. Many interesting places catering for all tastes only a short car journey away. Suitable for the business traveller, a place to unwind. 1 double, 1 twin en suite, 1 family, all with tea/coffee-making facilities and washbasins. Cot available. Dining room, lounge, TV. Open all year (closed Christmas Day & New Year).

---

② Far Baulker Farm, Oxton, Nottinghamshire NG25 0RQ

Janette Esam
☎ 01623 882375
🛏 From £16–£24
Sleeps 6
🐎 ♙ ♙ ♨ ♨ 🛁
Listed *Commended*

Far Baulker Farm is a 300-acre arable/livestock farm set in the heart of Sherwood Forest 10 miles north of Nottingham on the A614. One double en suite, one double with washbasin, one twin, tea/coffee-making facilities and TV in all rooms. Visitors lounge with TV/video. A welcome awaits you in our family home. Open all year.

---

③ Forest Farm, Mansfield Road, Papplewick, Nottinghamshire NG15 8FL

Mrs E J Stubbs
☎ 0115 9632310
🛏 From £16–£20
Sleeps 5
🐎 ⅍ 🛁
Listed *Commended*

Forest Farm is located on the A60 standing well back up the farm road away from traffic noise. Pleasant views from south-facing rooms, 1 double en suite, 1 single, 1 twin, all with tea-making facilities. TV in lounge/dining room. Midway between Mansfield and Nottingham, and ideal touring or business base. Open all year (closed Dec).

---

④ Jerico Farm, Fosse Way, Nr Cotgrave, Nottinghamshire NG12 3HG

Mrs Sally Herrick
☎/Fax 01949 81733
🛏 From £18–£20
Sleeps 6
🐎(5) ⅍ 🖭 ♨ ♨ 🛁 ✿
👄👄 *Commended*

A working farm with attractive accommodation surrounded by our own farmland with lovely views. Good firm beds, tea/coffee/chocolate trays and TVs in all bedrooms, (one en suite). Guests' sitting room. Good pubs nearby. Excellent location for visiting Nottingham, its universities, sports venues and tourist sites. Located down a farm drive off A46, 1 mile north of A46/A606 jct, south of Cotgrave village. Open all year (closed Christmas).

---

⑤ Manor Farm, Moorhouse Road, Laxton, Newark, Nottinghamshire NG22 0NU

Mrs Pat Haigh
☎ 01777 870417
🛏 From £16–£17
EM From £8
Sleeps 6
🐎 ♘ ♨ 🛁
Listed *Commended*

Manor Farm is a family-run dairy and arable farm of 137 acres, in the historic medieval village of Laxton, situated 10 miles north of Newark, and on the verge of the popular tourist area of Sherwood Forest in Nottinghamshire. 2 family rooms, 1 double room, tea/coffee-making facilities available. Visitors' lounge and dining room. Access to rooms at all times. Open all year (closed Christmas & New Year).

Norton Grange Farm, Norton, Cuckney, Mansfield, Nottinghamshire NG20 9LP ⑥

Fernie Palmer
☎ 01623 842666
BB From £17–£18
Sleeps 4
🐕 🐄 ■ ☂
🕮 *Commended*

Norton Grange is a Grade II listed farmhouse set in the heart of the Welbeck Estate, part of the world-famous Sherwood Forest. Ideally situated for overnight stops or touring the very beautiful countryside and the many attractions, in Nottinghamshire and Derbyshire. One double room and one twin room, both with washbasin and tea/coffee-making facilities. Open all year except Christmas & New Year.

SELF-CATERING

Blue Barn Cottage, c/o Blue Barn Farm, Langwith, Mansfield, Nottinghamshire NG20 9JD ①

June Ibbotson
☎/Fax 01623 742248
SC From £375–£400
Sleeps 8 + cot
🐕 ☂ ■ ◉
🔑 🔑 🔑 🔑 *Commended*

Do come and relax in peace and comfort on our family-run farm in Robin Hood country. Visit quiet villages, stately homes rich in history, ramble through country parks or hunt bargains in thriving market towns. Blue Barn is off the A616 near Cuckney. 4 bedrooms, bathroom, breakfast kitchen, dining room, lounge, TV, washing machine and dryer. CH and linen included. Open all year.

Foliat Cottages, c/o Jordan Castle Farm, Wellow, Newark, Nottinghamshire NG22 0EL ⑦

Mrs Janet Carr
☎/Fax 01623 861088
SC From £180–£325
Sleeps 6 + cot
🐕 ✂ ■ ☂
🔑 🔑 🔑 🔑 *Commended*

Close to the heart of Sherwood Forest, our renovated Edwardian cottages have beautiful pastoral views across our working family farm. Peaceful and cosy, with central heating, colour TV, microwave and washer/dryer. Each has 1 double and 2 twin bedrooms, with cot and highchair available. Enclosed south-facing gardens with patios. Linen provided. Brochure available. Open all year.

Foxcote Cottage, Foxcote Hill Farm, Stanton on the Wolds, Nottinghamshire NG12 5PJ ⑧

Joan Hinchley
☎ 0115 9374337
Fax 0115 9375193
SC £300
Sleeps 6
🐕 ■
🔑 🔑 🔑 *Commended*

Situated seven miles south of Nottingham, on the edge of the Vale of Belvoir, within easy reach of all attractions in the Midlands. The cottage stands well back from the A606 overlooking open countryside with views of lake, and is set in a private, well-maintained garden. The cottage is fully equipped to a high standard. All bedlinen and towels included. Open all year.

The Granary, Top House Farm, Lamins Lane, Mansfield Road, Arnold, Nottingham, Notts NG5 8PH ⑨

Mrs Ann Lamin
☎ 0115 9268330
SC From £250–£290
Sleeps 3/4
🐕 ✂
🔑 🔑 🔑 *Commended*

Charming granary flat with beams, open fireplace, CH. Lounge with colour TV, patio doors onto garden. Kitchen has electric and microwave ovens, use of automatic washer and dryer. Within easy reach of Nottingham, Newstead Abbey, Southwell Minster, the Dukeries, Sherwood Forest, Derbyshire and the National Watersports Centre. Open all year.

Shrewsbury, Ironbridge & Shropshire

Group Contact: *Mrs Janet Jones* ☎ *01939 220223*

Shropshire with its wealth of Historic Houses, Castles and Abbeys, is the largest landbound county. Medieval Shrewsbury the county town, and up to date Telford are the principle towns. With attractive market towns scattered around, leaving miles of unspoilt countryside to explore.

Don't miss Shrewsbury with it's historic buildings, passages and Castle. Famous for books and TV series about a medieval monk by Ellis Peters.

Ironbridge Gorge Museums and the world famous Iron Bridge, make this World Heritage site a must.

Hawkstone Park with its woodland fantasy of castles, cliffs and caves restored and open to the public for the first time in over 100 years.

Being so large the county caters for every need, with its own lake district at Ellesmere, hill country of South Shropshire. The Llangollen canal winding its way along and the Severn Valley Steam Railway at Bridgnorth to name but a few.

For the sports people: famous golf courses, fishing, horse riding and gliding.

Shropshire offers so much for everyone, seeing is believing!!!

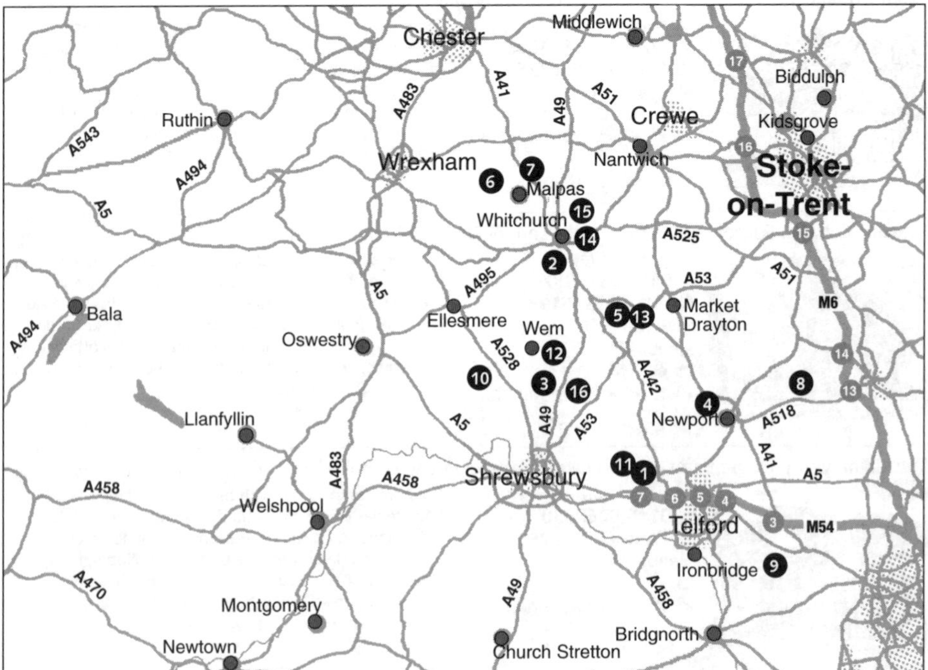

BED AND BREAKFAST
(and evening meal)

Church Farm, Wrockwardine, Wellington, Telford, Shropshire TF6 5DG ➊

Mrs Jo Savage
☎/Fax 01952 244917
BB From £20–£25
EM From £16
Sleeps 8
▣ ⚥ ♨ ◉
❀ ❀ *Highly Commended*

Down a lime tree avenue, in a peaceful village betwixt Shrewsbury and Telford, lies our superbly situated Georgian farmhouse. Mature gardens with medieval stonework, old roses and many unusual plants. Attractive bedrooms with TVs, tea/coffee/chocolate, some en suite with ground floor available. Enormous inglenook fireplace in spacious guests' lounge. Delicious breakfasts helped by free range hens! Minutes from Ironbridge, Shrewsbury and Telford. 1 mile M54 (J7) and A5. Open all year.

Dearnford Hall, Whitchurch, Shropshire SY13 3JJ ➋

Charles & Jane Bebbington
☎ 01948 662319
Fax 01948 666670
BB From £25–£30
Sleeps 4
✂ ▣ ♨ ✇ ◉
❀ ❀ *Highly Commended*

Relax and unwind in our beautiful 17th century farmhouse on the picturesque borders of Shropshire, Cheshire and the Welsh Marches in the heart of cheesemaking country. Log fires and CH, comfortable drawing room and lovely en suite bedrooms overlooking sweeping lawns and clematis-clad entrance. Stroll in the garden or enjoy outstanding fly-fishing at our own spring fed trout pool. Superb restaurants and pubs nearby to round off your day. Ample parking. Closed Christmas.

Grove Farm, Preston Brockhurst, Shrewsbury, Shropshire SY4 5QA ➌

Mrs Janet Jones
☎/Fax 01939 220223
BB From £17–£19
Sleeps 6
🐴 ✂ ♨ ◉
❀ *Highly Commended*

Step into Shropshire and enjoy quality accommodation and fine home cooking using local produce. Our 322-acre farm is set in a small village 7 miles north of Shrewsbury on the A49. The 17th century house is traditionally furnished and offers warmth and comfort after the day's activities. Ideally situated for Ironbridge World Heritage Site, Shrewsbury, Chester, Potteries and Wales. Brochures available. Open mid Jan–mid Dec.

Lane End Farm, Chetwynd, Newport, Shropshire TF10 8BN ➍

Mrs Janice Park
☎ 01952 550337
BB From £18–£20
EM from £11
Sleeps 4
🐴 🐾 ♨
❀ ❀ *Commended*

Relax and feel at home in our friendly, interesting farmhouse set amidst lovely countryside. Large bedrooms with en suite facilities. Good woodland walks nearby. Located on A41 two miles North of Newport; ideal for visiting Ironbridge, Weston Park, Cosford, Potteries, Chester, etc. Working sheep farm – see the lambs in spring! Open all year.

Mickley House, Faulsgreen, Tern Hill, Market Drayton, Shropshire TF9 3QW ➎

Mrs Pauline Williamson
☎/Fax 01630 638505
BB From £18–£26
Sleeps 6
⚤ 🐴 ✂ ⚥ ♨ ◉
❀ ❀ *Highly Commended*

In need of a break? We offer you peace, quiet and comfort in our home with its oak doors, beams, leaded windows. Tranquillity of the house spills out into landscaped gardens. Stroll through rose-scented pergolas to pools with trickling waterfall. Restful drawing room beckons after sightseeing and meal at local restaurants/pubs. Individually styled en suite bedrooms, master bedroom with Louis XIV king-size bed. Ground floor available. All facilities. 2 miles off A41. Closed Christmas.

6 Mill House, Higher Wych, Malpas, Cheshire SY14 7JR

Chris & Angela Smith
☎ 01948 780362
Fax 01948 780566
BB From £18
EM From £8
Sleeps 4
CN
Highly Commended

Modernised Mill House on the Cheshire/Clwyd border in a quiet valley, convenient for visiting Chester, Shrewsbury and North Wales. The house is centrally heated and has an open log fire in the lounge. Bedrooms have washbasins, radios and tea-making facilities. 1 bedroom has an en suite shower and WC. Reductions for children and senior citizens. Open Jan–Nov.

7 Millmoor Farm, Nomansheath, Malpas, Cheshire SY14 8ED

Mrs Sally-Ann Chesters
☎ 01948 820304
BB From £15–£20
EM From £10
Sleeps 6
Listed

Set amongst the beautiful valleys on the South Cheshire/Shropshire border, Millmoor Farm is a wonderful setting to escape the hurly burly of modern life. The 17th century farmhouse has recently been refurbished and boasts an exquisite en suite four-poster double bedroom. Within easy reach of Chester, North Wales and Shropshire's many attractions. Great pub meals within walking distance. Open all year.

8 Oulton House Farm, Norbury, Nr Stafford, Staffordshire ST20 0PG

Mrs Judy Palmer
☎/Fax 01785 284264
BB From £20–£25
Sleeps 6
Highly Commended

A 300-acre dairy farm situated on the Shropshire/Staffordshire border. Our large Victorian farmhouse offers warm, comfortable and well appointed en suite bedrooms, all with tea trays and TV. From your peaceful, rural base discover our many local attractions from the heritage of Ironbridge Gorge, the splendours of Shugborough to the bargains of the Potteries factory shops. Many local pubs and restaurants. Peace and quiet guaranteed. Open all year except Christmas.

9 Parkside Farm, Holyhead Road, Albrighton, Nr Wolverhampton WV7 3DA

Margaret Shanks
☎ 01902 372310
Fax 01902 375013
BB From £20–£23
Sleeps 6
Commended

There is always a friendly welcome at this traditional working farm set in rolling Shropshire countryside, with beautiful gardens which the guests are invited to enjoy at their leisure. Two comfortable family rooms, both with private bathroom, colour TV and tea/coffee facilities. Easy access to local attractions and motorway networks. Real ale restaurant/bar 2 minutes' walk. Business, leisure and tourist guests welcome all year round. Farmhouse breakfasts a speciality!

10 Petton Hall Farm, Petton, Burlton, Shrewsbury, Shropshire SY4 5TH

Mrs Mary Kennerley
☎/Fax 01939 270601
BB £18.50
Sleeps 2 + cot
Commended

Petton Hall Farm is situated between historic Shrewsbury and the beautiful meres of Ellesmere. A large Victorian furnished bedroom with en suite facilities offers privacy and comfort, with splendid views across old parkland. We welcome you to our 85-acre dairy farm and warm hospitality. Chester, Shrewsbury and North Wales within easy reach. Open Jan–Nov.

11 Red House Farm, Longdon on Tern, Wellington, Telford, Shropshire TF6 6LE

Mrs Mary Jones
☎ 01952 770245
BB From £18–£25
Sleeps 6
Commended

Our Victorian farmhouse is on a mixed farm. 2 double bedrooms have private facilities within 1 family room with separate bathroom, all large and comfortable. Excellent breakfast. Farm easily located, leave M54 (jct6), follow A442, take B5063. Central for historic Shrewsbury, Ironbridge Gorge museums or modern Telford. Several local eating places. Open all year.

Soulton Hall, near Wem, Shropshire SY4 5RS (12)

Ann Ashton
☎ **01939 232786**
Fax 01939 234097
BB **From £26–£33**
Sleeps 12
🐶 🐴 🖽 🎣 🥾 🎯 ⚓ 🎯
😊 😊 😊 *Commended*

Sample English country life in an Elizabethan manor house offering very relaxing holiday. Bird watching, fishing, riding. Good food, home produce where possible, super meals. Walled garden. Licensed bar. Direct dial telephones. We welcome you. Open all year.

Willow House, Shrewsbury Road, Tern Hill, Market Drayton, Shropshire TF9 3PX (13)

Mrs Moira Roberts
☎ **01630 638326**
BB **From £15–£18**
Sleeps 4
🐶 ✂ ⚓ 🎯
Listed *Commended*

A warm and friendly welcome awaits you at our modern farmhouse with 1 double, 1 twin room and guests' own bathroom/shower. Both rooms have hot drink facilities. Guests have a separate lounge with colour TV. A good base for touring Shropshire, Cheshire, Staffordshire and local attractions of Ironbridge, Hodnet gardens, Hawkstone Follies and the Potteries. Open all year.

Wood Farm, Old Wood Houses, Whitchurch, Shropshire SY13 4EJ (14)

Mrs Val Mayer
☎ **01948 871224**
BB **From £17**
Sleeps 6
🐶 ✂ ⚓ 🎯 🎯
Applied

Period farmhouse amid spacious gardens on a working dairy farm. Local produce freshly cooked. Tastefully decorated rooms using designer fabrics with antique country-style furniture, beamed ceilings and inglenooks, all combine to provide a warm, memorable welcome.

SELF-CATERING

Bradeley Green Cottage, Tarporley Road, Whitchurch, Shropshire SY13 4HD (15)

Ruth Mulliner
☎ **01948 663442**
SC **From £100–£180**
Sleeps 4
🐶 🐴 ✂ ⚓ 🎯 ⚓
🏠 🏠 🏠 *Commended*

One of two cottages in country lane with lovely views. Good parking. Kitchen, diner, electric cooker and fridge, comfortable sitting room with colour TV and open fire. Central heating. Logs provided (when available). Two bedrooms (twin & double), all bedding, towels are provided. Electricity by £1 meter. Bathroom with bath and shower. Ten minute walk for pub grub at the Willey Moor Lock on canal, set in open fields. Open all year.

The Granary, c/o Mill House, Higher Wych, Malpas, Cheshire SY14 7JR (6)

Chris & Angela Smith
☎ **01948 780362**
Fax 01948 780566
SC **From £75–£160**
Sleeps 4/5 + cot
🐶 ⚓
🏠 🏠 🏠 *Commended*

The Granary is a self-contained bungalow adjacent to Mill House. Sleeps 4/5 in 2 double bedrooms, kitchen/living area, shower and WC. TV. CH. Cot and babysitting available. Situated in a quiet valley with a small stream in the garden. Convenient for visiting Chester, Shrewsbury and North Wales. Open all year.

12 Keepers Cottage, Soulton Hall, Near Wem, Shropshire SY4 5RS

Ann Ashton
☎ 01939 232786
Fax 01939 234097
[SC] From £175–£396
Sleeps 6

Commended

Keepers Cottage nestles on south side of 50-acres of Oak woodland offering really relaxing holidays. Woodland and riverside walks, CH, TV, log fires in season. Evening meals available at Soulton Hall from £17.50, by arrangement. Shrewsbury, Chester, Ironbridge, North Wales, Potteries – all within easy reach. Open all year.

16 The Sett, Village Farm, Stanton-upon-Hine Heath, Shrewsbury, Shropshire SY4 4LR

Brenda & Jim Grundey
☎/Fax 01939 250391
[SC] From £160–£240
Sleeps 6

Applied

The Sett is a special place, share our secret. Escape for a well earned rest. Be warm and comfortable, hide yourselves away. We won't tell! Open all year.

8 Swallows Nest, Oulton House Farm, Norbury, Nr Stafford, Staffordshire ST20 0PG

Mrs Judy Palmer
☎/Fax 01785 284264
[SC] From £110–£250
Sleeps 4 + cot

Highly Commended

Swallows Nest has been designed with the comfort of our guests in mind. We think it is special. It is self-contained, fully equipped and all inclusive. An ideal base for a relaxing holiday: patchwork quilts, pine, pot pourri, peace and quiet – perfect. See why the swallows return! Open all year.

LET THE TELEPHONE RING!

Some farmhouses are big places. Let the telephone ring
long enough to give the owner time to answer it.

STAY ON A FARM GIFT TOKENS

If you have enjoyed your *Stay on a Farm*, why not treat your friends and relatives to *Stay on a Farm* gift tokens? Available from the Bureau office, telephone 01203 696909, they can be redeemed against accommodation booked on the majority of our farms

---

South Shropshire

Group Contact: *Mrs C Price* ☎ *01547 530249*

In an area of outstanding natural beauty, South Shropshire is full of contrasts; secluded and peaceful with rolling hills, high moorland and wooded valleys.

Shrewsbury lies in a loop of the River Severn and is entered by the English bridge or Welsh bridge and holds the keys to the mysteries of Brother Cadfael, Benedictine monk of Shrewsbury Abbey.

Ironbridge, birthplace of the Industrial Revolution has six separate museums including the famous Blists Hill Open Air Museum where craftsmen link bygone times to the present day.

The river flows South, passing through Bridgnorth. Here the Severn Valley Railway steams 16 miles along the valley through Bewdley and onto Kidderminster.

Ludlow, premier town of the Marches is the perfect historic town and the large ruined castle stands high above the River Teme and is the venue for an open air Shakespearian play each year. Along the Marches are many fortifications of which Stokesay Castle is a unique example of a fortified manor house.

South East Shropshire is dominated by the Limestone ridge of the Wenlock Edge described by the poet A E Housman in 'A Shropshire Lad'. Beneath this ridge the rich valley of Corvedale leads to the small market towns of Craven Arms and Church Stretton. Sheep farming country lies to the West with spectacular scenery on the Long Mynd Hills. Further west are the rugged outcrops of the Stiperstones and beyond them Bishop's Castle and the hills of Clun Forest. Here Offa's Dyke, an ancient earthwork divides England from Wales.

With this varied landscape seek out the wild places of South Shropshire. It's reputation as excellent walking country is growing and will suit all abilities – from gentle strolling to a full days ramble.

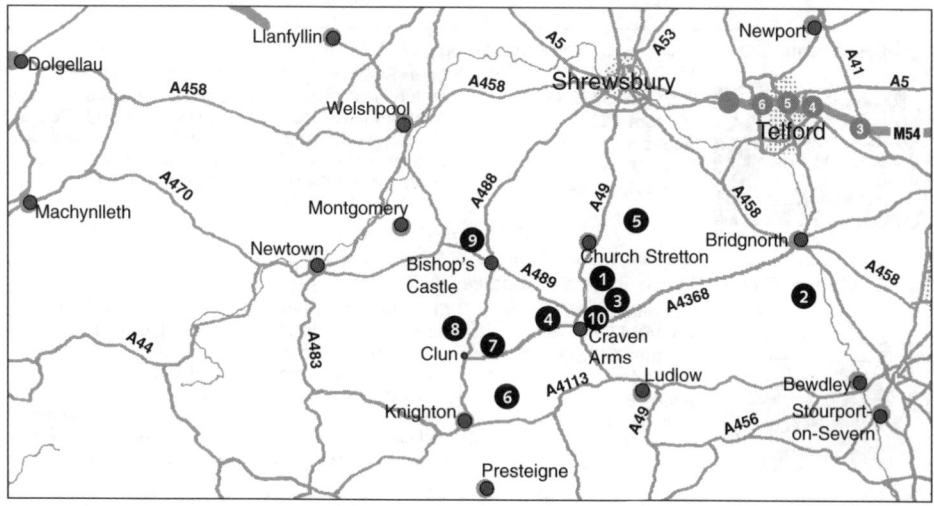

BED AND BREAKFAST

(and evening meal)

---

1 Acton Scott Farm, Church Stretton, Shropshire SY6 6QN

Mary Jones
☎ **01694 781260**
📖 From £15
Sleeps 6
🐕 🐎 ⊬ ⚓ ⛪ ◎
🍂🍂 *Commended*

Situated in beautiful countryside, adjacent to an historic working farm, the 17th century farmhouse of character has comfortable and spacious rooms, all with washbasin or en suite facilities. The spectacular hills and valley of Church Stretton are nearby and we are central for visiting Shrewsbury, Ludlow and Ironbridge. We look forward to welcoming you. Open mid Feb – mid Nov.

---

2 Billingsley Hall Farm, Covert Lane, Billingsley, Bridgnorth, Shropshire WV16 6PJ

Mrs Helen Sedgley
☎ **01746 861877**
📖 From £16–£20
Sleeps 6 + cot
🐕 🐎 ⊬ 🏕 ⚓ 🐾 ⛪ 🧳
Listed *Commended*

We welcome you to spacious accommodation on a 260-acre working farm with sheep, suckler cows and arable crops. We offer 2 double/family bedrooms, 1 twin room with guests' bathroom. Lounge with log fire, dining room. Guests can follow the many walks around the woods and farmland. Situated 6 miles from Bridgnorth on B4363 to Cleobury Mortimer road, ideal base for local attractions. Also luxury self-catering. Open all year.

---

3 Brereton House, Woolston, Church Stretton, Shropshire SY6 6QD

Joanna Brereton
☎ **01694 781201**
📖 From £17–£18
EM From £8.50
Sleeps 6
🐕 🐎 ⊬ ↩
🍂🍂 *Commended*

Our Victorian red brick farmhouse awaits you, with glorious views down the valley and extensive gardens. It is an ideal base for your Shropshire stay. Spacious bedrooms, two of which are en suite, are very comfortably furnished. Separate guests' lounge and dining room will help to make your stay enjoyable. Open Feb–Nov.

---

4 Castle Farm, Cheney Longville, Craven Arms, Shropshire SY7 8DR

Mrs Varny Jones
☎ **01588 673255**
📖 From £15
Sleeps 5
🐕 🐎 ⛪ 🧳
Listed *Approved*

Castle Farm is steeped in history. First built in the 9th century, and rebuilt in the 13th century, it stands in its own courtyard surrounded by many ancient buildings. Close to Stokesay, Ludlow and Powys Castle, our farm is ideal for a walking holiday over Offa's Dyke or the Long Mynd. One family and one double room. Peace and quiet in abundance. Open Mar–Nov.

✓ **5 Court Farm,** Gretton, Church Stretton, Shropshire SY6 7HU *Aug '92*

Mrs Barbara Norris
☎ **01694 771219**
📖 From £22.50–£25
EM £14
Sleeps 6
⊬ 🐎 🧳 ⛪ ◎
🍂🍂🍂 *Highly Commended*

Stone Tudor farmhouse on 325-acre arable stock farm in peaceful countryside, 1 mile off B4371, equal distance to Ludlow, Shrewsbury, Bridgnorth, Ironbridge. Spacious rooms, inglenook fireplace, full CH. 2 twin rooms, 1 double, all en suite with TV, shaving points and tea/coffee. Furnished to high standard. Warm welcome and high quality cuisine using home produce whenever possible. Midweek breaks available. Open Feb–Nov.

V. good breakfast.

The Hall, Bucknell, Shropshire SY7 0AA

⑥

Mrs Christine Price
☎/Fax 01547 530249
⒝⒝ From £17–£19
EM £10
Sleeps 6
⌖(7) ⌁ ▮
♥♥ *Commended*

The Hall is a working farm with spacious Georgian farmhouse and peaceful garden to relax in, after a day walking or exploring the Welsh Borderland with its historic towns and castles, also the black and white villages of North Herefordshire. Guest lounge, 1 twin en suite, 2 double with washbasins, shaving points. Colour TV and tea-making facilities. Open Feb–Nov.

Hurst Mill Farm, Clun, Craven Arms, Shropshire SY7 0JA

⑦

Joyce Williams
☎ 01588 640224
⒝⒝ From £17–£19
EM From £7
Sleeps 6
⌖ ⻗ ⼈ ⛏ ⩘ ⿄ ▮ ⛲ ⊚
♥♥ *Commended*

Winner of 'Shropshire Farm Breakfast Challenge'. A warm welcome to this working farm where the 'kettle's always on'. Well appointed bedrooms, double en suite. Riverside farmhouse and spacious gardens. Nestling in the delightful Clun Valley, between historic Clun and Clunton. Woodland and hills on either side. Two quiet riding ponies, kingfishers and herons. Pets welcome. Log fires. Also 2 luxury cottages. AA QQQ recommended. Open all year.

Llanhedric, Clun, Craven Arms, Shropshire SY7 8NG

⑧

Mrs Mary Jones
☎ 01588 640203
⒝⒝ From £16.50–£19
EM From £8.50
Sleeps 6
⌖ ⌁ ⛲ ▮ ⊚
♥♥ *Commended*

Relax in traditional style in characteristic farmhouse set in the splendours of the Clun Valley. Awake to the smell of good home cooking. Enjoy the life of a modern working farm, feel the fresh breeze as you explore the beautiful countryside, then unwind in the guests' lounge by a warm inglenook fire. Comfortable bedrooms overlooking attractive gardens, double en suite, tea/coffee facilities, CH. Open Apr–Nov.

Lower Broughton Farm, nr Bishop's Castle, Montgomery, Powys SY15 6SZ

⑨

Mrs Kate Bason
☎ 01588 638393
⒝⒝ From £16–£20
Sleeps 6
⌖ ⻗ ⌁ ▮
Listed *Commended*

A 140-acre cattle and sheep farm located near the Welsh border. The house is oak-framed and dates back to the 15th century. Traditional country house furnishings. Central heating. Comfortable bedrooms (one en suite) have washbasins and tea/coffee trays. Stroll around the farm and meet the animals or relax in the garden and enjoy the views. Open all year.

Strefford Hall Farm, Strefford, Craven Arms, Shropshire SY7 8DE

⑩

Mrs Caroline Morgan
☎/Fax 01588 672383
⒝⒝ From £18–£20
EM £10.50
Sleeps 6
⌁ ⌖ ⛲ ▮ ⊚
♥♥ *Commended*

Set in an Area of Outstanding Natural Beauty in the quiet hamlet of Strefford, against the wooded backdrop of the Wenlock Edge and with uninterrupted views of the Long Mynd and Church Stretton hills. Spacious accommodation in 2 doubles, 1 twin (all en suite) with tea/coffee and colour TV. Full English breakfast, special diets catered for. Evening meals by arrangement. Non smoking household. Closed Christmas and New Year.

NO ANSWER?

Farmers are mostly out and about during the day.
Try to telephone before 9.30am or after 4pm.

SELF-CATERING

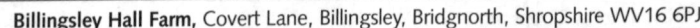

Billingsley Hall Farm, Covert Lane, Billingsley, Bridgnorth, Shropshire WV16 6PJ

Mrs Helen Sedgley
☎ 01746 861877
From £200–£280
Sleeps 6

Highly Commended

The Granary provides luxury accommodation for 4/5 people in spacious oak beamed rooms – a central feature of main bedroom. Fully carpeted and heated throughout. Modern fitted kitchen including washing machine. Guests can follow walks around the farm. Children catered for. Within easy reach many local attractions. Open all year.

FARM HOLIDAY BUREAU

Our Internet Address is
http://www.webscape.co.uk/farmaccom/

CONFIRM BOOKINGS

Disappointments can arise from misunderstandings over the telephone.
Please write to confirm your booking.

FINDING YOUR ACCOMMODATION

FARM HOLIDAY BUREAU

The Group contacts at the beginning of each section can always help you find a vacancy in your chosen area.

Herefordshire

Group Contacts: [BB] *Elizabeth Godsall* ☎ *01531 670408*
[SC] *Judy Wells* ☎ *01568 797347*

Herefordshire is a land of red earth, green meadows, quiet woods, streams and pretty black and white villages. This is the home of the world famous red and white Herefordshire cattle and a well-known centre for cidermaking. In the south are the spectacular gorges of the River Wye and the lovely woodland trails of the Forest of Dean; westward lies the tranquil Golden Valley leading into Offa's Dyke. To the east, Elgar country rises to the Malvern Hills with the finest ridge walk in England.

Herefordshire is rich in history and within reasonable travelling distance of the Black Mountains, Brecon Beacons and Elan Valley in Wales and the Clee Hills, Carding Mill Valley, Long Mynd and Wenlock Edge in South Shropshire. The county itself has a range of sights that span every period in British history from Iron Age hill forts, Roman remains, Norman castles and mediaeval manor houses to stately homes and their gardens and heritage museums. In the village of Kilpeck there are renowned 12th-century Herefordshire carvings and pagan Celtic figures.

You may also like to wander through the many street markets of the county. Hay-on-Wye is famous for its secondhand bookshops and Hereford is the home of a very large cattle market on Wednesdays.

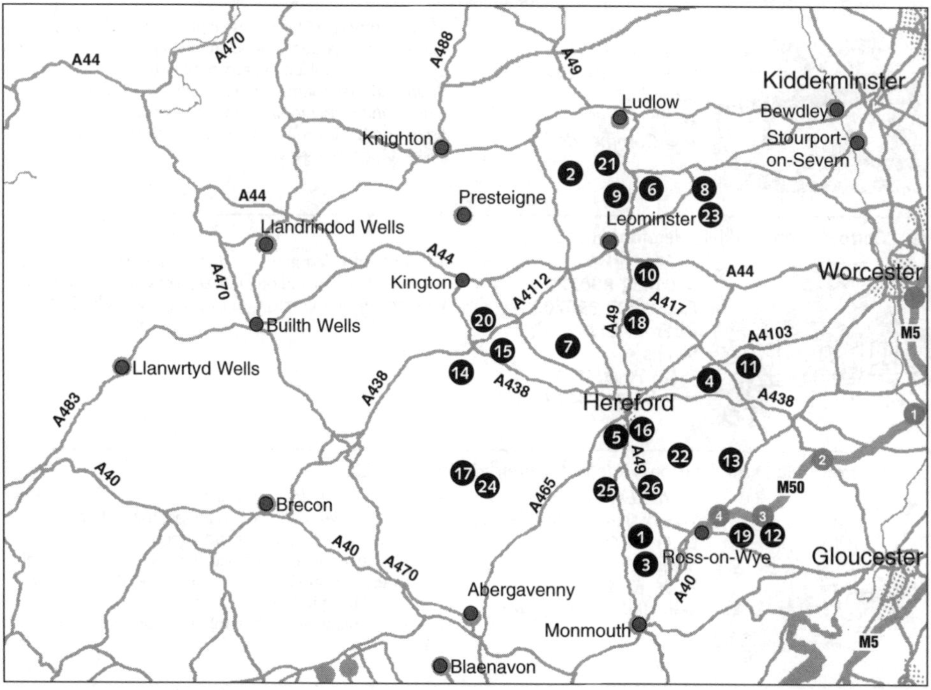

BED AND BREAKFAST

(and evening meal)

---

1 **Amberley,** Aberhall Farm, St Owen's Cross, Hereford HR2 8LL

Freda Davies
☎ 01989 730256
[BB] From £18–£20
Sleeps 4
✂ 🛄 ⊚
🍽🍽 *Highly Commended*

Savour the peace and tranquillity of our new home with panoramic views of the rolling countryside. 132-acre working family farm offering one ground floor en suite twin/double and, upstairs, one double with private bathroom. Guests'own lounge and dining room. Tea/trays, excellent cuisine, 'home from home'. Large garden with patio.

---

2 **The Barn Farm,** Leinthall Starkes, Ludlow, Shropshire SY8 2HP

Sylvia Price
☎/Fax 01568 770388
[BB] From £17–£20
EM £14
Sleeps 6
🐾 🐓 ✂ 🛄
🍽🍽 *Approved*

A warm welcome, comfort and a relaxed atmosphere await you. Our traditional mixed farm is 5 miles west of Ludlow. Cosy bedrooms, 2 double en suite, tea trays. Meals served in our conservatory dining room. Special diets. Guests' own sitting room.

---

3 **Brelston Court,** Marstow, Ross on Wye HR9 6HF

Jayne Rand
☎ 01600 890490
[BB] From £19–£22.50
Sleeps 4
🛄 ↩
🍽🍽 *Commended*

18th century listed farmhouse in the Wye Valley with lovely walled garden overlooking the Garron with views to Symonds Yat. Welcoming accommodation awaits offering double en suite rooms with tea/coffee trays. Guests' TV lounge and dining room. Farm provides idyllic walks and fishing on the Garron. Close by is Goodrich with its historic castle. Open Mar–Nov.

---

4 **Garford Farm,** Yarkhill, Hereford HR1 3ST

Helen Parker
☎ 01432 890226
Fax 01432 890707
[BB] From £17
Sleeps 4
🐾(2) 🐓 🛄 ↩ 🌴
🍽🍽 *Commended*

Timber-framed farmhouse in quiet location yet within easy reach of Hereford and other local places of interest. Pets welcome by arrangement and stabling available. Open all year.

---

5 **Grafton Villa Farm,** Grafton, Hereford, Herefordshire HR2 8ED

Jennie Layton
☎/Fax 01432 268689
[BB] From £19–£20
Sleeps 6
🐾 ✂ 🛄 🌴 ⚘
🍽🍽 *Highly Commended*

A farmhouse of great character and warmth set in an acre of beautiful lawns and gardens amidst the picturesque Wye Valley. Beautiful fabrics and antiques throughout, charming, peaceful en suite bedrooms with, TV and drinks tray. Guests' private bathroom or en suite. We offer our guests a relaxing holiday on a 'real farm', enjoying a sumptuous breakfast with farmhouse portions. Open Feb–Nov.

Haynall Villa, Little Hereford, Nr Ludlow, Shropshire SY8 4BG   6

Mrs Rachel Edwards
☎/Fax 01584 711589
[BB] From £17–£24
EM From £13
Sleeps 6
☆(6) 🐇 ⅛ 🐈 🏮
♥♥ *Commended*

1820s farmhouse nestling in Teme Valley 6m from historic Ludlow, ¾ from A456. Spacious bedrooms (1 en suite) offer comfort, views to 3 counties, vanity units, tea/coffee-making facilities. Guests' bathroom. Delicious farmhouse fayre (vegetarian and special diets). Relax in lounge with TV or attractive garden. Featured in Daily Telegraph. Open all year except Christmas and New Year.

Hill Top Farm, Wormsley, Hereford, Herefordshire HR4 8LZ   7

Mr & Mrs P Jennings
☎/Fax 01981 590246
[BB] From £16–£18
Sleeps 5
☆ 🐇 ⅛ 🏕 ⚙ 🏮 💼
♥♥ *Commended*

A working farm offering real peace and relaxation. Glorious views in all directions. The character farmhouse is fully modernised with rooms en suite or with private bathroom. Tea/coffee facilities. An abundance of flora and fauna and many walks and sports facilities locally, including golf. Our friendly welcome and personal attention will make your stay a delight. Open all year except Christmas.

The Hills Farm, Leysters, Leominster, Herefordshire HR6 0HP   8

Jane Conolly
☎/Fax 01568 750205
[BB] From £23–£25
EM £16
Sleeps 10
🐇 ⅛ 🖼 🏮
♥♥♥ *Highly Commended*

We have five charming, well equipped bedrooms – three are in delightfully converted barns, so you have your own front door! Scrumptious food including vegetarian is served, all home cooked. We try to offer everything for a comfortable, relaxing break, be it one night or many more. No smoking. Brochure. Open Mar–end Oct.

Home Farm, Bircher, Nr Leominster, Herefordshire HR6 0AX   9

Doreen Cadwallader
☎ 01568 780525
[BB] From £16–£20
Sleeps 6
☆ 🐇 ⅛ 🏕 ⚙ 🏮 🎪
♥ *Commended*

We welcome you to a traditional livestock farm offering you excellent service and accommodation. Set in a peaceful, secluded area on the Welsh Border, it's 4 miles north of Leominster, 7 miles south of Ludlow, and close to Croft Castle, Berrington Hall and other attractions. All rooms have tea/coffee-making facilities. TV and washbasins. Light evening meals by request. Open all year.

Little Wickton, Stoke Prior, Leominster HR6 0LL   10

Helena Mead
☎/Fax 01568 797292
mobile 0402 037119
[BB] From £18–£25
Sleeps 4
☆(8) ⅛ 💼
Applied

17th century timber-framed house with exposed timbers and inglenooks set in idyllic surroundings with abundant wildlife, peace and tranquillity. Beautiful antique furnishings. We offer one double en suite and one twin room. We are ideally placed for visiting Croft Castle, Berrington Hall, Ludlow (10 miles), Hereford (12 miles), Bromyard (8 miles). Guests' own sitting room. Light supper available on request. Open Mar–Nov.

Moor Court Farm, Stretton Grandison, Nr Ledbury, Herefordshire HR8 2TR   11

Elizabeth Godsall
☎ 01531 670408
[BB] From £17.50
EM From £12.50
Sleeps 6
🐇 🏮 🐈 🎪 🐾 ◉
♥♥♥ *Commended*

Relax and enjoy our beautiful 15th century timber-framed farmhouse with adjoining oast houses in a peaceful location. It's a traditional working Herefordshire hop and livestock farm, in scenic countryside central to the major market towns. Easy access to the Malverns, Wye Valley and Welsh borders. Spacious bedrooms, en suite or private bathroom, tea/coffee-making facilities. Oak beamed lounge and dining room. Open all year.

12 New House Farm, Barrell Lane, Longhope, Gloucestershire GL17 0LS

Mrs Elizabeth Beddows
☎/Fax 01452 830484
BB From £20–£25
EM From £12
Sleeps 6
🖙 🛏 🏕 ⚘ ◎
⚘⚘ *Commended*

Clive and Betty Beddows give you a warm welcome to their Georgian farmhouse set in 80 acres of farmland with many lovely walks. All bedrooms en suite with radio/alarms, TV, electric blankets and tea/coffee-making facilities. Five golf courses within ten mile radius. Beautiful walking area. Open all year.

13 New House Farm, Much Marcle, Ledbury, Herefordshire HR8 2PH

Mrs Anne Jordan
☎ 01531 660604
BB From £15
EM From £10
Sleeps 4
🖙(6) 🏕 🏇 ⚘ ◎
⚘ *Approved*

A friendly welcome awaits you at our delightful farmhouse enjoying panoramic views over Herefordshire, Worcestershire and Gloucestershire. Relax by a log fire on chilly evenings, or enjoy a swim in our outdoor pool during summer. Horses welcome by arrangement. Open all year.

14 Old Court Farm, Bredwardine, Herefordshire HR3 6BT

Sue Whittall
☎ 01981 500375
Mobile 0421 424575
BB From £20
EM From £15
Sleeps 4
🖙 ⚘ 🏇 ⚘ ⚘ 🏕 ⚘
⚘⚘ *Commended*

Old Court (featured on BBC Food programme) is a 14th century mediaeval manor situated on the banks of the River Wye. Ideal for the Wye Valley Walk. It has been carefully restored to preserve a wealth of beams and a 15ft fireplace. Central heating. Gardens enjoy beautiful views to the river. There are 2 four-poster bedrooms, 2 en suite and four-poster family room with private bathroom, all with teamakers. Evening meals. Phone for opening times.

15 Red Ley Farmhouse, Red Ley, Letton, Herefordshire HR3 6DT

Mary King
☎/Fax 01981 500438
BB From £17–£21
EM From £10
Sleeps 6
🖙(5) ⚘ 🏕 ◎
⚘⚘⚘ *Highly Commended*

Experience the friendly beamed atmosphere of Red Ley and its picturesque gardens, situated in the upper Wye Valley midway between Hay on Wye and Hereford. Safe parking, en suite rooms and delicious food. Open all year except Christmas.

16 Sink Green Farm, Rotherwas, Hereford HR2 6LE

David Jones
☎ 01432 870223
BB From £19–£25
Sleeps 6
🖙 🛏 ⚘ 🏕 ⚘
⚘⚘ *Commended*

Sink Green awaits you with a warm, friendly welcome to its 16th century farmhouse overlooking the River Wye and picturesque Herefordshire countryside yet only 3 miles from the cathedral city of Hereford. Comfortable bedrooms, one with four-poster bed, all en suite, tea/coffee-making facilities and colour TV. Large oak-beamed lounge and traditional farmhouse fare. Children welcome, pets by arrangement. AA listed. Open all year.

17 Upper Gilvach Farm, St Margarets, Vowchurch, Hereford HR2 0QY

Mrs Ruth Watkins
☎ 01981 510618
BB From £20–£28
EM From £12
Sleeps 6
🖙 🛏 ⚘ 🧍 🍴 🏕 ⚘
⚘⚘ *Commended*

Family-run farm between Golden Valley and Black Mountains. This 300-year-old farmhouse offers three spacious, attractively furnished bedrooms, all en suite with colour TV and hospitality trays. Peace and comfort in a relaxing atmosphere. Delicious evening meals and hearty farmhouse breakfasts using local wines and produce. Licensed, dinner optional. AA QQQQ Selected. Open all year.

The Vauld House Farm, Marden, Herefordshire HR1 3HA [18]

Mrs Judith Wells
☎ 01568 797347
Fax 01568 797366
BB From £20
EM From £13.50
Sleeps 5

🐴 ⅏ 🏕 ⚓ 🎿 🔱

♛♛ *Commended*

Situated 6 miles north of Hereford in beautiful countryside, this 17th century farmhouse offers traditionally furnished, comfortable en suite accommodation with guests' own lounge and dining room. Open log fires. All home cooking to a very high standard using fresh local produce. Guests may enjoy relaxing in the wooded and lawned gardens with carp ponds. Open all year except Christmas and New Year.

Warren Farm, Warren Lane, Lea, Ross on Wye, Herefordshire HR9 7LT [19]

Mrs Christine Whitehouse
☎/Fax 01989 750272
BB From £20–£24
Sleeps 6

🎿 ⚓

♛♛ *Commended*

A warm welcome awaits you in our beautifully restored 16th century Grade II listed farmhouse with a multitude of exposed beams and three inglenooks. Set in peaceful countryside on a mixed working farm. 1 double suite, 1 twin en suite, 1 double with private bathroom. All have TV, tea/coffee facilities. Two 18-hole golf courses within 3 miles and ideally situated for touring the Royal Forest of Dean, Wye Valley and the Vale of Leadon. Open Mar–Oct.

SELF-CATERING

Anvil Cottage, Grafton Villa, Grafton, Hereford, Herefordshire HR2 8ED [5]

Jennie Layton
☎/Fax 01432 268689
SC From £180–£300
Sleeps 5

🧍 🐕 ⅏ ⚓ 🎿 🐾

🐾 🐾 🐾 🐾 *Highly Commended*

Beams, natural wood and beautiful fabrics make our recently converted wainhouse into a very well equipped cottage for the discerning visitor. Comfortable, spacious twin and double bedded rooms, each en suite. Lovely open plan lounge leading to a sheltered patio. Suitable for disabled and wheelchair guests. Linen and electricity included. Open all year.

Apple Bough, Upper Newton Farmhouse, Kinnersley, Herefordshire HR3 6QB [20]

Pearl & Jon Taylor
☎/Fax 01544 327727
SC From £210–£290
Sleeps 4

🐴 ⅏ 🎿 ⚓ ◉

🐾 🐾 🐾 🐾

Highly Commended

Beautifully renovated stable block, with all modern amenities, four-poster, murals on walls, craftwork abounding. Sun patio, herb garden, ample parking, secluded and conveniently situated for black and white village trail, energetic and passive holiday activities! Please send for local interest brochures and further details. We look forward to meeting you. Open all year.
E mail: unewt@fclass.KC3Ltd.co.uk

Brooklyn, c/o Marlbrook Hall, Elton, Ludlow, Shropshire SY8 2HR [21]

Mrs Valerie Morgan
☎ 01568 770230
SC From £150–£280
Sleeps 6

🐴 🐎 🎿 ⚓

🐾 🐾 🐾 🐾 *Approved*

Situated on the Herefordshire/Shropshire border, ideal for exploring the market town of Ludlow, Mortimer Forest and Welsh Borders. Spacious accommodation consists of three bedroomed house with garden and garage. Fitted carpets and tastefully decorated. Colour TV, microwave oven, washing machine, tumble dryer, linen and towels included in price. Open all year.

22 Carey Dene and Rock House, Carey, c/o Folly Farm, Holme Lacy, Hereford HR2 6LS

Mrs Rita Price
☎ 01432 870259
SC From £160–£380
Sleeps 2–8 + cot
🐕 🐾 ✂ ◉
🔑🔑🔑–🔑🔑🔑🔑
Commended

Two oak-beamed cottages on traditional farm overlooking River Wye. Beautiful area between Hereford and Ross on Wye, for a peaceful holiday or short break. Access to the river, two minutes' walk to pub serving meals. Washing machine, microwave, colour TV, central heating. Electricity and linen included in charge. Open all year.

---

23 Mill House Flat, Woonton Court Farm, Leysters, Leominster, Herefordshire HR6 0HL

Mrs Elizabeth Thomas
☎/Fax 01568 750232
SC From £160–£250
Sleeps 3/4 + cot
🐕 🏃 🎿 🎵 ⊞ ▪
🔑🔑🔑🔑 *Commended*

Half-timbered brick and stone detached mill, recently converted to provide comfortable first floor self-contained accommodation. Open plan kitchen/dining room/ spacious sitting room, electric fire, colour TV. Night store heating and fitted carpets throughout. Linen/electricity included. Telephone. Sunny patio, parking, freedom to walk on the farm and enjoy a wealth of nature. Own farm produce. Short breaks. Open all year.

---

24 Moody Farm Cottage, Moody Farm, Longtown, Herefordshire HR2 0LW

Judy Stone
☎ 01873 860685
SC From £130–£285
Sleeps 4/5 + cot
🐕 ✂ ☕ 🎵 🎣
🔑🔑🔑 *Commended*

Swans on the lake, woodpeckers in the wood! Wonderful views and setting at foot of Black Mountains. Comfortable, very well equipped cottage, part of barn conversion. River, own lake, fishing and boating. Ideal for children. Walking, birdwatching and exploring castles. One double, one single, one single/twin. Open all year.

---

12 New House Farm Cottages, New House Farm, Barrell Lane, Longhope, Gloucestershire GL17 0LS

Mrs Elizabeth Beddows
☎/Fax 01452 830484
SC From £150–£350
Sleeps 4–5 + cot
🐕 🐾 🎵 ▪ ◉
🔑🔑
Commended

Newly converted cottages in peaceful surroundings. Well equipped with dishwashers, microwaves, TV, gas central heating, linen and electric all inclusive. Beautiful walking country. Evening meal available in farmhouse. Open all year.

---

25 Old Forge Cottage, Lyston Smithy, Wormelow, Nr Hereford HR2 8EL

Shirley Wheeler
☎ 01981 540625
SC From £160–£314
Sleeps 4 + cot
🐕 🐾 ▪
🔑🔑🔑🔑 *Commended*

The Forge cottage is all on one level and retains many original features. Large open plan living room, fully equipped kitchenette, one twin en suite, one double bedroom and bathroom. CH, telephone and TV. Linen included. 14 acres of gardens and grounds. 3 day breaks Nov–Mar. Open all year.

---

26 Poolspringe Farm Cottages, Much Birch, Hereford HR2 8JJ

David & Val Beaumont
☎/Fax 01981 540355
SC From £80–£285
Sleeps 1–7
🐕 🐾 ▪ ☕ 🎵
🔑🔑🔑🔑 *Approved*

Barn conversion on 17th century, 50-acre farm set in the orchards of south Herefordshire. Midway between Hereford and Ross on Wye. Indoor heated swimming pool, sauna, games room, large garden with games. Coarse fishing on farm. Dogs' walks. Pets very welcome. Reduced fees at Belmont Golf Course 7 miles away. Many excellent pubs for food. Lovely touring area within reach of Forest of Dean, Cotswolds and Wales. Open all year.

The Vauld House Farm, Marden, Hereford, Herefordshire HR1 3HA

Judith Wells
☎ 01568 797347
Fax 01568 797366
SC From £165–£280
EM From £13.50
Sleeps 2/5 + cot

⌖ ⋔ ⅄ ⌑ ⌑ ⌑
♟ ♟ ♟ ♟ *Commended*

Set amidst beautiful countryside on family stock farm midway between Hereford and Leominster, this skilfully converted Victorian hop kiln is spacious and well-equipped. Sleeps 5 + cot. Recently renovated 17th century Cider House, retaining character and charm. Ground floor sleeps 2. Lawned and wooded gardens with moat and ponds extend to over an acre. Open all year.

FOLLOW THE COUNTRY CODE

Leave nothing but footprints,
Take nothing but photographs,
Kill nothing but time!

Worcestershire

Group Contacts: 🅱🅱 *Mrs Pauline Grainger* ☎ *01299 404027*
🆂🅲 *Mr R Goodman* ☎ *01299 896500*

Worcestershire still has that flavour of Old England with flowering hedges, grazing pastures, rolling hills and bluebelled woodland, winding lanes and sleepy villages. To the north the Georgian town of Bewdley straddles the River Severn, fringed by the Wyre Forest where wild deer wander. Bromsgrove with its Georgian buildings and gabled houses and Droitwich Spa with the High Street of timber framed shops.

Follow the gentle flow of the Severn, Teme and Avon as they make their way through the county passing through Evesham, Pershore and Upton-on-Severn. Climb the rolling hills of Malvern, Abberley, Woodbury and Clee. Discover the market town of Tenbury Wells and Malvern with its Priory and famous drinking water flowing freely at St Annes Well and Holy Well. At the south-east tip of our county lies Broadway, the picturesque Cotswold village.

Worcestershire is steeped in history and where better to discover this than Worcester itself, the heart of our county. Dominated by its grand and beautiful cathedral, the city has many interesting museums, the Commandery with its Civil War connections, the Royal Worcester Porcelain factory and the Guild Hall.

The area offers great variety and you will be sure of a warm welcome.

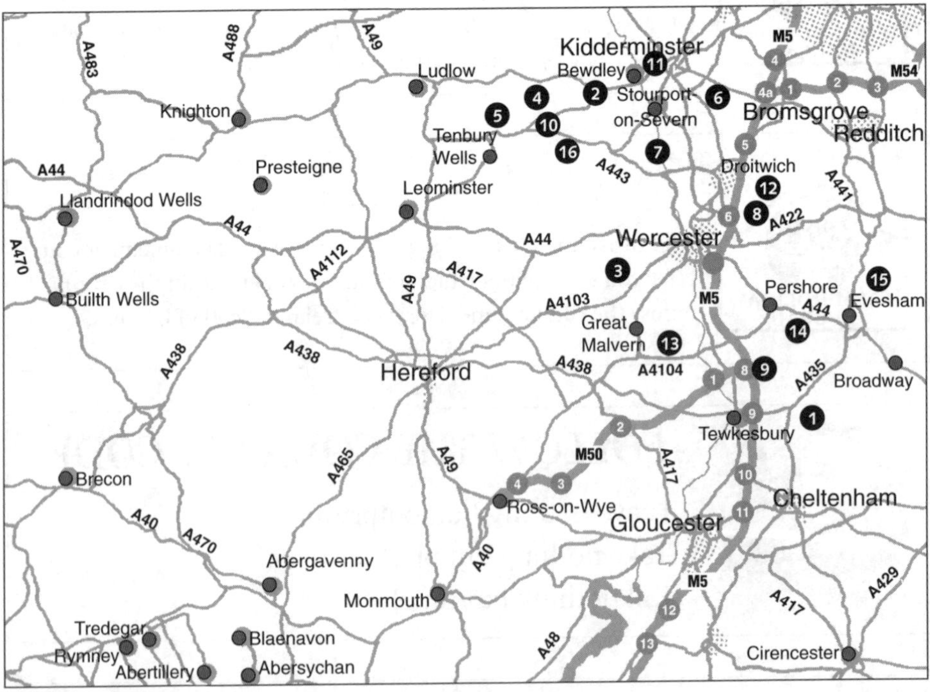

BED AND BREAKFAST
(and evening meal)

Alstone Fields Farm, Teddington Hands, Nr Tewkesbury, Gloucestershire GL20 8NG   **1**

Jane Rogers
☎ **01242 620592**
🅱 **From £20–£25**
Sleeps 12
🛏(3) ✂ 🏠 ♞
♛♛ *Highly Commended*

Enjoy the friendliest welcome on our traditional family farm, surrounded by sheep, horses and dogs. Wake up in pretty en suite suite rooms to splendid views of rolling countryside and the delicious smell of bacon! We promise a memorably peaceful holiday and a perfect base from which to explore the picturesque Cotswolds.

Bullockhurst Farm, Rock, Nr Bewdley, Worcestershire DY14 9SE   **2**

Margaret Nott
☎ **01299 832305**
🅱 **From £18.50**
Sleeps 4
🛏 🏠 ♞ ◉
♛♛ *Highly Commended*

Come and savour the peace and tranquillity of our Georgian farmhouse set in large gardens and beautiful undulating countryside. En suite facilities. Well situated for exploring the Wyre Forest, Bewdley with its Severn Railway and enjoying the panoramic views over the Worcestershire and Shropshire countryside. Excellent meals available in village. Children welcome. 1½ miles off A456.

Chirkenhill, Leigh Sinton, Malvern, Worcestershire WR13 5DE   **3**

Mrs Sarah Wenden
☎ **01886 832205**
🅱 **From £18**
Sleeps 6
🛏 🐕 🏠
♛♛ *Commended*

We welcome guests to Chirkenhill – or perhaps you will recognise us as 'Arkley House' in the ITV series 'Noah's Ark' broadcast last autumn. Come and relax in the peace and quiet of our lovely old farmhouse amidst some of Worcestershire's most beautiful countryside. Excellent walking or drive the 'Elgar Route'. Dogs/horses housed by arrangement. Open all year.

Clay Farm, Clows Top, Nr Bewdley, Worcestershire DY14 9NN   **4**

Mike & Ella Grinnall
☎ **01299 832421**
🅱 **From £17.50**
Sleeps 6
🛏(3) ⚓ 🚲 👜 🏠
♛♛ *Highly Commended*

Fully centrally heated farmhouse with outstanding views. Friendly atmosphere, homemade cakes and tea on arrival. En suite bedrooms with tea making facilities. Full English breakfast. Spacious TV lounge, log fires, sun lounge overlooking trout and coarse fishing pools. Close to Bewdley, Ludlow, Severn Valley Railway and many attractions. On Worcestershire and Shropshire borders on the B4202 Cleobury Mortimer Road. Open all year.

Clod Hall, Milson, nr Kidderminster, Worcestershire DY14 0BJ   **5**

Mrs C Morrison
☎ **01584 781421**
🅱 **From £17–£25**
Sleeps 3
🛏 🐕 🏠 ❀
Listed *Commended*

Comfortable house on road between Tenbury Wells and Cleobury Mortimer commanding beautiful views over woods and farmland. Horses are bred here. Near Clee Hills, historic town of Ludlow, market towns of Tenbury Wells and Leominster. CH. One double, one single, both with TV, tea/coffee. Generous breakfasts with homemade preserves. Packed lunches available and good local pubs. Children welcome. Open all year.

---

6   **The Durrance,** Berry Lane, Upton Warren, Bromsgrove, Worcestershire B61 9EL

Helen Hirons
☎/Fax 01562 777533
BB From £20–£25
EM From £7
Sleeps 6

Commended

We welcome you to our Victorian farmhouse in picturesque surroundings, set in large garden. Comfortably furnished en suite rooms, one downstairs bedroom and family accommodation. Full central heating, log fire in winter. Guests' lounge with colour TV. Convenient for NEC, 5 miles M5 J5, 7 miles M42 J1. Open all year.

---

7   **Eden Farm,** Ombersley, Nr Droitwich, Worcester WR9 0JX

Bill & Ann Yardley
☎ 01905 620244
BB From £20–£22
Sleeps 5

Commended

Come and enjoy our 17th century home with its lovely garden, fishing on the Severn and 5-acre marsh with over 100 species of flora. It's just off the A449 and the Wychavon Way, a wonderful centre for exploring the heart of England, with Worcester 7 miles, Droitwich 6 miles. Bedrooms are tastefully decorated, with bathrooms en suite, tea/coffee-making facilities and TV. Homemade produce and preserves used. Closed Christmas.

---

8   **The Green Farm,** Crowle Green, nr Worcester, Worcestershire WR7 4AB

Mrs Lucy Harris
☎/Fax 01905 381807
BB From £20–£22
Sleeps 3

Commended

A peaceful oak-beamed Grade II listed farmhouse set in large garden and surrounding farmland. Comfortable rooms with own basin, private bathroom, tea/coffee-making facilities and CH. Guests' also have sole use of lounge with wood-burning stove and colour TV. Excellent meals within easy walking distance at local country pub. Open all year.

---

9   **Home Farm,** Bredons Norton, Tewkesbury, Gloucestershire GL20 7HA

Mick & Anne Meadows
☎ 01684 772322
BB From £18–£20
EM From £15
Sleeps 6

Commended

Mixed 150-acre family-run farm with sheep, cattle and poultry. Situated in an extremely quiet, unspoilt little village nestling under Bredon Hill. Superb position for walking, an excellent base for touring or relaxing. The 18th century farmhouse is very comfortably furnished. All bedrooms have en suite bathrooms. Gas CH. Good home cooking, evening meal by arrangement. Lounge, TV. Children welcome. Open mid Jan–mid Dec.

---

10   **Hunt House Farm,** Frith Common, between Tenbury Wells and Bewdley, Worcestershire WR15 8JY

Chris & Jane Keel
☎/Fax 01299 832277
BB From £18
Sleeps 6
(8)

Highly Commended

This beautiful, 400-year old Elizabethan farmhouse, elevated amidst rolling hills on our arable and sheep farm, has incredible views. Relax and enjoy total peace, genuine hospitality, oak beams, an inglenook fireplace, antique furniture, en suite bedrooms, excellent local eating houses and tea and homemade cake on arrival. *'Which'* recommended. Closed Christmas and January.

---

11   **Lightmarsh Farm,** Crundalls Lane, Bewdley, Worcestershire DY12 1NE

Mrs Pauline Grainger
☎ 01299 404027
BB From £20–£25
Sleeps 4
(10)

Highly Commended

Small, pasture farm in elevated position with fine views. Ideal for walking, wildlife and exploring Heart of England. The house is approx 200 years old, with full CH and comfortable accommodation; TV lounge with inglenook fireplace. Both rooms have private facilities. Truly rural setting, only 1 mile from Bewdley's shops and restaurants, Severn Valley Railway and West Midland Safari Park. Brochure on request. Closed Christmas and New Year.

Phepson Farm, Himbleton, Droitwich, Worcestershire WR9 7JZ   (12)

David & Tricia Havard
☎ 01905 391205
[BB] From £20–£25
Sleeps 8
🐴 🐓 ⚡ 🧗 ⛴ 🚗 ◉
👹 👹 *Highly Commended*

In our 17th century oak beamed farmhouse we offer a warm welcome, good food and a relaxed and informal atmosphere. The recently converted Granary has two ground floor bedrooms whilst the farmhouse has double, and family accommodation. All rooms en suite with colour TV. Peaceful surroundings on family stock farm. Walking on Wychavon Way. Featured on 'Wish You Were Here'. Open all year except Christmas and New Year.

Tiltridge Farm & Vineyard, Upper Hook Road, Upton-on-Severn, Worcestershire WR8 0SA   (13)

Sandy Barker
☎ 01684 592906
Fax 01684 594142
[BB] From £19–£25
Sleeps 6
🐴 🐓 ⚡ ⛴ 🍴
👹 👹 *Highly Commended*

Period family farmhouse lying between the Malvern Hills and the attractive riverside town of Upton-on-Severn. Set in its own vineyard, the house is fully renovated with two doubles, one twin/family room. All rooms are en suite with TV. Warm welcome, bumper breakfast and plenty of our own wine available! New vineyard centre and vineyard walk open. Four minutes from the Three Counties Showground. Open all year.

SELF-CATERING

The Granary, c/o Phepson Farm, Himbleton, Droitwich, Worcestershire WR9 7JZ   (12)

David & Tricia Havard
☎ 01905 391205
[SC] From £160–£230
Sleeps 2/3
🐴 🐓 ⛴ 🚗 🍴 ◉
🎠 🎠 🎠 🎠
Commended

The recent conversion of the old granary is reached by an outside stone staircase. The light and airy flat is double-glazed and very comfortably furnished. Situated on working stock farm in peaceful surroundings. Entrance through stable door. Fitted kitchen, colour TV, double bedroom with en suite bathroom. Linen, electricity, night storage heating included. Open all year.

The Granary, Tibbitts Farm, Great Comberton, nr Pershore, Worcestershire WR10 3DT   (14)

Mrs Jenny Newbury
☎ 01386 710210
[SC] From £160–£260
Sleeps 3
🐴(5) ⚡ 🍴 🍴
🎠 🎠 🎠 🎠
Commended

The Granary is attached to 16th century farmhouse and reached by external stone stairs. Wealth of exposed beams with kitchen/dining area, lounge, bedroom and bathroom for 2/3. Peaceful village location, views to open countryside and walking directly to Bredon Hill. Central for Cotswolds, Malvern Hills and Stratford. Linen and electricity included. Open all year.

Hill Barn Orchard, Evesham Road, Church Lench, Evesham, Worcestershire WR11 4UB   (15)

Marlene Badger
☎ 01386 871035
[SC] From £252–£586
Sleeps 4/6
🐴 🐓 ⚡ 🧗 🚗 🚗 🍴 ⛴
🎠 🎠 🎠 *Commended*

Attractive, comfortably furnished house 4 miles from historic Evesham. On edge of village in quiet orchard setting. Views, lakes wildlife, trout fishing. Spring blossom trail, Elgar route, Cotswolds, Stratford, Ragley Hall. Ideal restful or touring holiday. Stratford 10 miles, Tewkesbury 12 miles, Broadway 12 miles. Open Easter–end Oct.

15   **Hill Barn Orchard – The Annexe,** Evesham Road, Church Lench, Evesham, Worcs WR11 4UB

Marlene Badger
☎ 01386 871035
[SC] From £196–£417
Sleeps 4
🐴 🐥 ✂ 人 🛋 🛍 ☂ ☂
🐾 🐾 🐾 *Commended*

Comfortably furnished, situated on the edge of village in quiet orchard setting, 4 miles from historic Evesham. Views, lakes, wildlife, trout fishing. Ideal for Cotswolds, Stratford, etc. One twin and one adjoining double room, both en suite. Lounge and kitchen diner on ground floor. Can be let in conjunction with Hill Barn Orchard (up to 10 people). Open all year.

16   **Old Yates Cottages,** Old Yates Farm, Abberley, Nr Worcester, Worcestershire WR6 6AT

Sarah & Richard Goodman
☎/Fax 01299 896500
[SC] From £125–£295
Sleeps 2/6
人 🐥 🐕 🛍 ☂ ☂ ◎
🐾 🐾 🐾 🐾 *Commended*

We invite you to enjoy the home comforts of our cottages, to experience their tranquil surroundings and to relax in our beautiful countryside. Games facilities and launderette on site. 1 mile from village; many restaurants, leisure and recreational facilities within easy reach. Please send for brochure. Open all year.

9   **Stable Cottage,** Home Farm, Bredons Norton, Tewkesbury, Gloucestershire GL20 7HA

Mick & Anne Meadows
☎ 01684 772322
[SC] From £200–£280
Sleeps 5
🐴 🐥 ✂ ☂ 🛍
🐾 🐾 🐾 🐾 *Commended*

Delightful Cotswold stone stable/barn conversion on a mixed working family farm in a quiet and picturesque village under Bredon Hill. Very cosy and tastefully furnished. Full central heating, lots of beams, own paddock. Perfect location for touring the Cotswolds, Severn Valley and Malverns with many wonderful walks. Open all year.

FINDING YOUR ACCOMMODATION

FARM HOLIDAY BUREAU

The Group contacts at the beginning of each section can always help you find a vacancy in your chosen area.

Warwickshire

Group Contact: *Miss Deborah Lea* ☎/Fax 01295 770652

The native county of William Shakespeare has a lot to offer. With its mediaeval castles, historic towns of Warwick, Stratford-upon-Avon, Leamington Spa, Rugby and Kenilworth and its delightful countryside.

Stratford-upon-Avon is the provincial home of the Royal Shakespeare Company who perform in the three theatres near the River Avon. There are many half-timbered buildings in the town, several of which have associations with the great bard and the shopping centre satisfies the most discerning shopper. A few miles up the River Avon lies the town of Warwick with its magnificent mediaeval castle brought to life by Madame Tussaud's vignettes.

At Kenilworth, the Castle can be seen. Close by is the Royal Showground which hosts the Royal Show every July and is a year-round agricultural centre. Royal Leamington Spa is an elegant Regency town with wide streets, crescents and fine gardens and famous for its healing waters.

There are also many pretty villages throughout the county and stately homes such as Packwood House, Ragley Hall, Charlecote Park, Baddesley Clinton and Coughton Court.

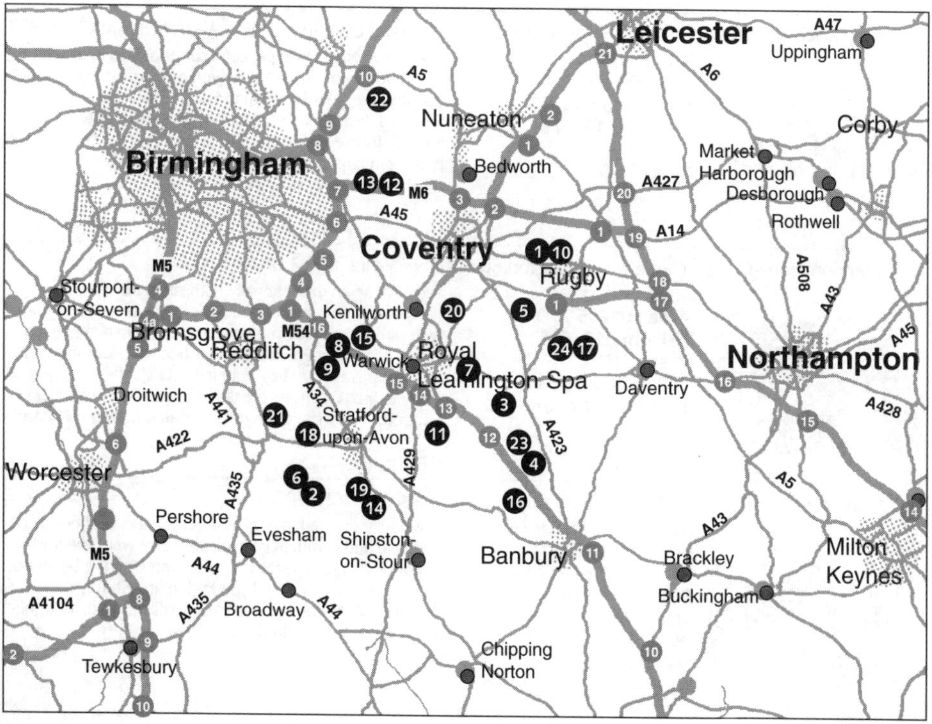

BED AND BREAKFAST

(and evening meal)

1   **The Byre,** Lords Hill Farm, Coalpit Lane, Wolston, Coventry CV8 3GB

Mrs Betty Gibbs
☎ 01203 542098
⊞ From £18–£25
Sleeps 6
♋(5) ✗ ✗ 🛄
🌠 *Commended*

A warm welcome awaits guests to our home set in a quiet country lane on a 200-acre sheep/arable farm. Attractive double/twin bedrooms, 1 en suite, 2 with washbasins. Dining and sitting room with colour TV and full CH. Ideally situated for visiting Rugby, Leamington, Warwick, Stratford, NEC and NAC. Numerous places nearby for evening meals. East of Fosse Way on Wolston crossroads. Non smokers only. Open all year except Christmas.

2   **Church Farm,** Dorsington, Stratford-upon-Avon, Warwickshire CV37 8AX

Mrs Marian J Walters
☎ 01789 720471
and 0831 504194
Fax 01789 720830
⊞ From £16.50–£19
Sleeps 14
👤 🐎 🐎 ← 🎪 🛄
🌠🌠 *Commended*

A warm welcome awaits you at our mixed working farm with lake, equestrian course and woodlands to explore. Situated on edge of quiet pretty village yet ideal for touring Stratford, Warwick, Cotswolds, NAC, NEC, Worcester and Evesham. Most bedrooms en suite, all with tea/coffee and TV. Stabling and fishing available. Open all year.

3   **The Coach House,** Snowford Hall Farm, Hunningham, Royal Leamington Spa, Warwickshire CV33 9ES

Rudi Hancock
☎ 01926 632297
Fax 01926 633599
⊞ From £18–£20
Sleeps 6
♋ 🛄 🍴
Applied

A warm welcome and peaceful surroundings in converted barn farmhouse on 200-acre working farm in rolling countryside. Near the Roman Fosse Way, ideal for visiting Stratford, Warwick, Leamington, Cotswolds, NAC and NEC. 2 double rooms en suite, 1 twin room with basin and bathroom next door. Singles extra. CH. Full breakfast. Open all year (closed Christmas & New Year).

4   **Crandon House,** Avon Dassett, Leamington Spa, Warwickshire CV33 0AA

Deborah Lea
☎/Fax 01295 770652
⊞ From £19–£25
Sleeps 10
♋(12) 🐎 💷 🎪 🛄
🌠🌠 *Highly Commended*

We offer an an exceptionally high standard of accommodation and a friendly welcome on our small farm with rare breeds. Set in peaceful countryside with beautiful views. Large garden. Full CH. 5 attractive bedrooms with en suite/private facilities, colour TV, tea/coffee tray and many extras. Extensive breakfast menu. Easy access to Stratford, Warwick, Cotswolds. Located between J11 and 12 on M40 (4 miles). Closed Christmas.

5   **Frankton Grounds Farm,** Frankton, Nr Rugby, Warwickshire CV23 9PD

Mrs Mary Pritchard
☎ 01926 632391
⊞ From £15–£17.50
EM From £8.50
Sleeps 4
♋ 🐎 🛄
Listed *Approved*

Beautifully situated in a mixed farm of horses, sheep, pedigree and commercial cattle. A warm welcome for the visitor who enjoys peace and quiet yet, with the benefit of easy access to Warwick, Leamington and Stratford. 2½ miles M45. Full CH, log fires, excellent food. 1 double with bathroom, 1 twin. Open all year.

Glebe Farm, Exhall, Alcester, Warwickshire B49 6EA
❻

John & Margaret Canning
☎/Fax 01789 772202
🅱🅱 From £17–£20
Sleeps 6
🐎 🐕 🎠 🛢
🦆 Commended

Shakespeare named our village 'Dodging Exhall' and it has somehow 'dodged' the passing of time, so if you want a true taste of rural England, come and relax in our quaint old farmhouse – parts of it dating from Tudor times – with its log fires, four-poster bed and country hospitality. 1 double, 1 twin, 2 singles, tea/coffee trays, electric blankets. Smoking in lounge. Payphone. Laundry. Ample parking. Open all year (closed Christmas & New Year).

Hill Farm, Lewis Road, Radford Semele, Leamington Spa, Warwickshire CV31 1UX
❼

Mrs Rebecca Gibbs
☎ 01926 337571
🅱🅱 From £17–£22
Sleeps 10
🐎 ⅍ 🚐 🛢
🦆🦆 Commended

Hill Farm is a comfortable, friendly farmhouse situated in 350 acres of mixed farmland. Excellent breakfasts, large garden, attractive double/twin/single bedrooms, some en suite, with CH and tea/coffee-making facilities. Comfortable TV lounge, quiet room, guests' bathroom. Children welcome. AA and Farm Holiday Guide award winner. Caravanning/Camping Club certificated site. Ideal for Shakespeare Country. Open all year (closed Christmas).

Holland Park Farm, Buckley Green, Henley in Arden, Nr Solihull, Warwickshire B95 5QF
❽

Mrs Kathleen Connolly
☎/Fax 01564 792625
🅱🅱 From £18–£25
Sleeps 6
🐎 🐕 🎠 🛢
🦆🦆 Commended

A Georgian style farmhouse, set in 300 acres of peaceful farmland, including the historic grounds of 'The Mount' and other interesting walks. Large garden with pond. Livestock includes cattle, sheep and Irish Draught horses. Ideally situated in Shakespeare's country, within easy reach of Birmingham International Airport, NEC, NAC, Stratford-upon-Avon, Warwick and the Cotswolds. Open all year.

Irelands Farm, Irelands Lane, Henley-in-Arden, Nr Solihull, Warwickshire B95 5SA
❾

Pamela Shaw
☎/Fax 01564 792476
🅱🅱 From £17.50–£20
Sleeps 6
🐕 ⅍ 🎠 🛢
🦆🦆 Highly Commended

If a quiet, relaxing holiday is what you are looking for, then visit our late Georgian farmhouse. Large rooms all with own bath/shower, TV, tea/coffee-making facilities, radio, CH. Set in 220 acres of peaceful farmland. Close to National Exhibition Centre, Stratford-upon-Avon, Warwick, National Agricultural Centre. Looking forward to meeting you. Open all year (closed Christmas & New Year).

Lawford Hill Farm, Lawford Heath Lane, Nr Rugby, Warwickshire CV23 9HG
❿

Mrs Susan Moses
☎ 01788 542001
🅱🅱 From £18–£25
Sleeps 10
🐎 🐕 ⅍ 🛢 ☕
🦆🦆 Commended

You will find a warm welcome at our Grade II listed Georgian farmhouse and converted stables set in an attractive garden, on a mixed family farm. Full CH, log fire, attractive double and twin bedrooms, some en suite. Fishing available. Situated two miles from Rugby. Easy access to Stratford, NAC and NEC. Open all year except Christmas and New Year.

Lower Watchbury Farm, Wasperton Lane, Barford, Warwickshire CV35 8DH
⓫

Valerie Eykyn
☎/Fax 01926 624772
🅱🅱 From £19.50–£22.50
Sleeps 5
🐎 ⅍ 🛢 🐎
🦆🦆 Highly Commended

In the heart of Shakespeare Country, we offer you a warm welcome in our luxurious accommodation with outstanding views over Warwickshire. 1 large twin/family en suite room with lounge area, 1 double en suite, 1 small double with own bathroom. All have colour TV, tea/coffee facilities. Excellent farmhouse breakfast. Village pubs for dinners. Large garden. Warwick, Stratford, NAC, NEC and Cotswolds nearby. Open all year except Christmas.

12 Maxstoke Hall Farm, Fillongley Road, Maxstoke, Nr Coleshill, Birmingham, Warwickshire B46 2QT

Mrs Heather Green
☎/Fax 01675 463237
[BB] £27
Sleeps 5
❦ ✂ ⚒ ♨ ⛺ ▲
♛♛ *Highly Commended*

Elegant farmhouse, built in 1632, and set in beautiful countryside. Bedrooms have en suite facilities, TV, hostess tray. Comfortable oak-beamed dining and sitting rooms for use by guests. Evening meals (from £13) by prior notice. Situated 3 miles from Coleshill, 5 mins from M6 and M42. 15 mins from National Exhibition Centre, Birmingham Airport and International Railway Station. Open all year (closed Christmas & New Year).

---

13 Packington Lane Farm, Coleshill, Warwickshire B46 3JJ

Constance Harcourt
☎/Fax 01675 462228
[BB] From £20–£25
Sleeps 5
❦ ✂ ✂ ⚒ ♨ ▲
♛♛ *Commended*

A warm welcome awaits you in a rural oasis when you stay in this charming 17th century farmhouse. Tastefully furnished, comfortable rooms. Full English breakfast served on fine china. Large gardens and parking on a working farm, with pleasant views over surrounding countryside. Within 4 miles of the National Exhibition Centre and Birmingham Airport. Easy access from M6 J4 and M42 J6 & 9.

---

14 The Poplars, Mansell Farm, Newbold on Stour, Stratford on Avon, Warwickshire CV37 8BZ

Judith Spencer
☎ 01789 450540
[BB] From £16–£18
EM From £9
Sleeps 6
❦ ✂ ✂ ▲
Listed *Commended*

A warm welcome awaits you on our working dairy farm. Enjoy the views of the Cotswolds from our modern farmhouse which is in easy reach of Sratford, Warwick, Oxford and NEC. 1 family and 1 twin, both en suite and 1 single with washbasin. All have TV, tea tray and CH. Good food or walk to local hostelry. Open all year except Christmas and New Year.

---

15 Shrewley Pools Farm, Haseley, Warwickshire CV35 7HB

Mrs Cathy Dodd
☎ 01926 484315
[BB] From £20–£25
EM From £10
Sleeps 6
❦ ✂ ⛺ ▲
♛♛ *Commended*

Why not sample the delights of staying in a beautiful 17th century traditional farmhouse? Set in an acre of landscaped garden with 4-acre pool. Shrewley Pools has many interesting features, including timbered barn, huge fireplaces, and beamed ceilings. 2 bedrooms, both en suite, with tea/coffee tray. As featured in *The Times*. Close to Warwick, Stratford-upon-Avon, the NEC and NAC. Open all year (closed Christmas).

---

16 Sor Brook House Farm, Horley, Banbury, Oxfordshire OX15 6BL

Yvonne Prickett
☎ 01295 738121
[BB] From £20–£25
EM From £15
Sleeps 4
❦(10) ✂ ⚒ ♨ ▲ ⚘

Tea and homemade cake await you in this charming stone farmhouse with oak beams and log fires. 1 twin with en suite, 1 twin with private bathroom. Full CH, colour TV, tea/coffee-making facilities. Guests' own sitting and dining rooms. Large, attractive gardens, peaceful walks. Stabling available.

---

17 Tibbit Farm, Nethercote, Flecknoe, Nr Rugby, Warwickshire CV23 8AS

Alison Mills
☎ 01788 890239
[BB] From £22.50–£25
Sleeps 4
❦ ✂ ✂ ▲ ⛺
♛♛ *Highly Commended*

Retreat from the trials of life to the seclusion and tranquillity of our 17th century farmhouse idyllically situated within acres of rolling countryside, where we offer luxurious bed and breakfast accommodation. The pretty bedrooms have en suite or private bathrooms, colour TVs, tea/coffee making facilities. Tibbits is ideally situated for exploring the many places of historic, scenic and cultural interest in the area.

Walcote Farm, Walcote, Haselor, Alcester, Warwickshire B49 6LY (18)

Prim & John Finnemore
☎/Fax 01789 488264
BB From £18–£19
Sleeps 4
🐎 🐓 ✂ ☕ 🎾 💼
🌸🌸 *Commended*

Come and enjoy the relaxing atmosphere at our attractive 16th century oak-beamed farmhouse with inglenook fireplaces, set in a tranquil, picturesque hamlet near Stratford-upon-Avon. En suite double and twin rooms with TV/Fastext, tea/coffee-making facilities and lovely views. Full central heating with log fires in winter. Ideal for Shakespeare's properties, Warwick Castle, NEC and the Cotswolds. Closed Christmas and New Year.

Whitchurch Farm, Wimpstone, Stratford-upon-Avon, Warwickshire CV37 8NS (19)

Mrs Joan James
☎/Fax 01789 450275
BB From £17–£18
EM From £10
Sleeps 6
🐎 ⚤ 📺 💼
🌸🌸 *Commended*

Lovely Georgian farmhouse set in park-like surroundings in peaceful Stour Valley 4½ miles from Stratford. Very convenient for Warwick Castle and Shakespeare properties. Ideal for touring the Cotswolds by car or rambling. The bedrooms are large and well furnished, all with en suite bathrooms, CH and tea/coffee-making facilities. Separate dining room and sitting room for guests. Open all year (closed Christmas Day).

SELF-CATERING

Furzen Hill Farm Cottages, c/o Furzen Hill Farm, Cubbington Heath, Leamington Spa, Warks CV32 6QZ (20)

Mrs Christine Whitfield
☎/Fax 01926 424791
SC From £100–£300
Sleeps 4/7
🐎 🐓 💼
🏠 🏠 🏠 *Commended*

Furzen Hill is a mixed farm. The cottage is part of 17th century farmhouse with a large shared garden. Sleeping 7. The Barn and Dairy Cottages, both recently converted, each sleep 4. Dairy Cottage has its own small garden. The Barn shares the Cottage garden. All have the use of tennis court. Situated within easy reach of NAC, NEC, Warwick and Stratford. Open all year.

The Granary, c/o Glebe Farm, Kinwarton, Alcester, Warwickshire B49 6HB (21)

Susan Kinnersley
☎/Fax 01789 762554
SC From £85–£140
Sleeps 2
✂ 💼 🎾
🏠 🏠 🏠 *Commended*

Off the beaten track, yet near the small market town of Alcester, this cottage retains many interesting features of the original granary combined with modern standards of warmth and comfort. The farm is bounded by the River Alne and there are a variety of attractive country walks in the area. Linen provided, colour TV. Car space. Short breaks by arrangement. Open all year.

Hipsley Farm Cottages, Hipsley Lane, Hurley, Atherstone, Warwickshire CV9 2LR (22)

Mrs Ann Prosser
☎/Fax 01827 872437
SC From £220–£340
Sleeps 2/4 + cots
♿ 🐎 🐓 ☕ – 🎾 💼
🏠 🏠 🏠 🏠
Highly Commended

Hipsley Farm is situated in beautiful rolling countryside. Very peaceful and quiet yet only 3 miles from jct10, M42/A5, so easy access to all the Midlands. The barns and cowshed have been carefully converted into 6 very comfortable, individually furnished cottages. Fully equipped including gas CH, colour TV, all bed linen and towels. Laundry facilities and putting green. Ample parking on site. Open all year.

(9) **Irelands Farm Cottages,** Irelands Lane, Henley in Arden, Warwickshire B95 5SA

Pamela Shaw
☎/Fax 01564 792476
[SC] From £130–£300
Sleeps 2/4
Highly Commended

Four attractively converted oak-beamed cottages in courtyard on 220-acre working farm. Very quiet location yet within 3 miles of M42/M40 junction. All cottages centrally heated and tastefully furnished, and equipped to a high standard. Linen provided. Private patios. Open all year except Christmas and New Year.

(23) **Knightcote Farm Cottages,** The Bake House, Knightcote, nr Leamington Spa CV33 0SF

Fiona Walker
☎ 01295 770637
Fax 01295 770135
[SC] From £280–£495
Sleeps 4/6
Highly Commended

Escape and relax to the quiet and historic village of Knightcote. These three newly converted cottages have been lavishly equipped and furnished to ensure you are cosy and comfortable. Explore the many beautiful lanes and footpaths. One cottage wheelchair friendly. Adjacent car parking. No smoking. Open all year.

(24) **Little Biggin,** c/o Broadwell House Farm, Broadwell, Rugby, Warwickshire CV23 8HF

Mrs Linda Denham
☎/Fax 01926 812347
[SC] From £200–£300
Sleeps 4
(12) *Commended*

Attractive stone cottage with exposed beams, well equipped and furnished, with full central heating. Radio and colour TV. Cosy double and twin bedrooms have sloping ceilings. Bathroom has shower. Gas hob, electric oven, microwave in modern kitchen. Ample parking. Outstanding views and tranquil walks. Peacefully situated. Linen, electricity and gas included. Open all year.

FARM HOLIDAY BUREAU

Please mention **Stay on a Farm** when booking

FARM HOLIDAY BUREAU

Our Internet Address is
http://www.webscape.co.uk/farmaccom/

CONFIRM BOOKINGS

Disappointments can arise from misunderstandings over the telephone. Please write to confirm your booking.

Cotswolds & Royal Forest of Dean

Group Contact: *Barbara Scudamore* ☎/Fax 01242 602344

The villages and scenic beauty of the Cotswolds are famed throughout the world. The many honey-coloured villages include Bibury, Broadway, Painswick and Lower Slaughter while some of the finest churches in the country are at Northleach, Fairford and Winchcombe which also has Sudeley Castle. Along the River Severn the villages have black and white half-timbered cottages and cattle graze peacefully in the orchards and meadows. Gloucester with its cathedral, the elegant Regency town of Cheltenham and picturesque Tewkesbury with its 12th century abbey are in the Severn Vale. There are numerous visitor attractions in the main towns and villages while further afield are Berkeley Castle and Sir Peter Scott's Wildfowl Trust at Slimbridge.

Bordered by two rivers, the Severn and the Wye, is the beautiful and romantic Forest of Dean, ancient hunting grounds of kings and still covered by oak woodlands.

Scattered through the Forest are mining towns such as Cinderford, Coleford and Lydney. Below Symonds Yat, the River Wye meanders dramatically in a most attractive wooded gorge.

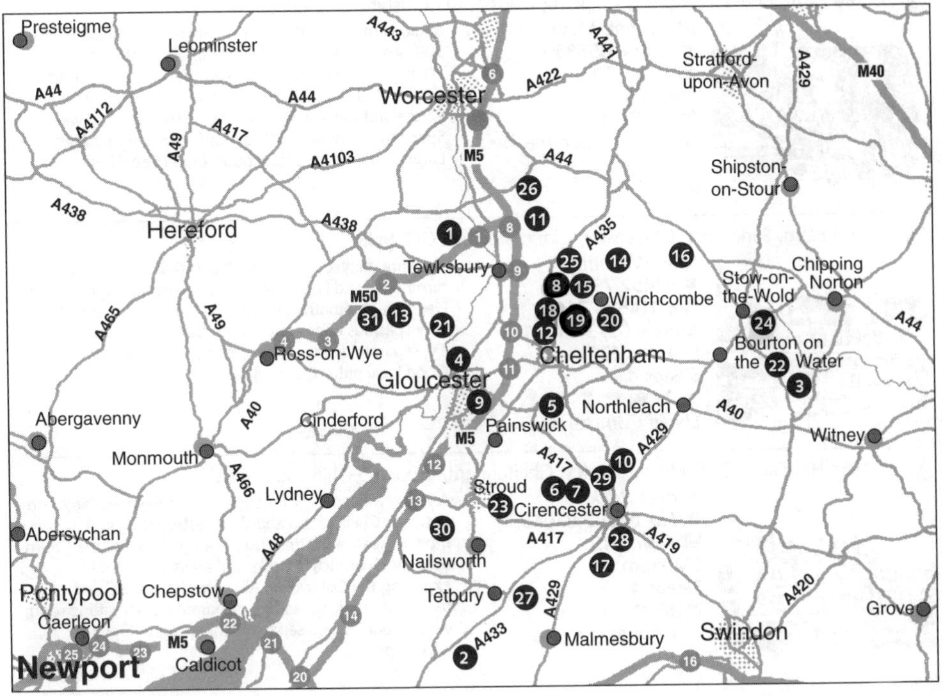

<figure>
Map showing the Cotswolds & Royal Forest of Dean region with numbered locations, including Presteigme, Leominster, Worcester, Stratford-upon-Avon, Hereford, Tewkesbury, Winchcombe, Stow-on-the-Wold, Chipping Norton, Ross-on-Wye, Gloucester, Cheltenham, Bourton on the Water, Cinderford, Northleach, Witney, Abergavenny, Monmouth, Lydney, Painswick, Stroud, Cirencester, Abersychan, Nailsworth, Pontypool, Chepstow, Tetbury, Malmesbury, Swindon, Grove, Caerleon, Newport, Caldicot.
</figure>

BED AND BREAKFAST

(and evening meal)

---

1 Abbots Court, Church End, Twyning, Tewkesbury, Gloucestershire GL20 6DA

Bernie Williams
☎/Fax 01684 292515
BB **From £16–£18**
Sleeps 15
🛏 🧒 🐕 🏇 ♨
🌸🌸 *Commended*

Lovely, quiet farmhouse in 350 acres between Cotswolds and Malverns. All bedrooms have colour TV, most en suite, tea-making facilities. Large lounge, separate dining room, excellent home cooked food. Licensed bar. 3 games rooms with pool table, table tennis, children's TV room, grass tennis court, bowling green, children's play area on lawn. Superb touring area. River and lake fishing on the farm. Open all year (except Christmas and New Year).

---

2 Avenue Farm, Knockdown, Tetbury, Gloucestershire GL8 8QY

Sonja King
☎ 01454 238207
Fax 01454 238033
BB **From £17.50–£20**
Sleeps 6
🛏 🐾 🏇
Listed *Commended*

Westonbirt Arboretum adjoins our farm with many miles of walks and a large summer programme of events. We are also near the cities of Bath and Bristol and delightful villages of Lacock and Castle Combe. 'Home from home' is our motto. Open all year.

---

3 Bould Farm, Bould, Nr Idbury, Chipping Norton, Oxfordshire OX7 6RT

Mrs Lynne Meyrick
☎ 01608 658850
BB **From £20–£25**
Sleeps 6
🛏 🐾 🏇 ♨
🌸🌸 *Highly Commended*

Bould Farm is a 17th century Cotswold farmhouse on a 300-acre family farm set in beautiful countryside, 10 minutes' drive from Stow-on-the-Wold and Bourton-on-the-Water and Burford. Within easy reach of Blenheim Palace and the Cotswold Wildlife Park. Children welcome. Spacious rooms with TV, tea/coffee-making facilities. Large garden. Good local pubs. Open Feb–Nov.

---

4 Brawn Farm, Sandhurst, Gloucester, Gloucestershire GL2 9NR

Sally Williams
☎ 01452 731010
Fax 01452 731102
Mobile 0973 313418
BB **From £20**
Sleeps 4
🛏 🧒 🐕 🐾 🏇 ♨ ◎
Listed *Commended*

Working dairy/corn farm with a 15th century listed farmhouse and large garden in an extremely quiet setting. Delightful footpaths through the farm and woods. Two very spacious bedrooms, comfortable sitting room with TV, separate dining room offering excellent breakfasts. Good local pubs. Open all year.

---

5 Butlers Hill Farm, Cockleford, Cowley, Cheltenham, Gloucestershire GL53 9NW

Bridget Brickell
☎/Fax 01242 870455
BB **From £15**
EM **From £7**
Sleeps 4
🛏(6) 🐾
🌸🌸 *Approved*

A warm welcome awaits you on this mixed working farm between Cheltenham and Cirencester. Relax in this modern spacious farmhouse, in a quiet part of the Churn Valley with attractive walks and an ideal centre for exploring the Cotswolds. All rooms have H&C and tea/coffee-making facilities, separate guests' sitting room with colour TV and separate dining room. Open Mar–Sept.

The Coach House, Middle Duntisbourne, Cirencester, Gloucestershire GL7 7AR 6

Mrs June Barton
01285 653058
From £17–£25
Sleeps 3
(13)
Approved

A warm welcome at the 17th century coachhouse by the River Dunt. Centrally situated in 400-acre arable and beef farm with lovely walks and ideal for visits to Bath, Oxford, Stratford and many pretty villages in and around Cirencester area. Pretty garden with country views. TV, tea/coffee-making facilities in bedrooms. Pleasant lounge with CTV. Always a choice of breakfast including English farmhouse breakfast. Open all year except Christmas.

Dix's Barn, Duntisbourne Abbots, Cirencester, Gloucestershire GL7 7JN 7

Mrs Rosemary Wilcox
01285 821249
From £17–£25
Sleeps 4
Commended

Dix's Barn is situated in an Area of Outstanding Natural Beauty. It has breathtaking views of the Cotswolds and one can take lovely walks in any direction. Ideally placed for touring by car. The farm is family run, being a mixture of arable, beef and sheep. Open all year except Christmas.

Elms Farm, Gretton, nr Winchcombe, Cheltenham, Gloucestershire GL54 5HQ 8

Rosemary Quilter
01242 620150
Mobile 0374 461107
From £17.50–£20
EM From £12.50
Sleeps 4
Commended

Relax and enjoy the Cotswolds in our farmhouse set on the outskirts of Gretton village, with picturesque views north and south. The 120-acre arable, sheep and mushroom farm adjoins some of the many footpaths in the area. Ideal for exploring those beautiful Cotswold villages, or just sitting and enjoying the peace and quiet. En suite rooms with TV and tea/coffee. Guests' lounge with log fire. Open all year except Christmas.

Gilbert's, Gilbert's Lane, Brookthorpe, Nr Gloucester, Gloucestershire GL4 0UH 9

Jenny Beer
/Fax 01452 812364
From £25–£35
Sleeps 6
Highly Commended

Gilbert's, which nestles beneath the Cotswolds close to Gloucester, is listed as an architectural gem. Whilst each room has modern comforts – WC, bath, shower, TV, telephone, etc. – the atmosphere is in keeping with the unpretentious nature of the house and organic smallholding. RAC Highly Acclaimed and *Which? Good Bed & Breakfast Guide*. Open all year.

Hartpury Farm, Chedworth, Nr Cheltenham, Gloucestershire GL54 4AL 10

Peter & Peggy Booth
01285 720350
From £15.50–£16.50
EM From £8
Sleeps 6
Listed *Approved*

Hartpury, lying centrally in the Cotswolds and in a quiet village, provides views across the valley. Good walking. Farm produce, provided by Jersey cows and organic gardening, cooked to traditional recipes. The beamed sitting room, vintage 1650, leads onto the garden where we often serve coffee. When we can, we help with excursions and local history. Open Apr–Oct.

Home Farm, Bredons Norton, Tewkesbury, Gloucestershire GL20 7HA 11

Mick & Anne Meadows
01684 772322
From £18–£20
EM From £15
Sleeps 6
Commended

Mixed 150-acre family-run farm with sheep, cattle and poultry. Situated in an extremely quiet, unspoilt little village nestling under Bredon Hill. Superb position for walking, an excellent base for touring or relaxing. The 18th century farmhouse is very comfortably furnished. All bedrooms have en suite bathrooms. Gas CH. Good home cooking, evening meal by arrangement. Lounge, TV. Children welcome. Open mid Jan–mid Dec.

12 Hunting Butts Farm, Swindon Lane, Cheltenham, Gloucestershire GL50 4NZ

Jane Hanks
☎ 01242 524982
Fax 01242 251507
BB From £18.50–£20
EM From £10
Sleeps 16
👤🐾🐴✄ 🏠
👑👑👑 *Commended*

Hunting Butts is a working 200-acre beef and arable farm on the edge of beautiful countryside overlooking the historic town of Cheltenham Spa, just 1½ miles from the town centre. Cheltenham Leisure Centre is a short walk away with swimming pools, squash courts, softball, etc. Children's playground, tennis courts, boating lake and golf course are again within easy walking distance. Open all year.

13 Kilmorie Guest House, Gloucester Road, Snigs End, Corse, Staunton, Nr Gloucester, Gloucs GL19 3RQ

Sheila Barnfield
☎ 01452 840224
BB From £14–£17
EM From £7.50
Sleeps 11
🛏(5) 🏹 🐾 🏠 🐕 ⊚
👑👑 *Approved*

Built in 1848 by the Chartists, Kilmorie is a Grade 2 listed smallholding keeping sheep, ponies, goats, ducks and hens. Children may help with animals. All accommodation is on ground floor, warm and cosy with CH, tea/coffee trays, colour TVs and washbasins. Relax in large garden or walk waymarked footpaths to discover the countryside. Good home cooking, full English breakfast, 3 course dinner. Ideal for Cotswolds, Malverns, Forest of Dean. Fishing nearby. Open all year (closed Christmas & New Year).

14 Lydes Farm, Toddington, Cheltenham, Gloucestershire GL54 5DP

Mrs R Sharpley
☎/Fax 01242 621229
BB From £17.50–£20
Sleeps 5
🛏(5) 🏹 🏠 🐾
👑 *Commended*

Comfortable farmhouse between Broadway and Winchcombe with panoramic views from every room. TV in bedrooms, separate dining room, garden. Dogs taken by arrangement. A grass farm grazed by cattle and horses; visitors are welcome to walk round. Ideal centre for exploring the North Cotswolds. Golf and riding nearby. Open Jan–Nov.

15 Manor Farm, Greet, Winchcombe, Cheltenham, Gloucestershire GL54 5BJ

Richard & Janet Day
☎ 01242 602423
BB From £25–£27.50
Sleeps 6
🐴🏹🐾🏠🔥
👑👑 *Highly Commended*

Luxuriously restored 16th century cotswold manor on mixed family farm, excellent views, near Sudeley Castle and steam railway. Convenient to Broadway, Cheltenham, Evesham, Tewkesbury and M5. 1½ miles from Cotswold Way and Wychavon Way. Large garden, croquet lawn, children welcome, horses can be accommodated. Self-catering cottages also available and camping space. Open Jan–Nov.

16 Manor Farm, Weston Sub-Edge, Chipping Campden, Gloucestershire GL55 6QH

Lucy Robbins
☎ 01386 840390
Mobile 0589 108812
BB From £20
Sleeps 6
🐴🏹🏠🔥
👑👑 *Commended*

Traditional 17th century farmhouse on a 600-acre mixed farm, an excellent base for touring the Cotswolds, Shakespeare Country and Hidcote Manor Gardens. Warm, friendly atmosphere with big hearty breakfasts. Beautiful walled garden. All rooms are en suite with tea/coffee making facilities, TV/radio. 1½ miles from Chipping Campden. Lots of excellent walks around beautiful countryside. Open all year.

17 Oakwood Farm, Upper Minety, Malmesbury, Wiltshire SN16 9PY

Mrs Katie Gallop
☎/Fax 01666 860286
Mobile 0385 916039
BB From £15
Sleeps 6
🐴🏹🔥
Listed *Commended*

A friendly farming couple welcome you to their working dairy farm overlooking Upper Minety church. Meander through the landscaped gardens or just relax on the croquet lawn under the old oak tree. Guests enjoy their own spacious wing with extra touches that make Oakwood Farm a special place to stay. Well situated for touring the Cotswolds, Heart of England and West Country. Open all year.

Pardon Hill Farm, Prescott, Gotherington, Cheltenham, Gloucestershire GL52 4RD

Mrs J Newman
☎/Fax 01242 672468
[BB] From £20–£25
Sleeps 5
🐴🐓🏹🚜🎯🎋💼🎿
🐚🐚 *Commended*

A quiet, family-run 300-acre livestock farm, set in the beautiful Cotswold hills just 6 miles from Cheltenham and 3 miles from Winchcombe. Double, twin and single rooms, all en suite with outstanding views. A marvellous base for walking, riding and touring holidays. Open all year.

Postlip Hall Farm, Postlip, Winchcombe, Cheltenham, Gloucestershire GL54 5AQ

Mrs Valerie Albutt
☎ 01242 603351
[BB] From £18–£30
Sleeps 6
🐴✂️🎋💼🐓
🐚🐚 *Highly Commended*

Spectacular situation, superb scenery in every direction. Set on side of Cleeve Hill off B4632, Winchcombe 1¾ miles. This working farm is a fantastic base for exploring Cotswolds, Warwick Castle, Blenheim Palace, Bath, Malverns. Great walking. Golf and horse riding nearby. Cosy, spacious en suite rooms, armchairs, colour TV. Beverages. Lovely welcoming atmosphere. Open all year except Christmas.

Sudeley Hill Farm, Winchcombe, Gloucestershire GL54 5JB

Barbara Scudamore
☎/Fax 01242 602344
[BB] From £22
Sleeps 6
🐴🎋💼
🐚🐚 *Highly Commended*

Delightfully situated above Sudeley Castle with panoramic views across the surrounding valley, this is a 15th century listed farmhouse with a large garden on a working mixed farm of 800 acres. Ideal centre for touring the Cotswolds. Family/twin, 1 double, 1 twin, all en suite. Comfortable lounge with TV and log fires. Separate dining room. Open all year except Christmas.

Town Street Farm, Tirley, Gloucestershire GL19 4HG

Sue Warner
☎ 01452 780442
Fax 01452 780890
[BB] From £18–£24
Sleeps 4
🐴🐓🐕💼
🐚🐚 *Commended*

Town Street Farm is a typical working family farm close to the River Severn, within easy reach of M5 and M50. The farmhouse offers a high standard of accommodation with en suite facilities in bedrooms and a warm and friendly welcome. Breakfast is served overlooking the lawns, flowerbeds and tennis court which is available for use by guests. Open all year except Christmas.

Upper Farm, Clapton-on-the-Hill, Bourton-on-the-Water, Gloucestershire GL54 2LG

Mrs Helen Adams
☎ 01451 820453
Fax 01451 810185
[BB] From £17–£20
Sleeps 8
🐴(6)✂️🎋
🐚🐚 *Highly Commended*

A mixed family farm of 140-acres in a peaceful, undiscovered village two miles from Bourton-on-the-Water. Our centrally heated period stone farmhouse has been tastefully restored and offers a warm, friendly welcome. Quality accommodation and hearty farmhouse fayre. We are centrally located for touring or walking and our hill position offers panoramic views over the surrounding Cotswold countryside. Open Mar–Nov.

Wickridge Court Farm, Folly Lane, Stroud, Gloucestershire GL6 7JT

Gloria & Peter Watkins
☎ 01453 764357
[BB] From £20
EM From £12
Sleeps 6
🐴🐓🎋💼◎
🐚🐚 *Commended*

Wickridge Court Farm is situated 1 mile from the B4070 holiday route. A farm of 250 acres with cattle and horses. The historic farmhouse is a sympathetically converted Cotswold stone barn offering all en suite rooms. It is a peaceful suntrap set in a fold of the beautiful Slad Valley offering excellent walks through National Trust woods; Stroud Leisure Centre with its heated pool is 1 mile, many places of interest within easy reach. Open all year.

24 Windrush Farm, Bourton-on-the-Water, Cheltenham, Gloucestershire GL54 3BY

David & Jenny Burrough
☎/Fax 01451 820419
BB From £20
Sleeps 4
✗ ♨ ♔
♔♔ Highly Commended

We look forward to welcoming you to our family-run arable farm in a delightful setting. 1½ miles from Bourton-on-the-Water. The Cotswold stone house has a lovely garden and panoramic views. Enjoy the beauty of the area, with its rolling hills, picturesque villages and places of interest. Our local 17th century pub is a stroll across the fields for evening meals. Open Mar–Dec except Christmas.

SELF-CATERING

25 Bangrove Farm, Teddington, Tewkesbury, Gloucestershire GL20 8JB

Pat Hitchman
☎ 01242 620223
SC From £260–£310
Sleeps 2/8
♨ ♔
♔ ♔ ♔ ♔ Commended

An attractive self-contained property part of 17th century oak-beamed farmhouse on arable/livestock farm in quiet rural setting near Cheltenham. Ideal for walking and touring Cotswolds. Comfortably furnished, fitted carpets throughout. 3 double bedrooms (1 with washbasin), large bathroom. Downstairs cloakroom, kitchen/diner, microwave, large lounge, TV. Linen/electricity/use of washing machine included. Children welcome. Garden, hard tennis court, barbecue. Golf/riding available. Open Mar–Oct.

26 Court Close Farm, Manor Road, Eckington, Pershore, Worcestershire WR10 3BH

Eileen Fincher
☎ 01386 750297
SC From £180–£285
Sleeps 5/6
♨ ✗ ♔ ♔ ♨
♔ ♔ ♔ ♔ Commended

A self-contained wing of our lovely 18th century farmhouse and garden on village edge, bordering Gloucestershire. Outstanding views of Bredon Hill. Attractive set dairy farm with meadows sloping to the Avon. Fishing by arrangement. Central for Shakespeare, Malvern and Cotswold jaunts. Convenient kitchen/diner and comfortable sitting room with TV, storage heat and electric fire. 3 bedrooms, linen provided. Closed Christmas.

27 Folly Farm Cottages, Malmesbury Road, Tetbury, Gloucestershire GL8 8XA

Julian Benton
☎ 01666 502475
Fax 01666 502358
SC From £90–£615
Sleeps 2–8
♨ ♔ ♘ ⚿ ♨
♔ ♔ ♔ – ♔ ♔ ♔ ♔
Commended

Close to Royal Tetbury, 10 superior 18th century cottages. Well furnished, fully equipped throughout. CH, CTV, microwave, linen provided. Some log fires. Games room, laundry, large gardens, barbecue and play area. Fishing, golf, riding, windsurfing nearby. Pubs 2 minutes walk. Resident host. Ideal for disabled and family reunions. Civilised pets and children welcome! Close to M4/M5. Open all year.

15 Manor Farm Cottages, Greet, Winchcombe, Cheltenham, Gloucestershire GL54 5BJ

Richard & Janet Day
☎ 01242 602423
SC From £200–£560
Sleeps 3/6
♨ ♘ ⚿ ♔ ♨
♔ ♔ ♔ ♔ Highly
Commended

Beautifully restored 15th century tithe house (pictured) also 'Shuck's Cottage' and 'Bread Oven Cottage', on family farm. Central for Tewkesbury, Broadway, Evesham, Cheltenham. Sleep 3–6, cot and high-chair available. Horses accommodated. Close to Cotswold Way and Wychavon Way, in sight of steam railway. Full central heating, every modern convenience. Camping space also available. Open all year.

Old Mill Farm, nr Cirencester, c/o Ermin House Farm, Syde, Cheltenham, Gloucestershire GL53 9PN **(28)**

Mrs Catherine Hazell
☎ 01285 821255
Fax 01285 821531
[sc] From £135–£500
Sleeps 2–7
ᵇ ♞ ♣ ⊕
ℐ ℐ ℐ ℐ *Commended*

Four superior barn conversions featuring Cotswold stone pillars and beams. Situated 4 miles from Cirencester on mixed farm beside River Thames and Cotswold Water Park for walking, birdwatching, fishing, sailing and jet skiing. Trains to London 1¼ hrs. Prices include full central heating, electricity, bed-linen, colour TV. Separate laundry room with pay-phone. Convenient for Stratford-upon-Avon, Oxford, Stonehenge, Bath and Tetbury. Open all year.

Stable Cottage, Home Farm, Bredons Norton, Tewkesbury, Gloucestershire GL20 7HA **(11)**

Mick and Anne Meadows
☎ 01684 772322
[sc] From £200–£280
Sleeps 5
ᵇ ♞ ✄ ⌂ ♣
ℐ ℐ ℐ ℐ *Commended*

Delightful Cotswold stone stable/barn conversion on a mixed working family farm in a quiet and pictuesque village under Bredon Hill. Very cosy and tastefully furnished. Full central heating, lots of beams, own paddock. Perfect location for touring the Cotswolds, Severn Valley and Malverns with many wonderful walks. Open all year.

Warrens Gorse Cottages, Home Farm, Warrens Gorse, Cirencester, Gloucestershire GL7 7JD **(29)**

John & Nanette Randall
☎ 01285 831261
[sc] From £140–£200
Sleeps 3–5
ᵇ ♞ ✄ ♣
ℐ ℐ ℐ *Approved*

2½ miles from Cirencester between Daglingworth and Perrotts Brook, these attractive whitewashed cottages are ideally situated for touring the Cotswolds. The cottages are personally attended by the owners and are comfortably furnished and well equipped. 100-acre sheep, cattle and corn farm. Golf club nearby. Water sports 5 miles. Open Mar–Oct.

Westley Farm, Chalford, Stroud, Gloucestershire GL6 8HP **(30)**

Julian Usborne
☎ 01285 760262
[sc] From £140–£300
Sleeps 2/4
ᵇ ♞ ⚘ ⌂
ℐ ℐ – ℐ ℐ ℐ *Approved*

Steep meadows of wild flowers and beech woods are the setting for this old fashioned 80-acre hill farm with breathtaking panoramic views over the Golden Valley. Children especially enjoy the donkey, calves, lambs and foals. Adults may prefer the complete tranquillity and abundant wildlife. Nearby horseriding, golf, gliding, watersports. Midway Cirencester – Stroud. Four cottages, two flats. Brochure available. Open Apr–Oct.

Windmill Annexe, Castle Fruit Farm, Castle Tump, Newent, Gloucestershire GL18 1LS **(31)**

Mrs Gilli Nicolson
☎/Fax 01531 890428
[sc] From £235–£350
Sleeps 4
♃ ᵇ ♞ ✄ ♣ ☞ ⌂
ℐ ℐ ℐ ℐ *Highly Commended*

Windmill Annexe is an extension to a beautiful Georgian country house. Designed on one level, it is spacious and opens on to large lawns and gardens. You are invited to seek secluded corners to relax in or wander through orchards. A unique windmill adds a majestic aspect to the tranquil setting. Open all year.

FARM HOLIDAY BUREAU

Please mention **Stay on a Farm** when booking

Lincolnshire

Group Contact: *Mrs Gill Grant* ☎ *01673 842283*

A frequent comment of first-time visitors to Lincolnshire is "I never realised there was so much to see and do". This doesn't surprise us for we know that Lincolnshire is a large unspoilt county, full of variety and contrast waiting to be discovered.

There are some attractions that you will not want to miss: for instance, Lincoln with its magnificent cathedral, castle and Museum of Lincolnshire Life; Belton House near Grantham; Stamford, a near perfect stone town or its brick-built equivalent, Louth; Elizabethan houses such as Doddington Hall and Burghley House.

The best way to enjoy the county is to get in your car and see it for yourself. Take your time though – slow down your pace of life to match that of Lincolnshire. Drive into the countryside where you will have miles of road to yourself. Try the twisting hidden lanes of Tennyson Country where villages have names such as Bag Enderby and Ashby Puerorum. Tennyson Country forms the southern part of the Lincolnshire Wolds, designated as an Area of Outstanding Natural Beauty. Visit one of the unspoilt market towns, or go for a walk along part of the Viking Way.

Then there is Boston and its Stump, the nearby Memorial marking the spot where the Pilgrim Fathers tried to leave England ... sorry no more space – you'll just have to come and see for yourself!

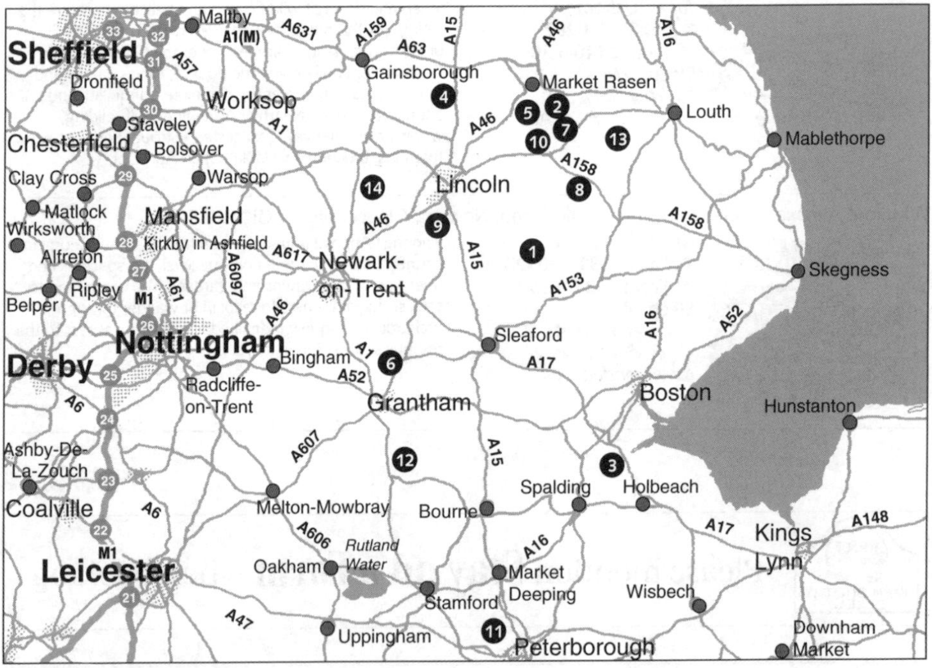

BED AND BREAKFAST

(and evening meal)

Beechwood Barn, North Moor Farm, Linwood Road, Martin, Lincoln LN4 3RA

Isobel Fletcher
☎ 01526 378339
[BB] From £18–£25
Sleeps 4
Listed *Commended*

We enjoy welcoming our guests to our delightful converted barn, still with its large open beams and memories of yesteryear. Right in the middle of Lincolnshire, ideal for touring. Cosy rooms, one double en suite with settee and one twin bedroom with washbasin adjacent to the bathroom. Choice of generous breakfasts. Open all year.

Bleasby House, Legsby, Market Rasen, Lincolnshire LN8 3QN

Janet Dring
☎ 01673 842383
[BB] From £20–£22
EM From £10–£12
Sleeps 5
🐕 *Highly Commended*

Enjoy a peaceful break in welcoming farmhouse at foot of Lincolnshire Wolds. Spacious en suite rooms with colour TV. Flower-filled sun lounge and large garden. Ideal for touring beautiful countryside, historic Lincoln, Cadwell Park. Fly fishing and hard tennis court on farm. Evening meals by arrangement. Open all year.

Cackle Hill House, Cackle Hill Lane, Holbeach, Lincolnshire PE12 8BS

Maureen Biggadike
☎ 01406 426721
Fax 01406 424659
[BB] From £18–£22
Sleeps 6
🐕(10) *Highly Commended*

We welcome you to our farm situated in rural position just off the A17. Comfortable accommodation (en suites and private facilities) and traditional farmhouse fare. Farm walks, large patio and gardens. Close to the shores of the Wash with its marshes, trails and mature reserves, Spalding, Boston, Norfolk and Cambridgeshire. Open all year.

Church Farm, Fillingham, Gainsborough, Lincolnshire DN21 5BS

Christine Ramsay
☎ 01427 668279
Fax 01427 668025
[BB] From £16–£19
EM From £11
Sleeps 6
🐕(5) Listed *Highly Commended*

Church Farm is an 18th century stone farmhouse set in a peaceful garden that has sweeping and well cut lawns – they are surrounded by flower-filled troughs and the only sound is of birdsong. All bedrooms have wonderful countryside views. Hemswell Antique Centre and Lincolnshire Showground close by. Open all year except Christmas and New Year.

East Farm House, Middle Rasen Road, Buslingthorpe, Market Rasen, Lincolnshire LN3 5AQ

Mrs Gill Grant
☎ 01673 842283
[BB] From £20
EM From £12
Sleeps 4
Highly Commended

Peace and relaxation await you in beamed 18th century listed farmhouse on 410 acre conservation award-winning farm with farm trail overlooking unspoilt countryside. Situated 4 miles SW of Market Rasen, ideal for rambling, touring beautiful Lincolnshire Wolds, coast, historic Lincoln and market towns. Wholesome farmhouse food, spacious bedrooms, TV and tea/coffee makers. 1 double en suite, 1 twin with private facilities. Guests' lounge. Business people welcome. Open all year.

6   **Gelston Grange Farm,** Nr Marston, Grantham, Lincolnshire NG32 2AQ

Janet Sharman
☎ 01400 250281
🅱 From £16–£25
Sleeps 6
👶(5) ⚹ ♿
👄👄 *Commended*

We are known for our welcome and homely atmosphere. Comfortable beds, 1 four poster en suite room, 1 double, 1 twin, all with HC, tea/coffee trays, TV, CH and tastefully decorated. Full English breakfast. Large garden. Lots of places to visit – Belton House, Lincoln, Newark, Boston and the coast, Robin Hood country. Northward on A1 take first right turn for Marston (after Grantham roundabout). Open all year except Christmas and New Year.

7   **The Grange,** Torrington Lane, East Barkwith, Nr Wragby, Lincolnshire LN8 5RY

Mrs Sarah Stamp
☎ 01673 858670
🅱 From £19–£24
Sleeps 4
👶 ⚹ 🖥 ☕ ♟ ♿
👄👄 *Highly Commended*

The Stamp family gives you a warm welcome to Grange Farm, a beautiful, spacious Georgian farmhouse peacefully situated with views of Lincoln Cathedral to the west and the Wolds to the east. Two double en suite rooms with TV and tea/coffee trays. Guests' sitting room, log fires. Lawn tennis. Unwind on the award winning farm trail, stopping for a break at the secluded trout lake.

8   **Greenfield Farm,** Minting, near Horncastle, Lincolnshire LN9 5RX

Judy Bankes Price
☎ 01507 578457
🅱 From £20–£25
Sleeps 6
👶(10) ⚹ ♟ ♿ ◎
👄👄 *Highly Commended*

Judy and Hugh welcome you to their comfortable farmhouse set in a quiet location yet central for all the major Lincolnshire attractions. Relax by the large garden pond or enjoy the forest walks that border the farm. Modern en suite shower rooms, heated towel rails, radios, tea/coffee facilities, CH. Excellent pub with traditional country cooking 1 mile. AA Selected QQQQ. Open mid Jan–mid Dec.

9   **The Manor House,** Manor Farm, Sleaford Road, Bracebridge Heath, Lincoln, Lincolnshire LN4 2HW

Mrs Jill Scoley
☎ 01522 520825
Fax 01522 542418
🅱 From £20–£26
Sleeps 6
👶(10) ⚹ ♿ ◎
👄👄 *Highly Commended*

Welcome to Lincolnshire. Stay in a lovely Georgian farmhouse situated in large walled garden. 3 miles south of Lincoln. Comfortable bedrooms two en suite, one with private facilities, all with radio, tea/coffee facilities. Large lounge with log fire for cooler evenings. Open all year (closed Christmas and New Year).

10   **The Manor House,** West Barkwith, Lincoln LN8 5LF

Mrs J A Hobbins
☎/Fax 01673 858253
🅱 £22.50
EM From £10.50
Sleeps 4
👶(12) ⚹
👄👄 *Highly Commended*

The Manor Farm is a 400-acre arable farm. The house stands in extensive landscaped grounds overlooking lawns, ornamental pond, rock garden and lake. Screened from the road by mature trees providing an attractive setting and seclusion. All rooms enjoy an uninterrupted view of the lake. An ideal base for touring the Wolds and historic Lincoln. Closed Christmas and New Year.

11   **Midstone Farmhouse,** Southorpe, Stamford, Lincolnshire PE9 3BX

Mr & Mrs C Harrison-Smith
☎/Fax 01780 740136
🅱 From £17.50–£30
EM From £10
Sleeps 6
👶 🐾 ⚹ ♿
Listed *Commended*

Midstone House is an 18th century farmhouse where a warm welcome awaits you. Many original features remain although we provide all the best modern standards of comfort and amenity. A private lounge is available for guests to use. We have a small herd of Dexter cattle, ponies, ducks and a potbellied pig named 'George'. Brochure on request. Open all year except Christmas.

Sycamore Farm, Bassingthorpe, Grantham, Lincs NG33 4ED (12)

Mrs Sue Robinson
☎ 01476 585274
🅱 From £20
EM From £10
Sleeps 6
🛏(12) ⌇ 🧳
🌼🌼 *Highly Commended*

Set in peaceful unspoilt countryside Sycamore Farm offers the perfect place to relax and unwind. Spacious, pretty bedrooms with en suite bathrooms (1 private), elegant guests' lounge, fresh flowers, log fires, fine views, books and board games. Ideally placed for A1 (4 miles), Stamford, Lincoln, historic Belton and Burghley and Geoff Hamilton's 'Barnsdale'. Open Mar–Nov.

SELF-CATERING

Bridle Cottage, Midstone Farmhouse, Southorpe, Stamford, Lincolnshire PE9 3BX   (11)

Mrs A Harrison-Smith
☎/Fax 01780 740136
🆂🅲 From £200–£250
Sleeps 2/3 + cot
🛏 🐴 ⌇ 🧳
🐾 🐾 🐾 *Highly Commended*

A former coachhouse and stables tastefully converted into a comfortable cottage providing ground floor accommodation close to the farmhouse. Our farm has a small herd of Dexter cattle and a pot-bellied pig named 'George'.

Mill Lodge, Benniworth House Farm, Donington on Bain, Louth, Lincs LN11 9RD   (13)

Mrs Pamela M Cade
☎/Fax 01507 343265
🆂🅲 From £150–£300
Sleeps 4
🛏 ⌇ 🧳
🐾 🐾 🐾 *Commended*

Ezra and Pamela Cade welcome you to a delightful cottage on a traditional farm/Nature reserve in the beautiful Bain valley. Spacious grounds with conservatory, patio, lawn, flowering shrubs and lock up garage. Lovely walks with well maintained footpaths. Many species, some rare. Children welcome. Open all year.

Red House Farm Cottage, Red House Farm, Spalford Lane, North Scarle, Lincoln LN6 9HB (14)

Mrs Helen Jones
☎ 01522 778224
🆂🅲 From £160–£260
Sleeps 6
🛏 🧳 🎣
🐾 🐾 🐾 *Commended*

Our brick and pantile cottage is ideally situated between Lincoln and Newark. The cottage offers spacious and comfortable accommodation with all modern amenities. Coarse fishing is available f.o.c. on our private lake. Colour brochure available. Open all year.

NO ANSWER?

Farmers are mostly out and about during the day.
Try to telephone before 9.30am or after 4pm.

Northamptonshire

Group Contact: *Mrs A M Singlehurst* ☎ *01832 205222*

Northamptonshire, the county of 'squires and spires', has houses, monuments and fine churches too numerous to mention. There's Sulgrave Manor, home of George Washington's ancestors; Rockingham Castle, built by William the Conqueror and lived in by the Watson family since 1530; Boughton House, modelled on Versailles and Althorp.

At the castle remains, by the River Nene in picturesque Fotheringhay, you may ponder upon the execution of Mary, Queen of Scots and the birth there of Richard III. The Battle and Farm Museum at Naseby will give you a taste of that decisive Civil War battle in 1645. A firm hold has been kept on our heritage and at Brixworth and Earls Barton you will be able to see possibly the country's finest examples of a Saxon church and tower. Many of the county's villages and towns have splendid churches dating from Norman times through to the 15th century.

Traditional methods of transport and entertainment are well preserved. The Waterways Museum at Stoke Bruerne gives you a fascinating insight into life on the canals, and there are boat trips along the Grand Union Canal. On the Nene Valley Steam Railway you can take a nostalgic trip down the line and study steam trains and rolling stock from all over the world. The world famous motor racing circuit at Silverstone is situated in the south of the county.

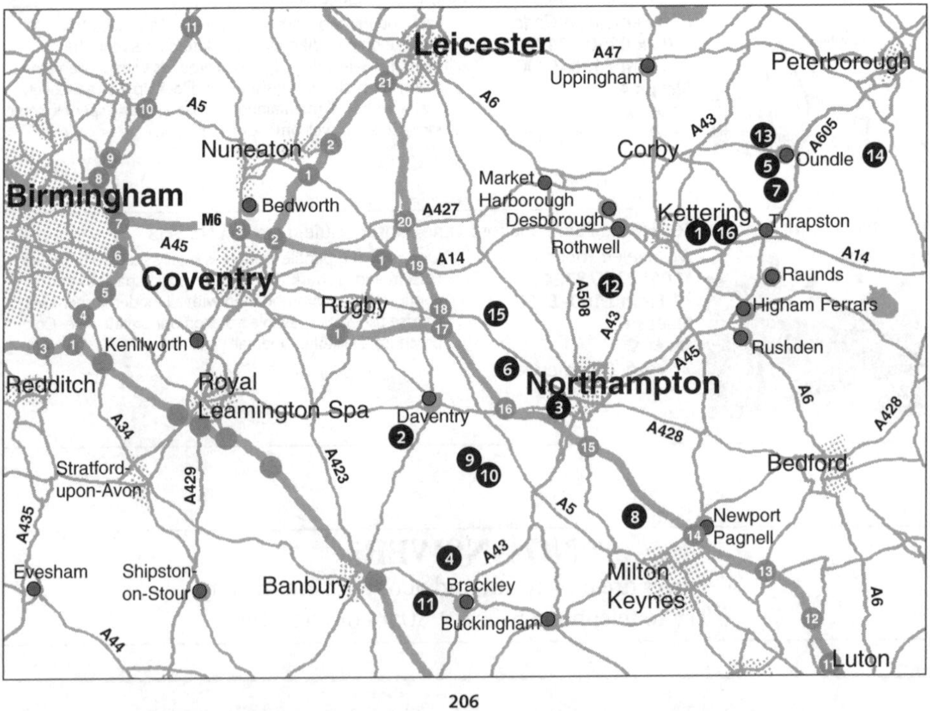

BED AND BREAKFAST
(and evening meal)

Dairy Farm, Cranford St Andrew, Kettering, Northamptonshire NN14 4AQ **1**

Audrey Clarke
☎ 01536 330273
🅱 From £20–£28.50
EM From £12
Sleeps 6
🐾 🐴 ☂ ▪
🌣 🌣 🌣 *Commended*

Enjoy a holiday in a comfortable 17th century farmhouse with oak beams and inglenook fireplaces. Four poster bed now available. Peaceful surroundings, large garden containing ancient circular dovecote. Dairy Farm is a working farm situated in a beautiful Northamptonshire village just off the A14 within easy reach of many places of interest or ideal for a restful holiday. Good farmhouse food and friendly atmosphere. Open all year except Christmas.

Drayton Lodge, Daventry, Northamptonshire NN11 4NL **2**

Ann Spicer
☎ 01327 702449
Fax 01327 872110
🅱 From £22.50–£25
EM From £12
Sleeps 8
🐾 🐴 ✂ ☂ 🐾 ▪
🌣 🌣 🌣 *Highly Commended*

Drayton Lodge is a secluded 18th century farmhouse set on the edge of Daventry to one side and rolling Northamptonshire countryside to the other. A warm, friendly welcome awaits you. Beautiful centrally heated bedrooms with en suite bathrooms and TVs. Championship golf course within ½ mile. Historical places of interest to visit. Full traditional English breakfast served. Open all year.

The Elms, Kislingbury, Northampton NN7 4AH **3**

Mrs Primrose Sanders
☎ 01604 830326
🅱 From £18.50
Sleeps 5
🐾 🐴 ✂ ☂ ▪
Listed *Commended*

A warm welcome awaits you in our Victorian farmhouse with views over the farm. Situated 2 miles from M1 junction 16 and 4 miles from Northampton. Convenient for business stopovers and touring Cotswolds, Stratford, Oxford and Cambridge. Nene Way Walk passes through the farm. Open all year.

Green Farm, Weedon Lois, Towcester, Northamptonshire NN12 8PL **4**

Mrs Paddy Elkington
☎/Fax 01327 860249
🅱 From £18.50–£21
Sleeps 6
🐾 ☕ ☂ ▪
Listed *Commended*

Green Farm is a comfortable 18th century farmhouse set in rolling countryside on a 550-acre mixed farm. You can enjoy private coarse fishing or visit the many local attractions, including Sulgrave Manor, Canons Ashby, and Silverstone Grand Prix circuit to name but a few! The M1 and M40 are both within 15 minutes. Open all year except Christmas.

Lilford Lodge Farm, Barnwell, Oundle, Peterborough, Northamptonshire PE8 5SA **5**

Trudy Dijksterhuis
☎/Fax 01832 272230
🅱 From £19
Sleeps 5
🐾 ☕ 🐾 ▪
🌣 🌣 *Commended*

Mixed farm set in the attractive Nene Valley situated on the A605, 3 miles south of Oundle and 5 miles north of the A14. Peterborough and Stamford are within easy reach. Guests stay in the recently converted original 19th century farmhouse. All bedrooms have en suite bathrooms, CH, radio and tea/coffee-making facilities. Comfortable lounge with satellite TV and separate dining room. Coarse fishing available. Open all year.

---

6   Murcott Mill, Long Buckby, Northamptonshire NN6 7QR

Carrie & Brian Hart
☎ 01327 842236
Fax 01327 844524
BB From £20–£22
EM From £7.50
Sleeps 6

Commended

Murcott Mill is an imposing Georgian mill house set within a working farm. It has a large garden and lovely outlook over open countryside. All rooms are en suite with colour TV. Central heating throughout and visitors have their own lounge and dining room with open log fires. An ideal stopover, close to M1 and good location for touring the area. Open all year.

---

7   Pear Tree Farm, Main Street, Aldwincle, Nr Kettering, Northamptonshire NN14 3EL

Mavis Hankins
☎ 01832 720614
Fax 01832 720559
BB From £20
Sleeps 8

Commended

Pear Tree Farm is a mixed 400-acre farm consisting of cattle, sheep, poultry and arable. Comfortably furnished with relaxed family atmosphere and excellent breakfasts. Four bedrooms. Excellent for walking, birdwatching, fishing. Large garden for relaxing. Open all year except Christmas and New Year (camping Feb–Sept).

---

8   Spinney Lodge Farm, Hanslope, Milton Keynes, Buckinghamshire MK19 7DE

Mrs Christina Payne
☎ 01908 510267
BB From £20–£22
EM From £8
Sleeps 4
☺(12)

Commended

Spinney Lodge is a arable, beef and sheep farm. The lovely Victorian farmhouse with its large garden and rose pergola has en suite bedrooms with colour TV and tea-making facilities. Evening meal by arrangement. M1 J15, 8 minutes, 12 minutes Northampton, 15 minutes Milton Keynes. Silverstone Circuit, Stowe Gardens and Woburn to visit in the area. Ideal base for touring. Open all year except Christmas.

---

9   Threeways House, Everdon, Daventry, Northamptonshire NN11 6BL

Elizabeth Barwood
☎ 01327 361631
Fax 01327 361359
BB From £20–£25
EM From £12
Sleeps 5
☺(4)

Highly Commended

Threeways is a character stone house set on the green of this charming and peaceful conservation village. All our rooms are en suite, well equipped and very comfortable with lovely views of our large, traditionally planted garden and the open countryside. We are 10 minutes from M1 J16 and 20 minutes from M40 J11. Open all year.

---

10   Tivy Farm, Litchborough, Towcester, Northamptonshire NN12 8JH

Mrs C Judge
☎ 01327 830874
BB From £18–£20
Sleeps 5

Listed *Highly Commended*

Find peace and quiet and a warm welcome at our comfortable, modern, stone farmhouse. Relax in large gardens with small lake or visit nearby Sulgrave Manor, Canons Ashby, Althorpe or Silverstone Circuit. Guests' own sitting room with colour TV and log-burner. 20 mins M40 J11, 10 mins M1 J16. Open all year except Christmas.

---

11   Walltree House Farm, Steane, Brackley, Northamptonshire NN13 5NS

Richard & Pauline Harrison
☎ 01295 811235
Fax 01295 811147
BB From £20–£30
EM From £10
Sleeps 18

Commended

Our home is in the middle of nowhere but at the centre of everything. Badger woods to explore, lovely walks. Historic places to visit. Individual ground floor rooms in the courtyard now with four new additional luxury rooms, others in the adjacent licensed Victorian farmhouse. Most rooms en suite. Nearby shopping, fishing, golf, gliding, Silverstone Circuit and leisure centres. Open all year except Christmas & New Year.

Wold Farm, Old, Northampton, Northamptonshire NN6 9RJ　⑫

Anne Engler
☎ 01604 781258
BB From £22–£24
EM From £15
Sleeps 10
🐕 🐴 ♿ 🖭
🌷🌷🌷 Commended

A friendly, informal atmosphere is offered at this 18th century farmhouse on 250-acre beef/arable farm. Main farmhouse offers attractive bedrooms. Hearty breakfast is served in oak-beamed dining room with inglenook fireplace. Relax by log fire or at snooker table. Recently converted barn provides en suite rooms overlooking pretty garden with colourful Pergola. Snacks or four course evening meals on request. Open all year.

SELF-CATERING

Granary Cottage, Brook Farm, Lower Benefield, Peterborough PE8 5AE　⑬

Mrs J Singlehurst
☎ 01832 205215
SC From £150–£250
Sleeps 4
🐕(4) ♿ 🌡
🔑 🔑 🔑 Commended

At the beginning of a gated road we offer peace and tranquillity with picturesque walks. Granary Cottage is warm, cosy and well equipped with linen provided. Close by are the historic market towns of Oundle and Stamford and the pretty village of Rockingham. Sorry no pets. Open all year.

Papley Farm Cottages, Papley Farm, Warmington, Peterborough PE8 6UU　⑭

Joyce Lane
☎/Fax 01832 272583
SC From £140–£380
Sleeps 2/5
🐕 🌡 ♿ 🖭
🔑 🔑 🔑 🔑 Highly
Commended

A warm welcome, peace and comfort await you tucked away in a fold of farming countryside. Choose a modern bungalow or one of four beautifully restored cottages where beams and inglenooks combine with today's luxuries in a large sunny garden – safe for children. All are warm, fully equipped and carefully prepared especially for you. Just bring your food, settle in and unwind! Near Oundle and Stamford, 5 miles A1. Free brochure. Open all year.

Rye Hill Country Cottages, Rye Hill Farm, Holdenby Road, East Haddon, Northants NN6 8DH　⑮

Michael & Margaret Widdowson
☎ 01604 770990
Fax 01604 770237
SC From £135–£395
Sleeps 2/6
🧍 🐴 ♿ 🌡 ♿ 🍴 🖭
🔑 🔑 🔑 🔑 Highly
Commended

Children are most welcome on our delightful, peaceful smallholding. They can help feed our farm animals, collect eggs and have fun in the play area and games room. Our 5 cottages have every modern convenience combined with beams, open fires and log burning stoves. Small licensed restaurant providing good country food and cream teas. Many places of interest for all the family. Open all year.

Villiers Suite, Cranford Hall, Cranford, Kettering, Northamptonshire NN14 4AL　⑯

Gayle Robinson
☎ 01536 330248
Fax 01536 330203
SC From £240–£250
Sleeps 5
🐕 🧍 🍴 ♿ 🌡 ♿ 🖭
🔑 🔑 🔑 🔑 Commended

Lovely Georgian mansion in the heart of a traditional estate village which is set in parkland amidst fine gardens. Many attractive walks and drives to be taken, together with historic spots to visit and a great range of cultural activities. The Villiers Suite is a stylish, self-contained apartment within the Hall.

(11) **Walltree House Farm,** Steane, Brackley, Northamptonshire NN13 5NS

Richard & Pauline Harrison
☎ **01295 811235**
Fax 01295 811147
SC **From £185–£460**
Sleeps 2/6

🐎 🔏 ♿ 🛋 ❦ ⊚
🐾 🐾 🐾 🐾 *Highly Commended*

We have converted the granary and stables into warm, comfortable, well-equipped, quiet cottages in a courtyard adjacent to the farmhouse, overlooking lawns and garden where you are welcome to relax. Near Cotswolds, Stratford, Warwick, Blenheim, Stowe, Waddesdon and other National Trust properties. Shopping, golf and leisure centres. Every activity you can think of. A peaceful haven to return to. Open all year except Christmas and New Year.

FARM HOLIDAY BUREAU

Our Internet Address is
http://www.webscape.co.uk/farmaccom/

CONFIRM BOOKINGS

Disappointments can arise from misunderstandings over the telephone. Please write to confirm your booking.

FINDING YOUR ACCOMMODATION

FARM HOLIDAY BUREAU

The Group contacts at the beginning of each section can always help you find a vacancy in your chosen area.

Leicestershire

Group Contact: *Janet S Clarke* ☎ *0116 260 0472*

Leicestershire is a land of transquil beauty spread with reminders of a turbulent history ... and it begins at every turn-off from any main road.

To find the true Leicestershire just travel over high horizons and narrow farm tracks, explore vast Rutland Water and the lazy green banks of the Grand Union Canal, take a nostalgic trip on our wealth of steam railways, walks in historic Bradgate Park or 'do battle' in Bosworth Field. Explore the counties curious customs which take place annually, such as Bottle Kicking and the Hare Pie Scramble between Hallata and Medbourne, or visit our castles and museums, timber framed cottages and grand mansions, theatres and theme parks.

Fun for the youngsters down on the farm – lambing Sundays and rare breeds; always wanted to touch the animals? – here you can. Spoil yourselves in our tea rooms, browse in the specialist shops and museums – all this and more in this green and undulating county.

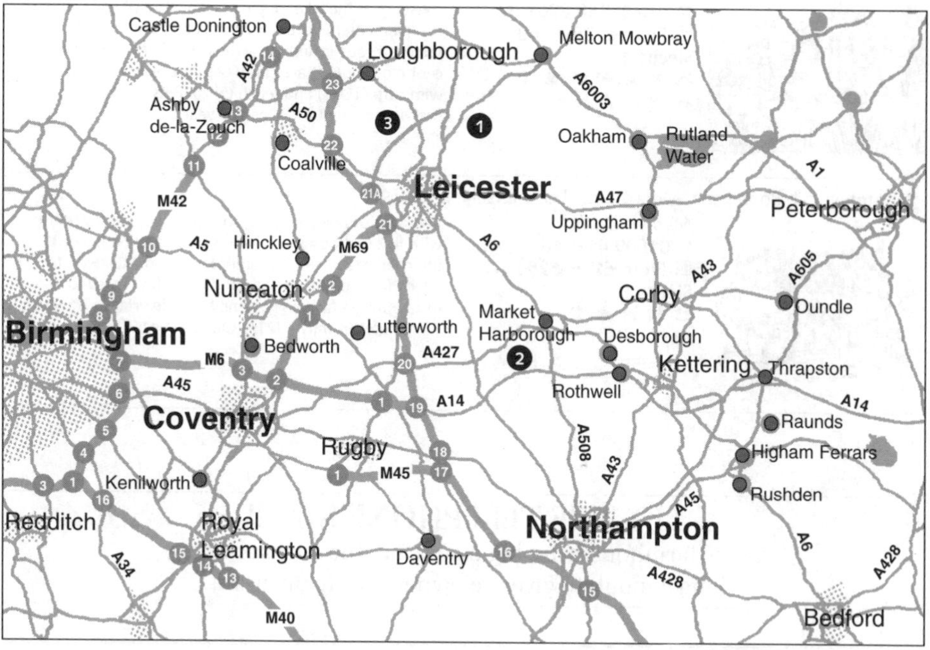

BED AND BREAKFAST

(and evening meal)

---

① Three Ways Farm, Melton Road, Queniborough, Leicester LE7 3FN

Mrs Janet S Clarke
☎ 0116 260 0472
[BB] From £17–£20
Sleeps 5
🐎 🐈 🛝 ⚓
Listed *Commended*

It's hard to believe you're only 6 miles north of Leicester in lovely Queniborough with its ancient church, thatched cottages and two good pubs. You'll be welcomed at the Clarke's bungalow in peaceful fields. All bedrooms have colour TV, tea/coffee facilities. West of Melton Road, ¼ m A607 Queniborough roundabout, connects with Leicester western bypass. Nottingham and Birmingham NEC 40 mins. Open all year except Christmas.

SELF-CATERING

---

② Brook Meadow Holiday Chalets, Welford Road, Sibbertoft, Market Harborough, Leicestershire LE16 9UJ

Mary and Jasper Hart
☎/Fax 01858 880886
[SC] From £125–£240
Sleeps 4
🐈 🐎 🏕 ⚓ 🛝 🐾 🌴
🐾 🐾 🐾 *Approved*

Relax in a rocking chair on the verandah watching the sunset over the lake, sipping a cool glass of wine from our complementary bottle. Each chalet is fully equipped for a family of four, including all the linen. They are in the centre of our 600-acre farm beside a 5-acre lake stocked with carp (18lbs) and tench (5lbs). Pets welcome. Brochure on request. Open all year.

---

③ Stonehurst, Bond Lane, Mountsorrel, Leicestershire LE12 7AR

Marilyn Duffin
☎ 01509 413216
[SC] From £175–£350
Sleeps 8
🐈 🐎 🏕 🛝 🌴
Applied

This comfortable, modern, well-equipped family house with five bedrooms, a private garden and barbecue is attached to Stonehurst Family Farm and Museum, to which free admission is given during stay. Teashop and restaurant on farm. All amenities in the village. The farm is 12 minutes from M1 J21A. Open all year.

LET THE TELEPHONE RING!

Some farmhouses are big places. Let the telephone ring
long enough to give the owner time to answer it.

Bedfordshire

Group Contact: *Mrs Pam Hutcheon* ☎ *01234 822344*

We invite you to spend some time in the County of Bedfordshire in the rural heartland of England, ideally situated between Oxford and Cambridge. The Great Ouse, with its quiet backwaters together with the Lakes at Stewartby, Wyboston and Grafham make ideal venues for the fisherman and the watersports enthusiast. Cyclists will appreciate the ease with which they can travel throughout the area, while walkers will find the Greensand Ridge Walk provides many routes. Golfers also have a wide choice of courses.

Stately homes include Woburn Abbey and Luton Hoo, plus pretty villages with thatched cottages and beamed Tudor buildings. The National Trust owns the extraordinary 16th-century stone dovecote and stables at Willington, plus 50 acres of hill country at Dunstable Downs.

Bedford Museum and John Bunyan Museum are well worth a visit. The Cecil Higgins Art Gallery enjoys an international reputation for the quality of its collections. Luton Museum and Art Gallery exhibit local and natural history, archaeology and lace, while Stockwood Park Craft Museum has exhibits relating to rural life and crafts.

Visit the Shuttleworth Collection of historic aeroplanes and road vehicles, or for garden enthusiasts there is the Swiss Garden and Wrest Park Gardens.

For the naturalist there is the RSPB nature reserve and headquarters at Sandy. For something more exotic, visit Whipsnade Zoo or the Wild Animal Kingdom at Woburn. Whatever your interests you'll enjoy your stay in Bedfordshire.

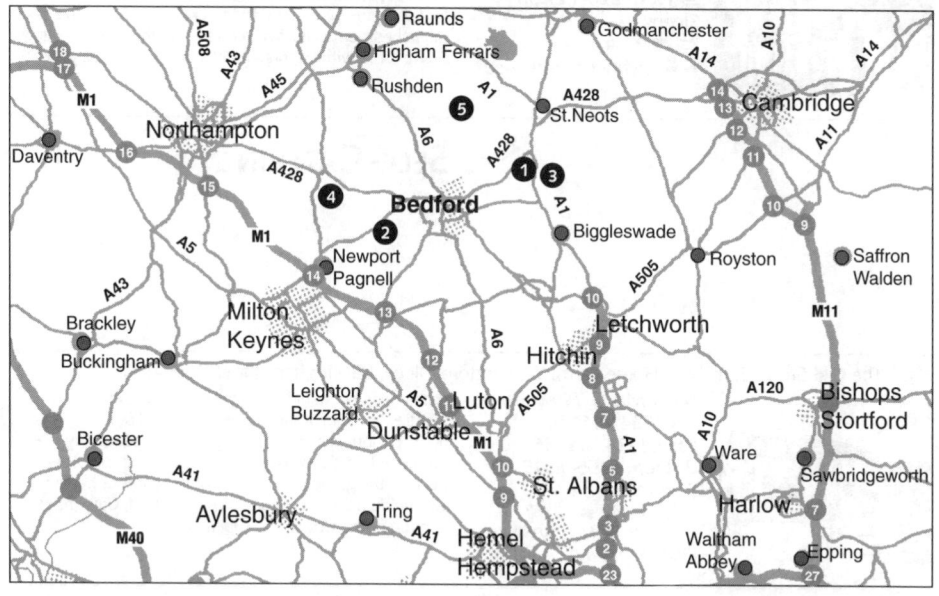

BED AND BREAKFAST
(and evening meal)

---

① Church Farm, High Street, Roxton, Bedford, Bedfordshire MK44 3EB

Janet Must
☎/Fax 01234 870234
[BB] From £18
Sleeps 6
🛌 🐴 🛴 ♨ ♨ ◉
❀ Commended

Set in a secluded village, Church Farm is a lovely 17th century farmhouse with Georgian facade. Guests' lounge and dining room are furnished with a pleasant mixture of family antiques. Local walks. Village inns for evening meals. Double, single and family accommodation available all year. Many guests return. Open all year.

---

② Firs Farm, Stagsden, Bedfordshire MK43 8TB

Mrs Pam Hutcheon
☎/Fax 01234 822344
[BB] From £17–£25
Sleeps 6
🛌 🐴 ♨ ♨
❀ ❀ Commended

Firs Farm is a family run arable farm, set in quiet surroundings ¼ mile south of A422. The farmhouse is timber framed and set in a large garden with swimming pool. Accommodation consists of 2 double (1 en suite) and 1 twin rooms with tea/coffee making facilities and guests' lounge with colour TV and log fire. A warm welcome awaits business and holiday guests. Open all year.

---

③ Highfield Farm, Great North Road, Sandy, Bedfordshire SG19 2AQ

Margaret Codd
☎ 01767 682332
Fax 01767 692503
[BB] From £20–£27.50
Sleeps 8
🛌 🐴 🛴 ♨
❀ ❀ Highly Commended

Tom and Margaret Codd welcome guests to their comfortable farmhouse. Just 1 mile north of Sandy on the A1, Highfield Farm is excellently situated for visiting Cambridge, Shuttleworth, the RSPB, Grafham Water and for taking the Greensand Ridge Walk. Family, double and single bedrooms, most with en suite bathroom. Guests' sitting room with log fire and colour TV. Open all year.

SELF-CATERING

---

④ 'The Old Stone Barn', c/o Home Farm, Warrington, Olney, Buckinghamshire MK46 4HN

Mr & Mrs G. Pibworth
☎ 01234 711655
Fax 01234 711855
[SC] From £155–£325
Sleep 1/6
🧍 🐴 🛴 ♿ ♨ ♨ ✂
🐾 🐾 🐾 🐾 Highly
Commended

A charming combination of old character and modern facilities, the Old Stone Barn is 3 ground floor and 3 first floor spacious self-contained apartments peacefully positioned on an arable farm 1½ miles north of Olney. Relax in the gardens, make use of the outdoor heated swimming pool or take day trips to Oxford, Cambridge, London or the Cotswolds. Open all year.

Scald End Farm, Scald End, Mill Road, Thurleigh, Bedford MK44 2DB   **5**

Jim Towler
☎ **01234 771996**
SC **From £100–£200**
Sleep 2–8
⌂ 🐄 🏠 ♨ ⊚
🐾 *Approved*

The Towler family provides self-catering accommodation in 16th century thatched cottages and modern barn conversions. The farm has cattle, horses, sheep, chickens, ducks and geese – so there is always something to see or do on the farm. The market town of Bedford is only about 15 minutes' drive away. Open all year.

STAY ON A FARM GIFT TOKENS

If you have enjoyed your Stay on a Farm, why not treat your friends and relatives to *Stay on a Farm* gift tokens? Available from the Bureau office, telephone 01203 696909, they can be redeemed against accommodation booked on the majority of our farms

THE 1000+ BUREAU MEMBERS OFFER A UNIQUE LINK TO CUSTOMERS ACROSS THE UK

All Bureau members belong to a local Group. Each member can refer you to an equally high quality member within the Group... or across the UK: England, Northern Ireland, Scotland, Wales.

FOLLOW THE COUNTRY CODE

Leave nothing but footprints,
Take nothing but photographs,
Kill nothing but time!

Hertfordshire & East Buckinghamshire

Group Contacts: ⓑⓑ *Mrs A Knowles* ☎ *01442 866541*
ⓢⓒ *Sally Smyth* ☎ *01763 281204*

Hertfordshire, a county of contrasts, is in the unique situation of being at the hub of the country's transport network whilst offering some truly unspoilt and varied rural landscapes. It well deserves the title it is often given:
'England's Best Kept Secret'.

Our area is rich in historical heritage with some important Roman sites: St Albans was the Roman town Verulamium, first recorded in 54BC. Those interested in history will enjoy many other sites including the Old Palace and House in Hatfield Park and Knebworth House.

Come and enjoy the Chiltern landscape including many picturesque villages such as Aldbury, Frithesden and The Lee. The 4,000 acres of ancient woodland of the National Trust's Ashridge Estate offer a wealth of wildlife including herds of wild deer.

Our farms can also offer the businessman or woman the chance to unwind in a homely atmosphere as little as half an hour by train from central London and close to the M1, M25 and four southern airports. A welcome change from the less individual hospitality of large hotels.

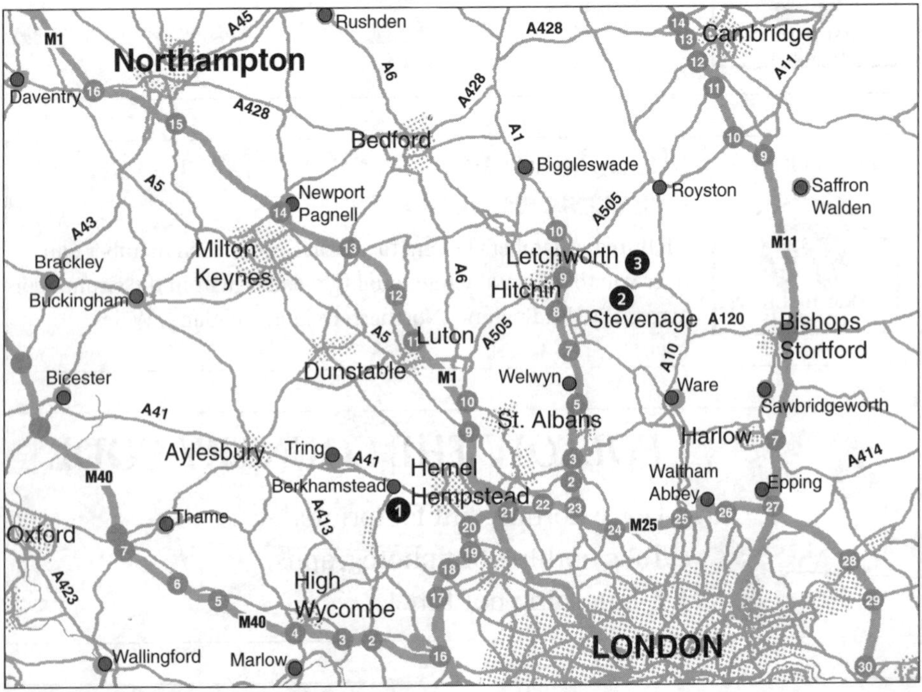

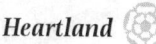
BED AND BREAKFAST

(and evening meal)

Broadway Farm, Berkhamsted, Hertfordshire HP4 2RR   ①

Mrs Alison Knowles
☎/Fax 01442 866541
[BB] From £20–£30
Sleeps 6
♿ ✗ ⅍ ☕ ♨
♥♥ *Commended*

Working arable farm with own fishing lake. 3 comfortable en suite rooms in recently converted buildings adjacent to farmhouse. Tea/coffee-making facilities, colour TV, CH. Everything for the leisure or business guest – the relaxation of farm life in an attractive rural setting, yet easy access to London, airports, motorways and mainline rail services. Open all year (closed Christmas).
E mail: a.knowles@broadway.nildram.co.uk

The Grange, Ardeley, Stevenage, Hertfordshire SG2 7AH   ②

Roger and Wendy Waygood
☎ 01438 861260
Fax 01438 861170
[BB] From £22.50
Sleeps 4
⅍ ♨ ♨
♥♥ *Commended*

Seeking traditional hospitality? Come to Ardeley, relax and enjoy the peace of a quiet, rural village setting. Overlooking our tranquil water garden are two recently converted luxury en suite bedrooms with TV, clock radio, CH, tea/coffee facilities. Situated midway A1 Stevenage and A10 Buntingford. No smoking. Regret no children or pets. Closed Christmas, New Year and Easter.

SELF-CATERING

Bluntswood Hall Cottages, Middle Farm, Throcking, Buntingford, Hertfordshire SG9 9RN   ③

Sally Smyth
☎/Fax 01763 281204
[SC] From £150–£250
Sleeps 4
♿ ♨
🔑 🔑 🔑 🔑 *Commended*

Stables recently converted into 2 cottages with lovely views over the countryside. Ideally situated for Cambridge, Duxford, Wimpole Hall or Knebworth Park. Each beamed cottage has double bedroom, bunk bedroom or single bed, bathroom, fitted kitchen and sitting room. R/C colour TV, CH. Linen and towels included in price. Children welcome. No pets. Open all year.

NO ANSWER?

Farmers are mostly out and about during the day.
Try to telephone before 9.30am or after 4pm.

Cambridgeshire

Group Contact: *Mrs Hilary Nix* ☎ *01353 778369*

Cambridgeshire is a county of contrasts, a county of quiet waterways, gentle hills, lanes, busy towns, attractions great and small, all presented with a friendly welcome for the visitor.

Best known is Cambridge itself, one of Britain's oldest university cities where the colleges in their architectural splendour rest near tranquil rivers overhung with willows, the city that inspired Brooke and Byron.

As well as Cambridge the county has many other attractions. North of Cambridge lies the strikingly flat landscape of the Fens. This once barren marshland was home to the 'Fen Tigers' who lived by cutting reeds and catching eels. Today, the landscape is crisscrossed with dykes which have vastly improved the drainage of this peaty area and made the land a valuable asset for farming.

For contrast there is the hustle and bustle of the modern city of Peterborough with its excellent shopping or the stately grandeur of Ely Cathedral, so called 'Ship of the Fens'.

Wherever you go in Cambridgeshire it is a beautiful county to explore with large towns and small villages, cathedrals and tiny churches and cricket on the village green.

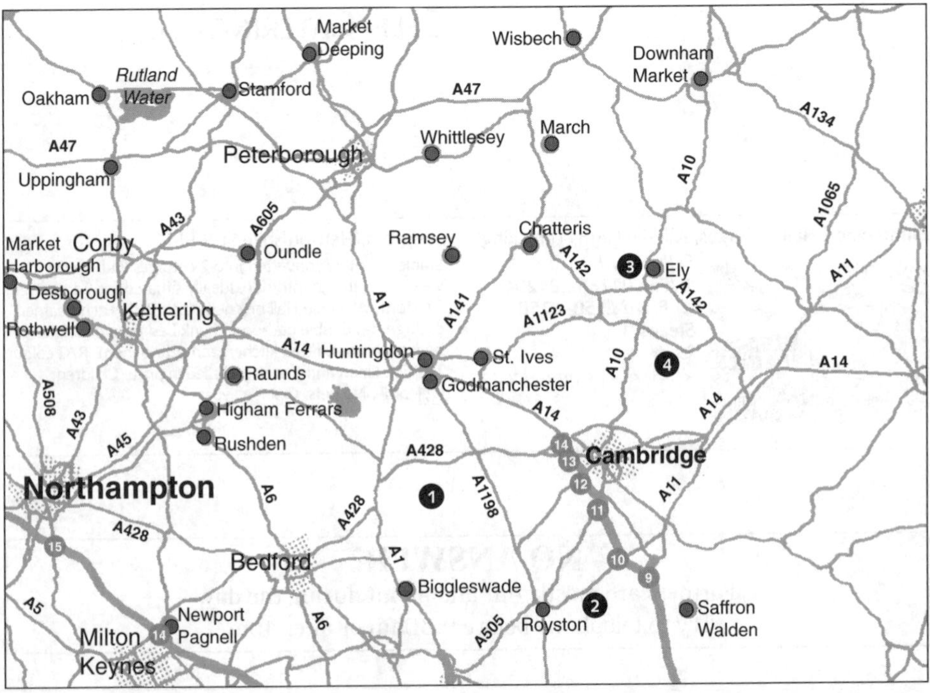

BED AND BREAKFAST

(and evening meal)

Gransden Lodge Farm, Little Gransden, Sandy, Bedfordshire SG19 3EB

Mrs Mary Cox
☎ **01767 677365**
Fax **01767 677647**
[BB] **From £16–£20**
Sleeps 6
🛇 🏇 ⅄ 🌣 ♿
🌸🌸 *Highly Commended*

A warm and friendly atmosphere awaits you at Gransden Lodge, where we have double, twin and single rooms with TV, clock-radio and tea/coffee-making facilities. Ample bathrooms and WCs. Dining room, also large lounge with TV. AA QQQ. Many local pubs and restaurants for evening meals. Situated on the B1046, west of Cambridge. London 50 miles. Also convenient for Stansted Airport (M11, J12). Open all year.

Hall Farm, Great Chishill, Nr Royston, Hertfordshire SG8 8SH

Mrs Jean Wiseman
☎/Fax **01763 838263**
[BB] **From £17.50–£25**
Sleeps 6
🛇 🏇 ⅄ 🌣 ♿
🌸 *Commended*

Beautiful, quiet farmhouse accommodation on a working arable farm. Set in secluded gardens on the highest point in Cambridgeshire. Great Chishill is 11 miles south of Cambridge on the B1039 midway between Saffron Walden and Royston on the Hertfordshire/Essex borders. Two double and one twin bedrooms, all with washbasins and share of guests' bathroom. All rooms have tea/coffee facilities and colour TV. Open all year except Christmas.

Hill House Farm, 9 Main Street, Coveney, Ely, Cambridgeshire CB6 2DJ

Hilary Nix
☎ **01353 778369**
[BB] **From £19–£20**
Sleeps 6
🛇(12) ⅄ 🏇 ♿ ◉
🌸🌸 *Highly Commended*

Spacious Victorian farmhouse in quiet fenland village, 3 miles west of the historic cathedral city of Ely. Open views of the surrounding countryside. Easy access to Cambridge, Newmarket & Huntingdon. Wicken Fen and Welney Wildfowl Trust are nearby. 3 tastefully furnished and decorated bedrooms, all en suite (1 on ground floor). All have own entrance, colour TV, etc full CH. Warm welcome. Open all year except Christmas.

Spinney Abbey, Wicken, Ely, Cambridgeshire CB7 5XQ

Mrs Valerie Fuller
☎ **01353 720971**
Fax **01353 720488**
[BB] **From £19–£20**
Sleeps 6
🛇(5) 🏇 ♿ ◉
🌸🌸 *Commended*

Enjoy the views across open pasture fields from our attractive Grade II listed Georgian farmhouse. Large garden with tennis court adjacent to our dairy farm which borders the National Trust nature reserve Wicken Fen. 1 double and 1 family room, both en suite and twin with private bathroom. All with TV and hospitality tray. Full CH. Guests' sitting room. Open all year except Christmas.

FARM HOLIDAY BUREAU

Please mention **Stay on a Farm** when booking

SELF-CATERING

③ Hill House Farm Cottage, 9 Main Street, Coveney, Ely, Cambs CB6 2DJ

Hilary Nix
☎ **01353 778369**
🆂 **From £180–£300**
Sleeps 6
🛏(8) ⚊ ✕ ⛴ ⊚
⚲ ⚲ ⚲ ⚲ *Highly Commended*

A tasteful barn conversion on our farm is now a comfortable cottage. Furnished and decorated to a high standard. Set in a quiet village location 3 miles west of Ely with open views of Ely Cathedral and the surrounding countryside. Ideally situated for touring Norfolk, Suffolk and Cambridgeshire. Easy access to Cambridge, Newmarket and Huntingdon. Access form A142 or A10. Regret no smoking, no pets. Open all year.

FARM HOLIDAY BUREAU

Our Internet Address is
http://www.webscape.co.uk/farmaccom/

CONFIRM BOOKINGS

Disappointments can arise from misunderstandings over the telephone. Please write to confirm your booking.

STAY ON A FARM GIFT TOKENS

FARM HOLIDAY BUREAU

If you have enjoyed your Stay on a Farm, why not treat your friends and relatives to *Stay on a Farm* gift tokens? Available from the Bureau office, telephone 01203 696909, they can be redeemed against accommodation booked on the majority of our farms

Norfolk & Suffolk

Group Contacts: 🅱 *Mrs Rosemary Bryce* ☎/Fax 01473 652253
🆂 *Mrs Margaret Langton* ☎/Fax 01473 652210

Have you discovered this unspoilt corner of England?

Make your visit one to remember by sharing our homes in the countryside. Choose from over 50 quality bed and breakfast or country properties.

We are easily accessible by A14, A11 & A12, Harwich and Stansted.

Explore our half timbered market towns, medieval churches and castles.

Experience the beauty of our coast and heathland, a birdwatcher's paradise.

Something for everyone – waymarked walks, easy cycling, stately homes and gardens.

You will find us ready to help with local knowledge for that stay with the personal touch.

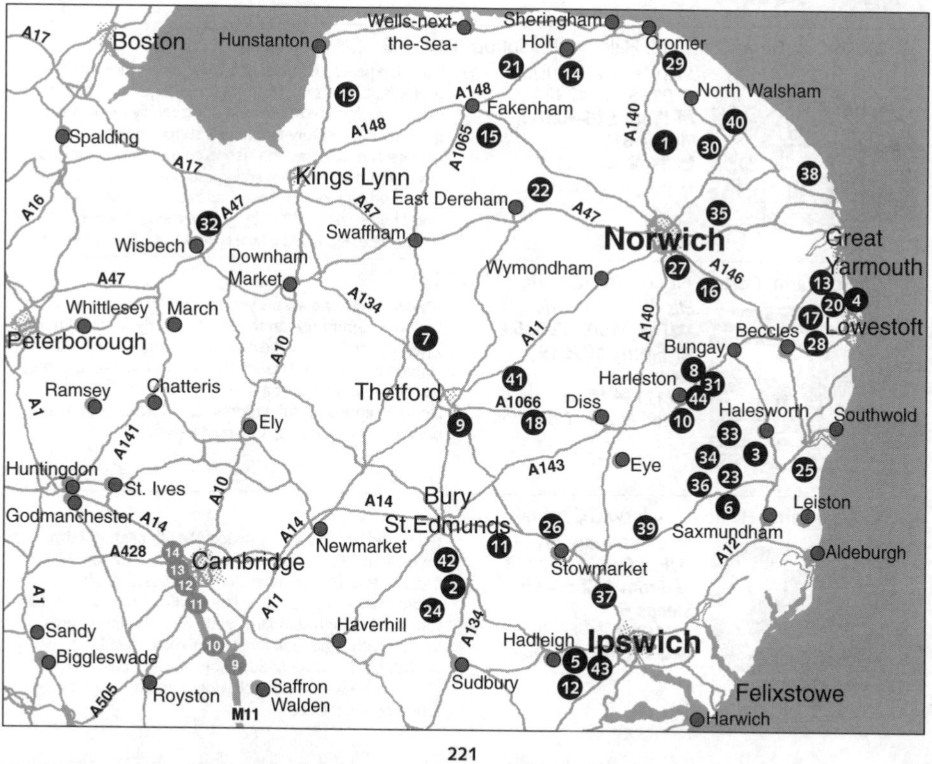

BED AND BREAKFAST

(and evening meal)

---

① Birds Place Farm, Back Lane, Coltishall Road, Buxton, Norwich NR10 5HD

Bill and Jenny Catchpole
☎ 01603 279585
🅱 From £18–£23
EM From £14
Sleeps 6
🏠(8) ⅍ 🐴 ♿
🐛🐛 *Commended*

Small family farm in the Bure Valley in beautiful Broadland countryside. Our 17th century farmhouse is licensed and we offer excellent cuisine, much of the produce home grown. Bedrooms comprise of 1 family and 1 double room en suite, 1 single with private bathroom, all with TV and tea/coffee-making facilities. We have riding stables plus public footpaths and fishing nearby. Open all year.

---

② Brighthouse Farm, Melford Road, Lawshall, near Bury St Edmunds, Suffolk IP29 4PX

Mr & Mrs Truin
☎ 01284 830385
🅱 From £18–£25
Sleeps 6
🏠⅍ Å 🐴 🏇 ♿ 🍴
🐛🐛 *Commended*

Timbered Georgian farmhouse, set in beautiful surroundings of the Suffolk countryside, 3 acres of picturesque gardens. We offer homely accommodation. Centrally heated throughout, log fires in TV room in winter. Two double rooms, one twin, all with en suite facilities. Historic Bury St. Edmunds/Lavenham close by. Good restaurants locally. Open all year.

---

③ Broad Oak Farm, Bramfield, Halesworth, Suffolk IP19 9AB

Mrs Patricia Kemsley
☎ 01986 784232
🅱 From £16–£20
Sleeps 6
🏠⅍ 🐴 🏇 ♿
🐛🐛 *Commended*

Enjoy the peace and quiet of a dairy farm, where the countryside meets the North-East Heritage Coast, only 8 miles from Southwold. Relax in our carefully modernised and spacious 16th century farmhouse, surrounded by attractive gardens and meadowland. Tennis court. One double and 2 twin rooms (2 en suite) and guests' bathroom. Separate guests' sitting room and beautiful beamed dining room. Good home cooking (EM by arrangement). Friendly, informal atmosphere. Bramfield village is on A144. Open all year.

---

④ Church Farm, Corton, Nr Lowestoft, Suffolk NR32 5HX

Elisabeth Edwards
☎/Fax 01502 730359
🅱 From £18–£19
Sleeps 6
🏠(12) ⅍ 🏇 ♿
Listed *Highly Commended*

A warm welcome awaits you to relax in our comfortable Victorian farmhouse on the most easterly farm in Britain. Within easy reach of the rural beach and clifftop walks, convenient driving distance for the Norfolk Broads, the Suffolk Heritage Coast and the fine city of Norwich. Double bedded en suite rooms. Quiet garden, ample parking. Non-smoking. Open Mar–Nov.

---

⑤ College Farm, Hintlesham, Ipswich, Suffolk IP8 3NT

Mrs Rosemary Bryce
☎/Fax 01473 652253
🅱 From £17.50–£21
Sleeps 6
🏠(10) 🏇 ⅍ 📺 ♿ ⊛
🐛🐛 *Highly Commended*

Relax and unwind at our peaceful 15th century farmhouse on 600-acre farm. Comfortable accommodation, hearty breakfasts and a warm welcome are assured. Three bedrooms (1 single, 1 double en suite, 1 family) tastefully furnished to high standards with every facility. Guests' lounge with inglenook fireplace. Explore nearby 'Constable Country' or Suffolk Heritage Coast. Countryside walks with golf, riding and fishing close by. Open Jan–mid Dec.

Colston Hall, Badingham, nr Framlingham, Woodbridge, Suffolk IP13 8LB   6

John & Liz Bellefontaine
☎/Fax 01728 638375
BB From £20–£30
Sleeps 6
🐕 🎯 ✗ 🏊 ⚙ ⛵ ⛴
🌷 *Commended*

Colston Hall, easily found just ½ mile from the A1120, is surrounded by beautiful, quiet countryside. Guests' can enjoy country walks, cycling, fishing, indoor bowling and Easter lambs. Our centrally heated Elizabethan farmhouse boasts a wealth of beams and brick flooring. We look forward to meeting you. Open all year.

Colveston Manor, Mundford, Thetford, Norfolk IP26 5HU   7

Mrs Wendy Allingham
☎ 01842 878218
Fax 01842 879218
BB From £20–£25
EM From £15
Sleeps 7
🐕(12) ✗ 🎯 🏊 ⚙ 🐎 ⛴
🌷🌷 *Highly Commended*

Peaceful 18th century farmhouse in delightful setting in heart of Breckland. Attractive bedrooms, some en suite. We specialise in delicious cooking from the Aga, using home-grown vegetables. NT properties, cathedrals, gardens and coast within easy reach. Brochure showing location available on request. Open all year.

Earsham Park Farm, Harleston Road, Earsham, Bungay, Suffolk NR35 2AQ   8

Mrs Bobbie Watchorn
☎/Fax 01986 892180
BB From £18.50–£30
EM £14.50
Sleeps 6
🐕 ✗ ⛴ ⛵ 🐎 🎯 ⊚
🌷🌷 *Highly Commended*

Delightful, quiet and friendly farmhouse with panoramic views over the Waveney Valley. Spacious and elegantly furnished en suite rooms (one four-poster bed) with extensive facilities. CH. Guests are welcome to use the large gardens and lovely farm walks. Indulge in the delicious, locally produced, huge Norfolk breakfasts. Evening meal available. Easy access coast/Norwich. Open all year.

East Farm, Euston Road, Barnham, Thetford, Norfolk IP24 2PB   9

Margaret Heading
☎ 01842 890231
Fax 01842 890457
BB From £20–£25
Sleeps 4
🐕 ✗ ⛴ ⛵
🌷 *Commended*

Relax and enjoy the comfort and warm welcome at East Farm in the village of Barnham. We're a 1,000-acre arable farm with beef and sheep and plenty of widlife on the edge of Breckland on Norfolk/Suffolk border between Thetford and Bury St Edmunds. A grey flint-faced house in peaceful surroundings with superb views. Spacious heated rooms with en suite bathrooms. Full English breakfast from local produce. Open all year except Christmas.

Elm Lodge Farm, Chippenhall Green, Fressingfield, Eye, Suffolk IP21 5SL   10

Sheila Webster
☎ 01379 586249
BB From £17–£21
EM £12
Sleeps 6
🐕(10) ✗ 🐎 ⛴
🌷🌷 *Commended*

This 112-acre working farm with early Victorian farmhouse overlooks a large common (SSSI) where animals graze in summer – the perfect spot for an after-dinner stroll. Spacious bedrooms (one en suite), separate dining and sitting rooms, log fires and excellent food ensure that a comfortable, relaxing holiday is enjoyed by all those we warmly welcome to this attractive and peaceful corner of Suffolk. AA QQQ Recommended. Open Mar–Nov.

Grange Farm, Woolpit, Bury St Edmunds, Suffolk IP30 9RG   11

Kathy Parker
☎ 01359 241143
BB From £20–£25
Sleeps 6
🐕 ✗ 🐎 🏊 ⚙ ⛵ ⛴
🌷🌷 *Commended*

Grange Farm is a Grade II listed Victorian house set in the heart of Suffolk, but only 1 mile from the A14 giving easy access. Ideal centre for exploring tranquil Suffolk villages or larger historic towns of Bury St Edmunds, Sudbury, Ely and Cambridge. Two en suite rooms and one with private bath/WC, all with TV and tea/coffee facilities. Guests' lounge and dining room with period furniture. Open all year except Christmas.

---

12 Grove Farm House, Little Wenham, via Colchester, Essex CO7 6QB

Mrs Monica Collins
☎ 01473 310341
BB From £17.50
EM From £7.50–£12
Sleeps 5
🐕(12) 🌿 🏛 🗱 ⊚
☙ *Commended*

Leave stress behind and enjoy warm hospitality in our 15th century farmhouse. Comfortable, centrally heated accommodation in 1 double, 1 twin and 1 single room all attractively furnished and overlooking open countryside. Cosy lounge with TV and charming dining room in which to enjoy excellent home-cooked meals. 1 mile off A12 giving easy access Constable Country, Ipswich, Harwich. Open all year except Christmas.

---

13 Hall Farm, Jay Lane/Church Lane, Lound, Lowestoft, Suffolk NR32 5LJ

Judith Ashley
☎ 01502 730415
BB From £16–£19
Sleeps 6
🐕 🗱 🌿 🏛 ⊚
Listed *Commended*

Share our peaceful, traditional Suffolk farmhouse 1½ miles from sea on 101-acre arable farm. Very clean, comfortable accommodation in two double rooms with en suite facilities and two pretty singles, tea/coffee. Excellent breakfast with our own farm eggs. Beamed lounge, colour TV and log fire. Convenient for Broads. Open Easter–Oct.

---

14 Hempstead Hall, Holt, Norfolk NR25 6TN

Lynda-Lee Mack
☎ 01263 712224
BB From £19–£25
Sleeps 6
🐕 🗱 🌿 ⌨ 🗱
☙☙ *Commended*

Attractive 19th century flint farmhouse peacefully set in beautiful surroundings. 300 acre arable farm with ducks, donkeys, large gardens, and country walks. Close to the Georgian town of Holt and the North Norfolk coast and its many attractions including steam train rides and boat trips to Blakeney Point Seal Sanctuary. En suite family room, double with private bathroom. Colour TV. Tea/coffee-making facilities in rooms.
E mail: www.broadland.com/hempsteadhall

---

15 Highfield Farm, Great Ryburgh, Fakenham, Norfolk NR21 7AL

Mrs E Savory
☎ 01328 829249
Fax 01328 829422
BB From £17–£22
EM from £10.50
Sleeps 6
🐕(12) 🌿 ⊞ 🗱 🏛 🗱
Listed *Commended*

Spacious, comfortable 19thC farmhouse on working farm 10 miles from the coast, set deep in countryside amidst 500 acres of rolling farmland. Central for historic houses and Pensthorpe. Ideal for birdwatchers. Sleeps 6 including twin en suite room, guests' sitting room and dining room, log fires, CH. Sweeping lawns. Evening meals by arrangement. Grass tennis court and croquet lawn, horse riding locally. Open all year except Christmas & New Year.

---

16 Hillside Farm, Welbeck Road, Brooke, near Norwich, Norfolk NR15 1AU

Mrs Carolyn Holl
☎ 01508 550260
BB From £18–£20
EM From £12
Sleeps 4
🐕 🗱 🌿 🏛 🤝 🗱 🗱
☙ *Commended*

This is a 350-acre arable and stock farm. A beautiful 16th century thatched and timber-framed house situated in a pretty village, 7 miles south of Norwich, within easy reach of coast and Broads. One twin/family room, 1 double/family room, both with private facilities. Large games barn with snooker, pool and table tennis. Five acre private lake for coarse fishing. Relaxed family atmosphere. Open all year except Christmas.

---

17 Laurel Farm, Hall Lane, Oulton, Lowestoft, Suffolk NR32 5DL

Janet Hodgkin
☎/Fax 01502 568724
BB From £17–£22
Sleeps 4
🐕 🌿 🏛 🗱 🗱
Listed *Highly Commended*

Attractive Georgian farmhouse set in mature gardens overlooking rural views. Spacious bedrooms each with private bathroom and tea/coffee facilities. Drawing room with TV for guests' use. A short drive from Oulton Broad where boat hire and river trips are available. Find the local marked footpaths or lose yourself in the Somerleyton Hall maze. A no smoking house. Open all year.

Malting Farm, Blo Norton Road, South Lopham, Diss, Norfolk IP22 2HT (18)

Cynthia Huggins
☎ 01379 687201
BB From £18–£21
Sleeps 6

☙ Commended

Situated on Norfolk/Suffolk border amid open countryside. A working dairy farm where cows can be seen being milked, and there are farmyard pets. Farmhouse is Elizabethan timber-framed (inside) with inglenook fireplaces. Central heating. Some four poster beds, some en suite. Easy reach Norfolk Broads, Norwich, Cambridge, Bressingham Steam Museum & Gardens. Cynthia is keen craftswoman in quilting, embroidery, spinning, weaving. Closed Christmas & New Year.

Marsh Farm, Wolferton, King's Lynn, Norfolk PE31 6HB (19)

Keith Larrington
☎ 01485 540265
Fax 01485 543143
BB From £20
Sleeps 6

☙ Commended

You can be assured of a warm welcome at our comfortable and relaxing farmhouse, with large garden, in the quiet village of Wolferton. This working arable farm is ideally situated for walking and exploring the countryside and North Norfolk coast. RSPB reserves nearby. Open all year except Christmas.

Oak Farm, Market Lane, Blundeston, Lowestoft, Suffolk NR32 5AP (20)

Julie and Keith Cooper
☎ 01502 731622
BB From £16–£20
Sleeps 4

Listed Commended

140-acre mixed farm set in peaceful countryside crossed by the Waveney Way footpath and 1½ miles from the sea. This Victorian house was originally farm cottages. We take a pride in our breakfast and local pubs offer other meals. Guests' stairs lead to a double and a twin room and a guests' bathroom. Tea/coffee facilities and colour TV in rooms. Children very welcome – reductions under 14. Closed Christmas & New Year.

Old Coach House, Thursford, Fakenham, Norfolk NR21 0BD (21)

Mrs Ann Green
☎ 01328 878273
BB From £17–£20
EM From £8
Sleeps 6

Listed Commended

Small peaceful working farm set in parkland with cows, sheep, ducks etc. Farmhouse is a converted 17th century coachhouse. Main bedroom has four-poster sharing bathroom with 1 twin-bedded room, also 1 twin-bedded room with en suite bathroom – all have washbasins and tea/coffee facilities. Farmhouse dining/kitchen, guests' own sitting room with TV and garden room. Close to Thursford Collection and within easy reach of sandy beaches. Open all year (closed Christmas).

Park Farm, Bylaugh, East Dereham, Norfolk NR20 4QE (22)

Mrs Jenny Lake
☎ 01362 688584
BB From £15–£20
EM From £9
Sleeps 6

☙ Commended

Charming old family farmhouse with picturesque setting in Wensum Valley, ideally situated for exploring the Norfolk countryside and visits to Norwich, the Norfolk Broads and North Norfolk coast. One large family room, one double and one twin, all en suite. Lounge with colour TV, dining room with inglenook. Children welcome, sorry no pets. Open all year.

Park Farm, Sibton, Saxmundham, Suffolk IP17 2LZ (23)

Margaret Gray
☎ 01728 668324
Fax 01728 668564
BB From £17–£19
EM From £11.50
Sleeps 6

☙☙ Commended

Do you want comfort, peaceful surroundings and delicious food? If so, enjoy friendly farmhouse hospitality at its best in our spacious 18th century house close to Heritage Coast. English breakfast and 3-course dinners imaginatively cooked from local produce. All tastes and special diets catered for. Two twins en suite; one double with private bathroom. Ideal for birdwatching, sightseeing or relaxing. Open all year except Christmas.

24   **Pear Tree Farm**, Hartest, Bury St Edmunds, Suffolk IP29 4EQ

Mrs Rachel White
☎ 01284 830217
▣ From £20–£21
Sleeps 4
↪(2) ⤬
♨♨ Commended

A warm welcome awaits you in our modern farm chalet bungalow on this arable family farm. Ideally situated for exploring Lavenham, Constable Country, and Cambridge. We have 1 double en suite, 1 twin en suite, both with TV and tea/coffee-making facilities. Guests' TV lounge. Children welcome. Open Mar–Nov.

---

25   **Priory Farm**, Darsham, Saxmundham, Suffolk IP17 3QD

Suzanne Bloomfield
☎ 01728 668459
Fax 01728 668744
▣ From £19–£25
Sleeps 4
↪(8) ⤬ ⊞ ⌂

♨♨ Commended

Comfortable 17th century farmhouse situated in peaceful countryside. An ideal base for exploring the Suffolk coast and heathlands and other numerous local attractions. Excellent pubs and restaurants nearby. 1 double, 1 twin, each with private facilities, tea/coffee making in all bedrooms. Separate guests' dining room. Cycle hire available at the farm. Open Mar–Oct.

---

26   **Red House Farm**, Station Road, Haughley, Nr Stowmarket, Suffolk IP14 3QP

Mrs Mary Noy
☎/Fax 01449 673323
▣ From £18–£20
Sleeps 6
↪(8) ⤬ ⋏ ⊞ ⌂
♨♨ Commended

A warm welcome and homely atmosphere awaits you at our attractive farmhouse set in the beautiful surroundings of mid Suffolk. Comfortably furnished bedrooms with en suite shower rooms, tea/coffee-making facilities. One double, one twin and two single rooms. CH. Guests' own lounge with TV and dining room. Ideal location for exploring, walking, cycling and birdwatching. No smoking or pets. Open Jan–Nov.

---

27   **Salamanca Farm Guest House**, 116–118 Norwich Road, Stoke Holy Cross, Norwich, Norfolk NR14 8QJ

Roy & Barbara Harrold
☎ 01508 492322
▣ From £18–£21
Sleeps 8
↪(6) ⤬ ⌂
♨♨ Commended

"Real experience of English hospitality" – "All we could have asked for" – just two comments from our visitors' book. The Harrold family have welcomed guests to their farm for 20 years. 4 miles from the cathedral city of Norwich, the valley of the River Tas, with the mill where Colmans began producing mustard, provides an attractive holiday base. All rooms have private facilities. Open 15 Jan–15 Dec.

---

28   **Shrublands Farm,** Burgh St Peter, nr Beccles, Suffolk NR34 0BB

Mrs Rachel Clarke
☎/Fax 01502 677241
▣ From £18
Sleeps 6
↪(5) ⌂
♨♨ Commended

Tranquillity, peaceful surroundings and a warm welcome at this attractive, homely farmhouse. Set in 550 acres of mixed working farmland in the Waveney Valley. Ideal base for touring Norfolk/Suffolk. 2 double/family en suite, 1 twin with private facilities, all with colour satellite TV and tea/coffee-making facilities. Excellent choice of home-cooked breakfast. Tennis court available. Swimming pool and food at River Centre nearby. Open all year.

---

29   **Shrublands Farm,** Northrepps, Cromer, Norfolk NR27 0AA

Mrs Ann Youngman
☎/Fax 01263 579297
▣ From £20–£26
EM by arrangement
Sleeps 6
↪(12) ⋈ ⋏ ⊞ ⤬ ♨ ⌂
♨♨ Highly Commended

A warm welcome awaits you at Shrublands Farm, an arable farm set in the village of Northrepps, 2½ miles SE of Cromer and 20 miles north of Norwich. The Victorian/ Edwardian house has 1 twin and 1 double with private bathrooms and 1 twin en suite. Separate sitting room and dining room for guests. Full central heating, log fires in chilly weather. Sorry, no pets. Open all year (closed Christmas & New Year).
E mail: www.broadland.com/shrublands

Sloley Farm, Sloley, Norwich, Norfolk NR12 8HJ ③⓪

Mrs Ann Jones
☎ **01692 536281**
Fax **01692 535162**
[BB] From **£17.50–£19**
Sleeps 6
ᕤ(4) ⅄ Å ⏁ ⏁
🌿🌿 *Commended*

Comfortable farmhouse on a mixed farm, 4 miles Norfolk Broads, easy reach of Norwich and the coast. Double/twin room with en suite, family and single rooms sharing guests' bathroom, colour TV, tea/coffee-making facilities. Sitting and dining rooms for guests. Sorry no pets and no smoking. Open all year (closed Christmas & New Year).

South Elmham Hall, St Cross, Harleston, Norfolk IP20 0PZ ③①

Mrs Jo Sanderson
☎ **01986 782526**
Fax **01986 782203**
[BB] From **£20–£25**
EM From **£12.50**
Sleeps 6
ᕤ ⅄ ⏁ ⏁ ⏁ ⏁ ⏁
🌿🌿 *Highly Commended*

Moated former bishop's palace with large gardens. Mixed farm, peaceful location with rare cattle and farm trails in historic landscape. Tastefully furnished comfortable rooms with tea/coffee tray. Kingsize bed, double antique brass bed and twin bedded rooms all with en suite facilities and views of the farm and garden. Guests' lounge and dining room with TV, full CH. Evening meals, cot and baby sitting by arrangement. Open all year.

Stratton Farm, West Drove North, Walton Highway, Norfolk PE14 7DP ③②

Derek & Sue King
☎ **01945 880162**
[BB] From **£20.70–£23**
Sleeps 6
♿ ᕤ(7) ⅄ ⏁ ⏁ ⏁ ⏁ ⏁
🌿🌿 *Highly Commended*

We invite you to stay on our peaceful farm which supports a prize winning herd of Shorthorn cattle. Meet our cows and calves, collect fresh eggs for your breakfast, or fish in our lake. All bedrooms have en suite facilities. Home produced sausages, bacon, eggs and marmalades. Open all year (including Christmas).

Walpole Old Hall, Walpole, Halesworth, Suffolk IP19 9AU ③③

Pauline & Rodney Winter
☎ **01986 284234**
Fax **01986 784538**
[BB] From **£18–£20**
EM From **£10**
Sleeps 6
⅄ Å ⏁ ⏁
🌿🌿 *Commended*

Walpole Old Hall is a dairy farm surrounded by meadowland. Double and twin en suite rooms with tea/coffee facilities. The 16th century farmhouse has exposed beams and listed chimneys and large lounge with colour satellite TV. Guests' own private dining room. Covered swimming pool (heated in season). Minsmere and coast 9 miles. Open Mar–Oct.

Watersmeet, Framlingham Road, Laxfield, nr Woodbridge, Suffolk IP13 8DH ③④

Mrs Margaret Jefferies
☎ **01986 798880**
[BB] From **£17–£22**
EM From **£10.50**
Sleeps 5–6
ᕤ(10) ⅄ ⏁ ⏁
🌿🌿 *Highly Commended*

Experience the warm welcome and relax at this comfortable, traditional farmhouse with log fires and wonderful food – English breakfasts, suppers and vegetarian too. Two doubles en suite. Small working farm on edge of pretty village with interesting church, museum and old inns. Cycle or ramble through this part of rural Suffolk. Treat yourself to a weekend or longer stay. Open all year.

Witton Hall Farm, Witton, Norwich, Norfolk NR13 5DN ③⑤

Jane Mack
☎ **01603 714580**
[BB] From **£18–£20**
Sleeps 6
ᕤ
🌿🌿 *Commended*

This elegant Georgian farmhouse on a dairy and arable farm is set in the heart of Norfolk, 5 miles east of Norwich and 12 miles from the coast, and 3 miles from the Broads. There are two acres of mature garden. Spacious bedrooms, all with TV and en suite bathrooms.

36 Woodlands Farm, Brundish, near Woodbridge, Suffolk IP13 8BP

Jill Graham
☎ 01379 384444
BB From £18–£20
EM From £12.50
Sleeps 6
☺(10) ⊁ ■
♥ ♥ Highly Commended

A friendly welcome and good home cooking assured in our comfortable, timber-framed farmhouse set in peaceful countryside near Framlingham. Within easy reach of the coast and numerous local attractions. One twin and 2 double bedrooms with en suite bathrooms, and tea/coffee facilities. Separate dining and sitting rooms with inglenooks. Centrally heated with log fires in cold weather. AA Selected QQQQ. Closed Christmas & New Year.

SELF-CATERING

37 Baylham House Farm Annexe and Flat, Mill Lane, Baylham, Suffolk IP6 8LG

Ann Storer
☎/Fax 01473 830264
SC From £110–£280
Sleeps 4+cot and 2+cot
☺ ⌁ ⚒ ■ ⚘
⚷ ⚷ ⚷ ⚷ Commended

Two self-contained units in old farmhouse. Small rare breeds farm on River Gipping with sheep, cattle, poultry, pigs and goats. Peaceful setting, good walks, good touring base. Fishing, garden, barbecue. Both fully equipped to high standard. Children welcome, sorry no pets. Please phone or write for further details. Open all year.

38 Burnley Hall, East Somerton, Great Yarmouth NR29 4DZ

Penny Beard
☎ 01493 393206
Fax 01493 393745
SC From £250–£500
Sleeps 4–8+cot
☺ ⚒
⚷ ⚷ ⚷ ⚷
Up to Highly Commended

Arable/livestock farm between Norfolk Broads and sea. We welcome families with children and well behaved dogs to our 4 holiday homes (own garden). Equipped to a high standard with comfortable beds (linen, towels, heat, electricity included). Three-mile private beach, nature reserve, footpaths, bicycles, access to Broads (boat available). Weekend breaks. Brochure in request. Open all year.

32 Carysfort Too, Stratton Farm, West Drove North, Walton Highway, Norfolk PE14 7DP

Derek & Sue King
☎ 01945 880162
SC From £142.50–£365
Sleeps 4
☺(8) ⊁ ⚒ ⌁ ⚒ ■ ⚘
⚷ ⚷ ⚷ ⚷
Highly Commended

We welcome you to our beautiful farm cottage boasting 2 en suite bathrooms. Relax in total comfort, peace and seclusion. You may meet the calves or walk for miles with only bird song for company. Come and catch a carp from the lake or plunge into our heated swimming pool. We can guarantee you a perfect holiday. Free secure parking for 2 cars. Open all year including Christmas.

39 The Coach House, Kenton Hall, Debenham, Stowmarket, Suffolk IP14 6JU

Sharon McVeigh
☎ 01728 860279
Fax 01728 861246
SC From £125–£410
Sleeps 8
☺ ⚒ ⊁ ■ ⚒
⚷ ⚷ ⚷ ⚷
Highly Commended

Part of beautiful moated Tudor hall set in the centre of our 460-acre arable farm. One double en suite, one bunk bedded room with bathroom and a large additional bedroom en suite to sleep up to 4. Bed linen, towels, electricity and CH all included. Well equipped kitchen/diner, comfortable sitting room, cloakroom. Centrally situated for touring Suffolk coast (½ hour drive). Sorry no pets and no smoking. Open all year.

Colston Cottage, Colston Hall, Badingham, Woodbridge, Suffolk IP13 8LB **6**

John & Liz Bellefontaine
☎/Fax 01728 638375
SC From £200–£400
Sleeps 6
🐎 ⚞ ⚺ Å ⚓ ▰ ☞
♟ ♟ ♟ ♟ ♟ ♟
Commended

Charming centrally heated cottage enjoying lovely views over the Alde Valley. Idyllically set in the tranquillity of the countryside, yet only minutes from the coast. Downstairs bedroom. Cot and high chair available. Dishwasher, washing machine, tumble drier, freezer, colour TV telephone. Coarse fishing and indoor bowls available. Open all year.

The Cottage, Red House Farm, Station Road, Haughley, Nr Stowmarket, Suffolk IP14 3QP **26**

Mrs Mary Noy
☎/Fax 01449 673323
SC From £150–£190
Sleeps 2/4
🐑(8) ⚺ Å ⚓ ▰
♟ ♟ ♟ *Commended*

Enjoy the peace and tranquillity of Suffolk staying in our charming cottage which adjoins the farmhouse. Very well furnished and equipped. Ideal location for exploring, cycling, birdwatching and walking. All linen and towels provided. Electricity and heating included. No smoking or pets. Open all year.

Dairy Farm Cottages, Dilham, North Walsham, Norfolk NR28 9PZ **40**

Annabel Paterson
☎ 01692 535178
Fax 01692 536723
SC From £200–£950
Sleeps 4–11 + cot
🐾 🐑 ⚞ ⊞ ⚔ ▰
♟ ♟ ♟ ♟ – ♟ ♟ ♟ ♟ ♟
Highly Commended

Relax at Dairy Farm in Broadland, mixed arable and stock farm. Superb walks, acres of woodland, Victorian folly – Dilham Islands. 15 minutes to coast. Top quality accommodation, each cottage sleeps 4 to 11, all bedrooms en suite. Full kitchen facilities, laundry facilities, games room, secure play area, wheelchair access. Pets welcome. Colour brochure available. Open all year.

Dolphin Lodge, Roudham Farm, Roudham, East Harling, Norfolk NR16 2RJ **41**

Mr & Mrs T Jolly
☎ 01953 717126
Fax 01953 718593
SC From £215–£340
Sleeps 5/6
🐑 ⚺ ▰ ☞
♟ ♟ ♟ ♟ *Highly*
Commended

Let us offer you a country retreat! Conveniently situated in central East Anglia, our cottages are home-from-home. Beautifully restored with beams and woodburning stoves, set in large garden by Thetford Forest. Carefully prepared for you and fully equipped. CH, Aga, washing machine, tumble drier, fridge, microwave, colour TV. Each cottage sleeps 5 in two bedrooms. Many local attractions. You choose, a quiet secluded holiday or a busy sightseeing one? Open all year.

Farm Cottage, Grange Farm, Woolpit, Bury St Edmunds, Suffolk IP30 9RG **11**

Mrs Kathy Parker
☎ 01359 241143
SC From £150–£200
Sleeps 2
⚞ ⚺ Å ⚓ ▰ ☞
♟ ♟ ♟ *Commended*

Farm cottage is adjacent to farmhouse in the heart of Suffolk, only one mile from A14 corridor giving easy access to East Anglia. Ideal for touring tranquil villages or visiting major towns and cities. The cottage, recently converted, consists of kitchen/diner, lounge, double bedroom, en suite shower room and balcony area. Patio with barbecue. Linen and towels provided. Open all year.

The Granary, Priory Fram, Darsham, Saxmundham, Suffolk IP17 3QD **25**

Suzanne Bloomfield
☎ 01728 668459
Fax 01728 668744
SC From £135–£295
Sleeps 4
🐑 ⚺ ▰
♟ ♟ ♟ *Commended*

17th century granary tastefully converted to provide comfortable accommodation. Situated in peaceful Suffolk countryside, an ideal base for touring Suffolk coast and heathlands and other local attractions. 1 double, 2 singles. Shower room, kitchen, dining room, sitting room. Storage heaters, colour TV, washing machine. Cycle hire. Sat–Sat. Weekend lets out of season. Open all year.

(2) **The Granary Suites,** Brighthouse Farm, Melford Road, Lawshall, near Bury St Edmunds, Suffolk IP29 4PX

Mr & Mrs Truin
☎ **01284 830385**
[SC] **From £160–£180**
Sleeps 2
🕿 🛆 ⊡ 🎄 ⚘ 🎣
🐾 *Commended*

Granary conversion to a high standard for self catering. Set in large landscaped gardens, small but cosy, comprising double bedroom, en suite shower, washbasin, toilet, kitchen, TV, linen etc. provided. No smoking. Open all year.

---

(22) **Meadow View,** Park Farm, Bylaugh, East Dereham, Norfolk NR20 4QE

Mrs Jenny Lake
☎ **01362 688584**
[SC] **From £100–£175**
EM From £9
Sleeps 2/3
🐾 ⚘
🐾 🐾 🐾 🐾 *Commended*

Attached to charming old family farmhouse with picturesque setting in Wensum Valley, Meadow View is a comfortable, well equipped one bedroom bungalow with lovely countryside views. Sleeps 2 adults plus cot/child's bed and includes living room, kitchen, bathroom, colour TV and heating. Evening meals available next door served in dining room with inglenook. Children welcome, sorry no pets. Linen provided and laundry service. Open all year.

---

(42) **Rowney Cottage,** Rowney Farm, Whepstead, Bury St Edmunds, Suffolk IP29 4TQ

Mrs Kati Turner
☎/Fax **01284 735842**
[SC] **From £180–£275**
Sleeps 5
🐾 🏹 ⚘
🐾 🐾 🐾 🐾 *Commended*

Situated atop the rolling countryside of West Suffolk the 500-acre farm is ideally placed for exploring this picturesque and historically fascinating part of East Anglia. The cottage is spacious and fully equipped, with 2 bedrooms, fully fitted kitchen and bathroom and a generous lounge. The farm is safely tucked away at the end of a private drive. Bury St Edmunds 6 miles, Cambridge 32. Linen and electricity included. Children and pets welcome. Open Apr–Oct.

---

(43) **Stable Cottages and The Granary,** Chattisham Place, Nr Ipswich, Suffolk IP8 3QD

Mrs Margaret Langton
☎/Fax **01473 652210**
[SC] **From £130–£350**
Sleeps 2/8
🏩 🐾 🏹 🎄 🎣 ⚘
🐾 🐾 🐾 – 🐾 🐾 🐾
Highly Commended

Come and enjoy the peaceful Suffolk countryside where we have something for everyone. Making our 3 beautifully converted cottages (en suites, dishwashers) your base with all home comforts, you can relax or explore Constable Country, Lavenham and the Heritage Coast. Borrow maps for waymarked walks or bring the family to share our heated outdoor pool, tennis court, games and studio/craft room. Wheelchair users welcome. Open all year.

---

(44) **Tom, Dick and Harry,** Church Farm, Withersdale, Mendham, Harleston, Norfolk IP20 0JR

Audrey & Kate Carless
☎/Fax **01379 588090**
[SC] **From £90–£225**
Sleeps 2 + cot
🐾 🏹 🎄 ⚘
🐾 🐾 🐾 *Commended*

Tom, Dick and Harry are three timber-framed converted farm buildings nestling by dewy pastures in the 'Valley of the Rams'. Walk the footpaths, watch birds, go fishing, cycle Norfolk and Suffolk's tranquil lanes, enjoy a coastal drive. Each cottage includes garden, linen/towels, electricity, open fire. Cot/high chair available, ample parking. Open all year.

LET THE TELEPHONE RING!

Some farmhouses are big places. Let the telephone ring
long enough to give the owner time to answer it.

Essex

Group Contact: *Tineke Westerhuis* ☎ *01763 838053*

Come and discover the real Essex. We are waiting to welcome you to our farmhouses and help you discover our hidden treasures. Travelling is easy from the coast to the capital on the motorways (M25 / M11), the port of Harwich or Stansted Airport.

Once off the beaten track you will be surprised by our pargetted cottages and unspoilt villages set in undulating countryside. We can cater for all tastes and interests whether you want to relax visiting stately homes and working museums or potter round gardens like Beth Chatto's.

Go back in time to Romans at Colchester Castle, the saxons at unique Greenstead Church and the Second World War airfields and Duxford Air Museum. The energetic may walk the Essex Way from Epping, via Constable Country to the coast where you can sail and birdwatch around the creeks and esturies. Come and share our homes in the heart of the countryside and experience a personal welcome.

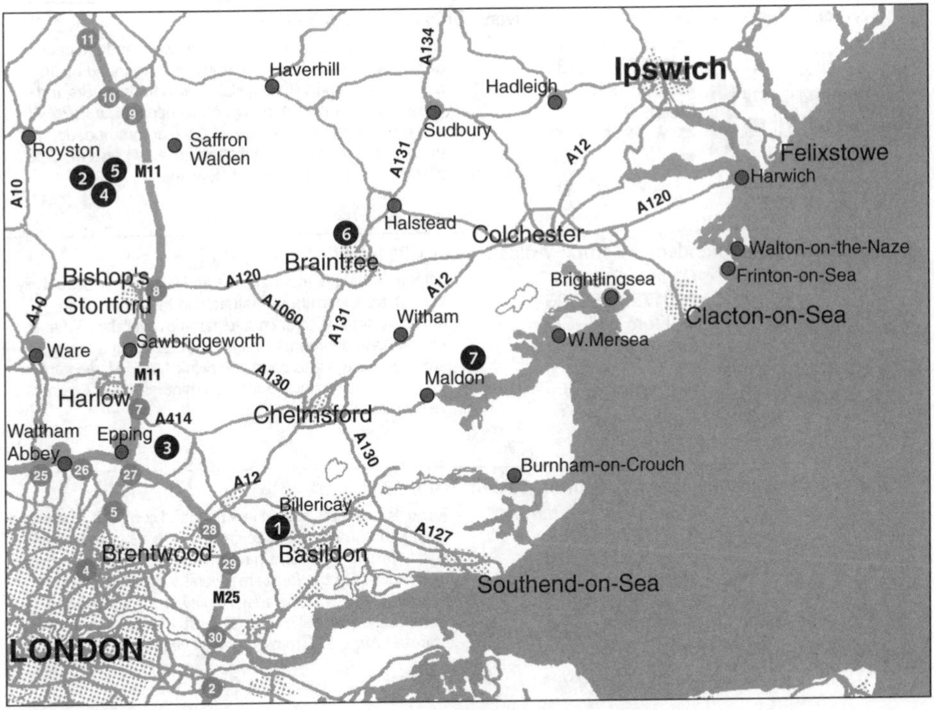

(map of Essex showing numbered locations, towns including Ipswich, Felixstowe, Harwich, Colchester, Chelmsford, Southend-on-Sea, Brentwood, Harlow, London, and road references M25, M11, A12, A120, A130, A131, A134, A127, A414, A10, A1060)

BED AND BREAKFAST

(and evening meal)

1 **Bonnydowns Farmhouse,** Doesgate Lane, Bulphan, Nr Upminster, Essex RM14 3TB

Rose Newman
☎ 01268 542129
BB From £20
EM From £8
Sleeps 6
🐎 ⚘ 🐈 🏛
Listed *Approved*

Large, comfortably furnished, pleasantly situated in large garden with lovely views. Close to Langdon Hills Country Park and Basildon New Town (modern shopping centre). Convenient for London, Southend, South East England via M25, A13, A127. Sheep/cattle kept on the farm. 2 twin, 1 family bedrooms, 1 bath with toilet/shower, 1 shower room with toilet. Tea/coffee trays. Good cooking. Open all year (closed Christmas).

2 **Duddenhoe End Farm,** Duddenhoe End, Nr Saffron Walden, Essex CB11 4UU

Peggy Foster
☎ 01763 838258
BB From £18–£22
Sleeps 6
🐎(12) ⚘
🌼 🌼 *Commended*

A warm welcome awaits you at this comfortable 17th century farmhouse situated in quiet rural area. All bedrooms have private or en suite bathrooms, tea/coffee-making facilities, TV and radio. Visitors' sitting room with TV. Ideally located for Cambridge, Audley End mansion, Duxford Air Museum and Stansted Airport. Central heating throughout. Non-smokers only. Open all year except Christmas.

3 **Newhouse Farm,** Mutton Row, Stanford Rivers, Ongar, Essex CM5 9QH

Mrs Beryl Martin
☎ 01277 362132
BB From £18
Sleeps 8
🐎 🏕 🐕 🏛 💼 🐈 🐾
🌼

Tudor farmhouse. with beams, inglenooks and bread oven on working arable farm. The house is surrounded by 10 acres of grassland with large lake with canoe, ducks and geese. Ideal for birdwatching and painting. Near Essex Way and open farmland. Specially adapted accommodation for disabled guests. Flashing light and fire alarm system. Open all year except Christmas and New Year.

4 **Parsonage Farm,** Arkesden, nr Saffron Walden, Essex CB11 4HB

Daniele Forster
☎ 01799 550306
BB From £15–£22
Sleeps 6
🐎 🐈 ⚘ 💼 🏛 🐾
🌼 *Commended*

After a hard day's touring come and relax in our beautifully kept Victorian farmhouse, situated in the centre of an attractive small village. En suite facilities available, TV and hot drinks in bedrooms. The farm is arable but a few pets are kept. Hard tennis court and picnic table in large garden. Excellent meals in local pub just 5 minutes' walk. Open all year except Christmas.

5 **Rockells Farm,** Duddenhoe End, Saffron Walden, Essex CB11 4UY

Mrs Tineke Westerhuis
☎ 01763 838053
BB From £17–£20
Sleeps 6
🐎 💼 🐾 🏛 🐾
🌼 🌼 *Commended*

Rockells is an arable farm in a beautiful corner of Essex. The Georgian house has a large garden with a 3-acre lake for coarse fishing. All rooms have private facilities, one room is downstairs. On the farm. are several footpaths, and beautiful villages in the area. Audley End, Duxford and Cambridge nearby. London is about 1 hour by car or train. Stansted Airport 30 mins. Open all year.

Spicers Farm, Rotten End, Wethersfield, Braintree, Essex CM7 4AL   6

Mrs Delia Douse
☎ **01371 851021**
🅱 **From £16–£20**
Sleeps 6
🐕 ♨ ♿
🐝 🐝 *Highly Commended*

Set in a delightful, peaceful position overlooking beautiful countryside. Comfortable and welcoming atmosphere. All rooms en suite with CH, tea/coffee-making facilities, colour TV, clock radio and lovely views. Convenient for Stansted, Harwich, Cambridge and Constable Country. Ideal for touring or walking. Open all year .

Wicks Manor Farm, Witham Road, Tolleshunt Major, Maldon, Essex CM9 8JU   7

Mary Howie
☎/Fax **01621 860629**
🅱 **From £15**
Sleeps 4
🐕 🐈 ✂ ♿
Listed *Commended*

Comfortable 17th century moated farmhouse set in large established garden. You are assured of a warm welcome on our mixed arable farm close to the River Blackwater estuary. Delicious traditional breakfasts or your own requirements. Guests' own bathroom and sitting room. Two attractive bedrooms with TV and tea/coffee-making facilities.

SELF-CATERING

The Byre, c/o Rockells Farm, Duddenhoe End, Saffron Walden, Essex CB11 4UY   5

Mrs Tineke Westerhuis
☎ **01763 838053**
🆂🅲 **From £140–£250**
Sleeps 3/5
🐕 🍴 🐕 🎿
🐾 🐾 🐾 *Commended*

The Byre is part of Rockells farmyard, an arable farm in a beautiful corner of Essex. Lounge with kitchen area has original wood panelling. The cottage is fully equipped to high standard. Garden with 3-acre lake for excellent fishing. In the area are several footpaths and beautiful villages with excellent pubs. Audley End, Duxford and Cambridge nearby. London is 1 hour by car or train, Stansted Airport 30 mins by car. Open all year.

Thames Valley

Group Contact: *Pat Hoddinott* ☎/Fax 01367 240175

The Thames Valley is at the heart of historical England. Farms and homes are situated in the area stretching from the Chiltern Hills above Henley through the rich farmland of the Vale of Aylesbury and on to the west of Oxford and the Cotswolds.

Oxford is at the centre of the region and its dreaming spires and great buildings, including mediaeval colleges and Renaissance masterpieces such as the Sheldonian Theatre, can provide great historical interest. You can take guided tours of Oxford, Windsor and Burford or enjoy browsing in antique shops and bookshops.

Woodstock has many historical associations and is the site of Blenheim Palace, the magnificent home designed by Sir John Vanbrugh for the Dukes of Marlborough. Sir Winston Churchill was born there and is buried in the nearby churchyard of Bladon. The area includes the moated castle at Broughton near Banbury and many other Tudor and 18th century manors and country houses.

Places of interest include the Cotswold Wildlife Park, Birdland, Cogges Farm Museum and a steam railway centre and activities such as boating, pony trekking and brass rubbing are available. Legoland has recently opened near Windsor.

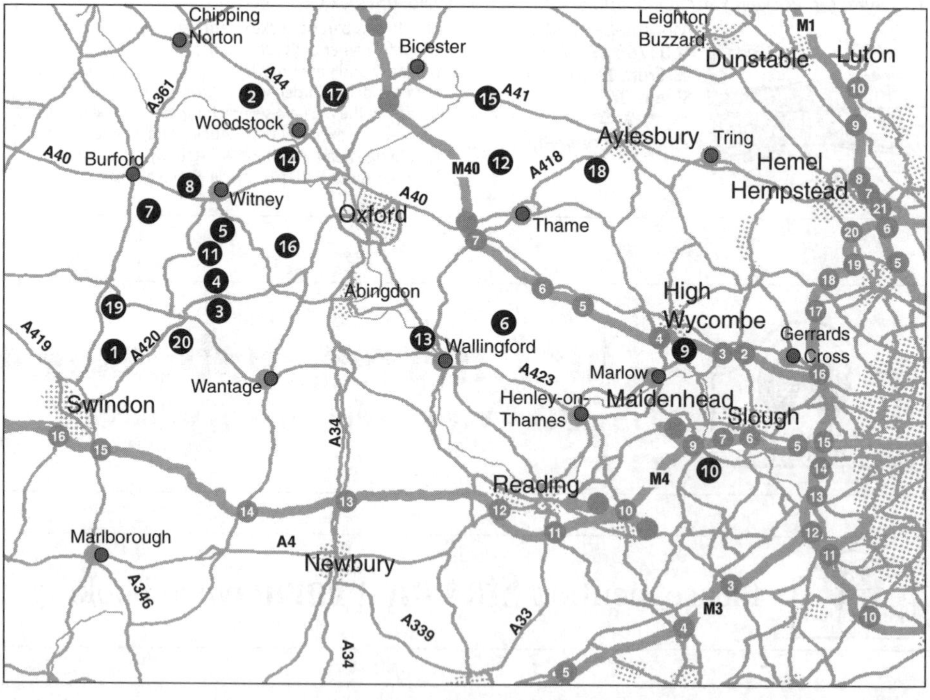

BED AND BREAKFAST

(and evening meal)

Ashen Copse Farm, Coleshill, Highworth, Nr Swindon, Wiltshire SN6 7PU   ①

Pat Hoddinott
☎/Fax 01367 240175
🅱 From £19–£22
Sleeps 6
🛋 ⅟ ☘ 💼 ◉
🦢🦢 *Commended*

Our National Trust beef/arable farm is an ideal setting for peace and quiet. Watch the wildlife during wonderful walks in beautiful countryside. Explore pretty Cotswold villages and attractions. Good food, golf and riding nearby. M4 11 miles. 1 family en suite, 1 twin and 1 single bedroom in comfortable 17th century farmhouse. Open all year except Christmas Day.

Banbury Hill Farm, Enstone Road, Charlbury, Oxford OX7 3JH   ②

Mrs Angela Widdows
☎ 01608 810314
Fax 01608 811891
🅱 From £16–£25
Sleeps 9
🛋 ⅟ 🐕 🐎 💼 ☘ 🦮
🦢🦢 *Commended*

Natural Cotswold stone farmhouse commanding spectacular view in AONB overlooking the small township of Charlbury with the ancient Wychwood Forest nestling against the River Evenlode. Large variety of animals around the farm. Ideally centred – midway Oxford, Stratford-on-Avon, near Blenheim, Burford and Chipping Norton. Family, double (3 en suite), twin or single rooms. Ideal for families. Also self-catering cottages available.

Bowling Green Farm, Stanford Road, Faringdon, Oxfordshire SN7 8EZ   ③

Della Barnard
☎ 01367 240229
Fax 01367 242568
🅱 From £20
Sleeps 6
🛋 ⅟ 🐎
🦢🦢 *Commended*

Attractive 18th century period farmhouse offering 20th century comfort situated in the Vale of the White Horse, just 1 mile south of Faringdon on the A417. Easy access to M4 for Heathrow Airport. A working farm breeding cattle and horses. Large twin/family room on ground floor en suite. All bedrooms have colour TV, electric blankets in winter, tea/coffee-making facilities and CH throughout. Open all year.

Chimney House, Chimney on Thames, Aston, Bampton, Oxfordshire OX18 2EH   ④

Mrs Jean Kinch
☎/Fax 01367 870279
🅱 From £21–£25
Sleeps 4
🛋(12) ⅟ 💼 ☘ ◉
🦢🦢 *Highly Commended*

Enjoy the peace and quiet of Chimney Farm, on the Thames path. Our recently renovated 100-year-old centrally heated farmhouse offers comfortable en suite bedrooms with TV, tea/coffee facilities and guests' lounge. Enjoy local walks and golf courses. In easy reach of Oxford, Blenheim and Cotswolds. A warm welcome awaits you. Open Mar–Nov.

Ducklington Farm, Coursehill Lane, Ducklington, Witney, Oxon OX8 7YG   ⑤

Mrs Stacey Strainge
☎ 01993 772175
🅱 From £19–£21
Sleeps 6
🛋 ⅟ 🐎 🦮 💼 ◉
🦢🦢 *Commended*

Looking forward to welcoming you to Ducklington Farmhouse. Our family-run mixed farm is situated 1½ miles from Witney on the edge of the Cotswolds. In this recently built house all rooms are en suite, have tea/coffee-making facilities and a TV. Pub meals available in village. Open all year except Christmas.

---

6 Fords Farm, Ewelme, Wallingford, Oxon OX10 6HU

Marlene Edwards
☎ **01491 839272**
🅱 **From £20–£28**
Sleeps 6
✌ ▦ ♞
🐝🐝 *Highly Commended*

500-acre mixed farm, arable beef and sheep. Attractive farmhouse set in historic part of village with famous church almshouses and school. Peaceful surroundings with good walks and good selection of pubs nearby. Easy access to Henley, Oxford, Reading, Windsor, Heathrow and London. Friendly and comfortable atmosphere. 3 twin rooms. Open all year.

7 Foxbury Farmhouse, Foxbury Farm, Burford Road, Brize Norton, Oxfordshire OX18 3NX

Mrs Di Dawes
☎/Fax **01993 844141**
🅱 **From £20**
Sleeps 6
🐴 ✌ ▦
Listed *Commended*

Come and relax at Foxbury Farm, an active mixed farm tucked in the country, yet only 10 minutes from Burford, and close to many of the Cotswold attractions. Spacious rooms with tea/coffee-making facilities and TV. The children will enjoy the lambs, chickens, donkey and other animals which surround our large lawn with outdoor play equipment. Good pub food nearby. Open all year except Christmas and New Year.

8 Hill Grove Farm, Crawley Road, Minster Lovell, Oxfordshire OX8 5NA

Mrs Katharine Brown
☎ **01993 703120**
Fax **01993 700528**
🅱 **From £19–£21**
Sleeps 4
🐴 ✌ 🚗 ♞ ▦ 🎾
🐝🐝*Highly Commended*

Hill Grove is a mixed, family-run 300-acre working farm situated in an attractive rural setting overlooking the Windrush Valley. Ideally positioned for driving to Oxford, Blenheim Palace, Witney (Farm Museum) and Burford (renowned as the Gateway to the Cotswolds and for its splendid Wildlife Park). New golf course 1 mile. Hearty breakfasts, friendly atmosphere. Children welcome. 1 double/private shower, 1 twin/double en suite. AA listed. Open all year (closed Christmas).

9 Monkton Farm, Little Marlow, Buckinghamshire SL7 3RF

Jane & Warren Kimber
☎ **01494 521082**
Fax **01494 443905**
🅱 **From £25**
Sleeps 6
🐴(5) ✌ Ⓐ 🚗 ▦
Listed *Commended*

A 150-acre working dairy farm with 14th century 'Cruck' farmhouse set in the beautiful Chiltern Hills, yet only 30 miles from London and 27 miles from Oxford. Heathrow 20 mins, 1 single, 1 double and 1 family room available. English breakfast served in the farm kitchen. Large choice of pubs and restaurants nearby. Open all year.

10 Moor Farm, Holyport, near Maidenhead, Berkshire SL6 2HY

Mrs G Reynolds
☎/Fax **01628 633761**
🅱 **From £20–£25**
Sleeps 6
🐴 ✌ ♞ ▦
🐝🐝 *Highly Commended*

In the pretty village of Holyport. Moor Farm is 4 miles from Windsor. The farmhouse is a timber-framed, 700-year-old 'listed' manor in a lovely country garden with charming en suite rooms, furnished with antiques. It is well placed for touring the Thames Valley and visiting London. Also close to Heathrow. Suffolk sheep and horses kept on farm. Open all year.

11 'Morar', Weald Street, Bampton, Oxfordshire OX18 2HL

Janet Rouse
☎ **01993 850162**
Fax **01993 851738**
🅱 **From £19–£22**
EM **From £13.50**
Sleeps 6
🐴(6) 🖰 ✌ ▦ ◎
🐝🐝 *Highly Commended*

A non-smoking farmhouse (retired from farming) where meat, vegetables, bread are nearly all home-produced and cooked to perfection. A member of The Guild of Master Craftsmen. Pet cats, sheep and goats will love your fuss and attention. Cotswolds, Oxford, Woodstock close by. We Morris dance, bellring, garden – and laugh! 1 twin, 2 doubles en suite. Spring breaks–4 nights BB EM £210 per couple inclusive. Open Mar–18 Dec.

New Farm, Oxford Road, Oakley, Aylesbury, Buckinghamshire HP18 9UR ⑫

Binnie Pickford
☎ **01844 237360**
BB **From £19–£25**
Sleeps 6
⏰(6) ◼ ⅄
Listed *Commended*

Friendly atmosphere in fully modernised farmhouse. Good food, comfortable bedrooms, views over 163 acres devoted to sheep, beef, arable. Situated on Oxfordshire/ Bucks boundary in peaceful surroundings. Walks in adjacent Bernwood Forest Nature Reserve. Golf course 1¼ miles. 7 miles Oxford, close to Waterperry Gardens, Waddesdon Manor, Quinton Railway Centre, Blenheim Palace and M40. Pubs and restaurants nearby. Open all year except Christmas.

North Farm, Shillingford Hill, Wallingford, Oxfordshire OX10 8NB ⑬

Hilary Warburton
☎ **01865 858406**
Fax 01865 858519
BB **From £22–£25**
Sleeps 4
⏰(8) ⅄ ☜ ☂ ◼
🌸🌸 *Highly Commended*

Attractive and quiet farmhouse in the middle of our 500-acre sheep and arable farm bordering the River Thames with a well-tended garden and hard tennis court. Pygmy goats and chickens. Lovely walks and private fishing available. Ideal for Oxford and Henley. One twin with private bathroom, one double en suite. Closed Christmas and New Year.

The Old Farmhouse, Station Hill, Long Hanborough, Oxfordshire OX8 8JZ ⑭

Vanessa Maundrell
☎ **01993 882097**
BB **From £19.50–£22**
Sleeps 4
⏰(12) ⅄ ⊙ ☂ ⚘ ◼
🌸🌸 *Highly Commended*

We welcome you to our former farmhouse dating from 1670 with many original features and charming bedrooms. Delicious breakfasts with freshly baked bread, homemade marmalade/jams and fresh orange juice (served in delightful cottage garden on summer mornings). Lovely country walks and good pubs within walking distance. Woodstock and Blenheim Palace nearby and Oxford a 10-minute train ride. Two doubles (one en suite). Closed Christmas.

Poletrees Farm, Ludgershall Road, Brill, Aylesbury, Buckinghamshire HP18 9TZ ⑮

Anita & John Cooper
☎/**Fax 01844 238276**
BB **From £20–£25**
EM From £12
Sleeps 8
⏰ ⅄ ◼ ☂ ◉
Listed *Commended*

A 16th century working beef and sheep farm with house of architectural interest. 2 quiet bedrooms, 1 double, 1 twin, both with H&C and tea/coffee-making facilities. Guests have own lounge. En suite barn conversion in garden for couples – suppers can be ordered. Many pubs and restaurants nearby. Places of interest include Waddesdon Manor, Claydon House, Stowe Gardens and Oxford and many others as seen under Thames Valley. Elizabeth Gundrey recommended. Open Feb–Dec.

Rectory Farm, Northmoor, Witney, Oxfordshire OX8 1SX ⑯

Mary Anne Florey
☎ **01865 300207**
Fax 01865 300559
BB **From £20–£22**
Sleeps 4
⅄ ☜ ☂ ◼
🌸🌸 *Highly Commended*

A 16th century farmhouse retaining old charm alongside modern comforts. Both rooms have en suite facilities, CH, tea/coffee-making facilities. Guests' own sitting room with woodburning stove. We are conveniently situated for Oxford (10m), the Cotswolds, Blenheim and the Thames path. A pot of tea, homemade shortbread, along with a warm welcome and a peaceful, comfortable stay await you at Rectory Farm. Open Feb–mid Dec.

Vicarage Farm, Kirtlington, Oxfordshire OX5 3JY ⑰

Mrs Judith Hunter
☎ **01869 350254**
BB **From £19–£20**
Sleeps 4
⅄ ☂ ◼ ◉
🌸 *Commended*

A no-smoking farmhouse, situated in a rural area, adjacent to an 18-hole golf course with driving range. Golf easily available. The well-furnished rooms have wonderful views. One twin and one double, both with colour TV and tea/coffee-making facilities. Woodstock and Blenheim Palace 4 miles, Oxford 8 miles, Stratford, Warwick and Silverstone within ½ hour's drive. Open Mar–Nov.

18 **Wallace Farm,** Dinton, Nr Aylesbury, Buckinghamshire HP17 8UF

Jackie Cook
☎ **01296 748660**
Fax **01296 748851**
🅱 From **£20–£28**
Sleeps 6
⌂ 🎫 🛏 ⛄ 🎪 🛉 ⑯
🌣 🌣 *Commended*

This 16th century listed farmhouse is situated in a quiet, rural setting in the Vale of Aylesbury, yet within easy reach of London, Oxford and Heathrow. A small family farm, rearing beef cattle and sheep, plus chickens, ducks and geese. Plenty of opportunities for country walks, coarse fishing or browsing through our extensive library. Open all year.

---

19 **Weston Farm,** Buscot Wick, Faringdon, Oxfordshire SN7 8DJ

Mrs Jean Woof
☎/Fax **01367 252222**
🅱 From **£20**
Sleeps 4
🌣(10) 🍴 ⛄ 🐎 ⑯
🌣 🌣 *Highly Commended*

Come and share our idyllic 17th century Cotswold farmhouse in peaceful surroundings. Period furniture and well maintained gardens. 500-acre mixed farm. CH, tea/coffee-making facilities and own TV, one four-poster and one twin room, each with private bathroom. Guests own dining and sitting rooms, with log fires. Ideally situated to explore this beautiful area. Open all year except Christmas.

SELF-CATERING

2 **Banbury Hill Farm,** Enstone Road, Charlbury, Oxford OX7 3JH

Mrs Angela Widdows
☎ **01608 810314**
Fax **01608 811891**
🆂🅲 From **£185–£295**
Sleeps 4/6
🌣 🛉 🎪
🏠 🏠 🏠 – 🏠 🏠 🏠 🏠
Highly Commended

Comfortable Cotswold farm cottages, well appointed with outstanding views in AONB between Oxford and Stratford-on-Avon. Variety of farm animals. Forest trail, play area, tennis and bike hire available. Ample parking. Open Mar–Nov.

---

10 **Courtyard Cottages,** Moor Farm, Holyport, near Maidenhead, Berkshire SL6 2HY

Mrs G Reynolds
☎/Fax **01628 633761**
🆂🅲 From **£225–£450**
Sleeps 2/4
🌣 🍴 🎪 🛏
🏠 🏠 🏠 🏠 *Highly Commended*

In the pretty village of Holyport, Courtyard Cottages are on the 700-year-old manor of Moor Farm and are conversions from a Georgian stable block and two small barns. They retain the charm of their original features and are furnished with antique pine. The 4 cottages are well placed for touring the Thames Valley and are 4 miles from Windsor and convenient for visiting London. Sheep and horses are on the farm. Open all year.

---

20 **Coxwell House,** Little Coxwell, Faringdon, Oxfordshire SN7 7LP

Elspeth Crossley Cooke
☎ **01367 241240**
Fax **01367 240911**
🆂🅲 From **£350–£695**
Sleeps 6
🌣 🛉 🛏 🐎 🎪 🛉 ⑯
🏠 🏠 🏠 🏠 *Highly Commended*

Coxwell House is the superb main 1760 part (self-contained) of a Georgian farmhouse set in an attractive, secluded walled garden. Every modern convenience. Tennis court, indoor swimming pool. Unspoilt stone walled farming village with thatched cottages and pub. Ideal for the Cotswolds, Oxford. 1½ miles Faringdon south of A420. Open all year. E mail: elspeth@coxwell.u-net.com

Rectory Farm Cottages, Northmoor, Nr Witney, Oxon OX8 1SX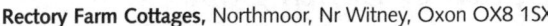

Mary Anne Florey
☎ **01865 300207**
Fax 01865 300559
⑤ From £210–£350
Sleeps 4
ఈ ⅟ ▲ ♥ ♨
♠ ♠ ♠ ♠ *Highly Commended*

Two delightful, warm, welcoming cottages tucked away on our farm in quiet village 10mw Oxford with south-facing enclosed gardens, field views and excellent walks. Each cottage is furnished in pine and has 1 double and 1 twin bedroom, bathroom, shower room, lounge with woodburner, TV, dining area and kitchen (washer/drier, dishwasher, electric cooker, fridge, microwave). CH, ample parking, linen/towels provided. Fully inclusive price. Open all year.

Wallace Farm Cottages, Dinton, Nr Aylesbury, Buckinghamshire HP17 8UF ⑱

Jackie Cook
☎ **01296 748660**
Fax 01296 748851
⑤ From £170–£270
Sleep 2–5
ఈ ♜ ⊞ ▲ ♥ ♨ ♈ ◉
♠ ♠ ♠ *Commended*

The Old Foaling Box and Keepers Cottage are two very charming cottages set across the courtyard of a 16th century farmhouse. These adjoining cottages are on one level and comfortably giving a feeling of cosiness and welcome. This conversion of a former stable block has been kept in complete harmony with the surrounding farm. Open all year.

FOLLOW THE COUNTRY CODE

Leave nothing but footprints,
Take nothing but photographs,
Kill nothing but time!

FINDING YOUR ACCOMMODATION

FARM HOLIDAY BUREAU

The Group contacts at the beginning of each section can always help you find a vacancy in your chosen area.

CONFIRM BOOKINGS

Disappointments can arise from misunderstandings over the telephone.
Please write to confirm your booking.

Hampshire

Group Contact: *Mrs Melanie Bray* ☎ *01705 631597*

Hampshire is a beautiful county of contrasts ... of creeks, harbours and beaches, grand rivers and sparkling streams, forests, and lush farmland with picturesque villages and hamlets.

The main centres of the county have all played an important role in history: the Saxons made Winchester their capital; Southampton bears witness to the Norman invasion, and Portsmouth is famous for its naval heritage with Nelson's HMS Victory, Henry VIII's Mary Rose and the first ironclad warship, HMS Warrior.

Hampshire has numerous other links with the past , Jane Austen's house at Chawton or Charles Dickens' birthplace in Portsmouth, for example, or enjoy the many rich treasures on show in the museums of the county's towns and cities.

In the New Forest there are plenty of quiet picnic spots and lots of ponies. Hampshire is served by a network of footpaths and bridleways and many country parks. There are long distance walks and guided walks which can take you round the towns and cities, along the Solent coastline or inland along the famous Test Valley. The country mansions of Broadlands, Breamore, Stratfield Saye and Highclere Castle and numerous gardens are open to the public.

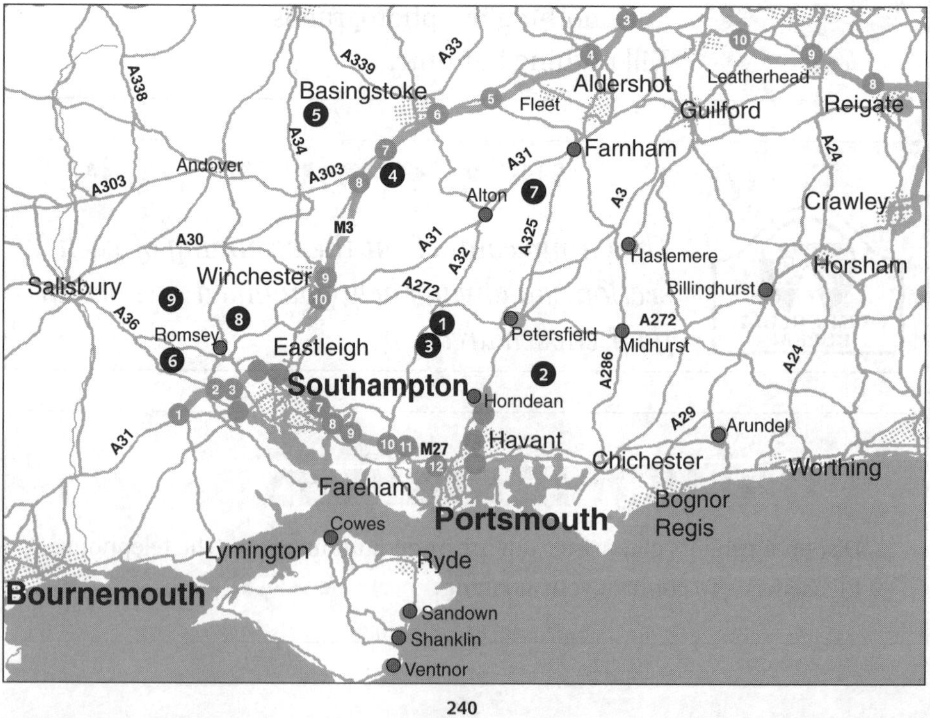

BED AND BREAKFAST
(and evening meal)

Brocklands Farm, West Meon, Petersfield, Hampshire GU32 1JN

Sue Wilson
☎ 01730 829228
BB From £18–£19.50
Sleeps 6
Listed *Commended*

Sue's home-baked bread and delicious preserves complement her warm hospitality in the unique, traditionally furnished, modern farmhouse. Lovely views of the countryside and a sheltered sunny terrace. Mown grass walks around the farm and into West Meon, a charming village with shops and 2 friendly pubs. TV in some rooms. There are badgers on the farm. Open all year except Christmas.

Compton Farmhouse, Church Lane, Compton, Nr Chichester, West Sussex PO18 9HB

Mrs Melanie Bray
☎ 01705 631597
BB £20
Sleeps 6
Listed *Commended*

Children are especially welcome (half-price) at our old, flint farmhouse. We are 200 yards up a track from the village square, next door to the church and are bordered by fields and woods. Lovely walks and plenty to do in our enclosed, child-orientated garden. Large family bedroom, own bathroom and sitting/dining room with drink-making facilities, fridge, TV. Open all year except Christmas.

Moortown Farm, Soberton, Droxford, Hampshire SO32 3QU

Rosemary Taylor
☎/Fax 01489 877256
BB £15–£25
Sleeps 6
Listed *Commended*

A friendly atmosphere is found at Moortown in the heart of the Meon Valley, an Area of Outstanding Natural Beauty. Crossed by the Warfarer's Walk and South Downs Way. 1 twin en suite, 1 4-bedded with private bathroom, both with TV and tea facilities. Set in a peaceful village within easy reach of Winchester, home of King Arthur's Round Table, Portsmouth, with the Mary Rose and Nelson's flagship, Chichester and the New Forest. Open all year.

Oakdown Farm Bungalow, c/o Oakdown Farm, Dummer, Basingstoke, Hampshire RG23 7LR

Mrs Elizabeth Hutton
☎ 01256 397218
BB From £16–£17
Sleeps 6
🐴(12) ▪ ⚘ ◉
⚘ *Commended*

Oakdown Farm Bungalow is on a secluded, private road, next to junction 7 on the M3, 1 mile south of Basingstoke and close to the village of Dummer. Excellent road communications to London, Winchester, South coast, the South-West, Oxford and the Midlands. Local historians welcome. B&B for horses. Wayfarer's Walk within 200 metres. Open all year.

Peak House Farm, Cole Henley, Whitchurch, Hampshire RG28 7QJ

Mrs Jenny Stevens
☎ 01256 892052
BB From £16–£18
Sleeps 6
Applied

Come and stay in our attractively furnished and decorated turn of the century farmhouse set in peaceful surroundings on working dairy farm close to Watership Down. Beautiful walks and horseriding nearby. Centrally based for New Forest, Winchester, Stonehenge, Legoland and Oxford. 1 twin en suite, 1 double and 1 twin with handbasin, all with colour TV, tea/coffee facilities. Lounge with log fire. Large garden, parking. Children welcome. Open all year.

6 **Pyesmead Farm,** Plaitford, Romsey, Hampshire SO51 6EE

Mrs Christina Pybus
☎ **01794 323386**
BB **From £15–£17.50**
Sleeps 6
😊 ⅍ 🏇 ↩ ♨
😊😊 *Commended*

A warm welcome awaits you, on the northern edge of the New Forest, at our family-run stock farm with its own coarse fishing lakes and indoor swimming pool. Many activities locally including horse riding, trout fishing, golf and forest walks. Within easy reach of Salisbury, Winchester, Southampton and the coast. Excellent pubs providing good food within ½ mile. Children welcome. Open all year except Christmas.

7 **Vine Farmhouse,** Isington, Alton, Hampshire GU34 4PW

Mrs G Sinclair
☎/Fax **01420 23262**
mobile **0467 767599**
BB **From £15–£20**
Sleeps 5
🏇 🐓 ⅍ ♨ ♨ 🎪 ⚘
Listed *Commended*

Vine Farmhouse is situated halfway between Alton and Farnham in its own farmland overlooking the River Wey. Gatwick and Heathrow are 1 hour by car as is London. Local attractions are Jane Austen's house, Birdworld, steam museum and railway and numerous gardens. Pubs and restaurants nearby. Open all year except Christmas.

SELF-CATERING

8 **Meadow Cottage,** c/o Farley Farm, Braishfield, Romsey, Hampshire SO51 0QP

Mrs Wendy Graham
☎ **01794 368265/368513**
Fax **01794 367847**
SC **From £160–£280**
Sleeps 5 + cot
😊 🐓 ♨ ♨
🐾 🐾 🐾 🐾 *Commended*

Well equipped, semi-detached cottage on a 400-acre beef and arable farm. Outstanding views of beautiful surrounding countryside. Ideal for walking or riding, or touring historic centres of Romsey, Winchester, Salisbury, Portsmouth, New Forest and coast. Cottage has CH, log fire, colour TV, downstairs WC, washer/dryer, cot. Garden with barbecue. Phone for brochure. Open Easter–Oct.

9 **Owl Cottage,** Lye Farm, West Tytherley, Romsey, Hampshire SP5 1LA

Maxine Vine
☎ **01794 341667**
SC **From £190–£290**
Sleeps 5
😊 🐓 ♨ 👤 🕭
Applied

Owl cottage has been skillfully converted from an old barn situated in one of the most beautiful parts of Hampshire. Outstanding views, close New Forest, Salisbury, Winchester. Location perfect for touring, walking, riding in southern England. Excellently equipped cottage, central heating, electric included, washer dryer, TV, cot. Peaceful and relaxing environment. Open all year.

NO ANSWER?
Farmers are mostly out and about during the day.
Try to telephone before 9.30am or after 4pm.

Isle of Wight

Group Contact: *Mrs Judy Noyes* ☎ *01983 852582*

The Isle of Wight with its sandy beaches and small secluded coves, and the sea never more than 15 minutes from wherever you may be, has a wide variety of holiday activities. With Cowes and the Royal Yacht Squadron, an international symbol of all that is finest in yachting, the Island is famous for its seafaring activities. A climate that tops the British Isles' Sunshine League makes the island particularly attractive in Spring or Autumn for short break holidays.

For the rambler, the birdwatcher, the angler and for those who merely wish to relax beside the splendours of ancient lighthouses or towering chalk cliffs, the Isle of Wight is the ideal holiday retreat with an internationally acclaimed network of well marked footpaths. For the more adventurous, the Island is a haven for hang-gliders, windsurfers, water skiers, canoe enthusiasts and deep sea fishermen.

Attractions for both children and adults include nature reserves, Butterfly World, the IOW Rare Breeds Park, Blackgang Chine with its history of smuggling and shipwrecks, a steam railway featuring some of the earliest steam engines, Roman remains, historic manors, mills, craft centres, and vineyards open for guided tours and wine tasting.

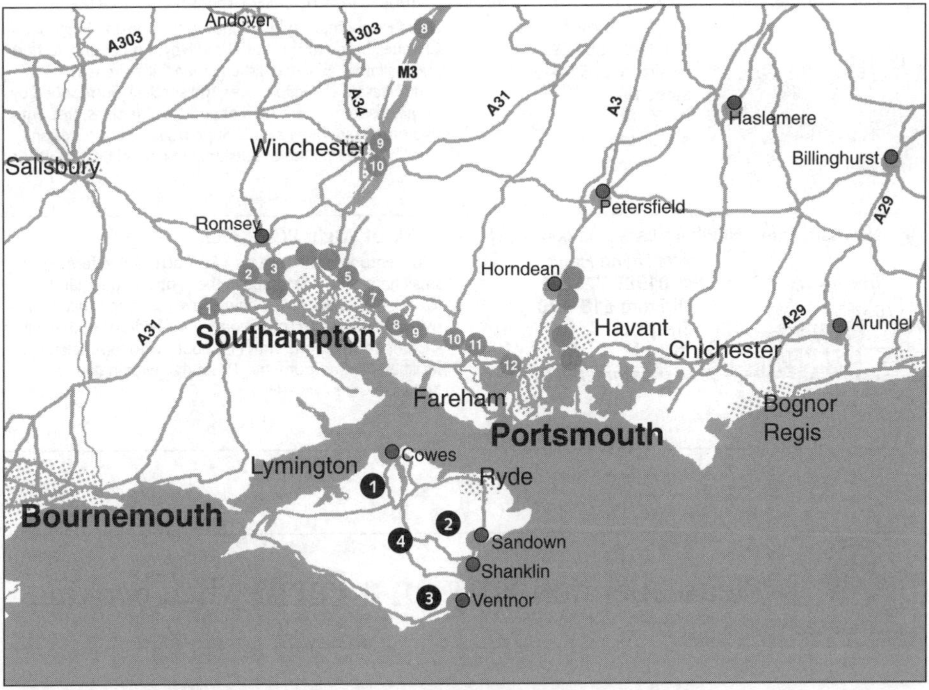

BED AND BREAKFAST

(and evening meal)

---

① Auld Youngwoods Farm, Whitehouse Road, Porchfield, Newport, Isle of Wight PO30 4LJ

Judith Shanks
☎/Fax 01983 522170
BB From £15–£19
Sleeps 5
☺(8) ✌ 亓 ♨ ♨ ☜
Listed *Commended*

A grassland farm set in open countryside. The 18th century renovated stone farmhouse retains its original character. The guest rooms are spacious and enjoy magnificent views of the West Wight (CH throughout). Close to Newtown Nature Reserve, an ideal base for the naturalist. Wild flowers. Red squirrels, owls and butterflies locally. Cowes sailing centre 4 miles. Open all year.

---

② Kern Farm, Alverstone, Nr Sandown, Isle of Wight PO36 0EY

Mrs Gaynor Oliver
☎ 01983 403721
BB From £18–£20
Sleeps 5
☺(10) ✌ 亓 ♨ ☜
♨ *Commended*

Quiet and secluded 16th century listed stone farmhouse nestling at the foot of the Downs on a mixed farm with wonderful views. Situated on Bembridge Trail. Sandy beaches 3 miles. One double and one triple bedroom – both en suite with tea and coffee-making facilities. Colour TV. Minimum 2 nights. Open all year.

---

③ Lisle Combe, Bank End Farm, Undercliff Drive, St Lawrence, Ventnor, Isle of Wight PO38 1UW

Hugh & Judy Noyes
☎ 01983 852582
BB From £16.50–£19
Sleeps 6
☺ ✌ ♨
♨ *Commended*

Listed Elizabethan style farmhouse overlooking English Channel, home of the late Alfred Noyes (poet and author) and his family. 5 acre coastal garden with rare waterfowl and pheasant collection (over 100 species). Surrounded by farmlands for owner's herd of pedigree Friesians, free entry to owner's rare breeds park. Superb sea views, coves and small beaches in area of outstanding natural beauty. Open all year.

---

④ Newbarn Farm, Newbarn Lane, Gatcombe, Newport, Isle of Wight PO30 3EQ

Mrs Diane Harvey
☎ 01983 721202
BB From £18–£20
Sleeps 6
☺(5) ✌ 亓 ♨
♨ *Commended*

17th century farmhouse on a 240-acre arable farm in the small hamlet of Gatcombe in the centre of the island. Wonderful walking area enjoying some spectacular views over the island and south coast. Two bedrooms, one with shower en suite, one with H/C, both with tea-making facilities. Dining room and TV lounge with inglenook fireplace. Open Mar–Nov.

FARM HOLIDAY BUREAU

Please mention **Stay on a Farm** when booking

SELF-CATERING

Lisle Combe Cottage, Bank End Farm, Lisle Combe, Underdiff Drive, St Lawrence, Ventnor, IOW PO38 1UW   3

Hugh & Judy Noyes
☎ **01983 852582**
🆂🅒 **From £160–£260**
Sleeps 5 + cot
🐕 💼
🔑 🔑 🔑 *Approved*

Listed cottage overlooking English Channel. Own garden within grounds of Lisle Combe. Large pheasant and waterfowl collection, free entry to owner's rare breed park. Many small beaches and coves for swimming or sunbathing. Colour TV, everything provided except linen. Fine coastal walks in area of outstanding natural beauty. Surrounded by 180-acre family farm with pedigree Friesian herd. Open all year.

The Stable, Newbarn Farm, Newbarn Lane, Gatcombe, Newport, Isle of Wight PO30 3EQ   4

Mrs Diane Harvey
☎ **01983 721202**
🆂🅒 **From £150–£425**
Sleeps 6
🐕 🎋 ½
🔑 🔑 🔑 🔑 *Highly Commended*

Beautiful converted stable offering high standard of accommodation for up to six people. Both bedrooms have double beds, one with 3 ft bunks, other with cot. Secluded valley setting, excellent walking. Centrally situated for island attractions. Enclosed patio and parking. Linen and electricity included. Beds made up on arrival. Open all year.

West Wing, Kern Farm, Alverstone, nr Sandown, Isle of Wight PO36 0EY   2

Mrs Gaynor Oliver
☎ **01983 403721**
🆂🅒 **From £250–£425**
Sleeps 6
🐕(10) 💼 🎋 🦞
🔑 🔑 🔑 *Commended*

Self-contained west wing of 16th century listed stone farmhouse on 250-acre mixed farm. Off beaten track, ideal for walking, painting or just relaxing. Two triple bedrooms. All linen provided. Log fire and CH. Regret no dogs or children under 10. Friday bookings. Open all year.

LET THE TELEPHONE RING!
Some farmhouses are big places. Let the telephone ring
long enough to give the owner time to answer it.

Sussex & Surrey

Group Contacts: *Sussex: Brenda Gough* ☎ *01273 478680*
Surrey: Mrs Gill Hill ☎ *01306 730210*

You've probably heard of 'Sussex by the Sea' so perhaps to you Sussex means the traditional attractions of the popular seaside resorts such as Brighton, Eastbourne, Hastings, Bognor Regis, Littlehampton and Worthing. What you may not know is that just inland there is a vast area of lovely downland punctuated with tiny villages and the occasional old market town. Further north busy towns such as Horsham, Crawley and East Grinstead are surrounded by lush green countryside. There is also a rich history here – Chichester with its famous Roman cross, nearby Fishbourne with the remains of a palace once ruled by a King Cogidubnus … really; and Hastings – 1066 and all that. Most towns in both counties have a wealth of antique shops.

In Surrey, the North Downs provide dramatic wooded hillsides with small, attractive towns and villages nestling in the valleys. Here you can walk along the track claiming to be the Pilgrim's Way which connects Winchester to Canterbury; clamber up famous heights like Leith Hill – just short of 1,000ft – or its neighbour Box Hill, coming down via the intriguingly named Zig Zag Hill.

Yet nowhere in these counties are you ever more than a couple of hours from central London should you wish to make a day trip there.

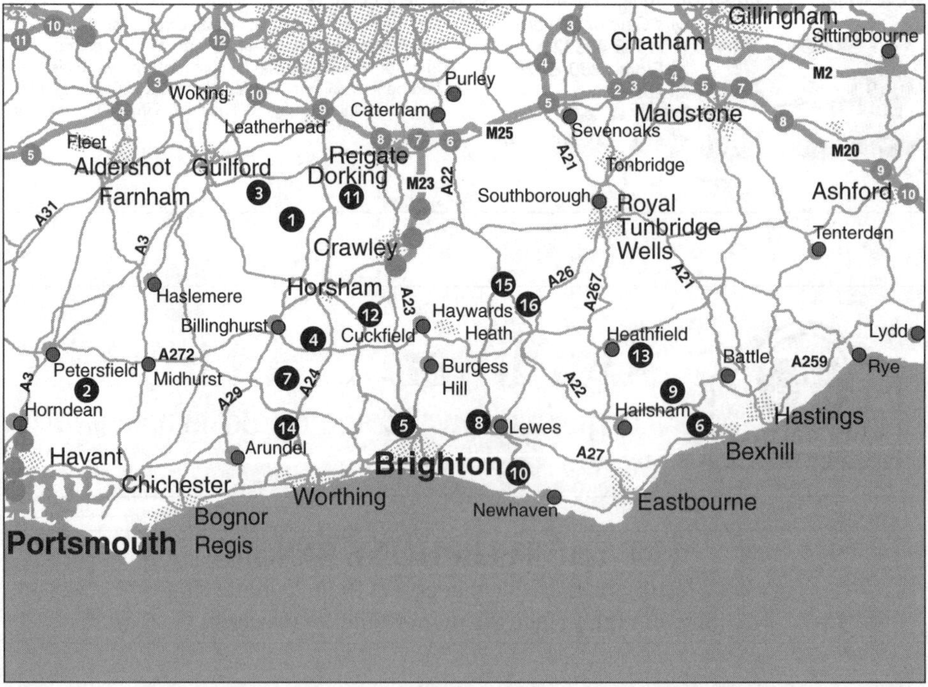

BED AND BREAKFAST

(and evening meal)

Bulmer Farm, Holmbury St Mary, Dorking, Surrey RH5 6LG ①

Gill Hill
☎ 01306 730210
⸬ From £19–£30
Sleeps 16
🐾 ☌(12) 🛏 🍽 🎩 🎺
Caravans £3.50
♨♨ *Commended*

Warm welcome guaranteed at our 30-acre farm in peaceful, picturesque Victorian village amid Surrey hills. 3 charming rooms in 17th century farmhouse; 5 en suite barn conversion, non-smoking rooms with TV around courtyard adjoining house. Homemade preserves. Large walled garden, woodland walk to award-winning lake. Good pubs nearby. Convenient for London, airports, Wisley, NT properties, sporting venues. Elizabeth Gundry recommended. Open all year.

Compton Farmhouse, Church Lane, Compton, Nr Chichester, West Sussex PO18 9HB ②

Mrs Melanie Bray
☎ 01705 631597
⸬ £20
Sleeps 6
☌ 🍽 🎩 🎺
Listed *Commended*

Children are especially welcome (half-price) at our old, flint farmhouse. We are 200 yards up a track from the village square, next door to the church and are bordered by fields and woods. Lovely walks and plenty to do in our enclosed, child-orientated garden. Large family bedroom, own bathroom and sitting/dining room with drink-making facilities, fridge, TV. Open all year except Christmas.

Crossways Farm, Raikes Lane, Abinger Hammer, Nr Dorking, Surrey RH5 6PZ ③

Sheila Hughes
☎ 01306 730173
⸬ From £18–£20
Sleeps 6
☌ 🛏 🎩 🎺 🍷
♨♨ *Commended*

Welcome to our 17th century listed farmhouse (book and TV setting) amidst the oustanding beauty of the Surrey hills. Good walks. Near A25 and Dorking/Guildford bus stop. Easy reach Gatwick, Heathrow, London, S Coast, Wisley. Large, comfortable rooms, washbasins, tea/coffee-making facilities, inglenooks, log fires, beams, colour TV. Walled garden, croquet. Laundry facilities. Elizabeth Gundry recommended. Open all year.

Goffsland Farm, Shipley, Horsham, West Sussex RH13 7BQ ④

Mrs Carol Liverton
☎/Fax 01403 730434
⸬ From £17–£19
Sleeps 5
☌ 🛏 🏇 Å 🎩 🎺 🍽
♨♨ *Commended*

A friendly welcome awaits you at our 17th century farmhouse on a working farm with sheep and dairy herd. Situated in the Sussex Weald central to Gatwick and the South coast. Family room has double bed and bunk beds with washbasin and tea/coffee-making facilities. Own bathroom with WC and own sitting/dining room with TV. Open all year.

Manor Farm, Poynings, Nr Brighton, West Sussex BN45 7AG ⑤

Mrs Carol Revell
☎/Fax 01273 857371
⸬ From £22–£25
Sleeps 6
Å 🎩 🍽
♨♨ *Commended*

260-acre family run sheep/arable farm with charming old manor house resting quietly in a green valley under the South Downs. An area of outstanding natural beauty, ideal for riders, walkers, golfers, hang gliders and country lovers. Plenty of country pubs and eating houses nearby. A23 5 mins, Hickstead 10 mins, Gatwick 30 mins, Brighton and Hove 15 mins. Evening meal by request only. Open Mar–Dec.

6 **Moonshill Farm,** The Green, Ninfield, Battle, East Sussex TN33 9LH

Mrs June Ive
☎/Fax 01424 892645
[BB] From £15–£17.50
Sleeps 6
♿(4) 🏨 🧍 🐕 🐎 🚲 💼 ℀
☙☙ *Commended*

In the heart of the '1066 Country' in the centre of Ninfield opposite pub. Farmhouse in 10 acres of garden, orchard, stables. Enjoy beautiful walks, golf and riding arranged. Comfortable rooms, 3 en suite, CH and electric fires, hospitality tray, TV, lounge, parking and garage, babysitting service. Every comfort in our safe, quiet and peaceful home. Reduced rates for weekly bookings. Open Jan–Nov.

---

7 **New House Farm,** Broadford Bridge Road, West Chiltington, Nr Pulborough, West Sussex RH20 2LA

Alma Steele
☎ 01798 812215
Fax 01798 813209
[BB] From £20–£25
Sleeps 6
♿(12) 💼 ℀
☙☙ *Commended*

Listed 15th century farmhouse with oak beams and inglenook fireplace, in the centre of the village, close to local inns which provide good food. A new 18 hole golf course, open to non-members, is only ¼ mile away. Many places of historical interest in the area including Goodwood House, Petworth House, Parham House, Arundel Castle. Gatwick 35 minutes. En suite facilities and colour TV in bedrooms. Open all year.

---

8 **Ousedale House,** Offham, Lewes, East Sussex BN7 3QF

Roland & Brenda Gough
☎ 01273 478680
Fax 01273 486510
[BB] From £23–£27
EM From £13
Sleeps 6
✂ 📧 💼 ⊛
☙☙ *Highly Commended*

You are warmly welcomed to our spacious Victorian house with its garden and panoramic views of the river valley. We are retired farmers who like music (Glyndebourne nearby/ speciality hampers prepared) and cooking, and are enthusiastic WI members/marketeers. Central for touring 'Sussex by the Sea'. Courtesy car – Lewes station. Open all year.

---

9 **The Stud Farm,** Bodle Street Green, Nr Hailsham, East Sussex BN27 4RJ

Philippa & Richard Gentry
☎/Fax 01323 833201
[BB] From £18
EM From £10 (by arrangement)
Sleeps 6
♿ ✂ 💼
☙☙ *Commended*

70 acre sheep and cattle farm situated in peaceful surroundings and beautiful countryside, ideal for walking. 8 miles from sea, Eastbourne, Hastings, South Downs in easy reach. Upstairs, family unit of double bedded room/twin bedded room, both with handbasins, and bathroom. Downstairs twin bedded room with shower, toilet, handbasin en suite. All bedrooms with colour TV and tea/coffee-making facilities. Guests' sitting room, colour TV. Sunroom. Open all year.

---

10 **Stud Farm House,** Telscombe Village, Lewes, East Sussex BN7 3HZ

Tim & Nina Armour
☎/Fax 01273 302486
[BB] From £18.50–£20
Sleeps 6
🧍 🐎 💼 🐕 🐈
Listed *Approved*

Family-run working 300-acre sheep farm and 17th century house in quiet hamlet on the South Downs Way in Glyndebourne and Bloomsbury area. Central for touring – Gatwick 30 mins, Brighton 15 mins, London 1 hour by train, Newhaven/Dieppe Sealink Ferries 10 mins. Guests' own 'unique' lounge. Cosy and comfortable, a relaxing break with a family atmosphere. Evening meal on request.

---

11 **Sturtwood Farm,** Partridge Lane, Newdigate, Dorking, Surrey RH5 5EE

Bridget MacKinnon
☎ 01306 631308
Fax 01306 631908
[BB] From £20–£30
EM From £8.50
Sleeps 5
♿ 🧍 ✂ 💼 🐎 ℀
☙☙ *Commended*

An attractive 18th century farmhouse in lovely countryside yet within 12 mins of Gatwick Airport. Many National Trust properties and gardens nearby. Also London, Brighton and several country towns. Open all year except Christmas.

SELF-CATERING

'Badgersholt' and 'Foxholme', c/o Bulmer Farm, Holmbury St Mary, Dorking, Surrey RH5 6LG ①

Gill Hill
☎ 01306 730210
SC From £150–£300
Sleeps 2/4
↟ ☄ ⛏ ⚄ ▪ ✂
↗ ↗ ↗ – ↗ ↗ ↗ ↗
Commended

Two delightfully cosy, single-storey cottages, sympathetically converted from a Surrey barn, forming a courtyard with the farmhouse. Fully carpeted, electric CH, colour TV and linen (beds made up). Communal laundry room, use of 2-acre farmhouse garden. Situated in picturesque, quiet valley. Ideal walking country. 'Badgersholt' sleeps 2 (also suitable disabled). 'Foxholme' sleeps 4 in 2 bedrooms. Open all year.

Black Cottage, c/o Newells Farm, Newells Lane, Lower Beeding, Horsham, West Sussex RH13 6LN ⑫

Vicky Storey
☎ 01403 891326
Fax 01403 891530
SC From £135–£260
Sleeps 4
↺ ⛏ ⌂ ⚘ ▪
↗ ↗ ↗ *Approved*

A delightful secluded cottage in the centre of a sheep and arable farm, with views to the South Downs. Surrounded by woods and lovely walks. Sleeps 4 in comfort. Recently modernised, it is 40 mins from Brighton, 20 mins from Gatwick, with fishing, golf and beautiful Sussex, Surrey and Kent gardens within easy reach. The ideal holiday cottage. Open all year.

Boring House Farm, Vines Cross, Heathfield, East Sussex TN21 9AS ⑬

Mrs Anne Reed
☎ 01435 812285
SC From £130–£190
Sleeps 6
↺ ⛏ ⌂ ⚘ ▪
↗ ↗ ↗ ↗
Commended

Peaceful farm cottage on sheep and beef farm. Marvellous views and walks, fishing available. Traditional local, good atmosphere/food in easy walking distance. Many beautiful places to visit. Beach within 15 miles. Accommodation (portion of farmhouse) comprises utility room, hall, WC, kitchen, dining room, sitting room, 3 bedrooms, 1 with shower, 1 with washbasin, bathroom and WC. Large garden. Open Mar–Nov.

Byre Cottages, c/o Sullington Manor Farm, Storrington, West Sussex RH20 4AE ⑭

Mrs G Kittle
☎ 01903 745754
Fax 01903 742469
SC From £120–£250
Sleep 2–6
↺ ⛏ ⚘ ▪ ⌂
↗ ↗ ↗ ↗ *Commended*

Mixed farm with many footpaths, including the South Downs Way, providing walks and beautiful views. The cottages have been converted from stables and overlook a shared lawn and 17th century tithe barn. An outdoor pool with springboard and children's slide may be used by guests. New tennis court for '98. Bike hire. Beaches approx 30 mins. Many historic houses, castles, places of interest and gardens.

---

2 High Weald Cottages, Chelwood Farm, Nutley, c/o Sheffield Park Farm, Nr Uckfield, E Sussex TN22 3QR ⑮

Mrs Nicky Howe
☎ 01825 790235/790267
Fax 01825 790151
SC From £180–£375
Sleeps 5 + cot
↺ ✂ ▪ ⚘
↗ ↗ ↗ ↗ *Commended*

Picturesque semi-detached farm cottage with garden on dairy farm adjacent Ashdown Forest. Comfortable accommodation comprises 1 double, 1 twin, 1 single room, bathroom, WC, sitting room (log fire, colour TV, phone), kitchen (fridge/freezer, auto washing machine, tumble dryer, electric cooker). Close Sheffield Park Gardens, Bluebell Railway. Easy reach Downs and coast. Cot/high chair available. Beds made up. No cot linen provided; towels on request. Open all year.

---

16 **2 Victoria Cottage,** c/o Hole and Alchorne Farm, Bell Lane, Nutley, East Sussex TN22 3PD

Pauline & Peter Graves
☎/Fax 01825 712475
ⓈⒸ **From £160–£300**
Sleeps 5
🛏 🍴 🎋
🔑 🔑 🔑 🔑 *Highly Commended*

A warm welcome awaits you at our comfortable, well-appointed semi-detached cottage, with lovely garden on our dairy farm. Near Ashdown Forest. 3 bedrooms (1 double, 1 twin, 1 single), bathroom, separate WC, sitting room with TV & phone, dining room, kitchen with electric cooker, microwave, fridge freezer, washing machine, tumble dryer. Beds made up. Towels on request. Ideal for visiting South Downs, castles and coast. Open all year.

STAY ON A FARM GIFT TOKENS

If you have enjoyed your Stay on a Farm, why not treat your friends and relatives to *Stay on a Farm* gift tokens? Available from the Bureau office, telephone 01203 696909, they can be redeemed against accommodation booked on the majority of our farms

THE 1000+ BUREAU MEMBERS OFFER A UNIQUE LINK TO CUSTOMERS ACROSS THE UK

All Bureau members belong to a local Group. Each member can refer you to an equally high quality member within the Group... or across the UK: England, Northern Ireland, Scotland, Wales.

FOLLOW THE COUNTRY CODE

Leave nothing but footprints,
Take nothing but photographs,
Kill nothing but time!

Kent

Group Contact: *Mrs Corrine Scutt* ☎ *01233 740596*

Kent is very much farming country, but the distinctive features are the many orchards, hop gardens and oast houses to be found in the aptly named 'Garden of England'. The hilly areas like the North Downs and the High Weald contrast with more lowlying parts such as the Low Weald and Romney Marsh. Each area has a distinct character which makes the Kent countryside very varied and attractive. Complementing the countryside are many historic towns and villages, among them the mediaeval port of Sandwich, Tenterden in the Weald with its wide tree-lined High Street, the traditional market town of West Malling, Cranbrook dominated by its splendid windmill, Rochester with its castle and cathedral and the hilltop village of Chilham built around a square and dominated by its castle.

Kent has a wealth of attractions for the visitor. Some of these, such as Dover Castle and Canterbury Cathedral, are well known. But there is much more – Roman remains, castles such as Leeds, Walmer and Deal, fortifications like the series of coastal Martello Towers built as a defence against Napoleon, historic houses like Hever Castle, where Henry VIII courted Anne Boleyn, Churchill's home at Chartwell, Penshurst Place and Knole set in a deer park on the outskirts of Sevenoaks. There are several vineyards open to the public, wildlife parks like Howletts and Port Lympne, the Whitbread Hop Farm, a working farm museum, three steam railways, numerous gardens and various country parks and picnic sites, all ideal for walks or family picnics.

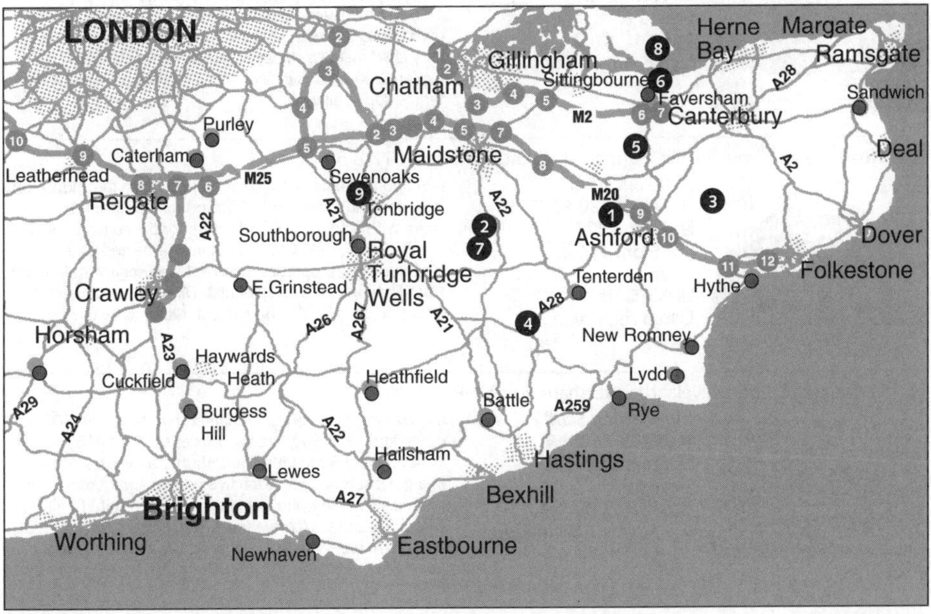

LONDON
Herne Bay · Margate · Ramsgate
Gillingham · Sittingbourne · Faversham
Chatham · Canterbury · Sandwich
Purley · M2 · Deal
Caterham · Maidstone · A2
Leatherhead · Sevenoaks · Canterbury
Reigate · M25 · M20 · Dover
Southborough · Tonbridge · Ashford · Folkestone
Royal Tunbridge Wells · Tenterden · Hythe
Crawley · E.Grinstead · New Romney
Horsham · Haywards Heath · Heathfield · Lydd
Cuckfield · Battle · Rye
Burgess Hill · Hailsham · Hastings
Lewes · Bexhill
Brighton · Eastbourne
Worthing · Newhaven

BED AND BREAKFAST
(and evening meal)

---

1 **Barnfield,** Charing, Ashford, Kent TN27 0BN

Mrs Phillada Pym
☎/Fax 01233 712421
BB From £20
Sleeps 6
Listed *Commended*

Charming and romantic Kent hall farmhouse built in 1420 with a wealth of character. A family home by a wildfowl lake amidst peaceful farmland. England at its very best. Excellent for Leeds Castle, Canterbury, Sissinghurst, Channel Tunnel and coastal ports. 1 family, 1 double, 1 twin and 2 singles. AA QQQ. Open all year.

---

2 **Great Cheveney Farm,** Marden, Tonbridge, Kent TN12 9LX

Mrs Diana Day
☎ 01622 831207
Fax 01622 831786
BB From £20–£25
Sleeps 3
(10) ⚡
Listed *Highly Commended*

We offer comfort and a friendly welcome in our 16th century farmhouse peacefully situated between Marden and Goudhurst villages on B2079. A perfect base for discovering Kent's attractive countryside, NT properties, gardens and coast. London and Le Shuttle 1 hour. Bedrooms with private facilities, guests' lounge, TV, spacious garden and parking. Open all year except Christmas & New Year.

---

3 **Great Field Farm,** Misling Lane, Stelling Minnis, Canterbury Kent CT4 6DE

Mrs Lewana Castle
☎/Fax 01227 709223
BB From £18
Sleeps 6
Listed *Highly Commended*

This comfortable, spacious farmhouse, with a wealth of old pine, sits amidst pleasant gardens and paddocks with friendly ponies. Three en suite rooms with colour TV, 1 double/family room with jacuzzi-style air bath, 2 have own lounges, 1 with kitchen. A warm welcome assured, very child friendly, all day access. Ideal location for exploring Kent, convenient for Canterbury, Chunnel and ferries. Open all year.

---

4 **Hoads Farm,** Crouch Lane, Sandhurst, Cranbrook, Kent TN18 5PA

Anne Nicholas
☎/Fax 01580 850296
BB From £17
EM From £11
Sleeps 6
Listed *Approved*

Bed and breakfast available in 17th century farmhouse on hop vine and sheep farm. Comfortable furnishings, sitting room with colour TV. Good centre for the coast, Bodiam Castle, Sissinghurst Castle, Scotney Castle and other National Trust properties. Excellent train service to London from Etchingham or Staplehurst. Dinner by arrangement. Dropside cot available on request. Open all year.

---

5 **Leaveland Court,** Leaveland, Faversham, Kent ME13 0NP

Mrs Corrine Scutt
☎ 01233 740596
BB From £20–£25
Sleeps 6
⚡ *Highly Commended*

Captivating 15th century timbered farmhouse on 300-acre downland farm. Easy access, 3 miles south of M2 junction 6, Faversham 5 minutes, Canterbury 20 minutes. Situated in a quiet setting with attractive garden and outdoor heated swimming pool. All rooms have en suite facilities, colour TV and tea/coffee trays. Traditional farmhouse food and warm welcome assured. Brochure available. Open Feb–Nov.

Pheasant Farm, Church Road, Oare, Faversham, Kent ME13 0QB   6

Lorna & Neville Huxtable
☎/Fax **01795 535366**
▦ **From £22.50–£26**
EM From £12
Sleeps 6
♫(5) ⅍ ⚘ ♨
Listed *Highly Commended*

14th century farmhouse on 210-acre working sheep farm, next to nature reserve and Swale estuary. All rooms are en suite with colour TV, tea/coffee-making facilities. Delightful sheltered garden with heated swimming pool. Ideal for visits to the continent and London. Historic cinque port town of Faversham 1½ miles, Canterbury 8 miles. A warm relaxing home from home. Open all year except Christmas and New Year.

Tanner House, Tanner Farm, Goudhurst Road, Marden, Tonbridge, Kent TN12 9ND   7

Lesley Mannington
☎ **01622 831214**
Fax 01622 832472
▦ **From £19–£21**
EM From £12.50
Sleeps 6
♫(5) ⅍ ⊞ ⅄ ⏚ ☞ ☂ ♨
♨♨ *Commended*

For a restful break, holiday or stop over, we are ideally placed in the beautiful Weald countryside. Our Tudor farmhouse in the centre of our working farm offers high standards of accommodation and cuisine. All our rooms are en suite, one with a genuine four-poster bed, and have colour TV, radio, tea/coffee-making facilities. We specialise in a countryside welcome. Visa/Access/Switch. Open all year except Christmas.

SELF-CATERING

'Birdwatcher's Cottage', c/o Newhouse Farm, Leysdown-on-Sea, Sheerness, Kent, ME12 4BA   8

Sally-Anne Marsh
☎ **01795 510201**
Fax 01795 880379
🆂 **From £170–£375**
Sleeps 2–8 + cot
♫ ⅍ ♨
🐾 🐾 🐾 🐾 *Highly Commended*

Come and relax in this peaceful, tucked away, quality country cottage on a sheep and arable farm. Panoramic views. Beamed ceilings, four bedrooms, CH. Large garden to sit in and daydream. Visit the nature reserves or wander along to the beach. Ideal touring base and a quiet hideaway. SAE for detailed leaflet. Open all year.

Golding Hop Farm Cottage, c/o Golding Hop Farm, Bewley Lane, Plaxtol, Nr Sevenoaks, Kent TN15 0PS   9

Jacqueline Vincent
☎ **01732 885432**
🆂 **From £140–£285**
Sleeps 5 + cot
♫ ⏚ ⅍ ☂ ♨ ☞
🐾 🐾 🐾 🐾
Highly Commended

13-acre farm producing Kent cobnuts for London markets. Surrounded by orchards and close to attractive village of Plaxtol. Secluded cottage, but not isolated. Sleeps 5, 2 double and 1 single, CH, colour TV, washer dryer and fridge/freezer, payphone. Horse riding, golf nearby. Car essential. Ample parking. Local station 2 miles with frequent trains to London. Motorway 4 miles. Dogs by arrangement only. Open all year.

Pheasant Farm, Church Road, Oare, Faversham, Kent ME13 0QB   6

Lorna & Neville Huxtable
☎/Fax **01795 535366**
🆂 **From £266**
EM From £12
Sleeps 2/3
♫(5) ⅍ ♨ ♨
🐾 🐾 *Highly Commended*

Attractive comfortable well-equipped beamed 14th century annexe to main farmhouse, bedroom, lounge shower, WC and kitchen, all with modern equipment. 210-acre working sheep farm next to nature reserve and Swale estuary. Delightful sheltered garden with heated swimming pool. Ideal for visits to continent and London, Faversham 1½ miles, Canterbury 8 miles. A warm relaxing home from home. Two nights £80. Open all year except Christmas.

Bath & Wells

Group Contact: *Mrs Jane Rowe* ☎ *01761 241294*

This area has a wealth of history going back to prehistoric times. The Druid Stones near Pensford are 600 years older than Stonehenge and there's always been a touch of magic and mystery in the air around Glastonbury, the ancient town and legendary Isle of Avalon, where it is rumoured King Arthur and his queen were buried.

The visitor is within easy striking distance of the beautiful city of Bath with its Regency architecture and older vestiges of civilisation like the Roman Baths. The whole town is alive with shops and pavement cafés. Another city within easy reach is Bristol, renowned as one of the world's leading ports. With Clifton Zoo, museums, theatres and marvellous shops, it's a visitor's delight. At the famous Wookey Hole Caves you can see the Witch of Wookey and visit a cave chamber in which the acoustics are said to be near perfection. Looking from Ebbor Gorge you will see what must be one of the grandest views in the world.

Interested in wine? There are vineyards at Pilton and North Wootton where you can taste the local brew. And, of course, if you fancy something stronger, there is always the renowned Somerset cider.

With the famous gorge and caves at Cheddar, the lovely cathedral city of Wells and the Mendip Hills, you will be spoilt for choice.

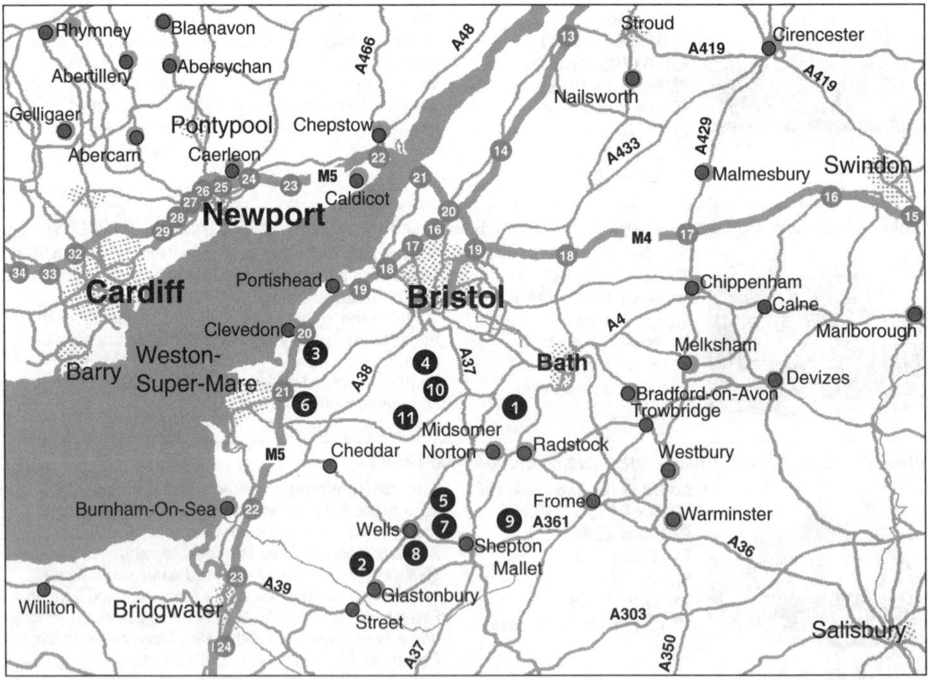

BED AND BREAKFAST

(and evening meal)

Barrow Vale Farm, Farmborough, Bath, BA3 1BL ①

Cherilyn Langley
☎ 01761 470300
From £17
Sleeps 6
🐎(5) ⅙ ♨ ▪
🌹🌹 *Commended*

Barrow Vale is a family-run dairy farm, situated between the historic cities of Bath and Wells. The farmhouse, which has been comfortably modernised, offers central heating, well furnished en suite bedrooms and guests lounge with TV. It is within easy reach of places of interest with local pubs and restaurants close by. Open all year (except Christmas and New Year).

Hartlake Farm, Hartlake, Nr Glastonbury BA6 9AB ②

Mrs Naomi Frost
☎ 01458 835406
From £17.50–£19.50
Sleeps 4
🐎 ⅙ ▪ ♨
🌹🌹 *Commended*

17th century farmhouse on a dairy/beef farm situated on the banks of the River Hartlake, overlooking the Somerset moors, with views of Glastonbury Tor and the Mendip Hills. An ideal touring area. Friendly welcome in relaxing accommodation and bountiful breakfasts. Open all year.

Icelton Farm, Wick-St-Lawrence, Weston-super-Mare, North Somerset BS22 0YJ ③

Mrs Elizabeth Parsons
☎ 01934 515704
From £16–£18
Sleeps 5
🐎(2) ▪
🌹 *Commended*

Icelton is a working dairy/sheep farm, just off the M5 (jct21). Ideal for touring Wells, Cheddar, and Mendip Hills. This listed farmhouse offers double room with H/C, family room with H/C and shower. Tea/coffee-making facilities. Oak-beamed dining room and lounge, both with inglenook fireplaces. English breakfast. Good pubs and restaurants close at hand. No dogs. Open Mar–Nov.

The Model Farm, Norton Malreward, Pensford, Bristol BS18 4HA ④

Margaret Hasell
☎ 01275 832144
From £16–£20
Sleeps 6
🐎 ▪ ◉
🌹🌹 *Commended*

The farmhouse is situated 2 miles off the A37 in a peaceful hamlet, nestling under the Dundry Hills. A working arable and beef farm in easy reach of Bristol, Bath, and many other interesting places. The accommodation consists of 1 family room en suite and 1 double room with washbasin. Guests' lounge and dining room. Open all year except Christmas and New Year.

Pantiles, Bathway, Chewton Mendip, Nr Bath, Somerset BA3 4NS ⑤

Pat Hellard
☎ 01761 241519
From £18–£20
Sleeps 6
🐎 ◉ 🐎 ⅙ ▪
🌹🌹 *Highly Commended*

Delightful house with views over Mendip countryside. Sample the locally baked bread and free range eggs. Ideal base for visits to Bath, Wells, Cheddar, Glastonbury. We offer 3 rooms all with private facilities, colour TV and hospitality trays. Early booking advised. Open all year.

---

6 **Purn House Farm,** Bleadon, Weston-super-Mare, North Somerset BS24 0QE

Thelma Moore
☎ 01934 812324
Fax 01934 811029
[BB] From £17.50–£22
Sleeps 20
🖧 🐂 🐈 🏕 ♨

🐝🐝 *Commended*

Peaceful 17th century farmhouse set at foot of Mendips. 3 miles from Weston-super-Mare. Five family rooms, (4 en suite, 1 ground floor). Games room. Pretty garden and pets' corner. Fishing available in River Axe which flows through the dairy farm. Riding nearby. Ideal base for Cheddar Gorge, Wells and Glastonbury. Open Feb–Nov.

---

7 **Redhill Farm,** Emborough, Nr Bath, Somerset BA3 4SH

Jane Rowe
☎ 01761 241294
[BB] From £18–£22
Sleeps 6
🖧 🍴 🏕 ◎

Listed *Commended*

Our listed farmhouse built in Cromwellian times is situated high on the Mendips between Bath and Wells. It is the perfect centre for outdoor activities and sightseeing. We are a working smallholding with a variety of animals to delight the children. CH. Guests' private bathroom. Fresh home produce. Tea/coffee-making facilities and washbasins in bedrooms. No dogs. Bath and West show ground 7 miles. Open all year except Christmas.

---

8 **Southway Farm,** Polsham, Wells, Somerset BA5 1RW

Anita Frost
☎ 01749 673396
Fax 01749 670373
[BB] From £19–£25
Sleeps 6
🖧 🏕

🐝🐝 *Commended*

A Georgian listed farmhouse situated halfway between Wells and Glastonbury overlooking Somerset levels and cider orchard. Accommodation is 3 comfortable and attractively furnished bedrooms, 2 with private bath, 1 en suite. A delicious full English breakfast is served. Guests may relax in the cosy lounge or pretty garden. Ideal location for touring the glorious West Country. Open Feb–Nov.

---

9 **Temple House Farm,** Doulting, Shepton Mallet BA4 4RQ

Mrs Veronica Reakes
☎ 01749 880294
Fax 01749 880688
[BB] From £18–£20
EM From £10
Sleeps 6
🖧(3) 🐄 🏕 🕭

🐝🐝 *Commended*

Temple House Farm is a family-run dairy farm situated on the eastern end of the Mendip Hills. A 400-year old listed farmhouse with all facilities, set in a rural area within easy reach of the Royal Bath and West Showground, Wells, Bath and many local attractions. All fresh produce used, hearty evening meals also available. Open all year.

---

10 **Valley Farm,** Sandy Lane, Stanton Drew, Nr. Bristol BS18 4EL

Mrs Doreen Keel
☎ 01275 332723
[BB] From £18–£22
Sleeps 6
🖧 🍴 🏕 🐂 🕭

🐝🐝 *Highly Commended*

Modern farmhouse situated on the edge of an ancient village near the river Chew with Druid Stones and many footpaths to walk. Near the Chew Valley Lakes renowned for trout fishing and in easy reach of Bath, Bristol, Wells and Cheddar. Stanton Drew is off A368 Bath to Weston-super-Mare road or the B3130 road. There are 2 rooms with double beds each with wash basins and coffee/tea making facilities. 2 en suite and 1 private bathroom. Open all year (except Christmas).

---

11 **Woodbarn Farm,** Denny Lane, Chew Magna, Bristol BS18 8SZ

Mrs Judi Hasell
☎/Fax 01275 332599
[BB] From £18–£22
Sleeps 6
🖧(3) 🍴 🏕

🐝🐝 *Commended*

Woodbarn is a working mixed farm. 5 minutes from Chew Valley Lake. Chew Magna is a large village with pretty cottages, Georgian houses and is central for touring. There are two en suite bedrooms, one double and one family, both with tea trays. Guests' lounge and dining room. Open Mar–Dec (closed Christmas).

Bath & Wiltshire

Group Contacts: 🆖 *Mrs Julie McDonough* ☎ *01225 891750*
🆖 *Mrs Janet Tyler* ☎ *01380 850523*

Easily accessible within 100 miles of London, the Midlands and the sea, Wiltshire offers the best of rural England, the marvellous scenery is its biggest surprise. Almost half the county is designated as an 'Area of Outstanding Natural Beauty'.

The wide peaceful downland is rich in historic interest: Stonehenge, Avebury and Silbury Hill stand out on the rolling green plain, with picturesque villages hidden away along the chalk stream valleys. Castle Combe and the National Trust village of Lacock are well known, but there are scores more waiting to be discovered. Six hundred years of building are displayed in the magnificent collection of historic homes, i.e. Longleat, Bowood House and Corsham Court and Sheldon Manor.

Walk the ancient Ridgeway Path, an important nomadic and trading route, or the Kennet and Avon Canal now restored along much of its route. Just over the county border the Romans built their city around the hot springs, and eleven centuries later Georgian architects created the elegant city of Bath. Whether you just stop for a short break or longer, the people of Wiltshire will welcome you.

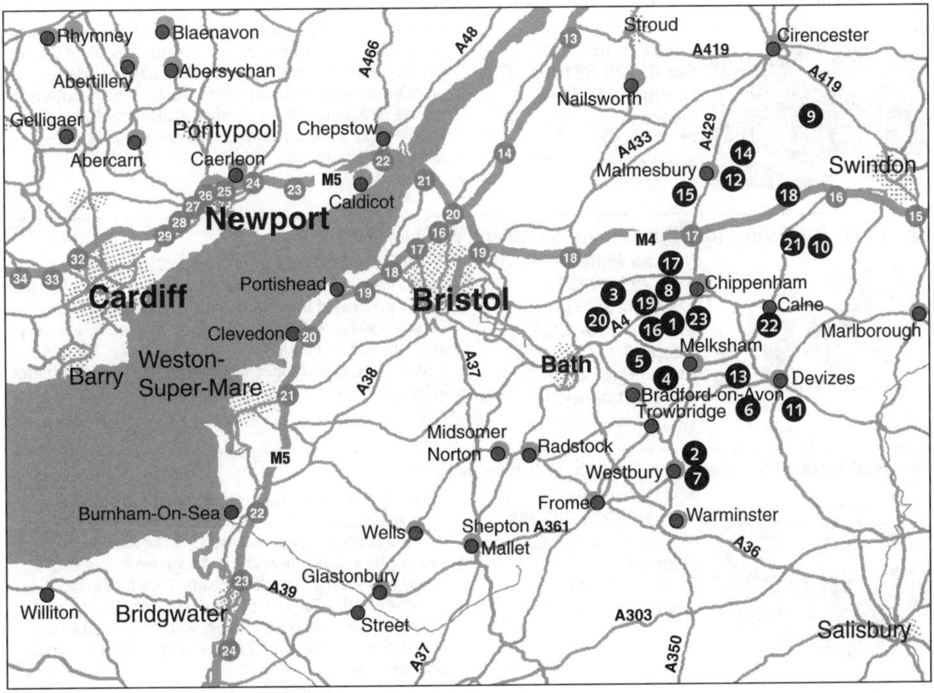

BED AND BREAKFAST

(and evening meal)

---

① **Boyds Farm,** Gastard, Nr Corsham, Wiltshire SN13 9PT

Dorothy Robinson
☎/Fax 01249 713146
🅱 From £18–£20
Sleeps 6
☺(5) ⚲ ⚘ ⛺ ◉
⚘⚘ *Highly Commended*

Enjoy a relaxing stay on our arable farm situated in the peace and tranquillity of the unspoilt Wiltshire countryside. Our delightful 16th century farmhouse, as featured by the *Daily Express*, accommodates families, couples and individuals, CH, H/C, tea/coffee-making facilities. Guests' own lounge with woodburning stove. Easy access to M4, Bath, Lacock, Castle Combe, Stonehenge, Bradford-on-Avon. Excellent pub food close by. Closed Christmas.

---

② **Church Farm,** Steeple Ashton, Trowbridge, Wiltshire BA14 6EL

Susan Cottle
☎ 01380 870518
🅱 From £17.50–£18.50
Sleeps 4
☺ ⚲ ⚘ ⛺ ▪ ◉
Listed *Commended*

Lovely old farmhouse dating back to 16th century in centre of beautiful village. Ideally situated for Bath, Salisbury, Longleat, Stourhead, Castle Combe. Lacock, Avebury. Spacious rooms, one double with H&C, one family, tea/coffee facilities. Guests' bathroom. Homely atmosphere, use of lounge, TV. Log fire in winter. Tea and homemade cake on arrival. No smoking in bedrooms. Open all year except Christmas and New Year.

---

③ **Fairfield Farm,** Upper Wraxall, Chippenham, Wiltshire SN14 7AG

Julie McDonough
☎ 01225 891750
Fax 01225 891050
🅱 From £17.50–£20
Sleeps 4
☺ ⛺ ▪ ◉
⚘⚘ *Commended*

Fairfield is a friendly family farmhouse in Beaufort country, 8 miles from Georgian Bath, 3 miles from beautiful Castle Combe on route for Bristol (12 miles). Large garden, wonderful views. 1 double/family room, 1 twin, both with private bathrooms and tea/coffee-making facilities. Excellent pubs nearby. A warm welcome awaits you. Closed Christmas.

---

④ **Frying Pan Farm,** Broughton Gifford, Melksham, Wiltshire SN12 8LL

Barbara Pullen
☎ 01225 702343
Fax 01225 793652
🅱 From £18–£22
Sleeps 6
☺(2) ⚲ ⛺ ▪
⚘⚘ *Commended*

A warm welcome awaits you at our 17th century farmhouse situated 1 mile from Melksham making it ideally positioned for visiting Bath, Bradford-on-Avon, Lacock and numerous National Trust properties. The cosy accommodation consists of 1 double en suite, 1 double/ 1 twin, all with tea/coffee facilities and TV. Good pub food in village 1 mile. Closed Christmas and New Year.

---

⑤ **Hatt Farm,** Old Jockey, Box, Nr Bath, Wiltshire SN13 8DJ

Mrs Carol Pope
☎/Fax 01225 742989
🅱 From £17.50–£20
Sleeps 4
☺ ⚲ ▪ ⛺ ◉
⚘⚘ *Commended*

Extremely comfortable Georgian farmhouse in peaceful surroundings. Scrumptious breakfasts served overlooking beautiful countryside views. What could be nicer than sitting by a log fire in winter or enjoying the garden in summer? Lovely walks and good golfing nearby. Ideal for touring Wiltshire and the Cotswolds yet close to Bath. One twin with en suite shower, one double/family with private bathroom, both with tea/coffee. CH. Guests' lounge. Closed Christmas and New Year.

Higher Green Farm, Poulshot, Devizes, Wiltshire SN10 4RW   6

Marlene & Malcolm Nixon
☎ **01380 828355**
BB **From £17**
Sleeps 6
⛄ 🐓 ⅄ 🐕
Listed *Commended*

Welcome to our peaceful 17th century timbered farmhouse facing village green and cricket pitch. Excellent traditional inn nearby. Our dairy farm is situated between Bath and Salisbury, close to many National Trust properties. Ideal for Stonehenge, Longleat, Avebury and Lacock. 1 double, 1 twin, 2 single rooms. Tea-making facilities. Guests' lounge, colour TV. Take A361 from Devizes, after 2 miles left to Poulshot, farm opposite Raven Inn. Open Mar–Nov.

Hillside Farm, Edington, Westbury, Wilts BA13 4PG   7

Carol Mussell
☎/Fax **01380 830437**
BB **From £16–£17**
Sleeps 4
⛄ 🐖 ◎
🐝 *Commended*

A warm welcome and wonderful views are yours on our small working farm nestled under the edge of Salisbury Plain. We have one double/family room and one twin room each with wash basins, colour TV and hospitality tray. Lovely conservatory for guests' use. Within easy reach of Bath and NT properties. Closed Christmas & January.

Home Farm, Harts Lane, Biddestone, Chippenham, Wilts SN14 7DQ   8

Ian & Audrey Smith
☎/Fax **01249 714475**
BB **From £15–£25**
Sleeps 6
⛄ ⅄ 🐖 🐎 ◎
🐝🐝 *Commended*

A warm welcome awaits you in this 17th century farmhouse on a family-run working mixed farm. Set in beautiful Biddestone just a stroll across village green from the pub. Ideally situated for Bath, Castle Combe and Lacock, Stonehenge, Avebury, Longleat, etc. Both rooms have colour TV, tea and coffee; one en suite, the other has private bathroom. Open all year.

Leighfield Lodge Farm, Cricklade, Swindon, Wiltshire SN6 6RH   9

Mrs Claire Read
☎/Fax **01666 860241**
BB **From £18.50–£25**
Sleeps 6
⛄ ⅄ 🐖 ◎
🐝🐝 *Commended*

Imagine a lovely old farmhouse in a truly rural setting. Step inside and discover comfortable en suite rooms with crisp cotton bedlinen. Relax in the sitting room in front of a warm fire, after explorong the Cotswolds or Wiltshire Downs. Children will enjoy meeting the Jersey cows and may even see the wild deer! Open all year except Christmas and New Year.

Little Cotmarsh Farm, Broad Town, Wootton Bassett, Swindon, Wiltshire SN4 7RA   10

Mary Richards
☎ **01793 731322 or 0831 090584**
BB **From £16–£18**
Sleeps 6
⛄ ⅄ 🐖 🐎 🍴
Applied

300 year old farmhouse with lots of character, situated 4 miles south of M4 J16 in peaceful hamlet. Comfortable attractive bedrooms with washbasins, one with toilet/shower en suite. All have tea/coffee-making facilities, heating and colour TV. Equal distance from Bath, Cotswolds and Oxford. Excellent amenities for wet days in and around Swindon. Good pub food locally. Open all year except Christmas.

Longwater Park Farm, Lower Road, Erlestoke, Nr Devizes, Wiltshire SN10 5UE   11

Pam Hampton
☎/Fax **01380 830095**
BB **From £21–£28**
EM **From £12**
Sleeps 12
♿ ⛄ 🐓 🐝 🐎 🐖 ◎
🐝🐝🐝 *Commended*

A peaceful retreat overlooking our own lakes and parkland with 2½ acre waterbird area and organic farm with rare sheep. Family suite, double/twin rooms all en suite, TV and tea-making facilities, CH. 2 ground floor bedrooms. Welcoming lounge, large conservatory, separate dining room. Traditional farmhouse fayre using local produce. Special diets. Local wines. Coarse fishing. Erlestoke Sands Golf Course adjacent. Open all year except Christmas and New Year.

12 Lovett Farm, Little Somerford, Nr Malmesbury, Wiltshire SN15 5BP

Susan Barnes
☎/Fax 01666 823268
BB From £18–£20
Sleeps 4
☺(4) ♞ ⅍ ♨ ⊛
♨♨ *Commended*

Enjoy traditional hospitality at our delightful farmhouse on a working farm with beautiful views. Two attractive double and twin en suite bedrooms each with tea/coffee-making facilities and colour TV. Full central heating. Guests' dining room/lounge. Log fires in winter. Convenient M4, Bath, Cotswolds, Lacock and Stonehenge. Excellent food pubs nearby. Open all year except Christmas.

13 Lower Foxhangers Farm, Rowde, Devizes, Wiltshire SN10 1SS

Cynthia & Colin Fletcher
☎/Fax 01380 828254
BB From £19–£25
Sleeps 6
☺ ♔ ♈ ⊶ **(touring & static)** ☞ ♞ ♨ ⊛
♨♨ *Commended*

We expectantly await your visit to our 18th century farmhouse alongside the canal with its gaily painted narrow boats. Assist boats through the locks whilst strolling to the pubs. Ideal for walking, cycling, fishing, boating. Easy reach Stonehenge/Bath. Also available for hire our new 40' narrowboat. Twin, double and family rooms, all en suite with TV and hospitality tray. Self-catering units and small campsite with electricity, toilets/shower. Open May–Oct.

14 Lower Stonehill Farm, Charlton, Malmesbury, Wiltshire SN16 9DY

Mrs Edna Edwards
☎/Fax 01666 823310
BB From £17.50–£20
Sleeps 6
☺ ♔ ♈ ♨
Listed *Commended*

Large Cotswold stone 15th century farmhouse on working dairy farm in the lush, rolling countryside on the Wilts/Glos border. Three comfortable rooms, 1 en suite, all with tea/coffee facilities. Children and dogs welcome. Delicious full English breakfast served in guests' sitting/dining room or garden if fine. Central for Oxford, Bath, Stratford, Stonehenge and the Cotswolds. On the B4040 3½ miles from historic Malmesbury. Open all year.

15 Manor Farm, Corston, Malmesbury, Wiltshire SN16 0HF

Mrs Ross Eavis
☎ 01666 822148
Fax 01666 826565
BB From £18–£26
Sleeps 12
☺(9) ⅍ ⊡ ♨ ⊛
♨♨ *Commended*

Manor Farm is very easy to find just 3 miles north of M4 J17. Cotswold stone farmhouse full of character and very homely. Six rooms, four en suite all with colour TV and hospitality tray. Large gardens to while away the time or visit local pub just down the road. As featured in the *Daily Express* and *Bella* magazine. Closed Christmas.

16 Manor Farm, Wadswick, Box, Corsham, Wiltshire SN13 8JB

Carolyn Barton
☎ 01225 810700
Fax 01225 810307
BB From £20
Sleeps 6
☺ ⅍ ♞ ⊡
♨♨ *Highly Commended*

Visit our arable, sheep and horse farm nestling in the quiet hamlet of Wadswick. We are only 7 miles from Bath yet close to Lacock and other beautiful villages. Our 16th century farmhouse has large, spacious rooms, all en suite with tea/coffee making facilities and colour TV. Stabling and riding by arrangement. Open Mar–Oct.

17 Oakfield Farm, Easton Piercy Lane, Yatton Keynell, Chippenham, Wiltshire SN14 6JU

Mrs Margaret Read
☎/Fax 01249 782355
BB From £17–£20
Sleeps 6
☺ ♔ ⅍ ♨ ⊛
Listed *Commended*

Friendly welcome in Cotswold stone farmhouse with fine views over open countryside. On working livestock farm in a quiet location, excellent for wildlife. One en suite double/family room, 1 double and 1 twin room, all with tea/coffee-making facilities and colour TV. Full central heating. Ideal base for visiting Bath, Castle Combe, Lacock and the Cotswolds. Open Mar–Nov.

Olivemead Farm, Olivemead Lane, Dauntsey, nr Chippenham, Wiltshire SN15 4JQ   (18)

Suzanne Candy
☎/Fax 01666 510205
Mobile 0378 667611
[BB] From £17–£20
Sleeps 6
♿ 🐎 ⅍ ▪ ☂ ◉
👜 *Commended*

Relax and enjoy the warm, informal hospitality at our delightful 18th century farmhouse on a working dairy farm. Thoughtfully decorated twin, double, family rooms with washbasin, colour TV. Tea/coffee facilities. Generous breakfasts. Oak beamed dining room/lounge for guests' exclusive use. Large garden, play area, cot, highchair. Convenient M4, Bath, Cotswolds, Salisbury. Open all year except Christmas and New Year.

Pickwick Lodge Farm, Guyers Lane, Corsham, Wiltshire SN13 0PS   (19)

Gill Stafford
☎ 01249 712207
Fax 01249 701904
[BB] From £18–£22
Sleeps 6
♿ ⅍ ▪ ☂ ◉
Listed
Highly Commended

Enjoy a stay at our beautiful home set in wonderful countryside where you can see rabbits, pheasant and occasionally deer. Relax in our garden having started the day with a hearty delicious breakfast. Local produce used when possible. Bath, NT properties, Corsham Court and many interesting villages nearby. Two well appointed and tastefully furnished rooms with en suite/private facilities, hospitality tray, home made biscuits. Closed Christmas and New Year.

Saltbox Farm, Drewetts Mill, Box, Corsham, Wiltshire SN13 8PT   (20)

Mary Gregory
☎ 01225 742608
[BB] From £17.50–£20
Sleeps 4
♿ ⅍ ☞ ☂ ▪ ◉
👜 *Commended*

Mary and Tony invite you to relax in their 18th century farmhouse surrounded by the unspoilt Box Valley, offering scenic walks in a wildlife and conservation area. Centrally situated for touring the West Country and Bath. One double room with en suite shower, one twin/family room with guests' bathroom, both with tea/coffee. Visitors lounge/diner with colour TV, CH. Special rates for 3/4 day breaks. Open all year except Christmas & New Year.

Tockenham Court Farm, Tockenham, Nr Swindon, Wiltshire SN4 7PH   (21)

Mrs Elizabeth Bennett
☎/Fax 01793 852315
☎ 0831 341310
[BB] From £18–£20
Sleeps 6
♿ 🐎 ⅍
👜👜 *Highly Commended*

Welcome to our Grade II listed 16th century court house. We have 1 double room with private shower room and toilet, 1 double room with private bathroom and toilet, 1 en suite room. CH, tea/coffee facilities and colour TV. Guests' own sitting room.

SELF-CATERING

Home Farm Barn and The Derby, Home Farm, Heddington, Nr Calne, Wiltshire SN11 0PL   (22)

Mrs Janet Tyler
☎/Fax 01380 850523
[SC] From £150–£350
Sleeps 2/5
🐎 ☂ ▪ ◉
🐾 🐾 🐾 🐾 *Commended*

Home Farm is a large dairy and arable farm in village centre with its own private lake and offering unbeatable downland walks with panoramic views (SSSI). Riding school and golf course adjoin the farm. Also bungalow-style stable conversion set in idyllic courtyard. Sleeps 2. Colour brochure. Open all year.
E mail: W.S.Tyler@farmline.comp

13 Lower Foxhangers Farm, Rowde, Devizes, Wiltshire SN10 1SS

Cynthia & Collin Fletcher
/Fax 01380 828254
From £160–£220
Sleeps 4/6
(touring and static)
Tourist Board Inspected

Enjoy your holiday with us on our small farm/marina with its diverse attractions. Relax on the patio of your rural retreat. We have four holiday mobile homes. Hear the near musical clatter of the windlass heralding the lock gate opening and the arrival of yet another narrow boat. Hire our new narrowboat 'Foxglove' and cruise to Bath and back. Also B&B and small campsite with electricity and facilities. Open Easter–Nov.

14 Stonehill Farm, Charlton, Malmesbury, Wiltshire SN16 9DY

Mrs Edna Edwards
/Fax 01666 823310
From £160–£210
Sleeps 2/3
Commended

Stonehill is a family-run dairy farm on the Wilts/Glos border, 3 miles from Malmesbury and 8 miles M4. The Cow Byre and Bull Pen are converted cowsheds, comfortably furnished with double bed, bathroom, fitted kitchen/diner and lounge. Full CH, colour TV, microwave, all power and linen included. Facing south-west with gravel patio and garden chairs. Open all year.

18 Swallow Cottage, Olivemead Farm, Olivemead Lane, Dauntsey, nr Chippenham, Wilts SN15 4JQ

Suzanne Candy
/Fax 01666 510205
Mobile 0378 667611
From £160–£350
Sleeps 4/6
Applied

Imagine a delightful, comfortable, well-equipped cottage on a working dairy farm. Newly converted to offer the luxuries of modern living but retaining its traditional features. Perfectly positioned for days out in Wiltshire, Bath and the Cotswolds. Plenty to do for all the family even on the wettest of days. Brochure available. Open all year except Christmas and New Year.

23 Wick Farm, Lacock, Chippenham, Wiltshire SN15 2LU

Philip and Sue King
01249 730244
Fax 01249 730072
From £170–£380
Sleeps 4/5 + cot
Highly Commended

Philip and Sue invite you to their working dairy farm in The Cheese House or Cyder House, where original cyder press remains, also stepped fireplace with woodburning stove. Some windows in Cheese have original shutters with gallery as extra seating area with portable TV. Both properties have exposed timbers, traditional furnishings. Linen and towels included. Coarse fishing on own lake. Brochure available. Open all year.

Heart of Dorset

Group Contact: *Rosemary Coleman* ☎ *01305 848252/Fax 01305 848702*

The Heart of Dorset Group offers you a range of holiday accommodation in the Dorset countryside. It is an area of outstanding natural beauty renowned for its beautiful villages, magnificent hills and lovely valleys.

Wherever you stay, the coast is but a short distance away with excellent swimming, sailing and fishing also excellent golf courses. For the country lover, the area has a wide choice of forest trails, nature reserves, coastal and inland walks, ancient monuments, historic houses and tropical gardens. Dorset's mild climate makes it an ideal location for a holiday all year round.

Dorset's most famous son, Thomas Hardy, was born within three miles of Dorchester; his rambling cottage, Higher Bockhampton is open to the public. Most of his books were based on villages and towns in the area, many of which still retain the rural atmosphere of Hardy's Wessex.

A romantic figure of more modern times is Lawrence of Arabia, who spent a number of reclusive years in his remote and rather bleak cottage, Clouds Hill, near Bovington Camp.

Corfe Castle, Brownsea Island, Lulworth Cove, Durdle Door ... even the Tolpuddle Martyrs' Museum are all here – you'll need more than a few days to discover Dorset!

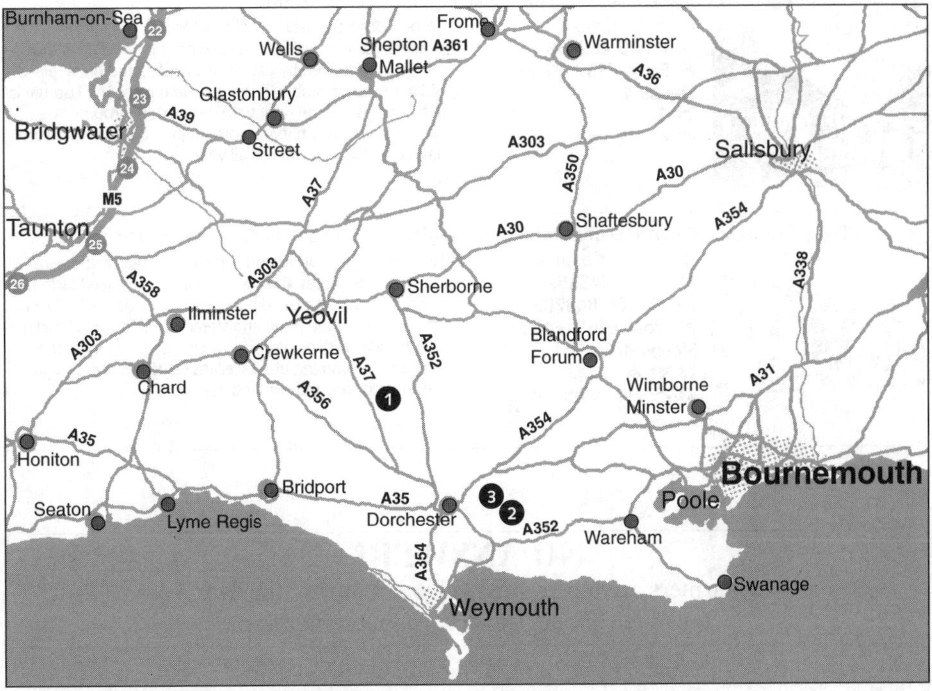

BED AND BREAKFAST
(and evening meal)

---

① Lamperts Farmhouse, 11 Dorchester Road, Sydling St Nicholas, Dorchester, Dorset DT2 9NU

Mrs Rita Bown
☎ **01300 341790**
BB **From £20**
EM From £12
Sleeps 4
🛏 🐾 ♿
🌾🌾 *Approved*

Enjoy home comforts in our thatched farmhouse in the unspoilt village of Sydling St Nicholas. Ideal for walking or touring. 1 double family room, 1 twin room, both with en suite bathroom. Guests' own lounge with inglenook fireplace, colour TV, tea/coffee-making facilities. Full CH. Open all year.

SELF-CATERING

---

② Glebe Cottage, c/o Glebe House, Moreton, Dorchester, Dorset DT2 8RQ

Carol Gibbens
☎ **01929 462468**
SC **From £130–£260**
Sleeps 4
🛏 ♿
🦮 🦮 *Approved*

Glebe Cottage is set in an old rectory garden in the peaceful farming village of Moreton, famous for its church windows engraved by Laurence Whistler and burial place of Lawrence of Arabia. It is a wildlife haven. The cottage is detached, is on one floor with 2 double bedrooms, kitchen, living room, bathroom, night storage heating and has its own garden. Open all year.

---

③ Old Dairy Cottage and Clyffe Dairy Cottage, c/o Clyffe Farm, Tincleton, Dorchester, Dorset DT2 8QR

Rosemary Coleman
☎ **01305 848252**
Fax 01305 848702
SC **From £160–£400**
Sleeps 3/6 + cot
🛏 🐾 ♿
🦮 🦮 🦮 *Commended*

Two attractively furnished character cottages with beams, inglenook fireplaces and own gardens. The mixed farm has cows, calves, horses, and beautiful woodland walks. Ducks and wildlife on the pond and streams. Fishing, ideal cycling countryside, within easy reach coast, golf, riding, leisure centre for swimming etc. Excellent value low season with OAP reductions and winter breaks. CH.

NO ANSWER?
Farmers are mostly out and about during the day.
Try to telephone before 9.30am or after 4pm.

Dorset

Group Contacts: [BB] *Jane Greening* ☎/Fax 01308 422884
[SC] *Su Read* ☎/Fax 01935 872150

Dorset may be described as a county for all seasons, with its mild south coast climate. It has so much to offer you whenever or wherever you choose to stay. West Dorset with pretty villages, interesting coastline and unspoilt countryside is where you may fish, enjoy watersports, hunt for fossils or wander the footpaths. North Dorset, with its unchanged pastureland and valleys may remind you of Thomas Hardy's Wessex. There are so many attractive places for you to visit, for instance Gold Hill at Shaftesbury and Milton Abbey. If you stay in East Dorset with its rolling downland you are within an easy distance of Blandford, Wimborne, Poole and Bournemouth to enjoy their attractions and theatres. South Dorset and the Isle of Purbeck have wonderful beaches, heathland and areas of historical interest.

The county footpath network is unsurpassed. You may meander through the country discovering hidden valleys, dramatic hills and unspoilt villages. Stroll the Coastal Way, along safe sandy beaches interspersed with rugged cliffs teeming with wildlife. This is all part of Dorset's charm.

'There never was a finer county' declared Charles II.

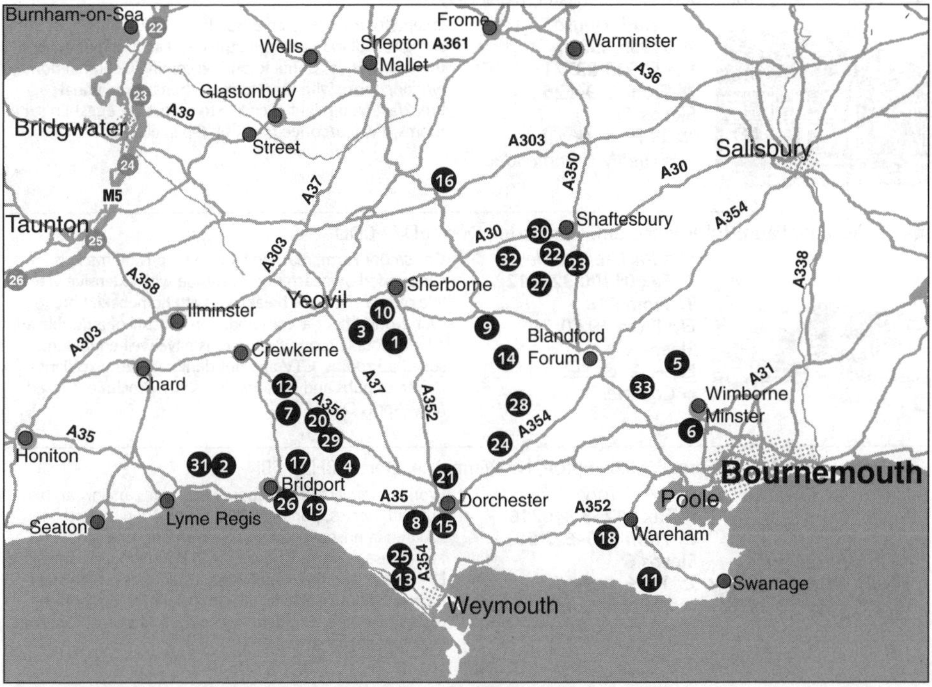

Burnham-on-Sea · Wells · Frome · Warminster · Shepton Mallet **A361** · **A36** · Glastonbury · **A39** · Bridgwater · Street · **A303** · **A350** · Salisbury · **A30** · **M5** · **A37** · **A354** · Taunton · **A303** · Shaftesbury · **A338** · **A358** · Ilminster · Yeovil · Sherborne · **A30** · **A30** · Crewkerne · Blandford Forum · **A31** · Chard · Wimborne Minster · Honiton · **A35** · Bridport · **A35** · Dorchester · **A352** · Poole · **Bournemouth** · Seaton · Lyme Regis · **A354** · Wareham · Weymouth · Swanage · **A352** · **A356** · **A37** · **A352**

BED AND BREAKFAST

(and evening meal)

---

1 Almshouse Farm, Hermitage, Sherborne, Dorset DT9 6HA

Mrs Jenny Mayo
☎/Fax 01963 210296
🅱 From £19–£22
Sleeps 6
🐎 🛠 🍳 🍴 🎪 ◎
🌠 *Highly Commended*

Spoil yourself and stay on our traditional working dairy farm situated in a totally unspoiled part of Dorset. Listed farmhouse retains its age and beauty whilst boasting every modern convenience. Wander the charming garden, surrounding fields or lanes and build an appetite for a real farmhouse breakfast. Golf, fishing and riding nearby. AA QQQQQ selected. Open Feb–Dec.

---

2 Cardsmill Farm, Whitchurch Canonicorum, Bridport, Dorset DT6 6RP

Mrs Sue M Johnson
☎/Fax 01297 489375
🅱 From £16–£20
Sleeps 6
🐎 🐕 🍴 🎪 ◎
🌠 *Commended*

Freedom to wander around and watch on this working family farm. Nature walks to the village and pub via the woods and fields. Ideal for family and friends to visit the beach, go fossil hunting, touring and walking. One double en suite and one family room with private bathroom. Lounge with CTV and inglenook fireplace. English and varied breakfasts. A warm welcome guaranteed. Open Feb–Nov.

---

3 Church Farm, Stockwood, Nr Dorchester, Dorset DT2 0NG

Mrs Ruth House
☎ 01935 83221
Fax 01935 83771
🅱 From £19–£25
Sleeps 6
🐎 🍴 ✂ 🎪 🍴 ◎
🌠 *Highly Commended*

Escape for a while to an unspoilt, peaceful landscape. Stroll along woodland paths, breathe clean air and rediscover the countryside. Come to our welcoming Georgian home, working farm, with tiny Norman church. Traditional breakfast, you might even like to collect the eggs! En suite rooms, TV, tea/coffee tray. CH. Open all year.

---

4 Colesmoor Farm, Toller Porcorum, Dorchester, Dorset DT2 0DU

Mrs Rachael Geddes
☎/Fax 01300 320812
🅱 From £18
EM From £9.50
Sleeps 4
🐎 ✂ 🎪 🍴 ◎
🌠 *Commended*

Colesmoor Farm, reached by its own private track, is surrounded by peaceful countryside with extensive views. We offer a choice of breakfasts with homebaked bread. Our ground floor accommodation consists of a double and a twin/double room. Both rooms have well-equipped en suite bathrooms, CTV and hot drink facilities. Excellent choice of pubs and restaurants nearby. Brochure. Closed Mar–Apr & Dec.

---

5 Hemsworth Manor Farm, Witchampton, Nr Wimborne, Dorset BH21 5BN

Mrs A C Tory
☎/Fax 01258 840216
🅱 From £20–£22.50
Sleeps 6
🐎 🐕 ✂ 🍴 🐾 🎪
🌠 *Highly Commended*

Working family farm of approx 800 acres, mainly arable, but with horses, ponies, cattle, sheep and pigs, and situated in unspoilt countryside with only one other farmhouse in sight! Easy access to Bournemouth, Salisbury, Dorchester and the New Forest. Three spacious en suite rooms, 2 double, 1 twin, all with colour TV, tea/coffee-making facilities. Excellent local pubs in the area. Open all year except Christmas.

Henbury Farm, Dorchester Road, Sturminster Marshall, Wimborne, Dorset BH21 3RN — 6

Sue & Jonathan Tory
☎ 01258 857306
Fax 01258 857928
BB From £20–£23
Sleeps 6
♿(10) ♨ ♣
☙ ☙ *Commended*

300-year-old farmhouse facing large front lawn and pond, situated on 200-acre dairy farm. Guests' lounge with colour TV. Near to New Forest and fifteen minutes from sandy beaches. Numerous local restaurants to meet your evening requirements. Many local attractions and country walks. Ideally situated for a great holiday. En suite facilities available. Open all year except Christmas.

Higher Langdon, Beaminster, Dorset DT8 3NN — 7

Judy Thompson
☎/Fax 01308 862537
BB From £18–£25
EM From £10
Sleeps 6
♞ ✆ ♨ ♣ ☂
☙ ☙ *Commended*

Escape to our farm set in acres of Dorset downland – not another house in sight, just dewy fields and grazing sheep. We can offer you a warm and tranquil break. If you have children, our farmyard animals together with a large playroom make sure everyone can relax! Fishing available. En suite rooms. Large sitting room with TV. Open all year.

Higher Park Farmhouse, Bats Lane, Martinstown, Dorchester, Dorset DT2 9TG — 8

Marigold King
☎ 01305 889362
Fax 01305 889541
BB From £20–£25
Sleeps 4
♿ ♣
☙ ☙ *Highly Commended*

Our farmhouse is at the centre of our 100-acre dairy farm, surrounded by fields. Rooms are en suite, peaceful and comfortably furnished, with TV, etc. Close to Dorchester, in Hardy Country with beautiful coastline and many places of interest. Start the day with a good breakfast, end it at one of the many local restaurants. Open all year except Christmas.

Holebrook Farm, Lydlinch, Sturminster Newton, Dorset DT10 2JB — 9

Charles Wingate-Saul
☎ 01258 817348
Fax 01258 817747
BB From £21–£34
EM From £13.50
Sleeps 16
♿ ♣ ☂ ✆ ♠ ♨ ♨
☙ ☙ *Highly Commended*

Situated in heart of Blackmore Vale and ideal as a central base for exploring Dorset, this is a family farm of 125 acres. Accommodation in 18th century farmhouse and delightfully converted stables, each with own sitting room, kitchen, shower, WC en-suite. Swimming pool, clay pigeon shooting, large games room with pool and table tennis. Comfortable, friendly atmosphere. Good home cooking, Licence. No dogs. Open all year.

Huntsbridge Farm, Leigh, Nr Sherborne, Dorset DT9 6JA — 10

Mrs Su Read
☎/Fax 01935 872150
BB From £20
Sleeps 6
♿ ✂ ▦ ♨ ♣ ◎
☙ ☙ *Highly Commended*

Family-run dairy and sheep farm situated in open countryside in the beautiful part of Dorset Thomas Hardy chose for his novel 'The Woodlanders'. Tastefully furnished bedrooms, 2 double and 1 twin, all en suite with tea/coffee facilities, colour TV, radio/alarm and full CH. Farmhouse breakfast served in conservatory overlooking garden and fields. So why not come and relax 'far from the madding crowd'?

Kimmeridge Farmhouse, Kimmeridge, Wareham, Dorset BH20 5PE — 11

Mrs Annette Hole
☎ 01929 480990
BB From £19–£20
Sleeps 6
♿(10) ✂ ♨ ♣
☙ ☙ *Highly Commended*

Picturesque 16th century farmhouse with views of Kimmeridge Bay across its 700 acres of farmland. Many spectacular coastal and inland walks. Lulworth Cove, Corfe Castle, Studland Bay, Poole and Bournemouth nearby. Many excellent local pubs and restaurants. Spacious, attractively furnished rooms, delicious breakfast with warm welcome at all times. Closed Christmas.

12 Kitwhistle Farm, Beaminster Down, Beaminster, Dorset DT8 3SG

Mrs Ann Hasell
☎ 01308 862458
BB From £15–£20
Sleeps 4
⛓ ⅍ 🏠
😊😊 *Approved*

A friendly welcome and a cup of tea await you at Kitwhistle Farm which is a working dairy farm on the peaceful Beaminster Downs. The historic town of Beaminster is just two miles away with its many eating houses. The perfect place to tour Hardy's coast and countryside. All facilities are on the ground floor. Open Mar–Oct.

13 Lower Farmhouse, Langton Herring, Weymouth, Dorset DT3 4JB

Mrs J Elwood
☎ 01305 871187
BB From £18–£20
Sleeps 6
⛓ ⅍ 🏠 🎿
😊😊 *Highly Commended*

16th century listed farmhouse quietly situated on the edge of the village with spectacular walks along the Dorset coastal footpath which passes through our farm. Traditional features including beamed sitting room with large open log fire and a secluded, pretty walled-in garden. Ideal for touring the wonderful sites of Thomas Hardy's countryside or for the local fishing and birdwatching. Open Feb–Nov.

14 Lower Fifehead Farm, Fifehead St Quinton, Sturminster Newton, Dorset DT10 2AP

Mrs Jill Miller
☎/Fax 01258 817335
BB From £17.50–£20
Sleeps 4
⛓ ⅍ 🏠 🐟 🎿
😊😊 *Commended*

Come and stay with us on a working farm in our 17th century listed farmhouse mentioned in Nicolas Pense's and Jo Draper's Dorset books for its architectural interest. En suite or private bathroom, tea/coffee, guests' sitting room. Large peaceful garden, green fields, ideal for relaxing, walking or touring Dorset beauty spots. Riding and golf easily arranged. Open all year.

15 Maiden Castle Farm, Dorchester, Dorset DT2 9PR

Hilary Hoskin
☎ 01305 262356
Fax 01305 251085
BB From £18–£22
Sleeps 6
⛓ ⅍ 🏠 @
😊😊 *Highly Commended*

Our large working farm, 1 mile from Dorchester and 7 miles from Weymouth in the heart of Hardy country, enjoys magnificent views of Maiden Castle and the surrounding countryside. En-suite bedrooms with CH, TV, tea-making facilities and a telephone for guests' use combine to offer comfort, peace and quiet – ideal for the perfect holiday. Babysitting by arrangement. Open all year.

16 Manor Farm, Manor Road, Mere, Warminster, Wiltshire BA12 6HR

Mrs Sarah Coward
☎ 01747 860242
BB From £17–£20
Sleeps 6
⛓ ⅍ 🏕 🚲 🏠
Listed *Commended*

Elegant manor house nestling under Wiltshire downland. Working family farm with pedigree Aberdeen Angus herd in an Area of Outstanding Natural Beauty. Large variety of family pets including hawk and falcons. Outdoor activities include clay pigeon shooting, horseriding, golf, hang gliding, walking, fishing. Excellent breakfasts and friendly hospitality. Open Jan–Nov.

17 New House Farm, Mangerton Lane, Bradpole, Bridport, Dorset DT6 3SF

Jane Greening
☎/Fax 01308 422884
BB From £17–£20
EM From £8
Sleeps 6
⛓ 🎿 🏠 @
😊😊 *Approved*

Modern, comfortable farmhouse set in the rural Dorset hills. Near coast (2½ miles). A warm welcome to guests. Family and double room, both en suite. Lots to do and see in this historically beautiful area. Evening meals available subject to prior reservation. Open Mar–Nov.

Priory Farm, East Holme, Wareham, Dorset BH20 6AG   18

Mrs Jenny Goldsack
☎/Fax 01929 553832
BB From £19–£23
Sleeps 6
Commended

A 16th century thatched family farmhouse in a quiet backwater of the Isle of Purbeck. It is here that our cows graze the water meadows of the Frome Valley and where we aim to provide you with a warm, friendly, relaxed atmosphere after your days out exploring coast and countryside. Open all year except Christmas and New Year.

Rudge Farm, Chilcombe, Bridport, Dorset DT6 4NF   19

Sue Diment
☎ 01308 482630
Fax 01308 482635
BB From £22
Sleeps 6
(10) *Highly Commended*

Peacefully situated in the beautiful Bride Valley, just over 2 miles from the sea. After a day spent exploring the lovely West Dorset countryside, relax in our comfortably furnished farmhouse. Then try one of the many good local pubs and restaurants. All rooms are en suite with TV and tea tray and have far reaching views. Open Mar–Oct.

Watermeadow House, Bridge Farm, Hooke, Beaminster, Dorset DT8 3PD   20

Mrs Pauline Wallbridge
☎/Fax 01308 862619
BB From £18–£24
Sleeps 6
Highly Commended

Watermeadow House stands amidst beautiful countryside on the edge of the small village of Hooke. All bedrooms enjoy splendid rural views and overlook the river Hooke which meanders close by the garden where guests are welcome to sit. Breakfast is served in the sunlounge which attracts the morning sun. Perfect for those seeking peace and quiet in a friendly atmosphere. Open Mar–Oct.

Yalbury Park, Frome Whitfield Farm, Dorchester, Dorset DT2 7SE   21

Tom and Ann Bamlet
☎ 01305 250336
Fax 01305 260070
BB From £20–£22
Sleeps 6
Highly Commended

Stone farmhouse with large garden in parkland to River Frome. Warm and welcoming for all country lovers. All rooms en-suite have TV, tea/coffee-making facilities, fridge, hairdrier. 1 double with french windows to garden, 2 family rooms. Traditional farmhouse breakfasts. Ideal for walking, beaches, fishing, riding and all country pursuits. Open all year.

Yew House Farm, Marnhull, Sturminster Newton, Dorset DT10 1PD   22

Gil Espley
☎ 01258 820412
Fax 01258 821044
BB From £20–£22
EM From £15
Sleeps 6
Highly Commended

Spacious family farmhouse of character in quiet location with superb views over open countryside. No longer a working farm, we welcome guests to enjoy our hospitality. Excellent area for walking, coarse fishing and sightseeing. Two double rooms, 1 twin, all en suite with tea/coffee-making facilities and colour TV. Home-cooked evening meals. Open all year.

Although the majority of farms will accept '*Stay on a Farm*' Gift Tokens, please check when booking to avoid disappointment.

SELF-CATERING

(23) Buddens Farm, Twyford, Shaftesbury, Dorset SP7 0JE

Sarah Gulliford
☎/Fax **01747 811433**
SC **From £100–£600**
Sleeps 2/6 + cot

Commended

HARRASSED? Have a real farm holiday, guests welcome to help feed pigs, sheep, chickens and goats and watch cows being milked. Pony rides over farm. Set in rolling hills and patchwork fields. Relax in superb farmhouse and cottage accommodation. Comfortably furnished, woodburners, dishwasher, colour TV, laundry room, outdoor swimming pool. Fully equipped for babies and children. Open all year.

(9) Dairy Cottages, Holebrook Farm, Lydlinch, Sturminster Newton, Dorset DT10 2JB

Charles Wingate-Saul
☎ **01258 817348**
Fax **01258 817747**
SC **From £145–£450**
Sleeps 2/4

Highly Commended

Beautifully converted, spacious cottages in old cow byre on working farm. Peaceful, quiet, well off beaten track. Exceptionally comfortable, oil CH, all modern appliances. Help with feeding animals or sleep all day. Games room with pool/table tennis, swimming pool, clay shooting, laundry room. Large garden for relaxing. Ideal base for exploring Hardy's Dorset. Licence. No dogs. Open all year.

(24) 2 Deverel Cottages, Deverel Farm, Milborne St Andrew, Blandford, Dorset DT11 0HX

Charlotte Martin
☎/Fax **01258 837195**
SC **From £150–£350**
Sleeps 6

Commended

In the midst of Hardy Country, 1 mile from Milborne St Andrew and just 2 miles from the picturesque village of Milton Abbas, the cottage is within easy reach of the coast. Situated at the edge of the farmyard, 150 yards from the A354, this modern 3 bedroom semi-detached cottage has a large, well fenced garden and views of rolling countryside. Open all year.

(25) Gorwell Farm, Abbotsbury, Weymouth, Dorset DT3 4JX

Mrs Mary Pengelly
☎ **01305 871401**
Fax **01305 871441**
SC **From £225–£480**
Sleeps 2/6 + cot

Commended

Gorwell Farm is the ideal place for you to relax, unwind and enjoy peaceful surroundings. A family dairy and sheep farm in its own scenic wooded valley with lambs in the spring and calves in the summer. Comfortable, well equipped accommodation for all times of the year. Just 2 miles from Abbotsbury and the Chesil Beach. Explore the coastal path crossing our farm. Winter short breaks. Open all year.

(26) Graston Farm Cottage, Graston Farm, Burton Bradstock, Bridport, Dorset DT6 4NG

Mrs Sylvia Bailey
☎ **01308 897603**
Fax **01308 897016**
SC **From £160–£460**
Sleeps 7–9

Approved

This spacious detached cottage is situated on a dairy farm in the beautiful Bride Valley one mile from Burton Bradstock and the sea. Three bedrooms (1 double, 1 double and single, 1 twin), sitting room with woodburning stove, large well equipped kitchen/dining room and a further room with bed-settee. Open all year.

Hartgrove Farm, Hartgrove, Shaftesbury, Dorset SP7 0JY — (27)

Mrs Susan Smart
☎/Fax 01747 811830
[SC] From £150–£495
Sleeps 2/5 + cot
♿ ☃ ♁ ♒ ⊞ ♈ ♟ ⚓ ⇦ ⊚
♞ ♞ ♞ ♞ Up to Highly
Commended

Far from the madding crowd! Discover this glorious, unspoilt corner of Dorset. Our family dairy farm has quite breathtaking views. 4 beautifully equipped, warm, character cottages. Old beams, log fires, laundry room, tennis, games barn, free swimming at leisure centre, fishing. Magnificent walking and wildlife. Children will enjoy cows, calves, sheep, pony, chickens. Pretty villages, good pubs, coast 30 mins. Open all year.

Higher Langdon Flat, Beaminster, Dorset DT8 3NN — (7)

Judy Thompson
☎/Fax 01308 862537
[SC] From £150–£200
Sleeps 2
☃ ⇦ ♟ ⚓ ♒
♞ Approved

On the first floor of our farmhouse (see B&B entry), set in 400 acres of Dorset countryside. The flat has sitting room/kitchen with colour TV and microwave. Linen, CH, double bedroom with bathroom en suite. Ideal for walkers – we are on the Wessex Way and 9 miles from heritage coastline. Fishing on farm. Relaxed atmosphere. Open all year.

Lower Fifehead Farm, Fifehead St Quinton, Sturminster Newton, Dorset DT10 2AP — (14)

Mrs Jill Miller
☎/Fax 01258 817335
[SC] From £100–£275
Sleeps 2/5
☃ ♈ ⚓ ♖ ♟
♞ ♞ ♞ Commended

Come and join us on our 400-acre dairy farm in beautiful, peaceful North Dorset staying in the cottage (sleeps 4/5) or flat (2/3). Situated in the heart of Hardy's Blackmore Vale within easy reach of many beauty spots. Large garden, friendly atmosphere.

Luccombe Farm, Milton Abbas, Blandford, Dorset DT11 0BE — (28)

Murray & Amanda Kayll
☎ 01258 880558
Fax 01258 881384
[SC] From £150–£500
Sleeps 2/4
♟ ☃ ♈ ▲ ♒ ⚓ ♖ ⇦ ⊚
♞ ♞ ♞ Up to Highly
Commended

Our traditional barn conversions lie in a secluded hidden valley, deep in rolling downland. Beauty, peace and history surround you. Comfortable, well equipped and sleeping 2/4, they stand around a pond in landscaped grounds. Riding, fishing, sailing, clay shooting, good walking, cycling, etc. on farm or locally. Telephone, games room, childcare, maid and laundry service all available. Open all year.

Orchard End, Hooke, Beaminster, Dorset DT8 3PD — (29)

Mrs Pauline Wallbridge
☎/Fax 01308 862619
[SC] From £180–£300
Sleeps 6
☃ ♈ ♟
♞ ♞ ♞ ♞ Approved

Stone-built bungalow on edge of small village of Hooke. Peaceful situation on our dairy farm, large garden, driveway and garage. Three comfortable bedrooms, 2 double, 1 twin. Large sitting room with dining area, well equipped kitchen. Lovely walking area. Price includes bedlinen, towels, electricity, VAT. Open all year.

Rudge Farm Cottages, Chilcombe, Bridport, Dorset DT6 4NF — (19)

Sue Diment
☎ 01308 482630
Fax 01308 482635
[SC] From £180–£495
Sleeps 2–6
♿ ☃ ♒ ♟ ⚓ ⊚
♞ ♞ ♞ ♞
Highly Commended

Rudge is a peacefully situated livestock farm in the beautiful Bride Valley, just over 2 miles from the sea. The old farm buildings have been converted into superbly comfortable cottages, around a flower-decked cobbled yard, enjoying open views towards our lake and the countryside beyond. Ideal for a family holiday or relaxing short break. Open all year.

30 Shire and Stable Cottages, Middle Farm, Fifehead Magdalen, Dorset SP8 5RR

Mrs Jo Trevor
☎ 01258 820220
Fax 01258 820200
℠ From £100–£300
Sleeps 4/6
🐕 🐎 🎿 ⛵ 🎣 ®
🎣 🎣 🎣 *Commended*

A 300-acre arable farm in small Dorset village. The self-catering cottages are located on the farm where we have coarse fishing, riding and walking for visitors. Full central heating, payphone, linen supplied. Easy reach of the local pubs and shops. One cottage suitable for the less able. Brochure available. Open all year.

31 Taphouse Farm, Whitchurch Canonicorum, Bridport, Dorset DT6 6RW

Mrs Sue M Johnson
☎/Fax 01297 489375
℠ From £160–£840
Sleeps 12 + 2cots
🐕 🐎 🎿 ⛵ ®
🎣 🎣 🎣 🎣 *Approved*

Stay at a quiet, comfortable farmhouse 4 miles from the coast. Five bedrooms, 2 bathrooms, kitchen/dining room 22'6x15' with oil-fired Rayburn, part CH, fridge/freezer, washing machine and payphone. Lounge with CTV and log fire, games room. Large garden, table, chairs and barbecue. Weekly bookings, short breaks, weekends available. Personal supervision and a warm welcome guaranteed. Open all year.

32 Top Stall, Factory Farm, Fifehead Magdalen, Gillingham, Dorset SP8 5RS

Kathy Jeanes
☎/Fax 01258 820022
℠ From £200–£380
Sleeps 5 + cot
♿ 🐕 🐎 ✂ ⛵ 🎿
🎣 🎣 🎣 *Commended*

Tastefully converted cow stall adjoining listed farmhouse on a dairy farm, formerly a woollen mill. 'Top Stall' has a walled garden with barbecue. It is well equipped throughout. Babysitting can be arranged. Ideal for fishing and walking or just relaxing. Longleat, Stourhead, Bath or the coast all within 30 miles. Open all year.

33 White Cottage, Tarrant Crawford, Blandford, Dorset DT11 9HY

Mrs Jan Tory
☎ 01258 857417
Fax 01258 857218
℠ From £210–£340
Sleeps 6
🐕 ✂ 🎿 ⛵
🎣 🎣 🎣 *Commended*

Enjoy a welcome in a modernised, extremely comfortable cob cottage with enclosed garden. On 550-acre family-run dairy/arable farm. Three bedrooms, CTV, CH, 2 WCs, washing machine, microwave. Ideal for exploring coast, National Trust properties – beach 20 mins. Children welcome, no pets please. Open May–Oct.

22 Yew House Cottages, c/o Yew House Farm, Marnhull, Sturminster Newton, Dorset DT10 1PD

Gil Espley
☎ 01258 820412
Fax 01258 821044
℠ From £95–£300
Sleeps 4/5
🐕 ⛵ 🎿 ®
🎣 🎣 *Commended*

Three timber cottages equipped to highest standard of comfort for summer or winter holidays. Situated in a secluded rural setting overlooking Blackmore Vale. Central heating, colour TV, linen inclusive. Excellent centre for sightseeing. Coarse fishing in Stour. Many good pubs for local beer and food. One cottage designed for disabled visitors. Colour brochure. Open all year.

LET THE TELEPHONE RING!
Some farmhouses are big places. Let the telephone ring
long enough to give the owner time to answer it.

Somerset

Group Contacts: BB *Jane Sedgman* ☎ *01458 223237/Fax 01458 223276*
SC *Robert Hembrow* ☎/*Fax 01823 490828*

Originally named by the Saxons as the 'Summer Land', come and experience a county full of contrasts from ancient gorges to the waterways of the Somerset Levels. Learn how traditional crafts still survive today, especially willow basket weaving, paper making, cheese making and the production of Somerset's finest cider from orchard to glass. We have a wealth of National Trust properties with beautiful buildings and fragrant gardens. For the energetic, go caving, cycling or ramble through our wonderful countryside and National Park. Remember those childhood days of steam trains? Come and book your tickets or simply wander around our rural museums.

Children can enjoy and thrill to the adventure of the legendary Witch of Wookey-Hole or have a 'bucket and spade' day at one of our coastal resorts and indulge in a delicious cream tea!

We will give you an insight into one of the most beautiful counties in England that we know you'll never forget !

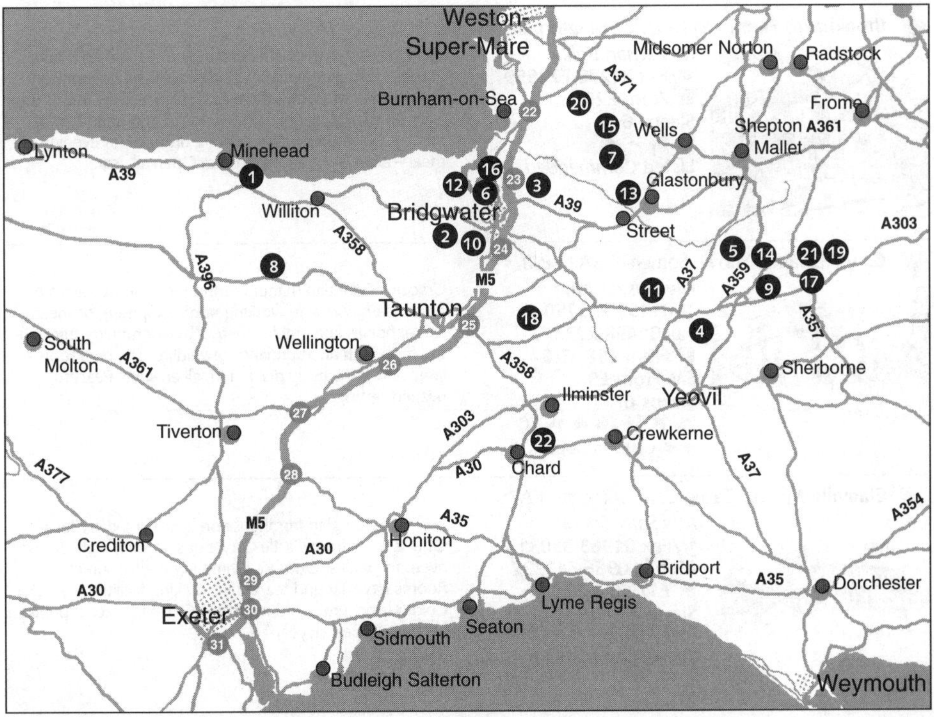

BED AND BREAKFAST

(and evening meal)

---

① Binham Farm, Old Cleeve, Minehead, Somerset TA24 6HX

Mrs S Bigwood
☎ 01984 640222
🛏 From £16–£19
Sleeps 6
🐕 🏇 ⅍ 🏏 ⚄ 🎠 🛢
🌸🌸 *Commended*

Predominantly 17th-century Jacobean farmhouse on a working family farm in an idyllic setting close to the Exmoor National Park and Quantock Hills. A few minutes walk across our fields to Blue Anchor sea front and the West Somerset Steam Railway. Comfortably furnished bedrooms with en suite facilities available, private lounge with colour TV, mediaeval dining hall. Full CH. Open all year.

---

② Blackmore Farm, Blackmore Lane, Cannington, Bridgwater, Somerset TA5 2NE

Mrs Ann Dyer
☎/Fax 01278 653442
🛏 From £19–£25
Sleeps 8
🕭 🐂 ⅍ 🍴 🛢 ⊛
🌸🌸 *Highly Commended*

A tastefully restored and furnished 14th century manor house, set in rolling countryside with views to the Quantock Hills. Rooms with oak bedsteads and four poster beds, all en suite. Facilities for disabled guests. As featured in *Country Living* magazine. Within easy reach of Exmoor, West Somerset coast, Taunton, Wells and Glastonbury. Open all year.

---

③ Brookhayes Farm, Bell Lane, Cossington, Bridgwater, Somerset TA7 8LW

Mrs Susan Bell
☎/Fax 01278 722559
🛏 From £20
Sleeps 6
🐂 🏇 ⅍ 🛢
Listed *Commended*

Working dairy farm with outstanding views over moors and hills. Situated between Bridgwater and Glastonbury on the edge of lovely village of Cossington. All rooms en suite plus family room. Large garden. Also good fishing nearby. Good pub within walking distance for evening meal – always a warm welcome. Open all year.

---

④ Cary Fitzpaine, Yeovil, Somerset BA22 8JB

Mrs Susie Crang
☎ 01458 223250
Fax 01458 223372
🛏 From £18–£20
EM From £9
Sleeps 6
🐂 🏇 ⅍ ⊞ 🛢 🐈 ⚒
🌸🌸 *Commended*

Gracious Georgian manor farmhouse set in two acres of gardens on 600-acre working farm comprising of sheep, cattle, horses and arable. There is a river running through the farm with an abundance of wildlife. The bedrooms are large and attractively decorated, all en suite. Peaceful, relaxed setting.

---

⑤ Clanville Manor, Castle Cary, Somerset BA7 7PJ

Mrs Sally Snook
☎/Fax 01963 350313
Mobile 0966 512732
🛏 £17.50–£20
Sleeps 6
🐂 ⅍ 🎠 🛢
Listed *Commended*

Stay in a Georgian farmhouse on a working dairy farm. Only 2 miles from Castle Cary, but secluded, with riverbank walks. Outdoor swimming pool in summer. Rooms have TV and tea/coffee-making facilities. Full CH. Colour brochure. Third night free Oct–Mar except public holidays. Open all year.

Cokerhurst Farm, 87 Wembdon Hill, Bridgwater, Somerset TA6 7QA   **6**

Derrick and Diana Chappell
☎/Fax 01278 422330
Mobile 0850 692065
BB From £20–£22.50
Sleeps 6
🐎 ⅔ ⬛ ◉
🥄🥄 *Highly Commended*

We would like to welcome you to our cheerful home, a 16th century Somerset longhouse. We have 3 pretty en suite bedrooms, all with comfortable beds, TV, CH, tea/coffee facilities. A good hearty breakfast is served to you in the dining room overlooking the garden and lake beyond. Good central location for exploring the 'Cider' county of Somerset. Open all year except Christmas.

Double-Gate Farm, Godney, Nr Wells, Somerset BA5 1RZ   **7**

Mrs H Millard
☎ 01458 832217
Fax 01458 835612
BB From £20
Sleeps 8
🐎 ⅔ ⬛
🥄🥄 *Highly Commended*

Situated on the banks of the River Sheppey, this lovely old Georgian farmhouse offers – comfortable guests' lounge, games room and en suite bedrooms with tea/coffee facilities, colour TVs and CH. Lovely flower garden, outdoor breakfast in summer. Ideal base for touring, cycling, birdwatching, etc. Evening meals available in nearby village inn. AA QQQ and RAC acclaimed. Open Feb–Nov.

Greenway Farm, Wiveliscombe, Taunton, Somerset TA4 2UA   **8**

Mrs M A Woollaston
☎ 01984 623359
Fax 01984 624051
BB From £17
EM From £7
Sleeps 6
🐎 🐴 ♨ ⬛
🥄 *Commended*

Comfort with peace and quiet. For those who prefer action, help us on the farm or take part in a country pursuit – excellent walks, rides, game or coarse fishing can be arranged and the coast is close. Good food, home-prepared menus, comfortable lounge, excellent views. Facilities for children. Open Apr–Oct.

Hill Ash Farm, Woolston, North Cadbury, Yeovil, Somerset BA22 7BL   **9**

Mrs Jane Pearse
☎ 01963 440332
BB From £20–£24
Sleeps 6
🐎 ⅔ ⛺ ♨ ⬛
🥄🥄 *Highly Commended*

This lovely thatched house, a listed building constructed in 1766, is set in a beautiful hamlet of south Somerset 1½ miles from A303. It is an ideal centre for visiting the many tourist attractions and NT gardens in Somerset and Dorset. 2 double en suite rooms and 2 singles, all with tea/coffee-making facilities, full central heating. Open Mar–Nov.

Lower Clavelshay Farm, Clavelshay, North Petherton, Bridgwater, Somerset TA6 6PJ   **10**

Sue Milverton
☎ 01278 662347
BB From £15–£18
Sleeps 6
🐎 🐴 ⅔ ⬛ ♣ ♨
Listed *Approved*

Badgers, buzzards and beautiful countryside surround our traditional 17th century farmhouse on 260-acre dairy farm. Spacious, comfortable rooms, beautiful views, peace and quiet. Ideally situated for exploring the Quantock Hills, Exmoor, Somerset Levels and coast. Close to Hestercombe Gardens. Warm welcome and relaxed family atmosphere. Open all year.

Lower Farm, Kingweston, Somerton, Somerset TA11 6BA   **11**

David & Jane Sedgman
☎ 01458 223237
Fax 01458 223276
BB From £19.50
Sleeps 5
🐎(6) ⅔ ♨ ⬛ ♨
🥄 *Commended*

This Grade II listed farmhouse, sited in a conservation area and overlooking a wide stretch of open country, was formerly a coaching inn and retains many of its original features. The attractively furnished rooms are all en suite, with tea/coffee-making facilities, colour TV and full central heating. Wells, Glastonbury, Cheddar, Wookey, Bath and Yeovil are within easy reach. Open all year except Christmas and New Year.

12 **Moxhill Farmhouse,** Combwich, Bridgwater, Somerset TA5 2PN

Carol Venner
☎ 01278 652285
mobile 0802 382870
[BB] From £19–£25
EM From £9.50
Sleeps 9
🐕 🐎 ✕ 🏕 ⛺ ◉
🏵🏵 *Highly Commended*

Relax in peaceful countryside in 17th century farmhouse. Excellent base for trips to the Quantock Hills and Somerset Levels. Double and family rooms, cot available and children very welcome. En suite bathrooms. Full farmhouse breakfast. Enjoy home prepared evening meals in our elegant licensed dining room. Non smokers only. We are situated 5 miles from Bridgwater just off the A39 Minehead Road. Open all year.

---

13 **New House Farm,** Burtle Road, Westhay, Nr Glastonbury, Somerset BA6 9TT

Mrs M Bell
☎/Fax 01458 860238
[BB] From £19–£21
EM From £10
Sleeps 5
🐕 🐎 ✕ ⛺
🏵🏵 *Highly Commended*

Large Victorian farmhouse on dairy farm. Central for touring Wells, Cheddar, etc. Accommodation comprises of double room and 1 family room both en suite with colour TV, tea/coffee facilities, hair drier, etc. Lounge with colour TV, separate dining room, also sun lounge, CH throughout, plenty of local fishing. Open all year except Christmas and New Year.

---

14 **Orchard Farm,** Cockhill, Castle Cary, Somerset BA7 7NY

Olive Boyer
☎/Fax 01963 350418
[BB] From £16–£18
EM From £10
Sleeps 5
🐕 🐎 🐈 ⛺ ⛺ ◉
🏵 *Commended*

Our pleasure is your comfort. We welcome you with tea and homemade cakes in the conservatory or garden. Quiet, beautiful surroundings. Two en suite bedrooms with radio, alarm clock, tea/coffee. Newspapers at breakfast. Bath, Longleat, Stourhead, Yeovilton Air and Haynes Motor Museums close, also many NT properties. Castle Cary with many shops and eating places 1½ miles. Open all year.

---

15 **Townsend Farm,** Sand, Wedmore, Somerset BS28 4XH

Sarah Willcox
☎ 01934 712342
[BB] From £16–£18
Sleeps 5
🐕(5) ✕ ⛺ ⚓ ☚ ⛺ 🎣
🏵🏵 *Commended*

Townsend Farm is a working dairy farm, set in peaceful countryside with views of the Mendip hills, close to Wells, Cheddar and Glastonbury, 6 miles from M5 (jct22). The spacious Victorian farmhouse offers comfortable accommodation and a friendly atmosphere, traditional English breakfast served in dining room, relaxing separate TV lounge. All bedrooms have TV, en suite available. Weekend breaks only until July. Open Apr–Nov.

---

16 **Wembdon Farm,** Hollow Lane, Wembdon, Bridgwater, Somerset TA5 2BD

Mrs Mary Rowe
☎ 01278 453097
mobile 0402 272755
Fax 01278 445856
[BB] From £18–£20
Sleeps 6
🐕(8) ✕ ⛺ ⛺ ◉
🏵🏵 *Highly Commended*

Enjoy a refreshing and memorable stay at our homely Georgian farmhouse situated near the Quantocks (AONB). We offer two romantic double en suite bedrooms, one pretty twin with private bathroom, all with tea/coffee, colour TV. Separate lounge and dining room for superb breakfasts. Landscaped gardens, off road parking. Tucked away yet easy to find, a place for all seasons.
E mail: mary.rowe@btinternet.com

> Although the majority of farms will accept '*Stay on a Farm*' Gift Tokens, please check when booking to avoid disappointment.

SELF-CATERING

Cockhill Farm & Orchard Farm, Cockhill, Castle Cary, Somerset BA7 7NY

Olive Boyer
☎/Fax 01963 350418
SC From £145–£380
Sleeps 5/7
🐎 🔥 🏠 🏛 ⊚
🔑 🔑 🔑 🔑 Commended

An attractive listed farmhouse overlooking beautiful countryside, with 3 bedrooms and fully equipped with TV, dishwasher, washing machine. Also 2 attractive cottages converted from a Somerset barn, both fully equipped, electricity and linen inclusive. Bath, Longleat, Stourhead, Yeovilton Air and Haynes Motor Museums and many NT properties nearby. Castle Cary with many shops and eating places 1½ miles. Open all year.

The Courtyard, c/o New House Farm, Burtle Road, Westhay, Nr Glastonbury, Somerset BA6 9TT

Mr & Mrs P Bell
☎/Fax 01458 860238
SC From £150–£400
Sleeps 6
🐎 🔥 🏠
🔑 🔑 🔑 🔑 Highly
Commended

The Courtyard is a converted barn which sleeps up to 4 adults and 2 children. Its situation on a dairy farm on the Somerset Levels makes it central for touring Wells, Cheddar, Bath, etc. Superbly equipped, including colour TV, washing machine, microwave, tumble dryer. Bed-linen, electricity and heating included. Good local fishing. Open all year.

Hale Farm, Cucklington, Wincanton, Somerset BA9 9PN

Mrs Pat David
☎ 01963 33342
SC From £95–£175
Sleeps 4
🐎 🔥 🏠
🔑 🔑 🔑 Approved

Set in a peaceful, but not isolated, position on edge of village, only 2 miles from A303. Ideal touring. Period converted former cowshed, comfortable and well equipped. 2 twin-bedded rooms, bathroom, kitchen, sitting room. All electric (coin meter). Linen supplied. Open all year.

Holly Farm, Holly Cottage, Stoke St. Gregory, Taunton TA3 6HS

Robert Hembrow
☎ 01823 490828
SC From £160–£370
Sleeps 4/6
🐎 🔥 🏠 🏛
🔑 🔑 🔑 – 🔑 🔑 🔑 🔑
Highly Commended

Come and stay in one of our 5 spacious cottages converted from old stone long barns. Each has its own private, enclosed garden and there is a games barn for the energetic. Plenty of fishing, horse riding or walking and an excellent selection of pub grub and restaurants nearby so give the cook a holiday too. Open all year.

Lois Barns, Lois Farm, Horsington, Templecombe, Somerset BA8 0EW ⑲

Paul & Penny Constant
☎/Fax 01963 370496
SC From £179–£375
Sleeps 4/6
🐎 🏛 🎋
🔑 🔑 🔑 🔑 Commended

In the heart of Blackmore Vale, Lois Barns are on a sheep farm surrounded by fields and footpaths. Light and spacious, both barns enjoy south-facing patios, beams in the bedrooms and are fully equipped. CH, electricity, linen and wood for the woodburner are all inclusive. Walk, bike, drive or simply relax in our rural landscape. Open all year.

(7) The Old Cart House, Double Gate Farm, Godney, Nr Wells, Somerset BA5 1RZ

Terry and Hilary Millard
☎ 01458 832217
Fax 01458 835612
SC From £175–£350
Sleeps 4/6
🛏 ✂ ▥
🐾 🐾 🐾 *Highly Commended*

First floor barn conversion, with lovely views of the Mendip Hills and Glastonbury Tor, offers excellent, well equipped accommodation including 2 en suite bedrooms. Heating, electricity and bedlinen included. Ground floor games room, open to all residents, with full-size snooker table, table tennis, darts,etc. Ideal for touring, cycling, birdwatching, fishing. Village inn nearby for those days when you don't want to cook! Open all year.

(20) Pear Tree Cottage, Northwick Farm, Mark, Highbridge, Somerset TA9 4PG

Mrs G Hunt
☎ 01278 641228
SC From £200–£350
Sleeps 4/6
🛏 🐓 🏕 ⏰
🐾 🐾 🐾 🐾 *Highly Commended*

Situated on the Somerset Levels in an area of outstanding natural beauty. Recent barn conversion. Luxurious and comfortable with beautifully co-ordinated fabrics and furnishings. Perfect for a peaceful relaxing holiday and an ideal base for touring this part of the West Country. Excellent facilities nearby for golf, fishing and riding and only 4 miles from coast. Open Mar–Nov.

(21) Pigsty, Cowstall & Bullpen Cottages, Barrow Lane Farm, Charlton Musgrove, Wincanton, Somerset BA9 8HJ

Mrs Chilcott
☎/Fax 01963 33217
SC From £150–£350
Sleeps 5–7 + cot
🛏 🐓 ❀ ◉
🐾 🐾 🐾 *Commended*

Pigsty, Cowstall and Bullpen Cottages are conversions from the appropriate farm buildings in rural Somerset. Pleasant garden, barbecue and games room. Pets welcome. Please send for brochure. Open all year.

(22) Rull Farm, Otterford, near Chard, Somerset TA20 3QJ

Mrs Pauline Wright
☎ 01460 234398
SC From £100–£170
Sleeps 5/6
🛏 🏕 ✂
🐾 🐾 *Commended*

We would like to welcome you to our family farm in the beautiful Blackdown hills with splendid scenic views. This accommodation is part of the farmhouse within easy reach of 5 local towns and coastal resorts. Open all year.

(5) The Tallet, Clanville Manor, Castle Cary, Somerset BA7 7PJ

Mrs Sally Snook
☎/Fax 01963 350313
Mobile 0966 512732
SC From £175–£325
Sleeps 4/5 + cot
🛏 ✂ ▥ 🎪
🐾 🐾 🐾 *Commended*

In summer, walk or picnic beside the river, swim in the pool or play games in the walled garden. Watch the milking, help collect the eggs. Escape for a break in winter and curl up in front of the fire! All inclusive rent with selection of optional hampers. Brochure. Open all year.

Please mention **Stay on a Farm** when booking

Exmoor National Park

Group Contacts: [BB] *Mrs Rosemary Pile* ☎ *01598 741236*
[SC] *Mrs Ann Durbin* ☎ *01643 831255*

Exmoor National Park is a very special place. Situated on the north coast of Somerset and north Devon, it has one of the finest stretches of unspoilt countryside in England.

The scenery here is varied and dramatic – expanses of wild heather moorland, deep wooded coombes and the highest seacliffs in the country. There are quiet coves and beaches and some 600 miles of waymarked walks.

The National Park is famous for herds of wild red deer, soaring buzzards and the Exmoor ponies which date back to the Ice Age.

Exmoor offers something for everyone – walking, riding, cycling, fishing – even surfing, hang gliding or hot air ballooning! There are many beautiful National Trust properties to visit, the West Somerset Steam Train operates from Minehead, and there are leisure centres in the towns for wet days.

Some of the most well-known spots are Lynton and Lynmouth, Tarr Steps, Porlock Weir, Selworthy, Dunster and, of course, the Doone Valley.

This is an area that has been slow to change – come and share our homes and cottages, take the opportunity to relax, unwind and enjoy this peaceful haven.

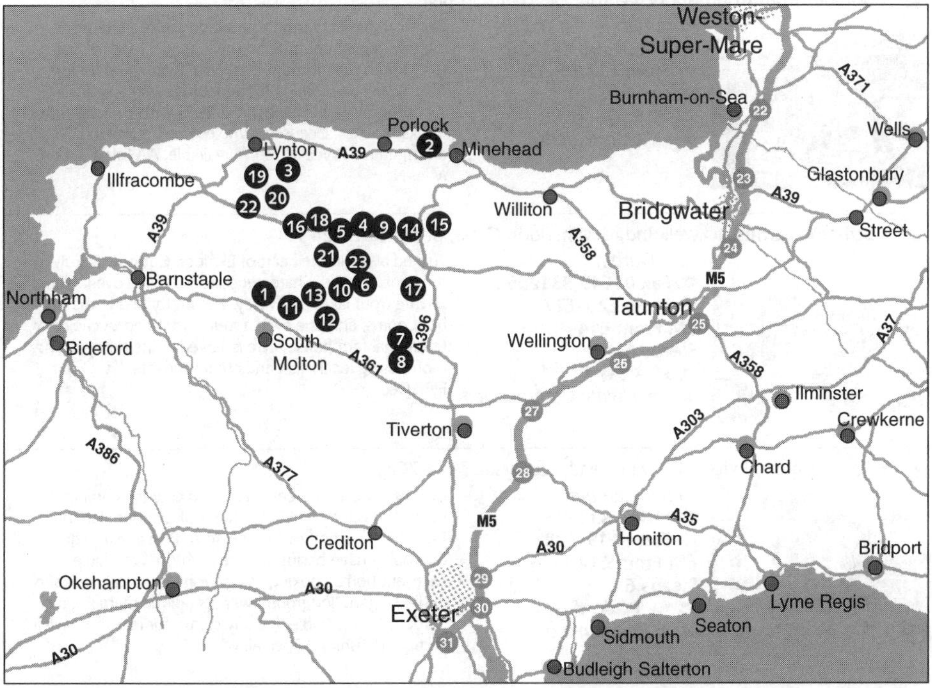

BED AND BREAKFAST

(and evening meal)

---

1 Barkham, Sandyway, South Molton, North Devon EX36 3LU

John Adie
☎/Fax 01643 831370
🅱🅱 From £19–£24
EM From £15
Sleeps 6
🛏 ⅍ 🛆 ⅍
♣ *Highly Commended*

Lovely rooms in an old farmhouse set in its own grounds in the Exmoor National Park with streams and woodland, tree house and croquet lawn. Wonderful walking/painting country. Families welcome and dinner available. En suite facilities, large drawing room with patio and excellent international cuisine. Open all year except Christmas.

---

2 Bossington Farm & Birds of Prey Centre, Allerford, Nr Porlock, Somerset TA24 8HJ

Cathy Powell
☎ 01643 862816
🅱🅱 From £17.50–£19.50
Sleeps 6
🛏 🐴 ⅍ 🛆 🐾 🐎 ◉
Listed *Approved*

Delightful character 15th century farmhouse with exposed beams and spacious rooms in quiet location at foot of wooded coombes on Exmoor, close to Minehead and Porlock. Ideal for birdwatchers, country lovers, riding and walking in National Trust area. Free entry to animals park. Exmoor activity breaks arranged. Open all year.

---

3 Coombe Farm, Countisbury, Lynton, Devon EX35 6NF

Rosemary & Susan Pile
☎/Fax 01598 741236
🅱🅱 From £17.75–£24
Sleeps 14
🛏 🐴 ⅍ 🛆 ◉
♣♣ *Commended*

Comfortable old farmhouse set on a hillside between picturesque Lynmouth and the legendary Doone Valley. Coast path runs through the farm. Riding and fishing nearby. Beamed dining room, lounge with colour TV. 2 bedrooms with shower en suite, 3 with H/C, all with hot drinks facilities. Licensed. Wholesome breakfasts. Dogs by arrangement. Weekly terms available. AA listed. Open Mar–Nov.

---

4 Cutthorne Farm, Luckwell Bridge, Wheddon Cross, Somerset TA24 7EW

Ann Durbin
☎/Fax 01643 831255
🅱🅱 From £20–£27
EM From £14
Sleeps 6
🐴 ⅍ 🥢 🛆 ⅍ ◉
♣♣♣ *Highly Commended*

Tucked away in the heart of Exmoor, Cuttorne is truly 'off the beaten track'. Share our peaceful home overlooking private trout lakes and valley. The pretty bedrooms all have bathrooms, and one even a four-poster bed. A choice of traditional farmhouse fayre is served in the sunny dining room, using local meat and organic vegetables. Open Feb–Dec.

---

5 Edgcott House, Exford, Nr Minehead, Somerset TA24 7QG

Gillian Lamble
☎ 01643 831495
🅱🅱 From £19–£22
EM From £12
Sleeps 6
🛏 ⓔ 🐴 🛆 ◉
♣♣ *Commended*

Country house of great charm and character amidst beautiful countryside in the heart of Exmoor National Park, ¼ mile from village of Exford. Peaceful and quiet. All bedrooms have basins, private bathroom available. Excellent home cooking using fresh local produce is served in the elegant 'longroom' with its unique murals. Large garden. Comfortable, friendly centre for relaxing, walking, riding and fishing. Open all year.

Highercombe Farm, Dulverton, Somerset TA22 9PT 6

Abigail Humphrey
☎/Fax 01398 323616
BB From £18–£25
EM From £12
Sleeps 6
(6)
Highly Commended

A 450-acre working farm on the edge of the moor. We have spectacular 60-mile views and red deer can often be seen from the farmhouse. Pretty en suite rooms with tea/coffee facilities and colour TV. Large guest lounge with inglenook and bay window where breakfast is served. A relaxed atmosphere, a friendly welcome, personal service and quality food. Complimentary farm tours. Open Mar–Nov.

Higher Langridge Farm, Exebridge, Dulverton, Somerset TA22 9RR 7

Gill Summers
☎ 01398 323999
BB From £17
EM From £12
Sleeps 6
Listed *Commended*

Charming old farmhouse on a 600-acre working farm situated in superbly peaceful countryside where elusive red deer and wildlife are often seen. For six generations our family has farmed here. Moorland market town of Dulverton 4 miles. Aga-cooked food a speciality. We look forward to welcoming you soon. Brochure. Open most of year.

Jubilee House, Highaton Farm, West Anstey, South Molton, North Devon EX36 3PJ 8

Lesley and Bill Denton
☎/Fax 01398 341312
BB From £17–£20
EM From £10
Sleeps 6
Listed *Commended*

We are close to the edge of Exmoor, situated on the Two Moors Walk. Peaceful surroundings but easily accessible. Stabling/grazing available. Single/double rooms all with scenic views, large lounge/dining room, gas CH and log fire. Excellent cuisine – home-grown vegetables/ preserves. Vegetarians catered for. Non-smokers. Open Apr–Oct.

Larcombe Foot, Winsford, Nr Minehead, Somerset TA24 7HS 9

Mrs Val Vicary
☎ 01643 851306
BB From £18
EM From £12
Sleeps 4
(8)
Highly Commended

Larcombe Foot is an attractive period house set in the beautiful, tranquil Exe Valley. Guests' comfort within a warm, happy atmosphere is paramount. A pretty garden to relax in, superb walks on the doorstep, Larcombe Foot makes an ideal base for exploring Exmoor and the scenic North Devon coast – 12 miles. Open Mar–Nov.

Springfield Farm, Ashwick Lane, Dulverton, Somerset TA22 9QD 10

Mrs Patricia Vellacott
☎ 01398 323722
BB From £17.50–£22.50
EM From £12
Sleeps 6
Commended

A warm welcome awaits you at our 270-acre working farm. Peacefully situated between Tarr Steps and Dulverton, overlooking the River Barle valley with magnificent moorland and woodland views. Comfortable accommodation and delicious farmhouse meals. All bedrooms have en suite or private facilities. Dining room with tea/coffee-making facilities, guests' sitting room with colour TV. Open Easter–Nov.

LET THE TELEPHONE RING!

Some farmhouses are big places. Let the telephone ring long enough to give the owner time to answer it.

SELF-CATERING

---

① Barkham, Sandyway, South Molton, North Devon EX36 3LU

John and Penny Adie
☎/Fax 01643 831370
🆂 From £190–£415
EM From £15
Sleeps 4/5/6

Up to Highly Commended

All three of our cottages have superb views down our private valley with its streams, woodland and wildlife – from deer to house martins. They are all attractively furnished and well equipped. We offer meals in the farmhouse. Tree house, croquet, colour TV, video, video library, babysitting and pets by arrangement. Open all year.

---

⑪ Churchtown Farm, West Anstey, South Molton, Devon EX36 3PE

Mrs Nicky Tarr
☎ 01398 341391
🆂 From £135–£420
Sleeps 8 + cot

Applied

Enjoy a characteristic, spacious and attractively furnished half of Devon longhouse set in 200 acres of working farm adjoining moorland. Farmyard animals and pony rides. Beautiful secluded garden, barbecue, stocked fish ponds. 3 bedrooms, lounge with TV and woodburner, dining hall, well equipped kitchen, bathroom, CH. Linen included. Washing/drying facilities. Babysitting. Ideal family/walking holiday destination. Open all year.

---

④ Cutthorne Farm, Luckwell Bridge, Wheddon Cross, Somerset TA24 7EW

Ann Durbin
☎/Fax 01643 831255
🆂 From £95–£475
Sleeps 4

Highly Commended

'What a wonderful position' – the most frequent comment we hear. Nestling in the heart of Exmoor, we offer two attractive barn conversions on side of farmhouse. These peaceful havens overlook our own trout lakes and valley. Close to Lynton and Lynmouth, Tarr Steps and Dunster, also small unspoilt beaches. Home-cooked meals may be taken in the farmhouse.Open all year.

---

⑫ Dunsley Farm, West Anstey, South Molton, Devon EX36 3PF

Mrs Mary Robins
☎ 01398 341246
🆂 From £90–£350
Sleeps 5

Commended

Self-contained cottage forming part of 16th century farmhouse, overlooks meadows and woodland valley. Access off a quiet country road. 2 bedrooms (accommodate 5 people), bathroom, large lounge/diner with colour TV. Large modern equipped kitchen, electric heating (£1 meter). Linen provided, pets welcome. Coarse fishing available on farm. Dulverton 6 miles. Open Mar–Nov.

---

⑬ Dunsley Mill, West Anstey, South Molton, Devon EX36 3PF

Helen Sparrow
☎/Fax 01398 341374
🆂 From £200–£450
Sleeps 6

Commended

Beautifully converted detached stone barn set in 30 acres in an idyllic riverside situation. Three bedrooms, 2 doubles, 1 twin. Dishwasher, microwave, electric oven, washing machine. Children, dogs and horses welcome. Bridleways adjoin the property. Fishing, hunting and shooting all in the vicinity. Open all year.

Highercombe Farm, Dulverton, Somerset TA22 9PT   6

Abigail Humphrey
☎/Fax 01398 323616
[SC] From £180–£320
Sleeps 5
☺ 🐴 🐾
🔑 🔑 🔑 🔑 *Commended*

Self-contained wing of large farmhouse on 450-acre working farm next to the moor. Well furnished in cottage style. Private entrance, large gardens, spectacular views. 2 bedrooms, bathroom, large lounge/dining room with colour TV, CD player/radio, woodburner. Modern pine kitchen. Linen, CH, hot water, logs included. Use of washing machine/dryer. Evening meals arranged, babysitting service. Electricity pound coin meter. Open all year.

Liscombe Farm, Winsford, Dulverton, Somerset TA22 9QA   14

Sally Wade
☎ 01643 851551
[SC] From £100–£600
Sleeps 6/9 + cot
☺ 🐴 ♿
Applied

Liscombe is a 385-acre beef and sheep farm in Exmoor National Park. Peaceful, spacious farmhouse and two converted barns, each furnished to a high standard with CH, dishwasher, washing machine, drier, hi-fi, video – everything to make a relaxing holiday. Perfect for walking, riding or fishing. Cosy log fires, garden, play area and barbecue. Stabling available. Open all year.

Pembroke, c/o Brake Cottage, Wheddon Cross, Minehead, Somerset TA24 7EX   15

Mrs J Escott
☎ 01643 841550
[SC] From £95–£350
Sleeps 5/6
☺ 🐴
🔑 🔑 🔑 🔑 *Commended*

Situated in a peaceful position with parking, private garden and splendid south–westerly views, detached cottage in the heart of the Exmoor National Park. Well equipped with microwave, automatic washing machine, tumble dryer. Linen included. Open Mar–Dec. No pets.

Riscombe Farm, Exford, Minehead, Somerset TA24 7NH   16

Leone & Brian Martin
☎/Fax 01643 831480
[SC] From £100–£370
Sleeps 2–7
☺ 🐴 🐈 🐾
🔑 🔑 🔑 🔑 *Commended*

Four comfortable cottages converted from stone barns set in attractive courtyard. Ample parking. Quiet, relaxed setting beside River Exe in centre of Exmoor National Park, 1½ miles from Exford village. Smallholding with ponies, chickens, ducks, etc. Microwaves, colour TV, bedlinen provided. Logburning fires. Payphone. DIY stabling. Brochure available. Open all year.

Week Farm, Bridgetown, Dulverton, Somerset TA22 9JP   17

Hilda England
☎ 01643 851289
[SC] From £100–£350
Sleeps 6
☺ 🐴 ♿ 🏹 🎾 ◎
🔑 🔑 🔑 🔑 *Commended*

Enjoy a break in our comfortable cottage on a sheep and beef farm adjoining moorland. Peaceful setting, magnificent views and excellent walks. TV, video, CD player, microwave, heating. Safe garden and barbecue. Cot, highchair, toys and babysitting. Linen inclusive. Ponies, chickens, geese etc. Pets welcome and stabling available. Brochure. Open all year.

Westermill Farm, Exford, Nr Minehead, Somerset TA24 7NJ   18

The Edwards family
☎ 01643 831238
Fax 01643 831660
[SC] From £140–£399
Sleeps 4/8
🧍 ☺ 🐴 🏹 🐈 🎾 ♿ 🐾 ◎
🔑 – 🔑 🔑 🔑 *Up to*
Commended

Six delightful log cottages (Silver winners, David Bellamy Conservation Award) in small grassy paddocks on side of valley by a river. Also bright, comfortable cottage adjoining the farmhouse overlooks the river. Patio, garage. Four waymarked walks over 500-acre farm in centre of Exmoor. 2½ miles shallow river, fishing, bathing. Laundry, payphone, information centre, seasonal small shop. Log cottages open Mar–Jan, cottage all year.

19 West Ilkerton Farm, Barbrook, Lynton, North Devon EX35 6QA

Chris & Victoria Eveleigh
☎ 01598 752310
SC **From £180–£440**
Sleeps 6 + cot
🛏 🐴 ⚒ 🏠 🍴 ☂ 🌿 ◉
𝄞 𝄞 𝄞 𝄞 𝄞 𝄞
Commended

Luxurious semi-detached cottage on secluded hill farm bordering open moor. Sheep, cattle, carthorses and Exmoor ponies. Coast 3 miles, riding ½ mile. 3 bedrooms (2 king size, 1 twin) 2 bathrooms, living/dining room, kitchen (Rayburn and full range of appliances). CH. TV, video. Baby equipment and evening babysitting. Children, dogs and horses welcome. Special winter breaks from £95. Ideal for walking, riding, family farm holidays. Open all year.

20 Whitefield Barton, Challacombe, Barnstaple, Devon EX31 4TU

Rosemarie Kingdon
☎ 01598 763271
SC **From £100–£340**
Sleeps 6
🛏 🐴 🍴 ☂ ⚒
𝄞 𝄞 𝄞 𝄞 *Commended*

Spacious characteristic accommodation in half of 16th century farmhouse with modern luxuries. Tastefully furnished to high standard. Warm cosy lounge, well equipped kitchen, family & twin rooms, bathroom/shower, babysitting. Ample parking. Private patio, BBQ, streamed garden. Linen & electricity incl. Peaceful surroundings with scenic walks and farm animals (cows, sheep, ponies). Central for beaches, moors. Open May–Dec.

21 Wintershead Farm, Simonsbath, Exmoor, Somerset TA24 7LF

Jane Styles
☎ 01643 831222
Fax 01643 831628
SC **From £120–£465**
Sleeps 2–6
🛏 🍴 ⚒
𝄞 𝄞 – 𝄞 𝄞 𝄞 𝄞 *Highly*
Commended

Forget the pressures of everyday life and unwind in one of our four comfortable cottages. Set high among the hills of Exmoor with breathtaking views across open moorland. Relax after a wonderful day out with comfy sofas, log fires, central heating, etc. Short breaks available Nov–Mar. Colour brochure. Open all year.

22 Yelland Cottage, c/o West Whitefield Farm, Challacombe, Barnstaple, Devon EX31 4TU

Jean Kingdon
☎ 01598 763433
SC **From £120–£270**
Sleeps 6
🛏 🍴 ☂
𝄞 𝄞 𝄞 *Approved*

Semi-detached cosy farm cottage on working hill farm amidst beautiful countryside within easy reach of village pub and shop. Log fire, Rayburn plus electric conveniences. Relaxing lounge, colour TV. Linen provided. Friendly, relaxed atmosphere with farm animals. Spacious garden with ample parking. Ideal for beaches, walking, fishing, riding and touring North Devon. Open all year.

CAMPING AND CARAVANNING

23 Halse Farm Touring Park, Winsford, Minehead, Somerset, TA24 7JL

Mrs Julia Brown
☎/Fax 01643 851259
SC **Tents From £5.50**
Caravans From £5.50
(per pitch + 2 persons)
44 pitches
🛏 🍴 ⛺ 🚐 ⚒ ☂
✓ ✓ ✓ ✓

Small, unique caravan and tent park on a working farm. Outstanding views and moorland walking within 400 yards. Quality heated loo, shower and laundry block with disabled facilities. Free showers. Excellent village shop and pub only one mile. An ideal setting for seeing Exmoor and all its wildlife. Open mid Mar–Oct.

Westermill Farm, Exford, Nr Minehead, Somerset TA24 7NJ   (18)

The Edwards family
☎ **01643 831238**
Fax 01643 831660
☒ **Tents: adult £3.50/child £1**
Car: £1, 2 adults + vehicle £8
(all prices per night)

Beautiful secluded site (David Bellamy Silver Award for Conservation) for 60 tents and dormobiles beside upper reaches of River Exe. Centre of Exmoor National Park. Four waymarked walks over 500-acre working farm. 2½ miles shallow river, fishing and bathing. Loo block, showers, laundry, washing up. Information centre, small shop, payphone. A site and farm to enjoy in the most natural way. Children's paradise. Open Mar–Nov.

STAY ON A FARM GIFT TOKENS

If you have enjoyed your Stay on a Farm, why not treat your friends and relatives to *Stay on a Farm* gift tokens? Available from the Bureau office, telephone 01203 696909, they can be redeemed against accommodation booked on the majority of our farms

THE 1000+ BUREAU MEMBERS OFFER A UNIQUE LINK TO CUSTOMERS ACROSS THE UK

All Bureau members belong to a local Group. Each member can refer you to an equally high quality member within the Group... or across the UK: England, Northern Ireland, Scotland, Wales.

CONFIRM BOOKINGS

Disappointments can arise from misunderstandings over the telephone. Please write to confirm your booking.

Exmoor Coast & Country

Group Contact *Tammy Cody-Boutcher* ☎/*Fax 01643 841249*

We invite you to stay for the Exmoor experience – to watch buzzards soar – spot the deer on the moor – take a trip on a steam train – walk the rugged south west coast path – amble through woods where bluebells grow – gallop by the purple heather on the moors – paddle on the seaside shore – watch a horse get new shoes – hum along with the brass band playing – maybe help out down on the farm – search for antiques – shop till you drop – crafts to see, do and buy – cream teas in thatched cottages – cricket on the village green – listen to the sky lark sing – ride at the fun fair – surf in the sea – catch a fish to take home for tea – gaze at a view from on top of a beacon – cycle on the beach – find the smallest church in England – surprise ponies roaming free – sit by a river under an old oak tree – marvel at the working mill – wonder at the castle hill – read Lorna Doone on a wet day – in the sunshine, smile as the lambs play – sip a cider – and oh! so much to welcome you, come share our hospitality in the home of the red deer – don't you wish you were here!

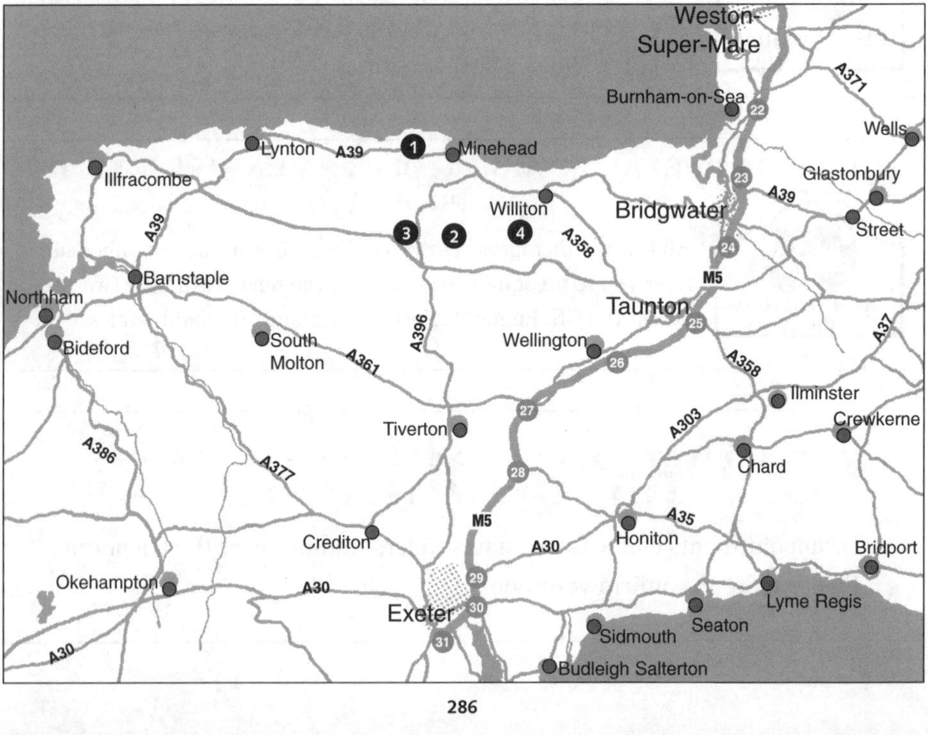

BED AND BREAKFAST

(and evening meal)

Hindon Farm, nr Minehead, Somerset TA24 8SH   ❶

Penny & Roger Webber
☎/Fax 01643 705244
[BB] From £18–£22
EM From £15
Sleeps 4
🛏 🐎 🖊 🐕 ♨ 🛢
Listed *Commended*

Escape to our working farm in peaceful Exmoor valley (Minehead 3 miles, Selworthy 1 mile for cream teas!) Wander our acres and adjoining heather moors to coast path. Relax by the stream while ducks dabble and donkeys dawdle. 18th century farmhouse with 20th century hospitality (own produce). Featured on TV *Getaways* and in *Which? Best B&B* and *Country Living*. Brochure.

Little Brendon Hill, Wheddon Cross, Nr Minehead, Somerset TA24 7BG   ❷

Mrs Shelagh Maxwell
☎/Fax 01643 841556
[BB] From £19.50
EM From £13
Sleeps 6
🛏(10) 🖊 🛢 ♨ 🐕 ◉
🌑🌑 *Highly Commended*

Enjoy a stay with us in our beautifully appointed farmhouse set in the peace and tranquillity of the Exmoor National Park. Three lovely en suite rooms with colour television. Log fires, cosy candlelit dinners. Central heating. Non-smoking. Short stay or long, a truly relaxing place to pursue country pastimes. You will be most welcome. Open all year except Christmas.

Little Quarme Farm, Wheddon Cross, Nr Minehead, Somerset TA24 7EA   ❸

Bob Cody-Boutcher
☎/Fax 01643 841249
[BB] From £18.50–£21
EM From £10
Sleeps 6
🛏 🖊 🐎 ♨ 🛢 ◉
🌑🌑 *Highly Commended*

Lovely old farmhouse in the heart of Exmoor in an outstanding situation with panoramic views. 2 double en suite bedrooms, 1 twin with private bathroom. Tea/coffee-making facilities. TV lounge with Sky TV, racing channel and video. 40' x 40' sun lounge. Friendly family atmosphere. Many animals, pony rides, stabling. Large garden and 18 acres. We are ¼ mile past Wheddon Cross on Exford road B3224. Open Mar–Nov.

Wood Advent Farm, Roadwater, Watchet, Somerset TA23 0RR   ❹

Diana Brewer
☎/Fax 01984 640920
[BB] From £18.50–£22.50
EM £12
Sleeps 8
🛏(10) 🐎 💷 👤 ♨ 🛢 ◉
🌑🌑🌑 *Commended*

Nestling at the foot of the Brendon Hills in the Exmoor National Park, a spacious listed farmhouse set in 340 acres of working farm. Relaxing en suite bedrooms with hospitality trays. Two large lounges to relax in with log fires and inglenook burners. Licensed dining room where wonderful country dishes can be assured. Grass tennis court, heated outdoor pool, clay pigeon shooting and waymarked walks from the farm. Perfect place to relax and enjoy the country life. Open all year.

NO ANSWER?

Farmers are mostly out and about during the day.
Try to telephone before 9.30am or after 4pm.

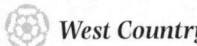

SELF-CATERING

---

① **Hindon Farmhouse Cottage,** Hindon Farm, Nr Minehead, Somerset TA24 8SH

Penny & Roger Webber
☎/Fax 01643 705244
[SC] **From £200–£490**
Sleeps 6
🛏 🐕 ⚰ 🐎 ☕ 🎿 ♨ 🌳
🐾 🐾 🐾 🐾 *Commended*

18th century cottage/wing of farmhouse situated between Minehead and Selworthy (short walk for cream teas!) Acres National Trust farm below heather moors and SW coast path – terrific views. Much farm and wild life. Tastefully furnished with original fireplace and log burner. Living/dining/kitchen, CH, TV, video and all mod cons. 1 double en suite, 2 twins with bathroom. Linen and towels provided. Baby listening. Breakfasts available. Featured on TV *Getaways*. Brochure with photos.

---

③ **Little Quarme Country Cottages,** Wheddon Cross, Nr Minehead, Somerset TA24 7EA

Tammy Cody-Boutcher & family
☎/Fax 01643 841249
[SC] **From £90–£460**
Sleeps 2/6
🛏 🐕 ⚰ 🐎 🎿 ♨ 💷 ◉
🐾 🐾 🐾 🐾 *Highly Commended to De Luxe*

Six stone cottages furnished and equipped to the highest standards in the heart of Exmoor. All have microwaves, colour TV, videos, bed linen and towels. Standing amid 18 acres and large informal gardens, direct access to footpaths and bridlepath. Traffic free tranquillity with panoramic southerly views. Ample parking, free laundry room, play area, pay phone, stabling. Many animals. Quality, comfort, cleanliness. Brochure available.

FOLLOW THE COUNTRY CODE

Leave nothing but footprints,
Take nothing but photographs,
Kill nothing but time!

North Devon

Group Contacts: [BB] *Pat Burge* ☎ *01598 710275*
[SC] *Ruth Ley* ☎ *01769 572337*

Welcome to North Devon – an area of tremendous contrasts. Miles of golden sands, surfed washed beaches, wide rolling hills and valleys of the Taw and Torridge stretching to the Tamar near the Cornish border. We span the land between two famous moors. Exmoor in the north with its magnificent rolling heather clad hills to Dartmoor in the south.

Here you can slow down, take time to marvel at our nature. Our winding country lanes filled with flowers. Our footpaths that link quaint villages with their thatch and white-washed cob-walled cottages. Henry Williamson wrote his book 'Tarka the Otter' here, and now the Tarka Trail joins our moors and coasts.

Clovelly with its steep cobbled street and picturesque cottages is delightful. While Heartland proudly shows off its dramatic cliff top.

Whether it's coast or country, whether you surf, walk, ride, play golf or like the easy life North Devon has so much to offer.

North Devon – an area you can rely on.

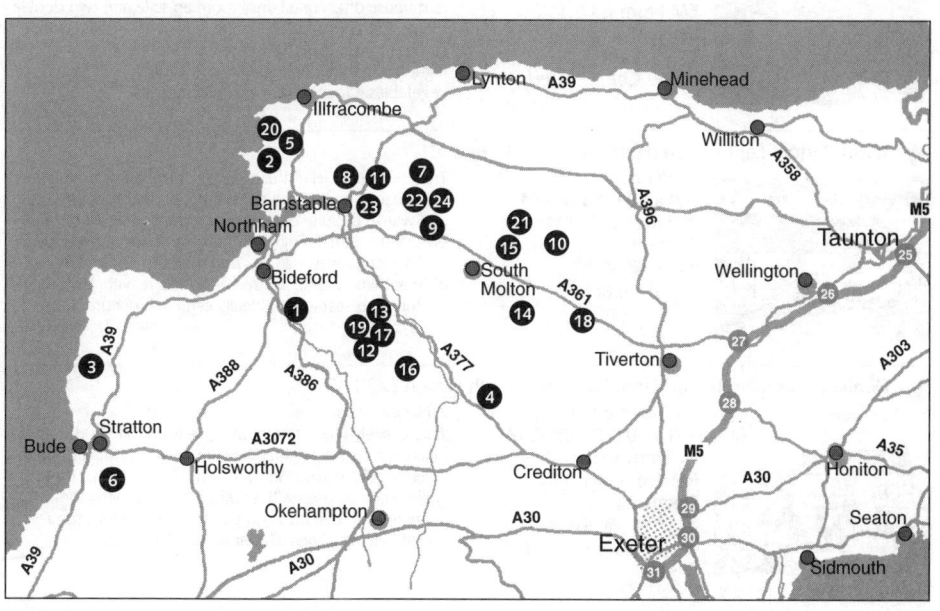

BED AND BREAKFAST

(and evening meal)

---

(1) Cleave Farmhouse, Weare Giffard, Nr Bideford, North Devon EX39 4QX

Liz Moore
☎ 01805 623671
Fax 01805 623235
🅱 From £20
Sleeps 4
🐕 ✂ 🛏 🌳 ✻
Listed *Commended*

Come to our beautiful village tucked away in heart of 'Tarka Country'. Panoramic views overlooking wooded valleys on a working dairy farm. Explore the lanes and walkable footpaths. Meet the badgers or rabbits and even deer on a nocturnal outing. Ring now for a brochure. Open Mar–Nov.

---

(2) Combas Farm, Putsborough, Croyde, North Devon EX33 1PH

Mrs Gwen Adams
☎ 01271 890398
🅱 From £18–£21
EM From £9
Sleeps 12
🐕 🐴 🏕 🛏 ◎
🐝 🐝 *Commended*

140-acre stock farm nestling in its own secluded valley, just 15 mins' walk from miles of golden sands (5 mins from the village pub!). Many repeat bookings confirm claims to a warm welcome and high standard of home cooking using home produce including unusual fruit and veg. Wisteria rambles over this 17th century longhouse overlooking a lovely garden and unspoiled view. In *'Which' Good B&B Guide*. Colour brochure. Closed Christmas & Jan.

---

(3) Cornakey Farm, Morwenstow, Bude, Cornwall EX23 9SS

Mrs Monica Heywood
☎ 01288 331260
🅱 From £16–£18
EM From £8
Sleeps 6
🐕 ✂ ✻ 🛏
Listed *Commended*

This is a 220–acre mixed coastal farm with extensive views of sea and Lundy island from bedrooms and bathroom. Good touring centre with easy reach of quiet beaches. The farmhouse offers one family room en suite and two double rooms. Bathroom, toilet, lounge (colour TV), dining room, games room. Children welcome at reduced rates. Cot, highchair, babysitting. Good home cooking with fresh vegetables. Open all year except Christmas.

---

(4) Court Barton, Lapford, Crediton, Devon EX17 6PZ

Sheila Mather
☎/Fax 01363 83441
🅱 From £17–£21
Sleeps 6
🐕 ✂ 🛏 ✻ ◎
🐝 🐝 *Commended*

Treat yourself. Delightful medieval farmhouse, undulating floorboards, beams and panelling. Quality bedrooms, cosy and warm. En suite or private bathrooms. Nibble or feast – breakfast's a treat. Enjoy our dairy farm and lovely local walks. Deer, foxes, badgers and buzzards abound. It's a different world here. Conservation village with 16th century pub/restaurant. Ideally central. Brochure. Open Jan–Nov.

---

(5) Denham Farm, North Buckland, Braunton, North Devon EX33 1HY

Mrs Jean Barnes
☎/Fax 01271 890297
🅱 From £25–£28
EM From £12
Sleeps 24
🐕 🎱 ✻ 🛏 ◎
🐝 🐝 🐝 *Commended*

A Happy Holiday Recipe
Take a lovely warm farmhouse, pretty en suite bedrooms, a pinch of fun and laughter, mix with nearby attractions and miles of golden sand. Surround with green fields, country walks, keep amused with small pets and games room. Serve up with delicious home cooking and return for a repeat helping. Open all year except Christmas.

Elm Park Farm, Bridgerule, Holsworthy, Devon EX22 7EL   6

Sylvia Lucas
☎ 01288 381231
BB From £15–£18
EM From £7
Sleeps 11
🐕 🐓 🐩 🏠
🌢🌢 Approved

Elm Park is 6 miles from Cornish surfing beaches at Bude and ideal for touring both Devon and Cornwall. Children are especially welcomed with pony and tractor and trailer rides. Twin and family rooms with en suite, colour TV and tea/coffee-making facilities. Ample 4-course dinners with freshly produced fare and delicious sweets. Big weekly reductions and everyone made most welcome and comfortable. Games room. Closed Christmas.

Haxton Down Farm, Bratton Fleming, Barnstaple, Devon EX32 7JL   7

Mrs Pat Burge
☎ 01598 710275
BB From £15–£17
EM From £8.50
Sleeps 5
🐕 🐓 🐩 🏠 ◎
🌢🌢 Commended

Relax among leafy lanes and wonderful scenery on our working stock farm nestling in a peaceful valley. 17th century farmhouse offers warmth and comfort with private or en suite facilities, CTV, tea trays and a warm welcome to all ages. Delicious food with hearty breakfasts and tempting 4-course dinners. Close to beach and moor and attractions galore. Give North Devon a try – you'll be pleased you did. Ring for brochure please. Open Easter–Nov.

Home Park Farm, Lower Blakewell, Muddiford, Barnstaple, North Devon EX31 4ET   8

Mrs Mari Lethaby
☎/Fax 01271 42955
BB From £15–£20
EM From £8.50
Sleeps 6
🐕 ✂ 🏠 ◎
🌢🌢 Commended

Paradise for a country and garden lover. Panoramic scenic views combined with warm hospitality, genuine farmhouse cuisine and a relaxing, tranquil atmosphere await you at Home Park. All rooms en suite, TV, hair dryer, hospitality tray. Four-poster beds. CH. Many extras including laundry. Conveniently positioned for Exmoor, N. Devon coast. Many repeat bookings confirm excellent accommodation. 2 miles north of Barnstaple. RAC acclaimed. AA QQQQ. Closed Christmas.

Huxtable Farm, West Buckland, Barnstaple, North Devon EX32 0SR   9

Jackie & Antony Payne
☎/Fax 01598 760254
BB From £23
EM £14
Sleeps 17
🐕 🏃 🏠 🎾 ◎
🌢🌢🌢 Commended

Enjoy a 4-course candlelit dinner of farm/local produce with a glass of complimentary homemade wine in the medieval dining room of this 16th century Devon longhouse. Secluded sheep farm with abundant wildlife. En suite bedrooms with TV. Log fires, fitness room, sauna, games room and tennis court. Reductions for short/long breaks out of season and for children (£10). Free informative brochure. Open all year (closed Christmas).

Kerscott Farm, Ash Mill, South Molton, North Devon EX36 4QG   10

Mrs Theresa Sampson
☎ 01769 550262
BB From £17.50
EM From £7.50
Sleeps 6
🐕(10) ✂ 🏠
🌢🌢🌢 Highly Commended

Peaceful, 16th century farmhouse and working farm mentioned in Domesday Book. Beautiful olde world antique interior and furnishings – a rare find. Superb elevated position overlooking Exmoor National Park and surrounding countryside. Pretty en suite bedrooms. Hearty, rustic farm cooking, homemade bread and preserves. Non-smokers only. AA QQQQQ Premier Selected. Open all year except Christmas.

Waytown Farm, Shirwell, Barnstaple, North Devon EX31 4JN   11

Hazel Kingdon
☎/Fax 01271 850396
BB From £17–£19.50
EM From £9
Sleeps 9
🐕 🏃 🏠 ◎
🌢🌢 Commended

A warm welcome awaits you on our family run beef and sheep farm set in beautiful countryside about 3 miles north of Barnstaple. Our 17th century farmhouse offers a warm and comfortable atmosphere with traditional farmhouse cooking. Double, family and twin bedrooms en suite and single bedroom, all with colour TV and beverage facilities. Brochure. Weekly terms available. Open all year except Christmas.

SELF-CATERING

5 **Barley Cottage & Old Granary,** c/o Denham Farm, North Buckland, Braunton, North Devon EX33 1HY

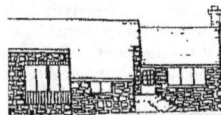

Jean Barnes
☎/Fax 01271 890297
£185–£610
EM From £12
Sleeps 4/6/8

Commended

Welcome to our cottages. Let us surround you with warmth, comfort, peace and green fields. Walk our country lanes or take a short drive to the nearby sandy beaches. Here you can be pampered by having a meal in our farmhouse or a drink in our bar. Come to Denham to see why everyone else does. Open all year.

---

12 **Beech Grove,** East Westacott, Riddlecombe, Chulmleigh, Devon EX18 7PF

Thomas & Joyce
Middleton
☎/Fax 01769 520210
From £150
Sleeps 4/6

Commended

Peace, comfort, charming surroundings and a lovely warm atmosphere make you quickly relax. 2 bedrooms, sleeping 4/6 (cot available). CH, cosy log fires in winter. Superbly equipped, even a dishwasher. Games room for all ages. Delightful views of rolling meadows, pretty gardens with sunny patio. Friendly hosts, 'home from home' comforts, Devon's magnificent scenery and a taste of farming life, all combined ensure many guests often return. Open all year.

---

13 **Bridleway Cottages,** Golland Farm, Burrington, Umberleigh, North Devon EX37 9JP

Diane and Robert Perry
☎/Fax 01769 520263
From £160
Sleeps 4/6

Commended

Secluded stone barn cottages, overlooking Taw Valley on our 16th century farm, offer you peace with every comfort including woodburners and many original features. Exclusive fishing on two lakes, wildlife and wildflower walks. Tarka Trail nearby. RHS Rosemoor 20 minutes. Between Dartmoor and Exmoor, a rural haven awaits you. Open all year.

---

14 **Crosse Farm,** Bishops Nympton, South Molton, North Devon EX36 4PB

Mrs Dawn Verney
☎ 01769 550288
From £140–£330
Sleeps 6 + cot

Approved

Wing of thatched 12th century Devon longhouse on 230-acre working farm. Magnificent views, unspoilt countryside, peace and tranquillity. Edge of Exmoor, 20 miles Golden Coast. 1 double en suite, 2 twins. Well equipped kitchen, microwave, dishwasher, washing machine. Lounge/diner with colour TV. Shower room. Enclosed garden. Electricity and linen included. Breakfasts and evening meals available.

---

15 **Drewstone Farm,** South Molton, North Devon EX36 3EF

Ruth Ley
☎ 01769 572337
From £160
Sleeps 6/7

Commended

Escape to farm tranquillity on edge of Exmoor. 16th century luxury cottage and converted barn with beams, woodburner, colour TV, fitted carpets, phone, dishwasher, washing machine. 3/4 bedrooms, bath-shower room. Fully equipped oak kitchen/diner and lounge with panoramic views. Enclosed lawn, children's games room, animals, freedom to explore the farm. Country walks, clay-pigeon shooting, trout lake. Open all year.

Hollacombe Barton, Hollacombe, Chulmleigh, Devon EX18 7QG   **16**

Christine Stevens
☎ 01837 83385
Fax 01837 83002
SC From £195
EM £6
Sleeps 2–8
⚘ ⚘ ⚘ ⚘ *Commended*

Children can roam and play in safety whilst parents relax in comfort in the conservatory while their evening meal is prepared. What more could you wish for? How about a superbly equipped farmhouse in beautiful countryside. Enjoy woodland walks, barbecues, quad bikes, pool table and pony rides.Watch the milking, make friends with our tame sheep, calves and Miss Piggy! Versatile accommodation and prices for couples or more. Suits all ages and interests. Brochure with pleasure.

Manor Farm, Riddlecombe, Chulmleigh, North Devon EX18 7NX   **17**

Eveline Gay
☎/Fax 01769 520335
SC From £160
Sleeps 7/8 + cot
⚘ ⚘ ⚘ ⚘ *Commended*

Picturesque farmhouse with cosy 3-bedroomed wing in idyllic setting, overlooking cows and sheep grazing in nearby fields. Meet Doris the cow, collect eggs, feed lambs, watch milking on our dairy/sheep farm. Outstanding games room – children call it 'Alladins cave'! Includes play cottage, tractor, trikes, slide, table tennis and much more. Excellent heating for all seasons. Illustrated brochure.

Nethercott Manor Farm, Rose Ash, South Molton, North Devon EX36 4RE   **18**

Carol Woollacott
☎/Fax 01769 550483
SC From £100–£425
Sleeps 4 and 7
⚘ ⚘ ⚘ *Approved*

Welcome to Nethercott! Situated in the heart of the Devonshire dales – explore the farm, Exmoor and beautiful coast. Three cottages within traditional thatched farmhouse. Comfortably furnished, cosy and warm atmosphere, woodburners, oak beams, nooks and crannies. Lawn tennis, trout pond, games room with skittles, pool table, tennis, darts. Barbecue or relax.

Northcott Barton Farm, Ashreigney, Chulmleigh, Devon EX18 7PR   **19**

Mrs Sandra Gay
☎/Fax 01769 520259
SC From £170
Sleeps 7/8 + cot
⚘ ⚘ ⚘ *Commended*

Unwind and relax country-style. Glorious countryside and farm to explore. Beautifully equipped, warm and comfy three bedroomed cottage offers character beams and log fire, plus video, microwave, washer, freezer, etc. Children love helping feed lambs and calves. Collect eggs for breakfast and see the cows come home for milking.

Pickwell Barton Holiday Cottages, Pickwell Barton, Georgeham, Braunton, North Devon EX33 1LA   **20**

Mrs Sheila Cook
☎ 01271 890987
SC From £160–£390
Sleeps 7/8
⚘ ⚘ *Commended*

Visit Pickwell Barton and you have the best of both worlds – gorgeous country walks with a fantastic view of Putsborough, Woolacombe beach. Stroll across our fields in the evening to view the sun setting into the ocean. Each cottage has 3 bedrooms on our sheep and arable farm just 20 minutes' walk to the golden, sandy beach. Warm, cosy open fires in winter. Open all year.

Stable Cottage, Pitt Farm, North Molton, North Devon EX36 3JR   **21**

Mrs Gladys Ayre
☎ 01598 740285
SC From £150–£380
Sleeps 5/6
⚘ ⚘ ⚘ ⚘ *Commended*

Enjoy peaceful surroundings at our charming cottage, set in unspoilt Exmoor countryside, 1 mile from village shops, pubs, garage, equipped to high standard with night storage heating throughout. 3 bedrooms. Bath/shower/beamed lounge with woodburner. Colour TV, oak fitted kitchen/diner. Autowasher, fridge, microwave, etc. Own patio. Barbecue. Pond with ducks and geese. Freedom to explore the farm. Open all year.

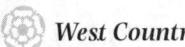
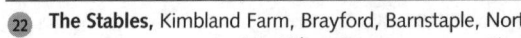

22 **The Stables,** Kimbland Farm, Brayford, Barnstaple, North Devon EX32 7PS

Mrs Hilary Ayre
☎ **01598 710352**
SC **From £160–£310**
Sleeps 4/6
♿ ⚑
♞ ♞ ♞ ♞ *Commended*

The Stables is set on a 210-acre beef and sheep farm with views over Exmoor. Tastefully converted with modern kitchen and bathroom, electric central heating on meter, woodburner in lounge. One double with shower, 1 twin and bedsetee in lounge. Excellent touring base. Peace and quiet with freedom to roam. Open all year.

23 **Willesleigh Farm,** Goodleigh, Barnstaple, North Devon EX32 7NA

*Charles and Anne
Esmond-Cole*
☎/Fax **01271 343763**
SC **From £154–£625**
Sleeps 6
♿ ♞ ⚑ ▪ ◎
♞ ♞ ♞ ♞ *Highly
Commended*

86-acre family-run dairy farm in glorious countryside, ½ mile from village, within ½ hour's drive of dramatic coastlines, Exmoor, glorious gardens, superb walks. Lovingly cared for, The Cottage and The Gatehouse welcome all ages and abilities to year-round comfort and peace. Enclosed heated swimming pool May–Oct.

CAMPING AND CARAVANNING

24 **Welcombe Farm,** Charles, Nr Barnstaple, North Devon EX32 7PU

Mrs Margaret Faulkner
☎/Fax **01598 710440**
SC **From £100–£250**
Sleeps 4/5
♿ ♞ ✂ ⊞ ▪
Tourist Board Inspected

Imaginative private setting for a luxury caravan holiday. Comfortable and peaceful, with full facilities, two bedrooms and heating throughout. Small, family run farm with dairy cows and sheep, on the foothills of Exmoor. Panoramic views of hills and valleys from enclosed garden. Close to Tarka Trail and easy reach of sandy beaches, moors and gardens. Wildlife in abundance. Open Easter–Oct.

FARM HOLIDAY BUREAU

Please mention **Stay on a Farm** when booking

FARM HOLIDAY BUREAU

DEVON FARMS

Availability of farms in Devon can be easily discovered by ringing **01548 550055**.

Heart & East Devon

Group Contact: 📖 *Jill Balkwill* ☎ *01548 550055/Fax 01548 550312*

With its thatched cottages, lush meadows, steeply wooded valleys, rivers and streams. It is unspoilt and rather special and includes designated Areas Of Outstanding Natural Beauty. This is a district of traditional family run sheep and cattle farms, each with their own individual characteristics. Many towns still hold their weekly market, where you can get the full flavour of the occasion, sampling fresh local produce. Lapped by the varying coastline with miles of sandy and pebble beaches, coves and harbours with the time honoured small fishing fleets.

This region has a colourful history and boasts Exeter Cathedral, with its replica at Ottery St Mary (birthplace of Samuel Taylor Coleridge), National Trust properties, the Grand Western Canal at Tiverton, delicate hand made lace at Honiton.

Walk along the coastal footpath or the East Devon Way, which meanders through quiet villages and open farmland, enjoy breathtaking views, flora and fauna.

However you care to spend your time, either an energetic outdoor sport or a leisurely candlelit meal, this corner of Devon will surpass all your expectations.

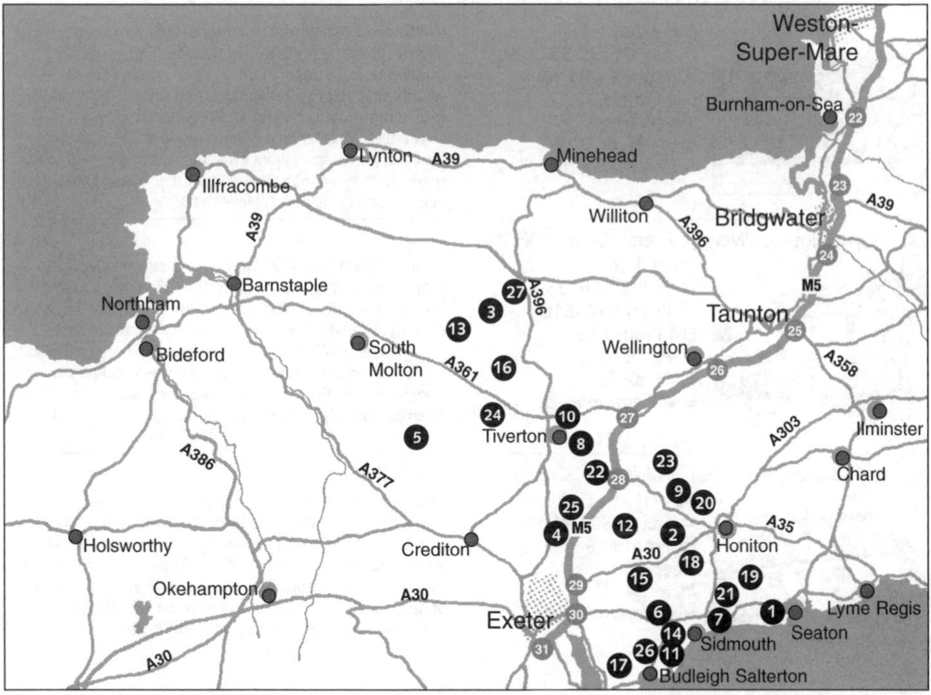

BED AND BREAKFAST

(and evening meal)

---

1 Gatcombe Farm, Seaton, Devon EX12 3AA

Julie Reed
☎ 01297 21235
Fax 01297 23010
🅱 From £15–£20
Sleeps 6
🐴✂☕🏛♿🎋
💐 *Commended*

Family-run dairy farm situated only 2 miles from sea in beautiful Axe Valley. Comfortable bedrooms, visitors' dining room and TV lounge with log fire and tea-making facilities. Large garden. Good walking area, restaurants and inns only 5 minutes' drive. Open Mar–Oct.

---

2 Godford Farm, Awliscombe, Honiton, Devon EX14 0PW

Sally Lawrence
☎/Fax 01404 42825
🅱 From £15–£21
Sleeps 6
🐴🏛♿ ⊚
💐💐 *Commended*

We invite you to stay on this family-run dairy farm, set in a beautiful river valley. Listed farmhouse with large sitting and dining rooms. Colour TV. Central heating. Drinks facilities in bedrooms. Large garden, play area, games barn. Delightful area for walking and wildlife. Cots and highchairs provided. Family and twin room, en suite/ private bathrooms. Child reductions. Brochure. Open Easter–Sept.

---

3 Harton Farm, Oakford, Tiverton, Devon EX16 9HH

Mrs Lindy Head
☎/Fax 01398 351209
🅱 From £14–£16
EM From £7
Sleeps 6
🐴(4) 🐕🏛♿🎋
💐 *Commended*

Welcome to our comfortable stone-built farmhouse dating from 17th century, situated in secluded but accessible position near Exmoor. 1 family, 1 twin room with washbasins. Hearty, traditional home baking using additive-free home-produced meat and organically grown vegetables. Vegetarian menu on request. Tea-making facilities, home-spun wool available. Farm walk with nature notes, friendly animals. Reduction for children. Open all year (closed Christmas & New Year).

---

4 Hayne House, Silverton, Exeter, Devon EX5 4HE

Mrs L Kelly
☎ 01392 860725
🅱 From £16–£18
EM From £10
Sleeps 6
🐴✂♿ ⊚
💐💐 *Commended*

Explore Devon from our spacious and elegant Georgian farmhouse in delightful rural location. Centrally situated for touring coast, moors and NT properties. Killertron House is close by. 1 family, 1 twin room, both with private bath, 1 single with H&C, all with tea/coffee. Separate drawing room with colour TV and dining room. Tea and homemade cake on arrival. Evening meal sometimes available by prior arrangement. Open Apr–Oct.

---

5 Hele Barton, Black Dog, Thelbridge, Crediton, Devon EX17 4QJ

Mrs Gillian Gillbard
☎/Fax 01884 860278
🅱 From £16
Sleeps 6
🐴✂♿ ⊚
💐💐 *Commended*

Relax amid peaceful surroundings with lovely views from our 17th century thatched farmhouse on family-run 273-acre beef and sheep farm. Ideal position just off B3042, 2 miles B3137 pub/restaurant just ½ mile. Double or twin rooms (en suite.available). Guests return year after year. Send for a brochure and the cream tea is waiting to welcome you. Open all year (closed Christmas).

Higher Coombe Farm, Tipton St John, Sidmouth, Devon EX10 0AX [6]

Kerstin Farmer
☎/Fax 01404 813385
[BB] From £16–£19
Sleeps 10
🐴 🎪 ♿ ⊛
Commended

Come and see the lambs born in spring, smell the hedgerow flowers, watch the soaring buzzard.
After a hearty breakfast explore the winding country lanes. Then unwind and relax in comfortable family, double and single rooms. (No smoking in bedrooms.) Guests' lounge. 4 miles from Sidmouth seafront. Open most of the year.

Higher Weston Farm, Weston, Nr Sidmouth, Devon EX10 0PH [7]

Sandy MacFadyen
☎ 01395 513741
[BB] From £16–£20
Sleeps 6
🐴 🐕 ✂ 🐄 🎪 ♿ 🎪 ⊛
Highly Commended

Enjoy a relaxed, comfortable holiday in superb Heritage coast location, 3 miles from Sidmouth. Fully equipped en suite rooms, comfortable lounge. Breakfast menu includes vegetarian. Lovely garden, croquet, badminton, stabling available. Conservation award winning, working farm. Fields extend to coastal footpath, superb views of Lyme Bay, and to unspoilt Combe and beach. Open Feb–Nov .

Hornhill Farm, Exeter Hill, Tiverton, Devon EX16 4PL [8]

Barbara Pugsley
☎/Fax 01884 253352
[BB] From £17.50–£21.50
EM From £12
Sleeps 6
🐴(12) 🐕 ✂ ♿ ⊛
Highly Commended

Overlooking beautiful Exe Valley, Hornhill is the perfect place to stay and relax. Explore our lovely county, return to comfort, warmth, delicious home cooking and a happy atmosphere. Peaceful bedrooms, one ground floor double, one with Victorian 4-poster, private, en suite bathrooms, heating, TV, tea/coffee. Log fires, large garden, ample parking. AA 5Q Premier Selected. Recommended by *Which? Good B&B Guide.* Open all year.

Lane End Farm, Broadhembury, Honiton, Devon EX14 0LU [9]

Mrs Molly Bennett
☎ 01404 841563
[BB] From £17–£20
EM From £10
Sleeps 6
🐴 🐕 🎪 ♿ ⊛
Commended

At Lane End Farm you will enjoy delicious home cooking in glorious surroundings. Panoramic views of the Blackdown Hills, an Area of Outstanding Natural Beauty. With cattle and sheep grazing, floral gardens all within walking distance of the unspoilt thatched village of Broadhembury. Tea/coffee facilities in bedrooms (2 en suite). CH, colour TV. Colour brochure. Children reduced rates. Evening meals optional. Open all year.

Lower Collipriest Farm, Tiverton, Devon EX16 4PT [10]

Mrs Linda Olive
☎/Fax 01884 252321
[BB] From £20
EM From £11
Sleeps 5
✂ ♿ 🎪 🐾 ⊛
Highly Commended

Come and relax and enjoy the beauty of the Exe Valley in our 17th century thatched farmhouse. Comfortable lounge with inglenook fireplace and oak beams. Colour TV. Central heating throughout. Twin/single rooms with bathroom en suite, tea/coffee-making facilities. Delicious, traditional fresh cooking with our/local produce. Lovely walks over 220-acre dairy farm, conservation pond/woodland area. An AA award-winning farm. Open Feb–Nov. Brochure available.

Lower Pinn Farm, Peak Hill, Sidmouth, Devon EX10 0NN [11]

Elizabeth Tancock
☎/Fax 01395 513733
[BB] From £17–£21
Sleeps 6
🐴 🐕 ♿ ⊛
Commended

A friendly welcome and comfortable, spacious rooms await you at Lower Pinn. 2 miles west of the coastal resort of Sidmouth. Many coastal and country walks. Bedrooms are en suite, fully centrally heated and have colour TV, hot drink making facilities. Own keys for access at all times. Guests' lounge, dining room with separate tables. Good hearty breakfasts. Ample parking. Several local pubs and restaurants. Open most of the year.

12 **Newcourt Barton,** Langford, Cullompton, Devon EX15 1SE

Mrs Helen Hitt
☎ 01884 277326
🛏 From £17–£18
Sleeps 6
Listed *Approved*

Newcourt Barton is an ideal base for touring the Devon coast and countryside. It is a working farm with sheep. The red brick farmhouse is surrounded by a large garden with grass tennis court. Situated in a quiet position 4 miles Cullompton, M5 J28. Coarse fishing on farm. 1 twin, 1 family, both en suite. Tea/coffee-making facilities, TV, lounge, dining room, full English breakfast. Local inn and restaurants for evening meal. Open all year.

13 **Newhouse Farm,** Oakford, Tiverton, Devon EX16 9JE

Mrs Anne Boldry
☎ 01398 351347
🛏 From £16–£20
EM £11
Sleeps 6
Commended

A perfect base for discovering Devon, our 17th century farmhouse is close to Exmoor. Tastefully and comfortably furnished featuring oak beams and inglenook. Bedrooms have CH, CTV, tea trays, en suite available. We aim to provide the best of farmhouse cooking and hospitality – home-baked bread our speciality! AA QQQQ Selected. Recommended by *Which? Good B&B Guide*. Open all year (closed Christmas).

14 **Pinn Barton Farm,** Pinn Lane, Peak Hill, Sidmouth, Devon EX0 0NN

Betty Sage
☎/Fax 01395 514004
🛏 From £19–£21
Sleeps 6
☺(3) 🏠 ⊚
Commended

Enjoy a warm welcome on our 330-acre farm by the coast, 2 miles from Sidmouth seafront. Lovely walks in Area of Outstanding Natural Beauty. Comfortable bedrooms (all en suite) with CH, colour TV, hot drink facilities, electric blankets, access at all times. TV lounge and dining room with separate tables. Substantial breakfast, bedtime drinks. Many restaurants, inns and places to visit nearby. Open most of the year.

15 **Pitt Farm,** Fairmile, Ottery St Mary, Devon EX11 1NL

Susan Hansford
☎ 01404 812439
🛏 From £17–£20
EM From £10
Sleeps 16
Commended

A warm family atmosphere awaits you at this 16th century thatched farmhouse which nestles in the picturesque Otter Valley ½ mile from A30 on B3176. Within easy reach of all East Devon resorts and pleasure facilities. Good home cooking using fresh local/own produce. A working cattle/arable farm surrounded by lovely countryside and rural walks. Family, double and twin rooms. Lounge with colour TV. Fire certificate. Closed Christmas & New Year.

16 **Quoit-at-Cross Farm,** Stoodleigh, Tiverton, Devon EX16 9PJ

Mrs Linda Hill
☎/Fax 01398 351280
🛏 From £17.50
Sleeps 6
Commended

Charming 17th century farmhouse in conservation village. Excellent accommodation, twin/double rooms, en suite, colour TV and tea/coffee-making facilities, delightful inglenook dining room and relaxing lounge. Full English breakfast. Heartbeat Award. Large garden, ample parking. Easy reach National Trust properties, beaches, etc. A361 2½ miles. Open from April.

17 **Rydon Farm,** Woodbury, Exeter, Devon EX5 1LB

Sally Glanvill
☎/Fax 01395 232341
🛏 From £19–£25
Sleeps 6
Highly Commended

Come and enjoy the peaceful tranquillity of our 16th century Devon longhouse on a working dairy farm. Exposed beams and inglenook fireplace. Bedrooms with tea/coffee facilities, hairdryers, full CH, private or en suite bathrooms. Romantic four-poster. Full English breakfast with free range eggs. Several local pubs and restaurants. AA QQQQ Selected. Open all year.

Skinners Ash Farm, Fenny Bridges, Honiton, Devon EX14 0BH   **18**

Mrs Jill Godfrey
☎ 01404 850231
BB £16
EM £8
Sleeps 6
Listed *Commended*

Enjoy a relaxing holiday on a family-run rare breeds farm. Two large family rooms with tea/coffee facilities, TV, private bathroom. Farmhouse cooking, cream teas. Farm walk, pony rides, egg collections. Lovely views. Near local beaches. Walk to two local inns. Please send for brochure. Open all year.

Smallicombe Farm, Northleigh, Colyton, Devon EX13 6BU   **19**

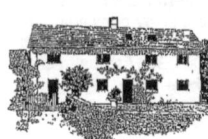

Maggie Todd
☎ 01404 831310
Fax 01404 831431
BB From £18.50–£21
EM From £9.50
Sleeps 6
Commended

Escape the fast lane to unwind in idyllic rural setting little changed since chronicled in the Domesday Book. Walk the coastal footpath or East Devon Way. Meet the prize-winning herd of rare breed pigs and other traditional farm animals. Family suite or ground floor twin/double room, all en suite. Laundry, games room. Open all year.

Stafford Barton, Broadhembury, Honiton, Devon EX14 0LU   **20**

Anne Barons
☎ 01404 841403
BB From £18–£22
EM From £10
Sleeps 6
Applied

Come and share our lovely home for a holiday treat. We are situated beneath the Blackdown Hills, ¼ mile from picturesque thatched village. Glorious walks through woodland and country lanes. Roam our farm and meet cows, sheep, horses and hens. Family, double, twin rooms, all en suite with colour TV, etc. Large lounge/ dining room overlooking beautiful garden. Delicious home cooking using own produce. Weekly terms. Brochure. Open Apr–Nov.

Wiscombe Linhaye Farm, Southleigh, Colyton, Devon EX13 6JF   **21**

Sheila Rabjohns
☎ 01404 871342
BB From £18–£22
EM From £9
Sleeps 6
ϕ ☜(8) *Commended*

A small working farm in the quiet countryside of East Devon but in reach of Sidmouth and Lyme Regis. A friendly atmosphere on this family farm with good home cooking from home/local produce. Two ground floor bedrooms with private bathroom, one en suite. Drink facilities, TV and hair dryers in all bedrooms. Colour TV in lounge and separate dining tables. Three double rooms. Open Mar–Nov.

Wishay Farm, Trinity, Cullompton, Devon EX15 1PE   **22**

Mrs Sylvia Baker
☎/Fax 01884 33223
BB From £16–£17
Sleeps 6
Commended

Comfortable and spacious 17th century farmhouse, set amid the peace and seclusion of the countryside. Ideal base for touring. Comfortable lounge with colour TV. Central heating. 1 family room with en suite bathroom, double with separate guests' bathroom, both with colour TV, fridge and tea/coffee-making facilities. Children welcome. Open Mar–Oct.

NO ANSWER?
Farmers are mostly out and about during the day.
Try to telephone before 9.30am or after 4pm.

SELF-CATERING

---

(18) Bertie and Porky's Barns, Skinners Ash Farm, Fenny Bridges, Honiton, Devon EX14 0BH

Mrs J S Godfrey
☎ 01404 850231
ⓢⓒ From £170–£410
EM £8
Sleeps 6/7
🐎 🐂 ⚰ 🎿 🧺 💼 ◉
🗝 🗝 🗝 🗝
Commended

Enjoy a relaxing holiday on a family-run rare breeds farm in a luxury flat and converted barn. Enjoy pony rides, farm walks, egg collections, Devonshire cream teas. Near local beaches and tourist attractions. On A30 Honiton to Exeter road. Please send for colour brochure. Open all year.

---

(23) Bodmiscombe Farm, Blackborough, Cullompton, Devon EX15 2HR

Mrs Brenda Northam
☎/Fax 01884 266315
ⓢⓒ From £115–£285
Sleeps 4 + cot
🐂 🐎 ⚰ 🎿 ♿ 🧺 💼 ◉
🗝 🗝 🗝 *Commended*

For three generations our family has been farming in this tiny peaceful hamlet set in the Blackdown Hills now designated an Area of Outstanding Natural Beauty. The self-contained part of our 17th century farmhouse with beamed ceilings is furnished to a high standard. Cleanliness and comfort guaranteed. Short breaks available to enjoy our 20-acre woodland walk or private coarse fishing. Weekend breaks from £60. Open all year.

---

(24) Cider Cottage, c/o Great Bradley Farm, Withleigh, Tiverton, Devon EX16 8JL

Mrs Sylvia Hann
☎ 01884 256946
ⓢⓒ From £150–£340
Sleeps 2–5 + cot
🐎 ⚰ ◉
🗝 🗝 🗝
Highly Commended

This charming cottage, its oak beams hung with cider jars, is cosy, warm, bright and comfortable. It has, we think, the best view in Devon, always changing with the light and seasons. Lean on the gate and watch the cows come home, or laze in the garden with a book. Then at the end of happy day out tuck freshly bathed children in bed, enjoy a glass of wine and relax. Lovely! Open all year.

---

(25) Hele Payne Farm, Hele, Exeter, Devon EX5 4PH

Irene and Sally Maynard
☎ 01392 881530/ 881356
Fax 01392 881530
ⓢⓒ From £170–£390
Sleeps 3/5/6
🐎 ⚰ 🧺 🎾 💼
🗝 🗝 🗝 🗝 *Up to Highly Commended*

Relax in our heated swimming pool and slip into the tranquillity of rural life as recently featured on BBC 1's *Holiday* programme. Explore our dairy farm – children may help to feed the baby calves. All three cottages are surrounded by beautiful gardens, ideal for barbecues, and have colour TV, bed linen, laundry room, cot, highchair and CH. Games barn with pool, table tennis etc provides fun for any age. Open all year.

---

(26) Lemprice Farm, Yettington, Budleigh Salterton, Devon EX9 7BW

Mrs Hanneke Coates
☎ 01395 567037
Fax 01395 567585
ⓢⓒ From £215–£480
Sleeps 4–6
♿ 🧍 🐎 🐂 🎾 💼
🗝 🗝 🗝 – 🗝 🗝 🗝 🗝
Highly Commended

Three south-facing stone barn cottages suitable for disabled. Exceptional walking area of outstanding natural beauty and scientific interest. Home of the rare barn owl. All cottage gardens overlook small lake and marshes abundant with wildlife, hills and open countryside beyond. All linen and electricity included. Dogs by arrangement only. Three miles to beach. Brochure. Winter short breaks. Open Mar–Nov.

Otter Holt and Owl Hayes, c/o Godford Farm, Awliscombe, Honiton, Devon EX14 0PW   2

Sally Lawrence
☎/Fax 01404 42825
SC From £120–£335
Sleeps 4 + cot
🐕 🎠 💼 ⊛
🐾 🐾 🐾 *Commended*

Come and see where the hayracks are in our beautiful barn cottages, one of the many features that make them unique. Each cottage has beamed lounge with colour TV, pine kitchen/diner with washer/dryer, microwave, fridge/freezer. CH. 2 bedrooms (linen incl). Walkers' paradise, wildlife abundant. Floral gardens, games barn, pets and calves to feed. Farm map. Children welcome, large play area. Cot available. Brochure. Open all year.

Smallicombe Farm, Northleigh, Colyton, Devon EX13 6BU   19

Maggie Todd
☎ 01404 831310
Fax 01404 831431
SC From £95–£625
Sleeps 2–8
♿ 🏡 🐕 💼 🎠 ⊛
🐾🐾🐾 –🐾🐾🐾🐾 *Commended*
– *Highly Commended*

Help collect your own eggs for breakfast. Join in feeding our friendly goats, sheep, cows and prize winning herd of rare breed pigs. Relax in converted barns in Area of Outstanding Natural Beauty, close to coast and glorious walks. Try Devon skittles in our games room. ETB 'England for Excellence' Award 1995. Holiday Care Service 'Best Self-Catering Accommodation' 1996. Open all year.

White Witches and Stable Lodge, Hele Barton, Black Dog, Crediton, Devon EX17 4QJ   5

Mrs Gillian Gillbard
☎/Fax 01884 860278
SC From £100–£450
Sleeps 6 + cot
🐕 💼 🍵 ⊛
🐾 🐾 🐾 🐾 *Commended –*
Highly Commended

Dream of a pretty, well-equipped thatched cottage in the country with a garden leading to fields with a river meandering by. Listen to the birds singing on a balmy summer evening or enjoy cosy nights by an open fire. Sounds like heaven? Well this is reality. Send for a brochure and we shall be here to welcome you. Open all year.

Wonham Barton, Bampton, Tiverton, Devon EX16 9JZ   27

Anne McLean Williams
☎/Fax 01398 331312
SC From £125–£280
Sleeps 4/6
🐕 🐎 🍴 🎠 💼 🎠
🐾 🐾 🐾 *Commended*

Conveniently explore sleepy Devon; Domesday hamlets, majestic moorland, dramatic coastlines. Enjoy active country pursuits and leisurely cream teas. Our comfortable 19th century farmhouse wing overlooks our valley with magnificent buzzards and Exmoor red deer; children marvel at our skilled Border collies and traditional shepherding on horseback; see our handsome Limousin cattle and roam 300 peaceful acres of pasture and woodland. Tell us when you are coming!

DEVON FARMS

Availability of farms in Devon can be easily discovered by ringing **01548 550055**.

Please mention **Stay on a Farm** when booking

Dartmoor, South & West Devon

Group Contact: ᴮᴮ *Jill Balkwill* ☎ *01548 550055/Fax 01548 550312*

Escape to the great outdoors on Dartmoor, 365 spectacular square miles stretching down to the coves and hamlets of the south coast.

The Dartmoor National Park is wild, open and free, offering delightful opportunities to walk, explore, ride, sit and see. Its boundaries are marked by Okehampton and Tavistock to the west, Ivybridge to the south and Bovey Tracey to the east. Now descend to the lowlands of South Devon with its pretty hamlets, thatched cottages around the green and hidden coves with beautiful sandy beaches. Ancient small country towns abound – Holsworthy, Hathersleigh, Totnes, Dartmouth, Ashburton – all unspoilt and tempting you to stop and browse. Come sample good food and drink, the wines, cider and ales, cream teas and country pubs. This is an area rich in the treasures of the National Trust, historic cities (Exeter, Plymouth) castles, abbeys, local crafts and cultures. Bustling seaside towns like Torquay, Paignton, Kingsbridge, Salcombe and Teignmouth are its hallmark. Our countryside is teeming with wildlife and woodlands, perfect for birdwatching, cycling, nature trails or just a quiet amble.

Come join us for a little bit of 'heaven in Devon'.

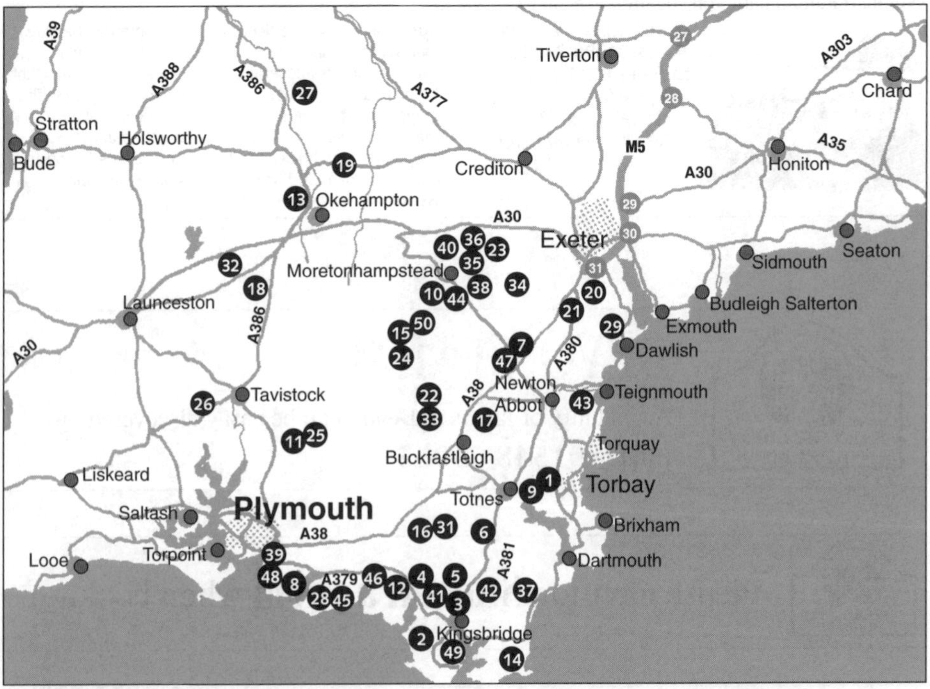

BED AND BREAKFAST

(and evening meal)

Berry Farm, Berry Pomeroy, Totnes, Devon TQ9 6LG   ❶

Mrs Geraldine Nicholls
☎ 01803 863231
🅱 From £16
EM From £10
Sleeps 6
♿(5) 🐈 ⅍ ▪ ⊚
Listed *Commended*

Large mixed working farm surrounded by lovely old cider orchards in village 1½ miles from Totnes town. Spacious rooms, tastefully decorated, with tea/coffee facilities, washbasins – 1 family, 1 double, 1 twin. Bathroom, shower, separate toilet. Guests' lounge, TV. Good local eating places, evening meal by arrangement. Parking. Ideal base for touring coast/moors. Open all year except Christmas.

Burton Farm, Galmpton, Kingsbridge, South Devon TQ7 3EY   ❷

Anne Rossiter
☎/Fax 01548 561210
🅱 From £21–£25
EM From £11
Sleeps 22
♿ ⅍ 🐎 ⊞ ▪ ♟ ⊚
👑👑 *Highly Commended*

Working dairy and sheep farm situated in the valley running towards Hope Cove. 3 miles from famous sailing haunt of Salcombe. Walking, beaches, sailing, windsurfing, bathing, diving, fishing. Guests welcome to enjoy the farm's activities when possible. Traditional farmhouse cooking, home produce (clotted cream, etc). 4 course dinner. Access to rooms at all times. En suite available and washbasins. Tea-making facilities, TV. Closed Christmas.

Coombe Farm, Kingsbridge, South Devon TQ7 4AB   ❸

Beni & Jonathan Robinson
☎ 01548 852038
🅱 From £18.50–£20
Sleeps 6
♿(12) ⅍ ☙ ▪
👑👑 *Commended*

Come and enjoy the peace and beauty of Devon in our lovely 16th century farmhouse. Wonderful breakfast, large elegant rooms each with own bathroom, colour TV, hot drink facilities. Artists have use of an art studio, and fisherman the well known Coombe Water fishery. Open all year except Christmas.

Court Barton Farmhouse, Aveton Gifford, Kingsbridge, Devon TQ7 4LE   ❹

John & Jill Balkwill
☎/Fax 01548 550312
🅱 From £20–£26
Sleeps 18
🐎 ⊞ ▪ ♟ ⚒ ⊚
👑👑 *Highly Commended*

Delightful 16th century listed manor farmhouse set in extensive gardens and situated on 40-acre farm. Seven bedrooms, mostly en suite, all with colour TV. Sunny breakfast room to enjoy delicious country farmhouse breakfasts and log fires in the comfortable lounge in colder weather. Close to moorland, beaches, ideal centre for walking, sailing, fishing, birdwatching. Open all year except Christmas.

Crannacombe Farm, Hazlewood, Loddiswell, Nr Kingsbridge, South Devon TQ7 4DX   ❺

Shirley & Stephen Bradley
☎ 01548 550256
🅱 From £17.50–£18.50
EM £10
Sleeps 6
🐎 ⅍ ♟ ⚒ ▪
👑👑 *Commended*

In an area of outstanding natural beauty near Kingsbridge. Working farm, Georgian farmhouse, comfortable, informal, absolutely peaceful. We have family/double bedrooms with private bathrooms and TV, hot drink facilities and a separate children's room sleeping 2. Lovely walks, stunning views and a clean river to paddle, play and picnic by. 15 minutes beach. Excellent food and cider.

---

6 **Foales Leigh,** Harberton, Totnes, Devon TQ9 7SS

Carol Chudley
☎ 01803 862365
BB From £17–£20
Sleeps 6
☺(5) ✂ ♣ ▥ ◉
♣♣ *Highly Commended*

A charming 16th century farmhouse in traditional courtyard setting. This family farm is situated in peaceful, unspoilt countryside within easy reach of beaches, moors and towns. Comfortable accommodation includes large oak-beamed lounge and 3 spacious bedrooms: 1 double, 1 family, 1 twin, all en suite with TV, CH and beverage trays. Delicious Aga-cooked breakfast. Closed Christmas & New Year.

---

7 **Frost Farm,** Hennock, Bovey Tracey, South Devon TQ13 9PP

Linda Harvey
☎/Fax 01626 833266
BB From £18–£20
EM From £10
Sleeps 6
☺ ✂ ▥
♣ *Commended*

A pretty, pink-washed, thatched old farmhouse on working farm in our green valley. Lovely for walking, bird watching, NT houses, gardens. Explore Dartmoor or seaside. Good farmhouse food, fresh meats, vegetables, fruits, local cream/ice creams. Large, spacious bedrooms en suite with tea/coffee facilities, colour TV, CH. Ground floor bedroom. Cosy, relaxed atmosphere. Open Mar–Nov.

---

8 **Gabber Farm,** Down Thomas, Plymouth, Devon PL9 0AW

Margaret MacBean
☎/Fax 01752 862269
BB From £16–£18
EM From £10
Sleeps 12
☺ ♞ ♣ ▥ ◉
♣♣ *Commended*

A warm welcome is assured on this working dairy farm in an area of outstanding natural beauty. Situated on the coast near Plymouth with lovely walks and within easy reach of the beaches. Good home cooking, hot drinks facilities in all rooms, double and family with en suite showers. Open all year.

---

9 **Great Court Farm,** Weston Lane, Totnes, Devon TQ9 6LB

Janet Hooper
☎ 01803 862326
BB From £16–£18.50
EM From £9
Sleeps 6
☺(5) ✂ ▥ ◉
♣ *Highly Commended*

Relax and enjoy the warm hospitality and country cuisine in our Victorian farmhouse overlooking the historic town of Totnes and surrounding countryside. Dairy farm with lanes and fields running down to River Dart. Ideal for coast and Dartmoor. Spacious double/family rooms have tea/coffee facilities, washbasins, TV, CH. Twin room en suite, WC and basin. Guests' bathroom, shower. Lounge, garden, evening meals by arrangement. Open all year.

---

10 **Great Sloncombe Farm,** Moretonhampstead, Newton Abbot, Devon TQ13 8QF

Mrs Trudie Merchant
☎/Fax 01647 440595
BB From £20–£21
EM From £11
Sleeps 6
☺(8) ♞ ✂ ♞ ◉
♣♣♣ *Highly Commended*

Share the magic of Dartmoor all year round whilst staying in our lovely 13th century farmhouse. A working dairy farm set amongst meadows and woodland, abundant in wild flowers and animals. A welcoming place to relax and explore Devon. Comfortable double and twin rooms all en suite with central heating, TV. Plenty of delicious home-cooked Devonshire food. Open all year.

---

11 **Greenwell Farm,** Nr Meavy, Yelverton, Plymouth, Devon PL20 6PY

Bridget Cole
☎/Fax 01822 853563
BB From £20–£23
EM From £12.50
Sleeps 6
☺ ▥ ◉
♣♣♣ *Commended*

Fresh country air, breathtaking views and scrumptious farmhouse cuisine. This busy farming family welcomes you to share the countryside and wildlife. Set in Dartmoor National Park, ideal for walking, visiting NT properties Plymouth, Cornwall and S Devon coast all only 8 miles Three spacious, comfortable en suite rooms. Licensed, weekly discunts, brochure available. Open all year (closed Christmas).

Helliers Farm, Ashford, Aveton Gifford, Kingsbridge, Devon TQ7 4ND   **12**

Christine Lancaster
☎/Fax 01548 550689
BB From £17–£22
Sleeps 9

Highly Commended

Small working sheep farm on a hillside set in the heart of Devon's unspoilt countryside. An ideal spot for touring the coast, Dartmoor, Plymouth, NT houses and walks. Family, double, twin and single rooms, all tastefully appointed with washbasins and tea/coffee facilities. Double and family have own private bathroom. Comfortable lounge with TV. Dining room where excellent breakfasts are served. Open all year except Christmas and New Year.

Higher Cadham Farm, Jacobstowe, Okehampton, Devon EX20 3RB   **13**

John & Jenny King
☎ 01837 851647
Fax 01837 851410
BB From £17–£23
EM From £10
Sleeps 17

Highly Commended

Superb farmhouse accommodation, tasty home cooking, and breathtaking Devon scenery, that's the appetising recipe on offer at Higher Cadham in the heart of Tarka Country. Facilities for the less agile, en suite, flexible meal times, riverside walks and lots more! Ring for a brochure and details of our special offers. Open all year except Christmas and New Year.

Higher Kellaton Farm, Kellaton, Kingsbridge, Devon TQ7 2ES   **14**

Mrs Angela Foale
☎/Fax 01548 511514
BB From £13.50–£20
EM From £8.50
Sleeps 6

Commended

Georgian farmhouse and spacious, mature garden, peacefully nestled in beautiful countryside on our cow, sheep and corn farm. Close to good beaches, walks and family attractions. Double en suite with TV, double and twin with washbasins. Guests' own bathroom and sitting room with TV. Tea/coffee-making facilities. Well furnished, comfortable and clean. Open Apr–Sept.

Higher Venton Farm, Widecombe-in-the-Moor, Newton Abbot, South Devon TQ13 7TF   **15**

Mrs Betty Hicks
☎ 01364 621235
BB From £16–£19
EM From £8
Sleeps 6

Listed Approved

A friendly welcome awaits you at Higher Venton Farm, a 16th century thatched farmhouse and working farm. Peaceful and relaxing, ideal for touring Dartmoor. Riding stables nearby. Coast 16 miles, ½ mile from Widecombe village. Good local eating places recommended. 1 double en suite, 1 double and 1 twin with washbasins. CH, tea/coffee-making facilities, lounge with colour TV. Open all year except Christmas.

Hillhead Farm, Ugborough, Ivybridge, Devon PL21 0HQ   **16**

Mrs J Johns
☎ 01752 892674
Fax 01752 690111
BB From £18–£20
EM From £10
Sleeps 6

Commended

Comfortable, welcoming family farmhouse. Guests' sitting room with TV and woodburner. 1 twin room, 2 double rooms both with TV and all with tea/coffee facilities and H&C. 2 en suite bathrooms, 1 private, also separate toilet. Full CH, open log fire in dining room. Good, home cooked and largely home produced food. Open all year except Christmas.

Kellinch Farm, Bickington, nr Newton Abbot, Devon TQ12 6PB   **17**

Debbie and Justin Dashwood
☎/Fax 01626 821252
BB From £17–£18
EM From £8.90
Sleeps 6

Commended

'What a glorious setting' is often heard as guests arrive. Breakfast in our sun-drenched conservatory. Listen to birdsong and enjoy tranquillity and breathtaking views of rolling Devon countryside. Relax with a game of tennis, badminton or pool. The children will have a ball in the games barn. Snuggle in front of our cosy logburner and picturesque inglenook. Open all year.

18   **The Knole Farm,** Bridestowe, Okehampton, Devon EX20 4HA

Mrs Mavis Bickle
☎ 01837 861241
BB From £17–£18
Sleeps 8
Highly Commended

Family working farm in area of outstanding beauty overlooking Dartmoor. Farmhouse with spacious rooms, large garden, sunlounge. Enjoy good home cooking. Ideally based to visit numerous places of interest with birdwatching, horseriding, fishing and walking for the energetic. En suite rooms available. Breakfast to your choice, four-course evening meal optional. Open Mar–Nov.

19   **Lower Nichols Nymet Farm,** North Tawton, Devon EX20 2BW

Mrs Jane Pyle
☎ 01363 82510
BB From £18–£19.50
EM From £11
Sleeps 6
Highly Commended

We offer a haven of comfort and rest on a modern working dairy farm and provide the perfect base for exploring the beauties of the West Country. Residents' lounge, colour TV. All rooms en suite, plus tea/coffee-making facilities. An ideal holiday centre – beaches, golf, good walks, riding, fishing, fine houses and gardens nearby to visit. Open Easter–Oct (incl).

20   **Lower Thornton Farm,** Kenn, Exeter, Devon EX6 7XH

Mrs Alison Clack
☎/Fax 01392 833434
BB From £17
Sleeps 4
Commended

Come and relax at our secluded family farm with panoramic views. Just 2 miles from A38. Ideal base to visit Exeter, Torquay, Dartmoor, coast and racecourse. Our ground floor bedrooms are spacious and comfortable. One room en suite opening onto patio and garden, other has private bathroom. Both with tea/coffee facilities. Guests' lounge, colour TV, CH throughout. Child reductions. Open Jan–Nov.

21   **Mill Farm,** Kenton, Exeter, Devon EX6 8JR

Delia Lambert
☎ 01392 832471
BB From £18
Commended

Mill Farm – a charming farmhouse with delightful, sunny en suite bedrooms with colour TV. Lovely rural setting. Ideal base to explore Devon. Good parking. Very easy to find. Don't miss out. Send for a brochure now! Closed Christmas.

22   **Mill Leat Farm,** Holne, Ashburton, Newton Abbot, Devon TQ13 7RZ

Dawn Cleave
☎/Fax 01364 631283
BB From £17–£19
EM From £8
Sleeps 6
Approved

120-acre hill farm situated on the edge of Dartmoor, an ideal place for touring Devon's beautiful countryside, moorland or beaches. Comfortable accommodation in 18th century farmhouse with large spacious bedrooms, en suite available, with tea/coffee facilities. Very peaceful surroundings, just right for relaxing. Closed Christmas.

23   **Moor Farm,** Dunsford, Exeter, Devon EX6 7DP

Mrs Joyce Dicker
☎ 01647 24292
BB From £14–£15
Sleeps 5
Listed *Commended*

The farmhouse is quietly situated on the edge of Dartmoor National Park with beautiful views of the surrounding Devon Hills and countryside. The guests have their own wing of the farmhouse, making it ideal for families. One family, one double room, each with tea/coffee-making facilities. Open Mar–Nov.

New Cott Farm, Poundsgate, nr Ashburton, Newton Abbot, Devon TQ13 7PD   24

Margaret Phipps
☎/Fax 01364 631421
BB From £18–£19
EM From £10.50
Sleeps 8
⚘ ☼(5) ⚘ ⚘ ⚘ ⚘ ◉
☙ ☙ *Commended*

A friendly welcome, beautiful views, pleasing accommodation at New Cott, a working farm in the Dartmoor National Park. Relax in our conservatory after enjoying the freedom and tranquillity of open moorland, the Dart Valley or one of the many attractions in Devon. Lots of lovely homemade food. Tea/coffee/chocolate in your en suite bedroom. Weekly reductions. Ideal for less able guests. Open all year except Christmas Day.

Peek Hill Farm, Dousland, Yelverton, Devon PL20 6PD   25

Justine Colton
☎/Fax 01822 854808
BB From £17–£20
EM From £10
Sleeps 6
☼ ☼ ⚘ ⚘ ⚘ ◉
☙ ☙ *Commended*

Situated on the southern slopes of Dartmoor with sweeping views to Cornwall and adjacent to wooded Burrator Lake. Comfortable, sunny bedrooms, with antique furniture and en suite bathrooms. Log fire in lounge and much more. Mountain cycle hire. We are friendly and informal and are easily located off B3212. Open all year.

Rubbytown Farm, Gulworthy, Tavistock, Devon PL19 8PA   26

Mary Steer
☎ 01822 832493
BB From £18.50–£19
EM From £12
Sleeps 6
☼(5) ⚘ ⚘ ⚘
☙ ☙ *Highly Commended*

Stay in our lovely old farmhouse and sleep in four-poster beds. Enjoy woodland walks. There is abundant wildlife, you may see deer if you are lucky and at dusk the foxes and badgers at play. Help with feeding the calves. Good farmhouse cooking with evening meals served by candlelight. St Mellion Golf and Country Club nearby. Upholstery classes are held locally. 2 double, 4 posters, en suite, 1 twin with private bathroom, games room. Evening meal served by candlelight by prior arrangement. Closed Christmas.

Seldon Farm, Monkokehampton, Winkleigh, Devon EX19 8RY   27

Mary Case
☎ 01837 810312
BB From £16
Sleeps 6
☼ ⚘ ⚘
☙ *Commended*

Relax in our delightful 17th century farmhouse situated in beautiful unspoilt part of the Devonshire countryside. Ideal for touring Dartmoor and Exmoor. Tarka Trail nearby, Rosemoor Gardens a short drive. Two double, one family room, all with H&C and tea/coffee-making facilities. Reductions for weekly bookings and children. Open Easter–Oct

Slade Barn, Netton Farm, Noss Mayo, Nr Plymouth, Devon PL8 1HB   28

Sandy Cherrington
☎/Fax 01752 872235
BB From £19–£21.50
EM From £8.50
Sleeps 6
☼(10) ⚘ ⚘ ⚘ ⚘
Listed *Commended*

Coastal South Devon beside the beautiful Yealm estuary. Lovely barn conversion. Indoor pool, games room, tennis court, gardens. Fabulous NT cliff walks, nearby sandy beaches. Double and 1 twin shared bathroom, CH, TV/radio, tea/coffee on request. Open all year.

Smallacombe Farm, Aller Valley, Dawlish, Devon EX7 0PS   29

Mrs Alison Thomson
☎ 01626 862536
BB From £16–£18
EM From £9
Sleeps 6
☼ ⚘
☙ ☙ *Commended*

Off the beaten track, yet only two miles from Dawlish and the beach. Enjoy the best of both worlds, 'country and coast'. Children play freely with no fear of busy roads. Meet our 3 friendly dogs. Relax in the peaceful surroundings and homely atmosphere. 2 double rooms, 1 twin room, family unit available, en suite. Fridges in bedrooms. Reductions for children, weekly discounts. Ring or write for brochure. Open all year.

DEVON FARMS

FARM HOLIDAY BUREAU

Availability of farms in Devon can be easily discovered by ringing **01548 550055**.

---

31 Venn Farm, Ugborough, Ivybridge, Devon PL21 0PE

Pat Stephens
☎ 01364 73240
BB From £20–£22
EM £11
Sleeps 12
☺(5) 🐴 ♿
🐛 *Commended*

Working farm amid peaceful scenery in the South Hams on edge of Dartmoor. Children encouraged to take an interest in farm life. The speciality of the house is 'carve your own roasts' and the atmosphere is friendly and relaxed. We have 2 family en suite rooms and separate garden cottage with 2 bedrooms, bathroom and picnic patio. Open Feb–Nov.

---

32 Week Farm, Bridestowe, Okehampton, Devon EX20 4HZ

Margaret Hockridge
☎/Fax 01837 861221
BB From £22–£24
EM From £11
Sleeps 12
🧍 ☺ 🐴 🍴 📷 ♿
🐛 *Commended*

Guests return annually to our 17th century farmhouse. Set in rolling countryside ¾ mile from old A30. Good home cooking and every comfort. Central for Dartmoor and coast, 8 miles Cornwall. Lounge with colour TV and log fires. 3 doubles, 2 family rooms all en suite (1 ground floor). Tea/coffee-making facilities, night storage heaters, colour TV. Heated outdoor swimming pool. Come and spoil yourselves. Fire certificate held. Open all year (closed Christmas).

---

33 Wellpritton Farm, Holne, Ashburton, South Devon TQ13 7RX

Sue Gifford
☎ 01364 631273
BB From £18
EM From £8
Sleeps 12
☺ 🐴 ♿ 🏇
🐛🐛 *Highly Commended*

A beautiful farmhouse on the edge of Dartmoor, where goats, horses and chickens are kept and sometimes sheep and cattle. Only ½ hour drive from Exeter, Plymouth and Torbay with riding, fishing, walking, sailing and golf nearby. Modernised to high standard – most rooms en suite, games room and swimming pool. Caring personal attention. Farm produced food. Weekly rates B&B & EM from £175. Open all year including Christmas.

---

34 Whitemoor Farm, Doddiscombsleigh, Nr Exeter, Devon EX6 7PU

Mrs Barbara Lacey
☎ 01647 252423
BB From £17.50–£18
EM From £8
Sleeps 6
☺ 🐴 🍴 🎾 ♿
🐛 *Approved*

Listed 16th century thatched farmhouse, set in seclusion of its own garden and farmland within easy reach of Exeter, coast, Dartmoor and forest walks. The Cobb House has exposed beams, log fires. Home made preserves. Good meals at local inn. Evening meal on request. Children and pets welcome. Swimming pool available. Open all year.

---

35 Wooston Farm, Moretonhampstead, Newton Abbot, Devon TQ13 8QA

Mary Cuming
☎/Fax 01647 440367
BB From £18.50–£21
Sleeps 6
☺(8) 🍴 ◎
🐛🐛 *Highly Commended*

Wooston Farm is situated above the Teign Valley in the Dartmoor National Park with views over open moorland. The farmhouse is surrounded by a delightful garden. There are plenty of walks on the moor and wooded Teign Valley adjoining farm. Good home cooking and cosy log fires await you at Wooston. 2 double en suite, 1 with four-poster, 1 twin room. Also mountain bikes available. AA listed QQQQ Selected. Open all year except Christmas.

Yarningale, Exeter Road, Moretonhampstead, Devon TQ13 8SW   **36**

Sarah Radcliffe
☎ **01647 440560**
BB **From £16–£17**
Sleeps 6
♨ 🐕 ♿ @
�
☕☕ *Approved*

A warm, friendly welcome at this secluded rural property with probably one of the best views in Dartmoor. Excellent facilities including stables/kennels, many walks/rides straight from the house. Large garden and patio for the less energetic! Evening meals/packed lunches available if required. Open all year.

SELF-CATERING

Alston Cottage, Alston Farm, Slapton, Kingsbridge, Devon TQ7 2QE   **37**

Mrs Suzanne Hutchings
☎ **01548 580337**
SC **From £130–£320**
Sleeps 5 + cot
♨ ▪
🍃 🍃 🍃 *Commended*

Alston is a family-run beef and arable farm tucked away between Dartmouth and Kingsbridge. Sea views. Alston Cottage is completely modernised, self-contained part of farmhouse. Separate driveway, entrance. Large garden. Ideal for a family holiday. Family and twin bedrooms, beds ready made. Well fitted kitchen, elegant lounge/diner, colour TV, NSH. Open all year.

Budleigh Farm, Moretonhampstead, Devon TQ13 8SB   **38**

Mrs Judith Harvey
☎ **01647 440835**
Fax 01647 440436
SC **From £95–£350**
Sleeps 2–6
♨ 🐕 ⚐ ⚐ 🍸 🎿 ▪ @
🍃 🍃 – 🍃 🍃 🍃
Commended

Seven cottages and flats, converted from barns, each with its own character, on a farm tucked into the end of the Wray Valley ½ mile from Moretonhampstead. Outdoor heated swimming pool, barbecue; table tennis and darts. Small campsite. A walker's dream – in the Dartmoor National Park. Open Jan–Dec.

Burton Farm Cottages, Burton Farm, Galmpton, Kingsbridge, South Devon TQ7 3EY   **2**

Anne Rossiter
☎/Fax **01548 561210**
SC **From £85–£475**
Sleeps 4/5 + cot
♨ 🐕 ⊞ 🍸 ▪ @
🍃 🍃 🍃 🍃
Commended

Situated in a pretty hamlet adjoining open farmland, 5 mins walk from farm, these cob and slate cottages are 5 miles from Kingsbridge, 3 miles from sailing haunt of Salcombe and 1 mile from lovely beaches of Hope Cove and Thurlestone. Decorated and furnished, many original features with stone-built fireplaces and electric heating. Guests welcome to enjoy farm activities. Meals (from £10.50) available on request. Open all year.

Coombe Farm Cottage, Wembury Road, Plymstock, Plymouth, Devon PL9 0DE   **39**

Suzanne MacBean
☎ **01752 401730**
SC **From £100–£350**
Sleeps 5/6
♨ 🐕 ✂ ▪
🍃 🍃 🍃 🍃 *Commended*

Coombe Farm dates back to the 14th century and is situated in a peaceful valley on the outskirts of Plymouth. An ideal centre for touring and within easy reach of moors and coast. The cottage is well equipped with two bedrooms, lounge, kitchen/diner, bathroom. Linen and electric included. Safe parking. Open all year.

32 **The Granary and Little Week Barns,** Week Farm, Bridestowe, Okehampton, Devon EX20 4HZ

Margaret Hockridge
☎/Fax 01837 861221
[SC] From £220–£595
Sleeps 5/8 + cot

Up to Highly Commended

A cream tea awaits you at these semi-detached barn conversions situated in a pretty part of Devon countryside where scenery, moorland and wildlife are magnificent. Near A30, ideal touring base for both coasts, Cornwall, Dartmoor and numerous attractions. Attractive garden with patio, BBQ, heated outdoor swimming pool. Well fitted kitchen, (washing machine, microwave, dish-washer, fridge freezer), lounge, colour TV. Open end May–end Oct.

---

40 **Great Howton Farm,** Moretonhampstead, Newton Abbot, Devon TQ13 8PP

Jane & Alastair Wimberley
☎/Fax 01647 440100
[SC] From £225–£475
Sleeps 6

Commended

Comfortable, well-designed barn conversion standing in its own garden. Spacious accommodation with well-equipped kitchen. Working livestock family farm with ponds, streams and woodland walks. Easy access to open moorland with its wonderful scenery, walking, cycling, horseriding, other outdoor pursuits and many tourist attractions. Open all year.

---

41 **Heath Farm,** Loddiswell, Kingsbridge, Devon TQ7 4EE

Ann Mulligan
☎ 01548 550565
[SC] From £150–£385
Sleeps 4

Commended

Unique rural retreat set in beautiful South Hams. Peaceful, sunny position amidst unspoiled countryside with cattle grazing surrounding fields. Enjoy rural walks, attractive villages, stunning coves and coastline – all within easy reach. Attached to main house, well-equipped, comfortable accommodation with pretty gardens. Electricity, CH, linen inclusive. Seasonal breaks. Open Whit–Sept.

---

42 **Ledstone Farm,** Ledstone, Kingsbridge, South Devon TQ7 2HQ

Ann Lidstone
☎ 01548 852662
[SC] From £175–£245
Sleeps 2/3

Highly Commended

In a tiny village near Kingsbridge we offer a choice of two converted haylofts. The Loft has two bedrooms and Swallow Barn one bedroom. Both have living rooms with corner kitchens, lots of extras. Lovely locations and a happy, comfortable atmosphere. Phone, towels, VCR, etc. Convenience and contentment guaranteed. Open all year.

---

43 **Longmeadow Farm,** Coombe Road, Ringmore, Shaldon, Teignmouth, Devon TQ14 0EX

Mrs Anne Mann
☎ 01626 872732
Fax 01626 872323
[SC] £140–£300
Sleeps 4

Approved

Enjoy the best of both worlds on our South Devon farm set in lovely countryside but less than a mile from the beach and Shaldon village. Comfortable accommodation (in two units each sleeping 4) adjoining traditional style farmhouse overlooking estuary. Garden, patio, barbecue. Ideal location for touring coast, moors. Walks, fishing, riding nearby. Ample parking. Brochure available. Open all year.

---

44 **Narramore Farm Cottages,** Narramore Farm, Moretonhampstead, Devon TQ13 8QT

Sue Horn
☎/Fax 01647 440455
[SC] From £100–£470
Sleeps 2/5

Commended to Highly Commended

Stressed out? Let Narramore work its magic on you! Six comfortable cottages situated on 107-acre horse stud/deer farm. A really warm pool, bubbling hot spa, satellite TV, games/laundry room, payphone, play area, fishing lake, boat, barbecue, small animals plus the opportunity to badgerwatch amidst glorious countryside – all these make us special. Colour brochure. Open all year.

Netton Farm Holiday Cottages, Netton Farm, Noss Mayo, Nr Plymouth, Devon PL8 1HA   45

Sandy Cherrington
☎/Fax 01752 872235
SC From £250–£1,300
Sleeps 2–12

Commended

Nestled into one of the most beautiful stretches of South Devon coastline, this small complex is ideally situated to cater for all tastes. Attractive, comfortable accommodation and warm, friendly atmosphere. Cottages sleep 2 to12. Use of lovely indoor pool, games room, tennis court, gardens. Rural and peaceful, superb coastal walks and nearby sandy beaches. SAE for colour brochure. Open all year.

Oldaport Farm Cottages, Modbury, Ivybridge, Devon PL21 0TG   46

Miss C Evans
☎ 01548 830842
Fax 01548 830998
SC From £149–£418
Sleep 2/6

Highly Commended

Oldaport is a small sheep farm of 70 acres, lying in the Erme Valley, and offering lovely views of the countryside. The four cottages, which sleep 2/6, were redundant stone barns which have been carefully converted into comfortable holiday homes. All fully equipped, heating in all rooms. Sandy beaches nearby, Dartmoor 8 miles. Excellent birdwatching. Brochure available. Open all year.

Shippen and Dairy Cottages, c/o Lookweep Farm, Liverton, Newton Abbot, Devon TQ12 6HT   47

Averil Corrick
☎ 01626 833277
SC From £150–£405
Sleeps 4/5 + cot

Commended

Come and relax in the peace and tranquillity of these two delightful barn converted cottages. Set within the Dartmoor National Park with easy access to the coast, golf, riding, walking and fishing locally. Sleeps 4/5, fully equipped and well furnished throughout. Own gardens with beautiful views. Ample parking. Use of outdoor heated swimming pool. High chairs, cots and linen available. Open all year.

Stick Wick Holiday Homes, c/o Frost Farm, Hennock, Bovey Tracey, South Devon TQ13 9PP   7

Linda Harvey
☎/Fax 01626 833266
SC From £125–£385
Sleeps 2–12

Commended

Three good country homes with excellent facilities. Long farmland views, garden, play area, games barn, friendly farm animals. 10 mins Bovey. Craft centre, working pottery/glass blowing, Becky Falls, Trago Mills, Dartmoor, Exeter. Seaside at Teignmouth. Golf, fishing, riding, swimming nearby. Come and join us and have fun in Devon. Open all year.

Traine Farm, Wembury, Plymouth, Devon PL9 0EW   48

Sheila Rowland
☎/Fax 01752 862264
SC From £105–£375
Sleeps 5 (+ 2) + cot

Commended

Come and enjoy a relaxed holiday in lovely surroundings, on dairy farm overlooking village of Wembury and beautiful heritage coastline. Ideal for families, children will love watching the milking, pony rides. Good centre for walking with waymarked trails through the farm. Sailing, diving, golf nearby. Short breaks. Open all year.

FARM HOLIDAY BUREAU

DEVON FARMS

Availability of farms in Devon can be easily discovered by ringing **01548 550055**.

49 **Withymore Cottage,** Withymore Farm, Malborough, Kingsbridge, South Devon TQ7 3ED

Mrs Jo Hocking
☎/Fax 01548 561275
[SC] From £130–£450
Sleeps 6 + cot
⌂ ⌂ ⌂ ⌂ ⌂
⌂ ⌂ ⌂ ⌂ *Commended*

Recently modernised cottage nestling in a peaceful valley on a family-run dairy farm within a short distance of Salcombe. Very comfortable and furnished to a high standard throughout. Colour TV, bed linen, CH. Well equipped kitchen. Large enclosed garden. Ideal centre for family holiday with many beaches, sailing, fishing, golf, horse riding and spectacular coastal walks. Open all year.

50 **Wooder Manor,** Widecombe-in-the-Moor, Newton Abbot, Devon TQ13 7TR

Mrs Angela Bell
☎/Fax 01364 621391
[SC] From £100–£800
Sleeps 2/12
⌂ ⌂ ⌂ ⌂ ⌂ ⌂ ⌂
⌂ ⌂ ⌂ – ⌂ ⌂ ⌂ ⌂
Commended

Cottages and converted coachhouse on 150-acre family farm, nestled in picturesque valley surrounded by unspoilt woodland, moors and granite tors. Central for touring Devon and exploring Dartmoor by foot or on horseback. Clean and fully equipped. Colour TVs, laundry facilities, microwaves, central heating. Gardens, courtyard for easy parking. Good food at local inn (½ mile). Choose a property to suit you from our brochure. Open all year.

DEVON FARMS

Availability of farms in Devon can be easily discovered by ringing **01548 550055**.

Our Internet Address is
http://www.webscape.co.uk/farmaccom/

STAY ON A FARM GIFT TOKENS

If you have enjoyed your Stay on a Farm, why not treat your friends and relatives to *Stay on a Farm* gift tokens? Available from the Bureau office, telephone 01203 696909, they can be redeemed against accommodation booked on the majority of our farms

Cornish Farm Holidays

Group Contact: *Pat Lutey ☎/Fax 01726 861200*

Cornwall has a coastline of 326 miles with its unique coastal footpath. It is a county of amazing contrasts with wonderful stretches of firm golden sands and soaring cliffs on the north coast, to tiny coves, picturesque fishing villages and sheltered, wooded estuaries on the south coast. Beaches from Bude to St Ives are famous for the wonderful Atlantic surf, whereas south coast resorts, such as Looe, Fowey, Mevagissey and Falmouth are ideal centres for sailing, fishing and windsurfing, with numerous safe bathing beaches spread all along this coast.

However, Cornwall has more than just the coastline to tempt you – there is a wealth of potteries and art galleries throughout the county (notably the Tate Gallery at St Ives). A wide choice of famous gardens and National Trust properties such as St Michael's Mount and Lanhydrock are open to the public. The atmospheric Bodmin Moor with mystical standing stones, Tintagel with King Arthur's Castle and the Iron Age village, Chysauster are just some of the fascinating places waiting for you to explore.

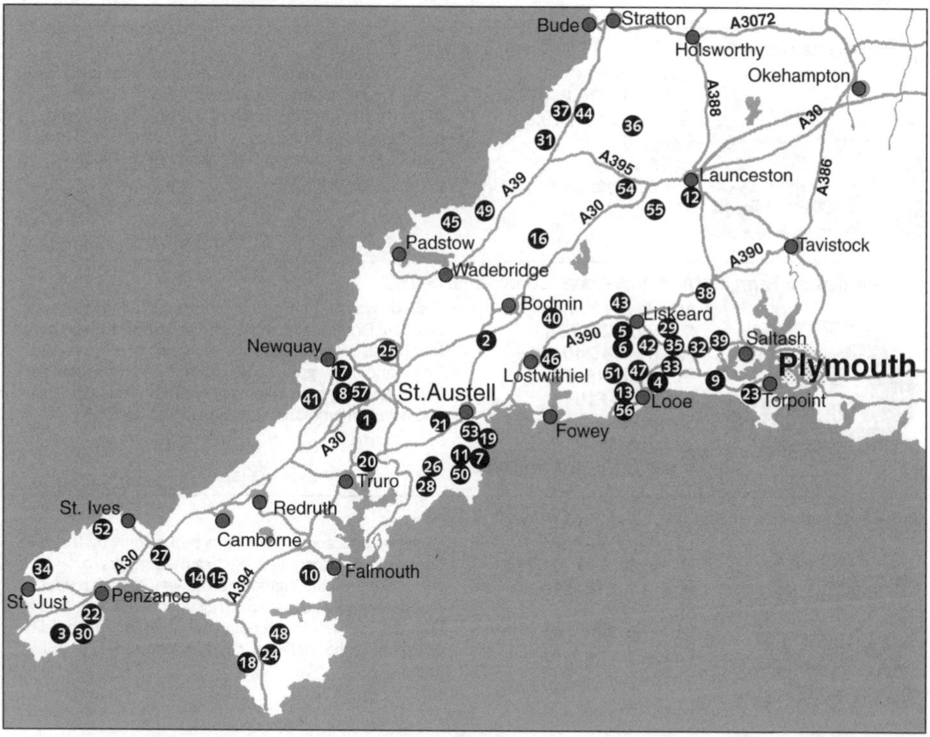

BED AND BREAKFAST

(and evening meal)

---

1   **Arrallas,** Ladock, Truro, Cornwall TR2 4NP

Mrs Barbara Holt
☎ 01872 510379
Fax 01872 510200
[BB] From £20–£24
EM £12
Sleeps 6
⚦ ▪ ⚒ ⊚
🐝🐝🐝 *Highly Commended*

Luxurious rooms, beautiful views, peaceful surroundings and the magic of birdsong make Arrallas something very special. The warm welcome, delicious meals and personal attention to our guests make your holiday with us one to remember. Come and be pampered, walk through our woods, watch for the barn owls. Listen for the woodpeckers, laze in the garden. Phone for directions. Open Feb–Oct.

---

2   **Bokiddick Farm,** Lanivet, Bodmin, Cornwall PL30 5HP

Gill Hugo
☎/Fax 01208 831481
[BB] From £19–£21
Sleeps 5
🐦(5) ⚦ ▪ ⚒ ⊚
🐝🐝 *Highly Commended*

Oak beams, wood panelling, magnificent views and a peaceful location make Bokiddick something special. Two pretty bedrooms, both en suite. Our 180-acre dairy farm is situated in central Cornwall and makes an excellent touring base for both coasts and moors.Close to National Trust Lanhydrock House. Delicious breakfasts cooked on the Aga. Warmest of welcomes awaits you. Open Mar–Oct.

---

3   **Boskenna Home Farm,** St Buryan, Penzance, Cornwall TR19 6DQ

Julia Hosking
☎/Fax 01736 810705
[BB] From £18–£19.50
Sleeps 6
🐦 ⚦ ▪ ⊚
🐝🐝 *Commended*

Our 17th century listed farmhouse which has been in our family for generations lies in the far west of Cornwall close to Land's End, nestling south of the rugged moorland, near the coastal path. Stay on our working dairy farm, with Guernsey cows, farm pets and Redde-Wood the pony. Open Mar–Oct.

---

4   **Bucklawren Farm,** St Martin-by-Looe, Cornwall PL13 1NZ

Mrs Jean Henly
☎ 01503 240738
Fax 01503 240481
[BB] From £19–£21
EM From £10
Sleeps 14
🐦 ⊞ ▪ ⚬ ⊚
🐝🐝🐝 *Highly Commended*

Tucked away in the Cornish countryside is Bucklawren, a beautiful Domesday hamlet. The delightful 19th century farmhouse enjoys spectacular sea views over Looe Bay. Come and enjoy good food, comfort and relaxation. An award-winning farm where every effort is made to ensure you have a memorable stay. Open Mar–Oct.

---

5   **Caduscott,** East Taphouse, Liskeard, Cornwall PL14 4NG

Lindsay Pendray
☎/Fax 01579 320262
[BB] From £16–£19.50
Sleeps 4/5
🐦 ⚦ ▪ ⊚
Listed *Commended*

Sweet dreams and restful nights broken only by the owl's hooting in the clear night sky; from stargazers to shellseekers, all the ingredients are here to match your mood! A positive approach to all your needs. Log fires to brighten your return after days spent on the rugged cliffs or exploring the sheltered valleys. Open Apr–Sept incl. Easter.

Carglonnon Farm, Duloe, Liskeard, Cornwall PL14 4QA **6**

Mrs Ann Bray
☎/Fax 01579 320210
[BB] From £16–£18
Sleeps 6
Commended

A lovely 18th century Georgian farmhouse which is part of the Duchy of Cornwall Estate. A working mixed farm of 230 acres, situated 4½ miles from fishing port of Looe. Forestry walks from farm. Golf, horse-riding, Theme Park, coastal walking, moors all nearby. Two doubles en suite. One twin with private bathroom. Tea/coffee-making facilities, central heating. Open Mar–Dec.

Coney Parc Farmhouse, Heligan, Pentewan, St Austell, Cornwall PL26 6EN **7**

Vicky Lobb
☎/Fax 01726 842001
[BB] From £18
Sleeps 6
Highly Commended

Unwind in our tastefully converted 18th century barn set amidst 700 acres of mixed farmland. Picturesque Mevagissey, beaches and footpaths nearby. After a hearty breakfast why not amble to the Lost Gardens of Heligan or explore our woodlands and trout lakes. Enjoy Cornwall in a real 'away from it all' setting. Open Apr–Sept.

Degembris Farmhouse, St Newlyn East, Newquay, Cornwall TR8 5HY **8**

Kathy Woodley
☎ 01872 510555
Fax 01872 510230
[BB] From £18–£20
EM From £10
Sleeps 12
Highly Commended

Degembris nestles in a south facing hillside overlooking a beautiful wooded valley. Its low beams and log fires make this listed 18th century farmhouse a delight. Come inside (mind your head!) and enjoy the charming Georgian surroundings, complete with creaky floorboards! Take a stroll along our farm trail that wanders through woodland and fields of corn. Open all year except Christmas.

Hendra Farm, Polbathic, Torpoint, Cornwall PL11 3DT **9**

Mrs A Hoskin
☎/Fax 01503 250225
[BB] From £15–£18
Sleeps 5
Commended

Hendra is a working farm situated in an area of outstanding natural beauty. The fishing port of Looe is 6 miles, and safe bathing beaches of Downderry and Seaton only 2 miles. The main shopping centre of Plymouth is within ½ hours travelling. TV lounge. Family room with en suite shower and WC. Babysitting. Open Mar–Nov.

Higher Kergilliack Farm, Budock, Falmouth, Cornwall TR11 5PB **10**

Jean Pengelly
☎ 01326 372271
[BB] From £17.50–£19.50
Sleeps 6
Commended

18th century Georgian listed farmhouse on 130-acre dairy farm, former residence of Bishop of Exeter. Overlooks Falmouth Bay and near the seal sanctuary. See the flowers in the hedgerows and daffodil fields. Trebah, Trelissick and Glendurgan Gardens 15 mins. 1 double with en suite WC and shower, 1 twin/family with en suite WC and bath. Take 2nd right on A39 at Hillhead roundabout. Open all year.

Kerryanna Country House, Treleaven Farm, Mevagissey, Cornwall PL26 6RZ **11**

Linda Hennah
☎/Fax 01726 843558
[BB] From £20–£25
EM From £11
Sleeps 14
Highly Commended

Surrounded by farmland, wildlife and flowers, the farm is only 8 minutes' walk from the centre of Mevagissey. Romantic en suite bedrooms with TV and beverage tray. Beautiful gardens with heated outdoor pool and stunning views. Games barn, putting green. Hearty breakfasts and delicious evening meals. A warm welcome assured. Mentioned in the *Daily Telegraph* and Gill Charlton's *A Week in Cornwall*. Open Mar–Oct.

12 Larrick Farm, South Petherwin, Launceston, Cornwall PL15 9LY

Michelle Tucker
☎/Fax 01566 772614
BB From £15
Sleeps 6
☒ ⅄ ♨ ✿
Listed *Commended*

Unwind in our characteristic traditional 16th century farmhouse, which is situated on a working dairy farm in peaceful rural countryside. Enjoy a hearty breakfast and a cosy log fire. The north and south coasts of Cornwall and the moors are easily accessible with a range of leisure facilities close by. Open all year.

---

13 Little Larnick Farm, Pelynt, Looe, Cornwall PL13 2NB

Angela Eastley
☎/Fax 01503 262837
BB From £18–£20
Sleeps 7
☒(3) ⅄ ◉
♨♨ *Commended*

Little Larnick is situated in a sheltered part of the West Looe river valley. Walk to the bustling fishing town of Looe from our working dairy farm and along the coastal path to picturesque Polperro. Popular with our guests is our new annexe bedroom with its separate entrance. Open Feb–Nov.

---

14 Little Pengwedna Farm, Helston, Cornwall TR13 0AY

Iris White
☎/Fax 01736 850649
BB From £18–£22
Sleeps 6
☒ ♨
♨♨ *Commended*

A friendly Cornish welcome and hearty home-cooked breakfast make a stay at this charming farmhouse a real treat. Ideally positioned for touring either coast, you'll find this 19th century granite house prettily and comfortably decorated with original paintings and fresh flowers. It's easily reached, on the B3302 between Helston and Hayle. Open all year including Christmas.

---

15 Longstone Farm, Trenear, Helston, Cornwall TR13 0HG

Gillian Lawrance
☎/Fax 01326 572483
BB From £16–£19
EM From £8.50
Sleeps 14
☒ ✝ ♨ ◉
♨♨ *Commended*

Enjoy the warm and friendly atmosphere of our home which is off the beaten track overlooking rolling fields and peaceful countryside. Central for sandy beaches and many attractions, particularly Flambards. All bedrooms en suite or private facilities. Delicious meals using local produce, attractively presented in our dining room overlooking spacious garden. Relax and unwind in our TV lounge and sunlounge. Open Mar–Nov.

---

16 Loskeyle Farm, St Tudy, Bodmin, Cornwall PL30 3PW

Mrs Sandra Menhinick
☎/Fax 01208 851005
BB From £15–£16
EM From £10
Sleeps 6
☒ ⅄ ♨ ◉
♨ *Commended*

Welcome to Loskeyle, a real 'home from home'. Wake up to a choice of breakfasts and home baked bread. Perfectly situated for touring, cycling and walking, then return to cosy log fires, a delicious supper, and listen out for our resident barn owls – a truly relaxing holiday. Open Mar–Nov.

---

17 Manuels Farm, Quintrell Downs, Newquay, Cornwall TR8 4NY

Mrs Jean Wilson
☎/Fax 01637 873577
BB From £18.50–£20
EM £12.50
Sleeps 10
☒ ✝ ⅄ ♥ ♠ ♨ ◉
♨♨ *Highly Commended*

A listed 17th century farmhouse situated in a sheltered valley, 2 miles from Newquay's magnificent beaches. Relax in peaceful countryside in this traditional Cornish farmhouse. Beautifully furnished, delicious plentiful farmhouse cooking. Log fires. Award winning garden. Children especially welcome. Nursery teas, free babysitting, play area, pony rides. Meet a whole variety of pets and farm animals on this friendly working farm. Open all year (closed Christmas).

Polhormon Farm, Polhormon Lane, Mullion, Helston, Cornwall TR12 7JE   **18**

Alice Harry
☎/Fax 01326 240304
[BB] From £15–£18
Sleeps 8
➴ ➴ ➴ ◉
❦ *Commended*

Treat yourselves to a relaxing Cornish break in our comfortable Georgian farmhouse. Spectacular views over the sea and sandy Poldhu beach on the unspoilt Lizard Peninsula. Watch the milking or help feed our newborn calves. Ideal base for beaches, cliffwalking or boat trips around Mullion Island with local fisherman, Barry. Scrumptious breakfasts. Open May–Nov.

Polrudden Farm, Pentewan, nr Mevagissey, St Austell, Cornwall PL26 6BJ   **19**

Mrs Jo Jackson
☎/Fax 01726 842051
[BB] From £18–£20
Sleeps 6
➴(10) ➴ ➴ ➴
❦ *Highly Commended*

Our farm, set in 80 acres of glorious countryside, enjoys magnificent sea views. The house and gardens lie on the site of the manor of Sir John Polrudden, and provide an excellent retreat in which to relax and savour peace and tranquillity. Excellent restaurants, delightful walks and many wonderful gardens to visit, including Heligan, make us an ideal base for exploring Cornwall. Open Mar–Nov.

Polsue Manor Farm, Tresillian, Truro, Cornwall TR2 4BP   **20**

Geraldine Holliday
☎ 01872 520234
Fax 01872 520616
[BB] From £17
EM From £9.50
Sleeps 14
➴ ➴ ➴ ➴ ➴ ◉
❦ ❦ *Commended*

The farmhouse on this 190-acre working farm, set in glorious countryside, overlooks the tidal Tresillian River and one of the prettiest parts of Cornwall, 'gateway' to the Roseland Peninsula. Beautiful cathedral city of Truro 2 miles. Centrally situated between north and south coasts, ideal centre for touring Cornwall. Delightful woodland and estuary walks. Traditional home cooking, comfortable, relaxed atmosphere. Open most of year.

Poltarrow Farm, St Mewan, St Austell, Cornwall PL26 7DR   **21**

Judith Nancarrow
☎/Fax 01726 67111
[BB] From £19–£22
EM From £10
Sleeps 12
➴ ➴ ➴ ➴ ➴ ➴ ➴ ◉
❦ ❦ *Highly Commended*

Our charming farmhouse is the ideal place for you to take time to relax. Tucked away, yet so central that you can do as much or as little as you want. Gardens in the spring, beaches in summer, the warm days of Autumn, but a log fire in the evenings. Open all year except Christmas.

Rose Farm, Chyanhal, Drift, Penzance, Cornwall TR19 6AN   **22**

Mrs Penny Lally
☎/Fax 01736 731808
[BB] From £19–£20.50
Sleeps 8
➴ ➴ ➴
❦ ❦ *Commended*

Rose Farm is a small working farm in a little hamlet close to the picturesque fishing villages of Mousehole and Newlyn and 7 miles from Lands End. The 200-year-old granite farmhouse is cosy with pretty, en suite rooms. 1 double, 1 family suite and a romantic 15th century four poster room in barn annexe. We have all manner of animals, from pedigree cattle to pot-bellied pigs! Open all year (closed Christmas).

Stone Farm, Whitsand Bay, Millbrook, Torpoint, Cornwall PL10 1JJ   **23**

Mrs Sarah Blake
☎/Fax 01752 822267
[BB] From £15–£18
Sleeps 6
➴ ➴ ➴ ➴ ➴
❦ ❦ *Highly Commended*

Dairy farm 400 yards from the cliff path leading to miles of sandy beaches in an Area of Outstanding Natural Beauty, with panoramic views from Rame to Looe. Large garden with croquet lawn. Everyone can help feed the animals or watch the milking. Children's pony rides and games room. Open all year except Christmas.

24 Tregaddra Farm, Cury, Cross Lanes, Helston, Cornwall TR12 7BB

June Lugg
☎/Fax 01326 240235
🅱 From £18.50–£20.50
EM From £9
Sleeps 13
🐎 🍴 💼 ⓦ
ⱳ ⱳ ⱳ *Highly Commended*

Unwind in this beautifully furnished 18th century farmhouse (1717) on working farm. Situated in an Area of Outstanding Natural Beauty, our views of rolling countryside are unrivalled. All-weather tennis court, heated outdoor pool and large garden. Pretty en suite bedrooms, two with balconies, one four-poster. Winter breaks, blazing inglenook fires and relaxed family atmosphere. Open all year.

25 Tregaswith Farmhouse, Tregaswith, near Newquay, Cornwall TR8 4HY

John & Jacqui Elsom
☎/Fax 01637 881181
🅱 From £22–£24
EM From £12
Sleeps 6
🐎 🐓 🍴 🐎 💼 ⓦ
ⱳ ⱳ ⱳ *Highly Commended*

Tregaswith is a small hamlet just outside Newquay, 5 minutes' drive to beaches and several National Trust properties near. The elegant farmhouse built over 250 years ago, now a smallholding with many friendly animals. Pony rides and an introduction to carriage driving can be arranged. We have a reputation for delicious food. 3 beautiful bedrooms, all en suite. Antiques and oak beams throughout. Open all year except Christmas.

26 Tregidgeo, Grampound, Truro, Cornwall TR2 4SP

Mrs Sally Wade
☎/Fax 01726 882450
🅱 From £19–£21
EM From £10.50
Sleeps 6
🐎(10) 🍴 💼
ⱳ ⱳ *Highly Commended*

Tregidgeo is a mixed farm of 216 acres. The elegant farmhouse is found in a beautifully secluded and peaceful setting overlooking lovely gardens, lake and countryside. Excellent spacious accomodation. Bedrooms all en suite with TV, beverage facilities and CH. Luxury four-poster. Delicious home cooking with fresh farm and local produce. Private coarse fishing. A very relaxing holiday. Open Feb–Nov.

27 Treglisson, Wheal Alfred Road, Hayle, Cornwall TR27 5JT

Carole Runnalls
☎/Fax 01736 753141
🅱 From £19–£24
Sleeps 15
🐎 🍴 🖽 🧍 🛋 💼 ♟ ⓦ
ⱳ ⱳ *Highly Commended*

Situated in the quiet Cornish countryside, Treglisson, a listed 18th century farmhouse, offers pretty en suite rooms with colour TV, tea/coffee, hairdrier and fresh flowers. Start the day with a swim in the heated indoor pool before tucking into a hearty breakfast served in the elegant dining room or conservatory. St Michael's Mount, St Ives, Lands End are all within easy reach. Open all year except Christmas and New Year.

28 Tregonan, Tregony, Truro, Cornwall TR2 5SN

Sandra Collins
☎/Fax 01872 530249
🅱 From £15
Sleeps 6
🐎 💼 ⓦ
ⱳ *Commended*

Discover Tregonan, tucked away down half-mile private lane. Comfortable, spacious farmhouse set in secluded garden, at centre of 300 acre arable and sheep farm. 6 miles west of Mevagissey, on threshold of renowned Roseland Peninsula. 2 beaches within 3 miles. All bedrooms H/C, beverage-making facilities, radio. Good selection of eating places locally. Open Apr–Oct. Advanced booking only Nov–Mar (closed Christmas and New Year).

29 Tregondale Farm, Menheniot, Liskeard, Cornwall PL14 3RG

Stephanie Rowe
☎/Fax 01579 342407
🅱 From £17.50–£19.50
EM From £10
Sleeps 6
🐎 🍴 ♟ 💼 ♣ ⓦ
ⱳ ⱳ *Highly Commended*

Feeling like a break? Relax in style in the peace of the countryside near the coast. Three charming en suite bedrooms with TV/radio. Home produce a speciality. Play tennis, explore the woodland farm trail. See pedigree cattle, lambs in spring amidst wildlife and flowers. Activities arranged, golf, cycling, walking and fishing. A warm welcome awaits you. Open all year.

Tregurnow Farm, St Buryan, Penzance, Cornwall TR19 6BL   30

Edwina Jeffery
☎/Fax 01736 810255
BB From £18–£23.50
Sleeps 6
🐎 🐔 ⅍ 🎠 ♨
😊😊 *Commended*

Our tastefully furnished farmhouse is situated in a magnificent coastal position above Lamorna Cove. Ideal base for the South West Way, Minack Theatre, Land's End, The Tate and beaches. Romantic four-poster. Spectacular views across Mount's Bay. Superb Aga-cooked breakfasts. We combine comfort and luxury with peace and tranquillity.

Trehane Farm, Trevalga, Boscastle, Cornwall PL35 0EB   31

Mrs Sarah James
☎/Fax 01840 250510
BB From £18–£20
EM From £11
Sleeps 6
🐎 🐔 ⅍ 🎠 🎠 ♨ 🐿 🔄
😊😊 *Commended*

Welcome to Trehane, a dairy farm on the spectacular North Cornwall heritage coast. Farmhouse set in magnificent position overlooking sea, superb coastal views. We offer a comfortable friendly atmosphere and wholesome nourishing food using fresh farm produce and home baked bread. Enjoy fine walks along the coast or inland on to Bodmin Moor. Learn to spin. Open Feb–Dec.

Tresulgan Farm, Nr Menheniot, Liskeard, Cornwall PL14 3PU   32

Mrs E Elford
☎/Fax 01503 240268
BB From £18–£20
EM From £9
Sleeps 6
🐎(2) 🐔 ⅍ ♨ 🔄
😊😊 *Highly Commended*

Relax and unwind at Tresulgan, our 17th century farmhouse on a livestock/arable farm enjoying picturesque views of the wooded Seaton Valley. Beamed dining room and attractive en suite bedrooms with tea/coffee facilities and colour TV. An ideal location for touring this most beautiful area. A friendly welcome is assured. Open all year.

Treveria Farm, Widegates, Looe, Cornwall PL13 1QR   33

Mrs J Kitto
☎/Fax 01503 240237
BB From £20–£22
Sleeps 6
🎠 ⅍ 🎠 ♨ 🔄
😊😊 *Commended*

Treveria is a delightful manor house set in a large garden overlooking the farm and surrounding countryside. A high standard of accommodation is offered with beautifully decorated en suite rooms, one with four-poster. All rooms have colour TV and beverage facilities. Looe and Polperro with their quaint harbours and excellent restaurants are only a short drive away. Open Easter–Nov.

Trewellard Manor Farm, Pendeen, Penzance, Cornwall TR19 7SU   34

Mrs Marion Bailey
☎/Fax 01736 788526
BB From £16–£20
Sleeps 6
🐎 ♨ 🔄
😊😊 *Commended*

The farm is situated in a superb coastal position between Lands End and St Ives. We offer a friendly, relaxed atmosphere with seasonal fires and CH. 3 bedrooms (1 en suite) all with tea/coffee facilities. Use of swimming pool (June–Sept) with good beaches within easy reach. Golf and coarse fishing available nearby. This is an outstanding area for walking, either inland or on the coast path. Open all year (closed Christmas).

Trewint Farm, Menheniot, Liskeard, Cornwall PL14 3RE   35

Elizabeth Rowe
☎/Fax 01579 347155
BB From £18
EM From £8
Sleeps 6
🐎 ⅍ 🎠 ♨ 🔄
😊😊 *Commended*

Ideally situated only minutes from the A38, yet in peaceful, tranquil surroundings, Trewint is a 200-acre working farm with pedigree cattle and sheep. Pony for the children, play area. En suite rooms with matching decor. Breakfast overlooking the garden watching the birds while you enjoy the farmhouse fare using home/local meats and produce. Open all year except Christmas and New Year.

36 **Wheatley Farm,** Maxworthy, Launceston, Cornwall PL15 8LY

Valerie Griffin
☎/Fax 01566 781232
BB From £18–£22
EM From £12
Sleeps 10
🐕 ⅍ ▥ 🎋 ◎
🏵🏵🏵 *Highly Commended*

Sample the delights of country living where the quality of life matters. Splendid food, hearty and healthy breakfasts, delicious dinners, only top-quality produce used. Enjoy your day exploring then return to our spacious Victorian farmhouse exclusively furnished with antiques. Crackling log fires, warm country bedrooms, one with romantic four-poster. Experience the warmth of true Cornish hospitality. Open Mar–Nov.

SELF-CATERING

29 **Beechleigh Cottage,** Tregondale Farm, Menheniot, Liskeard, Cornwall PL14 3RG

Stephanie Rowe
☎/Fax 01579 342407
SC From £145–£399
Sleeps 4 (+ cot)
🐕 🐈 🎋 ⇦ ◎
🔑 🔑 🔑 *Highly Commended*

In the leigh of our farmhouse beech tree, this peaceful, attractive character cottage nestles. Warm and cosy in winter, barbecue on the patio in summer, play tennis, golf (special rates), private fishing, explore the woodland farm trail. Hear birds singing, enjoy wild flowers and lambs in Spring. See pedigree South Devon cattle, naturally reared. A warm welcome awaits you – come and discover the beauty of Cornwall. Open all year.

2 **Bokiddick Farm,** Lanivet, Bodmin, Cornwall PL30 5HP

Gill Hugo
☎/Fax 01208 831481
SC From £100–£400
Sleeps 4
🐕 ⅍ ◎
🔑 🔑 🔑 *Commended*

When you arrive enjoy a cream tea in the lovely new conservatory of our country bungalow, overlooking its own secluded garden, with magnificent country views, our 180-acre dairy farm is in the heart of Cornwall making it an ideal touring base for both coasts and moors. Close to NT Lanhydrock House, it offers excellent walking. Open all year.

37 **Brevean,** Smallhill Barton, St Gennys, Bude, Cornwall EX23 0BQ

Mr & Mrs Harry Mead
☎/Fax 01840 230230
SC From £100–£375
Sleeps 6
🐕 🐈
🔑 🔑 🔑 *Highly Commended*

By the North Cornwall coast, between Bude and Tintagel and surrounded by rolling farmland, our spacious holiday cottage, standing in its own garden, offers a chance to relax in peace and comfort. Excellent home base from which to explore the mysteries and delights of this renowned and attractive area. Open all year.

4 **Bucklawren Farm,** St Martin-by-Looe, Cornwall PL13 1NZ

Mrs Jean Henly
☎ 01503 240738
Fax 01503 240481
SC From £120–£440
Sleeps 4/6
🐕 🐈 🖾 ⇦ ▪ ◎
🔑 🔑 🔑 *Highly Commended*

Step back in time and enjoy our character cottages, tastefully converted and furnished to a high standard. Come and enjoy our spectacular scenery with exceptional sea views. Plenty to do with walks, golf, fishing, all close by. An award-winning farm where you can come and discover a true Cornish farm holiday. Open Mar–Jan.

Cadson Manor Farm, Callington, Cornwall PL17 7HW

Brenda Crago
☎/Fax 01579 383969
sc From £150–£480
Sleeps 6 + cot
Highly Commended

Wing of manor house with large garden on 200-acre working farm set in the beautiful Lynher Valley with lovely views of two-acre fishing lake for guests' exclusive use. Three pretty bedrooms, bathroom, lounge/diner and separate kitchen, all tastefully decorated and equipped to a very high standard. Cosy and comfortable. Farm and river walks. Open all year.

The Coach House, c/o Lantallack Farm, Landrake, Nr Saltash, Cornwall PL12 5AE

Nichola Walker
☎/Fax 01752 851281
sc From £185–£520
Sleeps 6/7 + cot
Highly Commended

Georgian farm coach house, extremely comfortable with outstanding views across undulating countryside and wooded valleys. The perfect retreat for a relaxing holiday. We keep ponies, sheep, ducks and hens. Golf at St Mellion, 10 mins. away. Close to sea and moors. 2 bathrooms, log fire, CH, phone, microwave, dishwasher and games room. Linen/electricity inclusive. Open Mar–Oct.

Glynn Barton Farm Cottages, Glynn Barton, Cardinham, Bodmin, Cornwall PL30 4AX

Diana Mindel
☎/Fax 01208 821375
sc From £150–£540
Sleeps 2/6
Commended

Whatever the season, make the most of our comfortable cottages – four poster, wood beams and traditional cast iron stove. From your cottage enjoy beautiful views and take woodland or farmland walks. Play tennis or relax by heated pool in walled 'Mediterranean' atmosphere. Central for golf, beaches, cycling, fishing, horseriding and gardens. Open all year.

Hendra Farm, Rose, Truro, Cornwall TR4 9PS

Janet Symons
☎/Fax 01872 572273
sc From £250–£600
Sleeps 7 + cot
Commended

Spacious old farmhouse with pretty garden, two bathrooms and private coarse fishing in a secluded lake. Footpaths lead to the coast and glorious beaches. Tariff includes central heating, electricity, log fire, linen, well behaved pet.

Lodge Barton Farm, Liskeard, Cornwall PL14 4JX

Rosanne Hodin
☎/Fax 01579 344432
sc From £100–£400
Sleeps 2/5 + cot
Commended

Lodge Barton is set in a beautiful river valley flanked by woodland. We keep goats and also have ducks, hens and geese. Everyone can help collecting eggs and feeding. Our character cottages are luxuriously equipped including heating, woodburners, video, linen, laundry room, private gardens and playground. We are close to sea, moors, sailing, windsurfing, riding, fishing, golf. Open all year.

Lower Trengale Farm, Liskeard, Cornwall PL14 6HF

Louise Kidd
☎ 01579 321019
Fax 01579 321432
sc From £120–£480
Sleeps 4–6
Highly Commended

A small farm, set in beautiful countryside, offering three comfortable and well equipped cottages with woodburners, videos and dishwashers. Super for children with pony, playground and games room. Lovely views from the garden. Ideally located for beaches, moors, golfing, fishing and walking. All linen, cots, highchairs supplied. Open all year.

17 Manuels Farm, Quintrell Downs, Newquay, Cornwall TR8 4NY

Alan & Jean Wilson
☎/Fax 01637 873577
[SC] From £100–£450
Sleeps 2/5 + cot
♿ 🐕 🐎 🍴 ▪ ⦿
🐾 🐾 🐾 *Commended*

Imagine a family holiday close to Newquay's magnificent beaches but tucked away in your own quiet valley. Secluded from the crowd but perfectly placed for touring, walking and riding. Your own character cottage in the country, on the farm, with gardens, flowers, pets and farm animals around you. The children will enjoy the calves, tractor and ponies while you relax. Electricity and linen included. Short breaks available. Open all year.

44 Old Newham Farm, Otterham, Camelford, Cornwall PL32 9SR

Mrs Mary Purdue
☎ 01840 230470
Fax 01840 230303
[SC] From £120–£480
Sleeps 2/4/5
♿ 🐕 🐎 ← 🍴 ▪
🐾 🐾 🐾 🐾 *Approved*

Three individual stone and slate cottages around an old farmyard dating back to medieval times, at the end of a quiet country lane. Our 30-acre farm is managed in a traditional way with cattle, sheep and other small animals for the children. Here you can find the peace of the Cornish countryside yet be only 3 miles from the most spectacular coastline in the area. Cottages with character, open fire, CH. Open all year.

21 Poltarrow Farm , St Mewan, St Austell, Cornwall PL26 7DR

Judith Nancarrow
☎/Fax 01726 67111
[SC] From £100–£550
Sleeps 2/6
👤 ♿ 🐎 ⊞ 🐕 ← 🍴 ▪ ⦿
🐾 🐾 🐾 🐾 *Up to Highly Commended*

Tucked away in the countryside between Fowey and Mevagissey, discover your cottage, restored with care, with all the touches that make you feel at home. Wood fires for the coldest weather and summer barbecues. You'll find nature on your doorstep. Children love the animals, particularly Taffy the pony. Short breaks. Open all year.

45 Rooke Farm Cottages, Rooke Farm, Chapel Amble, Wadebridge, Cornwall PL27 6ES

Mrs Gill Reskelly
☎ 01208 880368
Fax 01208 880600
[SC] From £270–£850
Sleeps 2–7 (+ cot)
♿ 🍴 ▪ ⦿
🐾 🐾 🐾 🐾 🐾 *Highly Commended*

Something special – luxury country cottages set in 235 acres of Duchy of Cornwall farmland. On outskirts of the pretty Chapel Amble close to many golden beaches. Exclusively furnished and equipped with all that's required for a relaxing holiday. Pretty en suite bedrooms, log fires, dishwasher, satellite TV, hi fi and phone. Electricity heating, quality linen and towels inclusive. Each has private enclosed garden with barbecue. Brochure. Open all year.

46 Tredethick Farm Cottages, The Guildhouse, Tredethick, Lostwithiel, Cornwall PL22 0LE

Tim & Nicky Reed
☎/Fax 01208 873618
[SC] From £135–£540
Sleeps 35
♿ 🐕 ⚹ 🐎 ← 🍴 ▪ ⦿
🐾 🐾 🐾 🐾 *Highly Commended*

Award-winning cottages set amongst beautiful rolling countryside. Walk from your door through meadows and woods to the River Fowey and on to the quiet creekside village of Lerryn – the inspiration behind *The Wind in the Willows*. Ideal year round base for exploring the delights of coast and countryside or simply relaxing and enjoying the rural idyll. Open all year.

47 Tredinnick Farm, Duloe, Liskeard, Cornwall PL14 4PJ

Mrs Angela Barrett
☎ 01503 262997
Fax 01503 265554
[SC] From £150–£635
Sleeps 2/10 (+ cot)
♿ ▪ ⦿
🐾 🐾 🐾 🐾 *Highly Commended*

Beautiful springtime flowers, lazy summer days, leisurely autumn trips, warm and cosy winter fires. Whatever the time of year there should be something for everyone who stays in this extensive wing of Tredinnick House situated between the East and West Looe rivers. Open Mar–Jan.

Tregevis Farm, St Martin, Helston, Cornwall TR12 6DN 48

Julie Bray
☎/Fax 01326 231265
From £170–£425
Sleeps 6

Highly Commended

Come and relax at Tregevis, a working dairy farm in the picturesque Helford River area, just ½ mile from the little village of St. Martin and 5 miles from sandy beaches. The accommodation is a self-contained, spacious part of the farmhouse, very comfortable, well equipped and with a games room. The large lawn area with swings will prove popular with children, as will our farm animals. Open Easter–Oct.

Treharrock Farm Cottages, Treharrock Farm, Pendoggett, Port Isaac, Cornwall PL29 3TA 49

Linda Leigh-Firbank
☎/Fax 01208 880517
From £185–£495
Sleeps 2–6

Highly Commended

Take a relaxing break in one of our superbly equipped cottages on a family dairy farm with breathtaking views of countryside and coastline. Close to sandy beach and historic fishing port. Tastefully furnished with open fire. Ideal for all seasons. We provide a high standard of personal care, with many finishing touches to make your holiday extra-special. Open all year.

Treleaven Farm Cottages, Treleaven Farm, Mevagissey, Cornwall PL26 6RZ 50

Mrs Linda Hennah
☎/Fax 01726 843558
From £160–£575
Sleeps 4–6

Highly Commended

Surrounded by rambling countryside, wildlife and flowers, the farm is only 8 minutes' walk from the centre of Mevagissey. Each cottage has luxury pine fitted kitchen with dishwasher, microwave, fridge/freezer and cooker. Lovely bathroom with shower, cosy lounge with TV, some en suite bedrooms. CH included in winter. Linen and electricity inclusive. Laundry room. Ample parking. Games barn. Next to Heligan Gardens and central for touring. Open all year.

Tremadart Farm, Duloe, Liskeard, Cornwall PL14 4PE 51

Evelyn Julian
☎/Fax 01503 262855
From £150–£650
Sleeps 2–12

Commended

The wing of our Victorian farmhouse is situated in a secluded garden on a 330-acre working farm. Ideally located three miles from Looe for beaches and walking, cycling and fishing. Short breaks and smaller numbers welcomed in low season. Open all year.

Trevalgan Farm, St Ives, Cornwall TR26 3BJ 52

Jean Osborne
☎/Fax 01736 796433
From £150–£450
Sleeps 2/6

Commended

Trevalgan is a coastal stock-rearing farm surrounded by magnificent scenery, just 2 miles from St Ives. Enjoy walking our farm trail to the cliffs overlooking the sea, a paradise for nature lovers. Traditional granite barns have been carefully converted into 7 lovely holiday homes around an attractive courtyard. Land's End, St Michael's Mount, Mousehole and Lamorna within easy reach by car. Open all year (closed Feb).

Trevissick Manor, Trevissick Farm, Trenarren, St Austell, Cornwall PL26 6BQ 53

Mrs Pamela Treleaven
☎/Fax 01726 75819
From £120–£360
Sleeps 2–4 + cot

Commended

The east wing of the manor farmhouse on our coastal mixed farm is situated between St Austell and Mevagissey Bays. Spectacular views across the gardens down the valley to the sea. Ideal for a couple or family. Meet the animals, view the milking, play tennis or take the farm trail to Hallane Cove. Near sandy beaches, sailing, watersports, cycling, 18-hole golf. Heligan Gardens 5–10 mins. Open all year except Christmas.

34 **Trewellard Manor Farm,** Pendeen, Penzance, Cornwall TR19 7SU

Mrs Marion Bailey
☎/Fax 01736 788526
sc From £150–£375
Sleeps 4

Commended

In the heart of Poldark Country, between Land's End and St Ives, attractive stone cottages converted from old stables. Situated across courtyard from owner's farmhouse and swimming pool (June–Sept). On edge of village within easy reach of beaches and coast path. Special winter short breaks. Open all year.

54 **Trewithen Country Lodges,** Trewithen Farm, Laneast, Launceston, Cornwall PL15 8PW

Mrs Margaret Colwill
☎/Fax 01566 86343
sc From £90–£390
Sleeps 4

Commended

Come on down to our Cornish farm to stay,
Where the hedgerows are wonderful, changing each day,
Just two pine lodges, beautifully designed,
Away from the noise, relax and unwind,
Tastefully furnished and cosy as pie,
Fun for the family and jacuzzi to try,
Panoramic views of the surrounding moors,
Enjoy animals and walks in the great outdoors.

55 **Trotters,** Trevadlock Farm, Trevadlock, Congdon's Shop, Launceston, Cornwall PL15 7PW

Mrs Barbara Sleep
☎/Fax 01566 782239
sc From £200–£500
Sleeps 6 + cot

Highly Commended

We invite you to stay at Trotters, our tastefully restored character cottage set on beautiful farmland close to Bodmin Moor. See the animals, enjoy the local walks, return to our superbly equipped cottage with cosy rooms, original beams and open fires. Ideal touring base for north and south coasts and exploring both counties. Three excellent golf courses nearby. Open all year.

56 **West Kellow Farmhouse & Meadow Bank,** West Kellow, Lansallos, Looe, Cornwall PL13 2QL

Mrs E Julian
☎/Fax 01503 262855
sc From £100–£560
Sleeps 9/4

Up to Highly Commended

In a secluded position with panoramic views, our Victorian farmhouse and converted stone cottage are reached down a country lane. Visitors are welcome to walk around our 160-acre working beef and sheep farm. Close to the secluded bays of Lansallos and Lantivet with quiet, sandy beaches, we are just a mile from picturesque Polperro. Open all year.

36 **Wheatley Farm Cottages,** Maxworthy, Launceston, Cornwall PL15 8LY

Valerie Griffin
☎/Fax 01566 781232
sc From £90–£460
Sleeps 5/7

Highly Commended

Sample the delights of a little country living where the quality of life matters – the quiet peace of a golden sunset, crackling log fires, sweeping views of fine rolling countryside. These and much more can be found at Wheatley Farm. Two quality cottages of character and charm, lovingly restored. Near spectacular North Cornwall coast. Families very welcome. Open all year.

Although the majority of farms will accept *'Stay on a Farm'* Gift Tokens, please check when booking to avoid disappointment.

CAMPING AND CARAVANNING

Nancolleth Farm Caravan Gardens, Newquay, Cornwall TR8 4PN ⑤⑦

Joan Luckraft
☎ **01872 510236**
🆂 **From £115–£300**
Sleeps 4/6
🛏 ½ 🚐 🌐
✓✓✓✓✓

Nancolleth has a secluded, south-facing holiday park with just 6 Rose Award caravans in a garden setting. Enjoy the freedom of our spacious holiday homes, combining modern furnishings with practical layouts. With the use of a laundry room and phone. Relax in style, wander our country trail or explore Cornwall's delights. Open May–Oct.

CONFIRM BOOKINGS

Disappointments can arise from misunderstandings over the telephone. Please write to confirm your booking.

THE 1000+ BUREAU MEMBERS OFFER A UNIQUE LINK TO CUSTOMERS ACROSS THE UK

All Bureau members belong to a local Group. Each member can refer you to an equally high quality member within the Group... or across the UK: England, Northern Ireland, Scotland, Wales.

FINDING YOUR ACCOMMODATION

The Group contacts at the beginning of each section can always help you find a vacancy in your chosen area.

Isle of Anglesey

Group Contact: *Mrs Anne Astley* ☎ *01248 470278*

None of the epithets for the regions of Britain more accurately describes true character than that for Anglesey – the 'mother' of Wales.

The corner-stones of an agricultural way of life are to be seen everywhere – from the inland cornfields, set amongst trees and hedgerows, to the coastal pastures dotted with lambs, and from the whitewashed cottages of the smallholdings to the 'home farms' of the great country estates.

Holiday makers will find the island's lovely coast – much of it an Area of Outstanding Natural Beauty – includes some of Europe's most thrilling beaches.

It is said that Anglesey's history is written in stone. Prehistoric burial chambers and tall standing stones evoke ancient mysteries, Roman Walls tell a tale of bitter conquest, and the little churches and chapels are a reminder of the 5th-century saints. Archaeologists are beginning to reveal the influence of the Welsh Princes on medieval life, and the ramparts of Beaumaris Castle are reminders of the invaders from across the border.

The indomitable spirit survives in the songs of the island's choirs, the diligence of the farmer preparing his prize bull for the Agricultural Show, and the enthusiasm of the farmer's wife as she tells her guests about her wonderful island.

Croeso! Welcome to Anglesey.

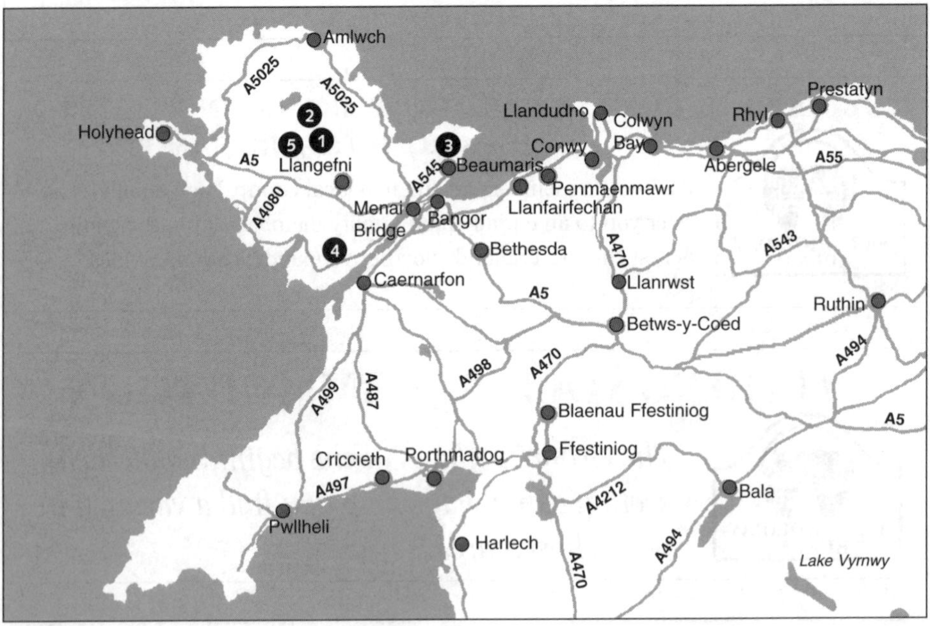

BED AND BREAKFAST

(and evening meal)

Drws-y-Coed, Llanerchymedd, Isle of Anglesey LL71 8AD

Mrs Jane Bown
☎ **01248 470473**
BB **From £20–£22.50**
EM From £12
Sleeps 6
➰ ✄ ⊞ ▪ ◉
❧ ❧ ❧ *De Luxe*

Beautifully appointed farmhouse on 550-acre beef, sheep and arable farm in peaceful wooded countryside with panoramic views of Snowdonia mountain range. Comfortable en suite bedrooms with all facilities. Inviting spacious lounge with log fire. Dining room with separate tables. Excellent food. Games room. Historic farmstead. Lovely private walks. Open all year except Christmas.

Llwydiarth Fawr, Llanerchymedd, Isle of Anglesey LL71 8DF

Mrs Margaret Hughes
☎ **01248 470321/470540**
BB **From £22.50–£25**
EM From £12.50
Sleeps 6
➰ ✄ ⊞ ⇄ ⇦ ♨ ▪ ◉
❧ ❧ ❧ *De Luxe*

Secluded Georgian mansion set in 850 acres of woodland and farmland. Ideal touring base for island's coastline, Snowdonia and North Wales coast. Nearby is Llyn Alaw for trout fishing. Reputation for excellent food using farm and local produce. En suite bedrooms. TV, CH, log fires. Walks and private fishing. Winner of the BBC 'Welsh Farm housewife of the Year' competition. Member of Taste of Wales. Warmest Welcome Award 1993. Closed Christmas.

Plas Cichle, Beaumaris, Isle of Anglesey LL58 8PS

Eirwen Roberts
☎ **01248 810488**
BB **From £20–£25**
Sleeps 6
➰(5) ⊞ ⅄ ▪ ♨ ◉
❧ ❧ *Highly Commended*

This beautiful period farmhouse offers accommodation in spacious double or family rooms, most en suite, all with TV and beverage tray. Close to historic town of Beaumaris, ideal base to enjoy the many local attractions and activities, or just to relax and enjoy the panoramic views. Start your day with a hearty Welsh breakfast, and in the evening, relax in our comfortable guest lounge. Brochure. Open Feb–Nov.

Plas Trefarthen, Brynsiencyn, Isle of Anglesey LL61 6SZ

Marian Roberts
☎ **01248 430379**
BB **From £19–£21**
Sleeps 14
➰ ⊞ ▪ ◉
❧ ❧ *Highly Commended*

Secluded Georgian house in glorious location in 200 acres on the shore of the Menai Strait. Outstanding views of Snowdonia and Caernarfon Castle, 6 miles Menai Bridge. Ideal base for touring Anglesey and Snowdonia, walking, birdwatching and visiting NT properties. Most bedrooms en suite with beverage tray, colour TV. Full size snooker table. Owned and run by Marian, a well-known soprano. Winner of Warmest Welcome Award for 1995. Closed Christmas.

Tre'rddôl Farm, Llanerchymedd, Isle of Anglesey LL71 7AR

Ann Astley
☎ **01248 470278**
Fax **01248 470276**
BB **From £19–£20**
EM From £11
Sleeps 6
➰ ✝ ⅄ ✄ ▪ ◉
❧ ❧ ❧ *Highly Commended*

If you are looking for freedom and relaxation, this family farm can oblige. Its historic 17th century house and country antiques add to the mystery and character of the past. Ornithologists' paradise, totally unspoilt countryside. Spacious, homely en suite bedrooms and log fire in lounge. Children enjoy pony rides and dabble in farm activities. Convenient to Holyhead Irish Ferry. Wales Farmhouse Award. Open Jan–Nov.

SELF-CATERING

(2) Llwydiarth Fawr Farm Cottages, Llanerchymedd, Isle of Anglesey LL71 8DF

Mrs Margaret Hughes
☎ **01248 470321/ 470540**
SC **From £100–£550**
Sleeps 4–9

Superbly furnished and equipped, beautifully positioned in the centre of Anglesey and surrounded by owner's farmland. Snowdonia and the coast within easy driving distance. Nearby is Llyn Alaw, excellent for trout fishing. In winter the cottages are warm and welcoming with log fires and CH. Well equipped kitchens have microwave, tumbledryer, washing machine, dishwasher. A warm Welsh welcome to guests who will enjoy our walks and private fishing. Open all year.

(4) Plas Trefarthen, Brynsiencyn, Isle of Anglesey LL61 6SZ

Marian Roberts
☎ **01248 430379**
SC **From £120–£310**
Sleeps 6

The wing of the Georgian house has large kitchen/diner with all mod cons, comfortable lounge, colour TV and three bedrooms with bath and shower. Large parking area. Located close to the Sea Zoo, Plas Newydd and Foel Open Farm. Ideal base for touring Anglesey and Snowdonia. Closed Christmas.

FARM HOLIDAY BUREAU

Our Internet Address is
http://www.webscape.co.uk/farmaccom/

CONFIRM BOOKINGS

Disappointments can arise from misunderstandings over the telephone. Please write to confirm your booking.

Llŷn Peninsula

Group Contact: *Mrs R. D. Wynne-Finch* ☎ *01758 770209*

With more than 70 miles of coastline, backed by the dramatic mountains of Snowdonia, this is an Area of Outstanding Natural Beauty where the warm waters of the Gulf Stream give a mild climate all year round. The Welsh language and way of life still flourish here and while you struggle with the seemingly impossible Celtic names, you will appreciate the very Welshness of it all.

It is also an area compact enough to travel around and get to know – and one that you will want to come back to time and time again.

No-one comes to this part of Wales without setting foot on mighty Mount Snowdon; and even if you only clamber for a relatively short distance you will be rewarded with views the like of which you will never have seen before. And you could always walk one way and take the famous narrow gauge railway the other!

Right at the foot of the Peninsula lies Bardsey Island – a bird sanctuary, place of pilgrimage and the legendary resting place of 20,000 saints.

Nestling on its own wooded peninsula you will find Portmeirion, the Italianate extravaganza created by the late Sir Clough Williams Ellis, full of delightful surprises in the shape of statues, follies and fake facades.

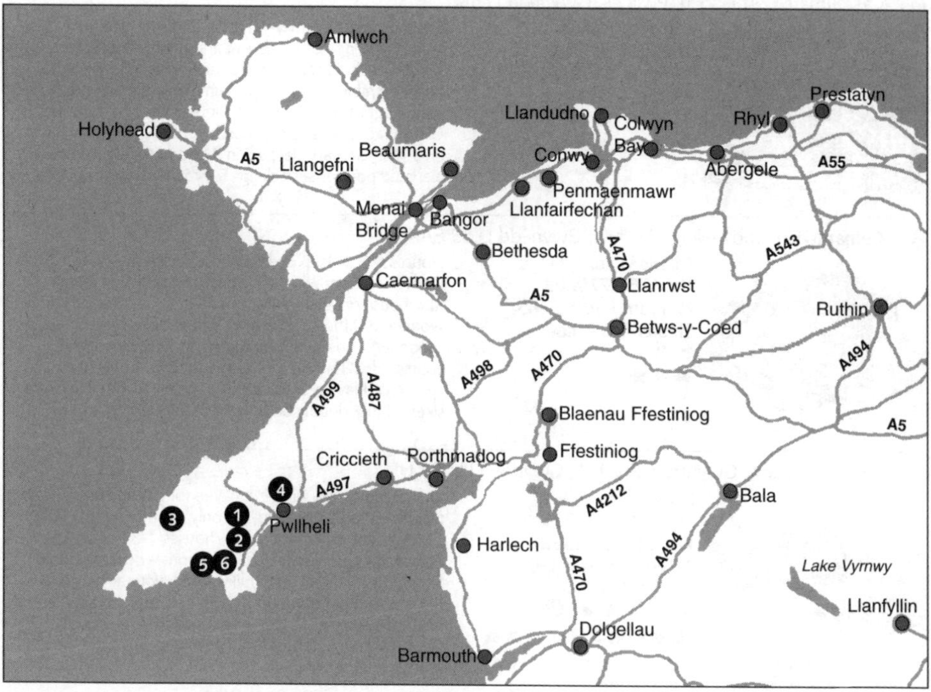

BED AND BREAKFAST

(and evening meal)

(1) Mathan Uchaf Farm, Boduan, Pwllheli, Gwynedd LL53 8TU

Mrs Jean Coker
☎ **01758 720487**
Fax 01758 720020
BB **From £16–£18**
Sleeps 6
🐕 🐈 ✂ ♿ ⚉
☙ *Highly Commended*

A 190-acre dairy farm, situated off the main Pwllheli to Nefyn road. Centrally positioned for northern and southern beaches of peninsula. Guests can participate in farm activities. Large garden provides safe play area. We have 1 dog who plays ball and a Shetland pony. 1 double room, 1 family room with washbasins, 1 twin bedded room. Dining room, sitting room with colour TV. Good food and friendly atmosphere are our aim. Farmhouse Award. Open Mar–Nov.

SELF-CATERING

(2) Castellmarch, Abersoch, Pwllheli, Gwynedd LL53 7UE

Mrs H M Jones
☎ **01758 712242**
SC **From £100–£330**
Sleeps 4/5 (+ cot)
🐕 🐈 ♿ ⚉
🌺🌺🌺 – 🌺🌺🌺🌺

Castellmarch, a family-run beef and sheep farm, 1 mile from the village of Abersoch, and minutes' walk from safe sandy beach. Listed 16th century farmhouse, once the home of fabled March Ap Meirchion – a man with horse's ears. Cegin-Isa (wing of farmhouse) sleeps 4 + cot (gas CH). All rooms have exposed beams, inglenook in living area. The Granary sleeps 5 in 2 bedrooms. A chalet set on elevated position also sleeps 5. Brochure. Open all year.

(3) Cefnamwlch, Tudweiliog, Pwllheli, Gwynedd LL53 8AX

Mrs R Wynne-Finch
☎ **01758 770209**
SC **From £100–£265**
Sleeps 4/6 + cot
🐕 🐈 ⚉
🌺🌺🌺

Houses 1 & 2 sleep 6 in 3 double bedrooms. Cot available. Converted from wing of owner's 17th century manor farmhouse on ancient Welsh estate. Situated in beautiful woodland setting 1 mile from village of Tudweiliog, along rhododendron drive. Easy reach sandy beaches, golf course. Ideal touring centre. Colour TV, tumble dryer and spindryer. Play area. Electric 50p meter. Ty Thimble Cottage sleeps 4 in 2 double bedrooms. Open Easter–end Oct.

(4) Gwynfryn Farm, Gwynfryn, Pwllheli, Gwynedd LL53 5UF

Sian B Ellis
☎ **01758 612536**
Fax 01758 614324
SC **From £94–£490**
Sleeps 2/8
🚶 🐕 🐈 🅿 ♿ ⚉
🌺🌺🌺🌺 – 🌺🌺🌺🌺🌺

Our **organic** dairy farm is a haven for nature lovers, away from the madding crowd, yet only 1½ miles from Pwllheli. Cottages for romantic couples/houses 4–8 persons, all personally supervised, WTB 5 dragons – quality assured. Snowdon 25 miles, sea 2 miles – vary your activity to suit the weather or your mood. Beds made up, storage/central heating. Mini breaks Oct–Mar. Cooked dishes to order. Gold Award Welcome Host. Farmhouse Award. Colour brochure. Open all year.

Rhydolion, Llangian, Abersoch, Pwllheli, Gwynedd LL53 7LR

Catherine Morris
☎/Fax 01758 712342
SC From £105–£380
Sleeps 6–8

Unwind and relax in our 'olde worlde' farmhouse and cottage (disabled facilities) offering all modern comfort. Exposed beams and stone walls, inglenook fireplaces, both 3-bedroomed. Four-poster in farmhouse, attractively furnished – all conjure up a cosy homestead. Surrounded by farm interest yet only ¾ mile from beach. Explore the peninsula on foot or bike. Sandy beaches, ideal sailing and surfing area. Colour brochure. Open Feb–New Year.

Tai Gwyliau Tyndon Holiday Cottages, c/o Penlan, Rhos Isaf, Caernarfon, Gwynedd LL54 7NG

Mrs Elisabeth Evans
☎ 01286 831184
SC From £99–£400
Sleeps 2/8

120 acre sheep farm on the beautiful Llŷn heritage coast. Peaceful and relaxing self-catering units. 1 mile from Llanengan with its country pub and 6th century church. Boating resort of Abersoch only 2 miles away. Beautiful sandy beach of Porthneigwl within 200 yards (with private access). Most cottages have glorious views of the bay. Ideal family holiday. Personal supervision. Free brochure. Short breaks. Open all year.

FOLLOW THE COUNTRY CODE

Leave nothing but footprints,
Take nothing but photographs,
Kill nothing but time!

STAY ON A FARM GIFT TOKENS

FARM HOLIDAY BUREAU

If you have enjoyed your Stay on a Farm, why not treat your friends and relatives to *Stay on a Farm* gift tokens? Available from the Bureau office, telephone 01203 696909, they can be redeemed against accommodation booked on the majority of our farms

---

FOLLOW THE COUNTRY CODE

Leave nothing but footprints,
Take nothing but photographs,
Kill nothing but time!

Snowdonia

Group Contact: *Mrs Jane Llewelyn Pierce* ☎/Fax 01248 670147

In Snowdonia those interested in history have a wealth of locations to visit, from the early 12th century Welsh fortresses at Dolbadarn and Dolwyddelan to the magnificent castles of Edward 1st at Caernarfon, Beaumaris, Harlech and Conwy. The National Trust's historic houses include Plas Newydd on Anglesey and Penrhyn Castle near Bangor. Segontium Fort at Caernarfon is witness to the four hundred years of Roman occupation and there is an interesting museum nearby.

Take a boat trip along the Menai Strait, a ride on a steam train into the mountains with the Talyllyn or Ffestiniog Railways, alongside Llanberis Lake or even up Mount Snowdon itself. Visit the heart of a Welsh slate cavern, take a trip to the theatre at Bangor or Harlech, or see craftsmen at work – some of the many choices available.

Add to this the Sports Council's excellent centres near Caernarfon and Capel Curig, heated swimming pools at Caernarfon, Bangor and Harlech, golf at one of the many courses with superb sea views, some really excellent restaurants and pubs and walks in the mountains or forests, and often a week is all too short a time to stay with us.

Most of us are Welsh speaking as Snowdonia is the heartland of the Welsh language and we will be very happy to teach you a few Welsh greetings or tell you more about our ancient language.

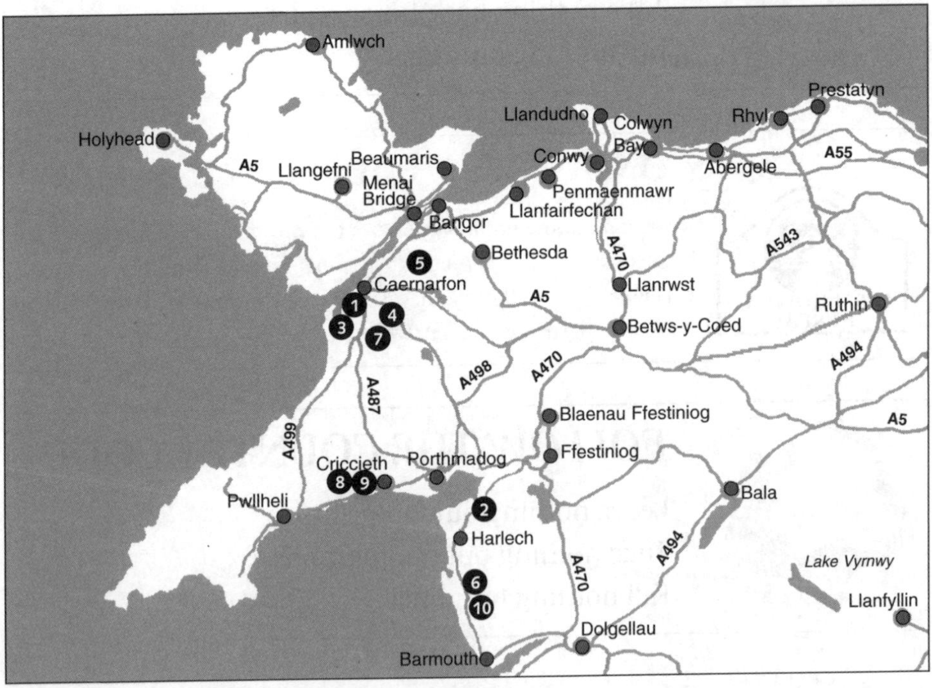

Amlwch

Llandudno · Colwyn · Rhyl · Prestatyn
Holyhead · Bay · Abergele · A55
A5 · Llangefni · Beaumaris · Conwy
Menai · Penmaenmawr
Bridge · Llanfairfechan
Bangor
⑤ Bethesda · A470
① Caernarfon · A5 · Llanrwst
③ ④ · Betws-y-Coed · Ruthin
⑦ · A494
A487 · A498 · A470
A499 · Blaenau Ffestiniog · A5
Criccieth · Porthmadog · Ffestiniog
⑧ ⑨ · Bala
Pwllheli · ② · A494
Harlech · Lake Vyrnwy
⑥ · A470 · Llanfyllin
⑩ · Dolgellau
Barmouth

BED AND BREAKFAST

(and evening meal)

Cae'r Efail, Llanfaglan, Caernarfon, Gwynedd LL54 5RE ①

Mrs Mari Williams
☎ 01286 676226/672824
Fax 01286 676226
BB From £18–£20
EM From £10
Sleeps 4
ど れ 🛋 ❦ ●
❦ ❦ ❦ *De Luxe*

Modernised farmhouse enjoying perfect tranquillity and seclusion with splendid views of Snowdonia and the Menai Strait. Central for Snowdonia, Isle of Anglesey, Llŷn Peninsula and all attractions of North Wales. Caernarfon only 2 miles. Homely atmosphere and warm welcome. Good home cooking. En suite bedrooms with colour TV, hairdryer and tea/coffee facilities. TV/video lounge and separate dining room. Open Easter–Oct.

Gwrach Ynys, Talsarnau, Nr Harlech, Gwynedd LL47 6TS ②

Mrs Deborah Williams
☎ 01766 780742
Fax 01766 781199
BB From £20–£23
EM From £12
Sleeps 15
ど(3) ⊛ ⅄ 🛋 ●
❦ ❦ ❦ *De Luxe*

Relax in the peace and comfort of our secluded Edwardian House. Conveniently located, close to sea and mountains with many tourist attractions nearby. Ideal golfing, rambling, birdwatching area. En suite bedrooms with TV, telephone, beverage facilities. Renowned for superb home cooking using fresh local produce. WTB Farmhouse Award. AA Selected. Open Mar–Oct.

Pengwern, Saron, Llanwnda, Caernarfon, Gwynedd LL54 5UH ③

G & J Lloyd Rowlands
☎/Fax 01286 831500
Mobile 0378 411780
BB From £20–£35
EM From £12.50
Sleeps 6
ど ⅄ 🛋 ♣ ❦ ●
❦ ❦ ❦ *De Luxe*

Charming, spacious farmhouse of character, situated between mountains and sea. Unobstructed views of Snowdonia. Well appointed bedrooms, all with en suite bathrooms. Set in 130 acres of land which runs down to Foryd Bay. Jane has a cookery diploma and provides the excellent meals with farmhouse fresh food, including home-produced beef and lamb. Excellent access. Open Feb–Nov.

Plas Tirion Farm, Llanrug, Caernarfon, Gwynedd LL55 4PY ④

C H Mackinnon
☎/Fax 01286 673190
BB From £20–£25
Sleeps 6
ど 🛋 ●
❦ ❦ *De Luxe*

Peacefully located in 300 acres of lowland pastures, commanding panoramic views of Snowdonia and historic Caernarfon. Ideally situated for touring North Wales. Traditional stone farmhouse, offering guests warm and comfortable accommodation. All en suite bedrooms with beverage facilities and TV. Recommended for wide range of breakfast dishes and packed lunches. Open May–Sept.

Ty Mawr Farm, Llanddeiniolen, Caernarfon, Gwynedd LL55 3AD ⑤

Mrs Jane Llewelyn Pierce
☎/Fax 01248 670147
BB From £18–£25
EM From £12.50
Sleeps 6
ど れ 🛋 ●
❦ ❦ ❦ *Highly Commended*

Charming, warm country farmhouse on 100-acre farm with superb views of Snowdonia mountain range. Ideal for touring North Wales and Anglesey. Caernarfon only 5 miles. All rooms have en suite bathrooms, TV and tea and coffee facilities. Two lounges with wood fires and a separate dining room. Good home cooking. Ample parking area. Open all year.

6   **Ystumgwern, Hall Farm,** Dyffryn Ardudwy, Gwynedd LL44 2DD

Jane E Williams
☎ **01341 247249**
Fax **01341 247171**
[BB] From £20–£22
Sleeps 16
🧍 🐕 🐎 🎿 🏠 🍽 ●
🌳 🌊 *De Luxe*

A warm Welsh welcome awaits you at Ystumgwern where the mountains of Snowdonia slope down to the sea. The traditional 16th century farmhouse has a wealth of antiques and heavy oak timbers creating a luxurious homely atmosphere. Each bedroom is charmingly decorated with many extras including the luxury of a well-equipped kitchen and its own lounge with colour TV and video. Farmhouse Award. Colour brochure sent with pleasure.

Self-Catering

7   **Bryn Beddau,** Bontnewydd, Caernarfon, Gwynedd LL54 7YE

Eleri Carrog
☎ **01286 830117/673795**
Fax **01286 675664**
[SC] From £80–£340
Sleeps 5
🐎 🐕 🎿 🏠 🍽
🏵 🏵 🏵 🏵

Cosy stone–built stable cottage with views of mountains and sea. Excellent centre for walks, touring, lovely beaches and Snowdonia. Secluded setting yet only 3 miles from Caernarfon. Lovely gallery bedroom with graceful arch windows, twin room, cot. Ideal for families or that romantic break. Spacious beamed lounge of great character and many books. Patio, barbecue. "Croeso Cymreig". Open all year.

8   **Chwilog Fawr,** Chwilog, Pwllheli, Gwynedd LL53 6SW

Catherine Jones
☎/Fax **01766 810506**
[SC] From £100–£450
Sleeps 2/6
🐎 🐕 🍴 👤 🐟 🍽 🏠 ●
🏵 🏵 🏵 🏵 – 🏵 🏵 🏵 🏵

Enjoy the comforts of a home from home holiday with panoramic views of the Welsh coastline while sheep and cattle graze peacefully nearby. Walk along the footpath past the fishing lake to the village or down to the beach (3 miles). Choice of accommodation to suit you. Request our colour brochure today. Open Mar–Nov.

9   **Dwyfach Cottages,** Pen-y-Bryn, Chwilog, Pwllheli, Gwynedd LL53 6SX

Mrs Sulwen Edwards
☎ **01766 810208**
Fax **01766 810064**
[SC] From £100–£475
Sleeps 2–8
🐎 🐕 🍴 👤 🏠 🏹 🐟 ●
🏵 🏵 🏵 🏵 🏵

We offer a choice of luxury accommodation for the discerning. Enjoy a memorable holiday in our tastefully restored farmhouse or bungalow. Both are set in their own garden with permanent barbecue and enjoy panoramic views of Cardigan Bay and Snowdonia. Here you will find peace and tranquillity yet be within easy reach of towns, beaches, tourist attractions, fishing and shooting, children's play area. Open all year.

5   **Hafod & Hendre,** c/o Ty Mawr Farm, Llanddeiniolen, Caernarfon, Gwynedd LL55 3AD

Mrs Jane Llewelyn Pierce
☎/Fax **01248 670147**
[SC] From £100–£400
EM From £12.50
Sleeps 3/5
🐎 🐎 🏠 ●
🏵 🏵 🏵 🏵 🏵

Two luxurious, self-catering converted granaries situated in a private courtyard on our working farm. Hafod sleeps 3 and Hendre 5. Camp beds are available for extra children. Both are centrally heated and have wood burning stoves. CH, electricity, towels and full bedding included in price. Caernarfon 5 miles, Snowdon 4 miles. Brochures available. Open all year.

Llys Bennar, Dyffryn Ardudwy, Gwynedd LL44 2RX (10)

Catrin Rutherford
☎/Fax 01341 247316
🅂🄲 From £130–£388
Sleeps 4/7
🐕🐏

✿✿✿✿

Attractive 18th century farm buildings converted into charming cottages, within a courtyard setting. They have retained the original charm of the oak beams, one with inglenook fireplace. All have nightstore heating. Laundry facility available. Ten minutes to village or to sandy beach. One mile from station. In Snowdonia National Park. Many attractions in the area. Open all year.

Ynys, Ystumgwern, Dyffryn Ardudwy, Gwynedd LL44 2DD (6)

Jane & John Williams
☎ 01341 247249
Fax 01341 247171
🅂🄲 From £130–£650
Sleeps 1/8
🐕🐏♿ ❉ ⚜ 🌐

✿✿✿✿✿

A taste of luxury with cosy, relaxed atmosphere. Situated between sea and mountains. 16th century farmhouse and barn conversions furnished and equipped to the highest standards. Kitchen/diner with dishwasher, microwave, oak beams. Lounge has gas, electric or open fire in inglenook fireplace. Laundry room. Barbecue and picnic tables. Ample parking via private drive. Farmhouse Award. Warm welcome to all. Colour brochure available. Open all year.

FARM HOLIDAY BUREAU

FINDING YOUR ACCOMMODATION

The Group contacts at the beginning of each section can always help you find a vacancy in your chosen area.

FARM HOLIDAY BUREAU

THE 1000+ BUREAU MEMBERS OFFER A UNIQUE LINK TO CUSTOMERS ACROSS THE UK

All Bureau members belong to a local Group. Each member can refer you to an equally high quality member within the Group... or across the UK: England, Northern Ireland, Scotland, Wales.

Heart of Snowdonia

Group Contacts: *Paula Williams* ☎/*Fax 01766 590281*
Olwen Davies ☎/*Fax 01678 520456*

A choice of quality, traditional Welsh farmhouses, ALL located in the Snowdonia National Park, an ideal base for exploring the whole of North Wales. Most have en suite bedrooms, tea trays, colour TVs, CH and provide full farmhouse breakfasts with optional evening meals.

There are numerous attractions within this area including the spectacular Ffestiniog Railway, Bala Lake Railway and the Welsh Highland Railway at Porthmadog. Slate is the theme at Blaenau Ffestiniog, where the Llechwedd Slate Caverns and Gloddfa Ganol Mountain Centre welcome thousands of visitors journeying into Victorian working conditions. Stroll through the unique Italianate village of Portmeirion. Try dry slope skiing at Trawsfynydd or pony trekking nearby. Bala Lake is renowned for its watersports, sailing and windsurfing, close to the white water canoe centre. Keen fishermen can fish at Bala Lake, Llyn Celyn and Trawsfynydd. Bodnant Garden in the Conwy valley is world acclaimed. There are many National Trust properties to visit as well as a great choice of historic and Roman ruins.

All this plus the mountains, lakes, waterfalls and fine beaches await you. Hear our language, listen to local choirs practising, above all relax, find peace and tranquillity in the resplendent beauty that surrounds you.

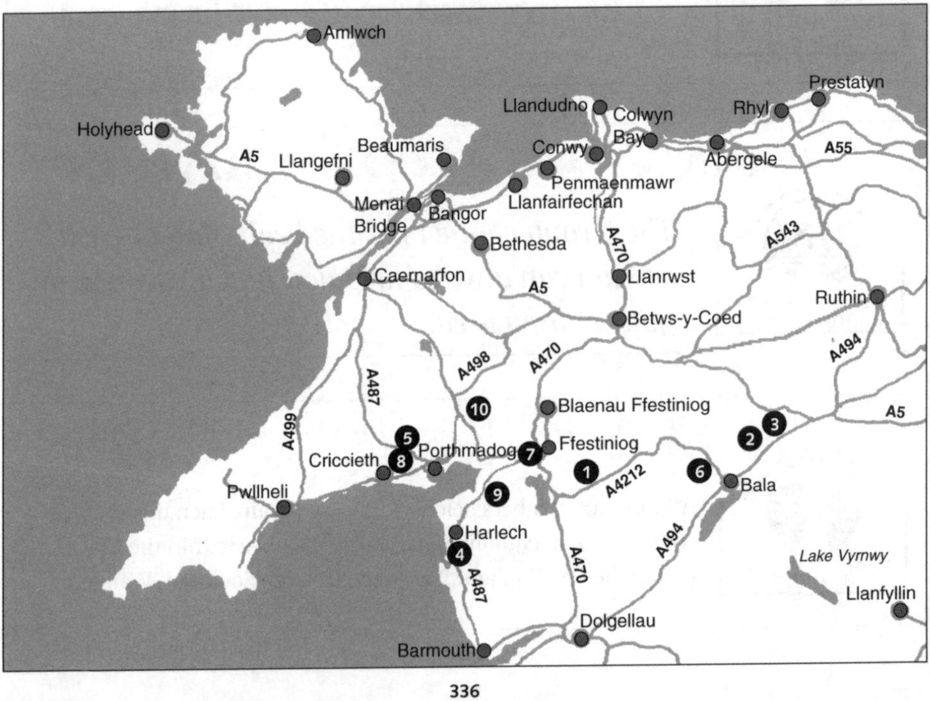

BED AND BREAKFAST
(and evening meal)

Bryn Celynog Farm, Cwm Prysor, Trawsfynydd, Gwynedd LL41 4TR ①

Mrs G E Hughes
☎/**Fax 01766 540378**
From £17.50–£19
EM From £11
Sleeps 6
☼ ♞ ☞ ☆ ▯ ◉
Highly Commended

Relax in peaceful setting with splendid views of Cwmprysor Valley, on 700-acre working beef and sheep farm 3 miles from Trawsfynydd village. Spacious twin, double and family bedrooms, one en suite, all with washbasins, beverage trays. Guests' lounge with colour TV, log fire. Reputation for excellent food and friendliness. Welsh speaking. WTB Farmhouse Award. Open all year except Christmas.

Cwm Hwylfod, Cefn-Ddwysarn, Bala, Gwynedd LL23 7LN ②

Joan Best
☎/**Fax 01678 530310**
From £16–£18
EM From £10
Sleeps 6
☼ ☆ ☞ ▯ ♘ ◉
Highly Commended

Set in hills near Bala, our 400-year-old farmhouse is warm and welcoming. The views are spectacular. Animals abound and everyone, especially children, can take part in farm activities. Bedrooms have washbasins and tea making facilities. The guest lounge has TV, books and games. Full central heating. For our home-cooked evening meals we use the best of local produce. All diets catered for. Taste of Wales. Open all year except Christmas Day.

Erw Feurig Farm, Cefn-Ddwysarn, Bala, Gwynedd LL23 7LL ③

Glenys Jones
☎ **01678 530262**
From £15–£18
Sleeps 9
☼ ▯ ☞ ◉
Highly Commended

Facing the Berwyn Mountains, Erw Feurig is a guesthouse set on the 200-acre family farm, 3½ miles from Bala. The old farm cottage has been extended to provide modern, comfortable accommodation in family, double and twin rooms, some en suite. All bedrooms have heating and tea/coffee. Separate guests' dining room and lounge. Good home cooking using local produce. Coarse fishing on the farm. Open all year except Christmas.

Hendy Farm, Llanbedr, Gwynedd LL45 2LT ④

Eirian Williams
☎/**Fax 01341 241263**
From £17.50
EM From £10
Sleeps 6
☼(4) ♞ ✂ ▯ ♙ ♿ ☆ ♘
Highly Commended

Hendy Farm is a 200-acre mixed working farm run by Welsh speaking family, located overlooking Cardigan Bay in Snowdonia. Convenient for walking, fishing, swimming, riding, golfing, etc. Good country food provided using fresh produce whenever possible. Three en suite bedrooms, all with tea/coffee facilities. A warm welcome awaits you. Open all year.

Llwyn Mafon Isaf, Criccieth, Gwynedd LL52 0RE ⑤

Mrs Buddug Anwyl Jones
☎ **01766 530618**
From £16–£18
Sleeps 6
☼ ♞ ♙ ♿ ▯ ◉
Highly Commended

Traditional 17th century farmhouse, sympathetically modernised and offering superb views of Cardigan Bay and the Snowdonia mountain range. Two double en suite bedrooms, a spacious single bedroom and 1 twin bedroom, both with private bathroom. Relax in the comfortable beamed lounge with colour TV and enjoy a hearty breakfast on separate tables in the dining room. Please ring for directions.

6 Rhydydefaid Farm, Frongoch, Bala, Gwynedd LL23 7NT

Olwen Davies
☎/Fax 01678 520456
BB £18
Sleeps 6
🐕 🐎 ✂ 🍴 🚲 ☕
👑 👑 *Highly Commended*

A true Welsh welcome awaits you at our traditional Welsh stone farmhouse. 3 miles from Bala in secluded position. 100-acre working farm. Oak beamed lounge with inglenook fireplace. Three comfortable bedrooms with CH, 1 with exposed beams and trusses, 2 en suite. All with tea/coffee-making facilities. Ideal for touring Snowdonia. Open all year except Christmas & New Year.

7 Tyddyn Du Farm, (b), Gellilydan, Ffestiniog, nr Porthmadog, Gwynedd LL41 4RB

Paula Williams
☎/Fax 01766 590281
BB From £17.50–£22.50
EM £11
Sleeps 8
🐕 🐎 ✂ 🍴 ☕ 💿
👑 👑 👑 *Highly Commended*

Located amidst spectacular scenery, guests are very welcome to enjoy the old world charm of our 400yr old farmhouse (WTB Farmhouse Award). Excellent central location. Most bedrooms en suite, superb private cottage and stable suites, all have TV and beverage facilities. CH with log fires. Delicious candle light dinners. Organic working farm with pony, ducks and bottle fed lambs. Weekly dinner B&B from £170– £205. Stamp please for brochure. Open all year.

8 Tyddyn Iolyn, Pentrefelin, Nr Criccieth, Gwynedd LL52 0RB

Maurice & Charlotte Lowe
☎/Fax 01766 522509
BB From £16–£21
EM From £11
Sleeps 12
🐕 🐎 ✂ 🍴 ☕ 💿
👑 👑 *Highly Commended*

Lovingly restored, secluded 16th century oak-beamed farmhouse, set in idyllic farmland. Breathtaking views of Snowdonia and coastline. Perfect base for exploring Portmeirion, Snowdonia, Llŷn Peninsula. Three en suites (family and 4-poster), twin with basin, all with beverage trays. Traditional cooking/vegetarian, candlelit dinners. Abundance of books/local information. Cats, chickens, pony. Farm Tourism Award. Open all year except Christmas.

SELF-CATERING

9 Caerwych Farmhouse, Llandecwyn, Near Harlech, Gwynedd LL47 6YT

Richard Williams-Ellis
☎ 01766 770913/771270
SC From £150–£400
Sleeps 9/10
🐕 🐎 ☕ ✄
👑 👑 👑

Secluded and set in marvellous scenic countryside with stupendous views to the sea. We are a typically traditional sheep farm but also breed horses and are replanting ancient woodlands. The stone farmhouse is old, large and handsome. Central heating throughout. Five bedrooms. Perfection for walkers. Accompanied trail riding in the mountains. Open all year.

10 Garth-y-Foel, Croesor, Penrhyndeudraeth, Gwynedd LL48 6SR

Richard Williams-Ellis
☎ 01766 770913
SC From £150–£350
Sleeps 7
🐕 🐎 ☕ ✄
Applied

Absolute seclusion! And set in its own gentle, park-like, miniature valley with views to the sea in this otherwise wild mountain landscape – an unexpected, special, compelling place. Own wooded 90 acres include river with falls, pools and firewood for free. Oil, Aga and CH. 3/4 bedrooms (plus there's a large bell tent). Be forewarned about the rough, narrow, gated and bridged access track.

Vale of Clwyd

Group Contact: *Mrs Elsie Jones* ☎ *01824 703142*

Clwyd – its northern boundary strung with seaside resorts – comes up with some surprising contrasts, from the sandcastle and holiday atmosphere of the coast to the fortresses left behind from mediaeval times. It is a beautiful county with a necklace of seaside towns and unspoilt inland scenery.

St Asaph, at the head of the Vale of Clwyd, might be just a large village, but it is also a cathedral city. The cathedral may be the smallest in the country but it is also one of the oldest in Wales, dating back to the 15th century. It houses some rare treasures like the original copy of William Morgan's Welsh translation of the Bible.

Further into the county lies Ruthin. Boasting a wealth of history including a castle which provides a very popular mediaeval banquet. Also there is the 'Maen Huail' stone where King Arthur is said to have beheaded his rival in love. The craft centre is well worth a visit, as are the ones at Afonwen and Llanasa. Crafts of a different nature are to be found in Llangollen where horse-drawn barges glide along the Shropshire Union Canal. Llangollen also hosts the International Musical Eisteddfod in early July.

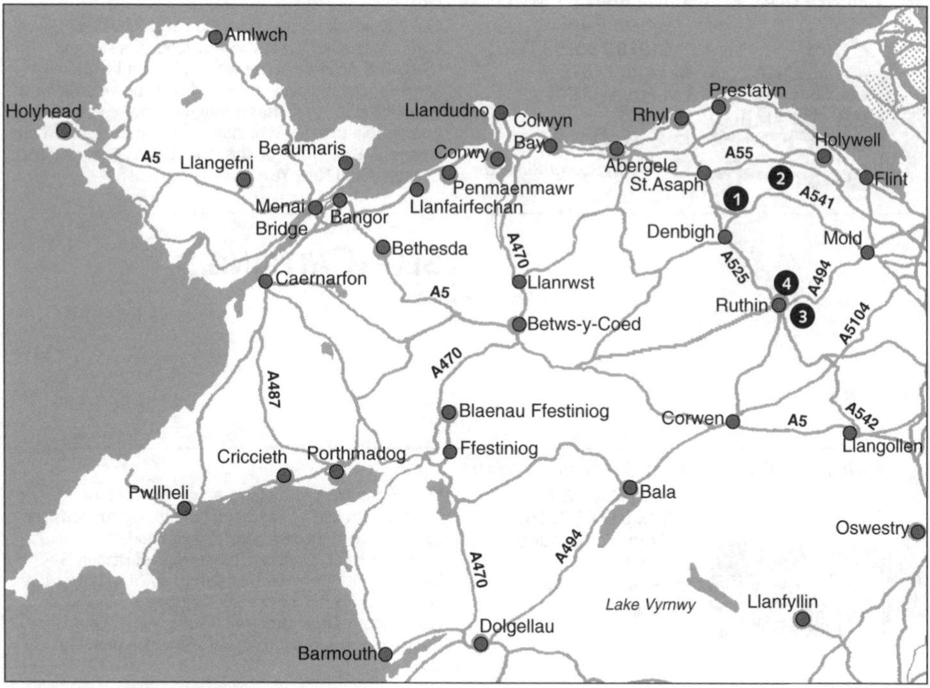

BED AND BREAKFAST
(and evening meal)

(1) Bach-y-Graig, Tremeirchion, St Asaph LL17 0UH

Anwen Roberts
☎/Fax 01745 730627
BB From £20
EM From £11
Sleeps 6

❄ 🐎 ♿ ☕ ☂ ●
🐛🐛🐛 *Highly Commended*

A 16th century listed farmhouse nestling at the foot of the Clwydian Range with beautiful views of the surrounding countryside. Highest standard of traditional furnishings and decor, en suite, TVs, tea/coffee-making facilities in bedrooms, full CH, beamed inglenook fireplace with log fires. Central for North Wales, Chester, coast 9 miles. Games room. 40 acre woodland trail. WTB Farmhouse Award. AA selected award. RAC acclaimed. Closed Christmas/New Year.

(2) Fron-Haul, Bodfari, Denbigh, Denbighshire LL16 4DY

Gwladys M Edwards
☎/Fax 01745 710301
BB From £17.50–£19
EM From £8.50
Sleeps 6

🐑 🐎 ❄ ☂ ♿ ●
🐛🐛 *Highly Commended*

Discover an oasis of calm and taste. Fron-Haul dominates the high ground above the Wheeler Valley with superb views of the Vale of Clwyd and Snowdonia. Easily accessible from the A55 expressway, just a short distance from Chester and the North Wales coast. The farm supplies the freshest, best quality vegetables, Welsh lamb, etc for the varied farmhouse menu. Truly a Taste of Wales. Open all year.

(3) Llainwen Ucha, Pentrecelyn, Ruthin, Clwyd LL15 2HL

Elizabeth Parry
☎ 01978 790253
BB From £15–£16
EM From £7.50
Sleeps 5

🐎 ❄ ♿ ●
☐ *Highly Commended*

Our 130 acre farm overlooks the beautiful Vale of Clwyd. Centrally situated to coast, Snowdonia, Chester and Llangollen. Modern house with 2 pleasant bedrooms to accommodate 5 persons. CH and good home cooking, a warm welcome to visitors throughout the year. Take A525 from Ruthin towards Wrexham; after 4 miles turn left after college, we are a mile up this road. Open all year except Christmas and New Year.

SELF-CATERING

(1) Bach-y-Graig, Tremeirchion, St Asaph LL17 0UH

Anwen Roberts
☎/Fax 01745 730627
SC From £110–£340
Sleeps 6 + cot

🐎 ❄ ♿ ☕ ☂ ●
🌼🌼🌼🌼🌼

Stay on a working dairy farm in this 16th century farmhouse, retaining the charm but offering comforts and convenience of modern living in high standard accommodation. Dark oak, fully equipped kitchen. 3 bedrooms, 1 four-poster bed. Bathroom with shower/bath. Downstairs toilet, CTV heating. Log fires. Linen provided. Games room, large garden with swings/slide. Central for Chester, Snowdonia and coastal resorts. No pets. Open all year.

Tyddyn Isaf, Rhewl, Ruthin, Clwyd LL15 1UH

④

Elsie Jones
☎ **01824 703142/703367**
[SC] **From £90–£240**
Sleeps 4/6 + cot

Stay in self-contained part of farmhouse or recently converted granary in picturesque Vale of Clwyd. Both fully equipped to high standard. Farmhouse has kitchen lounge/diner, 2 bedrooms sleeping 4/6, bathroom, separate toilet. Granary has 1 bedroom with vanity unit, sofa bed in lounge, sleeps 2/4, shower room. 3 miles from Ruthin and within easy reach of Chester, the coast, Snowdonia. Bedlinen provided. No pets. Open all year.

LET THE TELEPHONE RING!
Some farmhouses are big places. Let the telephone ring
long enough to give the owner time to answer it.

STAY ON A FARM GIFT TOKENS

If you have enjoyed your Stay on a Farm, why not treat your friends and relatives to *Stay on a Farm* gift tokens? Available from the Bureau office, telephone 01203 696909, they can be redeemed against accommodation booked on the majority of our farms

---

Our Internet Address is
http://www.webscape.co.uk/farmaccom/

Croeso Cader Idris

Group Contact: *Mrs Deilwen Breese* ☎ *01654 791235*

A true Welsh welcome 'croeso' is offered by the farming families around Cader Idris, one of the highest peaks in Wales; from the farms you can explore the coast and the countryside of this lovely area of Wales.

A vast area of green valleys and mountains criss-crossed by long distance footpaths, old drovers' lanes and mountain paths which provide some of the finest hill walking country in Britain. For the explorer and adventurer, fishing, golfing, riding, pony trekking, climbing, canoeing and a mountain bike safari ensure a wealth of activity.

Dolgellau, beneath the majestic peak of Cader Idris, and Fairbourne, with its beautiful beach, combined with a visit to a real gold mine at Ganllwyd is a day out to remember. The working demonstrations of wind, water and solar power at the National Centre for Alternative Technology near Machynlleth. At Machynlleth experience the mysterious and magical world of the Celts, a unique attraction telling the story of the Celtic people.

An exciting area of contrasts, from the golden beaches of the coast to the high mountains of the Snowdonia National Park, there is something for everyone, from craft workshops to forest visitor centres, towering castles to deep slate caverns.

The Welsh language is heard frequently, the farmers of Cader Idris have roots deep in the area. A warm welcome is extended to visitors to share the language, history, culture and hospitality of one of the loveliest areas of Wales.

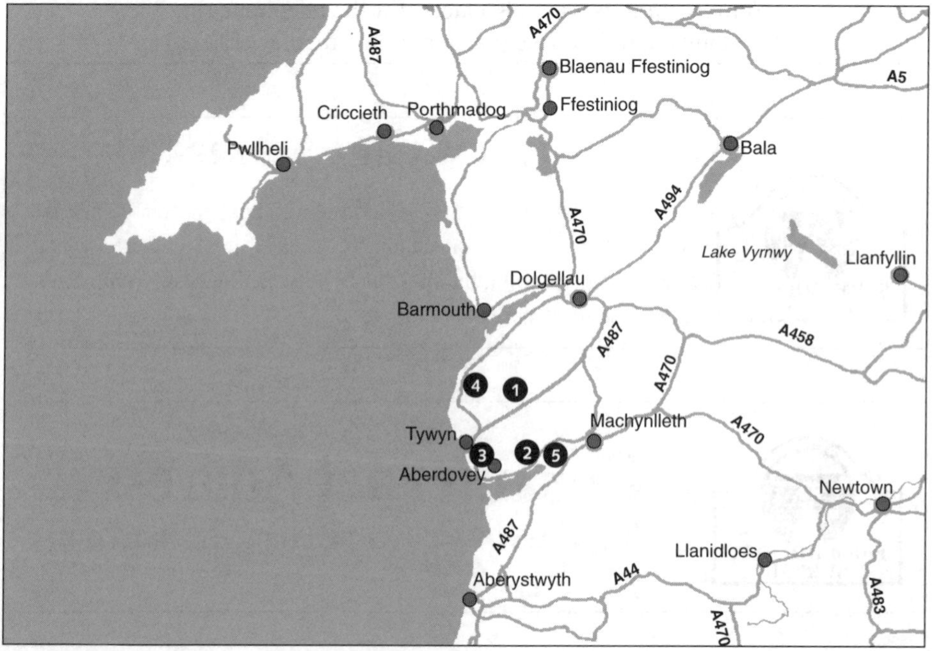

BED AND BREAKFAST

(and evening meal)

Eisteddfa, Bryncrug, Tywyn, Gwynedd LL36 9UP ①

Gweniona Pugh
☎ 01654 782228
🆒 From £15–£19
EM From £10.50
Sleeps 6

□ *Commended*

A newly-built bungalow situated in the picturesque Dolgoch Valley next to Tarycoed Ucha farmhouse overlooking the Talyllyn gauge railway which runs through our land. En suite bedrooms with tea/coffee, TV (one room suitable for disabled). Evening meal optional. Warm welcome. Log fires when cold and wet. Open Feb–Nov.

Gogarth Hall Farm, Pennal, Machynlleth, Powys SY20 9LB ②

E D Breese
☎/Fax 01654 791235
🆒 From £16–£19
EM From £8
Sleeps 6

😊😊😊 *Highly Commended*

It's a pleasure to welcome guests for a quiet, relaxing stay. Feel the warmth and quality of a Welsh welcome in traditional style on our farm in magnificent setting overlooking the Dovey estuary opening to Cardigan Bay. Aberdovey beach 4 miles. En suite facilities, guests' sitting and dining rooms. See the farm animals and wildlife (kites, barn owls, etc). Farmhouse Award. Brochure. Open all year.

Tyddyn Rhys Farm, Aberdovey, Gwynedd LL35 0PG ③

Mrs Mair Jones
☎ 01654 767533
🆒 £16–£18
Sleeps 5
😊(8) ✂ 🐎 🎋 🌐
😊😊 *Highly Commended*

A warm Welsh welcome awaits you at Tyddyn Rhys with its fantastic panoramic view of the Dovey Estuary and Cardigan Bay. Only ½ mile from the centre of Aberdovey with its beautiful sandy beaches. Full central heating with colour TV, tea/coffee-making facilities in bedrooms. One en suite, one double, one single. Also static caravan. Very nice walks in the area. Open Feb–Nov.

SELF-CATERING

Carn y Gadell Uchaf, c/o Henblas, Llwyngwril, Gwynedd LL37 2QA ④

Mrs Swancott Pugh
☎/Fax 01341 250350
🆒 From £144–£485
Sleeps 6

🌺 🌺 🌺 🌺 🌺

An historic 16th century farmhouse situated 1 mile from A493, a perfect retreat with panoramic views of Cardigan Bay. Stone spiral staircase, inglenook fireplace with log fire, 3 bedrooms, 2 bathrooms, colour TV, video, dishwasher, washing machine, fridge/freezer, microwave, games room, drying room. Excellent accommodation, ideal for exploring Snowdonia National Park. Welsh speaking family. No extra charges. Brochure. Open all year.

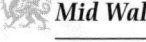
5 **Penmaenbach Farm Cottages,** Cwrt, Pennal, Machynlleth, Powys SY20 9LD

Mrs Shana Rees
☎/Fax 01654 791616
SC From £140–£400
Sleep 4/7

Come and stay in our newly converted stable or in our delightful 18th century keeper's cottage. Both provide an interesting blend of 'olde worlde' charm and every modern comfort. Ideally located with Aberdovey beach, Talyllyn Railway, Celtica, Centre for Alternative Technology and lots more all within 8 miles. Children are welcome to see the farm animals and feed the hens. Welsh speaking family. Brochure. Open all year.

CONFIRM BOOKINGS

Disappointments can arise from misunderstandings over the telephone. Please write to confirm your booking.

FINDING YOUR ACCOMMODATION

The Group contacts at the beginning of each section can always help you find a vacancy in your chosen area.

Please mention **Stay on a Farm** when booking

Montgomeryshire – Heart of Wales

Group Contact: *Mrs Gwyneth Williams* ☎ *01686 430285*

You'll find a warm welcome in the Heart of Wales!

By sharing our homes with you, we're upholding a centuries old Montgomeryshire tradition of hospitality – personal without being intrusive, friendly without being familiar, and above all genuine, with good old fashioned value-for-money and memories you can take home and treasure. That's what makes a Heart of Wales holiday special.

Whether it's angling for trout, riding a pony or a mountain bike, boarding the Great Little Trains of Wales, or searching the wide blue sky for the Red Kite, exploring the ancient castles or just bargain-hunting in the picturesque market towns of this historic region, you'll find the cosy farmhouses of the Heart of Wales combine the comforts of home with the perfect touring bases.

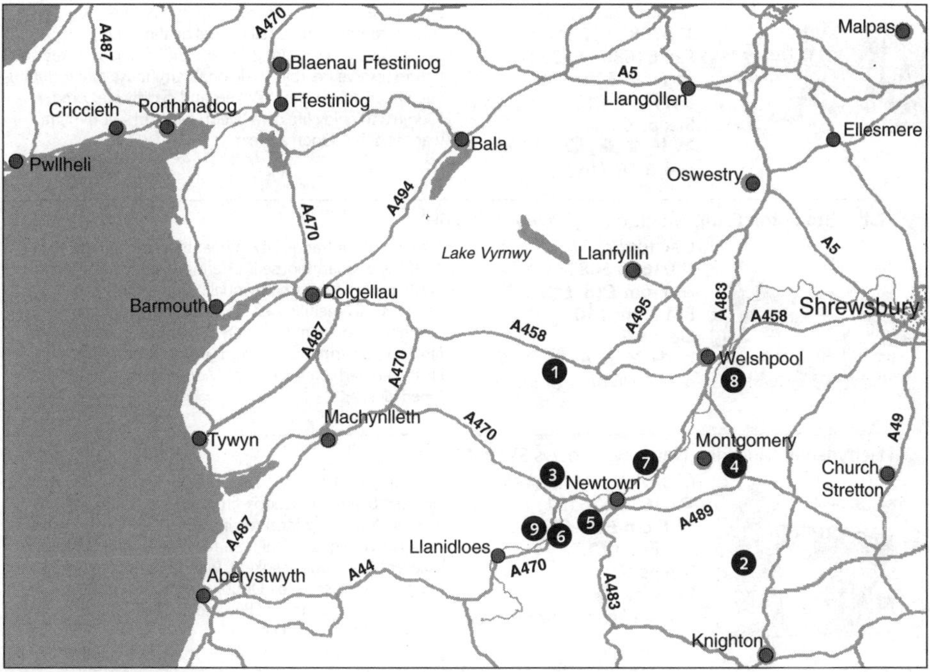

BED AND BREAKFAST

(and evening meal)

---

1 Cwmllwynog, Llanfair Caereinion,Welshpool, Powys SY21 0HF

Joyce Cornes
☎ 01938 810791
▣ From £18
EM From £10
Sleeps 4
♿ ⛄
♨♨ *Highly Commended*

Built in the early 17th century Cwmllwynog is a traditional long farmhouse of character on a working dairy farm. We have a spacious garden with a stream at the bottom and a lot of unusual plants. All bedrooms have colour TV and drink making facilities. Double room en suite, twin with hot and cold and private bathroom. Delicious home-cooked meals cooked. Just for you! We can help you with routes. Open Mar–Nov.

---

2 The Drewin Farm, Churchstoke, Montgomery, Powys SY15 6TW

Mrs Ceinwen Richards
☎ 01588 620325
▣ From £17–£19
EM From £10
Sleeps 6
♿ ⛄ ✂ ♟ ♨ ●
♨♨ *Highly Commended*

Relax in our friendly family run 17th century farmhouse with panoramic views. Bedrooms have TV, hairdryer and drinks facilities (en suite available). Games room with snooker table, dining room with inglenook, separate lounge, full CH. Good home cooking, vegetarian by request. Offa's Dyke footpath runs through our mixed farm. Featured on BBC Travel Show 1993. Warm Welsh welcome. AA Selected. WTB Farmhouse Award. Kettle always on the boil! Open Mar–Oct.

---

3 Dyffryn Farmhouse, Aberhafesp, Newtown, Powys SY16 3JD

Dave & Sue Jones
☎ 01686 688817
Fax 01686 688324
▣ From £22–£24
EM From £12
Sleeps 6
♿ ✂ ♟ ♨ ●
♨♨ *De Luxe*

Set on the banks of a stream, Dyffryn has luxurious, en suite accommodation, full central heating and pretty decor. Lovely walks along stream and in woods, lakes and nature reserve nearby. Traditional farmhouse fare including vegetarian specialities. Walkers and cyclists welcome. 'Come and enjoy life on a Welsh hill farm – you might want to stay!' Open all year.

---

4 Little Brompton Farm, Montgomery, Powys SY15 6HY

Gaynor Bright
☎ 01686 668371
▣ From £18–£19
EM From £10
Sleeps 6
♿ ⛄ ✂ ⚲ ⛽ ♨ ♟ ●
♨♨ *Highly Commended*

A true oasis of tranquillity in beautiful scenery and this 17th C stone farmhouse is offering friendly hospitality. Pretty rooms enhanced by quality furnishings and antiques, all amenities, en suites available. Traditional farmhouse cooking. Offa's Dyke footpath runs through farm. WTB Farmhouse Award. AA selected. Welcome Host. Situated 2 miles east of Montgomery on B4385. Open all year.

---

5 Llettyderyn, Mochdre, Newtown, Powys SY16 4JY

Mrs Margaret Jandrell
☎ 01686 626131
▣ From £18–£23
EM From £12
Sleeps 6
♿ ⛄ ♨ ●
♨♨ *Highly Commended*

Llettyderyn – a restored 18th century farmhouse with exposed beams, inglenook fireplace and traditional parlour. A working farm rearing sheep and beef. 2 miles from Newtown; an ideal base for touring Mid-Wales. Excellent farmhouse cooking, with home-made bread. Vegetarians catered for. Double and twin-bedded rooms en suite, tea-making facilities and TV. Full central heating. Ample parking. Open all year.

Lower Gwerneirin Farm, Llandinam, Powys SY17 5DD ⑥

Mrs A Brown
☎ **01686 688286**
🅱🅱 **From £17–£20**
EM From £10
Sleeps 6
🛏 🐾 ✂ 🛁 🎎 🐕 🌐
🌺🌺🌺 *Highly Commended*

Beautifully situated in the Severn Valley, the farmhouse is a spacious Victorian dwelling offering comfortable accommodation. All rooms have CH, drinks facilities and colour TV. One double and 1 twin en suite, 1 double with own bathroom. Guests lounge with log fire. Fishing in own trout pool. We have a wealth of wildlife. Ideally located for exploring Mid Wales. Large garden with beautiful views. Superb home cooking. Open all year.

Lower Gwestydd, Llanllwchaiarn, Newtown, Powys SY16 3AY ⑦

Iris Jarman
☎ **01686 626718**
🅱🅱 **From £18–£20**
EM From £10
Sleeps 4
🛏 🛁 🎎 🌐
🌺🌺 *Highly Commended*

Lower Gwestydd is a listed half-timbered farmhouse set on a quiet hillside 2 miles north of Newtown just off the B4568 road. Guests have own lounge and dining room. All rooms centrally heated, 2 bedrooms en suite, all have beverage trays. WTB Farmhouse Award, hygiene certificate, Hostess Award. Finalist in the Best British Breakfast 1991 competition. Large garden with beautiful views, own produce. Open all year.

Moat Farm, Welshpool, Powys SY21 8SE ⑧

Gwyneth Jones
☎ **01938 553179**
🅱🅱 **From £19–£21**
EM From £11
Sleeps 6
🛏 🎎 ✂ 🛁 🌐
🌺🌺 *Highly Commended*

Moat Farm is a 260-acre dairy farm set in the beautiful Severn Valley. The 17th century farmhouse offers warm and comfortable accommodation with good home cooking served in a fine timbered dining room, traditionally furnished with Welsh dresser. All rooms en suite with tea/ coffee facilities and colour TV. Quiet lounge, pool table and spacious garden. Good touring centre. Near Powis Castle. Golf, riding and fishing nearby. Open Mar–Nov.

SELF-CATERING

Red House, Trefeglwys, Nr Caersws, Powys SY17 5PN ⑨

Gwyneth Williams
☎ **01686 430285**
🆂🅲 **From £150–£270**
Sleeps 5 + cot
🛏 ✂ 🛁 🎎 🌐
🌺🌺🌺🌺

A highly furnished, self–contained part of the farmhouse, situated on a mixed working family farm. Panoramic views, unspoilt scenery and the tranquillity of the Trannon Valley. Ideal base for touring Mid Wales. Llanidloes 6 miles. Guests' comfort is the priority. Log fire, oak beams, garden furniture, ample parking and wildlife. Open all year.

NO ANSWER?
Farmers are mostly out and about during the day.
Try to telephone before 9.30am or after 4pm.

Radnor

Group Contact: *Mrs Gill Morgan* ☎ *01547 550219*

Mid Wales is an area of outstanding natural beauty; with rugged mountain scenery, lakes, gentle hills and beautiful valleys.

It is an area abounding in wildlife and natural history, providing a habitat for rare birds and flowers. It is still possible to see the Red Kite in its last stronghold in Wales.

This breathtaking scenery is perfect for walkers; from gentle rambles to exploring the long distance footpaths of Glyndwr's Way and the Upper Wye Valley; for the more experienced and adventurous, the remote areas of the vast Elan Valley watershed.

The area is steeped in history and includes Roman encampments, castles, caves, old mine workings, churches and monuments. It also offers practically every sport or pastime that requires an outdoor or country environment. This is a place to come to relax, to enjoy the peace, tranquillity and solitude of George Borrow's 'Wild Wales' and the place to recharge your batteries.

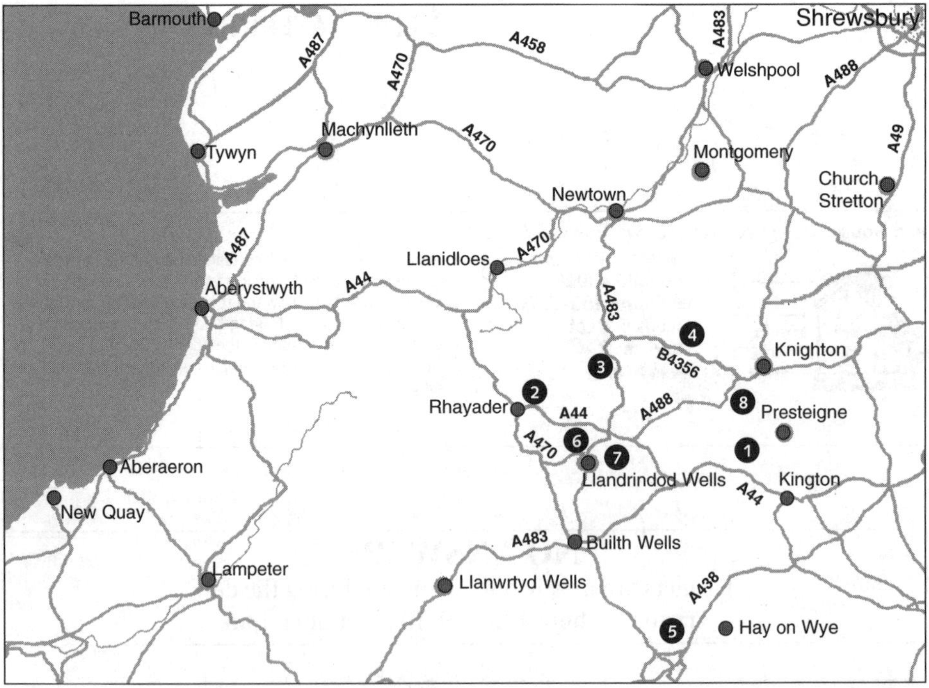

BED AND BREAKFAST

(and evening meal)

Bache Farm, New Radnor, Presteigne, Powys LD8 2TG   ①

May Hardwick
☎ **01544 350680**
🛏 **From £16–£18.50**
EM From £9.50
Sleeps 6
🛇 🛏 👝 🔥 ⚫
💐💐 *Highly Commended*

Situated near to the village of New Radnor – gateway to the heart of Wales. 'Bache', a family-run mixed farm with stone built farmhouse with exposed beams and log fires, offers an ideal base for walking/touring Mid Wales and the borders. Special diets catered for. Open all year except Christmas.

Beili Neuadd, Rhayader, Powys LD6 5NS   ②

Mrs Ann Edwards
☎ **01597 810211**
🛏 **From £19–£20**
EM From £9.50
Sleeps 6
🛇(8) 🛏 Å 👝 🔥 ⚫
💐💐 *Highly Commended*

An attractive 16th century stone-built farmhouse set amidst beautiful countryside in a quiet, secluded position approx. 2 miles from small market town of Rhayader. Guests are assured of every comfort with CH, log fires and well appointed accommodation in single, double and twin bedded rooms, all with private facilities. WTB Farmhouse Award winner. We look forward to welcoming you to this lovely part of Wales.

Bwlch Farm, Llananno, Llandrindod Wells, Powys LD1 6TT   ③

Dorothy Taylor
☎/Fax **01597 840366**
🛏 **From £18.50–£21**
EM From £10.50
Sleeps 6
🛇 🛏 🔥 ⚫
💐💐💐 *Highly Commended*

Come to the Bwlch and spend a peaceful holiday in our beautiful 16th century farmhouse. Go walking, birdwatching or touring or just laze and admire the magnificent views. You will be made welcome. We're ½ mile from A483 and 12 miles north of Llandrindod Wells. Open Easter–Oct.

Cefnsuran Farm, Llangunllo, Knighton, Powys LD5 1SL   ④

Gill & Gordon Morgan
☎/Fax **01547 550219**
🛏 **From £20–£25**
EM From £10.50
Sleeps 8
🛇(9) 👝 🔥 ⚫
💐💐 *Highly Commended*

Cefnsuran is a 16th century farmhouse set in isolated valley with large gardens and extremely picturesque countryside. 5 mins from A483. Recently refurbished, it retains its farmhouse feel with woodburning inglenook fireplaces and exposed beams. High standard of traditional cooking using fresh local produce whenever possible. Vegetarian and special diets. Open all year.

Ffordd-Fawr Farmhouse, Fforddfawr, Hay-on-Wye, Glasbury via Hereford HR3 5PT   ⑤

Mrs Barbara Eckley
☎/Fax **01497 847332**
🛏 **From £18–£20**
Sleeps 6
🛇(5) 🛏 🔥 ⚫
💐💐💐 *Highly Commended*

An attractive late 17th century farmhouse set in the beautiful Wye Valley, 3 miles from the bustling unspoilt border town of Hay-on-Wye where you will find the largest second-hand bookshops in the world. We offer superb accommodation decorated with flair. Peaceful, comfortable en suite bedrooms, all with colour TV and beverage tray. WTB Farmhouse Award winner. Open all year.

6   **Highbury Farm,** Llanyre, Llandrindod Wells, Powys LD1 6EA

Shirley Evans
☎/Fax 01597 822716
[BB] From £16–£19
EM From £9
Sleeps 6
🐕 ♻ ■ ⬤
👄👄 *Highly Commended*

Come and visit our comfortable Victorian farmhouse at our smallholding one mile from the spa town of Llandrindod Wells. Three tastefully decorated bedrooms with hospitality trays. TV lounge, separate dining room. WTB Farmhouse Award. Brochure available. Ideally situated for the Elan Valley dams and for touring the heart of Wales. Open Mar–Nov.

---

7   **Neuadd Farm,** Penybont, Llandrindod Wells, Powys LD1 5SW

Peter & Jackie Longley
☎/Fax 01597 822571
[BB] From £19.50
EM From £10
Sleeps 6
🐕(10) ✁ ■
👄👄 *Highly Commended*

Enjoy a relaxing break in our comfortably furnished 16th century farmhouse looking over the lovely Ithon Valley. Historic location with no traffic. Separate guests' sitting and dining rooms, both with inglenook fireplaces. Good traditional home cooking. Ideal for exploring Mid Wales or walk direct from our door. Brochure available. Open all year except Christmas.

---

8   **Pilleth Court,** Whitton, Knighton, Powys LD7 1NP

Mrs Heather Hood
☎/Fax 01547 560272
[BB] From £17–£25
EM From £8.50
Sleeps 6
🐕(9) ✗ ■ ⬥ ♻ ⬤
👄👄 *Highly Commended*

A listed Elizabethan house, tastefully furnished to retain its character and atmosphere, on a large working farm set in marvellous, unspoilt countryside. All guest rooms have panoramic views. One room is en suite and all rooms have tea/coffee-making facilities and TV. A wonderful centre for walking and touring. Open all year except Christmas.

Heart of Cardiganshire

Group Contact: *Carole Jacobs ☎ 01239 851261*

The magic of Cardiganshire will enchant you with its gentle mountains and unspoiled coastline encircling pastureland threaded with rivers famous for sewin and salmon.

This undiscovered part of West Wales, free of traffic and crowds, is home to the Red Kite. Otters have returned to the rivers; dolphins and seals play in Cardigan Bay; butterflies shelter among wild flowers. Here is the heartland of Welsh Cob breeding. Monthly horse sales are held in Llanybydder, trotting races at Tregaron and Synod Inn and pony trekking can be enjoyed in the mountains or along the coast.

Cardiganshire's 52 mile coastline has safe, sandy beaches and spectacular walks. It stretches from Cardigan to Aberystwyth, a university town and home to Wales' National Library and the thriving Arts Centre. The county's main river, the Teifi, is shared by fisherman, canoeists and the famous coracle men of Cenarth. There are well-stocked lakes to satisfy the angler. Here, in the ancient kingdom of Ceredigion, a rural way of life persists in the small farms and villages where Welsh is still the first language. Woollen mills, potteries and Celtic crafts reflect the traditional image of Cardiganshire.

Come and join us, the food is fresh, the beds are comfortable and the hearth is warm.

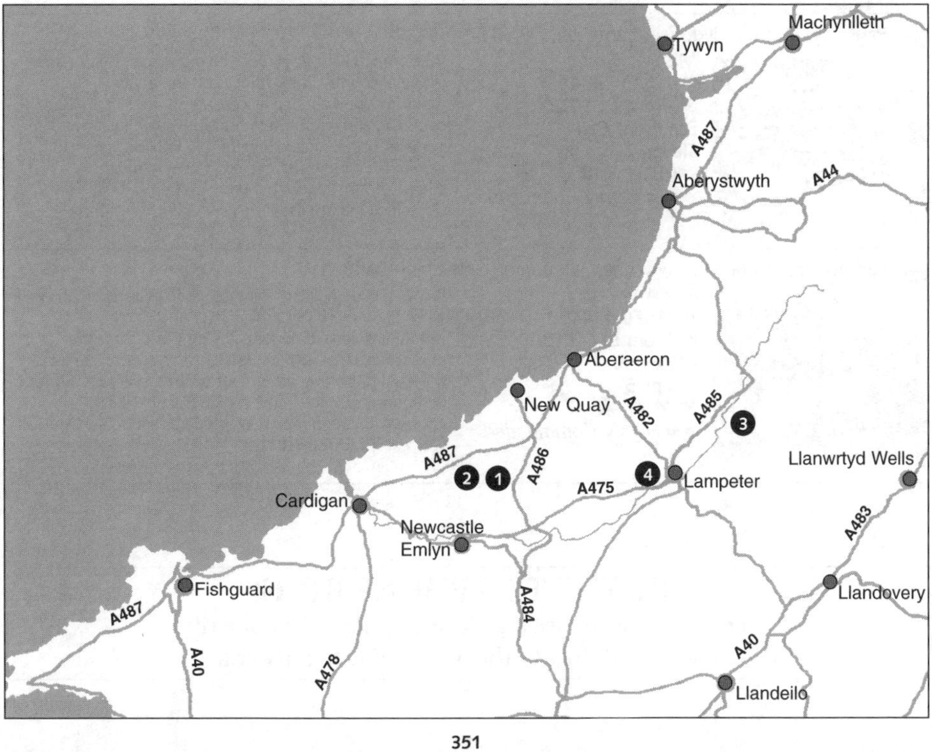

BED AND BREAKFAST
(and evening meal)

---

1 **Broniwan,** Rhydlewis, Llandysul, Cardiganshire SA44 5PF

Carole Jacobs
☎/Fax 01239 851261
🅱🅱 From £18.50
EM From £9.50
Sleeps 4
☺(7) 🐴 ⚹ 🛇 🐾 🐎 ⊙
♨♨ *Highly Commended*

Unwind in the peace of our small farm, 10 minutes' drive from National Trust beaches at Penbryn and close to River Teifi and Welsh Wildlife Centre. We offer cosy rooms, a warm hearth, good books and generous home cooking including vegetarian. Pretty garden, views of Preseli Hills. En suite/private facilities. Reduced weekly terms. WTB Farmhouse Award.

---

2 **Llwyn yr Eos,** Rhydlewis, Llandysul, Cardiganshire SA44 5QU

Judith Rodwell
☎ 01239 851268
🅱🅱 From £17.50
Sleeps 6
🐴 🛇 ⚹
♨♨ *Highly Commended*

Escape to our sheep farm in the beautiful Teifi valley. Comfortable, south-facing bedrooms with superb views. Watch buzzards and red kites on the farm or dolphins and seals off the coast 10 minutes' drive away. Good food using fresh local produce with fruit and vegetables from the garden. Open all year.

---

3 **Pant-Teg,** Llanfair Clydogau, Lampeter, Dyfed SA48 8LL

Mrs Pat Brown
☎ 01570 493416
🅱🅱 From £19–£20
EM From £10
Sleeps 7
☺(6) 🐴 ⚹ 🛇 🐾 ⊙
♨♨♨ *Highly Commended*

Welcome to Pant-Teg! Once an old stone hill farm, now a peaceful country home, it rests on the gentle mountainside with magnificent views. Red kites wheel overhead and wildlife surrounds us. Beautiful lawned gardens, pond, meandering brook. Enticing meals, vegetarian if preferred, served in our charming conservatory. Cosy woodburner and en suite facilities. Come and join us! Open all year exept Christmas.

---

4 **Pantycelyn,** Blaencwrt, Llanwnnen, Lampeter, Ceredigion SA48 7LW

Mrs Ann Jenkins
☎ 01570 434455
🅱🅱 From £16–£19
EM £9.50
Sleeps 5
🐴 ⚹ 🛇 ⊙
♨♨ *Highly Commended*

Enjoy relaxing holidays Pantycelyn, in peaceful countryside within easy reach of Cardigan Bay and Cambrian Mountains. Ideal base for enjoying Cardiganshire's attractions: birdwatching, fishing, riding, local markets, horse sales, trotting races, craft centres, potteries. En suite bedrooms, genuine home cooking, ample local information and our own Welsh Cobs and foals. Open all year except Christmas.

LET THE TELEPHONE RING!
Some farmhouses are big places. Let the telephone ring
long enough to give the owner time to answer it.

SELF-CATERING

Pant-Teg Studio Cottage, Llanfair Clydogau, Lampeter, Dyfed SA48 8LL ③

Mrs Pat Brown
☎ **01570 493416**
SC **From £150–£300**
Sleeps 4–6
🛏(6) 🐾 ✂ ▪ ❀ ⚫
❀ ❀ ❀ ❀

Set on the bank, its patio area next to our tumbling brook, and surrounded by meadows of grazing sheep, Pant-Teg Studio, tastefully converted, fully equipped and with en suite facilities, shares the beautiful views and tranquil gardens of the main farmhouse, whilst offering privacy and independence. Coast and countryside abound with wildlife and our peaceful haven is a perfect base from which to explore – or just relax! Brochure available. Open all year.

Although the majority of farms will accept '*Stay on a Farm*' Gift Tokens, please check when booking to avoid disappointment.

CONFIRM BOOKINGS

Disappointments can arise from misunderstandings over the telephone. Please write to confirm your booking.

FARM HOLIDAY
BUREAU

Our Internet Address is
http://www.webscape.co.uk/farmaccom/

Brecon

Group Contact: *Mrs Mary Adams* ☎ *01874 636505*

The Brecon Beacons welcome you to the great outdoors. This unspoilt countryside of mountains and forests, hills and valleys with rivers and lakes, caves and waterfalls, offers a great variety of country pursuits.

Enjoy cycling on graded tracks to suit different abilities with the National Park and also the Taff Trail. Visit Dan-yr-Ogof Show caves, take a trip on the Monmouth to Brecon canal or Brecon Mountain Railway. The hills delight climbers, walkers and pony trekkers and Red Kites are regularly seen. Fish in the rivers Wye and Usk or the many reservoirs. Guided walks start from the National Park Visitor Centre and Craig-y-Nos Country Park. On wet days visit Brecon Leisure Centre or Llangorse Rope Centre.

There are craft centres to visit, castles and historic sites. Browse around museums and secondhand bookshops and listen to the local choirs.

Sample home cooking at its best, and wherever you go you will be greeted by friendly, helpful people.

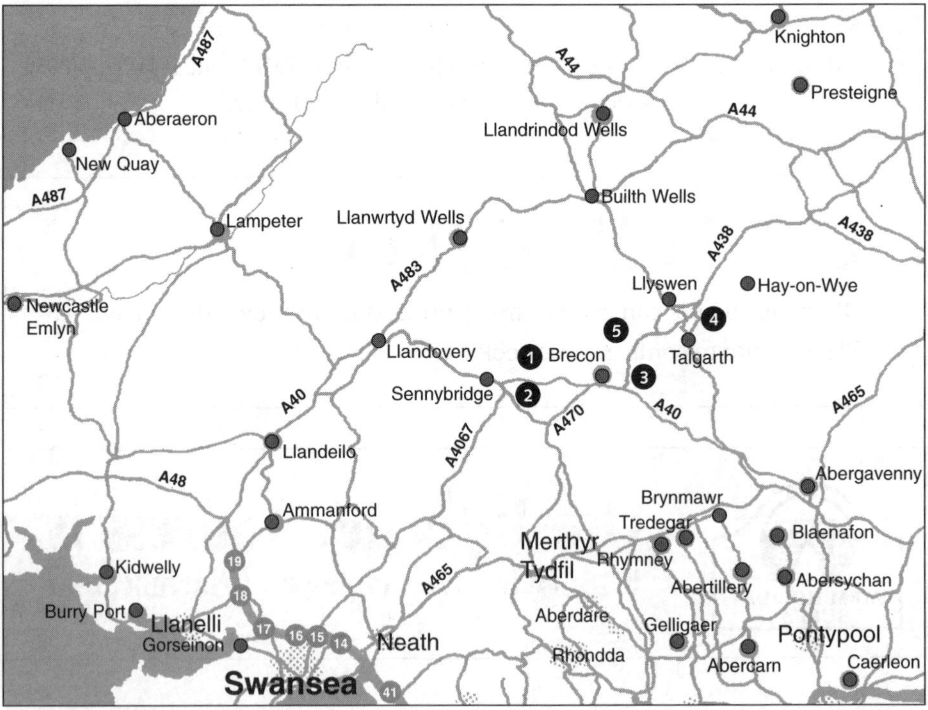

BED AND BREAKFAST

(and evening meal)

Brynfedwen Farm, Trallong Common, Sennybridge, Brecon, Powys LD3 8HW   **1**

Mrs Mary Adams
☎/Fax 01874 636505
[BB] **From £20**
EM From £10
Sleeps 6
🛏 🐕 ⅍ ♨ ●
🐚🐚 *Highly Commended*

Enjoy peace and quiet at Brynfedwen, a hill livestock farm situated between Brecon and Sennybridge overlooking the Brecon Beacons and Usk Valley. Lovely farm walks with wildlife. Comfortable, spacious en suite rooms including twin bedded apartment (equipped for disabled). TV lounge with log fire. Personal attention and good home cooking. Children welcome. Farmhouse Award. AA Selected.

Cwmcamlais Uchaf Farm, Cwmcamlais, Sennybridge, Brecon, Powys LD3 8TD   **2**

Mrs Jean Phillips
☎/Fax 01874 636376
[BB] **From £19–£20**
EM From £11
Sleeps 6
🐕(8) 🛏 ⅍ ← ♨ ●
🐚🐚🐚 *Highly Commended*

Cwmcamlais Uchaf is a working farm situated on the route of a popular walk in the Brecon Beacons National Park. 1 mile off the A40 between Brecon and Sennybridge. Our 16th century farmhouse has exposed beams and stonework, inglenook fireplace and tastefully decorated bedrooms, (2 en suite) with tea/coffee. The River Camlais with its waterfalls, flows through the farmland. A warm Welsh welcome awaits you. Open all year except Christmas.

Highgrove Farm, Llanhamlach, Brecon, Powys LD3 7SU   **3**

Mrs Ruth Williams
☎ 01874 665489
[BB] **From £18–£25**
Sleeps 6
🐕 ⅍ ♨ ♨ ⚒
🐚🐚 *Highly Commended*

Highgrove, situated between Brecon and Llangorse Lake in the National Park, is a 16th century farmhouse in a superb position overlooking the Brecon Beacons. Conservation award for renovation. An ideal base for a relaxing, touring or sporting holiday. Good choice of restaurants and pubs for evening meals nearby. Open all year except Christmas.

Lodge Farm, Talgarth, Brecon, Powys LD3 0DP   **4**

Mrs Marion Meredith
☎/Fax 01874 711244
[BB] **From £18–£21**
EM From £12
Sleeps 6
🐕 🛏 ⅍ ♨ ♨ ●
🐚🐚🐚 *Highly Commended*

Enjoy the tranquillity on this working farm nestling in the Brecon Beacons National Park. Relax in cottage-style garden with spectacular mountain views, wander along country lanes or climb well-known mountains. Return to 18th century house for interesting homemade meals including vegetarian. Dining room has inglenook and flagstone floor. Retire to cosy en suite period furnished bedrooms. Talgarth 1½ miles, Hay-on-Wye 8 miles. Open all year.

Trehenry Farm, Felinfach, Llandefalle, Brecon, Powys LD3 0UN   **5**

Mrs Theresa Jones
☎ 01874 754312
[BB] **From £20**
EM From £11
Sleeps 6
🐕 ♨ ●
🐚🐚🐚 *De Luxe*

Trehenry is a 200 acre mixed farm situated east of Brecon, 1 mile off A470. The impressive 18th century farmhouse with breathtaking views, inglenook fireplaces and exposed beams offers comfortable accommodation, good food and cosy rooms. TV lounge, separate dining tables, central heating, tea-making facilities, all rooms en suite. Brochure on request. Farmhouse Award winner. Open all year except Christmas.

SELF-CATERING

5 **Trehenry Farm,** Felinfach, Llandefalle, Brecon, Powys LD3 0UN

Mrs Theresa Jones
☎ **01874 754312**
☒ **From £300–£480**
Sleeps 8

For a holiday to remember then come to Trehenry 200 acre working farm. Tranquillity surrounded by breathtaking views. 17th century farmhouse modernised to a high standard with oak beams, inglenook fireplace. 3 bedrooms, 2 en suite, 1 private. Bed settee in second lounge. Very well equipped kitchen, lounge with TV, video, CH, wood stove. Price includes linen, electric, heating. Brochure. Open all year.

STAY ON A FARM GIFT TOKENS

If you have enjoyed your Stay on a Farm, why not treat your friends and relatives to *Stay on a Farm* gift tokens? Available from the Bureau office, telephone 01203 696909, they can be redeemed against accommodation booked on the majority of our farms

FOLLOW THE COUNTRY CODE

Leave nothing but footprints,
Take nothing but photographs,
Kill nothing but time!

THE 1000+ BUREAU MEMBERS OFFER A UNIQUE LINK TO CUSTOMERS ACROSS THE UK

All Bureau members belong to a local Group. Each member can refer you to an equally high quality member within the Group... or across the UK: England, Northern Ireland, Scotland, Wales.

Gwent

Group Contact: *Mrs Ann Ball* ☎ *01873 821236*

To the north of the county are the Black Mountains and the Brecon Beacons with majestic peaks and deep sheltered valleys. This area contains part of the Brecon Beacons National Park which provides opportunities for pony trekking, walking and many other activities.

Eastern Gwent is very different – the countryside is pastoral with undulating, wooded hills and the river valleys of the Usk and Wye. Ancient market towns and picturesque villages are dotted throughout this part of the county. Part of the Welsh Marches falls within this region and there are a number of strategically placed castles, including Raglan and Chepstow, reminders of less peaceful times. Tintern Abbey, immortalised by Wordsworth, shows a more tranquil face of the county.

Western Gwent can boast bracing, beautiful mountainsides, spectacular views and lovely walking country. It also has a rich industrial heritage with a wealth of attractions for those fascinated by the way we used to live.

Gwent is also an ideal base for exploring the interesting country and attractions in the South Wales and border areas. Brecon Beacons National Park, the Forest of Dean, the Mendip Hills, the Cotswolds, Bristol and Bath ... are all within 60 miles.

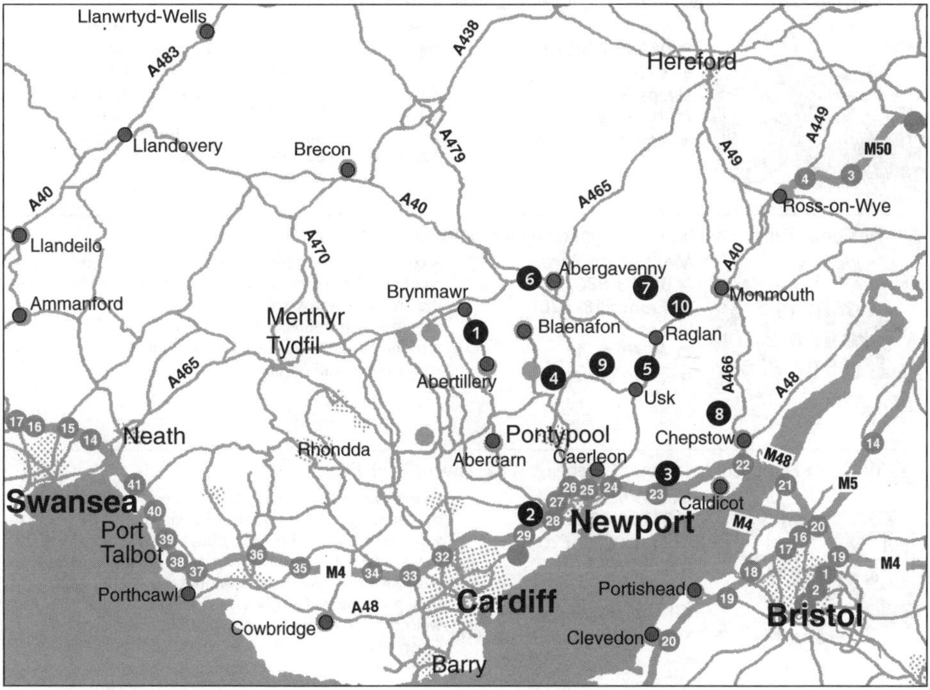

BED AND BREAKFAST
(and evening meal)

(1) Chapel Farm, nr Coalbrookvale, Blaina, Gwent NP3 3DJ

Mrs Betty Hancocks
☎ **01495 290888**
BB **From £18–£20**
EM From £7
Sleeps 6
🛏(4) ☂ ⚓ 🌐
🏵🏵 *Commended*

You will find traditional Welsh hospitality at Chapel Farm, a working sheep farm with panoramic views overlooking the towns of Blaina, Nantyglo and Brynmawr. The 15th century cruck farmhouse has been renovated to provide modern comfort yet keeping its old world charm. Home cooking, evening meals (pre-booked). Children welcome. Open all year except Christmas.

---

(2) Pentre-Tai Farm, Rhiwderin, Newport, Gwent NP1 9RQ

Susan Proctor
☎ **01633 893284**
BB **From £18**
Sleeps 6
🛏 ⚓ ✂ 🏃 🐕 🐾 🛆 ⚓ 🌾
🏵🏵 *Highly Commended*

Gateway to Wales. A warm welcome awaits you at our peaceful sheep farm located in the countryside yet only 3 miles from M4. Most rooms en suite, all with TV and beverage facilities. Children welcome at reduced rates. Ideal base for Wye Valley, Brecon Beacons, Cardiff, Museum of Welsh Life, St Fagans and magnficient Welsh castles. Open Feb–Nov.

---

(3) Penylan Farm, St Brides, nr Magor, Newport, Gwent NP6 3AS

A Arthur
☎ **01633 400267**
BB **£20**
Sleeps 6
🛏 🐕 ✂ ⚓ 🛆
🏵🏵 *Highly Commended*

Splendid Elizabethan farmhouse with oak beams and inglenook fireplaces. Set on hilltop overlooking beautiful St Brides Valley in rural setting, 2 miles from M4 and Wentwood Forest. Heated indoor swimming pool. Many golf courses (St Pierre, Celtic Manor), castles, excellent eating places. Good overnight stop for Irish ferries. Welsh hospitality assured. Open Apr–Nov.

---

(4) Ty-Cooke Farm, Mamhilad, Pontypool, Monmouthshire NP4 8QZ

Mrs Marion Price
☎ **01873 880382**
BB **From £18–£20**
Sleeps 6
🛏 ✂ ⚓ ⚓ 🛆
🏵 *Commended*

A comfortable 18th century farmhouse set in a cobbled courtyard. The family-run mixed farm is set on the edge of the Brecon Beacons National Park. Goytre Wharf on the Monmouthshire–Brecon Canal is ½ mile away. Ty-Cooke is the ideal centre for exploring the mountains and valleys of South Wales. Closed Christmas.

---

(5) Ty-Gwyn Farm, Cold Harbour, Gwehelog, Usk, Gwent NP5 1RT

Jean Arnett
☎ **01291 672878**
BB **From £15–£20**
EM From £11
Sleeps 6
🛏(5) ✂ ⚓ 🌐
🏵🏵 *Highly Commended*

Wake up and sit up to magnificent views of Brecon Beacons National Park from all 3 bedrooms (2 bath en suite with colour TV and hospitality tray). Hearty breakfasts and meals served in spacious dining room or conservatory overlooking secluded lawns. Mountains, castles, golf, fishing all nearby. Quality meals, vegetarians and own wine welcome. WTB Farmhouse Award. Brochure available. Open all year.

The Wenallt Farm, Gilwern, near Abergavenny, Gwent NP7 0HP   **6**

Janice Harris
☎ 01873 830694
🅱🅱 From £16.50–£20
EM From £11
Sleeps 7
🛏🐕🧍🏕🎃🍴 ●
♛♛♛ Commended

A 16th century Welsh longhouse set in 50 acres of farmland in the Brecon Beacons National Park commanding magnificent views over the Usk Valley. Retaining all its old charm with oak beams, inglenook fireplace, yet offering a high standard with en suite bedrooms, good food and a warm welcome. An ideal base from which to see Wales and the surrounding areas. Licensed. AA listed. Brochure available. Open all year.

Self-Catering

Granary & Coach House, Upper Cwm Farm, Brynderi, Llantilio Crossenny, Abergavenny, Mon. NP7 8TG   **7**

Ann Ball
☎ 01873 821236
🆂🅲 From £185–£350
Sleeps 6
🛏🐕🏕🎃 ●
🐾🐾🐾🐾

Holidays and short breaks in beautifully converted old barn on working sheep farm. Family accommodation with CH, TV, electricity, bed linen, towels included. Peaceful superb views, ideal for walking, birdwatching, exploring Welsh castles, Brecon Beacons, Wye and Usk Valleys. The Granary (upper) and Coach House (ground) each have 1 double and 2 twin bedrooms, lounge/dining/kitchen, bathroom with shower. Brochure. Open all year.

Parsons Grove, Earlswood, nr Shirenewton, Chepstow, Gwent NP6 6RD   **8**

Gloria Powell
☎/Fax 01291 641382
🆂🅲 From £110–£360
Sleeps 4/6
🏕🐾🏕

🐾🐾🐾🐾 – 🐾🐾🐾🐾🐾

On the edge of beautiful Wye Valley, set in 20 acres of peaceful countryside, with heated swimming pool. Three cottages, furnished to very high standard. Fully carpeted with colour TV, fitted kitchen, refrigerator, cooker, microwave, CH. All linen (duvets) and towels included. Panoramic views of beautiful valley and Wentwood Forest. Riding, golf and fishing nearby. Free use of barbecue, boules, croquet. Brochure. Open Mar–Nov.

Pentwyn Farm Stable Cottages, Pentwyn Farm, Little Mill, Pontypool, Gwent NP4 0HQ   **9**

Stuart & Ann Bradley
☎ 01495 785249
Fax 01495 785247
🆂🅲 From £160–£250
EM From £12
Sleeps 4/5
🏕🐾🎃🏕🍴 ●
🐾🐾🐾🐾

Relax in rural tranquillity in our delightfully converted stable cottages. Enjoy the castles, museums and water sports. Walk in the Black Mountains or along the canal bank. Each cottage has 2 bedrooms, a fully fitted kitchen and a large beamed sitting room with wood burner and wonderful views over the large garden with swimming pool and barbecue. Linen and electricity included. Meals available with house guests in farmhouse. Open all year.

Worcester House, Castle Farm, Raglan, Gwent NP5 2BT   **10**

Mrs Vivien Jones
☎ 01291 690492
🆂🅲 From £150–£250
Sleeps 6/7
🛏🐕🖼🎃🏕

Applied

Part of a 17th century manor house. The oldest brick building in Gwent. Easy access to Wye Valley, Brecon Beacons and Forest of Dean. Many castles and golf courses nearby. Raglan Castle 20 yards, overlooking picturesque village of Raglan. A 200-acre working dairy/arable farm with 3 bedrooms bathroom and separate shower room with WC. Living/dining room with french windows leading to large lawn, separate kitchen. Open Easter–Nov.

Carmarthenshire

Group Contact: *Marian Lewis* ☎ *01550 720410/Fax 01550 720262*

Carmarthenshire is a county of contrasts from the Black Mountain through the tranquil Towy Valley, to the picturesque coastal villages and golden sands of Carmarthen Bay.

It is at the heart of West Wales which means you can enjoy a different route every day to many and varied locations. Welsh is spoken throughout the county adding to the special Celtic atmosphere. Find the traditional markets and hear the farmers talk about the ups and downs of agricultural life.

All the main towns are steeped in history and many have their own castles, see especially Kidwelly and Llansteffan near the coast and Carreg Cennen in the hills.

For walking, choose coastal paths or cliffs, the magnificent scenery of the Towy, Teifi and Taf valleys, Brechfa forest, Brecon Beacons National Park or the Llyn Brianne reservoir with maybe the chance of sighting a rare Red Kite.

Every sport is catered for with excellent leisure centres, superb fishing and all country pursuits. Add to that the country parks, steam railway, crafts, antiques, agricultural shows, choirs and music festivals and soak up the warm Welsh welcome in our homes.

Croeso i Sir Gaerfyrddin.

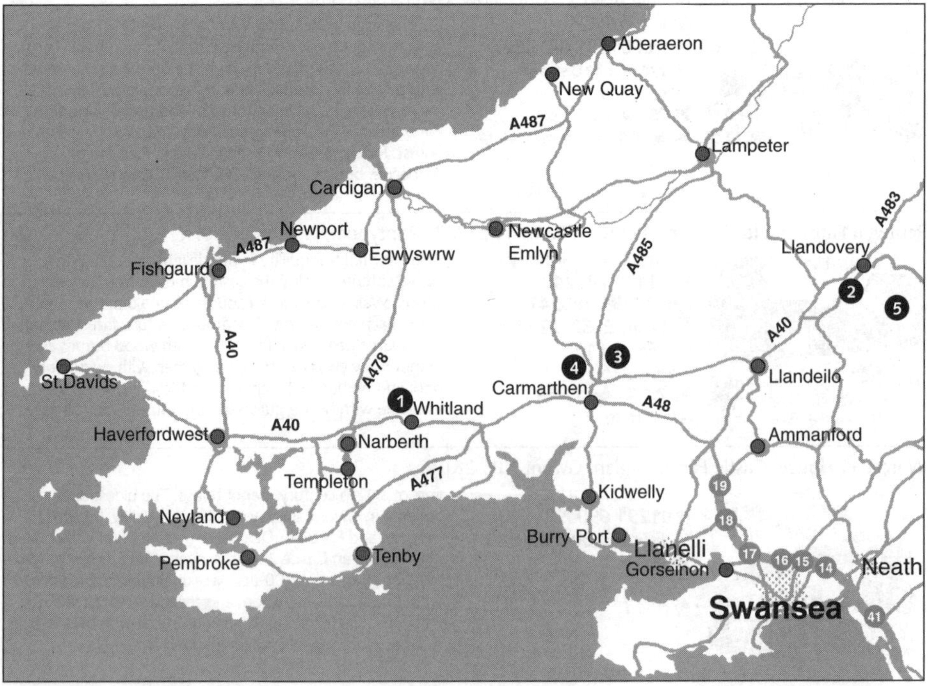

BED AND BREAKFAST

(and evening meal)

Cilpost, Whitland, Carmarthenshire SA34 0RP ①

Ann Lewis
☎ **01994 240280**
⒝ **From £16.50–£25.50**
Sleeps 18
👵 🐴 🛏 ⬅ 🏹
Applied

Our 300-year old farmhouse has been tastefully modernised to provide every modern amenity, including en suite facilities, central heating, colour TV in every bedroom, and is just 7 miles from the coast. The heated indoor swimming pool and snooker room are set amidst extensive lawns providing absolute safety for our younger visitors. You are warmly welcomed. Open Apr–Sept.

Cwmgwyn Farm, Llangadog Road, Llandovery, Carmarthenshire SA20 0EQ ②

Marian Lewis
☎ **01550 720410**
Fax 01550 720262
⒝ **£20**
Sleeps 6
👵 ⬅ 🌼
❦❦ *Highly Commended*

Welcome to the country on our livestock farm with superb views overlooking the River Towy, 2 miles from Llandovery on A4069. The 17th century farmhouse is full of charm and character with inglenook fireplace, exposed stonework and beams. 3 spacious luxury en suite bedrooms with bath/shower, hairdryer, TV, tea/coffee. Enjoy tranquil riverside setting from garden or picnic area. Ideal for touring mid/South Wales. Open Easter–Oct.

Pantgwyn Farm, Whitemill, Carmarthen, Carmarthenshire SA32 7ES ③

Tim Giles
☎ **01267 290247**
Fax 01267 290880
⒝ **From £23–£25**
EM From £18
Sleeps 6
👵 ⼚ ⬅ 🏹 🌼
❦❦❦ *De Luxe*

Restored 17th century farmhouse set in 12 acres, 5 miles from Carmarthen. Welsh winners 'Best Breakfast in Britain'. Reputation for enticing and imaginative food. Well-proportioned, individually furnished bedrooms, inglenook lounge, beamed dining room. Pony and donkey rides. Walking, riding, fishing, golf nearby. Peace and tranquillity assured. The perfect rural retreat – secluded but not isolated. Closed Christmas.

Trebersed Farm, St Peters, Travellers Rest, Carmarthen, Carmarthenshire SA31 3RR ④

Mrs Rosemary Jones
☎ **01267 238182**
Fax 01267 223633
⒝ **From £18–£20**
Sleeps 6
👵 🐴 ⼚ 🛏 🌼
❦❦ *Highly Commended*

A warm welcome awaits you at our working dairy farm. Wellingtons available! Excellent touring base overlooking thriving market town of Carmarthen, just off main A40. Three comfortable rooms, one family, all en suite, with tea/coffee tray, central heating, radio alarm and colour TV. Open all year except Christmas.

LET THE TELEPHONE RING!

Some farmhouses are big places. Let the telephone ring
long enough to give the owner time to answer it.

SELF-CATERING

5 **Gwydre Cottage,** Gwydre, Llanddeusant, Llangadog, Carmarthenshire SA19 9YS

Mrs D J Price
☎ 01550 740242
⟦SC⟧ From £180–£365
Sleeps 6
🐕 💼

🌼 🌼 🌼 🌼 🌼

Gwydre Cottage is situated at the foot of the Brecon Beacons on a working farm where you are welcome to lend a hand. With rolling acres to explore, feel the fresh hill breezes and see the breathtaking scenery. Ideal for birdwatching (red kites, etc). Safe, large lawn with children's play equipment. Open Mar–Nov.

1 **The Stable & Coach House,** Cilpost Farm, Whitland, Carmarthenshire SA34 0RP

Ann Lewis
☎ 01994 240280
⟦SC⟧ From £180–£580
Sleeps 4–8
🐕 🐴 💼 🍴 🏹
Applied

Just 7 miles from the Pembrokeshire coast, The Stable and Coach House are delightful stone-built cottages providing the most luxurious accommodation for eight and four people respectively. Guests are welcomed to use the indoor heated swimming pool and snooker room and, by arrangement, have breakfast or dinner in the main farmhouse. Early booking is recommended. Open Apr–Sept.

Pembrokeshire

Group Contact: *Mrs Vivienne Lockton* ☎/*Fax 01994 419327*

The spectacular coastline reflects Pembrokeshire's unique standing as Britain's only coastal National Park; the coast path offering 200 miles of varied walking and breathtaking views across the Irish sea. In contrast, the heart of the countryside with the tranquil, wooded creeks of the Cleddau estuary and the peaceful, rolling uplands of the Preseli Hills provide an idyllic, rural setting for a relaxing and stress-free holiday.

Pembrokeshire is rich in history with dramatic castles, stone circles and the beautiful cathedral at St David's. Explore unrivalled sandy beaches and enjoy a sunshine record which equals the best in the UK. Renowned for its flora and fauna, visit the bird sanctuary islands. Delight in the wild flowers which abound throughout the whole area or simply enjoy the peace.

For the more energetic, activities suit all ages – sailing, windsurfing, riding, fishing, walking, family attractions and theme parks.

Pembrokeshire has a special appeal in all seasons, to young and old and those of us who live here welcome you to share our treasures. Come and see us – soon.

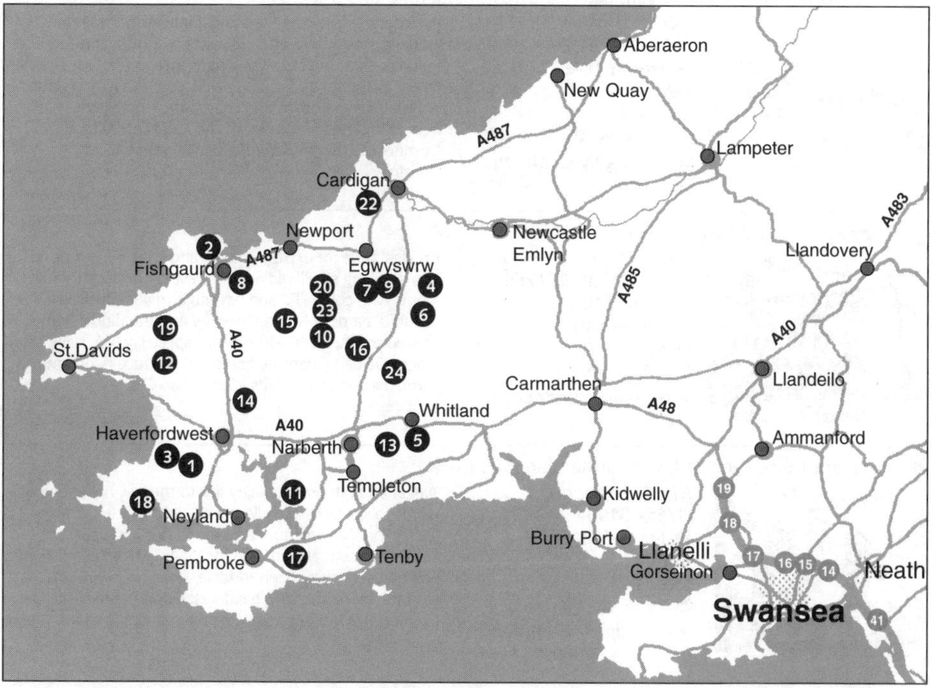

BED AND BREAKFAST

(and evening meal)

---

(1) Barley Villa, Walwyns Castle, Haverfordwest, Pembrokeshire SA62 3EB

Sandra Davies
☎ 01437 781254
BB From £15.50–£17
Sleeps 4
Commended

Our spacious family homestead and smallholding overlooks a nature reserve and woodland abundant with wildlife. Ideally situated for bird islands, sandy bays, coastal path and walks. Double and twin rooms with tea-making facilities, en suite available. TV lounge, parking, packed lunches, special diets. A non-smoking establishment. Warm welcome. Open Apr–Oct.

---

(2) Berry-Hill, Goodwick, nr Fishguard, Pembrokeshire SA64 0HG

Mrs Mayrid Rees
☎ 01348 872260
BB From £19–£20
Sleeps 4
Highly Commended

Smallholding of various animals magnificently positioned overlooking Fishguard harbour and Preseli Hills. Within two minutes' walk of some of Prembrokeshire's coastal walks. Bedrooms have sea views and en suite and tea/coffee-making facilities. Full central heating. Also ferry crossings. Open all year.

---

(3) The Bower Farm, Little Haven, Haverfordwest, Pembrokeshire SA62 3TY

John Birt-Llewellin
☎ 01437 781554
BB From £18–£27.50
EM £15
Sleeps 8
Highly Commended

An extensively modernised traditional farmhouse on working sheep farm offering peace, warmth, comfort and friendliness to the casual or longer stay visitor. Dogs, horses (livery available) and children welcome. Walking distance of Broad Haven beach and coast path. Impressive sea views over St Brides Bay and islands. All rooms en suite. Farmhouse Dragon Award. Open all year except Christmas.

---

(4) Bron-y-Gaer, Llanfyrnach, Pembrokeshire SA35 0DA

Mrs D Waghorn
☎/Fax 01239 831265
BB From £18
EM From £10
Sleeps 4
☎(12) ✄ ▪ ●
Highly Commended

An ideal base for exploring coast and country, our peaceful non-smoking smallholding offers every comfort. En suite rooms with colour TV and beverage-making facilities, beautiful gardens for you to enjoy and traditional home cooked meals. Gluten-free diets a speciality. We have Jacob sheep, Golden Guernsey goats and produce hand-spun garments and other crafts. Open Mar–Oct.

---

(5) Brunant Farm, Whitland, Carmarthenshire SA34 0LX

Mrs O Ebsworth
☎/Fax 01994 240421
BB From £18–£20
EM £12
Sleeps 6
Highly Commended

'Never enough time to enjoy this to the full, never enough words to say how splendid it was': John Carter, Thames TV (Wish You Were Here). Welcome to our 200 year old farmhouse centrally situated for touring, beaches, walking, golf or just relaxing. Comfortable, spacious bedrooms, all en suite, tea/coffee, TV, hairdriers. Good home cooking. Comfortable lounge, separate tables in dining room. Open Easter–Sept..

Castell Pigyn Farm, Llanboidy, Whitland, Carmarthenshire SA34 0LJ ⑥

Marian Davies
☎ **01994 448391**
Fax **01994 448755**
▨ **From £19–£21**
EM From £10
Sleeps 6
♿ ▓ ⓦ

ⓦⓦⓦ *Highly Commended*

Castell Pigyn is situated 4 miles north of Whitland in a peaceful area with fabulous views of undulating farmland. Accommodation with en suite bedrooms. Lounge with TV, dining room with family tables, good home cooking. CH throughout, ample parking. WTB Farmhouse Award, food hygiene certificate, residential licence. (Also self-catering cottage sleeping 4.) Brochure available. Closed Christmas and New Year.

Dolau Isaf Farm, Mynachlog-ddu, Clunderwen, Pembrokeshire SA66 7SB ⑦

Mrs V C Lockton
☎/Fax **01994 419327**
▨ **From £18–£20**
EM From £10
Sleeps 4
♿ ⚞ ⚟ ⚛ ▓ ⓦ

ⓦ *Highly Commended*

Nestling in the Preseli Hills we are centrally situated for exploring Pembrokeshire. You can see our sheep and mohair-producing goats from your bedroom window (1 en suite). Relax in our comfortable sitting room with its log fire. Enjoy your breakfast with fresh free-range eggs or sample our organic produce in season and have a happy, relaxed holiday in this idyllic setting. CH, TV. Walkers catered for. Riding and fishing nearby. WTB Farmhouse Award. Closed Christmas.

Gilfach Goch Farmhouse, Fishguard, Pembrokeshire, Dyfed SA65 9SR ⑧

June Devonald
☎/Fax **01348 873871**
▨ **From £23–£26**
EM £13
Sleeps 12
⚟ ▓ ⓦ

ⓦⓦⓦ *Highly Commended*

Charming farmhouse with attractive grounds in National Park for people who want somewhere relaxing, peaceful and very comfortable. Oak beams, stone walls, ingle-nook, pretty bedrooms (en suite), magnificent views to the sea. Small holding with friendly animals and friendly Welsh people too! Superb meals – own produce giving variety, quality and quantity. Residential licence, fire certificate, pay phone. Farmhouse Award. Open Easter–Nov.

Glandy Mawr, Efailwen, Clynderwen, Pembrokeshire SA66 7RS ⑨

Annabel Sampson
☎ **01994 419422**
▨ **From £16–£20**
Sleeps 6
♿ ⚟ ⊞ ▓ ⚛

Applied

A grass and arable farm of 140 acres, home to the Bluestone herd of suckler cows. Centrally located for all south-west resorts. Looking towards the Preseli Hills from which the Blue Stones were taken to Stonehenge. Spacious farmhouse, centrally heated, with guests' private lounge/dining room and comfortable en suite bedrooms. Closed Christmas and New Year.

Golwg-y-Foel, Maenclochog, Clynderwen, Pembrokeshire SA66 7LA ⑩

Gwyweth Williams
☎ **01437 532681**
▨ **From £15–£17**
EM From £9
Sleeps 5
♿(10) ⚟ ▓

☐ *Highly Commended*

Welcome to our smallholding located in a peaceful village at the foot of the Preseli Hills, 2 miles from Llys-y-fran dam and central to places of interest. Comfortable bedrooms and lounge. We offer hearty breakfasts in comfortable dining rom. Ring for directions. Open Mar–Nov.

Knowles Farm, Lawrenny, Kilgetty, Pembrokeshire SA68 0PX ⑪

Mrs Virginia Lort-Phillips
☎ **01834 891221**
Fax **01834 891344**
▨ **From £16–£20**
EM From £12.50
Sleeps 6
♿ ⚞ ⚟⚛ ⚟ ⚛ ▓ ⚓ ⓦ

ⓦⓦ *Highly Commended*

With land sloping down to the shores of the Upper Cleddau river, we provide the perfect base for boating, birdwatching, walking or fishing. Bedrooms all face south and are cosy and bright. All have tea/coffee-making facilities and are either en suite or with private bathroom. Woodland garden at its best in spring but with calming effect all year. Relax and unwind in total tranquillity. Open Easter–Oct.

12 **Lochmeyler Farm,** Llandeloy, Pen-y-Cwm, Nr Solva, Haverfordwest, Dyfed SA62 6LL

Mrs Morfydd Jones
☎ 01348 837724
Fax 01348 837622
BB From £15–£25
EM From £10
Sleeps 24
De Luxe

Lochmeyler is a 220-acre dairy farm in the centre of St David's Peninsula, 4 miles from Solva Harbour. Twelve en suite bedrooms (no smoking in bedrooms), TV. 4-poster beds available. Two lounges, 1 non-smokers. Choice of menus, traditional and vegetarian. RAC highly acclaimed. Member of Taste of Wales, WTB Farmhouse Award. RAC Guesthouse of the Year '93. Licensed, credit cards accepted. Open all year including Christmas.

13 **Lower End Town House,** Lampeter Velfrey, Narberth, Pembrokeshire SA67 8UJ

Judy Smith
☎ 01834 831738
BB From £19
EM From £10
Sleeps 4 + cot
Highly Commended

Beef and sheep farm owned and run by a young couple. Recent total refurbishment of the farmhouse has been aimed at recalling the peace and tranquillity of a bygone age whilst incorporating the comforts of a modern one. Easily accessible from the A40. Ideal for touring, walking or just unwinding. Evening meals by arrangement. Babies, dogs, and horses welcome. Open all year except Christmas & New Year.

14 **Lower Haythog,** Spittal, Haverfordwest, Pembrokeshire SA62 5QL

Nesta Thomas
☎/Fax 01437 731279
BB From £18.50
EM From £12.50
Sleeps 10–12
Highly Commended

For a taste of Wales and real country life join us on our friendly working farm 5 miles north of Haverfordwest. Tasteful and comfortable accommodation with CH and log fires. The well appointed bedrooms are in a 300 year old farmhouse, oozing with charm and character. Peaceful, entertaining with superb home cooking. Taste of Wales – Best Farmhouse Food Award 1996. WTB Farmhouse Award. Pretty landscaped gardens Pony rides. Trout fishing. Fire and basic food hygiene certificates. Open all year.

15 **Penygraig Farm,** Puncheston, Haverfordwest, Pembrokeshire SA62 5RJ

Betty Devonald
☎/Fax 01348 881277
BB From £16–£18
EM From £10
Sleeps 6
Highly Commended

A warm welcome awaits you at Penygraig, a working farm, situated near the picturesque Preseli Hills, with plenty of walks, natural trails and places of unspoilt beauty to be enjoyed. The rugged coastline of North Pembrokeshire being not far away. In the spacious dining room good wholesome cooking is served. There is 1 double room en suite, 1 family room. All rooms have tea trays, reductions for children sharing. Open Easter –Nov.

16 **Plas-y-Brodyr,** Rhydwilym, Llandissilio, Clynderwen SA66 7QH

Mrs Janet Pogson
☎/Fax 01437 563771
BB From £18
EM From £12.50
Sleeps 6
De Luxe

In hidden Rhydwilym Valley, Plas-y-Brodyr is the place to relax; walk, fish, enjoy outstanding views and the silence. Explore Pembrokeshire and West Wales and at the end of the day, relax by log fires in inglenook sitting room after delicious home cooking or walk the farm trail with Bob, our lovable sheepdog. Farmhouse Award. Open all year except Christmas.

17 **Poyerston Farm,** Cosheston, Pembroke, Pembrokeshire SA72 4SJ

Mrs Sheila Lewis
☎/Fax 01646 651347
Mobile 0973 907665
BB From £18–£20
EM From £11
Sleeps 12
Highly Commended

Welcome to Poyerston, a 300-acre dairy farm in unspoilt countryside, 2 miles east of Pembroke on A477. Tasteful, comfortable accommodation in 5 en suite bedrooms, CH throughout. Guests can relax in their own lounge or in our Victorian conservatory and dine in our attractive dining room. Good farmhouse cooking in friendly atmosphere. Spacious and attractive gardens. Ample parking. Central for beaches, castles, lily-ponds and inns nearby. Food hygiene certificate. AA QQQQ Selected. Brochure. Open Mar–Nov.

Skerryback, Sandy Haven, St. Ishmaels, Haverfordwest, Dyfed SA62 3DN   (18)

Mrs Margaret Williams
☎ **01646 636598**
Fax 01646 636595
BB **From £18**
EM From £12
Sleeps 4

Highly Commended

Warm Pembrokeshire welcome in 18th century farmhouse set in an attractive garden surrounded by farmland and the coastal footpath on the doorstep. A haven for walkers and bird lovers. All home comforts, home cooking, en suite available, tea-making facilities and central heating backed up by log fires on chilly evenings. Taste of Wales member.

Torbant Farmhouse, Croesgoch, Haverfordwest, Pembrokeshire SA62 5JN   (19)

Mrs Barbara Charles
☎ **01348 831276**
BB **From £18**
Sleeps 6

Commended

A warm welcome awaits you at Torbant, peacefully situated near St Davids, 1½ miles from sea. The Pembrokeshire Coast National Park is all around us. Two comfortable bedrooms, both en suite with tea/coffee tray and TV. Useful utility room and cosy lounge with log fire if needed. Open Easter–Oct.

Trepant Farm, Morvil, Rosebush, Nr Maenclochog, Pembrokeshire SA66 7RE   (20)

Marilyn Salmon
☎/Fax **01437 532491**
BB **From £16–£18.50**
EM From £10
Sleeps 6

Highly Commended

Nestling at the foot of the Preseli hills, our family farm offers a warm Welsh welcome. Ideal base for walking, cycling, pony trekking or just a leisurely drive through the quiet countryside, enjoying the unspoilt views and historical monuments. One double room with en suite facilities. Imaginative meals, including vegetarian, using the finest local produce. Food hygiene certificate.

SELF-CATERING

Castell Pigyn Cottage, Llanboidy, Whitland, Carmarthenshire SA34 0LJ   (6)

Mrs Marian Davies
☎ **01994 448391**
Fax 01994 448755
SC **From £100–£230**
Sleeps 4

Situated 4 miles north of Whitland in a peaceful area with views of undulating farmland, semi-detached to our farmhouse, the cottage is completely self-contained with 1 double and 1 twin bedded room, each with washbasins and shaver points, bedlinen and towels. Bathroom with bath and shower. Pine kitchen units and dining room furniture. Three piece suite, colour TV, fitted carpets. Own secluded garden with furniture, ample parking. Open all year.

FARM HOLIDAY BUREAU

Please mention **Stay on a Farm** when booking

22 Croft Farm and Celtic Cottages, Croft, Nr Cardigan, Pembrokeshire SA43 3NT

Andrew & Sylvie Gow
☎/Fax 01239 615179
SC From £145–£599
Sleeps 2/7

Croft Farm is situated amidst beautiful North Pembs countryside near unspoilt, sandy beaches, stunning coastal path and National Park. Farmhouse and slate cottages are lovingly furnished and fully equipped. Indoor pool, sauna, meeting room, gardens, orchard, patio, barbecue, play area. Help feed Tabitha (pig), Pearl and Hazel (goats) and other friendly animals. Open all year.

8 Gilfach Goch Farmhouse Cottages, Gilfach Goch, Fishguard, Pembrokeshire SA65 9SR

June Devonald
☎/Fax 01348 873871
SC From £175–£495
Sleeps 5/6

Choose from the 200 year old stone walls, beamed ceiling and inglenook of Garn Madog, or Edwardian elegance, vivid colours and style of Brynawelon, two outstanding renovations in quiet, sheltered location. Panoramic landscape of sea/hills. National Park. Each house has secluded private patio, lawns, parking, woodburner, elec heating, microwave, dishwasher, washing machine. Open all year.

23 Greenway Cottage, Greenway Farm, Rosebush, Clynderwen, Pembrokeshire SA66 7QY

Mrs Eirlys Davies
☎ 01437 532585
SC From £195–£480
Sleeps 8

17th century farm cottage in Preseli Hills within the National Park with views of Rosebush Reservoir and easy access to the coast. Recently renovated making the most of open beamed ceilings, stone walls and an inglenook fireplace with woodburner. The farm has sheep, sheepdogs, free-range poultry and waterfowl. Guests are welcome to watch sheepdogs being worked and trained. Open all year.

24 Gwarmacwydd, Llanfallteg, Whitland, Dyfed SA34 0XH

Mrs A Colledge
☎ 01437 563260
Fax 01437 563839
SC From £100–£398
Sleeps 22

Gwarmacwydd is a country estate of over 450 acres, set in the idyllic Taf river valley, with two miles of trout fishing, woodland and farm walks. Watch the milking and feed new born calves or lambs. Interesting and sandy local beaches at Saundersfoot and Pendine. The spacious character heated stone cottages are nicely furnished and equipped. Electricity and linen included. Open all year. E mail: Farm.Holidays@btinternet.com

25 Rogeston Cottages, Portfield Gate, Haverfordwest, Pembrokeshire SA62 3LH

John & Paula Rees
☎/Fax 01437 781373
SC From £133–£521
Sleeps 2–6

Enchanting smallholding tucked away in peaceful countryside yet only 1½ miles to glorious St Brides Bay and National Park coastal footpath. Our scrupulously clean 200-year old natural stone cottages are surrounded by delightful gardens, adjoining croquet and badminton lawns, boules pitch and barbecue area. Farm trail. Pet Jersey cows, hens, ducks. Mouthwatering food available. Open all year.

FARM HOLIDAY BUREAU

Please mention **Stay on a Farm** when booking

County Londonderry

Group Contact: *Mrs Heather Torrens* ☎ *012665 58245*

This is a fertile agricultural county with small farms scattered across the broad sweeping land and long Atlantic beaches.

The city of Londonderry (also known as Derry) is best known for its massive fortified walls which encircle the old city, a circuit of one mile. Two outstanding museums, two cathedrals and a lively cultural scene draw visitors from all over the north-west of Ireland. In the county's north-east corner is Coleraine (with one of the main campuses of the University of Ulster), conveniently close to the seaside resorts of Portstewart and Castlerock for sea angling, golf and children's amusements. For rewarding scenic drives the Sperrin Mountains are best approached from Limavady and the beautiful Roe Valley Country Park. The Bann river is noted for trout and salmon.

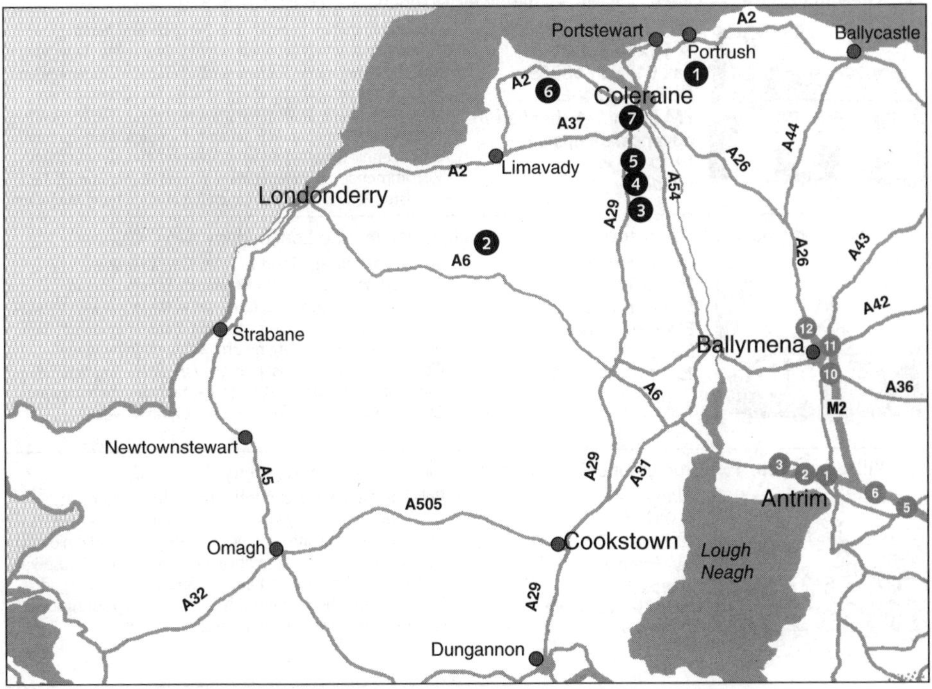

BED AND BREAKFAST

(and evening meal)

1 Brown's Country House, 174 Ballybogey Road, Coleraine, Co Londonderry BT52 2LP

Mrs Jean Brown
☎/Fax 012657
31627/32777
🅱 From £20
EM From £11
Sleeps 16
⬆ 🐗 ⅍ ■
Grade A

A chalet bungalow with spacious lawns. Central heating. Home baking. On Ballymoney – Portrush road (B62). 2 double bedrooms, 4 twin rooms, 1 family room, 3 ground floor, 1 single, all en suite. Tea/ coffee in all rooms. Babysitter. Dogs allowed (outside). Bushmills 4 miles, Coleraine and Portrush 5 miles. Open all year.

2 Drumcovitt House, 704 Feeny Road, Feeny, Londonderry BT47 4SU

Florence Sloan
☎/Fax 01504 781224
🅱 From £16–£20
EM From £8
Sleeps 6
🐗 🐓 ■ 🅳 🐝
Certified

Listed Georgian farmhouse with established gardens, 2 miles from Banagher Glen. Ideal centre for exploring Sperrins, Derry City, Donegal and the Causeway Coast. Fishing Roe, Faughan. Golf at Derry, Limavady. Archaelogical sites from pre-history onwards. Half mile east of Feeny on B74 off A6 Derry to Belfast. 1 family room, 1 twin, 1 single. Visa/Mastercard/Eurocard/Delta cards accepted. Open all year.
E mail: drumcovitt.feeny@btinternet.com

3 Greenhill House, 24 Greenhill Road, Aghadowey, Coleraine, Co Londonderry BT51 4EU

Mrs Elizabeth Hegarty
☎ 01265 868241
Fax 01265 868365
🅱 From £24–£29
EM From £16 (booked in advance) Sleeps 14
🕙 🐗 🅳 ■
Grade A

Georgian country guest house (with central heating). Good views across wooded countryside in the Bann Valley and the Antrim hills. Convenient to Giant's Causeway and north coast for golf, touiring, fishing. Six rooms are en suite with direct-dialling telephones, colour TV, tea/coffee. From Coleraine take A29 south for 7 miles, then turn left on Greenhill Road – B66 and Greenhill House is on right. Recommended in international guides. Egon Ronay, Taste of Ulster, AA Premier Selected QQQQQ. Open Mar–Oct.

4 Heathfield House, 31 Drumcroone Road, Garvagh, Coleraine, Co Londonderry BT51 4EB

Mrs Heather Torrens
☎ 012665 58245
🅱 From £18–£20
EM From £12
Sleeps 6
🐓 🐗 🅳 🧥 ♨ ■ 🐝
Certified

Winner of AIB Agr-Tourism Farm Guest House. Comfortable, spacious 17th century farmhouse on working beef and sheep farm, set in large garden in lovely countryside. Ideal base for touring Causeway coast. Golf, fishing and horse riding nearby. Walk country lanes. Central heating, guests' lounge with piano, log fire. En suite rooms, colour TV, tea/coffee facilities, hairdrier, etc. On A29 Garvagh-Coleraine road. Open all year.

5 Killeague Farm, 157 Drumcroone Road, Blackhill, Coleraine, Co Londonderry BT51 4HJ

Margaret Moore
☎ 01265 868229
🅱 From £20
EM From £12
Sleeps 6
🐗 🐓 ⅍ ■ 🐎 🧥
Certified

Relax and enjoy the comfort and warm welcome at Killeague Farm Bungalow. The 130-acre dairy farm is situated 5 miles south of Coleraine on A29, convenient to North Antrim coast, sandy beaches and Giant's Causeway. Stabling on the farm and horse riding can be arranged. Three en suite bedrooms with tea/coffee. TV lounge. Children welcome. Open all year.

The Poplars Guest House, 352 Seacoast Road, Limavady, Co Londonderry BT49 0LA   **6**

Mrs H McCracken
☎ **015047 50360**
▣ **From £16**
EM From £9
Sleeps 13
🚶 ⛄(13) 🔵 💷 🧳 ⬡
Grade B

Ten bed bungalow in gardens, views of Benevenagh, Donegal Hills. Fishing 14 mile, golf 6 miles, Roe Valley Country Park 7 miles, Ulster Gliding Club ½ mile. Five rooms en suite, one with wash hand basin. All home cooking. All ground floor. Babysitter available. Limavady 6½ miles, Coleraine 10 miles, Londonderry 24 miles. Open all year.

Tullans Farm, 46 Newmills Road, Coleraine BT52 2JB   **7**

Mrs Diana McClelland
☎ **01265 42309**
▣ **From £15–£17**
Sleeps 6
🐴 🐂 🧍 🚗 🧳
Certified

1 double room en suite, 1 family room with H&C. Farmhouse (central heating) 1 mile from Coleraine. Nearby fishing, swimming pool, bowling, ice-skating, horse riding and birdwatching. Babysitter. Dogs allowed outside. Portstewart/Portrush 5 miles. Golf and sandy beaches 5 miles. Turn off A29 Coleraine bypass (ring road), ½ mile past roundabout (junction A26) into Newmills Road. Open all year.

County Antrim

Group Contact: *Eileen P Duncan* ☎ *01232 825275*

To the south east of the county, Belfast provides excellent shopping and city entertainment while to the north west lies the Causeway Coast, a playground of holiday resorts, with the Giant's Causeway the dominant feature. Between lie the nine glens of Antrim and their quaint waterfoot villages, the spectacular coast road, Carrickfergus Castle, and inland towns like Antrim with its ancient round tower and splendid park. There's pony trekking near Ballycastle, a spectacular swinging rope bridge at Carrick-a-rede, golf at Royal Portrush, as well as bathing, boating and fishing along the hundred miles of shore. The Irish Linen Centre at Lisburn recreates Ulster's greatest industry and is a great place for souvenir shopping.

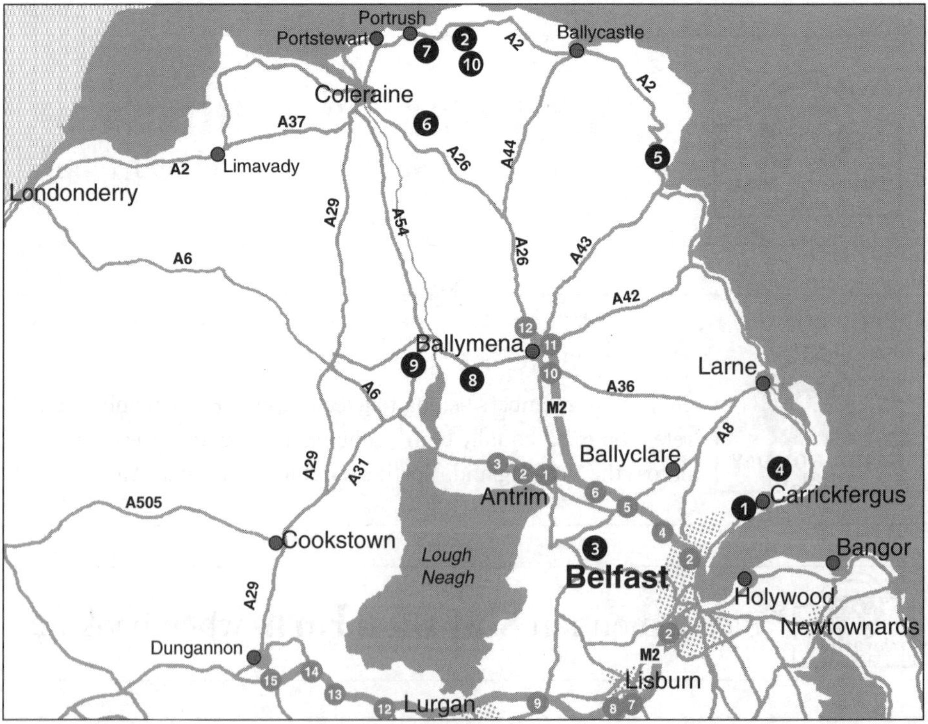

BED AND BREAKFAST

(and evening meal)

Beechgrove, 412 Upper Road, Trooperslane, Carrickfergus, Co Antrim BT38 8PW

Betta Barron
☎ 01960 363304
BB From £15–£17
EM From £9
Sleeps 13
Certified

A warm welcome awaits you at Beechgrove farmhouse (central heating) on 16 acre mixed farm near sea. Fishing, golf, riding. Knochagh monument, Belfast zoo, leisure centre nearby. 3 single, 1 double, 2 family rooms, 1 twin (all H/C). Babysitter. Dogs allowed (outside). Off A2, 1 mile south of Carrickfergus. Larne 10 miles. Belfast 10 miles. Carrickfergus 3 miles. Open all year.

Carnside Farm Guest House, 23 Causeway Road, Giant's Causeway, Bushmills, Co Antrim BT57 8SU

Frances Lynch
☎ 012657 31337
BB From £14–£18
EM From £10
Sleeps 15
Grade B

Farmhouse (central heating) on 200-acre dairy farm. Magnificent coastal view. Fishing, golf, water sports. Old Bushmills Distillery 2 miles has weekday tours. 1 single, 3 double (1 en suite), 1 twin, 3 family rooms (1 en suite), 2 on ground floor, all H&C. Babysitter. Dogs allowed (outside). Bushmills 2 miles, Ballycastle 12 miles, Giant's Causeway ¼ mile. Open Mar–Oct.

Clearsprings Farm, 9 Belfast Road, Nutts Corner, Crumlin, Co Antrim BT29 4TQ

Eileen P Duncan
☎/Fax 01232 825275
BB From £15–£17
Sleeps 6
Certified

Spacious, modernised house with 1 double en suite, 2 twin with H&C. Beautiful mature garden, ample parking. Rural setting, home from home atmosphere. All home cooking. Tea-coffee making facilities, electric blankets. 400 yards from Nutts Corner roundabout, 2nd house on right, A52 Belfast Road. 5 minutes Belfast International Airport. Pick-up service. Open all year.

Craig's Farm, 90 Hillhead Road, Ballycarry, Carrickfergus, Co Antrim BT38 9JF

Mrs J Craig
☎ 01960 353769
BB From £15
Sleeps 6
Certified

3 rooms, 1 twin with H&C, 1 family and 1 double both en suite, all with tea/coffee. Centrally heated farmhouse located in quiet rural surrounds. Convenient for golf, fishing, horse riding, walking. TV lounge. Babysitter. Dogs allowed outside. From Larne take the A2 towards Carrickfergus. Take 2nd right when you come through Glynn village. Signposted Ballycarry. Open all year.

Cullentra House, 16 Cloghs Road (off Gaults Road), Cushendall, Co Antrim BT44 0SP

Olive McAuley
☎/Fax 012667 71762
BB From £14–£16
Sleeps 6/8
Certified

Award-winning country house nestling amid breathtaking scenery of Glenballyeamon and Glenaan, overlooking Sea of Moyle. Golf course, Ballycastle and Giant's Causeway nearby. 1 family room, 1 double and 1 twin, all en suite. TV, tea/coffee-making facilities. Homely atmosphere and warm welcome extended to all guests. Last B&B on Cloghs Road. Open all year except Christmas.

---

6 **Hob Green Country House,** 41 Kirk Road, Ballymoney, Co Antrim BT53 8HB

Jean Johnston
☎/Fax 012656 62620
[BB] From £18.50–£20
EM From £8.50
Sleeps 10
Grade B

Modern bungalow in 2 acre garden, featured on TV for relaxing atmosphere. All rooms en suite with tea and coffee-making facilities. TV lounge and dining room for guests. Your own door keys to come and go as you please. Causeway coast, Antrim Glens, Giant's Causeway all within 15 miles, recreation centre 1 mile. Brochure on request. Open all year.

7 **Islay-View,** 36 Leeke Road, off Ballymagarry Road, Portrush, Co Antrim BT56 8NH

Eileen Smith
☎ 01265 823220
[BB] From £17.50
Sleeps 6
Certified

3 rooms, 2 doubles, 1 family or twin, all en suite. Chalet bungalow in quiet location, yet convenient to Giant's Causeway, Bushmills Distillery, Dunluce Castle and all amenities of Causeway Coast. TV lounge, tea/coffee-making facilities. Home baking. Wheelchair ramp. Off Ballymoney/Portrush road (B62). Portrush 2½ miles, Coleraine 6 miles. Open Easter–Sept.

8 **Neelsgrove Farm,** 51 Carnearney Road, Ahoghill, Ballymena, Co Antrim BT42 2PL

Mrs Margaret Neely
☎ 01266 871225
[BB] From £16–£18.50
EM From £10
Sleeps 6
Certified

Country house (central heating) in 1 acre of grounds on mixed farm. Home baking. Water skiing 2 miles. Sports complex 6 miles. 6 miles from Ballymena, 15 miles from International Airport. Convenient to Glens of Antrim and River Bann. Fishermen welcome, tackle space available. 1 double en suite, 1 double, 1 twin room with H/C. Dogs allowed outside. Open Jan–Nov.

9 **Sprucebank,** 41 Ballymacombs Road, Portglenone, Co Antrim BT44 8NR

Mrs Thomasena Sibbett
☎ 01266 822150
Fax 01266 821422
[BB] From £15.50–£17.50
Sleeps 8
Certified

Relax in the tranquil surroundings of our 18th century farmhouse conveniently situated for touring the province and on route to Ireland's north and west coast. Golf, fishing, forest and river walks nearby. One hour from ports of entry on A54, 1½ miles from Portglenone. Open Mar–Oct or by arrangement.

10 **Valley View,** 6a Ballyclough Road, Bushmills, Co Antrim BT57 8TU

Valerie McFall
☎ 012657 41608/41319
[BB] From £15–£16.50
Sleeps 18
Certified

Family-run with homely atmosphere and very comfortable accommodation. Convenient to all the North Antrim coastal attractions including Giant's Causeway. Beautiful views of mountains and Bush river valley. 6 rooms all en suite, 1 disabled, each with TV, coffee/tea-making facilities. Home cooking, tea on arrival. No smoking. Payphone. Families very welcome. Open all year except Christmas and New Year.

LET THE TELEPHONE RING!

Some farmhouses are big places. Let the telephone ring
long enough to give the owner time to answer it.

County Tyrone

Group Contact: *Mrs Louie Reid* ☎ *01662 841325*

Between the Sperrins in the north and the green Clogher Valley with its village cathedral in the south lies this region of great historical interest. The county's associations with the USA are recalled at the Ulster-American Folk Park near Omagh and Gray's old printing shop in Strabane still contains its 18th-century presses. The Ulster History Park, also near Omagh, offers a fascinating introduction to Ulster's past up to the 17th-century 'plantation' of Ulster. The story of the Lough Neagh fishing and eel industry is told at Kinturk Cultural Centre, east of Cookstown. A mysterious ceremonial site of stone circles and cairns at Beaghmore, between Cookstown and Gortin, has recently been uncovered and there are numerous Stone Age and Bronze Age remains in the area. There are forest parks, Gortin Glen and Drum Manor, for driving or rambling, excellent trout and salmon waters near Newtownstewart, and market towns for shopping and recreation. Dungannon is notable for its fine glassware, Tyrone Crystal.

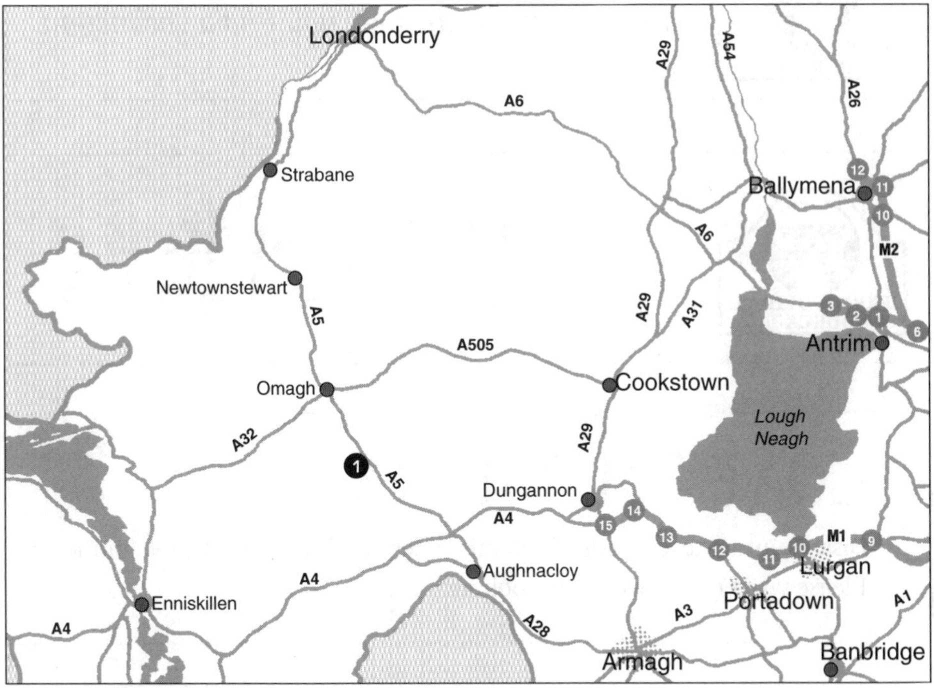

BED AND BREAKFAST

(and evening meal)

① Greenmount Lodge, 58 Greenmount Road, Gortaclare, Omagh, Co Tyrone BT79 0YE

Mrs F Louie Reid
☎ **01662 841325**
Fax **01662 840019**
ⓑⓑ **From £17.50–£21**
EM From £12
Sleeps 20
♿ 🐕 🐎 ✂ 🅴 💼
Grade A

Farm guest house on 150-acre farm. Superb accommodation, excellent cuisine. Central for sightseeing Fermanagh, Lakeland, the Sperrin Mountains. A5 from Ballygawley to Omagh, left before Carrick Keel pub at Fintona sign 1 mile. Open all year.

FINDING YOUR ACCOMMODATION

The Group contacts at the beginning of each section can always help you find a vacancy in your chosen area.

Our Internet Address is
http://www.webscape.co.uk/farmaccom/

CONFIRM BOOKINGS

Disappointments can arise from misunderstandings over the telephone. Please write to confirm your booking.

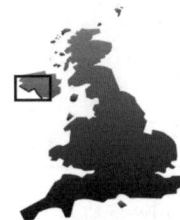

County Fermanagh

Group Contact: *Mrs Mary Fawcett* ☎ *01365 322725*

Ulster's Lakeland spreads its web of waterways, islands, forest and glen, castles and abbey ruins right across the county. Enniskillen, county town and shopping centre, strides the narrows between upper and lower Lough Erne, with the romantic silhouette of the Watergate a famous feature of the waterfront scene. Pleasure boats run daily cruises in summer and boats are available to hire. Golf, water-skiing and even pleasure flying are available nearby. Fishermen need no reminder that these are the waters where record catches are made. Two of Ulster's finest houses in National Trust care, Florence Court and Castle Coole, are in Fermanagh, and there is an underground boat trip at Marble Arch Caves. Visitors to the old pottery at Belleek can watch craftsmen at work on fine porcelain.

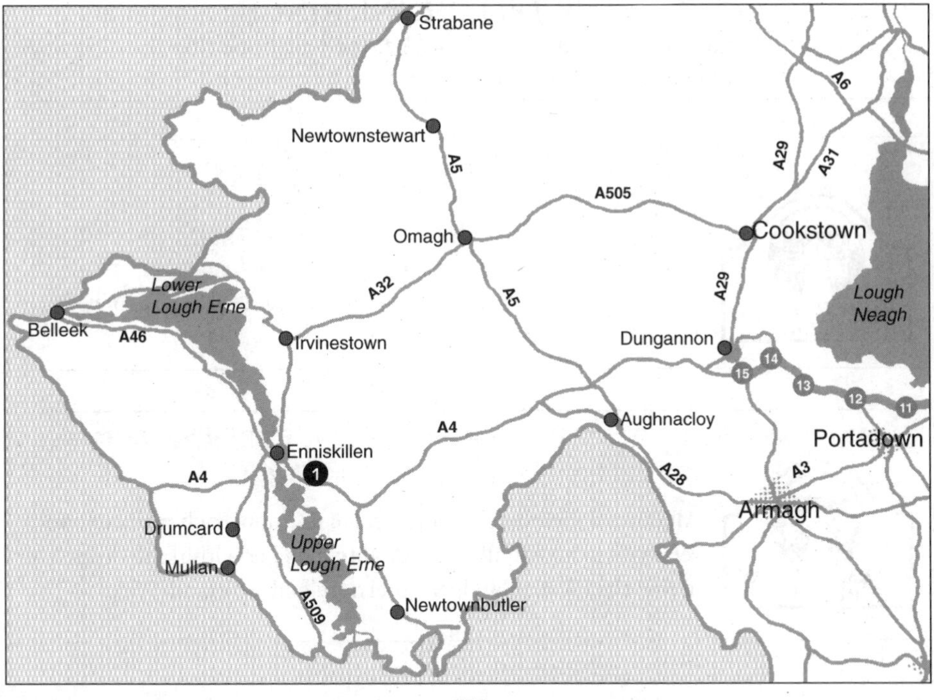

Strabane

Newtownstewart

A5

A505

A29 A31 A6

Omagh

Cookstown

Lower Lough Erne

A32

A5

A29

Lough Neagh

Belleek A46

Irvinestown

Dungannon

15 14

13 12 11

A4

Aughnacloy

Portadown

Enniskillen

A28

A3

Armagh

A4

Drumcard

Upper Lough Erne

Mullan

A509

Newtownbutler

BED AND BREAKFAST
(and evening meal)

 Riverside Farm Guest House, Gortadrehid Culkey Post Office, Enniskillen, Co Fermanagh BT92 2FN

Mrs Mary Isobel Fawcett
☎ **01365 322725**
🆔 **From £15–£17**
EM From £8
🐎 🏕 👶 🛏 ☕ 🏛 🛥
Grade B

Farmhouse (central heating) on 65-acre livestock farm. NT
properties, fishing, shooting, scenic drives, golfing nearby.
2 family rooms (1 en suite), 3 twin, 1 double, 1 single, all
H&C. Babysitter. Dogs allowed outside. Fire certificate.
Small parties catered for (max 25). Self-catering bungalow.
From Enniskillen take A4 for 1½ miles, left (A509) for
1½ miles. Enniskillen 3 miles. Open all year.

LET THE TELEPHONE RING!
Some farmhouses are big places. Let the telephone ring
long enough to give the owner time to answer it.

STAY ON A FARM GIFT TOKENS

If you have enjoyed your Stay on a Farm, why not treat your friends and
relatives to *Stay on a Farm* gift tokens? Available from the Bureau office,
telephone 01203 696909, they can be redeemed against accommodation
booked on the majority of our farms

THE 1000+ BUREAU MEMBERS OFFER A UNIQUE LINK TO CUSTOMERS ACROSS THE UK

All Bureau members belong to a local Group. Each member can
refer you to an equally high quality member within the Group... or
across the UK: England, Northern Ireland, Scotland, Wales.

County Armagh

Group Contact: *Elizabeth Kee* ☎ *01762 870081*

Northern Ireland's smallest county rises gently from Lough Neagh's banks, southward through apple orchards, farmland and hill forest to the rock summit of Slieve Gullion, mountain of Cuchulain. But the crown of Armagh is the city itself, a religious capital older than Canterbury, with two cathedrals, the Georgian Mall and a Planetarium and Observatory. Visit the famous hill fort known as *Emain Macha,* capital of the King's of Ulster from 600BC, which is interpeted at the Navan Centre just outside the city. Craigavon has a leisure centre and ski-slope, with lakes for water sports, and there is sailing on Lough Neagh and angling and canoeing on the Blackwater river.

BED AND BREAKFAST

(and evening meal)

---

① Ballinahinch House, 47 Ballygroobany Road, Richhill, Co Armagh BT61 9NA

Elizabeth Kee
☎ /Fax 01762 870081
🅱🅱 From £15
Sleeps 6
♿ 🐕 ✂ 🏕 🛄 🎪 🚲 ⚙

Grade B

Early Victorian farmhouse with traditional furnishings, landscaped lawns and rose garden. Tea/coffee-making facilities, home cooking. Shooting over farm. Pony riding, golf, fishing and NT properties nearby. From A3 turn off at junction B131 to Richhill. 2nd road left – Ballyleny Road – go to end, cross roads, straight across – Ballygroobany Road. House 1 mile on left. 1 single, 1 twin, 1 double, 1 family, 1 en suite.

---

② Ivanhoe, 10 Valley Lane, Waringstown, Craigavon, Co Armagh BT66 7SR

Mrs Frances Dewart
☎ 01762 881287
🅱🅱 From £14–£16
Sleeps 6
♿(2) 🐕 🛄 ⚙

Certified

Georgian farmhouse close to fishing, boating, golf, Craigavon lakes and leisure centre. 1 mile from Waringstown off Clare Road. 1 twin, 2 double rooms. Open all year.

FINDING YOUR ACCOMMODATION

FARM HOLIDAY BUREAU

The Group contacts at the beginning of each section can always help you find a vacancy in your chosen area.

FOLLOW THE COUNTRY CODE

Leave nothing but footprints,
Take nothing but photographs,
Kill nothing but time!

County Down

Group Contact: *Mrs Esther Kerr* ☎ *01806 24251*

This area includes the populous dormitory fringe along Belfast Lough (do not miss the Ulster Folk and Transport Museum at Cultra) and the ancient shrines of St. Patrick's Country round the cathedral hill at Downpatrick; the flat golden beaches of the Ards Peninsula and the mountainous Kingdom of Mourne, an ancient town with one of the richest heritages in Ireland including St Patrick's grave, a place of pilgramage on the Saint's day (17 March), in the cathedral grounds. Lively Newcastle with its seaside festival, and stately homes like Mount Stewart and Castle Ward open to visitors.

Horseriding, sailing, angling and golf are everywhere within reach, and there is motor racing at Kirkistown and sea angling in Strangford Lough and an intrguing aquarium at Portaferry.

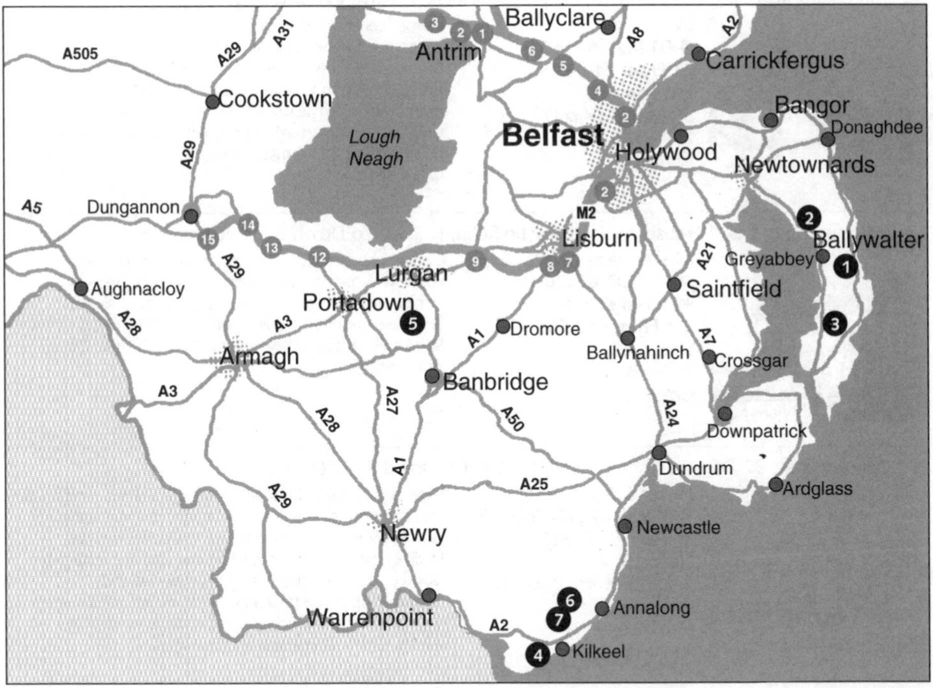

A505
A29
A31
Ballyclare
Antrim
A8
A2
Carrickfergus
Cookstown
Lough Neagh
Belfast
Holywood
Bangor
Donaghdee
Newtownards
A5
Dungannon
A29
M2
Lisburn
A21
Greyabbey
Ballywalter
Aughnacloy
A29
Lurgan
Portadown
A3
Saintfield
Armagh
A28
A1
Dromore
A7
Ballynahinch
Crossgar
Banbridge
A27
A24
A28
A50
Downpatrick
A29
A1
A25
Dundrum
Ardglass
Newry
Newcastle
Warrenpoint
A2
Annalong
Kilkeel

BED AND BREAKFAST

(and evening meal)

---

① Ballynester House, 1A Cardy Road, Greyabbey, Newtownards, Co Down BT22 2LS

Geraldine Bailie
☎/Fax 012477 88386
BB From £16–£20
EM From £10
Sleeps 6
Certified

Country house overlooking Strangford Lough and wildfowl refuge. Convenient to many tourist attractions. Mount Stewart House (NT) 3 minutes. Golf, sailing, horseriding and fishing within easy reach. 1 family, 1 double, both en suite with colour TV, 1 twin with bathroom with shower. In-house Aromatherapy and Reflexology also available. Please telephone for directions. Open all year.

---

② Beechhill Farm, 10 Loughries Road, Newtownards, Co Down BT23 8RN

Mrs Joan McKee
☎ 01247 818404
Fax 01247 812820
BB From £15–£17
EM From £10
Sleeps 6
Certified

Farmhouse on the Ards peninsula on a working farm. 1 double, 1 single, 1 family room (all H/C). Dogs allowed outside. A20 south from Newtownards, 2 miles left at Millisle signpost, right at T junction, left at Loughries School. Newtownards 4 miles, Bangor 8 miles. Open all year except Christmas.

---

③ Greenlea Farm, 48 Dunover Road, Ballywalter, Newtownards, Co Down BT22 2LE

Evelyn McIvor
☎ 012477 58218
BB From £14–£16
EM From £8
Sleeps 11 (+ cot)
Certified

Come feel at home in our friendly little home with the big welcome. 5 bedrooms, all with H&C. CH. Large dining room, guests' own sitting room with piano and TV. We provide good food, enjoy people and will make your stay memorable. ½ mile off A2. Yachting, fishing, golf, flying club, racing (Kirkiston), NT properties nearby. Bangor 10 miles, Portaferry 14 miles, Belfast City Airport 20 miles. Open all year.

---

④ Morne Abbey Guest House, 16 Greencastle Road, Kilkeel, Co Down BT34 4DE

Mrs Annabel Shannon
☎ 016937 62426
BB From £16–£17
EM From £10.50
Sleeps 10
Grade B

Country house on mixed farm in magnificent setting. A warm welcome assured, home cooking a speciality. Fishing, riding, tennis, bowls, golf nearby. 1 single, 2 twin, 1 double, 1 family room. All with H&C, 3 en suite. Sea 1 mile, Silent Valley 4 miles. Kilkeel ½ mile. Open Apr–Sept.

---

⑤ Mourneview, 32 Drumnascamph Road, Gilford, Co Down BT63 6DU

Esther & Nettie Kerr
☎ 01820 626270/624251
BB From £16–£20
Sleeps 8
Certified

Superbly appointed bungalow beautifully designed on 200 acre farm providing a welcoming homely atmosphere. Guests TV lounge, dining room, tea/coffee-making facilities, payphone. Health/hygiene and fire certificates. Good base for touring. Linen. Homelands and participating in the full range of leisure activities nearby. 4 en suite rooms which are also suitable for disabled guests. Open all year except Christmas.

Sharon Farmhouse, 6 Ballykeel Road, Ballymartin, Kilkeel, Co Down BT34 4PL   ⑥

M. Bingham
☎ 016937 62521
🅱🅱 From £15–£17
Sleeps 6
👤 🐕 🐎 🏠 ✂ ♨ ⬡
Certified

Farm bungalow – 1 family, 1 twin, 1 single, all with H/C and central heating. Guest bathroom/shower. With excellent sea and mountain views. Situated ideally for mountaineering and 10 minutes from beach. 2 miles from Kilkeel town and fishing port. The area is rich in varied birdlife. Good wholesome home cooked food served in abundance. A warm and welcoming atmosphere. Your comfort is our pleasure. Open all year.

Wyncrest, 30 Main Road, Ballymartin, Kilkeel, Co Down BT34 4NU   ⑦

Robert & Irene Adair
☎ 016937 63012/65988
Fax 016937 63012
🅱🅱 £21
EM £14
Sleeps 11
🐎 ⓔ 💷 🏠
Grade A

A warm welcome awaits you at our farm guesthouse where we are renowned for our food and hospitality. Enjoy a holiday in the beautiful 'Mourne' country, a rambler's paradise. Relax in our conservatory and sample our home baking. Most rooms en suite with tea/coffee facilities and colour TV. Visa/Mastercard accepted. Open Apr–Oct.

For information on farm holidays in various countries in Europe please contact the following:

GERMANY
Arbeitsgemeinschaft für Urlaub auf dem Bauernhof in der Bundesrepublik Deutschland e.V.
Godesberger Allee 142-148
53175 BONN
☎ [49] 228 81 98 220
Fax [49] 228 81 98 231

Deutsche Landwirtschafts gesellschaft
Eschborner Landstraße 122
60489 FRANKFURT
☎ [49] 69 247 880
Fax [49] 69 247 88 110

BELGIUM
Gîtes de Wallonie
Rue de Millénaire, 53
6941 VILLERS SAINTE GERTRUDE
☎ [32] 86 49 95 31
Fax [32] 86 49 94 07

FINLAND
Lomarengas
Malminkaari 23
00700 HELSINKI
☎ [358] 0 351 61 321
Fax [358] 0 351 61 370

FRANCE
Fédération Nationale des Gîtes de France
56, rue Saint Lazare
75009 PARIS
☎ [1] 49 70 75 75
Fax [1] 49 70 75 76

Agriculture et Tourisme
Assemblée Permanente des Chambres d'Agriculture
9, avenue George V
75008 PARIS
☎ [1] 47 23 55 40
Fax [1] 47 23 84 97

HUNGARY
Association of Village Farm Houses
Szoboszalai u. 2-4
1126 BUDAPEST
☎ [36] 1 155 533 312
Fax [36] 1 155 18 57

Hungarian Federation of Rural Tourism
Klauzal Ter 5
1072 BUDAPEST
☎/Fax [36] 1 268 05 92

ICELAND
Icelandic Farm Holidays
Hafnarstraeti 1
101 REYKJAVIK
☎ [354] 562 36 40
Fax [354] 562 36 44

IRELAND
Irish Farm Holidays
2 Michael Street
LIMERICK
☎ [353] 61 400 700
☎ [353] 61 400 707
Fax [353] 61 400 771

Irish Country Holidays
Rural Development Centre
ATHENRY CO GALWAY
☎ [353] 91 44 473
Fax [353] 91 44 296

ITALY
Agriturist
C. SO Vittorio Emmanuelle, 101
00186 ROMA
☎ [39] 66 85 23 42
Fax [39] 66 85 24 24

LUXEMBOURG
Association pour la Promotion du Tourisme
Rural au Grand-Duché du Luxembourg
c/o Centrale Paysanne
2980 LUXEMBOURG
☎ [352] 48 81 61
Fax [352] 40 03 75

PORTUGAL
Privetur
Nucleo Regional Do Minho E Litoral Norte
Largo das Pereiras
4990 PONTE DE LIMA
☎/Fax [351] 58 741 493

ROMANIA
Antrec
National Association of Rural, Ecological, Cultural, Tourism
B. P. 22-559
BUCAREST
☎/Fax [40] 1 222 83 22

Bran Imex
Bran Jud. Brasov
Str. dr. A. Stoian 395
☎ [40] 68 23 66 42
☎ [40] 1 666 59 48
Fax [40] 68 15 25 98

SLOVAKIA
Slovensky Zväz Vidieckej Turistiky A Agroturistiky
Trencianska 55
82101 BRATISLAVA
☎ [42] 7 215 800/209
Fax [42] 7 214 903

SPAIN
Red Andaluza de Alojamientos Rurales
Apartado Correos 2035
04080 ALMERIA
☎ [34] 50 26 50 18
Fax [34] 50 27 04 31

SWEDEN
The Sweddish University of Agricultural Sciences
Ala Box 7013
75007 UPPSALA
☎ [46] 18 67 19 12
Fax [46] 18 67 19 80

SWITZERLAND
Verein "Ferien auf dem Bauernhof"
Feierlenhof
8595 ALTNAU
☎/Fax [41] 72 65 23 72

Index to farms

SCOTLAND
Region/Farm

		Page no.	Accessible category	Caravans and/or camping	Working farm (p=participation)	Farm – non-working	En suite available	Business people welcome	Meeting room (capacity)	Gift tokens accepted
Aberdeen & Grampian										
B&B	The Bungalow	42			✔		✔	✔		
SC	Logie Newton	42	♠		✔			✔	✔(10)	
Angus & City of Dundee										
B&B	Blibberhill Farm	44		✔	✔		✔	✔	✔(20)	✔
	Brathinch Farm	44			✔P		✔	✔	✔(10)	✔
	Purgavie Farm	44		✔	✔		✔	✔	✔(10)	✔
	Wemyss Farm	44			✔P		✔	✔	✔(20)	✔
	West Mains of Turin	44			✔P		✔	✔		✔
	Wood of Auldbar	45			✔			✔		✔
SC	Purgavie Farm	45	♠	✔	✔			✔	✔(10)	✔
Argyll, Isles, Loch Lomond, Stirling & Trossachs										
B&B	Bandominie Farm	53			✔			✔		✔
	Easter Drumquhassle Farm	53		✔	✔		✔	✔		✔
	Inchie Farm	54			✔			✔		✔
	Lochend Farm (Carronbridge)	54		✔	✔			✔		✔
	Lochend Farm (Port of Menteith)	54			✔P		✔	✔		✔
	Lower Tarr Farm	54			✔		✔	✔	✔(10)	✔
	Mains Farm	39			✔					✔
	Ormsary Farm	39			✔		✔	✔		✔
	Shantron Farm	54			✔P		✔	✔		✔
	Thistle-Doo	39		✔			✔			
	The Topps Farm	55			✔		✔	✔	✔(20)	✔
	Wester Carmuirs Farm	55			✔			✔		✔
	West Plean	55				✔	✔	✔	✔(12)	✔
SC	Maymore	40			✔					✔
	Shemore Farm Cottage	55			✔P			✔		✔
	Torlochan	40			✔P			✔	✔(20)	✔
Ayrshire & Arran										
B&B	Auchencloigh Farm	67			✔			✔		✔
	Aulton Farm	67			✔P			✔	✔(6)	
	Blair Farm	70			✔P		✔	✔		✔
	Dunduff Farm	67			✔P		✔	✔		✔
	East Lochhead	67				✔	✔	✔		✔
	Fisherton Farm	67			✔P		✔	✔		
	Glen Cloy Farmhouse	68				✔	✔	✔		
	Glengennet Farm	70			✔		✔	✔		✔
	Muirhouse Farm	68			✔		✔	✔	✔(8)	
SC	Bothy Cottage	68			✔P		✔	✔		✔
	East Lochhead	68				✔		✔		✔
	Upper Barr Farm	71			✔			✔		✔
Dumfries & Galloway										
B&B	Airds Farm	70			✔		✔	✔		
	Broomlands Farm	73			✔		✔	✔		✔
	Coxhill Farm	73			✔			✔		✔
	Ericstane	73			✔		✔	✔		
	Rascarrel Cottage	70			✔		✔	✔		✔
SC	Kirkwood Cottages	73			✔P			✔		
Edinburgh & Lothians										
B&B	Bankhead Farm	57			✔P		✔	✔		

SCOTLAND
Region/Farm

		Page no.	Accessible category	Caravans and/or camping	Working farm (p=participation)	Farm – non-working	En suite available	Business people welcome	Meeting room (capacity)	Gift tokens accepted
Scottish Borders										
B&B	Cockburn Mill	61			✔P		✔	✔		
	Lyne Farm	61			✔			✔	✔(12)	✔
	Morebattle Tofts	61			✔		✔	✔		✔
	Overlangshaw Farm	61			✔P		✔			✔
	Wiltonburn Farm	61			✔P			✔	✔(6)	✔
SC	Bailey Mill	62,76	⚲		✔P		✔	✔	✔(24)	✔
	The Cottage	62			✔P			✔		
	Craggs Cottage	62			✔P			✔		
	Kerchesters	62			✔			✔		✔
	Lochton Farm Cottages	62			✔P			✔		✔
	Roxburgh Newtown Farm	63			✔			✔		✔
	Steading Cottage	63			✔			✔		
	Thirlestane Farm Cottages	63								✔

ENGLAND County/Farm		Page no.	Accessible category	Caravans and/or camping	Working farm (p=participation)	Farm – non-working	En suite available	Business people welcome	Meeting room (capacity)	Gift tokens accepted
Bath & North East Somerset										
B&B	Barrow Vale Farm	255			✔p		✔	✔		
	Woodbarn Farm	256			✔		✔	✔		✔
Bedfordshire										
B&B	Church Farm	214			✔			✔	✔(6)	✔
	Firs Farm	214			✔		✔	✔		✔
	Gransden Lodge Farm	219			✔		✔	✔		
	Highfield Farm	214			✔p		✔	✔		✔
SC	Scald End Farm	215			✔p			✔	✔(40)	
Berkshire										
B&B	Moor Farm	236			✔		✔	✔		
SC	Courtyard Cottages	238			✔			✔		
Bristol										
B&B	The Model Farm	255			✔		✔	✔		
	Valley Farm	256			✔		✔	✔	✔(12)	
Buckinghamshire										
B&B	Monkton Farm	236		✔	✔			✔	✔(40)	
	New Farm	237			✔			✔		
	Poletrees Farm	237			✔p			✔		
	Spinney Lodge Farm	208			✔		✔	✔		✔
	Wallace Farm	238			✔		✔	✔	✔(8)	✔
SC	The Old Stone Barn	214	♿		✔			✔		
	Wallace Farm Cottages	239			✔		✔	✔		✔
Cambridgeshire										
B&B	Hill House Farm	219			✔		✔	✔		✔
	Spinney Abbey	219			✔		✔	✔		✔
SC	Hill House Farm Cottage	220			✔			✔		✔
Cheshire										
B&B	Adderley Green Farm	148		✔	✔p		✔	✔	✔(12)	✔
	Ash House Farm	148			✔		✔	✔		✔
	Beechwood House	148			✔		✔	✔		✔
	Bridge Farm	148			✔p		✔	✔		✔
	Carr House Farm	148			✔			✔		✔
	Coole Hall Farm	149		✔	✔					✔
	Ford Farm	149						✔		
	Golden Cross Farm	149				✔		✔		✔
	Goose Green Farm	149			✔		✔	✔		✔
	Henhull Hall	149			✔p		✔	✔	✔(12)	✔
	Lea Farm	149			✔p		✔	✔	✔(12)	✔
	Little Heath Farm	150		✔	✔p		✔	✔	✔(12)	✔
	Lower Harebarrow Farm	150						✔		✔
	Manor Farm	150		✔	✔		✔	✔	✔(10)	✔
	Mill House	170					✔	✔		✔
	Millmoor Farm	170			✔p		✔	✔		✔
	Needhams Farm	145		✔	✔		✔	✔		✔
	Newton Hall	150			✔		✔			
	Oldhams Hollow Farm	150			✔			✔		✔
	Poole Bank Farm	150		✔	✔		✔	✔		✔
	Sandhole Farm	151	♿		✔		✔	✔	✔(15)	✔
	Sandpit Farm	151				✔	✔	✔		✔

ENGLAND County/Farm	Page no.	Accessible category	Caravans and/or camping	Working farm (p=participation)	Farm – non-working	En suite available	Business people welcome	Meeting room (capacity)	Gift tokens accepted
Cornwall (cont)									
Brevean	320			✔					
Bucklawren Farm	320			✔			✔	✔(16)	✔
Cadson Manor Farm	321			✔P			✔		✔
The Coach House	321			✔P			✔		
Glynn Barton Farm Cottages	321			✔P			✔		
Hendra Farm	321			✔P					
Lodge Barton Farm	321			✔P			✔		
Lower Trengale Farm	321			✔P			✔		
Manuels Farm	322			✔P			✔		✔
Old Newham Farm	322			✔P			✔		✔
Poltarrow Farm	322	⚇					✔		
Rooke Farm Cottages	322			✔		✔	✔		
Tredethick Farm Cottages	322			✔		✔	✔	✔(12)	✔
Tredinnick Farm	322			✔		✔	✔	✔	✔
Tregevis Farm	323			✔P					
Treharrock Farm Cottages	323			✔P					
Treleaven Farm Cottages	323			✔		✔	✔		✔
Tremadart Farm	323			✔P		✔	✔		
Trevalgan Farm	323			✔			✔		✔
Trevissick Manor	323			✔			✔		✔
Trewellard Manor Farm	324			✔			✔		
Trewithen Country Lodges	324			✔P					
Trotters	324			✔P		✔	✔		
West Kellow Farmhouse & Meadow Bank	324					✔			
Wheatley Farm Cottages	324			✔P			✔		✔
C&C Nancolleth Farm Caravan Gardens	325		✔	✔					✔
Cumbria									
B&B Augill House Farm	97			✔		✔	✔		
Bessiestown Farm	78			✔		✔	✔		✔
Birkrigg Farm	100			✔			✔		✔
Bridge End Farm	97			✔		✔	✔		✔
Cracrop Farm	78			✔P		✔	✔	✔(8)	✔
Craigburn Farm	78			✔		✔	✔	✔(50)	✔
Crossgill Farm	95			✔		✔	✔		
Fell Foot Farm	100			✔P		✔	✔		
Garghyll Dyke	137			✔			✔		✔
Garnett House Farm	104			✔		✔	✔		✔
Gateside Farm	104			✔		✔	✔		✔
High Gregg Hall	104			✔					
Howard House Farm	75			✔P		✔	✔		✔
Howe Farm	104			✔			✔	✔(6)	
Keskadale Farm	100		✔	✔			✔		
New Pallyards	75			✔P		✔	✔	✔(30)	✔
Park House Farm	97			✔		✔	✔		✔
Slakes Farm	97			✔			✔		✔
Stanger Farm	102			✔P			✔	✔(6)	✔
Stock Bridge Farm	104				✔		✔		

ENGLAND County/Farm		Page no.	Accessible category	Caravans and/or camping	Working farm (p–participation)	Farm – non-working	En suite available	Business people welcome	Meeting room (capacity)	Gift tokens accepted
Gloucestershire (cont)										
	Windmill Annexe	201	✻		✔P			✔	✔(15)	✔
Greater Manchester										
B&B	Boothstead Farm	145						✔		✔
	Globe Farm	145		✔		✔	✔	✔		✔
Hampshire										
B&B	Brocklands Farm	241		✔	✔			✔	✔(12)	✔
	Moortown Farm	241				✔	✔	✔		
	Oakdown Farm Bungalow	241			✔			✔		✔
	Peak House Farm	241			✔		✔	✔		✔
	Pyesmead Farm	242			✔P		✔	✔		✔
	Vine Farmhouse	242			✔		✔	✔		✔
SC	Meadow Cottage	242			✔			✔		✔
	Owl Cottage	242		✔	✔					
Herefordshire										
B&B	Amberley	178			✔		✔	✔		✔
	Brelston Court	178			✔			✔		
	Garford Farm	178			✔		✔	✔		
	Grafton Villa Farm	178			✔P		✔	✔		✔
	Hill Top Farm	179		✔	✔P		✔	✔		✔
	The Hills Farm	179			✔		✔	✔	✔(10)	✔
	Home Farm	179		✔	✔			✔		
	Little Wickton	179				✔	✔	✔		
	Moor Court Farm	179			✔P		✔	✔	✔(20)	✔
	New House Farm, Longhope	180				✔	✔	✔		✔
	New House Farm, Much Marcle	180			✔P			✔		✔
	Old Court Farm	180			✔P		✔	✔	✔(30)	✔
	Red Ley Farmhouse	180			✔		✔	✔	✔(20)	
	Sink Green Farm	180			✔		✔	✔	✔(6)	✔
	Upper Gilvach Farm	180		✔	✔P		✔	✔		✔
	The Vauld House Farm	181		✔	✔		✔	✔		✔
	Warren Farm	181			✔		✔	✔		
SC	Anvil Cottage	181	✻		✔P		✔	✔		✔
	Apple Bough	181			✔			✔	✔(10)	
	Carey Dene & Rock House	182			✔P					
	Mill House Flat	182		✔	✔			✔		✔
	Moody Farm Cottage	182			✔P			✔		
	New House Farm Cottages	182				✔		✔		✔
	Old Forge Cottage	182				✔	✔	✔		
	Poolspringe Farm Cottages	182			✔			✔		✔
	The Vauld House Farm	183		✔	✔			✔		✔
Hertfordshire										
B&B	Broadway Farm	217			✔		✔	✔	✔(10)	✔
	The Grange	217				✔	✔	✔		
	Hall Farm	219			✔			✔		✔
SC	Bluntswood Hall Cottages	217						✔	✔(100)	✔
Isle of Man										
B&B	Ballamadrell Farm	107			✔P			✔	✔(6)	✔
	Ballavell Farm	107			✔P			✔		✔
	Booilshuggel Farm	107			✔P			✔		✔

ENGLAND
County/Farm

County/Farm	Page no.	Accessible category	Caravans and/or camping	Working farm (p=participation)	Farm – non-working	En suite available	Business people welcome	Meeting room (capacity)	Gift tokens accepted
Lincolnshire (cont)									
East Farm House	203			✔		✔	✔		✔
Gelston Grange Farm	204			✔		✔	✔		
The Grange	204		✔	✔		✔	✔		
Greenfield Farm	204			✔		✔	✔		✔
The Manor House, Manor Farm	204			✔		✔	✔		✔
The Manor House, West Barkwith	204			✔		✔			
Midstone Farmhouse	204			✔P			✔		✔
Sycamore Farm	205			✔		✔	✔	✔(6)	✔
SC Bridle Cottage	205			✔P			✔		✔
Mill Lodge	205			✔			✔		
Red House Farm Cottage	205			✔			✔		
Norfolk									
B&B Birds Place Farm	222			✔P		✔	✔		✔
Colveston Manor	223		✔	✔P		✔	✔	✔(12)	✔
East Farm	223			✔		✔	✔	✔(10)	✔
Hempstead Hall	224		✔	✔		✔			✔
Highfield Farm	224			✔P		✔	✔	✔(10)	
Hillside Farm	224			✔		✔	✔		✔
Malting Farm	225			✔P		✔	✔		
Marsh Farm	225			✔P		✔	✔		✔
Old Coach House	225		✔	✔		✔	✔		
Park Farm	225			✔		✔	✔		✔
Salamanca Farm	226			✔		✔	✔	✔(14)	
Shrublands Farm	226		✔	✔		✔	✔		✔
Sloley Farm	227		✔	✔		✔	✔	✔(20)	✔
South Elmham Hall	227			✔		✔	✔		✔
Stratton Farm	227	♿		✔P		✔	✔	✔(10)	✔
Witton Hall Farm	227			✔		✔			
SC Burnley Hall	228			✔		✔			
Carysfort Too	228			✔P		✔	✔	✔(10)	✔
Dairy Farm Cottages	229	♿		✔		✔	✔	✔(15)	
Dolphin Lodge	229			✔			✔		
Meadow View	230			✔			✔		✔
Tom, Dick and Harry	230			✔			✔		✔
North Somerset									
B&B Icelton Farm	255			✔			✔		✔
Purn House Farm	256			✔		✔	✔	✔(12)	✔
North Yorkshire									
B&B Ainderby Myers Farm	118			✔P		✔	✔		✔
Barn Close Farm	123			✔P		✔	✔		
Bay Tree Farm	118			✔		✔	✔		✔
Beech Tree House Farm	123			✔P			✔		
Bewerley Hall Farm	115			✔		✔	✔		✔
Bushey Lodge Farm	111						✔		✔
Carr House Farm	118		✔	✔		✔	✔		✔
Church Farm	131			✔P		✔	✔		
Clough House Farm	115				✔	✔	✔		✔
Croft Farm	126			✔		✔	✔		
Cuckoo Nest Farm	131			✔			✔		

ENGLAND County/Farm	Page no.	Accessible category	Caravans and/or camping	Working farm (p=participation)	Farm – non-working	En suite available	Business people welcome	Meeting room (capacity)	Gift tokens accepted
Northumberland (cont)									
The Herdsman Cottage	87			✔					✔
Keepers Cottages	84			✔			✔		✔
Lumbylaw Cottage	84			✔					✔
Nos. 2 and 3 Cottages	84			✔					✔
Shepherd's Cottage	84			✔P			✔		✔
Nottinghamshire									
B&B									
Blue Barn Farm	166			✔		✔	✔		✔
Far Baulker Farm	166		✔			✔	✔		
Forest Farm	166			✔		✔	✔		
Jerico Farm	166			✔		✔	✔	✔(6)	
Manor Farm	166			✔			✔		
Norton Grange Farm	167			✔P			✔	✔(10)	
SC									
Blue Barn Cottage	167			✔			✔		✔
Foliat Cottages	167			✔			✔	✔(8)	✔
Foxcote Cottage	167			✔		✔	✔		
The Granary	167			✔			✔		
Oxfordshire									
B&B									
Banbury Hill Farm	235		✔	✔		✔	✔		
Bould Farm	196			✔		✔	✔		✔
Bowling Green Farm	235			✔		✔	✔		✔
Chimney House	235			✔		✔	✔		
Ducklington Farm	235		✔	✔		✔	✔		
Fords Farm	236			✔			✔		
Foxbury Farm	236			✔			✔		✔
Hill Grove Farm	236		✔	✔		✔	✔		
Morar	236				✔	✔	✔		✔
North Farm	237			✔P		✔	✔	✔(8)	✔
The Old Farmhouse	237				✔	✔	✔		✔
Rectory Farm	237			✔		✔	✔		✔
Sor Brook House Farm	192		✔	✔			✔		
Vicarage Farm	237				✔		✔		
Weston Farm	238			✔		✔			✔
SC									
Banbury Hill Farm	238			✔			✔		
Coxwell House	238			✔		✔	✔		
Rectory Farm Cottages	239			✔			✔		✔
Shropshire									
B&B									
Acton Scott Farm	174			✔		✔	✔		✔
The Barn Farm	178			✔		✔	✔		✔
Billingsley Hall Farm	174		✔	✔			✔	✔(12)	
Brereton House	174					✔			✔
Castle Farm	174						✔	✔(20)	
Church Farm	169			✔		✔	✔	✔(12)	✔
Court Farm	174			✔		✔	✔		✔
Dearnford Hall	169			✔		✔	✔	✔(10)	✔
Grove Farm	169			✔		✔	✔		✔
The Hall	175			✔		✔	✔		✔
Haynall Villa	179					✔	✔		✔
Hurst Mill Farm	175		✔	✔P		✔	✔		
Lane End Farm	169			✔P		✔	✔		✔

ENGLAND County/Farm		Page no.	Accessible category	Caravans and/or camping	Working farm (p=participation)	Farm – non-working	En suite available	Business people welcome	Meeting room (capacity)	Gift tokens accepted
Somerset (cont)										
SC	Cockhill Farm & Orchard Farm	277			✔P			✔		✔
	The Courtyard	277			✔			✔		✔
	Cutthorne Farm	282			✔			✔		✔
	Hale Farm	277				✔		✔		
	Highercombe Farm	283			✔P					
	Hindon Farmhouse Cottage	288			✔P		✔	✔	✔(12)	
	Holly Farm	277			✔			✔		✔
	Liscombe Farm	283			✔			✔		
	Little Quarme Country Cottages	288			✔			✔		
	Lois Barns	277			✔P		✔			
	The Old Cart House	278			✔		✔	✔		✔
	Pear Tree Cottage	278		✔	✔					
	Pembroke	283								
	Pigsty, Cowstall & Bullpen Cottages	278			✔					✔
	Riscombe Farm	283				✔				✔
	Rull Farm	278			✔					
	The Tallet	278			✔P		✔	✔		✔
	Week Farm	283			✔P			✔		
	Westermill Farm	283	🚶	✔	✔P			✔		
	Wintershead Farm	284					✔	✔		✔
C&C	Halse Farm Touring Park	284		✔	✔					
	Westermill Farm	285		✔	✔P			✔		
Staffordshire										
B&B	Brook House Farm	156			✔P		✔	✔		
	The Church Farm	156			✔			✔		
	Ley Fields Farm	157			✔P		✔	✔		✔
	Manor House Farm	162			✔		✔	✔		
	Oulton House Farm	170			✔		✔	✔		✔
	Ribden Farm	154			✔		✔	✔		
SC	Keepers Cottage	164			✔			✔		
	Lower Berkhamsytch Farm	159			✔			✔		✔
	Priory Farm Fishing House	154			✔		✔	✔		✔
	Swallows Nest	172			✔			✔		✔
Suffolk										
B&B	Brighthouse Farm	222		✔	✔		✔	✔		
	Broad Oak Farm	222			✔P		✔	✔		
	Church Farm	222			✔		✔	✔		
	College Farm	222			✔		✔	✔		✔
	Colston Hall	223		✔	✔		✔	✔	✔(6)	✔
	Earsham Park Farm	223			✔P		✔	✔	✔(12)	✔
	Elm Lodge Farm	223			✔		✔	✔		✔
	Grange Farm	223		✔	✔		✔	✔		✔
	Hall Farm	224			✔		✔	✔		
	Laurel Farm	224				✔		✔		✔
	Oak Farm	225			✔			✔		✔
	Park Farm	225			✔		✔	✔		✔
	Pear Tree Farm	226			✔		✔			
	Priory Farm	226		✔	✔			✔		
	Red House Farm	226		✔	✔		✔	✔		✔

WALES Region/Farm		Page no.	Accessible category	Caravans and/or camping	Working farm (p=participation)	Farm – non-working	En suite available	Business people welcome	Meeting room (capacity)	Gift tokens accepted
North Wales										
B&B	Bach-y-Graig	340			✔P		✔	✔		✔
	Bryn Celynog Farm	337			✔P		✔	✔		✔
	Cae'r Efail	333				✔	✔	✔		
	Cwm Hwylfod	337			✔P		✔	✔		✔
	Drws y Coed	327			✔P		✔	✔		✔
	Erw Feurig Farm	337			✔		✔	✔		✔
	Fron-Haul	340		✔	✔P		✔	✔	✔(25)	✔
	Gwrach Ynys	333				✔	✔	✔		
	Hendy Farm	337		✔	✔		✔			
	Llainwen Ucha	340			✔			✔		
	Llwydiarth Fawr	327		✔	✔P		✔	✔	✔(12)	
	Llwyn Mafon Isaf	337		✔	✔P		✔	✔		
	Mathan Uchaf Farm	330			✔P			✔		
	Pengwern	333			✔		✔	✔	✔(6)	
	Plas Cichle	327		✔	✔P		✔	✔		✔
	Plas Tirion Farm	333			✔P		✔	✔		✔
	Plas Trefarthen	327			✔		✔	✔	✔(12)	✔
	Rhydydefaid Farm	338		✔	✔		✔	✔		✔
	Tre'rddôl Farm	327		✔	✔P		✔	✔		✔
	Tyddyn Du Farm	338			✔P		✔	✔		✔
	Tyddyn Iolyn	338				✔	✔	✔	✔(20)	✔
	Ty Mawr Farm	333			✔		✔	✔	✔(8)	✔
	Ystumgwern	334	⚐		✔		✔	✔		✔
SC	Bach-y-Graig	340			✔P		✔	✔		✔
	Bryn Beddau	334						✔		
	Caerwych Farmhouse	338			✔					
	Castellmarch	330			✔P			✔		
	Cefnamwlch	330			✔					
	Chwilog Fawr	334		✔	✔			✔		✔
	Dwyfach Cottages	334		✔	✔P		✔	✔		✔
	Garth-y-Foel	338			✔					
	Gwynfryn Farm	330	⚐	✔	✔P			✔		✔
	Hafod and Hendre	334			✔		✔	✔		
	Llwydiarth Fawr Farm Cottages	328		✔	✔P		✔	✔		
	Llys Bennar	335				✔	✔			
	Plas Trefarthen	328			✔			✔	✔(12)	✔
	Rhydolion	331	♿	✔	✔P		✔			
	Tai Gwyliau Tyndon Holiday Cottages	331		✔	✔			✔		✔
	Tyddyn Isaf	341			✔			✔		✔
	Ynys	335			✔		✔	✔		✔
Mid Wales										
B&B	Bache Farm	349			✔		✔	✔		
	Beili Neuadd	349		✔			✔	✔		✔
	Broniwan	352			✔P		✔	✔	✔(6)	
	Bwlch Farm	349				✔	✔	✔		✔
	Cefnsuran Farm	349			✔P		✔	✔	✔(16)	✔
	Cwmllwynog	346			✔		✔	✔		✔
	The Drewin Farm	346			✔		✔	✔		✔

INDEX